Historic Documents
of 2014

SAGE was founded in 1965 by Sara Miller McCune to support the dissemination of usable knowledge by publishing innovative and high-quality research and teaching content. Today, we publish more than 750 journals, including those of more than 300 learned societies, more than 800 new books per year, and a growing range of library products including archives, data, case studies, reports, conference highlights, and video. SAGE remains majority-owned by our founder, and after Sara's lifetime will become owned by a charitable trust that secures our continued independence.

Los Angeles | London | New Delhi | Singapore | Washington DC | Boston

Historic Documents
of 2014

Heather Kerrigan, Editor

Los Angeles | London | New Delhi
Singapore | Washington DC | Boston

Los Angeles | London | New Delhi
Singapore | Washington DC | Boston

FOR INFORMATION:

CQ Press

An Imprint of SAGE Publications, Inc.

2455 Teller Road

Thousand Oaks, California 91320

E-mail: order@sagepub.com

SAGE Publications Ltd.

1 Oliver's Yard

55 City Road

London EC1Y 1SP

United Kingdom

SAGE Publications India Pvt. Ltd.

B 1/I 1 Mohan Cooperative Industrial Area

Mathura Road, New Delhi 110 044

India

SAGE Publications Asia-Pacific Pte. Ltd.

3 Church Street

#10-04 Samsung Hub

Singapore 049483

973

His

Associate Editor: Laura Notton

Managing Editor: Heather Kerrigan

Contributors: Alexis Atwater, Brian Beary, Anastazia Clouting, Melissa Feinberg, Sarah Gall, Linda Fecteau Grimm, Robert Howard, Heather Kerrigan

Editorial Assistant: Jordan Enobakhare

Production Editor: David C. Felts

Copy Editor: Deanna Noga

Typesetter: C&M Digitals (P) Ltd.

Proofreader: Lawrence W. Baker

Indexer: Joan Shapiro

Cover Designer: Michael Dubowe

Marketing Manager: Carmel Schrier

Cover images: AP Images.

"Award Ceremony Speech." December 10, 2014. © The Nobel Foundation 2014. Used with permission.

"Center for Reproductive Rights Statements on 2014 Anti-Choice Ballot Initiative Results." November 5, 2014. Center for Reproductive Rights. Used with permission.

"Joint Remarks with Prime Minister Najib Razak, Western Australia." April 3, 2014. Licensed from the Commonwealth of Australia under a Creative Commons Attribution 3.0 Australia License. The Commonwealth of Australia does not necessarily endorse the content of this publication. http://creativecommons.org/licenses/by/3.0/au/

"Radical Pro-Abortion Lobby Continues Effort to Silence TN Voters." Yes on 1. November 8, 2014. Used with permission.

"Radical Pro-Abortion Lobby Continues Effort to Silence TN Voters." November 8, 2014. Used with permission.

"OPEC 166th meeting concludes."Organization of Petroleum Exporting Countries. November 27, 2014. Used with permission.

"Speech on the occasion of Opening Ceremony—126th Session." February 4, 2014. Used with permission from the International Olympic Committee. www.olympic.org

"Statement of Mayor Martin J. Walsh on Gun Safety Legislation." August 1, 2014. City of Boston. Used with permission.

"Stinging Defeats for Radical Anti-Hunting and Gun Control Groups." National Rifle Association. Institute for Legislative Action. November 5, 2014. Used with permission.

"Touchdown! Rosetta's Philae Probe Lands on Comet." November 12, 2014. European Space Agency. Used with permission.

"Transcripts of remarks by CE at media session." August 31, 2014. Hong Kong SAR Government.

"Voters Across Country Accelerate Unprecedented Momentum to Legalize Marijuana, End Drug War." Drug Policy Alliance. November 5, 2014. Used with permission.

"Washington State Voters Overwhelmingly Approve Citizens' Initiatives to Expand Background Checks to All Gun Sales." Brady Campaign to Prevent Gun Violence. November 5, 2014. Used with permission.

AFL-CIO. "Working-Class Voters Put the Economy First." November 5, 2014. Used with permission.

Printed in United States of America

ISBN 978-1-4833-8052-0 (cloth)

This book is printed on acid-free paper.

SFI Certified Sourcing
www.sfiprogram.org
SFI-00453

15 16 17 18 19 10 9 8 7 6 5 4 3 2 1

Contents

JANUARY

FEBRUARY

Sochi; and the speech by IOC president Thomas Bach officially opening the Winter Games on February 7, 2014.

The edited text of the United Nation's summary report on suspected human rights abuses in North Korea, released on February 7, 2014; and a response to the UN report from North Korea on April 22, 2014.

A statement by U.S. secretary of state John Kerry on February 15, 2014, raising concern about the Venezuelan government's crackdown against protesters; and a statement from the Government of the Bolivarian Republic of Venezuela rejecting Kerry's statement and accusing the U.S. government of backing antigovernment movements in Venezuela.

MARCH

The edited text of the Supreme Court's May 4, 2014, decision in *Lawson v. FMR LLC*, in which the Court ruled 6–3 that the Sarbanes-Oxley Act of 2002 grants anti-retaliation protection to employees of a public company's private contractors or subcontractors.

The text of a statement by the acting president of Ukraine on March 6, 2014, regarding Crimea's plan to hold a secession referendum; the text of statements given at a signing ceremony admitting Crimea into the Russian Federation on March 21, 2014; and an April 1, 2014, statement from the NATO-Ukraine Commission on Russian military intervention in Ukraine.

A statement by current Malaysian prime minister Najib Razak on March 15, 2014, regarding the ongoing search for flight MH370; a statement by Australian prime minister Tony Abbott on March 24, 2014, on his nation's involvement in the search; a March 24, 2014, statement by Razak announcing the assumption that MH370 crashed, killing all onboard; and an April 3, 2014, joint statement by Abbott and Razak on the ongoing search for MH370 in the Indian Ocean.

A statement by President Barack Obama delivered on March 27, 2014, outlining proposals to revise the way in which the National Security Agency collects data.

APRIL

MAY

JUNE

JULY

AUGUST

of a statement delivered on September 30, 2014, by Julia Pierson, director, U.S. Secret Service, before the U.S. House of Representatives Committee on Oversight and Government Reform.

The text of the peace agreement signed by the Yemeni government and Houthi rebel group on September 21, 2014.

OCTOBER

The Bureau of Labor Statistics commissioner's statement on October 3, 2014, announcing September job growth; and a press release from the Federal Reserve on October 29, 2014, announcing the end of its quantitative easing program.

The text of a statement by Indiana governor Mike Pence on October 6, 2014, in favor of traditional marriage; a press release issued by the office of Utah governor Gary Herbert on October 6, 2014, responding to the Supreme Court's decision not to review same-sex marriage; and an October 7, 2014, press release from the office of Virginia governor Terry McAuliffe directing state agencies to comply with the same-sex marriage decision.

NOVEMBER

A statement by Speaker of the House John Boehner, R-Ohio, on November 4, 2014, on Republican election victories; and the text of a press conference with President Barack Obama on November 5, 2014, following the midterm elections.

Press releases from advocacy groups responding to state ballot measures including remarks from the Brady Campaign and the National Rifle Association on gun restrictions, both on November 5, 2014; a statement from the Drug Policy Alliance on November 5, 2014, in support of ballot initiatives on marijuana use; a November 5, 2014, press release from the AFL-CIO in support of the minimum wage increases that appeared before voters; and press releases from the Center for Reproductive Rights and Tennessee Yes on 1 advocacy group in response to abortion rights initiatives, on November 5, 2014, and November 8, 2014, respectively.

DECEMBER

in Greece; and a second statement by Moscovici on December 29, 2014, on general elections in Greece.

The findings and conclusions from the Senate Select Committee on Intelligence report on the Central Intelligence Agency's detention and interrogation program, printed on December 9, 2014.

The text of the Nobel Peace Prize award ceremony presentation, delivered by Norwegian Nobel Committee chair Thorbjørn Jagland on December 10, 2014.

A press release issued on December 16, 2014, by Pakistan's Ministry of Foreign Affairs on the terrorist attack in Peshawar; and a December 17, 2014, statement from the Pakistan prime minister's office on actions against extremists.

The text of an address delivered by President Barack Obama on December 17, 2014, regarding the restoration of diplomatic relations with Cuba.

Excerpts from a press conference held by Russian president Vladimir Putin on December 18, 2014, on the state of Russia's economy.

A December 19, 2014, press release from the Federal Bureau of Investigation on the outcome of its inquiry into the Sony hack; and a statement by North Korea's National Defence Commission on December 21, 2014, in response to allegations that it was behind the Sony attack.

The text of two statements, one from North Atlantic Treaty Organization secretary general Jens Stoltenberg, and one from U.S. secretary of defense Chuck Hagel, both released on December 28, 2014, in response to the end of formal combat missions in Afghanistan.

Thematic Table of Contents

AMERICAN LIFE

BUSINESS, THE ECONOMY, AND LABOR

ENERGY, ENVIRONMENT, SCIENCE, TECHNOLOGY, AND TRANSPORTATION

GOVERNMENT AND POLITICS

HEALTH AND SOCIAL SERVICES

INTERNATIONAL AFFAIRS
AFRICA

INTERNATIONAL AFFAIRS
ASIA

INTERNATIONAL AFFAIRS
EUROPE

INTERNATIONAL AFFAIRS
LATIN AMERICA AND THE CARIBBEAN

INTERNATIONAL AFFAIRS
MIDDLE EAST

INTERNATIONAL AFFAIRS
RUSSIA AND THE FORMER SOVIET REPUBLICS

INTERNATIONAL AFFAIRS
GLOBAL ISSUES

NATIONAL SECURITY AND TERRORISM

RIGHTS, RESPONSIBILITIES, AND JUSTICE

List of Document Sources

CONGRESS

EXECUTIVE DEPARTMENTS, AGENCIES, FEDERAL OFFICES, AND COMMISSIONS

INTERNATIONAL GOVERNMENTAL
ORGANIZATIONS

INTERNATIONAL NONGOVERNMENTAL ORGANIZATIONS

JUDICIARY

NONGOVERNMENTAL ORGANIZATIONS

NON-U.S. GOVERNMENTS

U.S. STATE AND LOCAL GOVERNMENTS

WHITE HOUSE AND THE PRESIDENT

Preface

President Barack Obama's executive orders on immigration, the wage gap, and LGBT employment protections amidst continued congressional gridlock and midterm elections, landmark Supreme Court rulings on campaign contributions and the Affordable Care Act's birth control mandate, the Supreme Court's rejection of same-sex marriage appeals, historic movement on climate change initiatives, reports on human rights violations across the globe, the momentous election of a new Indian prime minister while the military seizes power in Thailand, debate regarding Internet neutrality and the right to be forgotten in Google searches, an Ebola outbreak that caused international alarm, continued tensions in the Middle East and the compounded refugee crisis as the civil war in Syria marches on, the growing threat from terrorist groups ISIL and Boko Haram, and the secession of Crimea from Ukraine and subsequent sanctions against Russia by the United States and European Union are just a few of the topics of national and international significance chosen for discussion in *Historic Documents of 2014*. This edition marks the forty-third volume of a CQ Press project that began with *Historic Documents of 1972*. This series allows students, librarians, journalists, scholars, and others to research and understand the most important domestic and foreign issues and events of the year through primary source documents. To aid research, many of the lengthy documents written for specialized audiences have been excerpted to highlight the most important sections. The official statements, news conferences, speeches, special studies, and court decisions presented here should be of lasting public and academic interest.

Historic Documents of 2014 opens with an "Overview of 2014," a sweeping narrative of the key events and issues of the year, which provides context for the documents that follow. The balance of the book is organized chronologically, with each article comprising an introduction titled "Document in Context" and one or more related documents on a specific event, issue, or topic. Often an event is not limited to a particular day. Consequently, readers will find that some events include multiple documents that may span several months. Their placement in the book corresponds to the date of the first document included for that event. The event introductions provide context and an account of further developments during the year. A thematic table of contents (page xvii) and a list of documents organized by source (page xxiii) follow the standard table of contents and assist readers in locating events and documents.

As events, issues, and consequences become more complex and far-reaching, these introductions and documents yield important information and deepen understanding about the world's increasing interconnectedness. As memories of current events fade, these selections will continue to further understanding of the events and issues that have shaped the lives of people around the world.

How to Use This Book

Each of the seventy entries in this edition consists of two parts: a comprehensive introduction followed by one or more primary source documents. The articles are arranged in chronological order by month. Articles with multiple documents are placed according to the date of the first document. There are several ways to find events and documents of interest:

By date: If the approximate date of an event or document is known, browse through the titles for that month in the table of contents. Alternatively, browse the tables of contents that appear at the beginning of each month's articles.

By theme: To find a particular topic or subject area, browse the thematic table of contents.

By document type or source: To find a particular type of document or document source, such as the White House or Congress, review the list of document sources.

By index: The index allows researchers to locate references to specific events or documents as well as entries on the same or related subjects.

An online edition of this volume, as well as an archive going back to 1972, is available and offers advance search and browse functionality.

Each article begins with an introduction. This feature provides historical and intellectual contexts for the documents that follow. Documents are reproduced with the original spelling, capitalization, and punctuation of the original or official copy. Ellipsis points indicate textual omissions (unless they were present in the documents themselves indicating pauses in speech), and brackets are used for editorial insertions within documents for text clarification. The excerpting of Supreme Court opinions has been done somewhat differently from other documents. In-text references and citations to laws and other cases have been removed when not part of a sentence to improve the readability of opinions. In those documents, readers will find ellipses used only when sections of narrative text have been removed.

Full citations appear at the end of each document. If a document is not available on the Internet, this too is noted. For further reading on a particular topic consult the "Other Historic Documents of Interest" section at the end of each article. These sections provide cross-references for related articles in this edition of *Historic Documents* as well as in previous editions. References to articles from past volumes include the year and page number for easy retrieval.

Overview of 2014

In the United States, 2014 was a battleground of contentious November midterm election campaigns. President Barack Obama, frustrated by the lack of action in Congress, took a number of executive actions on issues ranging from protections from discrimination in the workplace based on gender identity or sexual orientation, to deferring the deportation of some of the eleven million illegal immigrants currently in the United States. Republicans seized the opportunity to paint the president as overstepping his authority. Both parties worked to prove that they could help grow the middle class, which suffered the greatest losses during the recession and has struggled to regain a foothold. After the November election, Republicans kept control of the House of Representatives and took control of the Senate. The party also won a majority of the governorships and state legislatures that were up for election. Overall, the federal and state victories were some of the largest ever for the party.

Internationally, the year was dominated by ongoing turmoil in the Middle East and tension between Russia and Ukraine. In the Middle East, Syria's civil war entered its fourth year, and despite months of negotiations, the rebels were unable to reach a meaningful peace agreement with the government of President Bashar al Assad. The ongoing fighting in the nation has displaced millions and led to the deaths of tens of thousands. The weakened Syrian state also gave rise to the Islamic State of Iraq and the Levant (ISIL), a militant group that claimed land in Syria and Iraq throughout 2014 with the intent of imposing strict seventh century Islamic Sharia law. The international community struggled with how best to thwart the group's rise. Israel and Palestine intended to work toward a peace agreement with each other, but with the April announcement that the Hamas and Fatah factions had formed a unity government in Palestine, Israel ended the talks indefinitely before any agreement could be reached. Tensions between Russia and Ukraine ignited in March when the Ukrainian peninsula of Crimea voted to become part of Russia. Russian president Vladimir Putin's government annexed the territory, which led to sanctions from the United States and European Union. Violence escalated along the border toward the end of the year as Russia funneled more troops into Ukraine, in support of new separatist movements that had sprung up in Eastern Ukraine. The continued isolation of Russia on the world stage had a significant impact on its economy, which was already struggling after the steep decline in oil prices in the second half of 2014.

DOMESTIC ISSUES

April marked the first enrollment deadline for the president's landmark piece of healthcare legislation, known as the Affordable Care Act. In total, more than eight million Americans were able to sign up for health insurance through the federal exchange or one of thirteen state-based exchanges. Republicans in Congress have fought since the law's inception to repeal it or roll back some of its provisions, and Republican control of the House and Senate beginning in 2015 will likely mean new attempts to repeal many parts of the law.

After months of gridlock and inaction in Congress, President Obama undertook a number of executive actions throughout the year. In April, in an attempt to close the wage gap between men and women, the president signed an executive order and presidential memorandum to enable employees of federal contractors to discuss their wages with colleagues and required employers to be more transparent about their compensation structure. In July, the president signed a pair of executive orders extending workplace and hiring protections with regard to gender identity and sexual orientation to federal employees and the employees of federal contractors. In the fall, the president undertook his most controversial executive actions that sought to address the approximately eleven million illegal immigrants currently living in the United States. The president's actions included improved border security and enforcement, as well as a program that would defer deportations for a specific portion of undocumented immigrants. Republicans accused the president of offering amnesty to all illegal immigrants currently in the country.

The Department of Veterans Affairs (VA) came under fire in April when a whistle-blower brought to light secret waiting lists at the Phoenix VA hospital, which had left hundreds of veterans without much-needed medical assistance and ultimately led to at least eighteen deaths. VA secretary Eric Shinseki ordered an internal audit of all VA facilities, which revealed widespread delays in care. Ultimately, on May 30, Shinseki resigned amid pressure from both parties in Congress for his failure to amend the shortcomings highlighted by the report. His interim successor, Sloan Gibson, told Congress that fixing the current problems at the VA will require hiring 1,500 new doctors and 8,500 new nurses and clinicians and would cost approximately $17.6 billion.

In May, the Federal Communications Commission (FCC) sparked a major debate when it released a Notice of Proposed Rulemaking for network neutrality, the idea that Internet service providers (ISPs) should not block or slow access to certain websites or content. The notice sought to gather public opinion on how best to protect an open Internet. Over the course of four months, the FCC received largely critical reaction, some of which came from telecommunications providers who argued that reclassifying ISPs as a utility would lead to burdensome and unnecessary regulations that would ultimately hurt the service provided to customers. The FCC received around four million comments in response to its proposed regulations.

The shooting of two unarmed black men by white police officers, in separate incidents in Ferguson, Missouri, and Staten Island, New York, brought race relations to the forefront. In both instances, the grand juries opted not to bring charges against the police officers involved in the shootings. This sparked protests across the country and calls for greater accountability for police departments. President Obama called on Attorney General Eric Holder to formulate a plan to open the lines of communication between the police and communities of color. The Department of Justice in December released revised regulations that prohibit officers from using racial profiling in certain federal law enforcement activities.

Following an admission by the CIA in July that it had hacked into Senate Select Committee on Intelligence computers, in December portions of the committee's report on CIA interrogation techniques were released. The report alleged that CIA officials had misled Congress and the White House about the effectiveness of "enhanced interrogation techniques," such as waterboarding, rectal feeding, and long-term isolation, which were being used to gain information from captured terrorists. According to the report, some of these potentially illegal techniques had not been approved or were being used outside the bounds of their original intent, and many failed to produce useful information. The CIA defended its programs, noting that the Senate report did not paint a complete picture.

In December, President Obama announced that he would work with Cuban leader Raúl Castro to normalize relations between the two countries, which had been estranged since the late 1950s. The normalization will include removing sanctions on exports to Cuba, lifting a travel ban for American citizens, and establishing a diplomatic presence in Cuba. The agreement also included the immediate release of two Americans who were detained in Cuba, along with the remaining three members of the Cuban Five. Many Republicans in Congress lashed out at the president's decision, arguing that the agreement gave too much power to a dictatorial state.

U.S. MIDTERM ELECTIONS

Ahead of the November midterm elections, Republicans and Democrats placed a heavy focus on which party could best help the middle class. In October 2014, the Bureau of Economic Analysis released its monthly jobs report, which showed that the September unemployment rate hit 5.9 percent, the lowest level in six years. It declined even further by December to 5.6 percent. However, despite continued job growth, wages had stagnated and the benefits of a growing economy unequally impacted the various classes.

A major upset occurred during primary season, when House minority leader Eric Cantor of Virginia lost to David Brat, a professor at Randolph-Macon College, despite outspending Brat by nearly $2 million. Cantor ultimately resigned his seat before the midterm election. Even after the loss, heading into November, Republicans were expected to retain control of the House of Representatives and potentially gain control of the Senate. Republicans needed a net gain of six seats to take majority control from the Democrats. When the final congressional race was decided on December 6, the Republican Party held all its seats and won nine new ones, including the unseating of incumbent Democrats in Alaska, Arkansas, Colorado, Louisiana, and North Carolina.

Shortly after their victory, Congressional Republicans began outlining some of their strategies for the next Congress, which would begin in January 2015. According to House Speaker John Boehner, R-Ohio, and soon-to-be majority leader Mitch McConnell, R-Ky. this included a vote to repeal the Affordable Care Act, also known as ObamaCare. Republican leadership also noted that they hoped to avoid some of the political brinksmanship that had plagued the past few Congresses and eroded public confidence.

The election, in which spending reached an all-time high of nearly $4 billion, also marked a major victory for the Republican Party in the states, where Republicans won a majority of the governorships and legislatures. Democrats suffered major losses in the historically Democratic states of Illinois, Maryland, and Massachusetts, where Republicans won the gubernatorial races.

Despite the gains made by largely conservative politicians, the electorate was decidedly more liberal in how it voted for the nearly 150 ballot initiatives that appeared in a number of states. These included votes to legalize recreational marijuana use in Alaska, Oregon, and Washington, D.C., and a vote in Washington State to increase background checks on gun purchasers. There were a variety of conservative issues on the ballot as well, which passed primarily in Republican-leaning states. These included a measure in Tennessee to add language to the state constitution that would allow the legislature to make decisions on changing, repealing, or enacting laws on abortion.

U.S. Supreme Court Decisions

The Supreme Court heard a number of polarizing cases during its 2013–2014 term. Perhaps its most impactful case of the year, however, came when the Court decided not to rule on same-sex marriage appeals. This effectively legalized same-sex marriage in a number of states. For the first time, following the Court's inaction, same-sex couples were able to marry in a majority of states.

On April 22, the Supreme Court issued its second major ruling on affirmative action in university admissions in less than a year. In *Schuette v. BAMN*, the Court looked at the constitutionality of a voter-passed Michigan constitutional amendment that prohibited the use of race in school admissions. In four separate opinions, the Court ruled 6–2 that the Michigan law should be upheld in an effort to avoid disempowering voters.

In May, the Court ruled on prayer in city council meetings in the case of *Town of Greece v. Galloway*. In its ruling, the Supreme Court looked specifically at the Establishment Clause of the First Amendment and whether it had been violated when town board meetings were opened with Christian prayers. The divided 5–4 ruling, written by Justice Anthony M. Kennedy, said there was no violation of the Constitution, noting that prayer before government meetings was instilled in the history and tradition of the United States.

Fourth Amendment rights were challenged in the June ruling of *Riley v. California* in which the Court was challenged with addressing search and seizure protections in the digital age. The Court ruled unanimously that police must obtain a warrant before searching the cell phone of someone who has been arrested. The case was considered a huge victory for digital privacy rights.

The issue of union dues was before the Supreme Court in 2014, specifically, whether quasi-government employees in Illinois could be forced to pay union dues for a union of which they choose not to be a full-fledged member. In its June 30 decision in *Harris v. Quinn*, the Court ruled 5–4 that the home care workers in the case could not be forced to pay union dues. The Court did not go as far as to determine whether other groups of public employees could also be forced to pay union dues, but the case left the door open for future litigation.

In 2010, the Supreme Court issued a controversial ruling on campaign finance in *Citizens United v. Federal Election Commission*. That ruling gave corporations and labor unions the ability to spend infinite amounts of money in support of or opposition to candidates for elected office. In April 2014, the Court followed with its ruling in *McCutcheon v. Federal Election Commission*, which eliminated a $123,000 cap on how much an individual can donate in total during one election cycle. The decision left intact the $5,200 limit on how much can be spent by an individual on any one candidate.

On the final day before its summer recess, the Supreme Court handed down its ruling in *Burwell v. Hobby Lobby Stores, Inc. et al.*, its second major decision on the Affordable Care Act of 2010. In this case, Hobby Lobby argued that the requirement for employers to provide contraceptive services violated the religious freedoms of closely held corporations that object to such items on religious grounds. The Court ultimately ruled 5–4 in favor of Hobby Lobby. Writing for the majority, Justice Samuel A. Alito Jr. said that the federal government could not force these corporations to provide coverage for methods of birth control that are in direct violation of the religious beliefs of the company's owner.

Foreign Affairs

Middle East Turmoil

Internationally, the year began with a flurry of activity surrounding the ongoing civil war in Syria. Violence began with the Arab Spring uprising in 2011, and when President Assad refused to resign and instead began cracking down on protests, rebel groups formed and for the past three years have clashed with the state military. The violence has killed tens of thousands and driven millions from their homes. In January and February, the United Nations sponsored two rounds of peace talks aimed at securing a ceasefire between the rebels and supporters of Assad. Despite two weeks of meetings, the more than forty participating countries were unable to negotiate any peace deal. An agenda for a third round of negotiations was drafted, but the talks remain in doubt as rebels continue to demand a transitional government that Assad does not head, while the president refuses to acquiesce to those he deems "terrorists."

In Egypt, another Middle Eastern nation that saw its government thrown into upheaval during Arab Spring, military chief Abdel Fattah el-Sisi won the May presidential election with 97 percent of the vote. His election came on the heels of the approval of a new Egyptian draft constitution. Sisi has consolidated power in the executive and pushed back indefinitely parliamentary elections that were scheduled for March 2015. Sisi's election has been questioned by international observers who note that his opponents have been arrested and prevented from casting a vote. To garner support within Egypt, Sisi has used the media to create a cult of personality that has allowed him to push through unpopular initiatives, including the slashing of oil subsidies.

The long-running tension between Israel and Palestine dragged on into 2014 as the two nations continued peace talks brokered by the United States. Israel criticized Palestine's decision to seek entrance into a variety of international organizations, including the International Criminal Court, as a clear indication of their unwillingness to compromise. Israel ultimately canceled the talks after Hamas and Fatah announced the formation of a Palestinian unity government in April. In June, three Israeli teenagers were kidnapped and murdered in the West Bank by a Hamas operative in what the UN classified as a war crime. In response, the Israeli military launched a seven-week assault, which led to rocket attacks by militants. In August, Egyptian mediators were able to secure a permanent ceasefire, but prospects for renewed negotiations on a final peace agreement between Israel and Palestine remain dim.

The nuclear talks between China, France, Germany, Russia, the United Kingdom, United States, and Iran continued into 2014 beginning with a three-day meeting in Vienna. The group set a July deadline for a final agreement to be reached with Iran that would limit its nuclear capabilities to only nonmilitary production, likely in exchange for a reduction in sanctions. Negotiators made some progress, but because of the ongoing disagreement between the two sides, the deadline was initially extended into November, and then again to June 30, 2015.

Human Rights Violations in North Korea

In February, the United Nations (UN) released an extensive report on "systematic, widespread and gross human rights violations" occurring in North Korea. The report, which was written with the assistance of confidential interviews with victims, details the crimes against humanity committed by the secretive state including "extermination, murder, enslavement, torture, imprisonment, rape, forced abortions and other sexual violence, persecution on political, religious, racial and gender grounds, the forcible transfer of populations, the enforced disappearance of persons, and the inhumane act of knowingly causing prolonged starvation." The report recommended that the UN Security Council refer North Korea to the International Criminal Court. The government of Kim Jong Un rejected the report's findings, calling it an attempt by the United States to further undermine and isolate the regime. North Korea released its own human rights report, noting the many freedoms instilled in the nation's constitution, and denying allegations in the UN report. When it appeared in October that the United Nations might take action related to the report, North Korea somewhat softened its stance, reopened high-level talks with South Korea, gave a rare briefing before the United Nations, released three American detainees, and opened the possibility of the UN's special rapporteur on human rights visiting North Korea and conducting a new investigation.

Terrorism in Africa

In April, the terrorist organization Boko Haram kidnapped more than 200 teenage girls from a school in northeastern Nigeria. The Islamic jihadist group's rise has displaced more than one million Nigerians and resulted in thousands of deaths. Citizens around the world called on the government of Goodluck Jonathan to act aggressively to secure the release of the schoolgirls. By the close of 2014, the girls had not been released, despite an agreement reached between the Nigerian army and Boko Haram. In December, the Taliban staged its own school attack when it entered a school for children of Pakistani military members and indiscriminately killed 132 students. This marked the worst attack carried out by the Taliban in Pakistan.

Political, Economic Challenges in Europe

In September, Scottish citizens went to the polls to vote on a referendum to make Scotland independent of the United Kingdom. Supporters of the measure argued that such a move would be financially beneficial for Scotland because it would be able to retain all the revenue from its offshore oil reserves. Opponents said devolution would hurt the country because oil revenue was steadily declining and it would need to seek entry into a variety of international organizations, such as the European Union. Ultimately, voters decided to remain a part of the United Kingdom, but Scottish leaders did secure some additional powers for Scotland, such as taxation and borrowing.

The European economy continued to struggle throughout 2014, and economic indicators released for the second quarter of the year showed slower than expected growth, some of which was caused by the ongoing tension along the Russia-Ukraine border in response to Crimea's decision to break away from Ukraine. The International Monetary Fund encouraged eurozone nations to take a new approach to recovery and focus on growth-promoting investments rather than austerity policies. Much of the debate over improving finances revolved around heavily indebted Greece, where the standing government lost a vote of confidence in December, which led to new elections.

Global Issues

Countries around the world came together to fight the Ebola virus as it spread across West Africa and ultimately into other nations including the United States and Spain. The outbreak that began in December 2013 was considered the deadliest since the virus was first discovered. The virus heavily impacted Guinea, Liberia, Mali, Nigeria, and Sierra Leone, and resulted in an estimated 10,000 deaths by early 2015. One person died from the disease in the United States after traveling from Liberia; two nurses also became infected but recovered.

The U.S.-led coalition combat mission in Afghanistan quietly came to an end in December 2014. Thousands of troops, many of them American, will remain in the country through 2016 as part of the Bilateral Security Agreement signed by U.S. and Afghan leaders. These troops will be responsible for training Afghan troops and assisting in counterintelligence measures.

Economically, one of the largest issues of 2014 was falling oil prices. The price of oil had hovered around $100 per barrel since 2010, but rapidly declined through the second half of 2014, down to $60 per barrel by December. The drop in prices was largely due to decreased demand following the global economic recession and greater attempts to reduce oil consumption in favor of more environmentally friendly fuels in a number of nations. Increased oil exploration in North America also contributed to the global oversupply. The Organization of the Petroleum Exporting Countries (OPEC) failed to take action to raise prices, largely because Saudi Arabia, a leading oil producer, feared that if it cut back production it would lose market share and struggle once the market picked up. Falling prices positively impacted consumers, but for oil producing giants such as Iran, Russia, and Venezuela declining revenue strained budgets.

TENSION RISES BETWEEN RUSSIA AND UKRAINE

In late 2013, under heavy pressure from Russia, Ukrainian president Viktor Yanukovych decided not to sign a free trade agreement with the European Union. The move, which was thought to be a first step toward eventual inclusion in the European Union, sparked months of protests between those who supported closer ties with the European Union and those who preferred to remain close to Russia. By mid-February, Yanukovych fled the country and was subsequently impeached. He was temporarily replaced by pro-European leader Oleksandr Turchynov. On May 24, Ukrainians elected a new leader, pro-Western former foreign affairs minister Petro Poroshenko.

In Crimea, the Ukrainian peninsula where Russia maintains a strategic military base, pro-Russian protests began following the February impeachment, and Russia reportedly sent additional troops into the region in violation of standing agreements. The peninsula's parliament voted to dissolve its local government and called a referendum on autonomy on March 16. Voters overwhelmingly approved the resolution in favor of breaking away from Ukraine and becoming part of Russia.

Russia considered the vote to be in accordance with international law and therefore signed a treaty with Crimea to outline how the peninsula, which is geographically separated from Russia, would be assimilated. Tensions between the two nations escalated, and Russian troops began moving into Eastern Ukraine, something Russian leaders fiercely denied despite photographic evidence that those involved in the fighting were wearing Russian uniforms. Russia and Ukraine agreed to a ceasefire on April 17, but fighting quickly resumed five days later when Ukraine accused Russia of violating the agreement. The situation grew direr in July when a passenger plane with 298 onboard was shot down over eastern Ukraine, reportedly by pro-Russian separatists using a weapon supplied by the Russian government. Another ceasefire followed in September, but after Russia supported new referendums in Eastern Ukraine for additional breakaway states, Russia again began building up its troops along the shared border.

The United States and European Union immediately sanctioned Russia following the annexation. In June, the Group of 8 refused to allow Russia to join its annual meeting of world leaders, and the member nations imposed a new round of travel and financial sanctions on President Vladimir Putin's government. The United States, European Union, and other nations added a third round of sanctions in September, and, in December, Congress quietly approved more sanctions and also authorized arms sales to Ukraine. Russia imposed its own sanctions on the United States and European Union in response, including banning the import of fruits and vegetables, a costly blow to EU nations. The mounting sanctions hurt the already weakened Russian economy, where, combined with falling oil prices, the country's currency lost nearly a fifth of its value by the end of the year.

ISIL Militants

Perhaps one of the biggest international challenges in 2014 was how to stop the rise of the militant group known as ISIL—the group is alternately referred to as the Islamic State of Iraq and Syria, or ISIS, and the Islamic State, or IS. The radical wing of al Qaeda began gaining power in 2013 in Syria, taking advantage of the weakened state to find supporters. It slowly moved into Iraq, where in 2014 it captured a number of strategically important cities including Fallujah, Mosul, and Ramadi. The Iraqi government struggled to respond and encouraged tribal leaders to take up arms to fight back. In Ramadi, this effort paid off. However, in Fallujah and Mosul, ISIL fighters, who number less than 3,000, were joined by sleeper cells and other insurgent groups who helped easily overrun Iraqi military units numbering in the tens of thousands.

The United States, which has an interest in fighting terrorism in the region, was cautious in its response because it did not want to re-involve itself in another ground war after officially ending its Iraq combat mission in 2011. Early in 2014, the United States served mainly in a support capacity, providing training and strategic assistance to the Iraqi military. The country also provided helicopters, missiles, and surveillance vehicles. In a televised address to the nation in August, President Obama announced that he had authorized airstrikes against ISIL militants in an effort to protect U.S. interests in Iraq. In September, the president approved nonmilitary actions including humanitarian assistance, sending 475 support troops to Iraq, and providing intelligence capabilities to stop the movement of militants across the region. Congress provided additional funds to help combat ISIL in December as part of its defense reauthorization.

The UN raised the alarm throughout the year that ISIL's rise was intensifying the refugee crisis in the region as more Iraqis and Syrians fled the violence. Many of these refugees fled to Mount Sinjar in Kurdistan, where they became trapped and dependent on American-led rescue missions. Others crossed the border into Turkey, where the government was struggling to keep up with the volume of refugees from Syria's civil war and had already invested billions into social services for its refugee population. The United Nations made a number of pleas to the international community to support the countries that were housing refugees.

—Heather Kerrigan

January

State of the Union Address and Republican Response

JANUARY 28, 2014

In his sixth State of the Union address, President Barack Obama chose the theme of "opportunity for all," reiterating a number of earlier proposals including increasing funding for Pre-K and higher education, raising the minimum wage, and ending the continuing disparity between economic classes. The president struck an individualistic tone, stating a number of times that he would use his executive power if Congress continued to fail to take action in a number of areas. It was likely that both parties in Congress would tread lightly throughout the year, with the impending November midterm elections. Still, President Obama said that 2014 should be "a year of action," adding, "that's what most Americans want, for all of us in this chamber to focus on their lives, their hopes, their aspirations."

Promoting Higher Education

President Obama covered a number of domestic affairs over the course of his sixty-five-minute speech, focusing primarily on how to grow the middle class. He allocated a significant amount of attention to education, both at the preschool and college levels. The president said that finding a way to get more young people into colleges and universities is key to helping impoverished youth climb into the middle class. Community colleges are especially important for this segment of the population, but many are struggling in light of significantly reduced state funding. In California, for example, community colleges across the state are turning away students. The president vowed to work with businesses to create more job training programs to make up for these cuts.

Obama also said he wanted to make "high-quality pre-K available to every 4-year-old." Last year, the president proposed adding $75 billion to the federal budget to expand pre-school programs, most of which would be covered by increased cigarette taxes. Despite the growing disparity in early education programs for lower- and middle-class families, analysts said Congress would be unlikely to take up an issue like this, which would increase spending during a midterm election year. With this knowledge, the president again promised to use the authority available to him to "pull together a coalition of elected officials, business leaders and philanthropists willing to help more kids access the high-quality pre-K they need."

Health Care and Immigration

Despite the president's overall victory with Congress and the courts in preserving most aspects of the Affordable Care Act (ACA), Obama devoted only a few sentences in his State of the Union to his landmark piece of legislation. He encouraged Republicans, after rounds of failed legislation and Supreme Court cases, to stop trying to repeal the bill and instead focus on the positive effects, including the "nine million." Americans who signed up for Medicaid or private coverage on the HealthCare.gov website. He added that many of those who signed up would have previously been unable to afford care or denied because of a preexisting condition.

Immigration, another contentious issue on which the president has attempted to make progress, also received little mention. The president did not endorse any of the proposals made by Congress regarding how to handle the estimated eleven million unauthorized immigrants currently in the United States, but instead simply called on Congress to act. "When people come here to fulfill their dreams—to study, invent, and contribute to our culture—they make our country a more attractive place for businesses to locate and create jobs for everybody. So let's get immigration reform done this year," the president said. Political analysts suggested that this was intended to provide Republicans room to negotiate a possible solution within their own party. In the summer of 2014, Speaker of the House John Boehner , R-Ohio, told the president that his chamber would not consider the issue because he was not confident that the president could uphold the current immigration laws. Obama responded by issuing an executive order in November that expanded the deferred deportation action program for children of illegal immigrants and their parents, a move that was viewed by his opponents as akin to granting permanent amnesty. By the end of the year, Congress had yet to take any action on immigration.

Improving the Economy

Similar to the proposal made during his 2013 address, Obama also called on Congress to pass a law to raise the minimum wage for all workers. But knowing that the legislative body would be unlikely to act, he stated, "To every mayor, Governor, State legislator in America, I say; You don't have to wait for Congress to act; Americans will support you if you take this on. And as a chief executive, I intend to lead by example." As such, the president's primary proposal with regard to the economy, which he presented during his State of the Union address, was raising the minimum wage nationally. The president said that he would issue an executive order in the coming days to raise the minimum wage to $10.10 for all federal contract workers. "If you cook our troops' meals or wash their dishes, you should not have to live in poverty," Obama said. Congress did not take action in 2014 on raising the minimum wage for all workers, but some states, such as Connecticut, Hawaii, Minnesota, and West Virginia, took action themselves to raise the minimum wage for those working within their borders.

Republicans were highly critical of the president's proposal, arguing that it would stifle job creation by hurting businesses. Before the president's speech, Boehner, a former small business owner, said, "When you raise the cost of something, you get less of it." He added that because the president's executive order would only apply to future federal contracts, it would have no immediate impact. "Let's understand something: This affects not one current contract," the Speaker said, adding, "I think the question is, how many people, Mr. President, will this executive action actually help? I suspect the answer is somewhere close to zero."

National Security and Diplomacy

Regarding foreign affairs, Obama asked for Congress to give diplomats room to maneuver, especially in nations like Iran, before speaking about or seeking a stronger response. "We must give diplomacy a chance to succeed," the president said. He added that he would veto a sanctions bill against Iran currently backed by fifty-nine lawmakers because he felt that it would derail denuclearization talks. But Obama said that if the diplomatic method failed he would impose sanctions and pursue other options to stop Iran from expanding its nuclear program. "If Iran's leaders do not seize this opportunity, then I will be the first to call for more sanctions," Obama said. Following the president's speech, Republicans noted that they don't disagree with the diplomacy route, but they do disagree with Obama's decision to lift economic sanctions already in place against Iran to secure the talks.

When the president was first elected in 2008, he promised to bring an end to the war in Afghanistan. And during his 2014 State of the Union, he was able to announce that "America's longest war will finally be over" by the end of 2014 when all combat forces come home. The president promised to keep "a small force" of troops on the ground as long as the Afghan government agrees to the Bilateral Security Agreement, which Afghan president Hamid Karzai has not yet signed despite the months that went into reaching the agreement. The president did not give any indication of how large or small the force might be, but White House officials said it would be less than 10,000. These troops would be responsible for training security forces and providing counter-terrorism assistance in combatting al Qaeda. And with the war in Afghanistan drawing to a close, the president asked Congress to lift "the remaining restrictions on detainee transfers" and "close the prison at Guantánamo Bay." The prison only holds around 150 prisoners, but the president said we must "counter terrorism not just through intelligence and military actions, but by remaining true to our constitutional ideals and setting an example for the rest of the world."

Obama defended his continuing use of drones to fight terrorists. He said these unmanned vehicles allow the United States to "fight the battles that need to be fought" while avoiding "large-scale deployments that drain our strength and may ultimately feed extremism." The president also added that the decision to strike using drones is not taken lightly and has been done with strict limits. "We will not be safer if people abroad believe we strike within their countries without regard for the consequences," he said.

Multiple Republican Responses

Rep. Cathy McMorris Rodgers, R-Wash., the highest ranking Republican female in the House of Representatives, was chosen by her party's leaders to give the official response to the State of the Union. Like Obama, she also focused on how to grow the middle class, but said that "the president's policies are making people's lives harder. Republicans have plans to close the gap." She held that the problem in the nation is not that of growing income inequality, but rather "opportunity inequality." She said that the Republican Party has "plans that focus on jobs first without more spending, government bailouts, and red tape." Without offering any specific proposals, Rodgers added that Republicans had solutions to help Americans save more of their money "through lower taxes, cheaper energy costs, and affordable health care."

Rodgers also spoke about the ACA and said that despite the president's appeal, Republicans would continue to fight to roll back the law. However, she said, it was not the intent of the Republican Party to entirely eliminate health care for the underserved individuals who have enrolled through the ACA. "No, we shouldn't go back to the way things were, but this law is not working," she said. Instead, "Republicans believe health care choices should be yours, not the government's."

Signaling the divide within the Republican party, three other responses were offered—one by Rep. Ileana Ros-Lehtinen of Florida who delivered most of Rodgers's address in Spanish; another by Sen. Mike Lee of Utah, who gave the response for the Tea Party Express; and a social media response by Sen. Rand Paul, R-Ky. Lee and Paul gave the most strongly worded responses to the president's address. Both focused primarily on economic issues, with Lee asking Republicans to develop a "conservative reform agenda" on federal spending, taxes, and regulatory policy. "We are facing an inequality crisis, one to which the president has paid lip service but seems uninterested in truly confronting," Lee said. Paul's ten-minute prerecorded speech called for a better antipoverty program. Paul said that "the ticket to the middle class is not higher taxes on the very businesses that must create jobs," adding that the economy would grow only when taxes are lowered for everyone.

The number of responses could be a reflection of how Republicans feel about their leaders. According to a *Washington Post-ABC News* poll taken shortly before the president's address, only 36 percent of Republicans polled were confident that their Congressional leaders will make the right decisions, while 63 percent are not confident.

—Heather Kerrigan

Following is the full text of the State of the Union Address delivered by President Barack Obama, and the Republican response given by Rep. Cathy McMorris Rodgers, R-Wash., both on January 28, 2014.

President Obama Delivers the State of the Union Address

January 28, 2014

Mr. Speaker, Mr. Vice President, Members of Congress, my fellow Americans: Today in America, a teacher spent extra time with a student who needed it and did her part to lift America's graduation rate to its highest levels in more than three decades. An entrepreneur flipped on the lights in her tech startup and did her part to add to the more than 8 million new jobs our businesses have created over the past 4 years. An autoworker fine-tuned some of the best, most fuel-efficient cars in the world and did his part to help America wean itself off foreign oil.

A farmer prepared for the spring after the strongest 5-year stretch of farm exports in our history. A rural doctor gave a young child the first prescription to treat asthma that his mother could afford. A man took the bus home from the graveyard shift, bone-tired, but dreaming big dreams for his son. And in tight-knit communities all across America, fathers and mothers will tuck in their kids, put an arm around their spouse, remember fallen comrades, and give thanks for being home from a war that after 12 long years is finally coming to an end.

Tonight this Chamber speaks with one voice to the people we represent: It is you, our citizens, who make the state of our Union strong.

And here are the results of your efforts: the lowest unemployment rate in over 5 years; a rebounding housing market; a manufacturing sector that's adding jobs for the first time since the 1990s; more oil produced at home than we buy from the rest of the world, the first time that's happened in nearly 20 years; our deficits cut by more than half. And for the first time in over a decade, business leaders around the world have declared that China is no longer the world's number-one place to invest, America is.

That's why I believe this can be a breakthrough year for America. After 5 years of grit and determined effort, the United States is better positioned for the 21st century than any other nation on Earth.

The question for everyone in this Chamber, running through every decision we make this year, is whether we are going to help or hinder this progress. For several years now, this town has been consumed by a rancorous argument over the proper size of the Federal Government. It's an important debate, one that dates back to our very founding. But when that debate prevents us from carrying out even the most basic functions of our democracy—when our differences shut down Government or threaten the full faith and credit of the United States—then we are not doing right by the American people.

Now, as President, I'm committed to making Washington work better and rebuilding the trust of the people who sent us here. And I believe most of you are too. Last month, thanks to the work of Democrats and Republicans, Congress finally produced a budget that undoes some of last year's severe cuts to priorities like education. Nobody got everything they wanted, and we can still do more to invest in this country's future while bringing down our deficit in a balanced way, but the budget compromise should leave us freer to focus on creating new jobs, not creating new crises.

And in the coming months, let's see where else we can make progress together. Let's make this a year of action. That's what most Americans want: for all of us in this Chamber to focus on their lives, their hopes, their aspirations. And what I believe unites the people of this Nation—regardless of race or region or party, young or old, rich or poor—is the simple, profound belief in opportunity for all: the notion that if you work hard and take responsibility, you can get ahead in America.

Now, let's face it, that belief has suffered some serious blows. Over more than three decades, even before the great recession hit, massive shifts in technology and global competition had eliminated a lot of good, middle class jobs and weakened the economic foundations that families depend on.

Today, after 4 years of economic growth, corporate profits and stock prices have rarely been higher, and those at the top have never done better. But average wages have barely budged. Inequality has deepened. Upward mobility has stalled. The cold, hard fact is that even in the midst of recovery, too many Americans are working more than ever just to get by, let alone to get ahead. And too many still aren't working at all.

So our job is to reverse these trends. It won't happen right away, and we won't agree on everything. But what I offer tonight is a set of concrete, practical proposals to speed up growth, strengthen the middle class, and build new ladders of opportunity into the middle class. Some require congressional action, and I am eager to work with all of you. But America does not stand still, and neither will I. So wherever and whenever I can take steps without legislation to expand opportunity for more American families, that's what I'm going to do.

As usual, our First Lady sets a good example. [Applause] Well—[applause]. Michelle's "Let's Move!" partnership with schools, businesses, local leaders has helped bring down childhood obesity rates for the first time in 30 years. And that's an achievement that will improve lives and reduce health care costs for decades to come. The Joining Forces alliance that Michelle and Jill Biden launched has already encouraged employers to hire or train nearly 400,000 veterans and military spouses.

Taking a page from that playbook, the White House just organized a College Opportunity Summit, where already, 150 universities, businesses, nonprofits have made concrete commitments to reduce inequality in access to higher education and to help every hard-working kid go to college and succeed when they get to campus. And across the country, we're partnering with mayors, Governors, and State legislatures on issues from homelessness to marriage equality.

The point is, there are millions of Americans outside of Washington who are tired of stale political arguments and are moving this country forward. They believe—and I believe—that here in America, our success should depend not on accident of birth, but the strength of our work ethic and the scope of our dreams. That's what drew our forebears here. That's how the daughter of a factory worker is CEO of America's largest automaker; how the son of a barkeep is Speaker of the House; how the son of a single mom can be President of the greatest nation on Earth.

Opportunity is who we are. And the defining project of our generation must be to restore that promise. We know where to start: The best measure of opportunity is access to a good job. With the economy picking up speed, companies say they intend to hire more people this year. And over half of big manufacturers say they're thinking of insourcing jobs from abroad.

So let's make that decision easier for more companies. Both Democrats and Republicans have argued that our Tax Code is riddled with wasteful, complicated loopholes that punish businesses investing here and reward companies that keep profits abroad. Let's flip that equation. Let's work together to close those loopholes, end those incentives to ship jobs overseas, and lower tax rates for businesses that create jobs right here at home.

Moreover, we can take the money we save from this transition to tax reform to create jobs rebuilding our roads, upgrading our ports, unclogging our commutes, because in today's global economy, first-class jobs gravitate to first-class infrastructure. We'll need Congress to protect more than 3 million jobs by finishing transportation and waterways bills this summer. That can happen. But I'll act on my own to slash bureaucracy and streamline the permitting process for key projects so we can get more construction workers on the job as fast as possible.

We also have the chance, right now, to beat other countries in the race for the next wave of high-tech manufacturing jobs. My administration has launched two hubs for high-tech manufacturing in Raleigh, North Carolina, and Youngstown, Ohio, where we've connected businesses to research universities that can help America lead the world in advanced technologies. Tonight I'm announcing, we'll launch six more this year. Bipartisan bills in both Houses could double the number of these hubs and the jobs they create. So get those bills to my desk. Put more Americans back to work.

Let's do more to help the entrepreneurs and small-business owners who create most new jobs in America. Over the past 5 years, my administration has made more loans to small-business owners than any other. And when 98 percent of our exporters are small businesses, new trade partnerships with Europe and Asia—the Asia-Pacific will help them create more jobs. We need to work together on tools like bipartisan trade promotion authority to protect our workers, protect our environment, and open new markets to new goods stamped "Made in the U.S.A."

Listen, China and Europe aren't standing on the sidelines, and neither should we. We know that the nation that goes all-in on innovation today will own the global economy tomorrow. This is an edge America cannot surrender. Federally funded research helped lead to the ideas and inventions behind Google and smartphones. And that's why Congress should undo the damage done by last year's cuts to basic research so we can unleash the next great American discovery.

There are entire industries to be built based on vaccines that stay ahead of drug-resistant bacteria or paper-thin material that's stronger than steel. And let's pass a patent reform bill that allows our businesses to stay focused on innovation, not costly and needless litigation.

Now, one of the biggest factors in bringing more jobs back is our commitment to American energy. The all-of-the-above energy strategy I announced a few years ago is working, and today, America is closer to energy independence than we have been in decades.

One of the reasons why is natural gas. If extracted safely, it's the bridge fuel that can power our economy with less of the carbon pollution that causes climate change. Businesses plan to invest almost $100 billion in new factories that use natural gas. I'll cut redtape to help States get those factories built and put folks to work, and this Congress can help by putting people to work building fueling stations that shift more cars and trucks from foreign oil to American natural gas.

Meanwhile, my administration will keep working with the industry to sustain production and jobs growth while strengthening protection of our air, our water, our communities. And while we're at it, I'll use my authority to protect more of our pristine Federal lands for future generations.

Well, it's not just oil and natural gas production that's booming, we're becoming a global leader in solar too. Every 4 minutes, another American home or business goes solar, every panel pounded into place by a worker whose job cannot be outsourced. Let's continue that progress with a smarter tax policy that stops giving $4 billion a year to fossil fuel industries that don't need it so we can invest more in fuels of the future that do.

And even as we've increased energy production, we've partnered with businesses, builders, and local communities to reduce the energy we consume. When we rescued our automakers, for example, we worked with them to set higher fuel efficiency standards for our cars. In the coming months, I'll build on that success by setting new standards for our trucks so we can keep driving down oil imports and what we pay at the pump.

And taken together, our energy policy is creating jobs and leading to a cleaner, safer planet. Over the past 8 years, the United States has reduced our total carbon pollution more than any other nation on Earth. But we have to act with more urgency, because a changing climate is already harming Western communities struggling with drought and coastal cities dealing with floods. That's why I directed my administration to work with States, utilities, and others to set new standards on the amount of carbon pollution our power plants are allowed to dump into the air.

The shift to a cleaner energy economy won't happen overnight, and it will require some tough choices along the way. But the debate is settled. Climate change is a fact. And when our children's children look us in the eye and ask if we did all we could to leave them a safer, more stable world, with new sources of energy, I want us to be able to say, yes, we did.

Finally, if we're serious about economic growth, it is time to heed the call of business leaders, labor leaders, faith leaders, law enforcement and fix our broken immigration system. Republicans and Democrats in the Senate have acted, and I know that members of both parties in the House want to do the same. Independent economists say immigration reform will grow our economy and shrink our deficits by almost $1 trillion in the next two decades. And for good reason: When people come here to fulfill their dreams— to study, invent, contribute to our culture—they make our country a more attractive place for businesses to locate and create jobs for everybody. So let's get immigration reform done this year. [Applause] Let's get it done. It's time.

The ideas I've outlined so far can speed up growth and create more jobs. But in this rapidly changing economy, we have to make sure that every American has the skills to fill those jobs. The good news is, we know how to do it.

Two years ago, as the auto industry came roaring back, Andra Rush opened up a manufacturing firm in Detroit. She knew that Ford needed parts for the best selling truck in America, and she knew how to make those parts. She just needed the workforce. So she dialed up what we call an American Job Center, places where folks can walk in to get the help or training they need to find a new job or a better job. She was flooded with new workers. And today, Detroit Manufacturing Systems has more than 700 employees. And what Andra and her employees experienced is how it should be for every employer and every job seeker.

So tonight I've asked Vice President Biden to lead an across-the-board reform of America's training programs to make sure they have one mission: train Americans with the skills employers need and match them to good jobs that need to be filled right now.

That means more on-the-job training and more apprenticeships that set a young worker on an upward trajectory for life. It means connecting companies to community colleges that can help design training to fill their specific needs. And if Congress wants to help, you can concentrate funding on proven programs that connect more ready-to-work Americans with ready-to-be-filled jobs.

I'm also convinced we can help Americans return to the workforce faster by reforming unemployment insurance so that it's more effective in today's economy. But first, this Congress needs to restore the unemployment insurance you just let expire for 1.6 million people.

Let me tell you why. Misty DeMars is a mother of two young boys. She'd been steadily employed since she was a teenager, put herself through college. She'd never collected unemployment benefits, but she'd been paying taxes. In May, she and her husband used their life savings to buy their first home. A week later, budget cuts claimed the job she loved. Last month, when their unemployment insurance was cut off, she sat down and wrote me a letter, the kind I get every day. "We are the face of the unemployment crisis," she wrote. "I'm not dependent on the government. Our country depends on people like us who build careers, contribute to society, care about our neighbors. I'm confident that in time, I will find a job, I will pay my taxes, and we will raise our children in their own home in the community we love. Please give us this chance."

Congress, give these hard-working, responsible Americans that chance. Give them that chance. [Applause] Give them the chance. They need our help right now. But more important, this country needs them in the game. That's why I've been asking CEOs to give more long-term unemployed workers a fair shot at new jobs, a new chance to support their families. And in fact, this week, many will come to the White House to make that commitment real. Tonight I ask every business leader in America to join us and to do the same, because we are stronger when America fields a full team.

Of course, it's not enough to train today's workforce. We also have to prepare tomorrow's workforce, by guaranteeing every child access to a world-class education. Estiven Rodriguez couldn't speak a word of English when he moved to New York City at age 9. But last month, thanks to the support of great teachers and an innovative tutoring program, he led a march of his classmates through a crowd of cheering parents and neighbors from their high school to the post office, where they mailed off their college applications. And this son of a factory worker just found out, he's going to college this fall.

Five years ago, we set out to change the odds for all our kids. We worked with lenders to reform student loans, and today, more young people are earning college degrees than ever before. Race to the Top, with the help of Governors from both parties, has helped States raise expectations and performance. Teachers and principals in schools from Tennessee to Washington, DC, are making big strides in preparing students with the skills for the new economy: problem solving, critical thinking, science, technology, engineering, math.

Now, some of this change is hard. It requires everything from more challenging curriculums and more demanding parents to better support for teachers and new ways to measure how well our kids think, not how well they can fill in a bubble on a test. But it is worth it, and it is working. The problem is, we're still not reaching enough kids, and we're not reaching them in time. And that has to change.

Research shows that one of the best investments we can make in a child's life is high-quality early education. Last year, I asked this Congress to help States make high-quality pre-K available to every 4-year-old. And as a parent as well as a President, I repeat that request tonight. But in the meantime, 30 States have raised pre-K funding on their own. They know we can't wait. So just as we worked with States to reform our schools, this year, we'll invest in new partnerships with States and communities across the country in a Race to the Top for our youngest children. And as Congress decides what it's going to do, I'm going to pull together a coalition of elected officials, business leaders, and philanthropists willing to help more kids access the high-quality pre-K that they need. It is right for America. We need to get this done.

Last year, I also pledged to connect 99 percent of our students to high-speed broadband over the next 4 years. Tonight I can announce that with the support of the FCC and companies like Apple, Microsoft, Sprint, and Verizon, we've got a down payment to start connecting more than 15,000 schools and 20 million students over the next 2 years, without adding a dime to the deficit.

We're working to redesign high schools and partner them with colleges and employers that offer the real-world education and hands-on training that can lead directly to a job and career. We're shaking up our system of higher education to give parents more information and colleges more incentive to offer better value so that no middle class kid is priced out of a college education.

We're offering millions the opportunity to cap their monthly student loan payments to 10 percent of their income, and I want to work with Congress to see how we can help even more Americans who feel trapped by student loan debt. And I'm reaching out to some of America's leading foundations and corporations on a new initiative to help more young men of color facing especially tough odds to stay on track and reach their full potential.

The bottom line is, Michelle and I want every child to have the same chance this country gave us. But we know our opportunity agenda won't be complete, and too many young people entering the workforce today will see the American Dream as an empty promise, unless we also do more to make sure our economy honors the dignity of work and hard work pays off for every single American.

Today, women make up about half our workforce, but they still make 77 cents for every dollar a man earns. That is wrong, and in 2014, it's an embarrassment. Women deserve equal pay for equal work. She deserves to have a baby without sacrificing her job. A mother deserves a day off to care for a sick child or a sick parent without running into hardship. And you know what, a father does too. It is time to do away with workplace policies that belong in a "Mad Men" episode. [Laughter] This year, let's all come together—Congress, the White House, businesses from Wall Street to Main Street—to give every woman the opportunity she deserves. Because I believe when women succeed, America succeeds.

Now, women hold a majority of lower wage jobs, but they're not the only ones stifled by stagnant wages. Americans understand that some people will earn more money than others, and we don't resent those who, by virtue of their efforts, achieve incredible success. That's what America is all about. But Americans overwhelmingly agree that no one who works full-time should ever have to raise a family in poverty.

In the year since I asked this Congress to raise the minimum wage, five States have passed laws to raise theirs. Many businesses have done it on their own. Nick Chute is here today with his boss, John Soranno. John's an owner of Punch Pizza in Minneapolis, and Nick helps make the dough. [Laughter] Only now he makes more of it. [Laughter] John just gave his employees a raise to 10 bucks an hour, and that's a decision that has eased their financial stress and boosted their morale.

Tonight I ask more of America's business leaders to follow John's lead: Do what you can to raise your employees' wages. It's good for the economy. It's good for America. To every mayor, Governor, State legislator in America, I say: You don't have to wait for Congress to act; Americans will support you if you take this on.

And as a chief executive, I intend to lead by example. Profitable corporations like Costco see higher wages as the smart way to boost productivity and reduce turnover. We should too. In the coming weeks, I will issue an Executive order requiring Federal contractors to pay their federally funded employees a fair wage of at least 10 dollars and 10 cents an hour. Because if you cook our troops' meals or wash their dishes, you should not have to live in poverty.

Of course, to reach millions more, Congress does need to get on board. Today, the Federal minimum wage is worth about 20 percent less than it was when Ronald Reagan first stood here. And Tom Harkin and George Miller have a bill to fix that by lifting the minimum wage to 10 dollars and 10 cents. It's easy to remember: 10–10. This will help families. It will give businesses customers with more money to spend. It does not involve any new bureaucratic program. So join the rest of the country. Say yes. Give America a raise. Give them a raise.

There are other steps we can take to help families make ends meet, and few are more effective at reducing inequality and helping families pull themselves up through hard work than the earned-income tax credit. Right now it helps about half of all parents at some point. Think about that: It helps about half of all parents in America at some point in their lives. But I agree with Republicans like Senator Rubio that it doesn't do enough for single workers who don't have kids. So let's work together to strengthen the credit, reward work, help more Americans get ahead.

Let's do more to help Americans save for retirement. Today, most workers don't have a pension. A Social Security check often isn't enough on its own. And while the stock market has doubled over the last 5 years, that doesn't help folks who don't have 401(k)s. That's why, tomorrow, I will direct the Treasury to create a new way for working Americans to start their own retirement savings: MyI—MyRA.

It's a new savings bond that encourages folks to build a nest egg. MyRA guarantees a decent return with no risk of losing what you put in. And if this Congress wants to help, work with me to fix an upside-down Tax Code that gives big tax breaks to help the wealthy save, but does little or nothing for middle class Americans. Offer every American access to an automatic IRA on the job so they can save at work just like everybody in this Chamber can.

And since the most important investment many families make is their home, send me legislation that protects taxpayers from footing the bill for a housing crisis ever again and keeps the dream of home ownership alive for future generations.

One last point on financial security: For decades, few things exposed hard-working families to economic hardship more than a broken health care system. And in case you haven't heard, we're in the process of fixing that. Now, a preexisting condition used to mean that someone like Amanda Shelley, a physician's assistant and single mom from Arizona, couldn't get health insurance. But on January 1, she got covered. On January 3, she felt a sharp pain. On January 6, she had emergency surgery. Just one week earlier, Amanda said, and that surgery would have meant bankruptcy.

That's what health insurance reform is all about: the peace of mind that if misfortune strikes, you don't have to lose everything. Already, because of the Affordable Care Act, more than 3 million Americans under age 26 have gained coverage under their parent's plan. More than 9 million Americans have signed up for private health insurance or Medicaid coverage. Nine million.

And here's another number: zero. Because of this law, no American—none, zero—can ever again be dropped or denied coverage for a preexisting condition like asthma or back pain or cancer. No woman can ever be charged more just because she's a woman. And we did all this while adding years to Medicare's finances, keeping Medicare premiums flat, and lowering prescription costs for millions of seniors.

Now, I do not expect to convince my Republican friends on the merits of this law. [Laughter] But I know that the American people are not interested in refighting old battles. So again, if you have specific plans to cut costs, cover more people, increase choice, tell America what you'd do differently. Let's see if the numbers add up. But let's not have another 40-something votes to repeal a law that's already helping millions of Americans like Amanda. The first 40 were plenty. [Laughter]

We all owe it to the American people to say what we're for, not just what we're against. And if you want to know the real impact this law is having, just talk to Governor Steve Beshear of Kentucky, who's here tonight. Now, Kentucky is not the most liberal part of the country. That's not where I got my highest vote totals. [Laughter] But he's like a man possessed when it comes to covering his Commonwealth's families. They're our neighbors and our friends, he said: "They're people we shop and go to church with, farmers out on the tractor, grocery clerks. They're people who go to work every morning praying they don't get sick. No one deserves to live that way."

Steve's right. That's why tonight I ask every American who knows someone without health insurance to help them get covered by March 31. [Applause] Help them get covered. Moms, get on your kids to sign up. Kids, call your mom and walk her through the application. It will give her some peace of mind, and plus, she'll appreciate hearing from you. [Laughter]

After all, that's the spirit that has always moved this Nation forward. It's the spirit of citizenship, the recognition that through hard work and responsibility, we can pursue our individual dreams, but still come together as one American family to make sure the next generation can pursue its dreams as well.

Citizenship means standing up for everyone's right to vote. Last year, part of the Voting Rights Act was weakened, but conservative Republicans and liberal Democrats are working together to strengthen it. And the bipartisan Commission I appointed, chaired by my campaign lawyer and Governor Romney's campaign lawyer, came together and have offered reforms so that no one has to wait more than a half hour to vote. Let's support these efforts. It should be the power of our vote, not the size of our bank accounts, that drives our democracy.

Citizenship means standing up for the lives that gun violence steals from us each day. I've seen the courage of parents, students, pastors, police officers all over this country who say, "We are not afraid." And I intend to keep trying, with or without Congress, to help stop more tragedies from visiting innocent Americans in our movie theaters, in our shopping malls, or schools like Sandy Hook.

Citizenship demands a sense of common purpose, participation in the hard work of self-government, an obligation to serve our communities. And I know this Chamber agrees that few Americans give more to their country than our diplomats and the men and women of the United States Armed Forces. Thank you.

Tonight, because of the extraordinary troops and civilians who risk and lay down their lives to keep us free, the United States is more secure. When I took office, nearly 180,000 Americans were serving in Iraq and Afghanistan. Today, all our troops are out of Iraq. More than 60,000 of our troops have already come home from Afghanistan. With Afghan forces now in the lead for their own security, our troops have moved to a support role. Together with our allies, we will complete our mission there by the end of this year, and America's longest war will finally be over.

After 2014, we will support a unified Afghanistan as it takes responsibility for its own future. If the Afghan Government signs a security agreement that we have negotiated, a small force of Americans could remain in Afghanistan with NATO allies to carry out two narrow missions: training and assisting Afghan forces and counterterrorism operations to pursue any remnants of Al Qaida. For while our relationship with Afghanistan will change, one thing will not: our resolve that terrorists do not launch attacks against our country.

The fact is, that danger remains. While we've put Al Qaida's core leadership on a path to defeat, the threat has evolved as Al Qaida affiliates and other extremists take root in different parts of the world. In Yemen, Somalia, Iraq, Mali, we have to keep working with partners to disrupt and disable those networks. In Syria, we'll support the opposition that rejects the agenda of terrorist networks. Here at home, we'll keep strengthening our defenses and combat new threats like cyber attacks. And as we reform our defense budget, we will have to keep faith with our men and women in uniform and invest in the capabilities they need to succeed in future missions.

We have to remain vigilant. But I strongly believe our leadership and our security cannot depend on our outstanding military alone. As Commander in Chief, I have used force when needed to protect the American people, and I will never hesitate to do so as long as I hold this office. But I will not send our troops into harm's way unless it is truly necessary, nor will I allow our sons and daughters to be mired in open-ended conflicts. We must fight the battles that need to be fought, not those that terrorists prefer from us: large-scale deployments that drain our strength and may ultimately feed extremism.

So even as we actively and aggressively pursue terrorist networks through more targeted efforts and by building the capacity of our foreign partners, America must move off a permanent war footing. That's why I've imposed prudent limits on the use of drones. For we will not be safer if people abroad believe we strike within their countries without regard for the consequence.

That's why, working with this Congress, I will reform our surveillance programs, because the vital work of our intelligence community depends on public confidence, here and abroad, that privacy of ordinary people is not being violated.

And with the Afghan war ending, this needs to be the year Congress lifts the remaining restrictions on detainee transfers and we close the prison at Guantanamo Bay. Because we counter terrorism not just through intelligence and military actions, but by remaining true to our constitutional ideals and setting an example for the rest of the world.

You see, in a world of complex threats, our security, our leadership, depends on all elements of our power, including strong and principled diplomacy. American diplomacy has rallied more than 50 countries to prevent nuclear materials from falling into the wrong hands and allowed us to reduce our own reliance on cold war stockpiles. American diplomacy, backed by the threat of force, is why Syria's chemical weapons are being eliminated.

And we will continue to work with the international community to usher in the future the Syrian people deserve, a future free of dictatorship, terror, and fear. As we speak, American diplomacy is supporting Israelis and Palestinians as they engage in the difficult but necessary talks to end the conflict there, to achieve dignity and an independent state for Palestinians and lasting peace and security for the State of Israel, a Jewish state that knows America will always be at their side.

And it is American diplomacy, backed by pressure, that has halted the progress of Iran's nuclear program and rolled back parts of that program for the very first time in a decade. As we gather here tonight, Iran has begun to eliminate its stockpile of higher levels of enriched uranium. It's not installing advanced centrifuges. Unprecedented inspections help the world verify every day that Iran is not building a bomb. And with our allies and partners, we're engaged in negotiations to see if we can peacefully achieve a goal we all share: preventing Iran from obtaining a nuclear weapon.

These negotiations will be difficult. They may not succeed. We are clear eyed about Iran's support for terrorist organizations like Hizballah, which threatens our allies. And we're clear about the mistrust between our nations, mistrust that cannot be wished away. But these negotiations don't rely on trust. Any long-term deal we agree to must be based on verifiable action that convinces us and the international community that Iran is not building a nuclear bomb. If John F. Kennedy and Ronald Reagan could negotiate with the Soviet Union, then surely a strong and confident America can negotiate with less powerful adversaries today.

The sanctions that we put in place helped make this opportunity possible. But let me be clear: If this Congress sends me a new sanctions bill now that threatens to derail these talks, I will veto it. For the sake of our national security, we must give diplomacy a chance to succeed. If Iran's leaders do not seize this opportunity, then I will be the first to call for more sanctions and stand ready to exercise all options to make sure Iran does not build a nuclear weapon. But if Iran's leaders do seize the chance—and we'll know soon enough— then Iran could take an important step to rejoin the community of nations, and we will have resolved one of the leading security challenges of our time without the risks of war.

Now, finally, let's remember that our leadership is defined not just by our defense against threats, but by the enormous opportunities to do good and promote understanding around the globe: to forge greater cooperation, to expand new markets, to free people from fear and want. And no one is better positioned to take advantage of those opportunities than America.

Our alliance with Europe remains the strongest the world has ever known. From Tunisia to Burma, we're supporting those who are willing to do the hard work of building democracy. In Ukraine, we stand for the principle that all people have the right to express themselves freely and peacefully and to have a say in their country's future. Across Africa, we're bringing together businesses and governments to double access to electricity and help end extreme poverty. In the Americas, we're building new ties of commerce, but we're also expanding cultural and educational exchanges among young people. And we will continue to focus on the Asia-Pacific, where we support our allies, shape a future of greater security and prosperity, and extend a hand to those devastated by disaster, as we did in the Philippines, when our Marines and civilians rushed to aid those battered by a typhoon, and who were greeted with words like, "We will never forget your kindness" and "God bless America."

We do these things because they help promote our long-term security, and we do them because we believe in the inherent dignity and equality of every human being, regardless of race or religion, creed or sexual orientation. And next week, the world will see one expression of that commitment, when Team U.S.A. marches the red, white, and blue into the Olympic Stadium and brings home the gold. [Laughter]

Audience members.
U.S.A.! U.S.A.! U.S.A.!

The President.
My fellow Americans, no other country in the world does what we do. On every issue, the world turns to us, not simply because of the size of our economy or our military might, but because of the ideals we stand for and the burdens we bear to advance them. No one knows this better than those who serve in uniform.

As this time of war draws to a close, a new generation of heroes returns to civilian life. We'll keep slashing that backlog so our veterans receive the benefits they've earned and our wounded warriors receive the health care—including the mental health care—that they need. We'll keep working to help all our veterans translate their skills and leadership into jobs here at home. And we will all continue to join forces to honor and support our remarkable military families.

Let me tell you about one of those families I've come to know. I first met Cory Remsburg, a proud Army Ranger, at Omaha Beach on the 65th anniversary of D-day. Along with some of his fellow Rangers, he walked me through the program and the ceremony. He was a strong, impressive young man, had an easy manner, he was sharp as a tack. And we joked around and took pictures, and I told him to stay in touch.

A few months later, on his 10th deployment, Cory was nearly killed by a massive roadside bomb in Afghanistan. His comrades found him in a canal, face down, underwater, shrapnel in his brain. For months, he lay in a coma. And the next time I met him, in the hospital, he couldn't speak, could barely move. Over the years, he's endured dozens of surgeries and procedures, hours of grueling rehab every day.

Even now, Cory is still blind in one eye, still struggles on his left side. But slowly, steadily, with the support of caregivers like his dad Craig and the community around him, Cory has grown stronger. And day by day, he's learned to speak again and stand again and walk again. And he's working toward the day when he can serve his country again. "My recovery has not been easy," he says. "Nothing in life that's worth anything is easy."

Cory is here tonight. And like the Army he loves, like the America he serves, Sergeant First Class Cory Remsburg never gives up, and he does not quit. Cory.

My fellow Americans, men and women like Cory remind us that America has never come easy. Our freedom, our democracy, has never been easy. Sometimes, we stumble, we make mistakes; we get frustrated or discouraged. But for more than 200 years, we have put those things aside and placed our collective shoulder to the wheel of progress: to create and build and expand the possibilities of individual achievement, to free other nations from tyranny and fear, to promote justice and fairness and equality under the law so that the words set to paper by our Founders are made real for every citizen. The America we want for our kids—a rising America where honest work is plentiful and communities are strong, where prosperity is widely shared and opportunity for all lets us go as far as our dreams and toil will take us—none of it is easy. But if we work together—if we summon what is best in us, the way Cory summoned what is best in him—with our feet planted firmly in today, but our eyes cast toward tomorrow, I know it is within our reach. Believe it.

God bless you, and God bless the United States of America.

SOURCE: Executive Office of the President. "Address Before a Joint Session of the Congress on the State of the Union." January 28, 2014. *Compilation of Presidential Documents* 2014, no. 00050 (January 28, 2014). www.gpo.gov/fdsys/pkg/DCPD-201400050/pdf/DCPD-201400050.pdf.

Rep. Rodgers Delivers Republican Response to the State of the Union Address

January 28, 2014

What an honor it is for me to be with you after the President's State of the Union.

Tonight we honor America—a nation that has witnessed the greatest rise of freedom and opportunity our world has ever seen.

A nation where we are not defined by our limits, but by our potential.

And a nation where a girl who worked at the McDonald's Drive-Thru to help pay for college can be with you from the United States Capitol.

But the most important moments right now aren't happening here.

They're not in the Oval Office or in the House Chamber.

They're in your homes.

Kissing your kids goodnight. . . .

Figuring out how to pay the bills. . . .

Getting ready for tomorrow's doctor's visit. . . .

Waiting to hear from those you love serving in Afghanistan, or searching for that big job interview.

After all, "We the People" have been the foundation of America since her earliest days—people from all walks of life, and from all corners of the world—people who come to America because here, no challenge is too great and no dream too big.

That's the genius of America.

Tonight the President made more promises that sound good, but won't solve the problems actually facing Americans.

We want you to have a better life. The President wants that too.

But we part ways when it comes to how to make that happen.

So tonight I'd like to share a more hopeful, Republican vision. . . .

One that empowers you, not the government. . . .

It's one that champions free markets—and trusts people to make their own decisions, not a government that decides for you.

It helps working families rise above the limits of poverty and protects our most vulnerable.

And it's one where Washington plays by the same rules that you do.

It's a vision that is fair and offers the promise of a better future for every American.

If you had told me as a little girl that one-day I would put my hand on the Bible and be sworn in as the 200th woman to serve in the House of Representatives, I never would've thought it possible.

I grew up working at my family's orchard and fruit stand in Kettle Falls, a small town in Eastern Washington—getting up before dawn with my brother to pick apples.

My dad drove a school bus and my mom worked as a part-time bookkeeper.

They taught me to work hard, help others, and always, always dream for more.

So, when I showed my 4H animals at the county fair, my parents used to say to me, "Cathy, you need to save this money so you can go to college one day!"

So I did—I saved, I worked hard, and I became the first in my family to graduate from college.

The chance to go from my Washington to this one was unexpected.

I came to Congress to help empower people, not politicians;

To grow the working middle class, not the government;

And to ensure that everyone in this country can find a job.

Because a job is so much more than just a paycheck—

It gives us purpose, dignity, and the foundation to build a future.

I was single when I was elected—but it wasn't long before I met Brian, a retired Navy commander, and now we have three beautiful children, one who was born just eight weeks ago.

Like all parents, we have high hopes and dreams for our children, but we also know what it's like to face challenges.

Three days after we gave birth to our son, Cole, we got news no parent expects.

Cole was diagnosed with Down syndrome.

The doctors told us he could have endless complications, heart defects, even early Alzheimer's.

They told us all the problems.

But when we looked at our son, we saw only possibilities.

We saw a gift from God.

Today we see a 6-year old boy who dances to Bruce Springsteen; who reads above grade level; and who is the best big brother in the world.

We see all the things he can do, not those he can't.

Cole, and his sisters, Grace and Brynn, have only made me more determined to see the potential in every human lifed—that whether we are born with an extra twenty-first chromosome or without a dollar to our name—we are not defined by our limits, but by our potential.

Because our mission—not only as Republicans, but as Americans, is to once again to ensure that we are not bound by where we come from, but empowered by what we can become.

That is the gap Republicans are working to close.

It's the gap we all face: between where you are and where you want to be.

The President talks a lot about income inequality.

But the real gap we face today is one of opportunity inequality. . . .

And with this Administration's policies, that gap has become far too wide.

We see this gap growing every single day.

We see it in our neighbors who are struggling to find jobs. . . .

A husband who's now working just part-time. . . .

A child who drops out of college because she can't afford tuition. . . .

Or parents who are outliving their life's savings.

Last month, more Americans stopped looking for a job than found one. Too many people are falling further and further behind because right now, the President's policies are making people's lives harder.

Republicans have plans to close the gap. . . .

Plans that focus on jobs first without more spending, government bailouts, and red tape . . . .

Every day, we're working to expand our economy, one manufacturing job, nursing degree and small business at a time.

We have plans to improve our education and training systems so you have the choice to determine where your kids go to school . . . so college is affordable . . . and skills training is modernized.

And yes, it's time to honor our history of legal immigration. We're working on a step-by-step solution to immigration reform by first securing our borders and making sure America will always attract the best, brightest, and hardest working from around the world.

And with too many Americans living paycheck to paycheck, we have solutions to help you take home more of your pay—through lower taxes, cheaper energy costs, and affordable health care.

Not long ago I got a letter from Bette in Spokane, who hoped the President's health care law would save her money—but found out instead that her premiums were going up nearly $700 a month.

No, we shouldn't go back to the way things were, but this law is not working. Republicans believe health care choices should be yours, not the government's.

And that whether you're a boy with Down syndrome or a woman with breast cancer . . . you can find coverage and a doctor who will treat you.

So we hope the President will join us in a year of real action—by empowering people—not making their lives harder with unprecedented spending, higher taxes, and fewer jobs.

As Republicans, we advance these plans every day because we believe in a government that trusts people and doesn't limit where you finish because of where you started.

That is what we stand for—for an America that is every bit as compassionate as it is exceptional.

If we're successful. . . .

Years from now our children will say that we rebuilt the American Dream.

We built a working middle class that could take in anyone, and a workforce that could take on the world.

Whether you're a girl in Kettle Falls or a boy from Brooklyn, our children should be able to say that we closed the gap.

Our plan is one that dreams big for everyone and turns its back on no one.

The President said many things tonight.

But now, we ask him to listen—to you—for the true state of the union lies in your heart and in your home.

Tomorrow, I'll watch my son Cole get on the school bus; others will wait in the doctor's office or interview for that first job.

Some of us will celebrate new beginnings. . . .

Others will face great challenges. . . .

But all of us will wake up and do what is uniquely American. . . .

We will look forward to the boundless potential that lies ahead.

We will give thanks to the brave men and women who have answered America's call to freedom, like Sgt. Jacob Hess from Spokane, who recently gave his life to protect all of ours.

So, tonight, I simply offer a prayer . . . .

A prayer for Sgt. Hess's family, your family, and for our larger American family.

That, with the guidance of God, we may prove worthy of His blessings of life . . . liberty . . . and the pursuit of happiness.

For when we embrace these gifts, we are each doing our part to form a more perfect union.

May God guide you and our President, and may God continue to bless the United States of America.

SOURCE: Office of the Speaker of the House John Boehner. "Full Text: 2014 Republican Address to the Nation." January 28, 2014. www.speaker.gov/press-release/full-text-2014-republican-address-nation.

OTHER HISTORIC DOCUMENTS OF INTEREST

FROM THIS VOLUME

FROM PREVIOUS *HISTORIC DOCUMENTS*

ISIL Captures Fallujah; U.S. Vows Support for Iraq

JANUARY 28, FEBRUARY 5, AND APRIL 9, 2014

Throughout 2013, a radical wing of al Qaeda known as the Islamic State of Iraq and the Levant (ISIL) began gaining power in Iraq with the aim of capturing major cities and turning them into Islamic caliphates. The group already held control of cities in Syria, and by moving into Iraq it was attempting to fan out across the region. The Iraqi government struggled to control the group's growth, and by January 2014, ISIL had taken control of Fallujah and Ramadi. The central government encouraged local tribal leaders to take up arms against the insurgents; however, some of these groups fractured and shifted support to ISIL. The United States, wary of entering another ground war, offered training and equipment support and worked through its regional partners to find assistance for Iraqi fighters.

The Rise of ISIL

ISIL's roots lie mainly in the fall of the regime of Saddam Hussein in 2003. At that time, the group functioned as al Qaeda in Iraq under the aim of combatting the United States and any new non-Islamic Iraqi government. The group's Jordanian leader, Abu Musab al-Zarqawi, carried out suicide bombings and ruthless attacks against U.S. and Iraqi troops and civilians. Zarqawi's methods were highly criticized by Iraqis, and when he was killed in 2006 by U.S. troops, his death was celebrated around the country. The group rebranded, calling itself the Islamic State in Iraq (ISI), under the leadership of Abu Omar al-Baghdadi. The new leader's plan was to make the group appear more nationalistic. Still, it struggled to gain credibility, and Baghdadi was killed in 2010 by U.S. and Iraqi forces. He was replaced by Awwad Ibrahim al-Badri al-Samarra (who changed his name in college to something more recognizable: Abu Bakr al-Baghdadi, the latter portion of which is meant to represent Baghdad). The new Baghdadi sought to expand the group's influence by any means necessary. In 2012, he used the Syrian civil war and the country's weakened state to gain power over Syrian cities.

ISI merged with the Nusra Front in 2012 to form ISIL (the group is alternately known as ISIS and the Islamic State). Ayman al-Zawahiri, the leader of al Qaeda, was critical of the merger between the two al Qaeda–inspired groups. In the following months, ISIL undertook a ruthless campaign in Syria, killing those who disagreed with its strict interpretation of Islam and any rivals who tried to stop it from capturing Syrian cities. Al Qaeda formally broke ties with ISIL in 2014, to which ISIL replied that al Qaeda had "deviated from the correct path." On its own, ISIL managed to become one of the most powerful fighting forces in the eastern and northern parts of Syria, even taking control of lucrative oil fields. In 2014, ISIL turned its attention to Iraq.

ISIL Fighters Take Fallujah

On January 1, 2014, ISIL moved into Anbar province's largest cities, Fallujah and Ramadi, systematically destroying key facilities such as police stations, and securing roads and other infrastructure for itself. The terrorist organization easily took control of both cities because the Iraqi army remained largely uninvolved and local police forces were too weak to withstand ISIL fighters who were armed with heavy weapons. Following its victory, ISIL declared Fallujah and Ramadi the newest part of the Islamic caliphate. It was the group's intent to impose on the cities a strict seventh-century interpretation of Islamic rule based on the teachings of the Prophet Muhammad. The laws under the caliphate would include amputations for stealing; a ban on alcohol, drugs, and tobacco; restrictions on women leaving their homes; and a ban on political or military groups that rival Baghdadi. ISIL's intent drew strong resistance around Anbar province.

The tribal leaders in Ramadi attempted to fight ISIL to regain control of their city. The Iraqi government offered them $17 million in humanitarian and rebuilding support and also armed the tribal groups. By February, Ramadi's efforts paid off and they were able to push ISIL back to the outskirts of the city.

Fallujah, however, proved a far more difficult undertaking. There, ISIL grew stronger as it joined forces with other insurgent groups and took control of the central city. The Iraqi army and government had greater difficulty using the Ramadi strategy in Fallujah because local leaders fractured, with some supporting an attack on ISIL while others vowed to work with ISIL. The Iraqi army tried to set up a perimeter around the city to protect surrounding areas and eventually stage an attack inside Fallujah to remove ISIL fighters. On January 26, a group of Iraqi soldiers were captured and later executed. A video of the execution was posted online by ISIL as a warning that the military should not make any attempt to infiltrate the city. The Iraqi army, however, continued to stay the course and work out a strategy to retake the city, partnering with local tribal leaders as it did in Ramadi. ISIL fighters are unlikely to quickly relinquish power since Fallujah is strategically significant because it is located less than thirty miles from the Iraqi capital of Baghdad.

The Iraqi government vowed to undertake any means necessary to stop ISIL from gaining any more ground. "Due to the war declared by this terrorist organization, the Iraqi government and basing on constitutional responsibility finds itself obliged to take all security and military measures to secure the return of things to normal and the protection of citizens in Fallujah and other Iraqi cities," the Ministry of Foreign Affairs said in a statement.

U.S. Support for Iraq

The United States continues to have an interest in fighting terrorism in Iraq and the surrounding region. Baghdadi has made it clear that his group intends to harm Americans. On January 21, he released a statement saying, "Soon we will be in direct confrontation, and the sons of Islam have prepared for such a day. So watch, for we are with you, watching." Even so, any action against ISIL is politically risky for the United States. President Barack Obama came to office in 2008 promising to end the war in Iraq, and he succeeded in finishing the combat mission in 2010. The United States currently serves in a support capacity, providing training and strategic assistance to the Iraqis. Putting more boots on the ground in a combat capacity would hurt the president and his party.

Despite access to the equipment left behind by U.S. troops, the Iraqi government struggled to arm local fighters, and it was clear to the United States that these groups were ill-prepared to fight ISIL. As such, the United States provided Apache helicopters through its Foreign Military Sales program, delivered seventy-five Hellfire missiles (with the potential to sell more), and surveillance UAVs. The United States has also increased its training for counterterrorism units through bilateral and regional partnerships with nations such as Jordan.

The United States has suggested that Iraq develop a holistic plan to fight ISIL over the long term by working with local tribal fighters to protect the most vulnerable areas of Anbar, Ninewa, and Salah Din provinces. During a Congressional hearing, Brett McGurk, a deputy assistant secretary at the Department of State, said that "security, economics, and politics, must be fused together" for any plan to be successful. Given the divisions within some of the tribal communities, this will be a difficult undertaking for the Iraqi government. To encourage local fighters to support the movement against ISIL, the government has promised to provide full state benefits to anyone hurt or killed in the fighting. The government has also said that it will allow any willing fighters to join the official state security body once the fight against ISIL is over.

REGIONAL INVOLVEMENT

The Middle Eastern region in which ISIL is attempting to gain control has been a tinderbox for decades, and many of the states were further weakened by the Arab Spring movement of 2010–2011. The instability in the region makes a response to ISIL, as well as the terrorist organization's growth, a precarious issue. Iran has the possibility to become a key player in the response to ISIL, because its Shiite-led government stands in stark contrast to ISIL's Sunni leadership. Iran is known to have large stocks of heavy weaponry, which it could provide to Iraqi fighters. This scenario, of course, is difficult for the United States, because Iran has been a major adversary. In Syria, the weakened Bashar al Assad regime has been criticized for allowing ISIL to gain power, while his focus has remained on continuing to fight the rebels who threaten his government.

Turkey has been accused of leveraging ISIL oil reserves and purchasing the resource at discount rates from the terrorist organization. However, Turkey is also allied with the United States, which has vowed to support the Iraqi government in the fight against the terrorist organization. Economically, Turkey has put itself in a difficult position because, by the second quarter of 2014, the country's growth rate slowed to 2.1 percent, less than the government's prediction of 4 percent, and well below the double-digit growth seen in the preceding years. Much of this decline was attributed to a reduction in exports to Iraq as well as a slowing of construction in Iraq, which is largely supported by Turkish workers. Although the country needs the savings from oil sales, it is not feasible for the government to put its support behind ISIL.

—Heather Kerrigan

Following is the text of a press release from the U.S. Embassy in Iraq on January 28, 2014, detailing the United States' ongoing commitment to helping Iraq secure its nation; the edited text of a statement before the House Foreign Affairs Committee on the resurgence of al Qaeda in Iraq, delivered on February 5, 2014; and remarks by the Iraqi government on April 9, 2014, on the deteriorating situation in Fallujah.

United States Discusses Continuing Commitment to Iraq

January 28, 2014

Deputy Secretary Burns met today in Baghdad with Prime Minister Nouri al-Maliki, Speaker of the Council of Representatives Osama Nujaifi, Foreign Minister Hoshyar Zebari, and National Security Advisor Faleh Fayyad. In all of these meetings, the Deputy Secretary confirmed the enduring U.S. commitment to Iraq as defined in the Strategic Framework Agreement.

Regarding the security situation, the Deputy Secretary stressed the importance of a holistic security and political strategy to isolate and defeat terrorist groups like the Islamic State of Iraq and the Levant (ISIL). He praised the strategy in Ramadi where local and tribal officials are playing a leading role in pushing terrorists out of the city, and encouraged the Government of Iraq (GOI) to follow through on its commitment to incorporate tribal fighters into the formal security structures of the state.

The Deputy Secretary also reviewed preparations for national elections to be held on April 30, noting the importance of holding elections on time and ensuring that those displaced from fighting in Fallujah and other cities in Anbar province are able to vote. He confirmed the U.S. commitment to Iraq's political process as defined in the Iraqi constitution and the right of all Iraqi citizens to hold their leaders accountable through regularly scheduled elections.

The Deputy Secretary finally reviewed the regional situation and noted strengthened relations over the past year between Iraq and its important neighbors Jordan and Kuwait. He further encouraged all relevant parties to conclude a framework agreement for exporting oil from the Iraqi Kurdistan Region to Turkey, noting the progress that has been made in recent talks between Baghdad and Erbil. He emphasized the serious risks to long-term stability should such exports begin before this deal is finalized.

The Deputy Secretary also commended the decision today by the Council of Ministers to contribute to the UN trust fund to cover costs of re-settling residents of Camp Liberty to a third country. He emphasized in all of his meetings the importance of close cooperation between the GOI, the United Nations Assistance Mission for Iraq (UNAMI), and the residents of Camp Liberty to ensure their safety and security pending their re-settlement outside of Iraq.

SOURCE: Embassy of the United States in Iraq. "Deputy Secretary William Burns Completes Visit to Iraq for Strategic Consultations." January 28, 2014. iraq.usembassy.gov/pr-012814b.html.

Congressional Testimony on Growing Terrorist Threat in Iraq

February 5, 2014

[Testimony delivered by Brett McGurk, Deputy Assistant Secretary for Iran and Iraq, Bureau of Near Eastern Affairs, Department of State.]

[Footnotes have been omitted.]

. . . I will begin with a brief overview of the security situation in 2011 and 2012, as it is important to understanding the current environment. In both years, 2011 and 2012, Iraq remained a very violent country. By our counts, 4,400 Iraqis were killed each year, most in attacks by extremist groups led by al-Qa'ida in Iraq (AQI).

While this violence was persistent and targeted, it did not threaten the stability of the state, or a rekindled civil war. Indeed, based on studies of historical parallels—civil wars and insurgencies—Iraq by 2012 had entered what is called a "low boil" stage of insurgency. A low boil insurgency reflects a level of violence that may not present a serious risk of state collapse, or rekindled broad scale reprisals, but rather a persistent tempo of attacks carried out by the hardened core of an insurgency—which, by historical examples, can take a decade to fizzle out.

These two years, 2011 and 2012, also witnessed the escalating civil war in Syria, inflamed by regional rivalry and opportunism by terrorist groups. The Asad regime's unwillingness to engage with the opposition in meaningful political dialogue and violent suppression of peaceful protests led to open, armed conflict. As the fighting has dragged on, the conflict has attracted terrorist groups seeking to take advantage of the loss of state authority, including in eastern Syria, leading to the rise of terrorist groups near the Iraq border.

The most organized and lethal of these groups—the al-Nusrah Front and ISIL—were franchises of AQI. They vary in their objectives: al-Nusrah has put greater priority on the toppling of Asad and working with other Syrian opposition groups, whereas ISIL has focused on a more regional agenda, with an aim to carve out an Islamic caliphate stretching from Baghdad to Lebanon. These dueling objectives have at times required direct mediation by Osama Bin Laden's former deputy, and now global head of al-Qa'ida, Ayman al Zawahiri. The debate has been a central focus among global jihadist networks, and has given ISIL, in particular, a global platform to propagate its agenda and recruit adherents.

Flush with resources, recruits, weapons, and training, ISIL slowly began to execute its strategy across the Syrian border in Iraq. Violence in Iraq ticked up towards the end of 2012, but did not accelerate until early 2013. This included a marked rise in suicide bombers. The majority of these suicide bombers, we believe, are foreign fighters, recruited through extremist propaganda. Suicide bombers are a key data point we track, as they have a pernicious effect on the stability of Iraq, and demonstrate a sophisticated global network that is able to recruit, train, and deploy human beings to commit suicide and mass murder. The suicide bombers are, in a twisted turn of logic, ISIL's most precious resource.

It was significant, therefore, that by early 2013, we began to see signs of ISIL shifting these resources from Syria to Iraq. In 2012, Iraq witnessed an average of 5–10 suicide attacks per month. By the summer of 2013, it was averaging 30–40 suicide attacks per month, and increasingly coordinated and effective attacks. On March 14, 2013, for example, five suicide bombers from ISIL attacked and took hostages in the Ministry of Justice in Baghdad, and controlled the building for several hours before detonating themselves. This was the first in a series of sophisticated military-style operations throughout 2013, with suicide bombers used to clear a path, followed by well-trained fighters to take and hold an objective.

By the summer of 2013, ISIL suicide bombers struck regularly, focused primarily on Shia civilian targets (playgrounds, funerals, markets), but also Sunni areas (to contest territory) and Kurdish areas (to spark ethnic conflict). In November 2013, Iraq witnessed 50 suicide attacks, compared with only three in November 2012. These attacks had a devastating effect on political discourse in the country, further fueling mistrust from political leaders to ordinary citizens, and making the tangible reforms that Iraq needs to reconcile its society even harder to reach.

Indeed, the violence may appear indiscriminate—but it is not. From what we are now seeing, ISIL attacks are calculated, coordinated, and part of a strategic campaign led by its Syria-based leader, Abu Bakr al-Baghdadi. This campaign has the stated objective to cause the collapse of the Iraqi state and carve out a zone of governing control in the western regions of Iraq and eastern Syria (an area known as the "Jazeera"). . . .

[A discussion of political instability in Iraq that allowed ISIL to grow and strengthen has been omitted.]

The Current Situation: Fallujah and Ramadi

On January 1, 2014, convoys of approximately 70–100 trucks with mounted heavy weapons and anti-aircraft guns, flying the black flag of al-Qa'ida, entered the central cities of Fallujah and Ramadi. They deployed to key objectives, destroyed most police stations, and secured vital crossways. The police in both cities nearly disintegrated. The Iraqi army, deployed in camps outside the cities, engaged some armed vehicles but generally chose not to get drawn into urban fighting.

The domination of these central cities was a culmination of ISIL's 2013 strategy to govern territory and establish 7th-century Islamic rule. Across the border in Syria, ISIL has governed the city of Raqqa (with a population of 220,000) for most of the past year. In Iraq, ISIL sees Ramadi and Fallujah as their new Raqqa. In Fallujah, days after seizing central areas, ISIL declared the city part of an Islamic caliphate. This message, however, is not popular in Anbar—and has bred fierce resistance.

In Ramadi, in the hours after ISIL arrived in force, tribal leaders organized and asked for funding and arms from the central government to retake their streets and protect their population. The GOI responded with $17 million to support urgent humanitarian assistance and reconstruction of areas damaged in fighting. It also began sending small and medium weapons to tribal fighters, with assurance that these fighters would be given full benefits of the state, as if they were soldiers.

I was in Iraq in early January as this effort got underway. In meetings with Maliki and other key leaders, I pressed the urgent message that without a broad base of support from the population in Ramadi, it would be impossible to root out the hundreds of ISIL fighters who had taken up positions in strategic areas. I also discussed the situation with former leaders of the Anbar awakening, such as Sheikh Abu Risha, and local officials in Ramadi, including Governor Ahmed Khalaf, who were focused on organizing tribal fighters to oust ISIL from populated areas.

Over the first two weeks of January, these local and tribal leaders made requests to the central government for additional resources, weapons, and a common strategy to reclaim the streets from ISIL and other militant groups. The GOI dispatched the acting Defense Minister, Sadoun Dulaimi, to fulfill these requests and finalize a military and political plan. (Dulaimi is from Anbar and a member of one of its largest tribes. He has been in Ramadi nearly full-time since this crisis began.)

These coordinated efforts have begun to produce results. Fighting continues in the outskirts of Ramadi, but the central city is increasingly secure with a critical mass of tribes having pledged to fight ISIL to ensure that they cannot return. This quick albeit fragile turnaround in Ramadi, with serious and regular coordination between local and national leaders, may provide a model for how we can best ensure that 2014 is a year in which the tide begins to turn once again against ISIL inside Iraq.

The Fallujah situation is far more serious, as hundreds of ISIL fighters have joined ranks with former insurgent groups to consolidate control of the inner city, and contest areas in small towns nearby. The Iraqi army is now working to establish a cordon from the outskirts of the city, in coordination with local tribes, but they face well-trained snipers armed with 50-caliber rifles. On January 26, approximately a dozen Iraqi soldiers were captured near Fallujah. Some were later paraded around the city in the back of a pickup truck flying the al-Qa'ida flag. The next day, ISIL posted a video showing their gruesome execution, daring the army to enter the city.

The army, thus far, has not taken the bait. It remains on the city's outskirts, working to execute a strategy similar to what proved effective in Ramadi. There had been reports of army units randomly shelling Fallujah's neighborhoods, but Iraqi commanders have denied this (blaming ISIL), and tribal figures have since confirmed that military operations are being coordinated with local actors.

At this moment, Fallujah is the scene of a tense standoff. Some tribes are ready and preparing to fight ISIL, others are working with ISIL (and forming "tribal councils" with declared intention to fight the army), and more are on the fence, waiting to see which side is likely to prevail in the end. Local leaders in Anbar, in coordination with the GOI, are working to recruit more tribes to enter, clear, and hold Fallujah, while ensuring civilians and families can leave the city.

This standoff will not last forever. The GOI has the responsibility to help local leaders secure the city and oust the militants now in control. Under the plan that is being developed by the GOI in coordination with local leaders, the army will seek to control outlying areas and cordon the city; tribal fighters will then seek to take the lead in securing populated areas, with military support when needed. We know from experience how difficult this will be, and U.S. military officers from the Office of Security Cooperation are in regular touch with their Iraqi counterparts to share lessons learned, offer advice, and make recommendations.

ISIL has also made its intentions clear: move from a new base of operations in Fallujah to Baghdad—a distance of under 30 miles. Its leader, Abu Bakr al-Baghdadi, had this to say in a rare audio statement issued on January 21:

"As for ISIS in Iraq: Be in the frontlines against the Shia, and march toward Baghdad and the South, keep the Shia busy in their own areas. Know that the entire Sunni population and the brothers in Syria are watching you."

Were there any doubt, moreover, of the threat Baghdadi and his network—now with approximately 2,000 fighters in Iraq—presents to the United States and our interests in the region, his statement said this in its concluding paragraph:

"Our last message is to the Americans. Soon we will be in direct confrontation, and the sons of Islam have prepared for such a day. So watch, for we are with you, watching."

DEVELOPING A LONG-TERM IRAQI STRATEGY: POLITICAL, ECONOMIC, SECURITY

Drawing on our own lessons learned, we are also encouraging the GOI to develop and execute a holistic strategy to isolate and defeat ISIL over the long-term. This strategy fuses political, security, and economic components with an immediate focus on incorporating tribal fighters to protect the population in towns and villages throughout the provinces of Anbar, Ninewa, and Sal ah Din. These tribal fighters would work in coordination with local officials, local police, and the army when needed, to deny space and sanctuary for an organized ISIL presence.

Such a strategy is extremely difficult to develop and execute in a dynamic tribal environment like Anbar province. But in recent weeks, we have seen a new level of commitment from the GOI to mobilize the local population against ISIL. Over the course of January, the GOI cabinet has allocated resources to ensure local people taking up arms against extremist groups enjoy full state benefits in the event they are killed or wounded. Importantly, the GOI has committed to incorporating these fighters into the security structures of the state once fighting concludes.

Regarding economic support, in January alone, the GOI allocated $18 million for rebuilding projects in Fallujah and Ramadi; $17 million for direct humanitarian assistance; and $3.4 million for direct payments to tribal fighters. As noted above, Sadoun Dulaimi has remained in Ramadi to oversee allocation of these resources. Our team in Baghdad is in direct and regular contact with all relevant actors, and urging them to ensure resources reach intended recipients as soon as possible. . . .

SECURITY MEASURES (AND FOCUSED U.S. SUPPORT)

Political and economic initiatives are necessary for defeating a network like ISIL. But they are not sufficient. From our own experience, we know that while success is impossible without mobilizing the population, such popular mobilization will not last absent focused and persistent security operations. The tribes will fight, but they must be confident that they are going to win *and* be recognized when the fighting is over—not left to the mercy of ISIL reprisals. For this to happen, ISIL networks must be constantly pressured, and their safe havens destroyed.

Consistent with ISIL's rise last summer, a series of armed camps—staging areas and training grounds—were spotted in western Iraq. The existence of these camps demonstrated a shortfall in the capacity of the ISF. Even where camps could be located, through persistent ISF reconnaissance platforms, such as manned King Air platforms, the ISF lacked the ability to target effectively, thereby providing ISIL safe haven just miles from populated areas.

Iraq's lack of armored helicopters was a glaring example. Iraqi pilots, over the course of 2013, often flew thin-skinned helicopters towards ISIL camps defended by PKC machine guns and anti-aircraft platforms. The result was helicopters shot up and crews (many of whom we had trained) suffering grievous wounds. This situation was not sustainable, and the GOI requested our urgent assistance.

I want to thank this Committee, in particular, for working so closely with us over the past six months to approve the Apache helicopter lease and sale through our Foreign Military Sales program. While this is not an immediate remedy to the current problem, they will provide the ISF with the most effective platform possible for denying ISIL a safe haven in the remote western deserts of Iraq. They will also ensure that we can provide effective oversight on the end use of attack helicopter systems, as well as influencing planning and operations.

Similarly, the Iraqis have recently proven effective at deploying Hellfire missiles against remote ISIL targets from a Caravan aircraft. The ISF have equipped Caravans to launch Hellfire strikes, but the overall supply of Hellfire missiles was not adequate to tackle the threat and number of targets they had located and surveyed. Again, thanks to close coordination with this Committee, this situation has begun to change. We delivered 75 Hellfire missiles in December, and have notified Congress of a potential sale of up to 500 more. Our objective is to ensure that ISIL can never again gain safe haven in western Iraq.

Consistent with this strategy, we will deliver 10 Scan Eagle surveillance UAVs this spring, and 48 Raven UAVs later this year, all of which, when used in combination with other platforms, can provide regular surveillance of the Jazeera region and the Iraq-Syria border. As Director of National Intelligence Clapper noted in recent testimony before the Senate Select Committee on Intelligence, the "greater two way flow of Sunni extremists between Syria and Iraq" has a direct bearing on ISIL's ability to conduct high-profile attacks in Iraq. To be successful, thus, a long-term strategy must focus on security and surveillance in these areas.

Finally, we have increased bilateral and regional training opportunities for Iraqi counterterrorism (CT) units, and expedited deliveries of key CT-related equipment for Iraq's most elite and disciplined units. U.S. trainers with the Embassy's Office of Security Cooperation are also conducting non-operational training with these high-end Iraqi operators, and Iraq and Jordan have discussed the possibility of advanced training for Iraqi forces in Jordan. We fully support this initiative.

All of this assistance comes in the context of the holistic strategy discussed above, short of which, long-term stability will not be possible. This was a point General Austin pressed home with Prime Minister Maliki and other key leaders in a visit to Baghdad last week: security, economics, and politics, must be fused together. . . .

SOURCE: U.S. Department of State. "Al-Qaeda's Resurgence in Iraq: A Threat to U.S. Interests." February 5, 2014. www.state.gov/p/nea/rls/rm/221274.htm.

Iraq Remarks on Security Situation in Fallujah

April 9, 2014

The situation in Anbar Province, especially in the city of Fallujah, is no longer a secret. The city of Fallujah is dominated by terrorist groups, particularly the Islamic State of Iraq and the Levant ISIL, it conducted acts of terrorism such as killing, kidnapping, and terrorizing the citizens, and spreading fear among them, as well as sabotaging public and private property, and destruction of infrastructure, including bridges connecting cities of Anbar province, to hinder the movement of citizens and prevent the delivery of aid to them.

The Iraqi government has sought from the beginning to form a committee in charge of providing the necessary needs, as the Independent High Electoral Commission started procedures necessary to ensure the participation of people of the province in the parliamentary elections scheduled late this month.

Not only did ISIL take the people of the city of Fallujah as human shields, but it committed other criminal acts by cutting the water of the Euphrates River through Fallujah dam and Nuaimiya dam, a thing that led to sinking villages and towns in Anbar province, and causing huge lack of water flowing towards the Central and Southern provinces, which threatens scarcity in drinking water and stop power plants, in addition to the damage that would be inflicted on the agricultural, animal, and environmental wealth.

Therefore, and due to the war declared by this terrorist organization, the Iraqi government and basing on constitutional responsibility finds itself obliged to take all security and military measures to secure the return of things to normal and the protection of citizens in Fallujah and other Iraqi cities.

SOURCE: Iraqi Ministry of Foreign Affairs. "Statement by MOFA." April 9, 2014. www.mofa.gov.iq/en/articles/print.aspx?id=ocsP0Pi3dGU=.

OTHER HISTORIC DOCUMENTS OF INTEREST

FROM THIS VOLUME

FROM PREVIOUS *HISTORIC DOCUMENTS*

United Nations-Brokered Syrian Peace Talks Conclude Without Agreement

JANUARY 31 AND FEBRUARY 15, 2014

In late January and mid-February 2014, the United Nations (UN) sponsored a round of talks aimed at securing a ceasefire in Syria between the rebels and the regime of President Bashar al Assad. The talks were rife with controversy from the beginning, after the UN extended and then rescinded an invitation to Iran to join the discussions. Despite meeting for more than two weeks, members were unable to reach a consensus with the Syrian government to end the civil war, which has killed more than 100,000 and displaced more than seven million since it began in March 2011.

PLANS FOR THE GENEVA II TALKS

Planning for UN-brokered peace talks began in 2012, when representatives from the United States, Russia, China, and Great Britain met with UN peace envoys to Syria and former UN secretary general kofi Annan. The group agreed that peace talks should produce a "transitional government body with full executive powers." Both members of the Assad government and the Syrian opposition could take part in this transitional body, but it was left unclear whether Assad would be required to step down. Russia was a strong proponent of allowing the president to remain in place, while the United States felt that peace could not be achieved while Assad was in power. Assad has made clear that he has no intent of leaving office, even announcing that he planned to run for reelection in 2014.

With the agreement in hand, Lakhdar Brahimi, who replaced Annan in August 2012 as peace envoy to Syria, began working to bring together all interested parties for peace talks. It took eight months of negotiation to persuade everyone invited to agree on the key provision of the conference, but progress toward setting up the meeting was accelerated after the alleged August 2013 chemical attack on Syrian civilians. According to Brahimi, the most difficult part of securing the meeting was getting all interested parties to agree that military action would not solve the conflict. "There is no military solution to this devastating conflict. Only a political solution will put an end to it," he said.

The Syrian government agreed to join the talks in July 2013. At the same time, the Syrian National Council split from the Syrian National Coalition over a disagreement regarding the peace talks; the latter of the two groups agreed to attend. Other smaller Syrian opposition groups announced that they would not attend and stated that they would not be bound by any agreement that was reached during negotiations.

Less than a week before the talks began, the UN issued an invitation to Iran to attend the conference under the assumption that it had accepted the terms of the 2012 agreement under which the conference was being held. Iran is Assad's main military backer, and some in the international community have argued that a true ceasefire cannot be reached without Iran at the table. The move drew instant backlash from both the United States and the coalition of Syrian forces fighting against the Assad regime. Both announced that they would not attend if Iran were present, which would have derailed the talks from the start.

Less than twenty-four hours after issuing the invitation, UN secretary general Ban Ki-moon rescinded it, noting that Iran had in fact not accepted the terms. Marzieh Afkham, a spokesperson for the Iranian Foreign Ministry, said that while the government had accepted the UN's invitation, it did "not accept any precondition to take part." Ban said that he was "deeply disappointed by Iranian public statements . . . that are not at all consistent with that stated commitment." Almost immediately, both the United States and the Syrian coalition agreed that they would attend the talks, slated to start later that week.

Negotiations Begin Amid Tension

After the debacle with Iran, it was clear that the talks were on rocky footing and that the United Nations held little power in the negotiations. Even so, on January 22, foreign ministers from more than forty nations gathered in Montreux, France, to discuss how to bring a peaceful end to Syria's civil war. The sessions in January marked the first direct talks between representatives for Assad and the Syrian opposition since the conflict began.

The nations participating in the event were offered the opportunity to make statements regarding the situation in Syria. "There is no way, no way possible, that a man who has led a brutal response to his own people can regain legitimacy to govern," said U.S. secretary of state John Kerry, reiterating the U.S. stance that Assad should step down. Kerry's statements were supported by those in the Syrian National Coalition, which called on the Assad regime to immediately hand over power to a transitional government. Syria's foreign minister also responded, saying, "No one in the world has the right to confer or withdraw the legitimacy of a president, a constitution or a law, except for the Syrians themselves."

Two days later, on January 25, representatives of the Assad regime and opposition forces met face-to-face with UN mediators in Geneva, Switzerland. These meetings continued through January 31, but produced no concrete results. Those with knowledge of the meetings said that the opposition would not accept any agreement that would allow Assad to remain in power. "The gaps between the sides remain wide; there is no use pretending otherwise," Brahimi said after the first round of negotiations.

Second Round Produces No Results

The second round of negotiations ran from February 10 to February 15, and again produced no results. Brahimi apologized to the Syrian people for the failure of the talks, saying, "I am very, very sorry, and I apologize to the Syrian people that . . . we haven't helped them very much." He called on both sides to regroup and decide whether they wanted negotiations to continue. Brahimi expressed his hope that the next round would be held in short order. "People are dying, the country is being destroyed. If this track aims at helping the Syrian people, then of course, the faster we achieve tangible results, the better," he said.

The talks did result in one positive change: UN and Red Crescent relief workers were allowed into the Old City of Homs, where thousands had been trapped in heavy fighting.

Brahimi said, however, that this agreement likely gave the people of Syria too much hope that more change would come. He blamed the collapse of the talks on the Syrian government's refusal to discuss opposition demands and its continued insistence on combatting "terrorists," the term it uses for opposition forces. The opposition, however, wanted to focus on forming a transitional government.

Brahimi presented an outline for an agenda for a third round of talks, which would see the first day focused on ending the bloodshed and combatting terrorism, while the second day would be about forming a transitional government. However, Brahimi said that the Syrian government refused this approach because it does not want to address the idea of a transitional government.

THIRD ROUND OF TALKS IN DOUBT

Since the Geneva talks concluded, the various opposition factions in Syria have further fractured, which hurts their ability to stand up to the Assad regime, and also makes a ceasefire ever more elusive. In March, Ban appealed to the United States and Russia to help restart the talks between Assad and the Syrian opposition. On the third anniversary of the start of the conflict, Ban said, "Syria is now the biggest humanitarian and peace and security crisis facing the world, with violence reaching unthinkable levels." UN diplomats had said that Brahimi was critical of the failure of the United States and Russia to put aside their own differences to end the war in Syria. Russia, with the help of China, has vetoed a number of resolutions put forth by the Security Council that would have placed sanctions on the Assad regime and has continuously stated that it does not believe it is the place of the Security Council to intervene in internal affairs. Others at the United Nations blamed a lack of progress in Syria on a shifting diplomatic focus to Ukraine and the Crimean decision to secede to Russia. Under the condition of anonymity, some diplomats said that the Ukraine crisis has taken up the time and effort that would have been reserved for Syria.

In November, Russia pushed for renewed talks. "It is important that constructive Syrian opposition forces restart political dialogue with official [representatives of] Damascus in the face of dangerous challenges posed by international terrorism," said Russian deputy foreign minister Mikhail Bogdanov. Moscow invited the Syrian foreign minister for private talks, saying they would be held "against the background of U.S. attempts to monopolize the right to decide on the goals and methods of anti-terrorist operations." Russia proposed late in the year that Assad should be allowed to remain in power for two years with a transitional government until fresh elections can be held, in which Assad would be allowed to run; the United States has rejected this idea. Assad's representative agreed to travel to Russia for the talks. No opposition leaders were invited to the meeting, nor was it made clear exactly what might be discussed or proposed.

—Heather Kerrigan

The following is the text of a statement delivered by Lakhdar Brahimi, the joint special representative to the UN-brokered Syrian peace talks, on the conclusion of the first round of negotiations on January 31, 2014; and a February 15, 2014, press release from the UN detailing Brahimi's apology to Syrians for failing to help the government and opposition forces reach an agreement during the second round of negotiations.

Peace Talks Conclude Without Consensus

January 31, 2014

At this first session of the Geneva Conference on Syria, the Syrian Government and the Syrian opposition met for the first time to discuss ending the war and finding a political solution to save their country. At Montreux, more than 40 countries, along with the United Nations and three regional organizations, came together to insist that the unspeakable suffering of the population of Syria must cease. They urged the two sides to come to a political settlement meeting the aspirations of the people of Syria and fully implementing the Geneva Communique of 30 June 2012.

Over the past eight days here in Geneva, the sides engaged each other through me. It was a difficult start. But the sides have become used to sitting in the same room. They have presented positions, and listened to each other. There have been moments where one side has acknowledged the concerns and point of view of the other. Progress is very slow indeed, but the sides have engaged in an acceptable manner. This is a modest beginning on which we can build.

The sides came here to discuss a political solution. But whenever Syrians meet, they cannot but discuss the terrible situation on the ground, and they did. I personally appealed for action to address the desperate humanitarian situation in Syria. Homs was extensively discussed, though unfortunately there has been no breakthrough yet. We also discussed access to other places, as well as the idea of a country-wide pause in the fighting to allow access to all areas. Some good news came yesterday with the delivery of humanitarian assistance to the Yarmouk camp for Palestinian refugees. But so much more is needed. Humanitarian discussions will continue on the ground; important countries are engaged; and there will be further push on humanitarian issues at a conference organized by Emergency Relief Coordinator Valerie Amos in Rome early next week.

In terms of the political settlement, I noted on the very first day that the sides were committed to discussing the full implementation of the Geneva Communique of 30 June 2012. Both sides have offered their overall vision on the future of Syria, and how this vision can be achieved through full implementation of the Geneva Communique. This week we started to discuss the specific areas of the cessation of violence in all its forms, including the fight against terrorism; and the transitional governing body exercising full executive powers. The gaps between the sides remain wide; there is no use pretending otherwise. Nevertheless, during our discussions, I observed a little bit of common ground—perhaps more than the two sides realize or recognize. I made a mental note of these points. I shared these points with the two sides today, and I thought perhaps I should share them with you:

- Both sides are committed to discussing the full implementation of the Geneva Communique to achieve a political solution in Syria. And they repeated that today.

- Both sides know that, to implement the Geneva Communique, they must reach agreement on a permanent and comprehensive end to the conflict and on the establishment of a Transitional Governing Body with full executive powers, as well as on subsequent steps. Chief amongst them; national dialogue, constitutional review, and elections.

- Both sides understand that the conflict in their country has imposed immense and unacceptable suffering on the Syrian people. Both sides recognize the urgent need to bring the violence to an end. We hope they will also redouble their efforts to seek early opportunities to reduce the level of violence on the ground.

- Both sides believe that the future of Syria can only be determined by the people of Syria, men and women, through peaceful means, without any external intervention and interference, direct or indirect.

- Both sides are committed to ensuring that the sovereignty, independence, territorial integrity and unity of Syria needs to be fully respected, and that no loss of territory will ever be accepted.

- Both sides foresee a future for the country that reflects the best of the historical and cultural traditions of Syria's diverse people and its history of harmony and tolerance.

- Both sides understand that the Syrian people are longing for a genuinely democratic Syria where governance is transparent and accountable and based on human rights and the rule of law.

- Both sides understand that the humanitarian situation of the population must be addressed rapidly, on the basis of need alone, wherever such need exists in the country. We hope they will act on this, and on the issue of detainees, the kidnapped, and the disappeared.

- Both sides recognize that the safety and security of all in Syria must be preserved and assured, along with the continued functioning and reform of State institutions and public services.

- Each side stated in no uncertain terms that they reject violent extremism and terrorism.

As I say, this is MY assessment of where I see the parties basically saying the same thing, or almost the same thing. And I hope that we can start to build more common ground when next we meet. We will now have a short break in the negotiations, to allow the sides to prepare their more detailed positions on the issues raised already, and on all other aspects of the Geneva Communique of 30 June 2012.

I suggested we resume, on the basis of an agreed agenda, on 10 February 2014. The delegation of the opposition agreed to this date. That of the government said they needed to consult with Damascus first.

For all the Syrians trapped in this war, our work here will seem far too slow. I understand that. But we are trying to overcome the very difficult issues that have led to this war, and this unfortunately takes time.

SOURCE: United Nations. News Centre. "Press statement of the Joint Special Representative Mr Lakhdar Brahimi on the conclusion of the first round of intra-Syrian talks—Geneva." January 31, 2014. © 2014 United Nations. Reprinted with the permission of the United Nations.www.un.org/apps/news/infocus/printfocusnews.asp?nid=1282.

UN Envoy Apologizes for Lack of Progress on Syria

February 15, 2014

Calling an end to the latest round of United Nations–backed talks in Geneva on Syria's civil war, Lakhdar Brahimi apologized to the Syrian people on Saturday for the lack of progress on halting the bloodshed in their country, and urged Government and opposition negotiators to go back to their bases and reflect on their responsibility and "on whether they want this process to continue or not."

"I am very, very sorry, and I apologize to the Syrian people that . . . we haven't helped them very much," said Mr. Brahimi, the United Nations/Arab League Joint Special Representative, telling a press conference that while no date was set to resume the talks, he presented both sides with an agenda for the next round, "so that we don't lose another week or 10 days as we have this time."

This is the second round of UN-sponsored direct talks between Government and opposition representatives—the first set of discussions took place in late January—to end a war which has killed well over 100,000 people and driven nearly 9 million others from their homes since the conflict erupted between President Bashar al-Assad and various groups seeking his ouster nearly three years ago.

"People are dying, the country is being destroyed. If this track aims at helping the Syrian people, then of course, the faster we achieve tangible results, the better," Mr. Brahimi said in response to a question, but added he has made it clear that "everybody needs to go back to their base and we will contact each other to determine the date [of the next round].

The talks have so far yielded only modest cooperation between the sides on allowing UN and Syrian Red Crescent relief workers access to thousands of people trapped in the long-besieged Old City of Homs, and Mr. Brahimi said today he felt "the little that has been achieved in Homs gave [the Syrian people] even more hope that maybe this is the beginning of the coming out of this horrible crisis—I apologize to them."

As for next steps, Mr. Brahimi said the parties agreed to his proposal that a new round of talks would focus on violence and terrorism, a transitional governing body, national institutions and national reconciliation. But he acknowledged that the main sticking point persisted: the Government side considers that the most important issue to be combatting terrorism; the opposition considers that the most important issue is forming a transitional governing authority.

"We suggested that the first day will be set for discussion on . . . ending violence and combating terrorism and the second day would be reserved for a discussion on the TGB [transitional governing body]," he explained, but while he had made clear that one day would not give enough time to conclude discussions on either issue, "unfortunately, the Government has refused [this approach], which raises the suspicion of the opposition that in fact the Government doesn't want to discuss the TGB at all."

"I very, very much hope that the two sides will reflect and think a little bit better and come back ready to engage seriously on how to implement the Geneva Communiqué," he said, referring to the 2012 action plan adopted at the first international meeting in Switzerland on the conflict and the full implementations of which is the basis of the current talks. "The Communiqué helps the two sides, and us sitting between them, to start the long road towards ending this crisis."

Of the fact that the two sides remain at odds over how to tackle his four-point proposal, Mr. Brahimi underscored that while they had "at least" agreed on an agenda: "It is not good for Syria that we come back for another round and fall in the same trap that we have been struggling with this week and most of the first round."

"I think it is better that every side goes back and reflect and take their responsibility: do they want this process to take place or not? I will do the same," he said, adding that [he] will head to New York to meet with UN Secretary General Ban Ki-moon, as well as United States Secretary of State John Kerry and Russian Foreign Minister Sergey Lavrov, the initiators of the Geneva talks.

He also plans to brief the other permanent five members of the Security Council—China, France and the United Kingdom—as well as the body's 10 non-permanent members.

"So I hope that this time of reflection will lead the Government side in particular to reassure the [opposition] that when they speak of implementing the Geneva Communiqué they do mean that a TGB exercising full executive powers will be the main objective to follow," said Mr. Brahimi, adding that ending violence and combating terrorism "is extremely important, indispensable."

Asked if he had a specific message for President Assad as the talks wrapped up, Mr. Brahimi said: "My message to everybody involved in this terrible crisis is to think of the Syrian people, to think of the immense suffering that has been imposed on [them], the destruction that has taken place in Syria, and to think of what anyone can contribute to pull Syria out of the ditch in which it has fallen."

To a question about the ongoing commitment of Russia and the US, he said he continued to believe the two countries are important partners with the United Nations. "There is no doubt—and I have said repeatedly—that the United Nations, the Russian Federation and the United States; none of them can turn a blind eye to this huge crisis in Syria."

SOURCE: United Nations. News Centre. "UN–Arab League envoy apologizes to Syrian people over stalemate in peace talks." February 15, 2014. © 2014 United Nations. Reprinted with the permission of the United Nations. www.un.org/apps/news/story.asp?NewsID=47152#.VH0zMItUxAg.

OTHER HISTORIC DOCUMENTS OF INTEREST

FROM PREVIOUS *HISTORIC DOCUMENTS*

February

Sochi Hosts the 2014 Winter Olympic Games

FEBRUARY 4 AND 7, 2014

In February 2014, the coastal resort city of Sochi, Russia, played host to the 22nd Winter Olympic Games. It was the first Olympics held in Russia since the Soviet Union dissolved in 1991, and the country—along with Russian president Vladimir Putin—was heavily invested in the games' success, hoping to impress the rest of the world. In the years and months preceding the games, political developments, security concerns, and allegations of corruption drew harsh scrutiny from outside Russia and increased speculation that the games could be a disaster.

INTERNAL TURMOIL

Perhaps chief among the concerns surrounding Russia's Olympics was ensuring the security of those attending the games. Sochi is located in a part of Russia that is close to the country's North Caucasus, which encompasses several regions with peoples who are seeking independence from Russia. Rebel leaders in these regions, particularly in Dagestan and Chechnya, have led an insurgency against the Russian government since the early 2000s, with some Islamic extremists declaring a jihad on the state. Russia has experienced an increase in related violent incidents since 2007.

In July 2014, Chechen insurgent leader Doku Umarov posted a video online that urged his followers to use "maximum force" to prevent the Olympics from happening, which was followed by a series of violent attacks. In October, for example, a female Dagestani suicide bomber killed six people in an attack on a bus in the Russian city of Volgograd. In December, a car bomb killed three in the city of Pyatigorsk. Then on December 29 and 30, a militant Islamist group orchestrated two suicide bombings in Volgograd. On December 29, eighteen people were killed and forty-four injured in an attack on the city's train station; the following day, sixteen people were killed and forty-one injured in a bombing of a trolleybus. The attacks heightened fears of the potential for similar terrorist acts to occur during the games, and so the Russian government placed an even greater focus on security needs. Russia ultimately deployed approximately 70,000 military and law enforcement personnel to Sochi, as well as warships, antimissile batteries, and drones. The United States also sent two warships to the Black Sea to provide assistance if necessary. For its part, the International Olympic Committee (IOC) offered assurances that no one would be harmed. Following the bombings in Volgograd, IOC president Thomas Bach condemned the "despicable attack on innocent people" and said he had confidence that Russia would deliver "safe and secure games in Sochi."

Beyond the security concerns, the games' location also created political sensitivities. A group of Muslim indigenous people called the Circassians, also from the Caucasus region, called for Russia to move or cancel the Olympics unless the country acknowledged and apologized for what they described as an act of genocide. In 1864, 300,000 of their ancestors who had been living in the Sochi area were killed during the end of the Russian-Circassian War; 2014 marked the 150th anniversary of the incident. The Circassians held protests to draw reaction from Russia, and in 2010, they presented Georgian lawmakers with a resolution asking them to recognize the incident as genocide. Russia made no such apology ahead of the games, and President Putin signed a security decree in August 2013 to prohibit demonstrations not connected to the Olympics for a two-month period that included February.

LGBT ISSUES

Another controversial matter for Russia proved to be its treatment of homosexuals. Antigay sentiment is strong there—even though homosexuality was legalized in 1994—and hate campaigns are allegedly carried out by local officials throughout the country. One group called Occupy Pedophilia, which has gangs in thirty Russian cities, films its members humiliating, beating, and torturing homosexuals, and then posts those videos online. Since President Putin's reelection in 2012, antigay sentiment has strengthened and given rise to new national laws. Putin often blames Russia's struggles on homosexuals and has said the country should "cleanse" itself of homosexuality.

In June 2013, Putin signed two new laws that prompted an international outcry. One of the laws classified "propaganda of non-traditional sexual relationships" as pornography, thus opening alleged disseminators of such propaganda to fines and arrest. The other authorized police to arrest tourists and foreign nationals whom they suspected of being homosexual, lesbian, or "pro-gay," and detain those individuals for up to fourteen days. Both laws used broad and vague language, creating significant concern that athletes, coaches, reporters, or others visiting the country for the Olympics could be detained, whether they were homosexual or merely tolerant of homosexuality.

These laws were followed by others that prohibit foreign gay couples who live in countries that allow same-sex marriage from adopting Russian-born children and forbid the sharing of "propaganda of non-traditional sexual relationships" among minors. One piece of legislation introduced in October would have permitted the state to forcibly remove children from the homes of their gay or lesbian parents because "nontraditional sexual orientation" was seen as equivalent to child abuse. This bill was later withdrawn due to growing international pressure to adopt a more tolerant stance ahead of the Olympics. More than 5,000 people were arrested during roughly 200 protests against these laws, with many homosexuals reportedly beaten and left without protection from police.

Amid harsh international criticisms, Putin offered assurances that Russia would protect athletes' safety at the Olympics, as long as they obeyed the country's laws. The IOC also issued a statement seeking to reassure athletes: "The IOC would like to reiterate our long commitment to non-discrimination against those taking part in the Olympic Games, the IOC is an open organization and athletes of all orientations will be welcome at the Games." World leaders, including U.S. president Barack Obama, denounced the laws, but did not support calls for a formal boycott of the games. However, President Obama, British prime minister David Cameron, French president François Hollande, and Canadian prime minister Stephen Harper were also among the world leaders who did not attend the Olympics's opening ceremony as national delegates. This prompted widespread speculation that their decision not to attend was a symbolic boycott. The United States also appointed openly gay athletes Billie Jean King, Brian Boitano, and Caitlin Cahow to serve in its delegation instead of the president. In discussing the selection, President Obama said, "There is no doubt we wanted to make it very clear that we do not abide by discrimination in anything, including discrimination on the basis of sexual orientation."

In September, IOC investigator Jean-Claude Killy told reporters that the IOC had no concerns "as long as the Olympic Charter is respected." At that time, the charter's "Fundamental Principles of Olympism" included the statement that "every individual must have the possibility of practicing sport, without discrimination of any kind," and that "any form of discrimination with regard to a country or a person on grounds of race, religion, politics, gender or otherwise is incompatible with belonging to the Olympic Movement." Killy's statement drew criticism from human rights organizations, including the Human Rights Campaign (HRC). "If this law doesn't violate the IOC's charter, then the charter is completely meaningless," said Chad Griffin, HRC's president. "The safety of millions of LGBT Russians and international travellers is at risk and by all accounts the IOC has completely neglected its responsibility to Olympic athletes, sponsors and fans from around the world," Griffin continued.

These concerns later led the IOC to add "sexual orientation" to its nondiscrimination principle and a human rights clause requiring respect for international standards on labor and environment rights to its host city contracts in 2014.

CONSTRUCTION PROBLEMS AND COST OVERRUNS

Russia faced challenges in building all the facilities and transportation infrastructure required to support the Olympics. The games were set to take place in two locations: a new Olympic Park on the Black Sea coast and in the resort settlement of Krasnaya Polyana, which is located in the mountains. There were also limited facilities available in the region at the time, so Russia needed to build nearly everything from scratch.

To complete building, the government brought in tens of thousands of construction workers, including approximately 16,000 non-Russian citizens, which in turn raised a number of labor-related issues. Human Rights Watch, for example, reported that the construction firms working to build event venues were cheating workers out of wages, forcing them to work long shifts and giving them little time off. The group also claimed that some companies had confiscated employees' passports and work permits to force them to stay on the job.

Russia's extensive construction needs also contributed to significant cost overruns. The country originally estimated a budget of $12 billion to host the games, but costs ultimately totaled more than $51 billion, making it the most expensive Olympics in history. Critics alleged that much of the ballooning cost could be attributed to corruption in Russia's system for awarding construction contracts. Opposition politicians Boris Nemtsov and Leonid Martynyuk, for example, claimed that a significant portion of the event's budget had been spent on "kickbacks and embezzlement" for close associates of Putin. A report they released concluded that "an absence of fair competition, clan politics and the strictest censorship about anything related to the Olympic Games have led to a sharp increase in costs and a low quality of work." Dmitry Kozak, Russia's deputy prime minister for Olympic preparations, argued that the $51 billion number was misleading because only $6 billion of that spending was directly related to the Olympics. He claimed that the rest of the money went to infrastructure and regional development projects that Russia would have completed anyway.

In 2012, law enforcement officials did file charges against contractors working on the Fisht Olympic Stadium and the bobsled course, alleging that they had inflated costs by filing false or unjustified project estimates. Putin also spoke out against the cost overruns and project delays, at one point in 2013 calling for a Russian Olympic Committee senior official to be fired for mismanagement.

Russia drew criticism for being unprepared for the influx of guests to Sochi in the days immediately preceding the games. Three of the nine hotels that had been designated for accredited media had not been finished, and many journalists who did have a room reported that they were dirty, did not have running water or safe drinking water, and were missing furniture and other amenities. Several of the dormitories that were meant to house the games' 25,000 volunteers had not been built yet. IOC president Bach defended Russia against the criticism, noting that only 3 percent of rooms had some kind of issue, while the other 97 percent were ready on time.

THE GAMES BEGIN

The 2014 Winter Olympic Games began on February 7 and continued through February 23. It featured ninety-eight events across fifteen sport disciplines, including new events such as biathlon mixed relay, women's ski jumping, mixed-team figure skating and luge, half-pipe skiing, ski and snowboard slopestyle, and the snowboard parallel slalom. Approximately 2,800 athletes from eighty-eight countries participated, setting a new record for a winter Olympics. This stood in stark contrast to the last Olympics Russia had hosted, the 1980 Summer Olympic Games, which sixty-five countries boycotted over the Soviet Union's invasion of Afghanistan.

Despite widespread and varied concerns, Russia's Olympics were deemed a success by many, including the IOC. Shortly before the closing ceremonies, IOC President Bach applauded President Putin and the Russian government for their involvement and support. "We saw excellent Games and what counts most is the opinions of the athletes, and they were enormously satisfied," Bach said. "You have to ask all those who criticized whether they change their opinions now."

FUTURE GAMES

Regardless of corruption charges, the significant cost of the Sochi and other recent games, prospective host countries around the world began to reconsider their bids to attract the next Olympics. In 2014, the cities of Oslo, Munich, Stockholm, St. Moritze, Krakow, and Lviv all withdrew their bids to host the 2022 Winter Olympics, leaving only Beijing, China and Almaty, Kazakhstan. In many cases, residents of these countries questioned how the new Olympic facilities would be used in the future and whether they were worth the investment. Indeed, Sochi's venues and facilities have largely gone unused since the end of the games, with the exception of the Formula-One Grand Prix race, which Russia hosted in October, and many of the hotels being built in the mountains around Sochi which were not ready in time for the games still have not opened.

—Linda Fecteau Grimm

The following is a statement by Russian president Vladimir Putin on February 4, 2014, officially opening the International Olympic Committee (IOC) session in Sochi; and the speech by IOC president Thomas Bach officially opening the Winter Games on February 4, 2014.

Putin Opens IOC Session in Sochi

February 4, 2014

Vladimir Putin spoke at the opening of the 126th session of the International Olympic Committee, held in Sochi ahead of the Winter Olympic Games.

PRESIDENT OF RUSSIA VLADIMIR PUTIN: Ladies and gentlemen, friends, President Bach,

I am truly happy to welcome you to Sochi, which is hosting the XXII Winter Olympic Games.

We are only three days away from the moment when the Olympic flame will light up Fisht Stadium and this grand global athletic celebration will begin.

Russia has been preparing for it with all the responsibility, thoroughness and enormous love for sports, with a lot of excitement and great hope.

We have strong memories of the emotional, uplifting enthusiasm we felt during the 1980 Moscow Olympics and we feel truly joyful and positive because the mighty, inspiring spirit of the Olympic Games is once again returning to our nation.

We are grateful to the International Olympic Committee for the opportunity to host the Winter Olympics. We understand how difficult it was to give Olympic hosting rights to a city that, at the time, had only ten or, at most, fifteen percent of the necessary infrastructure; but everyone believed in our potential and in the Russian character that could meet any challenges.

I should note that such challenges only serve to rally us. And here in Russia, we have a big, multi-ethnic family; it's hard to even count, but we have over 160 ethnic groups and peoples living in our nation. These challenges give all the Russian people powerful motivation to change the situation for the better, to prove that Russia is capable of overcoming any obstacle and successfully achieving the most ambitious goals, such as building elite sports facilities and all necessary city infrastructure in just five years, when it usually takes decades to complete this type of construction.

Today, each of you can see how the city of Sochi has been transformed over the last several years and ascertain for yourselves that our nation is prepared to make its contribution to the development of global sports. During our preparations for the Games, we gained extensive knowledge, which we are ready to share with all our friends and partners—members of the big Olympic Family, including in the area of education, in promoting the Olympic project itself as well as sports and the values of a healthy lifestyle.

Suffice to mention the largest media promotion programme in the history of preparing and holding the Olympic Games, the enormous number of bright cultural events that have united millions of citizens throughout Russia and, of course, the unique Olympic torch relay, whose duration and diversity reflected all the beauty and uniqueness of Russia, the largest country in the world in terms of territory.

In addition, hosts of future Olympic Games and other major athletic events will be interested in our experience of organising accommodation for Olympic athletes and the general plan we proposed for the Sochi Olympics.

These Olympic Games will also debut new types of sports, including the expanded freestyle skiing and snowboarding programmes, which are particularly popular among young people.

The Paralympic Games will open a little later, but I want to tell you right now that it is just as important for us to hold them at the highest level. I will note that many Russian media have expressed a desire and readiness to provide broad, detailed coverage of the brave Paralympic participants' athletic competitions. We hope this move will not only increase the Games' audience but also inspire thousands of young people to engage in sports.

Indeed, that is the very objective that many Olympians are pursuing, first and foremost, the legacy they leave behind.

This legacy is not just about inculcating the values of an active lifestyle, mutual respect, equality and fair competition in people's consciousness; it's also about more tangible areas. When the Games are over, the Olympic facilities and the infrastructure will serve as the foundation for the first Russian international winter sports centre, where Russia's national teams will train, where we will be happy to see not only our athletes, but our foreign colleagues and friends as well.

But most importantly, it will serve to train new generations of athletes: a Russian national children's sports education centre will be created on the basis of the Olympic facilities. So far, the practice of using Olympic facilities for children's sports has been a fairly uncommon thing around the world. However, it is entirely consistent with the spirit and the very idea of the Olympic and Paralympic legacy, which is essentially aimed toward future generations.

We also have high expectations for the Russian International Olympic University that has opened in Sochi and will train, with the IOC's support, sports managers from around the world, as well as actively develop the volunteer movement in Russia.

And naturally, the city of Sochi itself deserves special acknowledgement. It is largely thanks to the Olympic project that this gem on Russia's Black Sea will be able to fully realise its cultural and tourist potential, to attract guests not only with its unique natural environment but by also offering substantial infrastructure and hospitality options, a whole range of active recreation, educational and eco-tourism opportunities.

I want to stress again that in the years of implementing the Olympic project, a great deal of work has been done in all areas. On July 4, 2007, you, the members of the IOC, supported the Olympic dream of tens of millions of Russians; and for us, preparing and holding the Winter Olympic Games in Sochi, and doing it well, became a matter of honour.

I am confident that thanks to this extensive creative work—each of us has invested a part of our soul into it—the Games will remain in the memory of all Olympic athletes and guests. We hope that they will get to know better and appreciate the nature of modern Russia, to understand and appreciate our commitment to the Olympic Charter—Move forward and be open to the world—and, of course, our hospitality and kindliness, with which we always meet our good and true friends. I hope that each of you will feel it.

We consider everyone who has provided us full, comprehensive support during preparations for the Games in Sochi to be our friends. I want to thank you, Mr Bach, I want to thank Mr Rogge, Mr Killy, and all IOC members and staff, for your active assistance in implementing our Olympic project, fulfilling Russia's Olympic dream.

Please allow me to sincerely wish you success in your work.

Friends, ladies and gentlemen,

Please allow me to declare the 126th session of the International Olympic Committee open.

SOURCE: President of Russia. "Opening of International Olympic Committee Session in Sochi." February 4, 2014. http://eng.kremlin.ru/transcripts/6607.

IOC President Opens the Sochi Winter Olympics

February 7, 2014

Good evening Sochi
Good evening Russia
Good evening dear Athletes,
Mr President of the Russian Federation,
Mr Secretary General of the United Nations,
Dear Olympic friends and fans around the world!

Welcome to the 22nd Olympic Winter Games!

Tonight, we are writing a new page in Olympic history.

These are the first ever Olympic Games organised in the new Russia. We have come here with great respect for the rich and varied history of Russia, and for the many peoples who have always been part of this country. The Russians' deep desire for their own winter-sport resort was so great because of their passion for sports on snow and ice. What took decades in other parts of the world, has been achieved here in just seven years. This is a remarkable achievement.

I would like to thank in particular the President of the Russian Federation and his government, the Sochi Organising Committee, the Russian Olympic Committee and the IOC Members in Russia for their outstanding determination, commitment and their dedication to Olympic sports. Thank you to all the workers for your great contribution under sometimes difficult circumstances.

Thank you to all the people of Sochi and the Krasnodar region. Thank you for your patience, thank you for your understanding during these years of transformation. Now you are living in an Olympic Region. I am sure you will enjoy the benefits for many, many years to come.

Thousands of volunteers have welcomed us with the well-known warm Russian hospitality. Many thanks to all the volunteers. *Bolshoi spasiba, valantyoram!*

Russia and the Russians have set the stage for you, the best winter athletes on our planet. From this moment on you are not only the best athletes, you are Olympic Athletes. You will inspire us with your outstanding sports performances.

You have come here for sport.

You have come here with your Olympic dream.

The International Olympic Committee wants your Olympic Dream to come true.

This is why we are investing almost all of our revenues in the worldwide development of sports.

The universal Olympic rules apply to each and every athlete—no matter where you come from or what your background is. You are living together in the Olympic Village. You will celebrate victory with dignity and accept defeat with dignity. You are bringing the Olympic Values to life.

In this way, the Olympic Games, wherever they take place, set an example for a peaceful society. Olympic Sport unites the people.

This is the Olympic Message the athletes spread to the host country and to the whole world:

- Yes, it is possible to strive even for the greatest victory with respect for the dignity of your competitors.

- Yes, it is possible—even as competitors—to live together under one roof in harmony, with tolerance and without any form of discrimination for whatever reason.

- Yes, it is possible—even as competitors—to listen, to understand and to give an example for a peaceful society.

  Olympic Games are always about building bridges to bring people together.

  Olympic Games are never about erecting walls to keep people apart.

  Olympic Games are a sports festival embracing human diversity in great unity.

Therefore I say to the political leaders of the world:

- Thank you for supporting your athletes—they are the best ambassadors of your country.

- Please respect their Olympic Message of good will, of tolerance, of excellence and of peace.

- Have the courage to address your disagreements in a peaceful, direct political dialogue and not on the backs of these athletes.

To all sports officials and sports fans I say: Join and support our fight for fair play—the athletes deserve it.

And to you—my fellow Olympic Athletes—I say:

- Respect the rules

- Play fair

- Be clean

- Respect your fellow athletes in and out of competition.

We all wish you joy in your Olympic effort and a wonderful Olympic experience.

To all of you—Athletes, Officials, Spectators and Fans around our globe—I say: Enjoy the Olympic Winter Games in Sochi 2014!

And now I have the honour of inviting the President of the Russian Federation, Mister Vladimir Putin, to declare open the 22nd Olympic Winter Games, Sochi, Russia.

SOURCE: International Olympic Committee. "Speech on the occasion of Opening Ceremony Sochi 2014 Olympic Winter Games." February 7, 2014. www.olympic.org/Documents/Games_Sochi_2014/Speech_Games_Opening_IOC_President.pdf.

OTHER HISTORIC DOCUMENTS OF INTEREST

FROM PREVIOUS HISTORIC DOCUMENTS

United Nations Report on North Korea's Human Rights Abuses

FEBRUARY 7 AND APRIL 22, 2014

Often garnering critical attention for its pursuit of nuclear weapons capabilities, North Korea has also drawn international scrutiny for its treatment of its citizens. Human rights activists and members of the diplomatic community claim that North Korea's Communist party–led government has committed countless human rights abuses as it seeks to maintain military, political, and social control over the country, causing its people to face isolation, starvation, and the fear of imprisonment without trial. In February 2014, a United Nations (UN) commission published a landmark report detailing extensive human rights abuses and recommending that the UN Security Council refer the country to the International Criminal Court (ICC). North Korea condemned the report and denied its findings, but took several actions throughout the year that appeared aimed at easing international concerns, including raising the possibility of allowing a UN human rights investigator into the country.

THE UN REPORT

On February 7, 2014, the UN Commission of Inquiry on Human Rights in the Democratic People's Republic of Korea, an entity within the UN Office of the High Commissioner for Human Rights, released an extensive report detailing "systematic, widespread and gross human rights violations" that had been or were still being committed in North Korea. "The gravity, scale and nature of these violations reveal a state that does not have any parallel in the contemporary world," the report read. Since North Korea refused to cooperate with investigators and did not allow them to enter the country, the report was based on "first-hand testimony" from victims, witnesses, and interviews, collected through more than 240 confidential interviews over an eleven-month period.

Among its key findings, the report stated that political criminals "are 'disappeared,' without trial or judicial order, to political prison camps" where they are "incarcerated and held incommunicado." Others were executed without trial. Hundreds of thousands of political prisoners have reportedly died within this system of camps during the past fifty years. The report said inmates were subjected to starvation, forced labor, torture, rape, and, in the case of some female prisoners, forced to abort a pregnancy or commit infanticide. The commission wrote that these and other conditions were "deliberately imposed on suspects to increase the pressure on them to confess and incriminate other persons." It also noted that prison authorities "received orders to kill all prisoners in case of an armed conflict or revolution so as to destroy the primary evidence of the camps' existence."

Other report findings included that the North Korean government operates an "all-encompassing indoctrination machine," to which North Koreans are subject from birth to ensure their conformity and "obedience to the supreme leader." The government isolated citizens from each other and from the outside world, conducted surveillance on them, banned them from travelling, and prevented the dissemination of independent thought. The report also concluded that various government actions and decisions had knowingly caused the death of hundreds of thousands of people through starvation and "inflicted permanent physical and psychological injuries on those who survived." Further, the report noted that more than 200,000 people who had been brought to North Korea from other countries "may have become victims of enforced disappearance." In summary, the report stated:

> "crimes against humanity entail extermination, murder, enslavement, torture, imprisonment, rape, forced abortions and other sexual violence, persecution on political, religious, racial and gender grounds, the forcible transfer of populations, the enforced disappearance of persons and the inhumane act of knowingly causing prolonged starvation. The commission further finds that crimes against humanity are ongoing in the Democratic People's Republic of Korea because the policies, institutions and patterns of impunity that lie at their heart remain in place."

The report recommended several steps that North Korea could take to address these human rights issues, including implementing political reforms that would limit Supreme Leader Kim Jong Un's authority, establishing an independent judiciary, and allowing for the release of all political prisoners. Perhaps most notably, the report called for the UN Security Council to refer the situation to the ICC, writing, "The United Nations must ensure that those most responsible for the crimes against humanity committed in the Democratic People's Republic of Korea are held accountable." Such a referral would mark the strongest attempt yet by the international community to take action on North Korea's reported record of human rights abuses. The United Nations also sent a letter to Kim following the report's release, informing him that he could be held personally responsible for aiding crimes against humanity. Kim did not respond.

NORTH KOREA REACTS

The report drew a sharp response from North Korean officials. So Se Pyong, the country's ambassador to the United Nations, denounced its findings as "lies" and claimed the United States and "other hostile forces" had fabricated the report to "defame the dignified image of the Democratic People's Republic of Korea and eventually eliminate its social system." He also said the United States should be investigated for "egregious human rights violations." North Korea was not alone in criticizing the report. During a meeting of the UN Human Rights Council on March 17, China's UN representative said the report was "divorced from reality" and was unfair because of "the inability of the Commission to get support and cooperation from the country concerned." Notably, Chinese officials refused to collaborate with the UN commission, which requested meetings with the Chinese government and visits to the country's border with North Korea to inform the report. In a letter to the United Nations, China said it "opposed the politicization" of any country's human rights issues.

North Korea also took aim at Michael Kirby, who led the commission's investigation. An article published by the Korean Central News Agency (KCNA) in April claimed he "took the lead in cooking the 'report'" and described him as "a disgusting old lecher with a 40-odd-year-long career of homosexuality." Just over one week later, KCNA released another article titled "News Analysis on Poor Human Rights Records in U.S." The analysis claimed that the United States "is the world's worst human rights abuser and tundra of a human being's rights to existence," pointing to racial discrimination, unemployment, crime rates, surveillance of citizens, and poverty as evidence that the United States was a "living hell." That same day, North Korea released a white paper highlighting human rights concerns in South Korea, claiming it had the worst human rights record of any country and was "deprived of everything thanks to America."

As North Korea criticized other countries, it also defended itself. In September, the North Korean Association for Human Rights Studies published its own report analyzing the status of human rights in the country. The report included a long list of human rights that are included in North Korea's constitution, including freedoms of religion, speech, press, travel, and education. It also highlighted North Korea's compulsory education system, gender equality legislation, and labor regulations, among other items, as evidence that the country was in fact protecting human rights. The report further claimed that North Koreans enjoy "genuine human rights" and blamed the United States, European Union, Japan, and South Korea for fomenting unwarranted international criticism. It either ignored or dismissed claims and evidence put forward by the UN's report.

A UN Resolution Leads to Change

In October, amid growing speculation that the United Nations would consider a resolution referring North Korea to the ICC, the country appeared to soften its stance, if only slightly. Early in the month, North Korean officials announced they would resume high-level talks with South Korea, and they made a surprise appearance in the south for the Asian Games. Just a few days later, officials held a rare briefing at the United Nations to discuss the report. The country's UN representative, Choe Myong Nam, denied the existence of prison camps in the country and dismissed many criticisms as "wild rumors," but noted that North Korea was a society in transition and thus there was room for improvement. He also claimed that the country's faltering economy was due to "external factors," an apparent nod to economic sanctions.

The week of October 6, Japan and the European Union officially introduced a draft resolution to the UN General Assembly, calling for the Security Council to refer North Korea to the ICC for prosecution of crimes against humanity. The resolution was non-binding, but if passed was expected to put significant pressure on the Security Council. At least forty-two countries signed on in support within a week of the resolution's introduction, and it was set for a vote before the Third Committee of the UN General Assembly— which is responsible for social, humanitarian, and cultural issues—on November 18.

In the weeks preceding the vote, North Korea continued to act in a way that many diplomats and human rights investigators viewed as an effort to weaken the momentum behind the draft resolution. This included releasing three American detainees; demonstrating greater openness to engaging with the United States, Japan, and South Korea; sending a special envoy to Russia, which has veto power on the Security Council, to strengthen relations; and distributing a video discrediting an escaped prisoner who had become a vocal critic of North Korea's human rights record and had participated in the UN's report.

Then on October 27, North Korean officials met with Marzuki Darusman, the UN's special rapporteur on human rights in North Korea and said there could be an opportunity for him to visit the country—a major breakthrough for the diplomatic community.

Choe said North Korea was looking for a "new and objective report" from the United Nations because its previous reports "have been based on rumors and fabrications, as well as distortions." Darusman later told reporters that the officials requested that the General Assembly resolution be amended to not include the ICC referral request or a warning that Kim could be held personally accountable for the crimes, hinting that they would exchange an in-country visit for these changes.

On November 18, the Third Committee of the General Assembly passed the resolution by a vote of 111–19, with fifty-five abstentions. Choe denounced the resolution, saying it was "confrontational in nature" and would "only result in unpredictable and serious consequences." As of the end of 2014, the Security Council has yet to take up the matter and no arrangements have been made for a UN investigator to visit North Korea.

—Linda Fecteau Grimm

The following is the edited text of the United Nation's summary report on suspected human rights abuses in North Korea, released on February 7, 2014; and a response to the UN report from North Korea on April 22, 2014.

UN Report on North Korean Human Rights Violations

February 7, 2014

[The cover page, table of contents, introduction, report methodology, and footnotes have been omitted.]

III. PRINCIPAL FINDINGS OF THE COMMISSION

24. The commission finds that systematic, widespread and gross human rights violations have been and are being committed by the Democratic People's Republic of Korea. In many instances, the violations found entailed crimes against humanity based on State policies. The main perpetrators are officials of the State Security Department, the Ministry of People's Security, the Korean People's Army, the Office of the Public Prosecutor, the judiciary and the Workers' Party of Korea, who are acting under the effective control of the central organs of the Workers' Party of Korea, the National Defence Commission and the Supreme Leader of the Democratic People's Republic of Korea. . . .

A. Violations of the freedoms of thought, expression and religion

26. . . . The commission finds that there is an almost complete denial of the right to freedom of thought, conscience and religion, as well as of the rights to freedom of opinion, expression, information and association.

27. The State operates an all-encompassing indoctrination machine that takes root from childhood to propagate an official personality cult and to manufacture absolute

obedience to the Supreme Leader (*Suryong*), effectively to the exclusion of any thought independent of official ideology and State propaganda. Propaganda is further used by the Democratic People's Republic of Korea to incite nationalistic hatred towards official enemies of the State, including Japan, the United States of America and the Republic of Korea, and their nationals.

28. Virtually all social activities undertaken by citizens of all ages are controlled by the Workers' Party of Korea. Through the associations that are run and overseen by the Party, and to which citizens are obliged to be members, the State is able to monitor its citizens and to dictate their daily activities. State surveillance permeates the private lives of all citizens to ensure that virtually no expression critical of the political system or of its leadership goes undetected. Citizens are punished for any "anti-State" activities or expressions of dissent. They are rewarded for reporting on fellow citizens suspected of committing such "crimes."

29. Citizens are denied the right to have access to information from independent sources; State-controlled media are the only permitted source of information in the Democratic People's Republic of Korea. Access to television and radio broadcasts, as well as to the Internet, is severely restricted, and all media content is heavily censored and must adhere to directives issued by the Workers' Party of Korea. Telephone calls are monitored and mostly confined to domestic connections for citizens. Citizens are punished for watching and listening to foreign broadcasts, including foreign films and soap operas. . . .

31. . . . Apart from the few organized State-controlled churches, Christians are prohibited from practising their religion and are persecuted. People caught practising Christianity are subject to severe punishments in violation of the right to freedom of religion and the prohibition of religious discrimination.

B. Discrimination

32. . . . State-sponsored discrimination in the Democratic People's Republic of Korea is pervasive, but is also shifting. Discrimination is rooted in the *songbun* system, which classifies people on the basis of State-assigned social class and birth, and also includes consideration of political opinions and religion. *Songbun* intersects with gender-based discrimination, which is equally pervasive. Discrimination is also practised on the basis of disability, although there are signs that the State may have begun to address this particular issue. . . .

34. Early reforms aimed at ensuring formal legal equality have not resulted in gender equality. Discrimination against women remains pervasive in all aspects of society. Indeed, it might even be increasing, as the male-dominated State preys on both economically advancing women and marginalized women. . . .

35. The economic advances of women have not been matched by advances in the social and political spheres. Entrenched traditional patriarchal attitudes and violence against women persist in the Democratic People's Republic of Korea. The State has imposed blatantly discriminatory restrictions on women in an attempt to maintain the gender stereotype of the pure and innocent Korean woman. Sexual and gender-based violence against women is prevalent throughout all areas of society. . . .

36. Discrimination against women also intersects with a number of other human rights violations, placing women in a position of vulnerability. Violations of the rights to food and to freedom of movement have resulted in women and girls becoming vulnerable to trafficking and increased engagement in transactional sex and prostitution. . . .

C. Violations of the freedom of movement and residence

38. The systems of indoctrination and discrimination on the basis of social class are reinforced and safeguarded by a policy of isolating citizens from contact with each other and with the outside world, violating all aspects of the right to freedom of movement.

39. In the Democratic People's Republic of Korea, the State imposes on citizens where they must live and work, violating their freedom of choice. Moreover, the forced assignment to a State-designated place of residence and employment is heavily driven by discrimination based on *songbun*. This has created a socioeconomically and physically segregated society, where people considered politically loyal to the leadership can live and work in favourable locations, whereas families of persons who are considered politically suspect are relegated to marginalized areas. The special status of Pyongyang, reserved only for those most loyal to the State, exemplifies this system of segregation.

40. Citizens are not even allowed to leave their province temporarily or to travel within the country without official authorization. This policy is driven by the desire to maintain disparate living conditions, to limit the flow of information and to maximize State control, at the expense of social and familial ties.

41. In an attempt to keep Pyongyang's "pure" and untainted image, the State systematically banishes entire families from the capital city if one family member commits what is deemed to be a serious crime or political wrong. . . .

42. The State imposes a virtually absolute ban on ordinary citizens travelling abroad, thereby violating their human right to leave the country. Despite the enforcement of this ban through strict border controls, nationals still take the risk of fleeing, mainly to China. When they are apprehended or forcibly repatriated, officials from the Democratic People's Republic of Korea systematically subject them to persecution, torture, prolonged arbitrary detention and, in some cases, sexual violence, including during invasive body searches. Repatriated women who are pregnant are regularly subjected to forced abortions, and babies born to repatriated women are often killed. . . .

43. Despite the gross human rights violations awaiting repatriated persons, China pursues a rigorous policy of forcibly repatriating citizens of the Democratic People's Republic of Korea who cross the border illegally. China does so in pursuance of its view that these persons are economic (and illegal) migrants. However, many such nationals of the Democratic People's Republic of Korea should be recognized as refugees fleeing persecution or refugees *sur place*. . . .

44. Discrimination against women and their vulnerable status in the Democratic People's Republic of Korea, as well as the prospect of refoulement, make women extremely vulnerable to trafficking in persons. Many women are trafficked by force or deception from the Democratic People's Republic of Korea into or within China for the purposes of exploitation in forced marriage or concubinage, or prostitution under coercive circumstances. An estimated 20,000 children born to women from the Democratic People's Republic of Korea are currently in China. These children are deprived of their rights to birth registration, nationality, education and health care because their birth cannot be registered without exposing the mother to the risk of refoulement by China. . . .

D. Violations of the right to food and related aspects of the right to life

46. The rights to food, freedom from hunger and to life in the context of the Democratic People's Republic of Korea cannot be reduced to a narrow discussion of food shortages

and access to a commodity. The State has used food as a means of control over the population. It has prioritized those whom the authorities believe to be crucial in maintaining the regime over those deemed expendable.

47. Confiscation and dispossession of food from those in need, and the provision of food to other groups, follows this logic. The State has practised discrimination with regard to access to and distribution of food based on the *songbun* system. In addition, it privileges certain parts of the country, such as Pyongyang, over others. The State has also failed to take into account the needs of the most vulnerable. The commission is particularly concerned about ongoing chronic malnutrition in children and its long-term effects.

48. The State was aware of the deteriorating food situation in the country well before the first appeal for international aid in 1995. State-controlled production and distribution of food had not been able to provide the population with adequate food since the end of the 1980s. . . .

49. During the period of famine, ideological indoctrination was used in order to maintain the regime, at the cost of seriously aggravating hunger and starvation. The concealment of information prevented the population from finding alternatives to the collapsing public distribution system. It also delayed international assistance that, provided earlier, could have saved many lives. Despite the State's inability to provide its people with adequate food, it maintained laws and controls effectively criminalizing people's use of key coping mechanisms, particularly moving within or outside the country in search of food and trading or working in informal markets.

50. Even during the worst period of mass starvation, the State impeded the delivery of food aid by imposing conditions that were not based on humanitarian considerations. International humanitarian agencies were subject to restrictions contravening humanitarian principles. Aid organizations were prevented from properly assessing humanitarian needs and monitoring the distribution of aid. The State denied humanitarian access to some of the most affected regions and groups, including homeless children.

51. The State has consistently failed in its obligation to use the maximum of its available resources to feed those who are hungry. Military spending—predominantly on hardware and the development of weapons systems and the nuclear programme—has always been prioritized, even during periods of mass starvation. Nevertheless, the State still failed to feed the ordinary soldiers of its disproportionately large army. . . .

52. The State has also used deliberate starvation as a means of control and punishment in detention facilities. This has resulted in the deaths of many political and ordinary prisoners.

53. The commission found evidence of systematic, widespread and grave violations of the right to food in the Democratic People's Republic of Korea. While acknowledging the impact of factors beyond State control over the food situation, the commission finds that decisions, actions and omissions by the State and its leadership caused the death of at least hundreds of thousands of people and inflicted permanent physical and psychological injuries on those who survived.

54. In the highly centralized system of the Democratic People's Republic of Korea, decisions relating to food, including its production and distribution, State budget allocation, decisions relating to humanitarian assistance and the use of international aid, are ultimately made by a small group of officials, who are not accountable to those affected by their decisions. . . .

E. Arbitrary detention, torture, executions and prison camps

56. The police and security forces of the Democratic People's Republic of Korea systematically employ violence and punishments that amount to gross human rights violations in order to create a climate of fear that pre-empts any challenge to the current system of government and to the ideology underpinning it. The institutions and officials involved are not held accountable. Impunity reigns.

57. Gross human rights violations in the Democratic People's Republic of Korea involving detention, executions and disappearances are characterized by a high degree of centralized coordination between different parts of the extensive security apparatus. The State Security Department, the Ministry of People's Security and the Korean People's Army Military Security Command regularly subject persons accused of political crimes to arbitrary arrest and subsequent incommunicado detention for prolonged periods of time. Their families are not informed of their fate or whereabouts. Persons accused of political crimes therefore become victims of enforced disappearance. Making the suspect disappear is a deliberate feature of the system that serves to instil fear in the population.

58. The use of torture is an established feature of the interrogation process in the Democratic People's Republic of Korea, especially in cases involving political crimes. Starvation and other inhumane conditions of detention are deliberately imposed on suspects to increase the pressure on them to confess and to incriminate other persons.

59. Persons who are found to have engaged in major political crimes are "disappeared," without trial or judicial order, to political prison camps (*kwanliso*). There, they are incarcerated and held incommunicado. Their families are not even informed of their fate if they die. . . .

60. In the political prison camps of the Democratic People's Republic of Korea, the inmate population has been gradually eliminated through deliberate starvation, forced labour, executions, torture, rape and the denial of reproductive rights enforced through punishment, forced abortion and infanticide. The commission estimates that hundreds of thousands of political prisoners have perished in these camps over the past five decades. The unspeakable atrocities that are being committed against inmates of the *kwanliso* political prison camps resemble the horrors of camps that totalitarian States established during the twentieth century.

61. Although the authorities in the Democratic People's Republic of Korea deny the existence of the camps, this claim was shown to be false by the testimonies of former guards, inmates and neighbours. Satellite imagery proves that the camp system continues to be in operation. While the number of political prison camps and inmates has decreased owing to deaths and some releases, it is estimated that between 80,000 and 120,000 political prisoners are currently detained in four large political prison camps.

62. Gross violations are also being committed in the ordinary prison system, which consists of ordinary prison camps (*kyohwaso*) and various types of short-term forced labour detention facilities. The vast majority of inmates are victims of arbitrary detention, since they are imprisoned without trial or on the basis of a trial that fails to respect the due process and fair trial guarantees set out in international law. Furthermore, many ordinary prisoners are, in fact, political prisoners, who are detained without a substantive reason compatible with international law. Prisoners in the ordinary prison system are systematically subjected to deliberate starvation and illegal forced labour. Torture, rape and other arbitrary cruelties at the hands of guards and fellow prisoners are widespread and committed with impunity.

63. As a matter of State policy, the authorities carry out executions, with or without trial, publicly or secretly, in response to political and other crimes that are often not among the most serious crimes. The policy of regularly carrying out public executions serves to instil fear in the general population. . . .

F. Abductions and enforced disappearances from other countries

64. Since 1950, the Democratic People's Republic of Korea has engaged in the systematic abduction, denial of repatriation and subsequent enforced disappearance of persons from other countries on a large scale and as a matter of State policy. Well over 200,000 persons, including children, who were brought from other countries to the Democratic People's Republic of Korea may have become victims of enforced disappearance, as defined in the Declaration on the Protection of All Persons from Enforced Disappearance. . . .

65. For a nation State that seeks to live alongside others, the above-mentioned actions, in defiance of the sovereignty of other States and the rights of foreign nationals guaranteed under international law, are exceptional.

66. The vast majority of abductions and enforced disappearances are linked to the Korean War and the organized movement of ethnic Koreans from Japan that started in 1959. However, hundreds of nationals of the Republic of Korea, Japan and other States were also abducted and disappeared between the 1960s and 1980s. In more recent years, the Democratic People's Republic of Korea abducted a number of its own nationals and nationals of the Republic of Korea from China.

67. The Democratic People's Republic of Korea used its land, naval and intelligence forces to conduct abductions and arrests. Operations were approved at the level of the Supreme Leader. The vast majority of victims were forcibly disappeared to gain labour and other skills for the State. Some victims were used to further espionage and terrorist activities. Women abducted from Europe, the Middle East and Asia were subjected to forced marriages with men from other countries to prevent liaisons on their part with ethnic Korean women that could result in interracial children. Some of the abducted women have also been subject to sexual exploitation.

68. A number of the forcibly disappeared travelled to the Democratic People's Republic of Korea voluntarily. Others were abducted through physical force or fraudulent persuasion. Subsequently, they were all denied the right to leave the country. They have also been subject to severe deprivation of their liberty and freedom of movement within the Democratic People's Republic of Korea, denied the right to recognition as a person before the law, and the right not to be subjected to torture and other cruel, inhuman or degrading treatment. . . .

69. Ethnic Koreans from the Republic of Korea and Japan, forcibly disappeared by the Democratic People's Republic of Korea, have been discriminated against for their origins and background. . . .

70. Non-Korean abductees were not able to integrate into social and economic life in the Democratic People's Republic of Korea as they were detained in tightly controlled compounds. They were denied the right to work, to leave their place of residence or to move freely in society, and they were unable to choose educational opportunities for themselves and their children.

71. Family members abroad and foreign States wishing to exercise their right to provide diplomatic protection have been consistently denied information necessary

to establish the fate and whereabouts of the victims. Family members of the disappeared have been subjected to torture and other cruel, inhuman or degrading treatment. They have been denied the right to effective remedies for human rights violations, including the right to the truth. Parents and disappeared children have been denied the right to family life.

72. Despite admitting to the abduction of 13 Japanese nationals by agents of the State, the Democratic People's Republic of Korea has never adequately disavowed the practice of international abductions. Since the 1990s, its agents have abducted a number of persons from Chinese territory, including nationals of China, the Republic of Korea and, in at least one case, a former Japanese national. . . .

IV. Crimes against humanity

74. According to that standard, the commission finds that the body of testimony and other information it received establishes that crimes against humanity have been committed in the Democratic People's Republic of Korea, pursuant to policies established at the highest level of the State.

75. These crimes against humanity entail extermination, murder, enslavement, torture, imprisonment, rape, forced abortions and other sexual violence, persecution on political, religious, racial and gender grounds, the forcible transfer of populations, the enforced disappearance of persons and the inhumane act of knowingly causing prolonged starvation. The commission further finds that crimes against humanity are ongoing in the Democratic People's Republic of Korea because the policies, institutions and patterns of impunity that lie at their heart remain in place. . .

V. Conclusions and recommendations

80. Systematic, widespread and gross human rights violations have been and are being committed by the Democratic People's Republic of Korea, its institutions and officials. In many instances, the violations of human rights found by the commission constitute crimes against humanity. . . . The gravity, scale and nature of these violations reveal a State that does not have any parallel in the contemporary world. . . .

85. A number of long-standing and ongoing patterns of systematic and widespread violations, which were documented by the commission, meet the high threshold required for proof of crimes against humanity in international law. The perpetrators enjoy impunity. . . .

87. The United Nations must ensure that those most responsible for the crimes against humanity committed in the Democratic People's Republic of Korea are held accountable. Options to achieve this end include a Security Council referral of the situation to the International Criminal Court or the establishment of an ad hoc tribunal by the United Nations. Urgent accountability measures should be combined with a reinforced human rights dialogue, the promotion of incremental change through more people-to-people contact and an inter-Korean agenda for reconciliation.

88. On the basis of its findings and conclusions, the Commission makes the recommendations below.

89. The commission of inquiry recommends that the Democratic People's Republic of Korea:

(a) Undertake profound political and institutional reforms without delay to introduce genuine checks and balances upon the powers of the Supreme Leader and the Workers' Party of Korea; such changes should include an independent and impartial judiciary, a multiparty political system and elected people's assemblies at the local and central levels that emerge from genuinely free and fair elections; reform the security sector by vetting the entire officers' corps for involvement in human rights violations and by limiting the functions of the Korean People's Army to defending the nation against external threats; and dismantle the State Security Department and place the Ministry of Public Security under transparent democratic oversight. An independent constitutional and institutional reform commission, consisting of respected members of society in the Democratic People's Republic of Korea, should be constituted to guide this process and should be assisted by appropriate international experts;

(b) Acknowledge the existence of human rights violations, including the political prison camps described by the commission in the present report; provide international humanitarian organizations and human rights monitors with immediate access to the camps and their surviving victims; dismantle all political prison camps and release all political prisoners; and clarify with full detail the fate of any disappeared persons who cannot be readily traced;

(c) Reform the Criminal Code and Code of Criminal Procedure to abolish vaguely worded "anti-State" and "anti-People" crimes and to fully enshrine the right to a fair trial and due process guarantees articulated in the International Covenant on Civil and Political Rights; enforce existing provisions in the Criminal Code and the Code of Criminal Procedure that prohibit and criminalize the use of torture and other inhuman means of interrogation that are illegal under international law; reform the ordinary prison system so as to ensure humane conditions of detention for all inmates deprived of liberty; end reprisals against persons on the basis of guilt by association; and abolish immediately the practice of forcibly resettling the families of convicted criminals;

(d) Declare and implement an immediate moratorium on the imposition and execution of the death penalty, followed without undue delay by the abolition of the death penalty both in law and in practice;

(e) Allow the establishment of independent newspapers and other media; allow citizens to freely access the Internet, social media, international communications, foreign broadcasts and publications, including the popular culture of other countries; and abolish compulsory participation in mass organizations and indoctrination sessions;

(f) Introduce education to ensure respect for human rights and fundamental freedoms; and abolish any propaganda or educational activities that espouse national, racial or political hatred or war propaganda;

(g) Allow Christians and other religious believers to exercise their religion independently and publicly, without fear of punishment, reprisal or surveillance;

(h) End discrimination against citizens on the basis of their perceived political loyalty or the sociopolitical background of their families, including in matters of access to education and employment. . . .

(i)   Take immediate measures to ensure gender equality in practice, such as by providing equal access for women in public life and employment; eradicate discriminatory laws, regulations and practices affecting women. . . .

(j)   Ensure that citizens can enjoy the right to food and other economic and social rights without discrimination. . . .

(k)   In the light of the past expenditures by the leadership, the military and security apparatus, realign priorities and dedicate the resources made available to ensure, as necessary, freedom from hunger and other essential minimum standards for citizens, including those citizens serving in the armed forces;

(l)   Where necessary to ensure the right to food, seek international humanitarian assistance without delay; provide international humanitarian organizations with free and unimpeded access to all populations in need, including for the purposes of effective monitoring; and hold accountable State officials who illegally divert humanitarian aid for improper purposes;

(m)   Abolish the de facto prohibition on foreign travel imposed on ordinary citizens; decriminalize illegal border crossings and introduce border controls that conform to international standards. . . .

(n)   Provide the families and nations of origin of all persons who have been abducted, or otherwise forcibly disappeared, with full information on their fate and where-abouts, if they have survived. . . .

(o)   Allow separated families to unite, including by allowing citizens to travel or emi-grate where they choose; and immediately provide such persons with facilities for unmonitored communications by way of mail, telephone, email and any other means of communication;

(p)   Prosecute and bring to justice those persons most responsible for alleged crimes against humanity. . . .

(q)   Take immediate steps to end all other human rights violations and to address the human rights concerns raised by the commission in the present report. . . .

(r)   Ratify without delay the International Convention for the Protection of All Persons from Enforced Disappearance, the Convention on the Rights of Persons with Disabilities, the Rome Statute of the International Criminal Court and the fundamental conventions of the International Labour Organization;

(s)   Accept immediately a field-based presence and technical assistance from the Office of the United Nations High Commissioner for Human Rights and other relevant United Nations entities to help to implement the above-mentioned recommendations.

90.   The commission of inquiry recommends that China and other States:

(a)   Respect the principle of non-refoulement and, accordingly, abstain from forcibly repatriating any persons to the Democratic People's Republic of Korea, unless the treatment there, as verified by international human rights monitors, markedly improves. . . .

(b) Provide the Office of the United Nations High Commissioner for Refugees, and relevant humanitarian organizations, full and unimpeded access to all persons from the Democratic People's Republic of Korea seeking such contact;

(c) Request technical assistance from the United Nations to help to meet the obligations imposed under international refugee law, and ensure the effective protection of persons from trafficking;

(d) Adopt a victim-centric and human rights-based approach to trafficking in persons. . . .

(e) Regularize the status of women and men from the Democratic People's Republic of Korea who marry or have a child with a Chinese citizen; and ensure that all such children may realize their rights. . . .

(f) Take immediate measures to prevent agents of the Democratic People's Republic of Korea from carrying out further abductions from Chinese territory. . . .

94. With regard to the international community and the United Nations, the commission makes the following recommendations:

(a) The Security Council should refer the situation in the Democratic People's Republic of Korea to the International Criminal Court for action in accordance with that court's jurisdiction. The Security Council should also adopt targeted sanctions against those who appear to be most responsible for crimes against humanity. . . .

(b) The General Assembly and the Human Rights Council should extend the country-specific human rights monitoring and reporting mechanisms on the Democratic People's Republic of Korea that predate the establishment of the commission. . . .

(c) The United Nations High Commissioner for Human Rights, with full support from the Human Rights Council and the General Assembly, should establish a structure to help to ensure accountability for human rights violations in the Democratic People's Republic of Korea, in particular where such violations amount to crimes against humanity. . . .

(d) The High Commissioner should continue the engagement of OHCHR with the Democratic People's Republic of Korea, offering technical assistance and enhancing advocacy initiatives. . . .

(e) The High Commissioner should periodically report to the Human Rights Council and other appropriate United Nations organs on the implementation of the recommendations contained in the present report;

(f) The Human Rights Council should ensure that the conclusions and recommendations of the commission do not pass from the active attention of the international community. . . .

(h) States that have historically friendly ties with the Democratic People's Republic of Korea, major donors and potential donors, as well as those States already engaged with the Democratic People's Republic of Korea in the framework of the six-party talks, should form a human rights contact group to raise concerns about the situation of human rights in the Democratic People's Republic of Korea and to provide support for initiatives to improve it;

(i)   States should not use the provision of food and other essential humanitarian assistance to impose economic or political pressure on the Democratic People's Republic of Korea. Humanitarian assistance should be provided in accordance with humanitarian and human rights principles. . . .

[The remainder of the report, including correspondence between the United Nations and North Korean and Chinese officials, and appendices reflecting the commission's detailed findings, has been omitted.]

SOURCE: United Nations. Office of the High Commissioner for Human Rights. "Report of the Commission of Inquiry on Human Rights in the Democratic People's Republic of Korea." © 2014 United Nations. Reprinted with the permission of the United Nations. www.ohchr.org/Documents/HRBodies/HRCouncil/CoIDPRK/Report/A.HRC.25.63.doc.

DOCUMENT

North Korea Responds to UN Human Rights Report

April 22, 2014

Michael Kirby, chairman of the "Commission of Inquiry (CI)" on human rights situation in the DPRK, called a press conference at the UN headquarters on April 17.

He told reporters of different countries, skeptical about the truth of CI's "human rights report," that it was based on "testimonies" by "defectors." With such awkward excuse, he asserted it is high time that a UNSC was called to discuss the DPRK's "human rights issue" and bring it to the International Criminal Court.

His rash act is a last-ditch effort intended to lend credence to the "report" peppered with fabrications and create an atmosphere of international pressure on the DPRK in this regard.

Lurking behind it is a dishonest and political purpose of the U.S. and its followers seeking to undermine the ideology and social system of the DPRK.

Now, the forces hostile toward the DPRK regard the "human rights issue" as a main lever for stifling it since they had no way out over the "nuclear issue."

After all, such political swindlers as Kirby were mobilized so as to internationalize the nonexistent "human rights issue" of the DPRK.

As for Kirby who took the lead in cooking the "report," he is a disgusting old lecher with a 40-odd-year-long career of homosexuality. He is now over seventy, but he is still anxious to get married to his homosexual partner.

This practice can never be found in the DPRK boasting of the sound mentality and good morals, and homosexuality has become a target of public criticism even in Western countries, too. In fact, it is ridiculous for such gay to sponsor dealing with others' human rights issue.

As been already known, what was put up by Kirby and his group as data is all testimonies made by those "defectors," who are runaways or terrorists as they betrayed their country and nation after committing indelible crimes.

However, the Kirby group styling itself a judge accepted such unconfirmed data to cook up the "report." This makes one question if the group has an elementary legal sense. After all, they changed their position as judges with money paid by the U.S. and its followers.

At present, many countries and even Western media and personages are astonished at the Kirby group's "report" presented to a sacred UN body, terming it a replica of Nazi-style arbitrariness.

It is so pitiable for the U.S. and its followers to attempt to frighten the DPRK by letting such dirty swindlers, ready to do anything for money, invent an anti-DPRK false document.

The army and people of the DPRK reject the fabricated document as a foul crime unprecedented in the world history of human rights and will surely force them to pay dearly for it.

Source: Korean Central News Agency. "KCNA Commentary Slams Artifice by Political Swindlers." April 22, 2014. www.kcna.co.jp/item/2014/201404/news22/20140422-02ee.html.

Venezuelan Government Cracks Down on Protests Amid U.S. Concern

FEBRUARY 15 AND 16, 2014

Less than one year after a new leader was elected following the death of long-time president Hugo Chavez, the people of Venezuela took to the streets to protest the government of President Nicolas Maduro. Citizens blamed the president for failure to alleviate high crime rates, growing food shortages, and an unstable power grid. The government responded by violently cracking down on protesters and jailing those who spoke out against Maduro. The United States, which has long had an unstable relationship with the South American nation, raised concerns about potential human rights violations occurring at the hands of the Maduro government. Venezuela struck back, accusing the United States of backing a coup d'état.

Chavez and His Successor

The late president of Venezuela and former leader of the United Socialist Party of Venezuela (PSUV), Hugo Chavez, cemented his legacy as a populist anti-American icon through flamboyant rhetoric and preferential aid to allied countries. Venezuelan largess was distributed through his PetroCaribe program, which offered discounted oil exports. He also redirected energy revenues to expand social spending. After taking office in 1999, President Chavez alienated the middle and upper classes, whose living standards fell in response to rolling blackouts, rising shortages, inflation, and crime. This development contrasted with widespread support in poorer neighborhoods, which benefited from government transfers. Separately, international observers expressed concern regarding reports of increasing suppression of the opposition, with U.S. diplomatic cables describing attempts to support independent civic groups in the country through collaboration and funding. President Chavez frequently suggested that the United States was attempting to covertly destabilize the country.

A short-lived coup against the president in April 2002 further soured bilateral relations, because Venezuela accused the United States of withholding information regarding dissident officers who had been plotting his removal. The U.S. government replied that it had informed the opposition that it would not offer material support for any attempt to remove the government and that it was not obligated to provide information to its Venezuelan counterpart. Given the ideological gulf between the two countries, protests of U.S. disinterest were met with skepticism, with President Chavez repeatedly referring to then-U.S. president George W. Bush as "the devil." Venezuela's "Bolivarian" brand of populist socialism advanced with the removal of term limits via referendum in 2009, following an earlier defeat of the measure in December 2007.

Despite controversy regarding Chavez's bids to centralize political power and deteriorating economic conditions, his death in March 2013 after an extended, private battle with cancer provoked an outpouring of grief. Chavez's designated successor and former vice president, acting president Maduro, leveraged public attachment to the late president as well as the benefits of incumbency to secure the position after early elections were held in April that year. His closest rival, Henrique Capriles, campaigned on a center left platform similar to the Brazilian model. In contrast, Chavez had viewed himself as the ideological heir of the Cuban revolution. The opposition objected to the ruling party's close links to Cuba and argued that Venezuelan policy was being overseen by the government of Fidel Castro.

Protests Ignite in 2014; Government Responds

The government has since described international criticism of its policies as an attempt to undermine its sovereignty, deflecting grievances regarding enduring crime and inflation. In 2013, Venezuela was estimated to have one of the highest murder rates in the world, at seventy-nine per 100,000 residents, while inflation averaged more than 60 percent the following year. Domestic discontent grew as grocery shortages, power outages, and insecurity persisted. The murder of a former Miss Venezuela, Monica Spear, and her ex-husband in front of their five-year-old daughter during a carjacking in January 2014 underscored public vulnerability to violent crime. This perception deepened with official indifference to an attempted assault on a university student in San Cristobal, an opposition stronghold near the Colombian border. A violent crackdown on related protests in February 2014 prompted an expansion of demonstrators' complaints, which included suppression of the opposition, criminal impunity, and worsening economic conditions. Participants also claimed that government-sponsored *colectivo* militias instigated violence during the unrest.

For its part, the government blamed "fascists" for violence during the unrest and accused the opposition of destroying private property, as well as schools and health clinics. President Maduro called for the arrest of Leopoldo López, the leader of the opposition Popular Will (VP) party, charging him with inciting bloodshed and vandalism. López is seen as a more radical alternative to Capriles, in that he advocates street action given successive opposition defeats at the ballot box under disputed conditions. Confronting government claims, López urged supporters to attend a rally dressed in white to symbolize their commitment to nonviolence prior to his dramatic public surrender to authorities in February. He remained imprisoned for the duration of the year.

Notwithstanding setbacks for the opposition, protests spread throughout the country by April 2014, prompting the government to convene Vatican-mediated discussions with the opposition coalition, Democratic Unity Roundtable (MUD). These talks halted in response to mass arrests after the breakup of student protest camps in May. The demonstrations, which largely failed to animate the disgruntled blue-collar workers necessary for a successful national movement, eased from June but continued through 2014. International reports indicated that some working class protesters had traveled to demonstrate in more affluent areas barricaded against government forces to avoid being punished by progovernment paramilitary groups active in their local neighborhoods.

International Response

Venezuela echoed its traditional dismissal of the United States' calls for greater representation for the opposition, citing a democratic mandate to "build our country's destiny in a sovereign manner." The United States, for its part, rejects the characterization of Lopez as a violent ringleader and calls for other parties to join it in supporting Lopez's release, as well as greater protection for political rights in Venezuela.

International bodies including the European Union and the United Nations affirmed calls for Lopez's release, an end to violence, and greater dialogue between the parties. Observers also called for the release of the mayor of San Cristobal, Daniel Ceballos, also of the VP party, who was arrested in March 2014. Former president Luis Lula da Silva of Brazil, a regional power and model for moderate leftists, called for discussion and praised restraint by factions of the opposition, including supporters of Capriles, who favored greater engagement with the government. Members of the Bolivarian Alliance for the Americas (ALBA), including Cuba and Bolivia, have strong ties to the Chavista movement and endorsed Venezuela's official response to the protests. Political mediation was briefly facilitated by the Vatican until talks were suspended in May 2014 in response to the government's crackdown on protest camps.

The United Nations reiterated calls for the release of at least sixty-nine political prisoners in October 2014, characterizing the detention of López and Ceballos as "arbitrary." The United Nations High Commissioner for Human Rights argued that the detentions, which affected an estimated 3,300 people between February and June, prolonged political instability and undermined the rule of law. An additional forty-three deaths were reported during the unrest, as well as 150 abuse cases and widespread intimidation of independent media.

Venezuela's election to the UN Security Council that month was not expected to prompt a shift in domestic policy. The country also was seen as a likely advocate for Russian and Iranian interests within the body, because it has built alliances centered on shared opposition to perceived U.S. imperialism with both countries in recent years.

GOVERNMENT REMAINS SECURE

Notwithstanding external criticism and recent unrest, the Chavez-inspired Bolivarian system is viewed as reasonably secure in Venezuela. It is supported by political appointments in all the branches of government, as well as the loyalty of the military and the formerly destitute working class. A reversal of concentrated executive power would be opposed by widespread patronage networks and would require a series of electoral victories by the opposition, which is unlikely under the current institutional framework.

With little prospect of economic revival or concessions to the opposition, social division is expected to endure. The middle and upper classes, which have not benefitted from increased social entitlements, will maintain their opposition to the government. Discontent will likely be greater in border regions such as San Cristobal, where informal exports of subsidized goods to Colombia have exacerbated shortages. Meanwhile, the ruling party will continue to adopt a nationalist stance to rally Venezuelans against perceived external intervention in the face of declining living standards and worsening crime. Assuming the continuation of welfare payments, it will maintain the support of the working classes, which are emotionally invested in the legacy of Chavez and viewed recent demonstrations as a threat to their interests. This constituency will continue to value material provision over freedom of expression and could afford the government a claim to a genuine mandate, despite ongoing detention of political prisoners.

Regional influence, however, could be affected by fluctuating oil revenues, which could limit Venezuela's ability to offer subsidized exports to client states. Despite an assertive posture toward the United States, economic conditions are also likely to increase dependence on other major powers. In 2013, Venezuela was estimated to have a debt-to-gross domestic product (GDP) ratio of 70 percent, and in 2014 the ratings agency Standard and Poor's graded its sovereign debt as CCC+, or "junk" status. Inflation was expected to remain above 30 percent through 2017. Venezuela will require development aid from other states, because private investors remain wary of its business environment. The bilateral relationship with China is increasingly important: as of September 2013, China had invested billions of dollars in Venezuela's energy and mining sectors as part of an oil-for-aid arrangement. However, the United States will remain the most credible threat to Venezuelan sovereignty in the nation's official rhetoric.

—Anastazia Clouting

The following is a statement by U.S. secretary of state John Kerry on February 15, 2014, raising concern about the Venezuelan government's crackdown against protesters; and a statement from the Government of the Bolivarian Republic of Venezuela on February 16, 2014, rejecting Kerry's statement and accusing the U.S. government of backing antigovernment movements in Venezuela.

Secretary Kerry Raises Concern About Crackdown on Venezuelan Protesters

February 15, 2014

The United States is deeply concerned by rising tensions and violence surrounding this week's protests in Venezuela. Our condolences go to the families of those killed as a result of this tragic violence.

We are particularly alarmed by reports that the Venezuelan government has arrested or detained scores of anti-government protestors and issued an arrest warrant for opposition leader Leopoldo Lopez. These actions have a chilling effect on citizens' rights to express their grievances peacefully.

We join the UN High Commissioner for Human Rights, Secretary General of the Organization of American States, EU High Representative for Foreign Affairs, and others in condemning this senseless violence. We call on the Venezuelan government to provide the political space necessary for meaningful dialogue with the Venezuelan people and to release detained protestors. We urge all parties to work to restore calm and refrain from violence.

Freedoms of expression and peaceful assembly are universal human rights. They are essential to a functioning democracy, and the Venezuelan government has an obligation to protect these fundamental freedoms and the safety of its citizens.

Source: U.S. Department of State. "Recent Violence in Venezuela." February 15, 2014. www.state.gov/secretary/remarks/2014/02/221693.htm.

Venezuelan Government Accuses United States of Supporting Coup

February 16, 2014

On Sunday, the Bolivarian Government rejected statements made by U.S. Secretary of State John Kerry about the fascist, violent acts carried out in the past few days by right-wing groups in the country. The Bolivarian Government considers his statements to be a U.S. ploy to promote destabilization in Venezuela.

The following is a translation of the complete text:

The Government of the Bolivarian Republic of Venezuela strongly rejects statements made by the United States Secretary of State, John Kerry, given that they constitute yet another maneuver by the Government in Washington to promote and legitimize attempts to destabilize Venezuelan democracy unleashed by violent group in the past few days.

The Barack Obama Administration lies when it questions our country's record of human rights and democratic guarantees. The institutions of the Bolivarian Republic of Venezuela, established through the rule of law and justice, guarantee the exercise of political rights to all its citizens under a wide-ranging framework of civil liberties that are constitutionally consecrated.

The U.S. Government lies when it denounces the arrest of peaceful, anti-government protestors. The Venezuelan State has acted and will continue to act against violent actions perpetrated by extreme right splinter groups that dangerously conspire against democratic freedoms in threatening the lives of our fellow citizens and their freedom to peacefully exercise their rights, as well as against public and private property through vandalism that is punishable by law.

Secretary of State John Kerry, on behalf of his government, comes to the defense of violent leader Leopoldo López. The world should know that there is enough evidence that the groups which perpetrated the violence of the past days are led by Mr. Leopoldo López, and a legal arrest warrant has been issued for him to be placed in the custody of the authorities. No type of force or extortion will stop this decision by Venezuelan authorities, a decision that is needed to restore peace to our Homeland.

The Government of the United States should take responsibility, in front of the Venezuelan people and the world, for allowing U.S. institutions and individuals to finance, legitimize and promote actions by persons and groups that violently threaten Venezuelan society and attempt to twist the democratically expressed will of our people to build our country's destiny in a sovereign manner.

The Venezuelan people and Government, in hand with every State institution and organizations of people's power, will imperturbably continue exercising all the actions which, under the framework of the Constitution, laws and principles of a true people's democracy, are necessary to guarantee the normal function of society, and to defeat the agenda of violence openly promoted by the imperial government of the United States.

We call upon the most active solidarity of independent governments and peoples of the world against this grave U.S. intervention.

SOURCE: U.S. Department of Justice. Foreign Agents Registration Act. "Venezuela Rejects U.S. Ploy to Promote a Coup d'état." February 16, 2014[1]. www.fara.gov/docs/5957-Supplemental-Statement-20140429-9.pdf.

OTHER HISTORIC DOCUMENTS OF INTEREST

FROM PREVIOUS *HISTORIC DOCUMENTS*

- International Leaders Respond to Death of Venezuelan Leader Hugo Chavez, *2013*, p. 84
- Organization of American States on the Recall Vote in Venezuela, *2004*, p. 548
- U.S. Government, OAS on Failed Coup in Venezuela, *2002*, p. 201

NOTE

1. The original document, which begins on page 16 of the Department of Justice filing, was published on February 16, 2014. However, the larger Department of Justice filing was published on April 29, 2014.

March

Supreme Court Rules on Whistleblower Protection

MARCH 4, 2014

Whistleblower laws provide protection from workplace retaliation to employees who publically disclose information about ("blow the whistle on") their employer's illegal or dangerous activity. The laws are designed to encourage employees to raise their concerns without fear of losing their jobs. In 2002, in the wake of the scandal and collapse of the Enron Corporation, Congress passed the Sarbanes-Oxley Act to restore public confidence in financial markets and to protect investors in public companies. The act contains a whistleblower protection whose interpretation was the subject of the Supreme Court case *Lawson v. FMR LLC,* decided on March 4, 2014. The case hinged on the statutory meaning of a single word in the legislation—"employee"—that was subject to multiple interpretations. Writing the majority opinion, Justice Ruth Bader Ginsburg adopted an expansive reading of the word and concluded that the Sarbanes-Oxley Act extends its whistleblower protections not just to the employees of public companies, but also to the employees of the private contractors and subcontractors of public companies. This decision expanded the reach of corporate whistleblower protections to the employees of millions of small businesses, including law and accounting firms. Chief Justice John G. Roberts Jr. and Justices Stephen G. Breyer and Elena Kagan joined the majority opinion. Justices Antonin Scalia and Clarence Thomas joined in principal part, writing a separate concurring opinion. Justice Sonia Sotomayor, joined by Justices Anthony M. Kennedy and Samuel A. Alito Jr. dissented, objecting to the "stunning reach" of the majority's interpretation.

Enron and the Sarbanes-Oxley Act of 2002

The energy company Enron Corporation was the nation's seventh largest publicly traded corporation when, in 2001, it collapsed into what is still the biggest business bankruptcy ever, amidst charges of massive shareholder fraud. Passed the following year, the Sarbanes-Oxley Act of 2002, according to Senate reports, aimed to "prevent and punish corporate and criminal fraud, protect the victims of such fraud, preserve evidence of such fraud, and hold wrongdoers accountable for their actions." According to the legislative history of the act as cited by the Supreme Court, Congress had found that Enron's fraud was due in large part to a "corporate code of silence" that served to "discourage employees from reporting fraudulent behavior not only to the proper authorities . . . , but even internally." Contractors to Enron, including the accounting firm Arthur Andersen, were found to be participants in the fraud and cover-up. Congress documented that when employees of either Enron or of Arthur Andersen attempted to report corporate misconduct, they faced retaliation and discharge.

The petitioners in *Lawson v. FMR LLC* were Jackie Hosang Lawson and Jonathan M. Zang, investment advisors who worked for privately held companies (collectively FMR) that contracted with the Fidelity family of mutual funds to provide advisory and management services. The Fidelity mutual funds are public companies and therefore subject to the Sarbanes-Oxley Act. As is the practice in the industry, the mutual funds themselves have no employees, but rely instead on contractors like the petitioners to manage day-to-day operations. These two contract investment advisors each separately raised concerns about alleged fraud relating to the mutual funds. Lawson, who had worked for FMR for fourteen years, questioned certain cost accounting methodologies, believing that they overstated expenses. She alleged that after doing so she suffered workplace harassment that led to her resignation. Separately, Zang, a portfolio manager for several funds, alleged that FMR fired him in retaliation for raising concerns about inaccuracies in a draft Securities and Exchange Commission (SEC) statement concerning certain Fidelity mutual funds. They both sued in the U.S. District Court for the District of Massachusetts.

FMR argued that the suits should be dismissed because the Sarbanes-Oxley whistle-blower provisions only protect the employees of public companies and that, as employees of private companies contracting with public entities, these former employees had no right to sue. The District Court sided with the employees and denied the dismissal; it was then appealed to the First Circuit Court of Appeals. There, a divided Court agreed with FMR that the words "an employee" in the statute refer only to employees of public companies and do not cover the employees of contractors to the public company.

In an unrelated case several months later, the U.S. Department of Labor's Administrative Review Board came to the opposite conclusion, holding that the employees of contractors rendering services to public companies may be protected as whistleblowers. The Supreme Court agreed to hear the appeal from the First Circuit to resolve these conflicting interpretations of the same law.

Supreme Court Vastly Extends the Scope of Whistleblower Protection

Section 1514A of the Sarbanes-Oxley Act protects corporate whistleblowers from workplace retaliation. Under the heading "(a) WHISTLEBLOWER PROTECTION FOR EMPLOYEES OF PUBLICLY TRADED COMPANIES," relevant parts of the law read:

> No [public] company . . . , or any officer, employee, contractor, subcontractor, or agent of such company, may discharge, demote, suspend, threaten, harass, or in any other manner discriminate against an *employee* in terms and conditions of employment because of [whistleblowing or other protected activity]. [emphasis added]

Lawson v. FMR LLC posed the question: Whose employees are protected by this law? The provision is capable of two interpretations. The private company FMR argued before the Supreme Court that the word "employee" in this provision referred only to the employees of public companies, as indicated by the heading. The employees who had been fired by FMR argued that they should be protected even though they work for a private contractor providing service to the public company. They argue that the word includes employees of any of the entities listed as prohibited from taking retaliatory action, including any public company, officer, employee, contractor, subcontractor, or agent.

Whenever the Supreme Court has to resolve an issue of statutory interpretation, it looks first to the ordinary meaning of the provision's language. Here, the Court noted that when you take away unnecessary language, the provision can be rewritten as: "No . . . contractor . . . may discharge . . . an employee." The Court found that the "ordinary meaning" of the provision, written this way, applies to the contractor's own employees. To create an interpretation like that held by FMR would require inserting the words "of a public company" after "an employee." The Court concluded that the language "means what it appears to mean: A contractor may not retaliate against its own employee for engaging in protected whistleblowing activity." The majority rejected the argument that the law's heading should be dispositive, citing earlier cases where less weight has been placed on headings that are not intended to replace the detailed provisions of the text.

The Court went on to find that this textual analysis fit in with the purpose of the whistleblower provision in the Sarbanes-Oxley act, which was to avoid another "Enron debacle." The Court cited the legislative record of the act to show that Congress was "as focused on the role of Enron's outside contractors in facilitating the fraud as it was on the actions of Enron's own officers."

Holding otherwise, the Court concluded, would lead to the implausible result that Congress meant to insulate the entire mutual fund industry from whistleblowing protections. Virtually all mutual funds have no employees of their own but depend exclusively on independent investment advisors. These investment advisors would, in most instances, be the only firsthand witnesses to shareholder fraud involving mutual funds.

In a vigorous dissent, Justice Sotomayor objected that the majority's interpretation of Section 1514A gives it a "stunning reach" leading to "absurd results." According to the dissent, the majority's broad interpretation transforms the law into "a sweeping source of litigation that Congress could not have intended." Under the majority's formulation, the dissent argues that the whistleblower law would be stretched to provide federal redress to babysitters and gardeners and any other low-level personal employees of the millions of employees of public companies. Additionally, Sotomayor wrote, the majority opinion threatens "to subject private companies to a costly new front of employment litigation" by opening up the prospect of federal retaliation claims filed by the employees of the hundreds of thousands of small businesses that contract with public companies, for example, a cleaning service that contracts with Starbucks coffee shops or the babysitter of a checkout clerk at Petco.

"There is scant evidence," the majority said in dismissing the dissenters' objections, "that these floodgate-opening concerns are more than hypothetical." The majority rejected the notion that it should adopt an interpretation of Section 1514A that thwarts the aims of Congress by letting contractors retaliate against their whistleblowing employees "just to avoid the unlikely prospect that babysitters, nannies, gardeners, and the like will flood OSHA with Section 1514A complaints." In any event, the Court stated that if it is wrong, Congress could fix the problem by amending the law with various "limiting principles" suggested by the solicitor general that could limit the types of contractors covered by the law and the type of complaints that would provide whistleblowers with protections.

IMPACT OF THE DECISION

This decision greatly expands the scope of the whistleblowing protections of the Sarbanes-Oxley financial reform law. No longer will the provision cover only the employees of approximately 5,000 public companies, but instead, it will provide protections to the employees of millions of private companies, including small businesses, that may contract or subcontract to perform services for public companies. The practical result will be that privately owned businesses contracting with public companies will need to revamp their human resources policies to prevent retaliation against employees raising concerns about the legality of business practices.

Reaction to the decision was mixed. Business groups were critical, predicting a costly flood of new opportunistic and frivolous lawsuits. According to Karen Harned, the executive director of the National Federation of Independent Business Small Business Legal Center, the Supreme Court "is downplaying the reality that this decision gives plaintiffs' attorneys additional incentives to pursue aggressive litigation against independent companies." Supporters argued that the case closes a loophole in corporate whistleblowing protection and makes another scandal like Enron less likely because now accountants and other contractors don't need to close their eyes to fraud to keep their jobs. In a statement released after the ruling, Stephen M. Kohn, executive director of the National Whistleblowers Center, described it as "a big win for every person who invests money through mutual funds." Companies will no longer be able to "manipulate the employee relationship to have the employee lose whistleblower protections," he added.

In 2014, the Supreme Court went on to hear two additional cases involving the rights of whistleblowers, although in different contexts and involving different statutes. In June, the Court decided *Lane v. Franks* in favor of a whistleblower who testified about corruption and misuse of funds in a public program and was consequently fired by his public employer. In this case, the unanimous Court held that the First Amendment protects public employees who provide truthful testimony, compelled by a subpoena, about a matter of public concern. And in November, the Court heard oral arguments in *Department of Homeland Security v. MacLean,* a case involving an air marshal who had been briefed about the threat of a terrorist attack, but then was told that the Transportation Security Administration (TSA) would cut back protections due to budget restraints. After his concerns were dismissed by his bosses, he spoke with a reporter for MSNBC and was subsequently fired. This case pitted the legitimate governmental interest in protecting sensitive security information against the interests of a whistleblower who highlighted potentially deadly deficiencies in air travel security (that have since been corrected). A ruling on this case is likely in early 2015.

—Melissa Feinberg

Following is the edited text of the Supreme Court's May 4, 2014, decision in Lawson v. FMR LLC, *in which the Court ruled 6–3 that the Sarbanes-Oxley Act of 2002 grants anti-retaliation protection to employees of a public company's private contractors or subcontractors.*

DOCUMENT   *Lawson v. FMR LLC*

March 4, 2014

No. 12–3

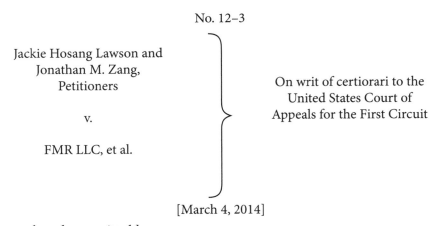

Jackie Hosang Lawson and
Jonathan M. Zang,
Petitioners

v.

FMR LLC, et al.

On writ of certiorari to the
United States Court of
Appeals for the First Circuit

[March 4, 2014]

[Footnotes have been omitted.]

JUSTICE GINSBURG delivered the opinion of the Court.

To safeguard investors in public companies and restore trust in the financial markets following the collapse of Enron Corporation, Congress enacted the Sarbanes-Oxley Act of 2002, 116 Stat. 745. See S. Rep. No. 107–146, pp. 2–11 (2002). A provision of the Act, 18 U. S. C. §1514A, protects whistleblowers. Section 1514A, at the time here relevant, instructed:

> No [public] company . . . , or any officer, employee, contractor, subcontractor, or agent of such company, may discharge, demote, suspend, threaten, harass, or in any other manner discriminate against an employee in the terms and conditions of employment because of [whistleblowing or other protected activity]. §1514A(a) (2006 ed.).

This case concerns the definition of the protected class: Does §1514A shield only those employed by the public company itself, or does it shield as well employees of privately held contractors and subcontractors—for example, investment advisers, law firms, accounting enterprises—who perform work for the public company?

We hold, based on the text of §1514A, the mischief to which Congress was responding, and earlier legislation Congress drew upon, that the provision shelters employees of private contractors and subcontractors, just as it shelters employees of the public company served by the contractors and subcontractors. We first summarize our principal reasons, then describe this controversy and explain our decision more comprehensively.

Plaintiffs below, petitioners here, are former employees of private companies that contract to advise or manage mutual funds. The mutual funds themselves are public companies that have no employees. Hence, if the whistle is to be blown on fraud detrimental to mutual fund investors, the whistleblowing employee must be on another company's payroll, most likely, the payroll of the mutual fund's investment adviser or manager.

Taking the allegations of the complaint as true, both plaintiffs blew the whistle on putative fraud relating to the mutual funds and, as a consequence, suffered adverse action by their employers. Plaintiffs read §1514A to convey that "[n]o . . . contractor . . . may . . . discriminate against [its own] employee [for whistleblowing]." We find that reading consistent with the text of the statute and with common sense. Contractors are in control of their own employees, but are not ordinarily positioned to control someone else's workers. Moreover, we resist attributing to Congress a purpose to stop a contractor from retaliating against whistleblowers employed by the public company the contractor serves, while leaving the contractor free to retaliate against its own employees when they reveal corporate fraud.

In the Enron scandal that prompted the Sarbanes-Oxley Act, contractors and subcontractors, including the accounting firm Arthur Andersen, participated in Enron's fraud and its coverup. When employees of those contractors attempted to bring misconduct to light, they encountered retaliation by their employers. The Sarbanes-Oxley Act contains numerous provisions aimed at controlling the conduct of accountants, auditors, and lawyers who work with public companies. See, *e.g.,* 116 Stat. 750–765, 773–774, 784, §§101–107, 203–206, 307. Given Congress' concern about contractor conduct of the kind that contributed to Enron's collapse, we regard with suspicion construction of §1514A to protect whistleblowers only when they are employed by a public company, and not when they work for the public company's contractor . . ..

[Section I, detailing the Sarbanes-Oxley Act of 2002 and background of the case, has been omitted.]

II

A

In determining the meaning of a statutory provision, "we look first to its language, giving the words used their ordinary meaning." *Moskal v. United States*, 498 U. S. 103, 108 (1990) (citation and internal quotation marks omitted). As Judge Thompson observed in her dissent from the Court of Appeals' judgment, "boiling [§1514A(a)] down to its relevant syntactic elements, it provides that 'no . . . contractor . . . may discharge . . . an employee.'" 670 F. 3d, at 84 (quoting §1514A(a)). The ordinary meaning of "an employee" in this proscription is the contractor's own employee.

FMR's interpretation of the text requires insertion of "of a public company" after "an employee." But where Congress meant "an employee of a public company," it said so: With respect to the actors governed by §1514A, the provision's interdictions run to the officers, employees, contractors, subcontractors, and agents "of such company," *i.e.*, a public company. §1514A(a). Another anti-retaliation provision in Sarbanes-Oxley provides: "[A] broker or dealer and persons employed by a broker or dealer who are involved with investment banking activities may not, directly or indirectly, retaliate against or threaten to retaliate against any securities analyst *employed by that broker or dealer or its affiliate. . . .*" 15 U. S. C. §78*o*–6(a)(1)(C) (emphasis added). In contrast, nothing in §1514A's language confines the class of employees protected to those of a designated employer. Absent any textual qualification, we presume the operative language means what it appears to mean: A contractor may not retaliate against its own employee for engaging in protected whistle-blowing activity.

Section 1514A's application to contractor employees is confirmed when we enlarge our view from the term "an employee" to the provision as a whole. The prohibited retaliatory measures enumerated in §1514A(a)—discharge, demotion, suspension, threats, harassment, or discrimination in the terms and conditions of employment—are commonly actions an employer takes against its *own* employees. Contractors are not ordinarily positioned to take adverse actions against employees of the public company with whom they contract. FMR's interpretation of §1514A, therefore, would shrink to insignificance the provision's ban on retaliation by contractors. The dissent embraces FMR's "narrower" construction.

FMR urges that Congress included contractors in §1514A's list of governed actors simply to prevent public companies from avoiding liability by employing contractors to effectuate retaliatory discharges. FMR describes such a contractor as an "ax-wielding specialist," illustrated by George Clooney's character in the movie *Up in the Air*. Brief for Respondents 24–25 (internal quotation marks omitted). As portrayed by Clooney, an ax-wielding specialist is a contractor engaged only as the bearer of the bad news that the employee has been fired; he plays no role in deciding who to terminate. If the company employing the ax-wielder chose the recipients of the bad tidings for retaliatory reasons, the §1514A claim would properly be directed at the company. Hiring the ax-wielder would not insulate the company from liability. Moreover, we see no indication that retaliatory ax-wielding specialists are the real-world problem that prompted Congress to add contractors to §1514A.

Moving further through §1514A to the protected activity described in subsection (a)(1), we find further reason to believe that Congress presumed an employer-employee relationship between the retaliator and the whistleblower. Employees gain protection for furnishing information to a federal agency, Congress, or "a person with supervisory authority over *the employee* (or such other person working for *the employer* who has the authority to investigate, discover, or terminate misconduct)." §1514A(a)(1) (emphasis added). And under §1514A(a)(2), employees are protected from retaliation for assisting "in a proceeding filed or about to be filed (*with any knowledge of the employer*) relating to an alleged violation" of any of the enumerated fraud provisions, securities regulations, or other federal law relating to shareholder fraud. §1514A(a)(2)(emphasis added). The reference to employer knowledge is an additional indicator of Congress' expectation that the retaliator typically will be the employee's employer, not another entity less likely to know of whistleblower complaints filed or about to be filed.

Section 1514A's enforcement procedures and remedies similarly contemplate that the whistleblower is an employee of the retaliator. As earlier noted, see *supra,* at 6, §1514A(b)(2)(A) provides that a claim under §1514A "shall be governed under the rules and procedures set forth in section 42121(b) of title 49," *i.e.,* AIR 21's anti-retaliation provision. Throughout §42121(b), the respondent is referred to as "the employer." See 49 U. S. C. §42121(b)(2)(B)(ii) (The Secretary shall not conduct an investigation into a retaliation claim "if the employer demonstrates, by clear and convincing evidence, that the employer would have taken the same unfavorable personnel action in the absence of that behavior."); §42121(b)(2)(B)(iv) ("Relief may not be ordered . . . if the employer demonstrates by clear and convincing evidence that the employer would have taken the same unfavorable personnel action in the absence of that behavior.").

Regarding remedies, §1514A(c)(2) states that a successful claimant shall be entitled to "reinstatement with the same seniority status that the employee would have had, but for the discrimination," as well as "the amount of back pay, with interest." As the Solicitor General, for the United States as *amicus curiae,* observed, "It is difficult, if not impossible, to see how a contractor or subcontractor could provide those remedies to an employee of a public company." Brief for United States as *Amicus Curiae* 15. The most sensible reading of §1514A's numerous references to an employer-employee relationship between the respondent and the claimant is that the provision's protections run between contractors and their own employees.

Remarkably, the dissent attributes to Congress a strange design. Under the dissent's "narrower" construction, a public company's contractor may not retaliate against a public company's employees, academic here because the public company has no employees. According to the dissent, this coverage is necessary to prevent "a gaping hole" that would allow public companies to "evade §1514A simply by hiring a contractor to engage in the very retaliatory acts that an officer or employee could not." This cannot be right—even if Congress had omitted any reference to contractors, subcontractors, or agents in §1514A, the remaining language surely would prohibit a public company from directing someone else to engage in retaliatory conduct against the public company's employees; hiring an ax-wielder to announce an employee's demotion does not change the fact that the public company is the entity commanding the demotion. Under the dissent's reading of §1514A, the inclusion of contractors as covered employers does no more than make the contractor secondarily liable for complying with such marching orders—hardly a hole at all.

There would be a huge hole, on the other hand, were the dissent's view of §1514A's reach to prevail: Contractors' employees would be disarmed; they would be vulnerable to retaliation by their employers for blowing the whistle on a scheme to defraud the public company's investors, even a scheme engineered entirely by the contractor. Not only would mutual fund advisers and managers escape §1514A's control. Legions of accountants and lawyers would be denied §1514A's protections. Instead of indulging in fanciful visions of whistleblowing babysitters and the like, the dissent might pause to consider whether a Congress, prompted by the Enron debacle, would exclude from whistleblower protection countless professionals equipped to bring fraud on investors to a halt.

B

We turn next to two textual arguments made by FMR. First, FMR urges that "an employee" must be read to refer exclusively to public company employees to avoid the absurd result of extending protection to the personal employees of company officers and employees, e.g., their housekeepers or gardeners. Plaintiffs and the Solicitor General do not defend §1514A's application to personal employees. They argue, instead, that the prohibition against an "officer" or "employee" retaliating against "an employee" may be read as imposing personal liability only on officers and employees who retaliate against other public company employees. FMR calls this reading "bizarre," for it would ascribe to the words "an employee" in §1514A(a) "one meaning if the respondent is an 'officer' and a different meaning if the respondent is a 'contractor.'"

We agree with FMR that plaintiffs and the Solicitor General offer an interpretation at odds with the text Congress enacted. If, as we hold, "an employee" includes employees of contractors, then grammatically, the term also includes employees of public company officers and employees. Nothing suggests Congress' attention was drawn to the curiosity its drafting produced. The issue, however, is likely more theoretical than real. Few housekeepers or gardeners, we suspect, are likely to come upon and comprehend evidence of their employer's complicity in fraud. In any event, FMR's point is outweighed by the compelling arguments opposing FMR's contention that "an employee" refers simply and only to public company employees (limiting principles may serve as check against overbroad applications). . . .

III

A

Our textual analysis of §1514A fits the provision's purpose. It is common ground that Congress installed whistleblower protection in the Sarbanes-Oxley Act as one means to ward off another Enron debacle. S. Rep., at 2–11. And, as the ARB observed in *Spinner*, "Congress plainly recognized that outside professionals—accountants, law firms, contractors, agents, and the like—were complicit in, if not integral to, the shareholder fraud and subsequent cover-up [Enron] officers . . . perpetrated." ALJ No. 2010–SOX–029, pp. 12–13. Indeed, the Senate Report demonstrates that Congress was as focused on the role of Enron's outside contractors in facilitating the fraud as it was on the actions of Enron's own officers. See, e.g., S. Rep., at 3. . . .

Also clear from the legislative record is Congress' understanding that outside professionals bear significant responsibility for reporting fraud by the public companies with whom they contract, and that fear of retaliation was the primary deterrent to such reporting by the employees of Enron's contractors. Congressional investigators discovered ample evidence of contractors demoting or discharging employees they have engaged who jeopardized the contractor's business relationship with Enron by objecting to Enron's financial practices. . . .

In the same vein, two of the four examples of whistleblower retaliation recounted in the Senate Report involved outside professionals retaliated against by their own employers. S. Rep., at 5 (on Andersen and UBS Paine-Webber employees); see also *id.,* at 4–5

(Andersen employees who "attempted to report or 'blow the whistle' on [Enron's] fraud . . . were discouraged at nearly every turn"). Emphasizing the importance of outside professionals as "gatekeepers who detect and deter fraud," the Senate Report concludes: "Congress must reconsider the incentive system that has been set up that encourages accountants and lawyers who come across fraud in their work to remain silent." *Id.*, at 20–21. From this legislative history, one can safely conclude that Congress enacted §1514A aiming to encourage whistleblowing by contractor employees who suspect fraud involving the public companies with whom they work. . . .

B

Our reading of §1514A avoids insulating the entire mutual fund industry from §1514A, as FMR's and the dissent's "narrower construction" would do. As companies "required to file reports under section 15(d) of the Securities Exchange Act of 1934," 18 U. S. C. §1514A(a), mutual funds unquestionably are governed by §1514A. Because mutual funds figure prominently among such report-filing companies, Congress presumably had them in mind when it added to "publicly traded companies" the discrete category of companies "required to file reports under section 15(d)."

Virtually all mutual funds are structured so that they have no employees of their own; they are managed, instead, by independent investment advisers. The United States investment advising industry manages $14.7 trillion on behalf of nearly 94 million investors. These investment advisers, under our reading of §1514A, are contractors prohibited from retaliating against their own employees for engaging in whistleblowing activity. This construction protects the "insiders [who] are the only firsthand witnesses to the [shareholder] fraud." S. Rep., at 10. Under FMR's and the dissent's reading, in contrast, §1514A has no application to mutual funds, for all of the potential whistleblowers are employed by the privately held investment management companies, not by the mutual funds themselves. See Brief for Respondents 45 (describing this glaring gap as "merely a consequence of the corporate structure" of mutual funds). . . .

Indeed, affording whistleblower protection to mutual fund investment advisers is crucial to Sarbanes-Oxley's endeavor to "protect investors by improving the accuracy and reliability of corporate disclosures made pursuant to the securities laws." 116 Stat. 745. As plaintiffs observe, these disclosures are written, not by anyone at the mutual funds themselves, but by employees of the investment advisers. "Under FMR's [and the dissent's] proposed interpretation of section 1514A, FMR could dismiss any FMR employee who disclosed to the directors of or lawyers for the Fidelity funds that there were material falsehoods in the documents being filed by FMR with the SEC in the name of those funds." Reply Brief 13. It is implausible that Congress intended to leave such an employee remediless.

[Sections IIIC, D and IV, further detailing FMR's argument and the protections of Sarbanes Oxley, have been omitted.]

* * *

For the reasons stated, we hold that 18 U. S. C. §1514A whistleblower protection extends to employees of contractors and subcontractors. The judgment of the U. S. Court of Appeals for the First Circuit is therefore reversed, and the case is remanded for further proceedings consistent with this opinion.

It is so ordered.

[The concurring opinion of Justices Antonin Scalia and Clarence Thomas has been omitted.]

JUSTICE SOTOMAYOR, with whom JUSTICE KENNEDY and JUSTICE ALITO join, dissenting.

Section 806 of the Sarbanes-Oxley Act of 2002, 116 Stat.802, forbids any public company, or any "officer, employee, contractor, subcontractor, or agent of such company," to retaliate against "an employee" who reports a potential fraud. 18 U. S. C. §1514A(a). The Court recognizes that the core purpose of the Act is to "safeguard investors in public companies." *Ante,* at 1. And the Court points out that Congress entitled the whistleblower provision, "Protection for Employees of Publicly Traded Companies Who Provide Evidence of Fraud." §806, 116 Stat. 802. Despite these clear markers of intent, the Court does not construe §1514A to apply only to public company employees who blow the whistle on fraud relating to their public company employers. The Court instead holds that the law encompasses any household employee of the millions of people who work for a public company and any employee of the hundreds of thousands of private businesses that contract to perform work for a public company.

The Court's interpretation gives §1514A a stunning reach. As interpreted today, the Sarbanes-Oxley Act authorizes a babysitter to bring a federal case against his employer—a parent who happens to work at the local Walmart (a public company)—if the parent stops employing the babysitter after he expresses concern that the parent's teenage son may have participated in an Internet purchase fraud. And it opens the door to a cause of action against a small business that contracts to clean the local Starbucks (a public company) if an employee is demoted after reporting that another nonpublic company client has mailed the cleaning company a fraudulent invoice.

Congress was of course free to create this kind of sweeping regime that subjects a multitude of individuals and private businesses to litigation over fraud reports that have no connection to, or impact on, the interests of public company shareholders. But because nothing in the text, context, or purpose of the Sarbanes-Oxley Act suggests that Congress actually wanted to do so, I respectfully dissent.

[The remainder of the dissent has been omitted.]

SOURCE: U.S. Supreme Court. *Lawson v. FMR LLC,* 571 U.S.__(2014). www.supremecourt.gov/opinions/13pdf/12-3_4f57.pdf.

OTHER HISTORIC DOCUMENTS OF INTEREST

FROM PREVIOUS *HISTORIC DOCUMENTS*

- General Accounting Office on Failures by the SEC, *2002,* p. 1032

Crimea Votes to Secede From Ukraine

MARCH 6 AND 21, AND APRIL 1, 2014

After Ukraine's parliament ousted its president in February 2014, the pro-Russian peninsula of Crimea staged a referendum on whether the area should secede from Ukraine and instead join the Russian Federation. The referendum was passed overwhelmingly and was followed by a vote in parliament to allow Crimea to become a Russian territory. Western nations and the central Ukrainian government called the vote a sham and refused to recognize the decision. Russia, however, quickly annexed Crimea. Following the referendum, pro-Russian separatists in other parts of Ukraine began seizing government buildings and infrastructure, calling themselves sovereign entities. These forces are thought to be backed by Russian militia who were fighting with the support of the Russian government. Russia's government has denied such claims, but fighting continued across Ukraine throughout 2014.

RUSSIAN INTEREST IN UKRAINE AND A FAILED FREE TRADE AGREEMENT

Following the collapse of the Soviet Union in 1991, Russia has maintained close ties with Ukraine, but the two governments have increasingly been at odds with each other. In the past, disputes mainly arose over gas reserves, but over the past decade they have been largely related to trade and Ukraine's cooperation with international bodies such as the European Union and the North Atlantic Treaty Organization (NATO). In 2008, animosity between the two governments grew stronger when Ukraine threw its support behind Georgia in the Russo-Georgian War.

In 2010, Viktor Yanukovych was elected president of Ukraine. Much to the dismay of many Ukrainians, this new pro-Russian leader agreed to allow Russian troops to train in parts of the country and also renewed a lease of the port of Sevastopol, allowing Russian troops to remain in Crimea indefinitely. Yanukovych was wildly unpopular with the public, who often accused him of violating the constitution and using false pretenses to jail his opponents.

For several years, the Ukrainian government had been negotiating a free trade agreement with the European Union, much to the dismay of Russia. The agreement was expected to be signed in November 2013. Russia pressured Ukraine to walk away from the agreement and imposed import restrictions on certain products, also indicating that harsher penalties would be enforced. "Ukrainian authorities make a huge mistake if they think that the Russian reaction will become neutral in a few years from now. This will not happen," said Sergei Glazyev, an adviser to Russian president Vladimir Putin. Glazyev added that if the agreement was signed, Russia could no longer guarantee the treaty that kept the two nations separate, which would allow Russian troops to enter Ukraine. Under heavy pressure, Yanukovych decided not to sign the trade agreement.

PROTESTS LEAD TO A PRESIDENTIAL OUSTER

Yanukovych's decision to pull out of the trade agreement at the last minute sent shockwaves across Ukraine, where many citizens had hoped the agreement would be the first step toward securing inclusion in the European Union. This sparked months of protests, which became known as the Euromaidan movement. The first citizens to join the protests on November 21, 2013, demanded that the Ukrainian government return to the table and seek closer ties with the European Union. On November 30, protesters were violently removed from their posts by government forces, leading an even greater number of Ukrainians to join the movement. The protesters began demanding the resignation of Yanukovych, arguing that he had abused his power, violated human rights, and installed a corrupt government.

In mid-February, the protesters called on parliament to restrict the president's powers by changing the constitution to its pre-2004 form. Parliament did not give in to this demand, and the protests grew stronger. Riot police clashed with protesters in Kiev, resulting in a number of casualties. On February 21, the protest movement announced that it would take up arms at 10:00 a.m. on February 22 if Yanukovych refused to resign. In response, the president and many of his close advisors fled the country. On February 23, Yanukovych was impeached, the constitution was reverted to its pre-2004 form, and the president was replaced by a pro-European interim government led by Oleksandr Turchynov.

The United States and European Union recognized the government of Turchynov, while Russia declared it illegitimate, considering it the result of a coup d'état. In Ukraine's Crimean Peninsula, pro-Russian protests sprung up in the city of Sevastopol, where Russia keeps a strategic military base. On February 26, additional Russian forces began entering the peninsula and occupying strategic locations. According to Ukraine's Defense Minister, Russia placed 22,000 troops in Crimea, violating agreements that limit this number to 12,500.

Referendum for Secession

As more Russian forces entered Crimea, the peninsula's parliament voted to dissolve the Crimean government and called for a referendum on Crimea's autonomy. The referendum, which was called for March 16, posed the question, "Do you support the idea of Crimea becoming part of Russian Federation?" The interim Ukrainian government immediately called the referendum illegal and suspended the decision of the Crimean parliament to hold such a vote, saying, "It contradicts the will of the Ukrainian people and the interests of Crimean citizens. Ukraine's territory within the boundaries recognized by the whole world is inviolable and sovereign."

The vote proceeded despite Turchynov's objections. Western nations, led by the United States, called the election a sham that was held under the duress of military incursion. Still, more than 83 percent of the eligible population turned out, with 96.77 percent voting in favor of joining Russia while only 2.51 percent opposed such action. One day later, the Crimean parliament voted to secede from Ukraine and join the Russian Federation. The decision was met with celebrations in the streets of Crimea.

Immediately following the decision, the United States and some European nations issued travel bans, placed financial sanctions on Russian and Ukrainian leaders who were behind the vote, and said that they would not recognize the referendum. The United States also banned certain Russian officials from entering the United States and froze all U.S. assets held by Russian government officials or anyone with close ties to a list of more than eleven people, including Putin. In a statement from the White House, the United States warned that Russia faced "additional costs" that would be imposed if Putin did not seek "a clear path for resolving this crisis diplomatically." President Barack Obama added that "the international community will continue to stand together to oppose any violations of Ukrainian sovereignty and territorial integrity; and continued Russian military intervention in Ukraine will only deepen Russia's diplomatic isolation and exact a greater toll on the Russian economy."

With the referendum passed, it was up to Putin to decide how to proceed. Although Western nations encouraged the Russian president not to allow Crimea to join Russia and disregard the decision, Putin called it "fully consistent with international law and the U.N. Charter." Putin added that it was his belief that Russian-speaking residents of Crimea were being terrorized by ultranationalist Ukrainian groups.

For its part, the new government in Ukraine vowed to prosecute those who led the referendum movement and "bring them to justice in Ukrainian and international courts." Ukraine's parliament voted to dissolve the Crimean parliament in an effort to void the secession vote; however, that move was largely ignored in Crimea.

Ongoing Conflict

In its agreement to fold Crimea into the Russian Federation, the two nations signed a treaty outlining a number of conditions, including preferential treatment for the Tatars and Ukrainian ethnic minorities in Crimea. It will take time for the Russian government to fully integrate Crimea into its nation, and there are still a number of remaining questions about how Russia plans to govern a state from which it is geographically disconnected. Crimea will need to pass local laws to adopt the ruble, Russian tax policies, and social regulations. Russia promised funding to its new territory to assist with the transition and immediately began issuing Russian citizenship to all those who did not opt out. Crimean officials were given the opportunity to retain their roles under the new Russian government, and elections were set for September 2014 to seat a new Crimean government.

The fledgling Ukrainian government faces challenges of its own. Shortly after Yanukovych's government dissolved, unrest sprung up in eastern Ukraine's Donbass region. Those in support of the new government clashed with the opposition, the latter of which temporarily took control of government buildings in Donetsk. By late spring, the opposition declared itself the Donetsk People's Republic. The group is considered a terrorist organization by the central government, and its claim to territory is not recognized by any state. Russian citizens joined the fight and even recruited volunteers for the insurgency. Russia has denied any direct involvement with the situation in Donbass. "There are no armed forces, no 'Russian instructors' in Ukraine—and there never were any," Putin said in an interview with a French television station. However, local media reports suggest that this recruiting has been happening openly across Russia. The Ukrainian government released photos of insurgents, and analysis by the United States indicated that they were members of the Russian Special Forces. According to U.S. secretary of state John Kerry, the insurgents "were equipped with specialized Russian weapons and the same uniforms as those worn by the Russian forces that invaded Crimea."

On July 17, a Malaysia Airlines passenger plane was shot down over Ukrainian airspace, killing the nearly 300 passengers and crew onboard. Accusations flew regarding whether the plane had been downed by Ukrainian separatists or Russian forces. Igor Girkin, the leader of the Donbass separatist movement, immediately claimed credit for the crash. However, he quickly withdrew his comments, which appeared on a social media site, after it was discovered that the plane was carrying civilians. U.S. and German intelligence agencies said they had evidence that indicated the plane was shot down by the pro-Russian separatists, using a surface-to-air missile likely provided by Russia. In turn, Russia blamed the Ukrainian government for the downing of the plane, while the Ukrainian government issued a statement indicating that the downing was done by "Russian professionals and coordinated from Russia." An independent investigation into the accident is being led by the Dutch Safety Board and the final report is expected to be released in August 2015.

—Heather Kerrigan

Following is the text of a statement by the acting president of Ukraine on March 6, 2014, regarding Crimea's plan to hold a secession referendum; the text of statements given at a signing ceremony admitting Crimea into the Russian Federation on March 21, 2014; and an April 1, 2014, statement from the NATO-Ukraine Commission on Russian military intervention in Ukraine.

DOCUMENT

Acting President of Ukraine on Crimea Referendum

March 6, 2014

The Verkhovna Rada of Crimea being totally controlled by servicemen of the Russian Armed Forces has made an illegal decision to hold a referendum. The referendum in Crimea on the question: "Do you support the idea of Crimea becoming part of Russian Federation?"

This decision is illegitimate and void.

It contradicts the will of the Ukrainian people and the interests of Crimean citizens. Ukraine's territory within the boundaries recognized by the whole world is inviolable and sovereign.

Under Article 73 of the Constitution of Ukraine, issues relating to borders and territories should be discussed only at a nationwide referendum.

By the way, it's impossible to hold even a local, Crimean referendum in ten days. So this is not a referendum. This will be a farce, this will be falsity and this will be a crime against the state organized by servicemen of the Russian Federation.

In accordance with the powers conferred on me, I have suspended the decision of the Crimean Parliament.

The Verkhovna Rada of Ukraine will initiate the dissolution of the Parliament of the Autonomous Republic of Crimea. We will protect the inviolability of our territory. We will protect the sovereignty of our country.

I am confident that Ukrainian citizens who live in Crimea will contribute to this in every way possible.

SOURCE: Official Website of the President of Ukraine. "Chairman of the Verkhovna Rada of Ukraine, Acting President of Ukraine Oleksandr Turchynov makes a statement to Ukrainian people regarding the situation in the Autonomous Republic of Crimea." March 6, 2014. www.president.gov.ua/en/news/30135.html.

Crimea Admitted Into the Russian Federation

March 21, 2014

A ceremony signing the laws on admitting the Republic of Crimea and the city of Sevastopol to the Russian Federation took place at the Kremlin.

PRESIDENT OF RUSSIA VLADIMIR PUTIN: Colleagues,

This is a big and important event. We are completing today the legal procedures for admitting Crimea and Sevastopol to the Russian Federation.

I want to thank the State Duma deputies and members of the Federation Council for their thorough and at the same time quick examination of these very important documents, ratifying the agreement on Crimea and Sevastopol's accession to the Russian Federation, and passing the Constitutional Law on admitting new constituent entities to the Russian Federation.

I congratulate all of you, all people of Russia and all residents of Crimea and Sevastopol on this occasion, which is with no exaggeration a momentous event.

Ms Matviyenko, please, go ahead.

SPEAKER OF THE FEDERATION COUNCIL VALENTINA MATVIYENKO: Mr President, colleagues,

It is probably deeply symbolic that we are meeting here in the Catherine Hall, and on the spring equinox, which marks the turn towards the sun and the dawn. I think that Russia's people are full of just such sunny and celebratory feelings today at this reunification with our brothers in Crimea. 250 years ago, during the reign of Catherine the Great, the famed land of Taurida became part of Russia. Crimea's long history, which is filled with difficult times and tragic events, is a part of our history too.

There were many attempts to take Crimea from Russia, many attempts to prevent Russia from having access to the Black Sea. The heroic defence of Sevastopol during the Crimean War and the city's immortal feat during the battle against Nazism are engraved forever in our history's chronicles.

Crimea's recent history has been difficult too and has unfolded before our very eyes. Crimea's tragic history began not with the Kiev Maidan, but with Khrushchev's arbitrary decision, taken in violation of the Soviet Union's constitution.

Crimea's drama continued a quarter of a century later with the Belavezha Accords. Already back in 1992, the people of Crimea wanted to hold a referendum but were unable to do so. Their 20 years of struggle have finally ended in success: they have held a referendum in which the region's peoples expressed their unanimous will.

The historic event that we are witnessing today was made possible by this unanimous decision by the people of Crimea, and thanks to our President's firm resolve and the support from people throughout our whole country.

Mr President, I want to inform you that the Federation Council unanimously passed two laws today that complete the legal procedure for Crimea's reunification with Russia.

I think this is good reason to congratulate everyone, congratulate people in Crimea and in Russia on this exceptional victory and great historic event. Mr President, on Monday, the flags of our two new constituent entities will fly on the Federation Council building, together with the flags of our other regions, and a new map will be on display in the building, showing Crimea as part of our country. I hope that four senators from our two new constituent entities will also soon join us in the Federation Council.

Mr President, thank you for your will and courage and for not giving in to any pressure. I hope that you felt our constant support over this time.

SPEAKER OF THE STATE DUMA SERGEI NARYSHKIN: Mr President, colleagues,

We are filled with genuine pride today at these historic events and decisions. Mr President, we are grateful to you for your firm stand that has reminded many that Russia's greatness lies not just in the past or in the future, but is with us in the present too.

Many of the State Duma deputies visited Crimea over this last month and saw in the eyes of people there at first the hope and then the joy of having Russia's support. This support gave them confidence and they made a clear and unambiguous choice to return to their homeland, and their homeland was waiting.

The State Duma deputies understood the situation very clearly and understood the mood of people in Crimea and why they made such a resolute decision. Yesterday, to the sound of Russia's national anthem, State Duma deputies from all four parliamentary parties passed the law on ratifying the agreement to admit to the Russian Federation two new constituent entities and approved the federal constitutional law on this matter.

It is perfectly clear to us that Russia and the people of Crimea acted in strict accordance with international law. Those who have doubts on this point should refresh their memories and read the United Nations Charter and other basic texts of international law.

VALENTINA MATIVIYENKO: Excuse me, Mr President, but when deputies from the Crimea and Sevastopol legislative assemblies visited us, Nikolai Ryzhkov [a member of the Federation Council] said, "We will never give you away anymore." Thank you.

< . . . >

VLADIMIR PUTIN: Colleagues,

I have signed several executive orders today, including one on establishing a new federal district—the Crimea Federal District, and have appointed Oleg Belaventsev Presidential Plenipotentiary Envoy to the new federal district.

We have a lot of work ahead to integrate Crimea into the Russian legal, economic and social systems. I discussed these issues yesterday with the Government and again today with the Security Council, and I ask the State Duma deputies and members of the Federation Council and the Federal Assembly as a whole to take an active part in this work and do everything within your power to ensure this process not only goes smoothly but benefits everyone in Russia and in Crimea.

Thank you very much for this joint work.

SOURCE: President of Russia. "Ceremony signing the laws on admitting Crimea and Sevastopol to the Russian Federation." March 21, 2014. http://eng.kremlin.ru/news/6910.

NATO-Ukraine Commission Remarks on Russian Military Intervention in Ukraine

April 1, 2014

We, the Foreign Ministers of the NATO-Ukraine Commission, are united in our condemnation of Russia's illegal military intervention in Ukraine, and Russia's violation of Ukraine's sovereignty and territorial integrity. We do not recognize Russia's illegal and illegitimate "annexation" of Crimea. We will continue to work together to reach a political and diplomatic solution which respects international law and Ukraine's internationally recognized borders.

We call on Russia to de-escalate by reducing its troops in Crimea to pre-crisis levels and withdrawing them to their bases; to reduce its military activities along the Ukrainian border; to reverse the illegal and illegitimate "annexation" of Crimea; to refrain from any further interference and aggressive actions in Ukraine; to respect the rights of the Ukrainian population including the Crimean Tatars; and to fulfil its international obligations and to abide by international law.

We support the deployment of an OSCE monitoring mission to Ukraine.

We commend the Armed Forces of Ukraine for their courage, discipline and restraint, in the face of provocation.

As a tangible demonstration of Allied commitment to the Distinctive Partnership between NATO and Ukraine, we have agreed on concrete measures to enhance Ukraine's ability to provide for its own security.

NATO and Ukraine will intensify cooperation and promote defence reforms through capacity building and capability development programmes. NATO Allies will also reinforce the NATO Liaison Office in Kyiv with additional experts.

Allies will continue working together with the Ukrainian government, the Verkhovna Rada and civil society to strengthen civilian control over the armed forces and related security sectors.

Allies support the measures taken by the Ukrainian government to advance reforms and to promote an inclusive political process, based on democratic values, respect for human rights, minorities and the rule of law.

We welcome Ukraine's signature of the political chapters of the Association Agreement with the European Union on 21 March.

An independent, sovereign and stable Ukraine, firmly committed to democracy and the rule of law, is key to Euro-Atlantic security. Allies firmly support Ukraine's sovereignty and territorial integrity. We call on Russia to abide by these principles.

SOURCE: North Atlantic Treaty Organization. "Statement of the NATO-Ukraine Commission." April 1, 2014. www.nato.int/cps/en/natolive/news_108499.htm.

OTHER HISTORIC DOCUMENTS OF INTEREST

FROM THIS VOLUME

■ International Leaders Announce Sanctions Against Russia, p. 375

FROM PREVIOUS *HISTORIC DOCUMENTS*

■ Yanukovych on His Victory in Ukrainian Presidential Election, *2004,* p. 1001

Disappearance of Malaysian Airlines Flight

MARCH 15 AND 24, AND APRIL 3, 2014

On March 9, 2014, Malaysian Airlines Flight 370 disappeared en route from Kuala Lumpur to Beijing. When the flight dropped off radar and did not appear at its destination, an international search began to find the missing plane, focused on the Indian Ocean. Aviation experts charted potential flight patterns based on the last known location of the flight, but as of the printing of this edition, neither the plane nor any of its wreckage has been located. Conspiracy theories abound about whether the plane was hijacked and flown to a secret location, intentionally crashed, or unintentionally crashed following a loss of cabin pressure or functionality. The Malaysian government was heavily criticized for its response and has been accused of withholding vital information that could lead to locating the plane. Given that no evidence has been found, officials assume that all 239 passengers and crew were killed, marking one of the largest aviation incidents involving a Boeing 777.

CHRONOLOGY OF EVENTS

Malaysia Airlines Flight 370 (MH370) departed Kuala Lumpur en route to Beijing on March 8, 2014. The last known communication from the cockpit with air traffic control occurred an estimated one hour after takeoff. The plane was last plotted by military radar just after 2:00 a.m. over the Andaman Sea. Questions remain about why the plane was reported missing by the airline only after an additional four hours elapsed. The aircraft was carrying twelve Malaysian crew members and 227 passengers from fourteen countries including: China, Malaysia, Indonesia, Australia, India, France, the United States, New Zealand, Ukraine, Canada, Russia, Taiwan, the Netherlands, and Iran. The majority of passengers held Chinese passports.

At the time of its disappearance, with the presumption of a loss of all lives aboard, MH370 would have been the deadliest aviation incident in the history of Malaysia Airlines and the deadliest incident in aviation history involving a Boeing 777. These numbers have since been surpassed by the crash of Malaysia Airlines Flight 17, also a Boeing 777, on July 17, 2014, which killed all 298 people aboard when the plane was shot down in Ukraine.

The Malaysian government released initial reports concerning the fate and mysterious whereabouts of MH370, though details remain scarce. International involvement in the location of the plane escalated amid claims that the Malaysian government may not have the resources or experts for a search of such a magnitude and concerns that the Malaysian government may deliberately withhold information regarding the search due to historical tensions with China.

In a press statement on March 15, 2014, Prime Minister Najib Razak revealed two possible flight scenarios based on satellite information. He stated:

Due to the type of satellite data, we are unable to confirm the precise location of the plane when it last made contact. However, based on this new data, the aviation authorities of Malaysia and their international counterparts have determined that the plane's last communication with the satellite was in one of two possible corridors: a northern corridor stretching approximately from the border of Kazakhstan and Turkmenistan to northern Thailand, or a southern corridor stretching approximately from Indonesia to the southern Indian ocean.

As it became clear that countries in the northern corridor had not detected the plane, the focus shifted to the Indian Ocean off of the coast of Australia.

In a statement on March 24, 2014, Prime Minister Tony Abbott of Australia made mention of objects that had been located in the Indian Ocean, believed to a portion of the wreckage. The objects were later identified as unrelated to the crash. Nearly two weeks after the initial disappearance, with no confirmed wreckage discovered, MH370 was declared crashed. Many expressed outrage that the news was reported via news outlets prior to the completion of official notifications of next of kin for all aboard. The government also faced criticism for notifying next of kin via text message.

THEORIES AND POSSIBLE CONSPIRACY

The investigation into the missing plane is still ongoing, but it is believed that the flight ended at a location in the Indian Ocean when the plane depleted all fuel aboard. A singular explanation for the original deviation from the flight plan has yet to emerge. Even among experts tasked with locating the plane, consensus remains elusive.

Equipment malfunction is suspected by some, citing similar problems with other Boeing 777s, including a cockpit fire in 2011 on an EgyptAir flight caused by faulty wiring. The EgyptAir incident occurred while the plane was still on the ground. Both the plane involved in the 2011 fire and flight MH370 were manufactured around the same time. A fire in the air could have resulted in catastrophic failure of the plane; such a fire would likely destroy the flight controls and flight instruments. According to experts, a fire of this kind while in flight is unlikely to be contained.

Soon after the disappearance of MH370 speculation began that the plane may have been hijacked, which was echoed in a statement made by Malaysia's prime minister when he said, "These movements are consistent with deliberate action by someone on the plane." Advocates of such a theory have identified in excess of 500 small runways, many on remote islands, where the plane could be landed by a terrorist group either to demand a ransom or to store the plane for a future attack. With the discovery of two Iranian nationals traveling with stolen passports onboard MH370, several American politicians joined those suggesting terrorist involvement. U.S. senator John Cornyn, R-Texas, tweeted a link showing runways where it would have been possible for the plane to land. However, with no group stepping forward to claim responsibility, a terrorist scenario has become increasingly unlikely.

Former Malaysian prime minister Mahathir Mohamad suggested that the autopilot system onboard may have been accessed by Boeing or a U.S. government agency, such as the Central Intelligence Agency (CIA), through available channels, effectively electronically hijacking the plane. In a blog post, the former prime minister wrote:

Airplanes can go up and stay up for long periods of time. But even they must come down eventually. They can land safely or they may crash. But airplanes don't just disappear. Certainly not these days with all the powerful communication systems, radio and satellite tracking and filmless cameras which operate almost indefinitely and possess huge storage capacities.

Mohamad later added, "Someone is hiding something. . . . For some reason the media will not print anything that involves Boeing or the CIA." No concrete evidence has come to light to support his claims. His sentiments are echoed by those who share his disbelief concerning such a disappearance in an age of advanced technology. In a report by the BBC, a lawyer commenting on what is believed to be the first lawsuit related to the disappearance of MH370, stated, "A big plane missing in this age of technology is really unacceptable." The lawsuit was brought against the Malaysian civil aviation department, alleging negligence. The suit contends that action should have been taken as soon as the plane disappeared from radar rather than hours later.

Some conspiracy theorists suggest that MH370 may have been flown to a U.S. military base on the atoll of Diego Garcia. The Diego Garcia landing theory gained traction after it was discovered that the pilot of MH370 had practiced landing on a similar runway using his in-home flight simulator. The records of practice flights on shorter runways were recovered from the in-home flight simulator by investigators, though the records had been deleted by the user. Theorists saw this as possible confirmation that the plane had been purposely diverted by the pilot as part of a larger clandestine operation. This theory was raised and quickly dismissed at a daily press briefing at the White House on March 18, 2014. Another theory suggests that the pilot may have purposely crashed the plane as part of a suicide plan.

Other less plausible theories range from a government shoot down to prophetic lyrics. American conservative commentator Rush Limbaugh initially suggested that the airplane may have been shot down by an "unfriendly country," though he has since retracted such comments. There is no evidence at this time that MH370 was shot down either purposely or accidentally. Following this line of thought, some speculate that Malaysian Airlines Flight 17, which was shot down over Ukraine in July 2014, may actually be the missing Flight 370. Conspiracy theorists claim that MH17 may have been captured, while MH370 was shot down as a double citing photographic evidence of subtle structural differences between the two 777s. Experts have dismissed this claim.

International Cooperation and Status of the Search

In his statement to the press on March 15, 2014, current Malaysian prime minister Razak stated:

> I instructed the Malaysian authorities to share all relevant information freely and transparently with the wider investigation team; and I requested that our friends and allies join the operation. As of today, fourteen countries, 43 ships and 58 aircraft are involved in the search.

Though critics may question the level of transparency from the Malaysian government, the search for MH370 has expanded to become the largest international search effort ever attempted incorporating multiple government and private entities for an unprecedented operation to locate the missing plane. In the early stages of the search, efforts focused on the area where radar contact was lost. The search area shifted as an analysis of possible flight paths was conducted using data from satellites. The focus ultimately shifted to an area of the Indian Ocean west of Perth, Australia.

The search resumed on October 5, 2014, after a four-month period during which several crews worked to update maps of the seabed in the expected search area. The search site covers approximately 23,000 square miles along the route where experts believe the plane may have run out of fuel. Teams aboard the Malaysian contracted GO Phoenix and two ships known as team Fugro and hired by the Australian authorities through a Dutch contractor are conducting the search. Five independent teams of investigators made up of officials from Boeing, Inmarsat, France's Thales Group, the United States' National Transportation Safety Board, and the Australian Defence Science and Technology Organisation were enlisted to define the area for the search. As a result of their findings, the ships will examine two distinct areas. The experts are split in their opinion regarding the probable crash site. One group made calculations based on the assumption that the autopilot function on the plane was still engaged. The other group made no such assumptions. Using these differing variables, two areas have been selected for the search. The GO Phoenix will scan the more northern search area, while the Fugro team will search the southern site.

The search effort is planned to last 300 days and will be the most expensive search in history. Sonar will be towed far beneath the surface of the water. These sonar devices also have a sensor attached to detect jet fuel, and cameras will be used to investigate any anomalies based on the sonar data. According to an interview with Chief Commissioner Martin Dolan of the Australian Transport Safety Bureau, it is estimated that currently committed government funding will run out before the areas are completely searched. Dolan believes that, at most, 80 percent of the area will be searched. It is not yet clear if other nations will contribute additional funding to bridge the gap.

—Sarah Gall

The following is a statement by current Malaysian prime minister Najib Razak on March 15, 2014, regarding the ongoing search for flight MH370; a statement by Australian prime minister Tony Abbott on March 24, 2014, on his nation's involvement in the search; a March 24, 2014, statement by Razak announcing the assumption that MH370 crashed, killing all onboard; and an April 3, 2014, joint statement by Abbott and Razak on the ongoing search for MH370 in the Indian Ocean.

Prime Minister Razak on the Search for MH370

March 15, 2014

Seven days ago Malaysia Airlines flight MH370 disappeared. We realise this is an excruciating time for the families of those on board. No words can describe the pain they must be going through. Our thoughts and our prayers are with them.

I have been appraised [sic] of the on-going search operation round the clock. At the beginning of the operation, I ordered the search area to be broadened; I instructed the

Malaysian authorities to share all relevant information freely and transparently with the wider investigation team; and I requested that our friends and allies join the operation. As of today, 14 countries, 43 ships and 58 aircraft are involved in the search.

I wish to thank all the governments for their help at such a crucial time. Since day one, the Malaysian authorities have worked hand-in-hand with our international partners—including neighbouring countries, the aviation authorities and a multinational search force—many of whom have been here on the ground since Sunday.

We have shared information in real time with authorities who have the necessary experience to interpret the data. We have been working non-stop to assist the investigation. And we have put our national security second to the search for the missing plane.

It is widely understood that this has been a situation without precedent.

We have conducted search operations over land, in the South China Sea, the Straits of Malacca, the Andaman Sea and the Indian Ocean. At every stage, we acted on the basis of verified information, and we followed every credible lead. Sometimes these leads have led nowhere.

There has been intense speculation. We understand the desperate need for information on behalf of the families and those watching around the world. But we have a responsibility to the investigation and the families to only release information that has been corroborated. And our primary motivation has always been to find the plane.

In the first phase of the search operation, we searched near MH370's last known position, in the South China Sea. At the same time, it was brought to our attention by the Royal Malaysian Air Force that, based on their primary radar, an aircraft—the identity of which could not be confirmed—made a turn back. The primary radar data showed the aircraft proceeding on a flight path which took it to an area north of the Straits of Malacca.

Given this credible data, which was subsequently corroborated with the relevant international authorities, we expanded the area of search to include the Straits of Malacca and, later, to the Andaman Sea.

Early this morning I was briefed by the investigation team—which includes the FAA, NTSB, the AAIB, the Malaysian authorities and the Acting Minister of Transport—on new information that sheds further light on what happened to MH370.

Based on new satellite information, we can say with a high degree of certainty that the Aircraft Communications Addressing and Reporting System (ACARS) was disabled just before the aircraft reached the East coast of peninsular Malaysia.

Shortly afterwards, near the border between Malaysian and Vietnamese air traffic control, the aircraft's transponder was switched off.

From this point onwards, the Royal Malaysian Air Force primary radar showed that an aircraft which was believed—but not confirmed—to be MH370 did indeed turn back. It then flew in a westerly direction back over peninsular Malaysia before turning northwest. Up until the point at which it left military primary radar coverage, these movements are consistent with deliberate action by someone on the plane.

Today, based on raw satellite data that was obtained from the satellite data service provider, we can confirm that the aircraft shown in the primary radar data was flight MH370. After much forensic work and deliberation, the FAA, NTSB, AAIB and the Malaysian authorities, working separately on the same data, concur.

According to the new data, the last confirmed communication between the plane and the satellite was at 8:11AM Malaysian time on Saturday 8th March. The investigations team is making further calculations which will indicate how far the aircraft may have flown after this last point of contact. This will help us to refine the search.

Due to the type of satellite data, we are unable to confirm the precise location of the plane when it last made contact with the satellite.

However, based on this new data, the aviation authorities of Malaysia and their international counterparts have determined that the plane's last communication with the satellite was in one of two possible corridors: a northern corridor stretching approximately from the border of Kazakhstan and Turkmenistan to northern Thailand, or a southern corridor stretching approximately from Indonesia to the southern Indian ocean. The investigation team is working to further refine the information.

In view of this latest development the Malaysian authorities have refocused their investigation into the crew and passengers on board. Despite media reports that the plane was hijacked, I wish to be very clear: we are still investigating all possibilities as to what caused MH370 to deviate from its original flight path.

This new satellite information has a significant impact on the nature and scope of the search operation. We are ending our operations in the South China Sea and reassessing the redeployment of our assets. We are working with the relevant countries to request all information relevant to the search, including radar data.

As the two new corridors involve many countries, the relevant foreign embassies have been invited to a briefing on the new information today by the Malaysian Foreign Ministry and the technical experts. I have also instructed the Foreign Ministry to provide a full briefing to foreign governments which had passengers on the plane. This morning, Malaysia Airlines has been informing the families of the passengers and crew of these new developments.

Clearly, the search for MH370 has entered a new phase. Over the last seven days, we have followed every lead and looked into every possibility. For the families and friends of those involved, we hope this new information brings us one step closer to finding the plane.

SOURCE: Office of the Prime Minister of Malaysia. "Prime Minister's Statement on Flight MH370." March 15, 2014. www.pmo.gov.my/home.php?menu=news&news_id=12606&news_cat=4&page=17 29&sort_year=2014&sort_month=03.

Australian Prime Minister on Involvement in the Search for MH370

March 24, 2014

Thank you, Mr. Acting Deputy Speaker.

Mr. Acting Deputy Speaker, I wish to update the House with the latest developments in the search for ill-fated flight MH370. The Australian Maritime Safety Authority has advised that objects have been located by a Royal Australian Air Force P3 Orion and I can advise the House that HMAS Success is on scene and is attempting to locate and recover these objects.

The objects were spotted in the search area about 2500 kilometres southwest of Perth at about 2.45pm our time.

The crew on board the Orion reported seeing two objects, the first a grey or green circular object and the second an orange rectangular object. These are separate to the objects reported earlier today by a Chinese search aircraft.

I can advise the House that US Navy Poseidon, a second Royal Australian Air Force Orion and a Japanese Orion are also on route to or in the search area. Planes and ships continue to search the area for any sign of the missing aircraft.

I caution again, Mr. Acting Deputy Speaker, that we don't know whether any of these objects are from MH370. They could be flotsam. Nevertheless we are hopeful that we can recover these objects soon and that they will take us a step closer to resolving this tragic mystery.

This is an extraordinary mystery. An absolutely baffling mystery. But as I've said before, Mr. Acting Deputy Speaker, let me reiterate to this House we owe it to the families of those on board, we owe it to the loved ones on board, we owe it to all the people who are concerned about the fate of this aircraft to do whatever we reasonably can to find anything that is out there, to test it and to see what we can learn about what so far is one of the great mysteries of our time.

SOURCE: Prime Minister of Australia. "Statement to the House of Representatives Regarding Flight MH370." March 24, 2014. Licensed from the Commonwealth of Australia under a Creative Commons Attribution 3.0 Australia Licence. The Commonwealth of Australia does not necessarily endorse the content of this publication. www.pm.gov.au/media/2014-03-24/statement-house-representatives-regarding-flight-mh370–0.

Prime Minister Razak Announces the Assumption that MH370 Crashed

March 24, 2014

This evening I was briefed by representatives from the UK Air Accidents Investigation Branch (AAIB).

They informed me that Inmarsat, the UK company that provided the satellite data which indicated the northern and southern corridors, has been performing further calculations on the data.

Using a type of analysis never before used in an investigation of this sort, they have been able to shed more light on MH370's flight path.

Based on their new analysis, Inmarsat and the AAIB have concluded that MH370 flew along the southern corridor, and that its last position was in the middle of the Indian Ocean, west of Perth.

This is a remote location, far from any possible landing sites. It is therefore with deep sadness and regret that I must inform you that, according to this new data, flight MH370 ended in the southern Indian Ocean.

We will be holding a press conference tomorrow with further details. In the meantime, we wanted to inform you of this new development at the earliest opportunity.

We share this information out of a commitment to openness and respect for the families, two principles which have guided this investigation.

Malaysia Airlines have already spoken to the families of the passengers and crew to inform them of this development.

For them, the past few weeks have been heartbreaking; I know this news must be harder still. I urge the media to respect their privacy, and to allow them the space they need at this difficult time.

SOURCE: Office of the Prime Minister of Malaysia. "PM Najib Razak's Press Statement on MH370." March 24, 2014. www.pmo.gov.my/home.php?menu=news&news_id=12634&news_cat=4&page=1729&sort_year=2014&sort_month=03.

Abbott and Najib Hold Joint Press Conference on Search for MH370

April 3, 2014

PRIME MINISTER ABBOTT (AUSTRALIA):

Ladies and gentleman, it is a real honour for me to be here again for the second time in four days to thank all of the personnel from many countries for the work that is being done in searching for and recovering ill-fated flight MH370.

This is a remarkable international cooperation—a truly remarkable international cooperation.

It's great to be here with my friend and colleague Prime Minister Najib Razak of Malaysia, but it's really good to be here with the service personnel of Australia, of Malaysia, of China, of Japan, of Korea, of the United States and of New Zealand.

To have the military forces of so many countries working together for our common humanity shows what we can do. It shows what we can do and if anyone would ever be unhappy or distraught about the prospects for international peace and harmony this operation is a marvellous antidote to pessimism—a marvellous antidote to pessimism.

So thank you for your commitment. Thank you for professionalism. Thank you for your idealism.

I am confident that everything that possibly can be done to find this aircraft will be done. We cannot be certain of success, but we can be certain of the professionalism and the effort that will be brought to the task.

Thank you.

PRIME MINISTER NAJIB (MALAYSIA):

Prime Minister Tony Abbott, Ministers, ladies and gentlemen. I am delighted to be here at the Royal Australian Air Force Base in Pearce to personally thank everyone involved in this gigantean task to find missing MH370.

When Prime Minister Tony Abbott called me a few days ago I was both relieved and thankful that Australia is willing to be very forthcoming to step up and offer their assistance to locate the missing aircraft. As the saying goes—a friend in need is a friend indeed. So Australia has proven to be a very reliable and a true friend to Malaysia. So thank you very much Prime Minister Abbott.

I am also delighted that Prime Minister Abbott has appointed Air Marshal Angus Houston, whom I know personally—a man of great experience and skill—and I'm confident that he's providing the true professional leadership of this Joint Action Coordination

Centre which requires true coordination among so many personnel from many countries, as well as other agencies involved in this search operation.

I would also like to thank all the countries involved. It was a very heart-warming experience to be introduced to the leaders of the various countries—from China, from the United States, from New Zealand, from Japan from the Republic of Korea, from New Zealand and of course from both Australia and Malaysia.

Indeed this is probably the largest mission put together by so many countries to locate an aircraft and your commitment is very, very much appreciated by Malaysia and by the world.

We owe it to the grieving families to give them comfort and closure to this rather tragic event and the world expects us to do our level best and I'm very confident that you will indeed show what we can do together as a group of nations that we want to find answers. We want to provide comfort to the families and we will not rest until answers are indeed found.

I'm very confident with the level of professionalism shown as alluded to by Prime Minister Abbott that indeed in due time we will provide a closure to this event, or this tragedy.

So once again, thank you very much to all of you. I know it is a daunting task to go out there in very inclement weather, in very challenging circumstances. Malaysia is indeed grateful for your courage and for your commitment.

And above all, I'd like to thank Prime Minister Abbott once again and the Australian Government for your steadfast commitment to the search mission and together let us work hand-in-hand to provide answers in what is probably the biggest mystery in aviation history thus far.

Thank you once again.

Source: Prime Minister of Australia. "Joint Remarks with Prime Minister Najib Razak, Western Australia." April 3, 2014. www.pm.gov.au/media/2014-04-03/joint-remarks-prime-minister-najib-razak-western -australia.

President Obama's National Security Agency Reform Proposal Released

MARCH 27, 2014

Throughout 2014, the United States continued its examination of intelligence-gathering procedures, particularly the National Security Agency's (NSA) "bulk telephony metadata" collection program. The program had been the subject of one of the most significant national security leaks in U.S. history in 2013 when former government contractor Edward Snowden provided media with classified documents outlining the program. Public backlash prompted officials to conduct a formal review of the program and identify opportunities for reform. President Barack Obama announced his own reform proposals in January 2014. While some immediate changes were made to the program, further changes are pending congressional approval of related legislation.

CONTROVERSY PROMPTS CALL FOR REFORM

The most recent controversy over U.S. intelligence gathering ignited during the summer of 2013 when government contractor Edward Snowden leaked a series of documents detailing top-secret surveillance programs conducted by the United States and Britain that involved collecting electronic communications in bulk, without individual warrants. Published by outlets including the *Guardian* and the *Washington Post,* the documents revealed that the NSA was collecting the phone records of millions of Verizon's U.S. customers on an "ongoing, daily basis," regardless of whether the individual callers were suspected of wrongdoing. This included phone numbers, location data, call duration, time of the calls, and any other unique identifiers, although it did not include the contents of phone messages or subscribers' personal information. The collection had been authorized by the U.S. Foreign Intelligence Surveillance Court (FISA Court), which is charged with reviewing and approving federal law enforcement agencies' requests for surveillance warrants against foreign targets who are suspected of espionage or terrorism. Other revelations included a program called PRISM, through which the NSA and Federal Bureau of Investigation (FBI) were directly tapping in to the servers of companies such as Google and Facebook to collect bulk information, and also that the United States had been monitoring allied heads of state and their staffs.

The documents caused a public outcry, raising concerns of privacy violations and prompting the government to reexamine its intelligence operations. In August 2013, President Obama created a formal panel to review and consider changes to the "bulk telephony metadata" collection program, sometimes known as the 215 Program after Section 215 of the Patriot Act. The program was initially established to analyze links between callers in an effort to determine whether an individual had any hidden terrorist associates and, if so, who they were. The Review Group on Intelligence and Communications Technologies was tasked with identifying opportunities for the U.S. government to better protect civil liberties while maintaining national security through its surveillance programs.

On December 18, the Review Group released its report, "Liberty and Security in a Changing World: Report and Recommendations of the President's Review Group on Intelligence and Communications Technologies," which outlined a total of forty-six non-binding recommendations. Among the most notable, a recommendation that the government transition from storing the phone metadata itself to a system in which the information is held by a private company. The government could query that information whenever necessary for national security purposes, but would need to identify a specific suspicion motivating a search before conducting such a query. The Review Group also recommended requiring the government to get an order from the FISA Court for each search, which was not previously mandated. In addition, the Review Group proposed new restrictions on the FISA Court's ability to compel third parties, such as phone service providers, to disclose private information to the government, and similar limitations on the FBI's use of National Security Letters to compel businesses to share private records. The group also called for legislation that would require the government to make information about surveillance programs available to Congress and the public to the greatest extent possible, as well as legislation authorizing communications providers to publicly disclose general information about the related orders they receive from the government. Companies were previously prohibited from making such orders and letters public.

The President's Proposal

After considering the Review Group's recommendations, President Obama offered his proposals for NSA reform during a speech at the Department of Justice on January 17. His plan largely adopted or modified the Review Group's recommendations, involving a transition in intelligence gathering that would "end the metadata program as it existed." President Obama directed Attorney General Eric Holder and the intelligence community to develop an alternative approach to metadata collection and monitoring that would match the capabilities of the NSA's current metadata program without requiring the government to store the data. They were tasked with providing options for consideration before March 28, the date when the metadata program was set for reauthorization. In the meantime, the government would continue to collect and store the data status quo.

Also of note, Obama called for requiring intelligence officials to obtain advance approval from the FISA Court each time they wanted to search a person's phone data, except in emergency situations, ensuring they would have to make a compelling case for why an individual represented a legitimate security concern. These searches would also be scaled back, with officials allowed to examine personal connections "two hops" removed from a target rather than the previously established "three hops." Obama also said the United States would end surveillance of its allies' heads of state and proposed new privacy protections for non-U.S. citizens, including reducing the length of time the NSA can keep its communications data and limiting the use of such surveillance to national security reasons such as counter-spying, counterterrorism, and cybersecurity. Additionally, Obama created a new yearly review process for surveillance operations and ordered a continued review of the FISA Court's classified opinions to determine whether certain opinions could be made public, particularly those with broad privacy implications. His plan included some organizational changes as well. He announced that the State Department would designate a senior officer to coordinate diplomacy on issues related to technology and signals intelligence, and that the White House would appoint a senior official to implement new privacy safeguards. Furthermore, he proposed creating a panel of expert advocates on privacy and technology issues that could be called before the FISA Court to testify in "novel" cases.

Obama did not adopt the Review Group's recommendation to require the FBI to obtain the FISA Court's approval before issuing National Security Letters, but he did call for Attorney General Holder to make the process more transparent and to allow companies that received letters to make more information about the orders public. He also did not address the Review Group's recommendations to prevent the NSA from undermining commercial software or exploiting flaws in such software in order to carry out cyberattacks or surveillance.

If authorized by Congress, the implementation of his proposals would mark the most significant changes to the U.S. surveillance program in more than ten years. "The reforms I'm proposing today should give the American people greater confidence that their rights are being protected, even as our intelligence and law-enforcement agencies maintain the tools they need to keep us safe," Obama said. Some lawmakers, including those on key congressional committees, offered strong praise for the proposals. Sens. Ron Wyden, D-Ore., Mark Udall, D-Colo., and Martin Heinrich, D-N.M., issued a joint statement describing the decision to move metadata storage from the NSA "a major milestone." Others were more measured in their response. "When lives are at stake, the president must not allow politics to cloud his judgment," said House Speaker John Boehner, R-Ohio. "I look forward to learning more about how the new procedure for accessing data will not put Americans at greater risk." Sen. Dianne Feinstein, D-Calif., and Rep. Mike Rogers, R-Mich., also noted the importance of maintaining an efficient search process while requiring prior court approval for searches: "If instituted, that approval process must be made faster in the future than it was in the past—when it took up to nine days to gain court approval for a single search," they said in a joint statement. "We encourage the White House to send legislation with the president's proposed changes to Congress so they can be fully debated."

On February 5, the FISA Court approved the president's requests to require court approval of each query and to limit the breadth of searches and began implementing those changes. Through February and March, the Obama administration reportedly consulted with members of Congress, including those on the House and Senate Judiciary and Intelligence Committees, private sector representatives, and privacy and civil liberties groups to help identify alternatives to government storage of the metadata. On March 27, President Obama issued a statement saying he had determined the best approach would be for the metadata to remain with the phone companies. He also said the companies should continue to hold the data for the length of time they currently do (approximately eighteen months). The government would then be able to query the necessary data once it received FISA Court approval. "I believe this approach will best ensure that we have the information we need to meet our intelligence needs while enhancing public confidence in the manner in which the information is collected and held," he said. "I am confident that this approach can provide our intelligence and law enforcement professionals the information they need to keep us safe while addressing the legitimate privacy concerns that have been raised."

SURVEILLANCE REFORM GOES BEFORE CONGRESS

Before the president's proposals could be implemented, Congress had to pass legislation that would permit the government to collect intelligence information with the speed and in the manner necessary to make the new approach work. More than twenty different pieces of legislation aimed at reforming intelligence gathering practices have been introduced since the 2013 document leak.

Chief among them is the USA Freedom Act, a bill introduced in both the House and Senate in October 2013 by Rep. James Sensenbrenner, R-Wis., and Sen. Patrick Leahy, D-Vt. As originally proposed, the bill would have ended the NSA's bulk collection of metadata, leaving the information with the phone companies; required preapproval from the FISA Court on all queries and that intelligence officials make a stronger case for why the search was necessary; limited the NSA's retention of "incidentally" gathered data on American citizens; created a special privacy advocate at the FISA Court; and required greater disclosure and transparency around FISA Court orders and decisions. The bill was widely supported by a variety of interest groups, ranging from the American Civil Liberties Union to the National Rifle Association. However, in May 2014, the House passed an amended version of the bill that broadened the scope of searches that intelligence officials would be permitted to conduct, including those based on geographic region, and did not explicitly prohibit the NSA from searching for Americans' information within the gathered data without a warrant. The changes caused many privacy advocates to pull their support for the bill, amid concerns that it did not go far enough to end the metadata program.

In July, Sen. Leahy introduced to the Senate a new, compromise version of the bill that would place greater limits on government queries of databases; require officials to report the number of queries run on Americans and how many Americans' data may have been collected as part of broader searches; and expand companies' ability to publicly report on government requests for information, among other provisions. While backed by the White House, the bill has not progressed through the Senate.

Other legislative proposals included the FISA Transparency and Modernization Act, introduced by Reps. Rogers and C. A. "Dutch" Ruppersberger, D-Md., which would keep metadata with phone companies but allow the government to subpoena records without prior judicial review and approval. Instead, the FISA Court would review search requests after they had been conducted and could expunge the data if it did not meet search standards. The bill remains before the Subcommittee on Crime, Terrorism, Homeland Security, and Investigations. As of publication, Congress has yet to approve any NSA-related legislation.

—Linda Fecteau Grimm

The following is a statement by President Barack Obama delivered on March 27, 2014, outlining proposals to revise the way in which the National Security Agency collects data.

President Obama Remarks on NSA Data Collection

March 27, 2014

Earlier this year in a speech at the Department of Justice, I announced a transition that would end the section 215 bulk telephony metadata program as it previously existed and that we would establish a mechanism to preserve the capabilities we need without the

Government holding this bulk metadata. I did so to give the public greater confidence that their privacy is appropriately protected, while maintaining the tools our intelligence and law enforcement agencies need to keep us safe.

In that January 17 speech, I ordered that a transition away from the prior program would proceed in two steps. In addition to directing immediate changes to the program, I also directed the intelligence community and the Attorney General to use this transition period to develop options for a new approach to match the capabilities and fill gaps that the section 215 program was designed to address without the Government holding this metadata. I instructed them to report back to me with options for alternative approaches before the program comes up for reauthorization on March 28th. As part of this process, we consulted with the Congress, the private sector, and privacy and civil liberties groups and developed a number of alternative approaches.

Having carefully considered the available options, I have decided that the best path forward is that the Government should not collect or hold this data in bulk. Instead, the data should remain at the telephone companies for the length of time it currently does today. The Government would obtain the data pursuant to individual orders from the Foreign Intelligence Surveillance Court (FISC) approving the use of specific numbers for such queries if a judge agrees based on national security concerns. Legislation will be needed to permit the Government to obtain this information with the speed and in the manner that will be required to make this approach workable.

I believe this approach will best ensure that we have the information we need to meet our intelligence needs while enhancing public confidence in the manner in which the information is collected and held. My team has been in touch with key Congressional leadership—including from the Judiciary and Intelligence Committees—and we are committed to working with them to see legislation passed as soon as possible. Given that this legislation will not be in place by March 28 and given the importance of maintaining this capability, I have directed the Department of Justice to seek a 90-day reauthorization of the existing program including the modifications I directed in January. I am confident that this approach can provide our intelligence and law enforcement professionals the information they need to keep us safe while addressing the legitimate privacy concerns that have been raised.

SOURCE: Executive Office of the President. "Statement on the National Security Agency's Section 215 Bulk Telephony Metadata Program." March 27, 2014. *Compilation of Presidential Documents* 2014, no. 00213 (March 27, 2014). www.gpo.gov/fdsys/pkg/DCPD-201400213/pdf/DCPD-201400213.pdf.

OTHER HISTORIC DOCUMENTS OF INTEREST

FROM PREVIOUS *HISTORIC DOCUMENTS*

April

Supreme Court Rules on Campaign Contributions

APRIL 2, 2014

With its ruling in *McCutcheon v. Federal Election Commission*, decided on April 2, 2014, the U.S. Supreme Court struck down a Watergate-era law that had put a cap, currently $123,000, on the aggregate amount of money an individual can donate to candidates and political parties in any one election. The decision, however, has for now left in place the current $5,200 base limit on how much a person can contribute to any one candidate during a particular election cycle. This was the latest in a series of decisions to have eroded the reach of federal campaign finance legislation and it reflected the same reasoning used in 2010 in the *Citizen's United* case, which struck down limits on independent campaign spending by corporations and unions, ruling that they had the right to spend unlimited sums of money to influence elections. Also like *Citizen's United*, this case was decided 5–4 with the conservative block of the Court in the majority over a strongly worded dissent by the Court's more liberal justices. The majority and dissenting opinions in the *McCutcheon* case reflect a deep and fundamental conflict in the Court about the application of the First Amendment to donating money in politics. The majority of the justices believe that contributing money to a candidate is a form of political expression and an exercise of the right to participate in the electoral process—both deeply important First Amendment rights. By contrast, the dissenters were concerned with the corrupting impact of so much money on the very "integrity of our public governmental institutions."

LEGAL BACKGROUND

In 1971, Congress passed the Federal Election Campaign Act ("FECA"), and then in 1974, amidst the wave of reactions to the Watergate scandal, strengthened the Act requiring, among other things, disclosures of campaign financing, the creation of the Federal Election Commission, and putting limits on contributions to campaigns. In a 1976 case, *Buckley v. Valeo*, the Supreme Court struck down several provisions of the law but upheld the original contribution caps. The most recent overhaul to FECA was the Bipartisan Campaign Reform Act of 2002, often referred to as the McCain-Feingold law after the two senators who sponsored it. The overhaul continued the regulations on campaign contributions, both on how much an individual could contribute to each candidate and how much could be contributed overall.

Shaun McCutcheon is a businessman from Alabama. In the 2011–2012 election cycle, he contributed to sixteen different federal candidates, giving no more than allowed by the base contribution limits to each candidate. He said that he wanted to contribute to twelve additional candidates but was prevented from doing so by the aggregate limit on total contributions to candidates. He also donated to several political committees in compliance with the rules but was unable to contribute further because he had reached the aggregate limit allowed by law. McCutcheon did not seek to give more than allowed to each candidate or committee, but he wanted to be able to give to more campaigns, in excess of the aggregate limits. He sued along with the Republican National Committee in the district court for the District of Columbia. The district court found that the aggregate limits survived First Amendment challenge. McCutcheon appealed directly to the Supreme Court.

CAMPAIGN CONTRIBUTIONS A FORM OF FREE EXPRESSION

Chief Justice John G. Roberts Jr. wrote the controlling decision, joined by Justices Antonin Scalia, Anthony M. Kennedy, and Samuel A. Alito Jr. He overturned the result of *Buckley v. Valeo* to reach his broad conclusion that all aggregate campaign limits violate the First Amendment. Justice Clarence Thomas concurred with the judgment but wrote separately and alone to argue for a more expansive ruling that would require all contribution limits to be struck down under the strictest First Amendment scrutiny.

The chief justice forcefully argued that the right to donate to campaigns fits squarely among the most important rights protected by the First Amendment: "There is no right more basic in our democracy than the right to participate in electing our political leaders." To contribute money, he reasoned, is to participate in the electoral process both through political expression and political association—rights safeguarded by the First Amendment. Whether an individual can merely hand out leaflets for a candidate or can give substantial sums for communicating ideas through "sophisticated" means, that individual is participating in the electoral debate in a way that is "integral to the operation of the system of government established by our constitution."

The opinion recognized that the First Amendment right to participate in democracy through political contributions is not absolute and can be regulated. But, he emphasized that the only legitimate reason for the government to restrict campaign finances is to prevent corruption or the appearance of corruption. Moreover, the only type of corruption that Congress may legitimately target is *quid pro quo* corruption, that which involves "a direct exchange of an official act for money." Chief Justice Roberts explicitly rejected the idea that giving large sums of money to a candidate in the hope of gaining influence or access could constitute corruption. That kind of influence or access is "a central feature of democracy" as "constituents support candidates who share their beliefs and interests, and candidates who are elected can be expected to be responsive to those concerns." He also rejected any effort to regulate for the purpose of "leveling the playing field," or "equalizing the financial resources of candidates." The First Amendment, he states, prohibits "legislative attempts to fine tune the electoral process no matter how well intentioned." Perhaps nodding to the fact that polling has consistently shown that *Citizens United* was a deeply unpopular opinion, Roberts recognized that "money in politics may at times seem repugnant to some, but so too does much of what the First Amendment vigorously protects." He cited flag burning and Nazi parades as other unpopular spectacles that are protected free speech.

The majority found any argument that the aggregate campaign limits at issue in this case could be justified as a way to stop *quid pro quo* corruption to be far too speculative. He wondered how it could be "perfectly fine to contribute $5,200 to nine candidates but somehow corrupt to give the same amount to a tenth." He compared restricting how many candidates or causes a donor can support with telling a newspaper how many candidates it can endorse.

Because they are protected by the First Amendment and the regulation serves no legitimate purpose, the five justices in the majority struck down all aggregate limits on the amount an individual can donate to a candidate or a political party.

REGULATION OF MONEY IN POLITICS NECESSARY FOR DEMOCRACY

Justice Stephen G. Breyer wrote the dissent in which he was joined by Justices Ruth Bader Ginsburg, Sonia Sotomayor, and Elena Kagan. Signally sharp disagreement, he read from his dissent in open court. The dissent lamented that the *McCutcheon* decision "eviscerates our Nation's campaign finance laws" and imperils our country's ability to deal with "the grave problems of democratic legitimacy that those laws were intended to resolve." . . . "If the court in *Citizens United* opened a door," he continued, "today's decision may well open a floodgate."

Justice Breyer disagreed with the majority's narrow description of the kind of corruption necessary to justify any regulation of campaign contributions. In his view, nothing in the First Amendment limits the legitimate purpose of regulation to preventing *quid pro quo* corruption, which he described as something akin to bribery. Instead, "the anticorruption interest that drives Congress to regulate campaign contributions is a far broader, more important interest than the plurality acknowledges." "It is an interest," he argues, "in maintaining the integrity of our public governmental institutions." Indicating that people lose faith in a political process that seems to only pay attention to big-money donors, he wrote, "Where enough money calls the tune, the general public will not be heard."

LIKELY IMPACT OF *MCCUTCHEON*

The Supreme Court's earlier decision in *Citizens United* (2010) led to an explosion of election spending, with a recent Brennan Center analysis revealing, among other results, a major increase in the influence of a few wealthy donors. *National Journal* reported that through their various organizations, the Koch brothers alone spent $100 million in the 2014 election cycle. The *McCutcheon* decision is likely to lead to a still further increase in the money in politics because now people with more money to give in elections will have more ways to spend it.

Reaction to the decision was as divided as the Court was, with some viewing it optimistically as a triumph of individual rights. For example, RNC chairman Reince Priebus reacted to the decision: "People should have the right to give their money and exercise free speech to as many candidates and as many political committees and PACs as they want." By contrast, those opposed to the ruling tended to view the decision more cataclysmically. Fred Wertheimer, president of Democracy 21, an advocacy group analyzing the role of money in politics, described the Court as "simply ignoring all the lessons of history" and "creating a new class of American political oligarchs and that is coming at the expense of the voices and interests of more than 300 million Americans." Senator Charles Schumer, D-NY, warned that the decision is in itself "a small step, but another step on the road to ruination."

The decision leaves in place the caps on the amount an individual can give to one campaign or committee, only striking down the aggregate limit on how much an individual can give in an election cycle. This means that, after this ruling, wealthy individuals can give to as many candidates as they would like as long as they don't give more than $5,200 to any single candidate.

The likely impact of this decision will be to embolden people to challenge other election financing regulations, and campaign finance experts are predicting that the individual limits will be challenged next. These would have a larger practical impact on the amount of money in the political system because only a few wealthy individuals ran up against the $123,200 aggregate limits, but many more give up to the individual $5,200 limit. Justice Thomas has already written his position that all limits are unconstitutional, but no other justice signed on to his concurring opinion. However, Chief Justice Roberts is clear in his view that spending money in campaigns is political speech and, as such, entitled to full First Amendment protections. Going forward, it will likely continue to be hard for any regulation of campaign contributions to survive a constitutional challenge. Senator John McCain, R-Ariz., a sponsor of the 2002 Bipartisan Campaign Finance Reform Act, predicted that *McCutcheon* may be only a step in a broader restructuring of American elections when he stated that the ruling "may represent the latest step in an effort by a majority of the court to dismantle entirely the long-standing structure of campaign finance law erected to limit the undue influence of special interests on American politics."

—Melissa Feinberg

Following is the edited text of the Supreme Court decision in McCutcheon v. FEC *in which the Court ruled 5–4 to strike down the overall campaign contribution limits on individual donors in each election cycle.*

McCutcheon v. FEC

April 2, 2014

No. 12-536

Shaun McCutcheon,
et al., appellants

v.

Federal Election
Commission

On appeal from the
United States District
Court for the District
of Columbia

[April 2, 2014]

CHIEF JUSTICE ROBERTS announced the judgment of the Court and delivered an opinion, in which JUSTICE SCALIA, JUSTICE KENNEDY, and JUSTICE ALITO join.

There is no right more basic in our democracy than the right to participate in electing our political leaders. Citizens can exercise that right in a variety of ways: They can run for office themselves, vote, urge others to vote for a particular candidate, volunteer to work on a campaign, and contribute to a candidate's campaign. This case is about the last of those options.

The right to participate in democracy through political contributions is protected by the First Amendment, but that right is not absolute. Our cases have held that Congress may regulate campaign contributions to protect against corruption or the appearance of corruption. See, *e.g., Buckley* v. *Valeo*, 424 U. S. 1, 26–27 (1976) (*per curiam*). At the same time, we have made clear that Congress may not regulate contributions simply to reduce the amount of money in politics, or to restrict the political participation of some in order to enhance the relative influence of others. . . .

Many people might find those latter objectives attractive: They would be delighted to see fewer television commercials touting a candidate's accomplishments or disparaging an opponent's character. Money in politics may at times seem repugnant to some, but so too does much of what the First Amendment vigorously protects. If the First Amendment protects flag burning, funeral protests, and Nazi parades—despite the profound offense such spectacles cause—it surely protects political campaign speech despite popular opposition. See *Texas v. Johnson*, 491 U. S. 397 (1989); *Snyder v. Phelps*, 562 U. S. ___ (2011); *National Socialist Party of America v. Skokie*, 432 U. S. 43 (1977) (*per curiam*). Indeed, as we have emphasized, the First Amendment "has its fullest and most urgent application precisely to the conduct of campaigns for political office." *Monitor Patriot Co. v. Roy*, 401 U. S. 265, 272 (1971).

In a series of cases over the past 40 years, we have spelled out how to draw the constitutional line between the permissible goal of avoiding corruption in the political process and the impermissible desire simply to limit political speech. We have said that government regulation may not target the general gratitude a candidate may feel toward those who support him or his allies, or the political access such support may afford. "Ingratiation and access . . . are not corruption." *Citizens United v. Federal Election Comm'n*, 558 U. S. 310, 360 (2010). They embody a central feature of democracy—that constituents support candidates who share their beliefs and interests, and candidates who are elected can be expected to be responsive to those concerns.

Any regulation must instead target what we have called "*quid pro quo*" corruption or its appearance. See *id.,* at 359. That Latin phrase captures the notion of a direct exchange of an official act for money. See *McCormick v. United States*, 500 U. S. 257, 266 (1991). "The hallmark of corruption is the financial *quid pro quo*: dollars for political favors." *Federal Election Comm'n v. National Conservative Political Action Comm.*, 470 U. S. 480, 497 (1985). Campaign finance restrictions that pursue other objectives, we have explained, impermissibly inject the Government "into the debate over who should govern." *Bennett, supra,* at ___ (slip op., at 25). And those who govern should be the *last* people to help decide who *should* govern.

The statute at issue in this case imposes two types of limits on campaign contributions. The first, called base limits, restricts how much money a donor may contribute to a particular candidate or committee. 2 U. S. C. §441a(a)(1). The second, called aggregate limits, restricts how much money a donor may contribute in total to all candidates or committees. §441a(a)(3).

This case does not involve any challenge to the base limits, which we have previously upheld as serving the permissible objective of combating corruption. The Government contends that the aggregate limits also serve that objective, by preventing circumvention of the base limits. We conclude, however, that the aggregate limits do little, if anything, to address that concern, while seriously restricting participation in the democratic process. The aggregate limits are therefore invalid under the First Amendment.

[Sections I and II, containing background on the case, have been omitted.]

III

The First Amendment "is designed and intended to remove governmental restraints from the arena of public discussion, putting the decision as to what views shall be voiced largely into the hands of each of us, . . . in the belief that no other approach would comport with the premise of individual dignity and choice upon which our political system rests." *Cohen v. California*, 403 U. S. 15, 24 (1971). As relevant here, the First Amendment safeguards an individual's right to participate in the public debate through political expression and political association. See *Buckley*, 424 U. S., at 15. When an individual contributes money to a candidate, he exercises both of those rights: The contribution "serves as a general expression of support for the candidate and his views" and "serves to affiliate a person with a candidate." *Id.*, at 21–22.

Those First Amendment rights are important regardless whether the individual is, on the one hand, a "lone pamphleteer[ ] or street corner orator[ ] in the Tom Paine mold," or is, on the other, someone who spends "substantial amounts of money in order to communicate [his] political ideas through sophisticated" means. *National Conservative Political Action Comm.*, 470 U. S., at 493. Either way, he is participating in an electoral debate that we have recognized is "integral to the operation of the system of government established by our Constitution." *Buckley*, *supra*, at 14.

Buckley acknowledged that aggregate limits at least diminish an individual's right of political association. As the Court explained, the "overall $25,000 ceiling does impose an ultimate restriction upon the number of candidates and committees with which an individual may associate himself by means of financial support." 424 U. S., at 38. But the Court characterized that restriction as a "quite modest restraint upon protected political activity." *Ibid.* We cannot agree with that characterization. An aggregate limit on *how many* candidates and committees an individual may support through contributions is not a "modest restraint" at all. The Government may no more restrict how many candidates or causes a donor may support than it may tell a newspaper how many candidates it may endorse.

To put it in the simplest terms, the aggregate limits prohibit an individual from fully contributing to the primary and general election campaigns of ten or more candidates, even if all contributions fall within the base limits Congress views as adequate to protect against corruption. The individual may give up to $5,200 each to nine candidates, but the aggregate limits constitute an outright ban on further contributions to any other candidate (beyond the additional $1,800 that may be spent before reaching the $48,600 aggregate limit). At that point, the limits deny the individual all ability to exercise his expressive and associational rights by contributing to someone who will advocate for his policy preferences. A donor must limit the number of candidates he supports, and may have to choose which of several policy concerns he will advance—clear First Amendment harms that the dissent never acknowledges.

It is no answer to say that the individual can simply contribute less money to more people. To require one person to contribute at lower levels than others because he wants to support more candidates or causes is to impose a special burden on broader participation in the democratic process. And as we have recently admonished, the Government may not penalize an individual for "robustly exercis[ing]" his First Amendment rights. *Davis* v. *Federal Election Comm'n*, 554 U. S. 724, 739 (2008).

The First Amendment burden is especially great for individuals who do not have ready access to alternative avenues for supporting their preferred politicians and policies. In the context of base contribution limits, *Buckley* observed that a supporter could vindicate his associational interests by personally volunteering his time and energy on behalf of a candidate. See 424 U. S., at 22, 28. Such personal volunteering is not a realistic alternative for those who wish to support a wide variety of candidates or causes. Other effective methods of supporting preferred candidates or causes without contributing money are reserved for a select few, such as entertainers capable of raising hundreds of thousands of dollars in a single evening. Cf. *Davis*, *supra*, at 742 . . .

IV

A

With the significant First Amendment costs for individual citizens in mind, we turn to the governmental interests asserted in this case. This Court has identified only one legitimate governmental interest for restricting campaign finances: preventing corruption or the appearance of corruption. See *Davis, supra,* at 741; *National Conservative Political Action Comm.,* 470 U. S., at 496–497. We have consistently rejected attempts to suppress campaign speech based on other legislative objectives. No matter how desirable it may seem, it is not an acceptable governmental objective to "level the playing field," or to "level electoral opportunities," or to "equaliz[e] the financial resources of candidates." *Bennett,* 564 U. S., at ___ (slip op., at 22–23); *Davis, supra,* at 741–742; *Buckley, supra,* at 56. The First Amendment prohibits such legislative attempts to "fine-tun[e]" the electoral process, no matter how well intentioned. *Bennett, supra,* at ___ (slip op., at 21).

As we framed the relevant principle in *Buckley,* "the concept that government may restrict the speech of some elements of our society in order to enhance the relative voice of others is wholly foreign to the First Amendment." 424 U. S., at 48–49. . . .

Moreover, while preventing corruption or its appearance is a legitimate objective, Congress may target only a specific type of corruption—"*quid pro quo*" corruption. As *Buckley* explained, Congress may permissibly seek to rein in "large contributions [that] are given to secure a political *quid pro quo* from current and potential office holders." 424 U. S., at 26. In addition to "actual *quid pro quo* arrangements," Congress may permissibly limit "the appearance of corruption stemming from public awareness of the opportunities for abuse inherent in a regime of large individual financial contributions" to particular candidates. *Id.,* at 27; see also *Citizens United,* 558 U. S., at 359 ("When *Buckley* identified a sufficiently important governmental interest in preventing corruption or the appearance of corruption, that interest was limited to *quid pro quo* corruption").

Spending large sums of money in connection with elections, but not in connection with an effort to control the exercise of an officeholder's official duties, does not give rise to such *quid pro quo* corruption. Nor does the possibility that an individual who spends large sums may garner "influence over or access to" elected officials or political parties . . . .And because the Government's interest in preventing the appearance of corruption is equally confined to the appearance of *quid pro quo* corruption, the Government may not seek to limit the appearance of mere influence or access. See *Citizens United,* 558 U. S., at 360.

The dissent advocates a broader conception of corruption, and would apply the label to any individual contributions above limits deemed necessary to protect "collective speech." Thus, under the dissent's view, it is perfectly fine to contribute $5,200 to nine candidates but somehow corrupt to give the same amount to a tenth. . . .

The line between *quid pro quo* corruption and general influence may seem vague at times, but the distinction must be respected in order to safeguard basic First Amendment rights. In addition, "[i]n drawing that line, the First Amendment requires us to err on the side of protecting political speech rather than suppressing it." *Federal Election Comm'n* v. *Wisconsin Right to Life,* 551 U. S. 449, 457 (2007) (opinion of ROBERTS, C. J.).

The dissent laments that our opinion leaves only remnants of FECA and BCRA that are inadequate to combat corruption. See *post,* at 2. Such rhetoric ignores the fact that we leave the base limits undisturbed. Those base limits remain the primary means of regulating campaign contributions—the obvious explanation for why the aggregate limits received a scant few sentences of attention in *Buckley.*

B

1

"When the Government restricts speech, the Government bears the burden of proving the constitutionality of its actions." *United States* v. *Playboy Entertainment Group, Inc.*, 529 U. S., at 816. Here, the Government seeks to carry that burden by arguing that the aggregate limits further the permissible objective of preventing *quid pro quo* corruption.

The difficulty is that once the aggregate limits kick in, they ban all contributions of *any* amount. But Congress's selection of a $5,200 base limit indicates its belief that contributions of that amount or less do not create a cognizable risk of corruption. If there is no corruption concern in giving nine candidates up to $5,200 each, it is difficult to understand how a tenth candidate can be regarded as corruptible if given $1,801, and all others corruptible if given a dime. And if there is no risk that additional candidates will be corrupted by donations of up to $5,200, then the Government must defend the aggregate limits by demonstrating that they prevent circumvention of the base limits.

The problem is that they do not serve that function in any meaningful way. In light of the various statutes and regulations currently in effect, *Buckley*'s fear that an individual might "contribute massive amounts of money to a particular candidate through the use of unearmarked contributions" to entities likely to support the candidate, 424 U. S., at 38, is far too speculative. And— importantly—we "have never accepted mere conjecture as adequate to carry a First Amendment burden." *Nixon* v. *Shrink Missouri Government PAC*, 528 U. S. 377, 392 (2000).

[A discussion of possible ways to bypass base limits has been omitted.]

* * *

For the past 40 years, our campaign finance jurisprudence has focused on the need to preserve authority for the Government to combat corruption, without at the same time compromising the political responsiveness at the heart of the democratic process, or allowing the Government to favor some participants in that process over others. As Edmund Burke explained in his famous speech to the electors of Bristol, a representative owes constituents the exercise of his "mature judgment," but judgment informed by "the strictest union, the closest correspondence, and the most unreserved communication with his constituents." The Speeches of the Right Hon. Edmund Burke 129–130 (J. Burke ed. 1867). Constituents have the right to support candidates who share their views and concerns. Representatives are not to follow constituent orders, but can be expected to be cognizant of and responsive to those concerns. Such responsiveness is key to the very concept of self-governance through elected officials.

The Government has a strong interest, no less critical to our democratic system, in combatting corruption and its appearance. We have, however, held that this interest must be limited to a specific kind of corruption—*quid pro quo* corruption—in order to ensure that the Government's efforts do not have the effect of restricting the First Amendment right of citizens to choose who shall govern them. For the reasons set forth, we conclude that the aggregate limits on contributions do not further the only governmental interest this Court accepted as legitimate in *Buckley*. They instead intrude without justification on a citizen's ability to exercise "the most fundamental First Amendment activities." *Buckley*, 424 U. S., at 14.

The judgment of the District Court is reversed, and the case is remanded for further proceedings.

It is so ordered.

[The concurring judgment of Justice Thomas has been omitted.]

JUSTICE BREYER, with whom JUSTICE GINSBURG, JUSTICE SOTOMAYOR, and JUSTICE KAGAN join, dissenting.

Nearly 40 years ago in *Buckley* v. *Valeo*, 424 U. S. 1 (1976) (*per curiam*), this Court considered the constitutionality of laws that imposed limits upon the overall amount a single person can contribute to all federal candidates, political parties, and committees taken together. The Court held that those limits did not violate the Constitution. *Id.*, at 38; accord, *McConnell* v. *Federal Election Comm'n*, 540 U. S. 93, 138, n. 40, 152–153, n. 48 (2003) (citing with approval *Buckley's* aggregate limits holding).

The *Buckley* Court focused upon the same problem that concerns the Court today, and it wrote:

"The overall $25,000 ceiling does impose an ultimate restriction upon the number of candidates and committees with which an individual may associate himself by means of financial support. But this quite modest restraint upon protected political activity serves to prevent evasion of the $1,000 contribution limitation by a person who might otherwise contribute massive amounts of money to a particular candidate through the use of unearmarked contributions to political committees likely to contribute to that candidate, or huge contributions to the candidate's political party. The limited, additional restriction on associational freedom imposed by the overall ceiling is thus no more than a corollary of the basic individual contribution limitation that we have found to be constitutionally valid." 424 U. S., at 38.

Today a majority of the Court overrules this holding. It is wrong to do so. Its conclusion rests upon its own, not a record-based, view of the facts. Its legal analysis is faulty: It misconstrues the nature of the competing constitutional interests at stake. It understates the importance of protecting the political integrity of our governmental institutions. It creates a loophole that will allow a single individual to contribute millions of dollars to a political party or to a candidate's campaign. Taken together with *Citizens United* v. *Federal Election Comm'n*, 558 U. S. 310 (2010), today's decision eviscerates our Nation's campaign finance laws, leaving a remnant incapable of dealing with the grave problems of democratic legitimacy that those laws were intended to resolve.

I

The plurality concludes that the aggregate contribution limits "'unnecessar[ily] abridg[e]'" First Amendment rights. Ante, at 8, 30 (quoting *Buckley, supra*, at 25). It notes that some individuals will wish to "spen[d] 'substantial amounts of money in order to communicate [their] political ideas through sophisticated' means." *Ante*, at 14– 15 (quoting *Federal Election Comm'n v. National Conservative Political Action Comm.*, 470 U. S. 480, 493 (1985) (NCPAC)). Aggregate contribution ceilings limit an individual's ability to engage in such "broader participation in the democratic process," while insufficiently advancing any legitimate governmental objective. *Ante*, at 16, 21–29. Hence, the plurality finds, they violate the Constitution.

The plurality's conclusion rests upon three separate but related claims. Each is fatally flawed. First, the plurality says that given the base limits on contributions to candidates and political committees, aggregate limits do not further any independent governmental objective worthy of protection. And that is because, given the base limits, "[s]pending large sums of money in connection with elections" does not "give rise to . . . corruption." *Ante*, at 19. In making this argument, the plurality relies heavily upon a narrow definition of "corruption" that excludes efforts to obtain "'influence over or access to' elected officials or political parties." Ibid. (quoting *Citizens United, supra*, at 359); accord, ante, at 18–20, 22–29.

Second, the plurality assesses the instrumental objective of the aggregate limits, namely, safeguarding the base limits. It finds that they "do not serve that function in any meaningful way." *Ante*, at 22. That is because, even without the aggregate limits, the possibilities for circumventing the base limits are "implausible" and "divorced from reality." *Ante*, at 23, 24, 28.

Third, the plurality says the aggregate limits are not a "'reasonable'" policy tool. Rather, they are "poorly tailored to the Government's interest in preventing circumvention of the base limits." *Ante*, at 30 (quoting *Board of Trustees of State Univ. of N. Y. v. Fox*, 492 U. S. 469, 480 (1989)). The plurality imagines several alternative regulations that it says might just as effectively thwart circumvention. Accordingly, it finds, the aggregate caps are out of "'pro portion to the [anticorruption] interest served.'" *Ante*, at 30 (quoting Fox, supra, at 480).

II

The plurality's first claim—that large aggregate contributions do not "give rise" to "corruption"—is plausible only because the plurality defines "corruption" too narrowly. The plurality describes the constitutionally permissible objective of campaign finance regulation as follows: "Congress may target only a specific type of corruption—'quid pro quo' corruption." *Ante*, at 19. It then defines quid pro quo corruption to mean no more than "a direct exchange of an official act for money"—an act akin to bribery. *Ante*, at 2–3. It adds specifically that corruption does not include efforts to "garner 'influence over or access to' elected officials or political parties." *Ante*, at 19 (quoting *Citizens United, supra*, at 359). Moreover, the Government's efforts to prevent the "appearance of corruption" are "equally confined to the appearance of quid pro quo corruption," as narrowly defined. *Ante*, at 19. In the plurality's view, a federal statute could not prevent an individual from writing a million dollar check to a political party (by donating to its various committees), because the rationale for any limit would "dangerously broade[n] the circumscribed definition of quid pro quo corruption articulated in our prior cases." Ante, at 37.

This critically important definition of "corruption" is inconsistent with the Court's prior case law (with the possible exception of *Citizens United*, as I will explain below). It is virtually impossible to reconcile with this Court's decision in *McConnell*, upholding the Bipartisan Campaign Reform Act of 2002 (BCRA). And it misunderstands the constitutional importance of the interests at stake. In fact, constitutional interests—indeed, First Amendment interests—lie on both sides of the legal equation.

A

In reality, as the history of campaign finance reform shows and as our earlier cases on the subject have recognized, the anticorruption interest that drives Congress to regulate campaign contributions is a far broader, more important interest than the plurality acknowledges. It is an interest in maintaining the integrity of our public governmental institutions. And it is an interest rooted in the Constitution and in the First Amendment itself.

Consider at least one reason why the First Amendment protects political speech. Speech does not exist in a vacuum. Rather, political communication seeks to secure government action. A politically oriented "marketplace of ideas" seeks to form a public opinion that can and will influence elected representatives.

This is not a new idea. . . .

[The remainder of the dissent has been omitted.]

SOURCE: U.S. Supreme Court. *McCutcheon v. FEC.* 572 U.S.__(2014). www.supremecourt.gov/opinions/13pdf/12-536_e1pf.pdf.

OTHER HISTORIC DOCUMENTS OF INTEREST

FROM PREVIOUS *HISTORIC DOCUMENTS*

- Supreme Court on Campaign Contributions, *2010,* p. 23
- Supreme Court on Regulation of Issue Ads, *2007,* p. 296
- Supreme Court on Federal Election Campaign Financing, *1976,* p. 71

U.S., Palestinian, and Israeli Leaders Remark on Peace Process

APRIL 6, 9, AND 17, AND AUGUST 1, 2014

In 2014, the United States again worked to bring together Israel and Palestine to secure a peace agreement that would establish a ceasefire ultimately leading to greater stability and cooperation in the region. As expected, the parties remained too far apart to reach any meaningful agreement. Perhaps the greatest breakthrough in this round of talks came on August 1 when Israel and Palestine agreed to a three-day humanitarian ceasefire in Gaza. By the end of the year, however, fighting had resumed, and the prospects of future peace negotiations were called into question after the collapse of the Israeli government.

U.S. INVOLVEMENT IN THE PEACE PROCESS

The Israeli-Palestinian peace process has animated regional politics for decades. Reconciliation between the state of Israel and the occupied Palestinian territories has eluded successive teams of negotiators since the 1967 Six-Day War, which altered the borders of Israel after its founding in 1948. The United States, Israel's most powerful ally, has promoted several attempts to resolve the conflict. These include the Camp David talks in 1978 and 2000, the 1993 Oslo Accords that secured Israel's withdrawal from the West Bank and Gaza territories in exchange for Palestinian recognition, and the 2003 Road Map initiative to establish a Palestinian state by 2005.

The United States' influence with Israel is supported by its role as the latter's most important military partner: $3.1 billion in U.S. military aid to Israel was allocated for FY 2014. Bilateral relations have been strained during the administration of President Barack Obama, however. President Obama favors a more liberal and internationalist stance than his predecessor, George W. Bush. Obama has been comparatively forceful in publicly calling for Israeli concessions to support continuation of the peace process, including a halt to settlement construction, a long-held Palestinian demand. Israeli premier Benyamin Netanyahu rejected Obama's proposal that Israel withdraw to its pre-1967 borders in November 2011. During negotiations, Netanyahu continued to acknowledge nationalist sentiment within Israel, which is traditionally governed by multi-party coalitions.

Relations soured markedly in 2014 as U.S. officials insulted members of the Israeli government, charging that the premier's sole redeeming quality was his wariness toward new wars. Leaked diplomatic cables also revealed U.S. skepticism regarding a preventative Israeli strike on sites hosting Iran's nuclear program, with both governments viewing their counterparts as less assertive than their predecessors. Given rhetorical distancing between the two allies, Israel could increasingly turn to pragmatic Gulf States that place greater emphasis on mutual strategic concerns, including the spread of local extremism and the influence of Russian, Iranian, and Syrian clients in the region.

NEGOTIATIONS FOR A COMPREHENSIVE PEACE PLAN

Given recent tensions, expectations for an agreement at the outset of talks in July 2013 were subdued. Both parties aimed to garner international favor with the announcement of concessions beforehand, including Israel's release of 104 Palestinian prisoners. Palestinian representatives also offered to delay or suspend efforts to secure international recognition from various countries and international organizations. Israeli officials later disclosed that they were considering ceding parts of the Arab-majority "Arab Triangle" in the north of the country in exchange for land in the West Bank, in line with previous international proposals for land and population swaps based on majority demographics in given areas.

In 2014, Israel and Palestine maintained divergent stances on most issues, including the right of return for descendants of Palestinians evicted from their homes; the ongoing construction of settlements for Israelis in Palestinian territories; and the final status of Jerusalem, a site sacred to all Abrahamic religions. Israeli construction of settlements in contested East Jerusalem is a particular point of contention, because a Jewish majority would undermine Palestinian claims to that section of the city. These concerns directed discussions in the four more recent peace talks. The nine-month series of negotiations through April 2014 aimed to settle all questions, with Israelis preferring to address the issues simultaneously, while the Palestinians prioritized resolution of security and border concerns. Prior to the conclusion of talks, Israel's foreign minister noted earlier land concessions, as well as peace deals with Egypt and Jordan, as evidence of sincere interest in regional peace. But Netanyahu indicated on April 6 that Palestine's decision to "unilaterally request to accede to 14 international treaties" showed unwillingness on their part to negotiate within the bounds set by the United States and agreed to by all involved in the peace talks.

All parties were urged to maintain the confidentiality of the talks by U.S. secretary of state John Kerry and his chief deputy in the talks, Martin Indyk, the former U.S. ambassador to Israel. Public disclosures had been seen as complicating factors in the collapse of past negotiations. Some positions were disclosed, however. Israel insisted on recognition of its right to exist as "the national state of the Jewish people," contrary to the doctrine of Hamas, the militant wing of the Palestinian leadership. Israel's paramount concern is the security of its borders and an end to rocket attacks on Israeli cities. The chair of the Palestinian Liberation Organization (PLO), Mahmood Abbas, publicly maintained that Palestine aimed for the complete withdrawal of Israeli security forces from its claimed territories.

Division between the PLO—led by the comparatively mainstream Fatah—and the more radical Hamas movement was previously seen as an obstacle to a diplomatic breakthrough given the difficulty of enforcing a comprehensive settlement. However, more recent cooperation between the parties is also a concern because Hamas rejects the legitimacy of the Israeli state as acknowledged by the PLO in the 1993 Oslo Accords. Hamas is also listed internationally as a terrorist organization. In 2007, the two factions briefly fought for control of the Gaza Strip. Hamas and Fatah announced the formation of a unity government in April 2014. The announcement prompted Israel to suspend the latest round of peace talks with Fatah. Israeli public opinion requires acknowledgment of a State of Israel by all concerned parties as a precondition for any diplomatic breakthrough.

The United States, for its part, expressed disappointment with the development but acknowledged Israel's wariness toward negotiating with a group committed to its disintegration. Secretary Kerry characterized actions by both parties as "unhelpful" in furthering the scuppered negotiations, citing earlier decisions by Israel to extend settlement construction and limit prisoner releases during the talks.

After the collapse of U.S.-sponsored peace talks, an offer to host negotiations came from a surprising source. During Pope Francis's visit to the region in May 2014, the pontiff invited the Palestinian president, Mahmood Abbas, and the outgoing Israeli president, Shimon Peres, to pray for peace at the Vatican, marking the first concrete papal engagement in the conflict. Peres was presumably invited instead of the prime minister because Netanyahu is viewed as less optimistic regarding the efficacy of additional talks.

Notwithstanding external diplomatic efforts, tensions rose markedly from mid-2014. The kidnapping and murder of three Israeli teenagers by a Hamas operative in the West Bank in June renewed intermittent war between the parties. The Israeli military launched seven weeks of attacks under Operation Protective Edge on July 8, which were responded to with rocket attacks by militants. The conflict resulted in more than 2,000 casualties, the majority of whom were Palestinian, when a permanent ceasefire secured with Egyptian mediation was announced on August 26.

Prospects for renewed negotiations remain limited. Israel insists on the suspension of rocket attacks supported by Hamas, as well as the destruction of cross-territory tunnels used to provide staples as well as arms for the militant group. The tunnels were heavily targeted during the summer of 2014, with Israel claiming that thirty-two of an unknown total had been demolished. Hamas, for its part, demands an end to the blockade of Gaza, citing supply shortages as a justification for the existence of the tunnels, which provide access to daily necessities for the general population as well as weapons for fighters. In a possible bid to limit the moral appeal against the blockade, the United States allocated $47 million in aid to support Palestinian residents in advance of the August ceasefire.

Hamas has also asked for the release of additional prisoners who are viewed by the Israeli government as security risks. The most fundamental obstacle to peace, however, remains Israel's requirement that Hamas recognize it as a legitimate and Jewish state. The outgoing Israeli government sought to have the country's Jewish identity codified in its Basic Law to allow this requirement to be met by default in any formal treaty between the two governing authorities. Although it provided a potential opportunity for both parties to retain credibility with their domestic audiences, the legislation was not expected to be fast-tracked after the election of a new government in snap elections scheduled for March 2015.

CONSEQUENCES AND OUTLOOK

The right-leaning government led by the Likud Party under Netanyahu collapsed in December 2014 after the prime minster failed to gain guaranteed support for his agenda from his centrist partners, Hatnua, led by Tzipi Livni, and Yesh Atid, led by Yair Lapid. Netanyahu opted to call early elections rather than attempt to constitute a new government within the existing legislature. Hatnua and Yesh Atid, meanwhile, declined to support initiatives such as the Basic Law amendment outlining the country's Jewish identity, which represented a possible setback for liberal, secular groups. The governing partners also largely failed to gain concessions on minority issues, settlement construction, or tax policy. A strengthened conservative government would reduce the likelihood of major compromises with Palestinian interests. In a departure from tradition, the U.S. government was expected to eschew implicit endorsements of any parties in the election, as the center-left options likely favored by the Obama administration could be undermined by its support, given its lack of credibility with the Israeli public.

Meanwhile, the elections scheduled to be held by the Palestinian unity government by the end of the year were postponed indefinitely, lengthening the odds that the next Israeli government would have a politically stable negotiating partner if talks resumed. Palestine was expected to continue its campaign for legitimacy through alternative means, including securing recognition from a growing list of countries and international bodies. In November 2014, Sweden became the 135th country to acknowledge a State of Palestine. Palestine also accepted the jurisdiction of the International Criminal Court (ICC) in January 2015, with the aim of reviewing alleged Israeli war crimes in Gaza during Operation Protective Edge in the preceding summer. This particular objective may be undermined by Israeli diligence in conducting its own investigations. As of January 2015, Israel had closed nine cases of reported misconduct and planned to investigate an additional ninety-seven cases.

The United States rejected recent overtures by Palestinian officials to the international community as unilateral measures that undermined the resumption of the peace process. Separately, the United States was expected to continue strategic cooperation with Israel on a range of issues, including regional intelligence, the Syrian conflict, and the Iranian nuclear program.

—Anastazia Clouting

Following is an April 6, 2014, statement by Israeli prime minister Benjamin Netanyahu on the peace talks with Palestine; statements by U.S. secretary of state John Kerry and Israeli foreign minister Avigdor Lieberman on April 9, 2014, on the peace process; a statement from Palestine's minister of information on April 17, 2014, on Israeli occupation; and an August 1, 2014, statement by Secretary Kerry on a ceasefire in Gaza.

Israeli Prime Minister on Negotiations with Palestine

April 6, 2014

In recent months the State of Israel has conducted negotiations with the Palestinians in order to reach a peace agreement. Israelis expect peace, a genuine peace, in which our vital national interests are assured, with security first and foremost. During these talks we carried out difficult steps and showed a willingness to continue implementing moves that were not easy, in the coming months as well, in order to create a framework that would allow for putting an end to the conflict between us. Just as we were about to enter into that framework for the continuation of the negotiations, Abu Mazen hastened to declare that he is not prepared even to discuss recognizing Israel as the national state of the Jewish People, which we have made clear to both the President of the United States and to other world leaders as well.

To my regret as we reached the moment before agreeing on the continuation of the talks, the Palestinian leadership hastened to unilaterally request to accede to 14 international treaties. Thus the Palestinians substantially violated the understandings that were reached with American involvement. The Palestinians' threats to appeal to the UN will not affect us. The Palestinians have much to lose by this unilateral move. They will achieve a state only by direct negotiations, not by empty statements and not by unilateral moves. These will only push a peace agreement farther away and unilateral steps on their part will be met with unilateral steps on our part. We are ready to continue the talks but not at any price.

SOURCE: Benjamin Netanyahu Official Website. "Prime Minister Netanyahu made the following remarks today at the start of the weekly Cabinet meeting 6.4.14." April 6, 2014. www.netanyahu.org.il/en/news/889-prime-minister-netanyahu-made-the-following-remarks-today-at-the-start-of-the-weekly-cabinet-meeting-6-4-14.

Secretary Kerry and Israeli Foreign Minister Speak on Peace Process

April 9, 2014

SECRETARY KERRY: Good afternoon, everybody. It's my great privilege to welcome Avigdor Lieberman, the foreign minister of Israel, here to the State Department and to Washington. We have gotten to see each other at a number of different places now. We most recently were in Rome together where we talked about the issues before both our countries and the region.

And today, I'm really happy to be able to welcome him here. Obviously, we are working hard to try to find a way forward. And both parties indicate they would like to find a way to go forward in the talks. We obviously want to see that happen. We think it's important for them and for the region. So we will, needless to say, talk about that.

But we also have many other issues to work on and cooperate on together. We will talk about Iran and the challenge of the Iranian nuclear program. The talks have been going on even this week, so we have a considerable amount to try to digest with respect to that process. And also the region, obviously, faces enormous challenges. Syria remains a humanitarian catastrophe, and it has a profound impact on Israel, on Jordan, on Lebanon, on the region as a whole. And we continue to face the challenge of removing the chemical weapons from Iran. I just literally hung up the phone a few minutes ago before I came out to meet the foreign minister. I was talking to Foreign Minister Lavrov and we were talking about the need for movement in Syria and the ability to complete the task.

So I'm very happy that the foreign minister is here today. This is an important time. The issues between us are of concern to both of us, are of enormous importance. And I want to affirm this: Our relationship with Israel, as everybody knows, is an historic and deep one. We remain totally committed to the security of Israel. We have a friendship that is, I believe, a bond that's unbreakable, and I'm really happy to have the foreign minister here at this important time. Thank you.

FOREIGN MINISTER LIEBERMAN: Thank you. First of all, thank you for the very warm welcome, and as you mentioned, we have a lot of items on our bilateral agenda. But first of all, I would like to express my appreciation for your efforts, for your commitment to our state, your efforts to resolve our long dispute with the Palestinians. We know and everybody in Israel knows that you are really a very close friend, reliable friend, and now we're in the midst of a very crucial process.

And I think that you and us have the same desire to achieve comprehensive solution, to achieve final status agreement. We're ready to sacrifice a lot for this goal. We proved our desire to achieve real peace with our neighbors, not only as a lip service, but in all our agreements that we signed with Egypt, with Jordan. We gave up territories three and a half times more than our territory today—Sinai, half of Judea Samaria, Gaza Strip. And I think that we really—we are looking for the same positive approach from the other side, and we think that any unilateral steps, they only can undermine all our efforts.

Of course, the biggest challenge for us, for all our region, is the Iranian issue, and I hope that we will discuss, of course, the Iranian issue. And of course we are (inaudible) now to the huge concern with Syria and what happens within Syria. The spillover of the Syrian conflict is all around us. And we are monitoring and following the situation in Syria, of course, and it's a new—a very serious challenge for our country, and again, thank you for your efforts and for your commitment. . . .

SOURCE: U.S. Department of State. "Remarks with Israel Foreign Minister Avigdor Lieberman Before Their Meeting." April 9, 2014. www.state.gov/secretary/remarks/2014/04/224611.htm.

Palestinian Minister of Information on Israeli Occupation

April 17, 2014

Deputy Minister of Information Dr. Mahmoud Khalefa said that the arrogance-driven language inhibiting the Israeli occupation continues to vessel extremism Israeli right wing leaders that mouth arrogance instead of rational constructive statements. Dr. Khalefa said that the statements of the Israeli Foreign Minister alleging that the Israeli occupation isn't dealing with "a Palestinian leadership that condemns aggression, and is dealing with a people, many of whom don't resent terror," a statement that Dr. Khalefa considered as erroneous and full of fact distortions in an attempt to blame others for Israel's own faults.

In a press statement by Dr. Khalefa today 17 April 2014, he pointed out that Liberman and Netanyahu's statements and their occupation army generals establish once again that occupation is the root problem and mother of evils; occupation resulted in barbaric massacres that left behind thousands of martyrs, wounded and prisoners for no reason other than their steadfastness in their own land and rejection to the practices of the Israeli occupation.

Dr. Khalef added that Liberman is fully aware that he is a foreign minister for a state that occupies others' territory since two centuries, making it the longest occupation in contemporary history; an evil that can only end by ending that occupation. He further added that throughout the many Israeli waves of Israeli terror that continued since the last century, we never heard from the Israeli occupation, foreign Minister and his predecessors anything but more of their incitement, unfounded accusations against the victims and exonerating murderer occupation officers of crimes committed upon direct orders of the Israeli occupation government and army generals.

Dr. Khalefa concluded by noting that Liberman's statements and call for recognizing the Jewish character of Israel are nothing but hallucination and evading requisites for the peace process, in addition for using such statements to cover up the crime of settlement and land theft; adding that We remind of what President Abu Mazen repeated in several meetings with Israeli and European leaders that the UN is the address for states to change their names and characters.

The developments on the ground clearly indicate that Israel is evading its commitments for the peace process and that the Israeli unilateral actions and sanctions will only make the Palestinian side seek accession for more of the UN organizations.

SOURCE: Ministry of Information. State of Palestine. "Khalefa: Lieberman's Profanity stinking blemish." April 17, 2014. www.minfo.ps/English/index.php?pagess=main&id=2149&butt=5.

Secretary Kerry Remarks on the Ceasefire in Gaza

August 1, 2014

Good morning. I'm sorry to get you all up at this hour. I'm not going to take any questions, but I think a few of the staff will be around to answer a few questions for you, and I'll just make a brief statement.

This morning, Israel and the Palestinian factions have agreed that they are now prepared to implement a 72-hour unconditional humanitarian cease-fire. So starting later this morning at 8:00 August 1st, the parties are expected to cease all offensive military activities, and neither side will advance beyond its current locations. They will stay where they are in place. Israel will be able to continue its defensive operations for those tunnels that are behind its lines, and the Palestinians will be able to receive food, medicine, and additional humanitarian assistance, as well as to be able to tend to their wounded, bury their dead, be able to in safe areas travel to their homes, and take advantage of the absence—hopefully, hopefully—of violence for these 72 hours.

Then, as soon as the cease-fire is underway tomorrow morning—I talked to the Egyptian foreign minister tonight—Egypt will issue invitations to the parties to come to Cairo immediately in order to engage in serious and focused negotiations with Egypt to address the underlying causes of this conflict. And we hope and we expect both sides to raise all the topics of concern. The parties, obviously, need to find a way to address Israel's security concerns and to ensure that the people of Gaza can live in safety and in dignity. And for our part, the United States will be sending a small delegation to Cairo to assist and take part in these negotiations.

As I said, this will last for 72 hours—three days—precious time. It is a lull of opportunity, a moment for the sides and the different factions to be able to come together with the state of Israel in an effort to try to address ways to find a sustainable cease-fire and then, obviously, ultimately, over a longer period of time, address the underlying issues. Let me also add that tomorrow morning the United States will also join in the effort to provide humanitarian assistance. President Obama has made available some $47 million to help ensure that some of the relief is able to come in, and many of our international partners have also made commitments over the course of the last weeks.

Now, obviously, while we are grateful that the violence and the bloodshed has the opportunity to stop for more than 24 hours, it is up to the parties—all of them—to take advantage of this moment. There are no guarantees. This is a difficult, complicated issue, years and years in the building, and I think everyone knows it has not been easy to get to this point. And everyone knows that it will not be easy even to get beyond this point, but it is imperative that people make the best effort to try to find common ground and do so.

A lot of folks have been working hard at this effort. I want to thank Prime Minister Netanyahu, who I know wants to see the people of Israel live in security, free from rockets, free from attacks from tunnels. And I know he has worked hard at this. We've had many phone calls, sometimes in the middle of the night, and I'm pleased that he thought this moment was an appropriate one to embrace this effort, this cease-fire. I want to thank UN Secretary-General Ban Ki-moon and Special Coordinator Serry for their continuous efforts to try to help create a framework as well as the call for a cease-fire, and helping to galvanize the international community. And I'm grateful also to President al-Sisi and to Foreign Minister Sameh Shoukry, who has been consistently on the phone working this, and Egypt will host these talks. And this effort is built on the original Egyptian initiative that began the talk of a cease-fire. So Palestinian President Abbas has been consistently working behind the scenes, sending his emissaries to various places to work effectively, and I appreciate his leadership in this effort.

Now, I want to re-emphasize: This is not a time for congratulations and joy, or anything except a serious determination, a focus by everybody to try to figure out the road ahead. This is a respite. It's a moment of opportunity, not an end; it's not a solution. It's the opportunity to find the solution. And President Obama hopes that all the parties will work diligently to do so. From the moment the President asked me to travel some 12 days or so ago, the President has been consistently on the phone, tracking this, talking with the prime minister and others in an effort to help to move us to this place.

But we have to understand: Both parties have—all the people involved in this have strong demands and strong visions about what the future should look like. Israel has to be able to live in peace and security, without terror attacks, without rockets, without tunnels, without sirens going off in the day. And Palestinians need to be able to live with the opportunity to educate their children and move freely and share in the rest of the world, and to lead a life that is different from the one they have long suffered. So we hope that this moment of opportunity will be grabbed by the parties, but no one can force them to do that, obviously.

So we come at it with sober reflection about the lives lost and the violence suffered; the soldiers killed, the individuals killed; the three kids who were kidnapped and murdered in the beginning of this, and then a retribution killing. There's been too much of it for most people's judgment here, and our hope is that reason could possibly prevail to find the road forward. And with that, I'll leave you to the folks who might give you a little more sort of background and everything else. Thank you all very much.

SOURCE: U.S. Department of State. "Remarks on Humanitarian Cease-fire Announcement in Gaza." August 1, 2014. www.state.gov/secretary/remarks/2014/08/230072.htm.

OTHER HISTORIC DOCUMENTS OF INTEREST

FROM THIS VOLUME

FROM PREVIOUS *HISTORIC DOCUMENTS*

President Obama Signs
Wage Gap Executive Order

APRIL 8, 2014

In the spring of 2014, one of the major issues facing U.S. policymakers was compensation discrimination, that is, the reported disparity between what male and female employees were paid for doing similar jobs. According to the U.S. Census Bureau, in 2012 full-time working women earned an average of 77 cents to every dollar earned by men. Since 2009, Congress considered various iterations of the Paycheck Fairness Act, legislation intended to complement existing equal pay laws and provide additional protections for employees. The most recent draft of the bill, sponsored by Sen. Barbara Mikulski, D-Md., and Rep. Rosa DeLauro, D-Conn., was introduced in January 2013 but languished in committee until April 2014. Amid congressional inaction, President Barack Obama issued an Executive Order and signed a presidential memorandum to enable employees of federal contractors to disclose and discuss their compensation with colleagues, and to require employers to provide more data about their compensation structure. Acknowledging that his actions were just one part of the solution, the president also called on Congress to extend such provisions to the broader workforce by passing the Paycheck Fairness Act.

PRESIDENT OBAMA'S EQUAL PAY INITIATIVES

The Obama administration pursued several initiatives related to compensation equality in the years leading up to 2014. In fact, the first bill Obama signed into law after taking office was the Lilly Ledbetter Fair Pay Act of 2009. The bill was named for former Goodyear employee Lilly Ledbetter, who one day received an anonymous note from a colleague informing her that she was making a significant amount less than the men working in her same position. Ledbetter filed a discrimination case against the company, which she initially won, then lost on appeal. Over the course of eight years, her case progressed all the way to the U.S. Supreme Court. In May 2007, the Court ruled in favor of Goodyear, stating that employees cannot challenge ongoing pay discrimination if the employer's original discriminatory pay decision occurred more than 180 days earlier, even if the employee continues to receive paychecks that have been discriminatorily reduced. This outcome raised concerns that the Court's ruling could incentivize employers to hide discriminatory practices until after the 180-day period had passed and that it could allow discrimination to continue indefinitely. Ledbetter continued to advocate for changed policies after losing her case and championed her namesake equal pay legislation, supported by both Republicans and Democrats. The law gives employees more time to file pay discrimination suits against employers by resetting the 180-day limit on filing claims with each discriminatory paycheck.

In addition, Obama established the National Equal Pay Task Force in 2010 and charged it with improving enforcement of equal pay laws and promoting efficiency and efficacy through greater interagency collaboration. The group consists of representatives from the U.S. Equal Employment Opportunity Commission (EEOC), Departments of Justice and Labor, and the Office of Personnel Management, whose recommendations for resolving compensation issues have included improving data collection on the private workforce to better understand the existing pay gap and inform allocation of enforcement resources. Other initiatives included the Department of Labor's 2012 "Equal Pay App Challenge," through which software developers were invited to create apps that provide greater access to data to inform pay negotiations.

PAY DISCRIMINATION BILLS BEFORE CONGRESS

Obama continued to call on Congress to pass the Paycheck Fairness Act—an item included in both his 2013 and 2014 State of the Union addresses. As written, the act would require employers to prove that any differences between employees' pay was based on each individual's background and skills rather than their gender; enable employees to discuss their compensation with colleagues, without fear of retaliation; allow employees to sue for punitive damages in cases of alleged sexual discrimination and be a part of class action suits; and require the EEOC to collect compensation data in addition to information about employees' sex, race, and nationality to help enforce laws prohibiting pay discrimination. The act would also establish a grant program within the Department of Labor that would support training programs for women and girls on negotiation skills, as well as a Secretary of Labor National Award for Pay Equity in the Workplace to recognize an employer who has made substantial efforts to eliminate pay disparities.

The bill initially passed in the House of Representatives in 2009, when the Democratic Party was in the majority, but it failed to progress in the Senate, due in part to Senate Republicans' efforts to prevent the bill from getting a vote. Many Republicans argued that the law was unnecessary because the Equal Pay Act of 1963 and Title VII of the Civil Rights Act of 1964 already required that men and women in the same workplace receive equal pay for equal work and made it illegal to discriminate against someone based on their sex. Instead of passing a new law, they argued, enforcement of existing laws should be strengthened. "All of us support equal pay for equal work," said then-House majority leader Eric Cantor, R-Va. "Let's put the politics aside, and let's get to work to see how we can make sure if there are problems with the law being implemented that we can address that."

Others shared concerns that the bill could unreasonably burden employers and lead to an increase in frivolous lawsuits and said the focus should be on passing measures that could stimulate job growth and provide more opportunities and choices in the labor market. "We don't think America suffers from a lack of litigation," said Senate minority leader Mitch McConnell, R-Ky. "We have a jobless problem. We have a debt problem. We have a deficit problem. We got a lot of problems. Not enough lawsuits is not one of them."

Still others challenged the U.S. Census data used by Democrats and the president to support the need for the legislation, noting that the purported 33-cent-per-dollar gap in earnings became much smaller when comparing men and women in a single occupation, or once factors such as education, family status, and number of hours worked were taken into account. Some also challenged the Obama administration on its own compensation issues after the American Enterprise Institute released a study in January 2014 that found female White House employees make 88 cents for every dollar male employees do. White House press secretary Jay Carney dismissed the criticisms, saying that "men and women in equivalent roles here earn equivalent salaries" and that more of the lower-paying jobs were filled by women. "Some of the most senior positions in the White House are filled by women, including national security adviser, homeland security adviser, White House counsel, communications director, senior adviser, deputy chief of staff," Carney added.

In January 2013, Mikulski and DeLauro reintroduced the bill, which was referred to the Senate Committee on Health, Education, Labor, and Pensions and the House Committee on Education and the Workforce. Both bills stalled in committee, until Democrats began pushing for a vote in 2014 ahead of the midterm elections. Passing the Paycheck Fairness Act was part of their 2014 agenda, titled "A Fair Shot for Everyone," that also included raising the minimum wage and allowing students to refinance federal loans, among other measures. The push prompted Kirsten Kukowski, spokesperson for the Republican National Committee, to characterize the bill as "a desperate political ploy and Democrats are cynically betting that Americans aren't smart enough to know better."

Obama Signs Executive Order 13665

While the bill was delayed in Congress, Obama decided to take several steps of his own to try to address pay discrimination. On April 8, 2014, he issued Executive Order 13665, known as Non-Retaliation for Disclosure of Compensation Information. The order enabled employees of federal contractors to inquire about, disclose, and discuss their compensation with coworkers, and prevented employers from firing or otherwise punishing the employees who did so. "Pay secrecy fosters discrimination, and we should not tolerate it, not in Federal contracting or anywhere else," Obama said before signing the order. "America should be a level playing field, a fair race for everybody, a place where anybody who's willing to work hard has a chance to get ahead. And restoring that opportunity for every American—men and women—has to be a driving focus for our country."

The president claimed that by helping make information about pay differences more accessible, employees would be more inclined to take action and seek more equitable pay. He also argued that it would help make the federal contracting labor market more efficient; enhancing the availability of compensation information to participants in the labor pool would increase the likelihood that the most qualified and productive workers would be hired at the market efficient price. Importantly, the order did not apply to the broader workforce and was not meant to protect employees who had access to other employees' compensation information and shared that information with colleagues unless they were required to by some legal reason.

Ledbetter, who introduced the president before he gave his remarks, said that such protections would have made a difference in her experience. "I didn't know I was being paid unfairly and I had no way to find out. I was told in no uncertain terms that Goodyear, then and still a government contractor, fired employees who shared their salary information. It was against company policy."

On the morning of his wage gap signing, Obama also signed a presidential memorandum directing the Department of Labor to require federal contractors to provide data about their employee compensation to help identify pay discrimination. "This is not just an issue of fairness, it's also a family issue and an economic issue, because women make up about half of our workforce and they're increasingly the breadwinners for a whole lot of families out there," Obama said. He also noted that the next day, the Senate would have an opportunity to vote on the Paycheck Fairness Act and called on senators to pass it to extend the protections included in his Executive Order to the broader workforce.

REPUBLICANS VOTE NO

Despite the urging of the president and others, Senate Republicans again prevented the Paycheck Fairness Act from advancing, voting against the bill on April 9. Several Republicans cited the unwillingness of Senate majority leader Harry Reid, D-Nev., to allow votes on several Republican-sponsored amendments as their reason for voting against the legislation, although Reid argued that many of those amendments were unrelated to the underlying bill. Reid ultimately switched his vote to no to preserve the option to bring the bill up for another vote, which he did on September 15, when Republicans voted against it for a second time. By the conclusion of the 113th Congress, the bill had not been reconsidered.

—Linda Fecteau Grimm

Following is the text of President Barack Obama's April 8, 2014, executive order on Non-retaliation for Compensation Disclosure, as well as his remarks during the signing ceremony.

President Obama Signs Wage Gap Legislation

April 8, 2014

By the authority vested in me as President by the Constitution and the laws of the United States of America, including the Federal Property and Administrative Services Act, 40 U.S.C. 101 *et seq.*, and in order to take further steps to promote economy and efficiency in Federal Government procurement, it is hereby ordered as follows:

Section 1. Policy. This order is designed to promote economy and efficiency in Federal Government procurement. It is the policy of the executive branch to enforce vigorously the civil rights laws of the United States, including those laws that prohibit discriminatory practices with respect to compensation. Federal contractors that employ such practices are subject to enforcement action, increasing the risk of disruption, delay, and increased expense in Federal contracting. Compensation discrimination also can lead to labor disputes that are burdensome and costly.

When employees are prohibited from inquiring about, disclosing, or discussing their compensation with fellow workers, compensation discrimination is much more difficult to discover and remediate, and more likely to persist. Such prohibitions (either express or tacit) also restrict the amount of information available to participants in the Federal contracting labor pool, which tends to diminish market efficiency and decrease the likelihood that the most qualified and productive workers are hired at the market efficient price. Ensuring that employees of Federal contractors may discuss their compensation without fear of adverse action will enhance the ability of Federal contractors and their employees to detect and remediate unlawful discriminatory practices, which will contribute to a more efficient market in Federal contracting.

Sec. 2. Amending Executive Order 11246. Section 202 of Executive Order 11246 of September 24, 1965, as amended, is hereby further amended as follows:

(a) Paragraphs (3) through (7) are redesignated as paragraphs (4) through (8).

(b) A new paragraph (3) is added to read as follows:

"The contractor will not discharge or in any other manner discriminate against any employee or applicant for employment because such employee or applicant has inquired about, discussed, or disclosed the compensation of the employee or applicant or another employee or applicant. This provision shall not apply to instances in which an employee who has access to the compensation information of other employees or applicants as a part of such employee's essential job functions discloses the compensation of such other employees or applicants to individuals who do not otherwise have access to such information, unless such disclosure is in response to a formal complaint or charge, in furtherance of an investigation, proceeding, hearing, or action, including an investigation conducted by the employer, or is consistent with the contractor's legal duty to furnish information."

Sec. 3. Regulations. Within 160 days of the date of this order, the Secretary of Labor shall propose regulations to implement the requirements of this order.

Sec. 4. Severability. If any provision of this order, or the application of such provision or amendment to any person or circumstance, is held to be invalid, the remainder of this order and the application of the provisions of such to any person or circumstances shall not be affected thereby.

Sec. 5. General Provisions. (a) Nothing in this order shall be construed to limit the rights of an employee or applicant for employment provided under any provision of law. It also shall not be construed to prevent a Federal contractor covered by this order from pursuing a defense, as long as the defense is not based on a rule, policy, practice, agreement, or other instrument that prohibits employees or applicants from discussing or disclosing their compensation or the compensation of other employees or applicants, subject to paragraph (3) of section 202 of Executive Order 11246, as added by this order.

(b) Nothing in this order shall be construed to impair or otherwise affect:

(i) the authority granted by law to a department, agency, or the head thereof; or

(ii) the functions of the Director of the Office of Management and Budget relating to budgetary, administrative, or legislative proposals.

(c) This order shall be implemented consistent with applicable law and subject to the availability of appropriations.

(d) This order is not intended to, and does not, create any right or benefit, substantive or procedural, enforceable at law or in equity by any party against the United States, its departments, agencies, or entities, its officers, employees, or agents, or any other person.

Sec. 6. Effective Date. This order shall become effective immediately, and shall apply to contracts entered into on or after the effective date of rules promulgated by the Department of Labor under section 3 of this order.

BARACK OBAMA
The White House,
April 8, 2014.

Source: Executive Office of the President. "Executive Order 13665—Non-Retaliation for Disclosure of Compensation Information." April 8, 2014. *Compilation of Presidential Documents* 2014, no. 00250 (April 8, 2014). www.gpo.gov/fdsys/pkg/DCPD-201400250/pdf/DCPD-201400250.pdf.

President Obama Remarks on Signing Wage Gap Legislation

April 8, 2014

The President. Thank you, everybody. All right. Well, thanks to my friend, Lilly Ledbetter, not only for that introduction, but for fighting for a simple principle: equal pay for equal work. It's not that complicated. And, Lilly, I assure you, you remain the face of fair pay. [*Laughter*] People don't want my mug on there. [*Laughter*] They want your face.

As Lilly mentioned, she did not set out to be a trailblazer. She was just somebody who was waking up every day, going to work, doing her job the best that she could. And then one day, she finds out, after years, that she earned less than her male colleagues for doing the same job. I want to make that point again. [*Laughter*] Doing the same job. This—sometimes, when you—when we discuss this issue of fair pay, equal pay for equal work, and the pay gap between men and women, you'll hear all sorts of excuses about: Now, well, they're childbearing, and they're choosing to do this, and they're this, and they're that and the other. She was doing the same job, probably doing it better. [*Laughter*] Same job. Working just as hard, probably putting in more hours. But she was getting systematically paid less.

And so she set out to make sure this country lived up to its founding, the idea that all of us are created equal. And when the courts didn't answer her call, Congress did.

The first time Lilly and I stood together in this room was my 10th day in office, and that's when we signed the Lilly Ledbetter Fair Pay Act. First bill I signed into law. And some of the leaders who helped make that happen are here today, including Leader Pelosi and Senator Mikulski and Congresswoman DeLauro. I want to thank all the Members of Congress and all the State legislators who are here and all the advocates who are here, because you all contributed to that effort. And I want to give a special thanks to the members of the National Equity Pay—Equal Pay Task Force, who have done outstanding work to make workplaces across America more fair.

Now, we're here because today is Equal Pay Day. [*Applause*] Equal Pay Day. And it's nice to have a day, but it's even better to have equal pay. And our job is not finished yet. Equal Pay Day means that a woman has to work about this far into 2014 to earn what a man earned in 2013. Think about that. A woman has got to work about 3 more months in order to get what a man got, because she's paid less. That's not fair. That's like adding an extra 6 miles to a marathon. [*Laughter*] It's not right.

Audience member. Ain't right.

The President. Ain't right. [*Laughter*] It's not right, and it ain't right. [*Laughter*]

America should be a level playing field, a fair race for everybody, a place where anybody who's willing to work hard has a chance to get ahead. And restoring that opportunity for every American—men and women—has to be a driving focus for our country.

Now, the good news is, today our economy is growing. Businesses have created almost 9 million new jobs over the past 4 years. More than 7 million Americans have signed up for health care coverage under the Affordable Care Act. [*Applause*] That's a good thing too.

And I know it's Equal Pay Day and not "Obamacare day"—[*laughter*]—but I do want to point out that the Affordable Care Act guarantees free preventive care, like mammograms and contraceptive care, for tens of millions of women and ends the days when you could be charged more just for being a woman when it comes to your health insurance. And that's true for everybody. That's just one more place where things were not fair.

We'll talk about drycleaners next, right—[*laughter*]—because I know that—I don't know why it costs more for Michelle's blouse than my shirt. [*Laughter*]

But we've got to make sure that America works for everybody. Anybody who is willing to work hard, they should be able to get ahead. And we've got to build an economy that works for everybody, not just those at the top. Restoring opportunity for all has to be our priority. That's what America is about. It doesn't matter where you started off, what you look like; you work hard, you take responsibility, you make the effort, you should be able to get ahead.

And we've got to fight for an opportunity agenda, which means more good jobs that pay good wages and training Americans to make sure that they can fill those jobs and guaranteeing every child a world-class education and making sure the economy rewards hard work for every single American.

And part of that is fighting for fair pay for women, because when women succeed, America succeeds. When women succeed, America succeeds. [*Applause*] It's true. I believe that. It's true. It's true. [*Applause*] It's true.

Now, here's the challenge: Today, the average full-time working woman earns just 77 cents for every dollar a man earns; for African American women, Latinas, it's even less. And in 2014, that's an embarrassment. It is wrong. And this is not just an issue of fairness, it's also a family issue and an economic issue, because women make up about half of our workforce and they're increasingly the breadwinners for a whole lot of families out there. So when they make less money, it means less money for gas, less money for groceries, less money for child care, less money for college tuition, less money is going into retirement savings.

And it's all bad for business, because our economy depends on customers out there, and when customers have less money, when hard-working women don't have the resources, that's a problem. When businesses lose terrific women talent because they're fed up with unfair policies, that's bad for business. They lose out on the contributions that those women could be making. When any of our citizens can't fulfill their potential for reasons that have nothing to do with their talent or their character or their work ethic, we're not living up to our founding values. We don't have second-class citizens in this country and certainly not in the workplace.

So tomorrow the Senate has the chance to start making this right by passing a bill that Lilly already alluded to: the Paycheck Fairness Act. They've got a chance to do the right thing. And it would put sensible rules into place, like making sure employees who discuss their salaries don't face retaliation by their employers.

And it's—here's why this is important. There are women here today who worked in offices where it was against the rules for employees to discuss salaries with one another. And because of that, they didn't know they were being paid less than men—just like Lilly didn't know—for doing the exact same work. For some, it was years before they found out. And even then, it only happened because a manager accidentally let it slip or, as in Lilly's case, a sympathetic coworker quietly passed a note. She only found out she earned less than her male colleagues for doing the same work because somebody left an anonymous note.

We can't leave that to chance. And over the course of Lilly's career, she lost more than $200,000 in salary, even more in pension and Social Security benefits—both of which are pegged to salary—simply because she was a woman.

And Lilly and some of the other women here decided it was wrong, set out to fix it. They went to their bosses; they asked for a raise. That didn't work. They turned to the law; they filed suit. And for some, for years after waiting and persisting, they finally got some justice.

Well, tomorrow the Senate could pay tribute to their courage by voting yes for paycheck fairness. This should not be a hard proposition. This should not be that complicated.

And so far, Republicans in Congress have been gumming up the works. They've been blocking progress on this issue and, of course, other issues that would help with the economic recovery and help us grow faster. But we don't have to accept that. America, you don't have to sit still. You can make sure that you're putting some pressure on Members of Congress about this issue. And I don't care whether you're a Democrat or a Republican. If you're a voter—if you've got a daughter, you've got a sister, you've got a mom—I know you got a mom—[*laughter*]—this is something you should care about.

And I'm not going to stand still either. So in this year of action I've used my executive authority whenever I could to create opportunity for more Americans. And today I'm going to take action—executive action—to make it easier for working women to earn fair pay. So first, I'm going to sign an Executive order to create more pay transparency by prohibiting Federal contractors from retaliating against employees who discuss their pay with each other.

Audience member. Excellent!

The President. Right? Pay secrecy fosters discrimination, and we should not tolerate it, not in Federal contracting or anywhere else.

Second, I'm signing a Presidential memorandum directing the Department of Labor and our outstanding Secretary of Labor, Tom Perez, to require Federal contractors to provide data about their employee compensation so pay discrimination can be spotted more easily.

Now, I want to be clear: There are great employers out there who do the right thing. And there are plenty of employers out there who are absolutely certain that there's no pay discrimination happening in their offices. But then sometimes, when the data is laid out, it paints a different picture. Many times, they then do everything they can to fix the problem, and so we want to encourage them to fix these problems if they exist by making sure that the data is out there.

So everybody who cares about this should pay attention to how the Senate votes tomorrow on this payness—Paycheck Fairness Act, because the majority of Senators support this bill, but 2 years ago, a minority of Senate Republicans blocked it from getting a vote. Even worse, some commentators are out there saying that the pay gap doesn't even exist. They say it's a myth. But it's not a myth, it's math. [*Laughter*] You can look at the paychecks. You can look at the stubs.

I mean, Lilly Ledbetter didn't just make this up. [*Laughter*] The court, when it looked at the documents, said, yes, yes, you've been getting paid less for doing the same job. It's just the court then said, you know, it's been—as Lilly said—it's been happening so long, you can't do anything about it anymore, which made no sense, and that's why we had to sign another bill. It's basic math that adds up to real money. It makes a real difference for a lot of Americans who are working hard to support their families.

And of course, the fact that we've got some resistance from some folks on this issue up on Capitol Hill just fits with this larger problem, this vision that the congressional Republicans seem to be continually embracing, this notion that, you know what, you're just on your own, no matter how unfair things are. You see it in their budget. The budget the Republicans in Congress just put forward last week, it's like a bad rerun. It would give massive tax cuts to households making more than a million dollars a year, force deep cuts to things that actually help working families, like early education and college grants and job training.

And of course, it includes that novel idea of repealing the Affordable Care Act. [*Laughter*] Fiftieth time they've tried that, which would mean the more than 7 million Americans who've done the responsible thing and signed up to buy health insurance, they'd lose their health insurance, and the 3 million young adults who've stayed on their parent's plan, they'd no longer have that available; take us back to the days when insurers could charge women more just for being a woman.

On minimum wage, three out of four Americans support raising the minimum wage. Usually, when three out of four Americans support something, Members of Congress are right there. [*Laughter*] And yet here, Republicans in Congress are dead set against it, blocking a pay raise for tens of millions of Americans, a majority of them women. This isn't just about treating women fairly, this is about Republicans seemingly opposing any efforts to even the playing field for working families.

And I was up in Michigan last week, and I just asked, I don't understand the—fully the theory behind this. I don't know why you would resist the idea that women should be paid the same as men and then deny that that's not always happening out there. If Republicans in Congress want to prove me wrong, if they want to show that they, in fact, do care about women being paid the same as men, then show me. They can start tomorrow. They can join us in this, the 21st century, and vote yes on the Paycheck Fairness Act. [*Applause*] Vote yes.

And if anybody is watching or listening, if you care about this issue, then let your Senators know where you stand, because America deserves equal pay for equal work.

This is not something we're going to achieve in a day. There's going to be a lot of stuff that we've got to do to close the pay gap. We got to make it possible for more women to enter high-paying fields that up until now have been dominated by men, like engineering and computer science. Women hold less than 6 percent of our country's commercial patents. That's not good enough. We need more parents and high school teachers and college professors encouraging girls and women to study math and science. We need more businesses to make gender diversity a priority when they hire and when they promote. Fewer than 5 percent of Fortune 500 companies have women at the helm.

I think we'd all agree that we need more women in Congress. [*Applause*] You know? Fewer than 20 percent of congressional seats are held by women. Clearly, Congress would get more done if the ratio was—[*laughter*]—evened out a little bit. So we've got to work on that.

And we've all got to do more to make our workplaces more welcoming to women. Because the numbers show that even when men and women are in the same profession and have the same education, there's still a wage gap, and it widens over time. So we're going to keep making the case for why these policies are the right ones for working families and businesses. And this is all going to lead up to this first-ever White House Summit on Working Families on June 23.

So ultimately, equal pay is not just an economic issue for millions of Americans and their families. It's also about whether we're willing to build an economy that works for everybody and whether we're going to do our part to make sure that our daughters have the same chances to pursue their dreams as our sons and whether or not we're willing to restore to the heart of this country that basic idea: You can make it, no matter who you are, if you try.

And that's personal for me. I've said this before: I've got two daughters, and I expect them to be treated just like anybody's sons. And I think about my single mom working hard, going to school, trying to raise two kids all at the same time. And I think about my grandmother trying to work her way up through her career and then hitting the glass ceiling. And I've seen how hard they've worked, and I've seen how they've sucked it up. And they put up with stuff, and they don't say anything, and they just take care of their family, and they take care of themselves, and they don't complain a lot. But at a certain point, we have the power to do something about it for the next generation. And this is a good place to start.

So for everybody out there who's listening, ask your Senator where you stand on paycheck fairness. If they tell you that there's not a pay gap out there, you tell them to look at the data, because there is. It's time to get this done. And I'm going to do my small part right now by signing these Executive orders and Presidential memoranda.

All right. Scoot on over here guys. Come on, let's scoot in here. Scoot in here. All right.

[*At this point, the President signed the Executive order.*]

The President. There you go. That's done right there.
All right, and then I got another one. This is for you, Tom. [*Laughter*]

[*The President signed the memorandum.*]

The President. There you go.

SOURCE: Executive Office of the President. "Remarks on Signing an Executive Order on Non-Retaliation for Disclosure of Compensation Information and a Memorandum on Advancing Pay Equality Through Compensation Data Collection." April 8, 2014. *Compilation of Presidential Documents* 2014, no. 00249 (April 8, 2014). www.gpo.gov/fdsys/pkg/DCPD-201400249/pdf/DCPD-201400249.pdf.

OTHER HISTORIC DOCUMENTS OF INTEREST

FROM THIS VOLUME

■   State of the Union Address and Republican Response, p. 3

Supreme Court Rules on Affirmative Action in Higher Education

APRIL 22, 2014

On April 22, 2014, the Supreme Court handed down its ruling in *Schuette v. BAMN*, its second major decision regarding the use of affirmative action in university admissions in less than one year. The first case, *Fisher v. University of Texas*, upheld the principle that race could be permissibly considered in admissions decisions if certain rigorous conditions were satisfied. By contrast, the *Schuette* case involved the constitutionality of a state constitutional amendment, passed by a voter initiative in Michigan, which prohibited the consideration of race in governmental decisions, particularly school admissions. Instead of focusing on the question of whether a state could use race-conscious criteria in college admissions, this case focused on the opposite question: whether a state could ban the use of race in such admissions. The Court's answer to this question was fractured into four separate opinions with no one opinion gaining a majority of votes for its rationale, but six justices agreed with the result: that the Michigan law should be upheld. The controlling plurality opinion, written by Justice Anthony M. Kennedy and joined by Chief Justice John G. Roberts Jr. and Justice Samuel A. Alito Jr., viewed this as an issue of disempowering voters and supported the Michigan voters' right to weigh in on "the national dialogue regarding the wisdom and practicality of race-conscious admissions policies in higher education."

LEGAL BACKGROUND

The subject of race-conscious admissions policies in Michigan schools has been to the Supreme Court multiple times in the past dozen years. Two major cases in 2003, *Gratz v. Bollinger* and *Grutter v. Bollinger*, addressed the role of affirmative action in admissions at the University of Michigan. In these cases the Court reemphasized that "universities cannot establish quotas for members of certain racial groups" and struck down the University of Michigan's undergraduate admissions program in which students, evaluated on a 150-point scale, were granted twenty points for being a member of an underrepresented minority group. However, the Court upheld Michigan's law school admissions program, which took race into account without a numerical scale, allowing universities to continue to "consider race or ethnicity more flexibly as a 'plus' factor in the context of individualized consideration." As long as schools do not use numerical quotas, the justices, by a 5–4 majority, allowed schools to take race into account as just one factor among many.

After the Supreme Court declined to reject all affirmative action programs on federal constitutional grounds, a coalition of disappointed anti-affirmative action advocates were able to put a statewide referendum on the November 2006 Michigan ballot to amend the Michigan Constitution to ban affirmative action programs. Similar to a law passed in California, Michigan's Proposal 2 provided that: "The state shall not discriminate against, or grant preferential treatment to any individual or group on the basis of race, sex, color, ethnicity, or national origin in the operation of public employment, public education or public contracting." The ballot proposal passed with 58 percent of the vote.

A collection of interest groups and individuals brought suit in federal district court, arguing that the newly passed part of the Michigan Constitution violates the United States Constitution. The district court judge rejected these arguments and upheld Proposal 2. On appeal, a panel of judges from the Sixth Circuit Court of Appeals overturned that decision, concluding that Proposal 2 impermissibly alters the political process in violation of the Equal Protection Clause. The attorney general of Michigan petitioned for an *en banc* review of this decision—that is, a review by all the judges of the Sixth Circuit together.

The Sixth Circuit granted an *en banc* review, and by a vote of 8–7 affirmed that Proposal 2 was unconstitutional. The case had strong political undertones because all eight of the judges who found the law unconstitutional had been appointed by Democratic presidents and the seven dissenting judges were appointed by Republicans. In overturning the Michigan law, the majority relied on a thirty-year-old theory known as the "political process doctrine," which finds violations of the Equal Protection Clause of the Fourteenth Amendment when the political system is restructured to put special burdens on a minority group's ability to achieve its goals through that process. The Supreme Court had most recently articulated this theory in *Washington v. Seattle School District*, a 1982 decision that struck down a voter-approved statewide law barring busing only when that busing was used to achieve racial integration, but not for any other purpose. In explaining why it thought the Michigan law was in violation of the political process doctrine, the Sixth Circuit opinion imagined two different prospective university students in Michigan. The first one is a nonminority applicant who wants the university admissions office to give greater weight to her family's alumni connections. This student could lobby the admissions committee, petition the leadership of the university or seek to influence the school's governing board, or, if necessary, campaign and vote for new members of the board who are more amenable to her position. By contrast, the second imagined student, a black student who wants race factored into his application in a constitutionally permissible way, does not initially have any of these avenues open to him. This student must first attempt to amend the Michigan Constitution, a process that is, as the court describes, "lengthy, expensive and arduous." Only after successfully altering the state constitution "would our now-exhausted citizen reach the starting point of his neighbor who sought a legacy-related admissions policy change." This added burden placed only on racial minorities seeking the opportunity to get the state government to even consider a policy change in their favor, the court concluded, makes the political process itself unequal.

The Supreme Court agreed to hear an appeal of this decision.

Court Reverses the Sixth Circuit and Upholds the Michigan Law

There were four decisions in this case and no single decision had the full support of more than three justices. Six justices agreed that the Michigan law should stand. The opinion written by Justice Kennedy was joined only by Chief Justice Roberts and Justice Alito but is the controlling plurality opinion because Justices Antonin Scalia and Clarence Thomas wrote separately, but concurred in the judgment. Justices Scalia and Thomas would have, however, gone much further, rejecting any policy that takes race into account unless it is a direct remedy for intentional discrimination. Justice Stephen G. Breyer also wrote a concurring opinion, and Justice Sonia Sotomayor wrote a dissent that was joined by Justice Ruth Bader Ginsburg. Justice Elena Kagan did not take part in the case.

In the controlling opinion, Justice Kennedy first described what this case is not about: "It is not about the constitutionality, or the merits, of race-conscious admissions policies in higher education." Rather, this case addresses "whether, and in what manner, voters in the States may choose to prohibit the consideration of racial preferences in governmental decisions, in particular with respect to school admissions," he continued. Justice Kennedy noted with approval that states have been "engaged in experimenting with a wide variety of alternative approaches" to "this contested and complex question" of race-conscious admissions policies.

The opinion then examined all the political process doctrine precedents and concluded that they had been interpreted too broadly. The earlier precedents involved instances of political restrictions created to encourage infliction of injury by reason of race; Justice Kennedy did not see such an injury in this case. In his view, the Sixth Circuit expanded the precedents to require strict scrutiny of any state action with a "racial focus" that makes it "more difficult for certain racial minorities than for other groups" to "achieve legislation that is in their interest." This, according to Justice Kennedy, would impermissibly put the Court in the position of determining which policies serve the "interest" of a racially defined group, an inquiry that would require relying on racial stereotypes and assumptions that all "members of the same racial group—regardless of their age, education, economic status, or the community in which they live—think alike, share the same political interests, and will prefer the same candidates at the polls." Justice Kennedy feared that starting down this road would have no limiting principle, potentially exempting tax policy, housing subsidies, wage regulations, and even the naming of public schools and highways from the power of voters to decide. Were the Court to accept the Sixth Circuit's broad interpretation of the political process doctrine, according to Justice Kennedy, "racial division would be validated, not discouraged," leading to "racial antagonisms and conflict."

At the same time, Justice Kennedy expressed confidence in the voters' ability to decide an issue of this sensitivity on "decent and rational grounds." While public debate of issues involving racial preferences may shade into rancor, he concluded that this "does not justify removing certain court-determined issues from the voters' reach. Democracy does not presume that some subjects are either too divisive or too profound for public debate."

Dissenting Opinions

"The stark reality that race matters is regrettable," Justice Sotomayor read in open court from her passionate dissent that was longer than the rest of the opinions put together, a rare move that signals deep disagreement. While she shares the plurality's faith in the democratic process, she added that it cannot be without limits because, without constitutional checks, democratically approved legislation can oppress minority groups. She agreed with the analysis of the Sixth Circuit that Michigan's constitutional amendment prohibiting race-conscious university admissions violated the political process doctrine of the Equal Protection Amendment by changing the rules in the middle of the game to disadvantage racial minorities. There are now two processes through which Michigan citizens can influence the admissions policies at their schools: those for people seeking race-sensitive admissions and those for everyone else. While athletes, those from underrepresented parts of the state, or children of alumni can lobby university officials to give their applications special weight, only those seeking a race-sensitive admissions policy have the added burden of amending the state constitution. The Constitution "does not guarantee minority groups victory in the political process," the dissent argues, but "it does guarantee them meaningful and equal access to that process."

Justice Sotomayor's dissent included charts detailing the drop in admissions of minorities after the passage of Michigan's law and a similar law in California, and she spoke directly to the justices who would strike down any race-conscious admissions policies:

"[That view] ignores the importance of diversity in institutions of higher education and reveals how little my colleagues understand about the reality of race in America." In a 2007 decision striking down Seattle's attempt to integrate schools by taking race into account in school assignments, Chief Justice Roberts wrote that "[t]he way to stop discrimination on the basis of race is to stop discriminating on the basis of race." Justice Sotomayor reworked the line to read: "The way to stop discrimination on the basis of race is to speak openly and candidly on the subject of race, and to apply the Constitution with eyes open to the unfortunate effects of centuries of racial discrimination."

STATE AFFIRMATIVE ACTION BANS

Currently, eight states have affirmative action bans similar to the one at issue in this Michigan case, including California, Florida, and Washington. These states have seen steep drops in black and Hispanic student enrollment following the bans while at the same time the number of minorities enrolled in colleges across the country has increased. Michigan's first graduating class that was admitted since the passage of its ban was markedly different than that of the previous year's graduating class, with the lowest percentage of black students since 1991. Nina Robinson, the associate president and chief policy adviser for the University of California system, described the numerous experimental race-neutral approaches the various UC campuses had tried to improve their diversity. Nonetheless, UC officials were forced to admit in court documents that "those efforts have had disappointing results."

It is possible that the *Schuette* case will energize those opposed to affirmative action in college admissions to organize for similar bans in other states. Currently there are plans to put such a ban before the voters in Missouri, Ohio, and Utah.

—Melissa Feinberg

Following is the edited text of the Supreme Court decision in Schuette v. BAMN *in which the Court ruled 6–2 on April 22, 2014, that upheld Michigan's ban on use of affirmative action in college admissions.*

DOCUMENT *Schuette v. BAMN*

April 22, 2014

[Footnotes have been omitted.]

Bill Schuette, Attorney General of Michigan, Petitioner	No. 12-682	
v.		On writ of certiorari to the United States Court of Appeals for the Sixth Circuit
Coalition to Defend Affirmative Action, Integration and Immigrant Rights and Fight for Equality By Any Means Necessary (BAMN), et al.	[April 22, 2014]	

JUSTICE KENNEDY announced the judgment of the Court and delivered an opinion, in which THE CHIEF JUSTICE and JUSTICE ALITO join.

The Court in this case must determine whether an amendment to the Constitution of the State of Michigan, approved and enacted by its voters, is invalid under the Equal Protection Clause of the Fourteenth Amendment to the Constitution of the United States. . . .

The ballot proposal was called Proposal 2 and, after it passed by a margin of 58 percent to 42 percent, the resulting enactment became Article I, §26, of the Michigan Constitution. As noted, the amendment is in broad terms. Section 26 states, in relevant part, as follows:

> "(1) The University of Michigan, Michigan State University, Wayne State University, and any other public college or university, community college, or school district shall not discriminate against, or grant preferential treatment to, any individual or group on the basis of race, sex, color, ethnicity, or national origin in the operation of public employment, public education, or public contracting." . . .

Before the Court addresses the question presented, it is important to note what this case is not about. It is not about the constitutionality, or the merits, of race-conscious admissions policies in higher education. The consideration of race in admissions presents complex questions, in part addressed last Term in *Fisher* v. *University of Texas at Austin*, 570 U. S. —— (2013). In *Fisher*, the Court did not disturb the principle that the consideration of race in admissions is permissible, provided that certain conditions are met. In this case, as in *Fisher*, that principle is not challenged. The question here concerns not the permissibility of race-conscious admissions policies under the Constitution but whether, and in what manner, voters in the States may choose to prohibit the consideration of racial preferences in governmental decisions, in particular with respect to school admissions. . . .

In holding §26 invalid in the context of student admissions at state universities, the Court of Appeals relied in primary part on *Seattle*, *supra*, which it deemed to control the case. But that determination extends *Seattle*'s holding in a case presenting quite different issues to reach a conclusion that is mistaken here. . . .

[In *Seattle*], the school board adopted a mandatory busing program to alleviate racial isolation of minority students in local schools. Voters who opposed the school board's busing plan passed a state initiative that barred busing to desegregate. The Court first determined that, although "white as well as Negro children benefit from" diversity, the school board's plan "inures primarily to the benefit of the minority." 458 U. S., at 472. The Court next found that "the practical effect" of the state initiative was to "remov[e] the authority to address a racial problem—and only a racial problem—from the existing decisionmaking body, in such a way as to burden minority interests" because advocates of busing "now must seek relief from the state legislature, or from the statewide electorate." *Id.*, at 474. The Court therefore found that the initiative had "explicitly us[ed] the racial nature of a decision to determine the decisionmaking process."

Seattle is best understood as a case in which the state action in question (the bar on busing enacted by the State's voters) had the serious risk, if not purpose, of causing specific injuries on account of race . . . . Although there had been no judicial finding of *de jure* segregation with respect to Seattle's school district, it appears as though school segregation in the district in the 1940's and 1950's may have been the partial result of school board policies that "permitted white students to transfer out of black schools while restricting the transfer of black students into white schools." *Parents Involved in Community Schools* v. *Seattle School Dist. No. 1*, 551 U. S. 701, 807–808 (2007) (BREYER, J., dissenting). In 1977, the National Association for the

Advancement of Colored People (NAACP) filed a complaint with the Office for Civil Rights, a federal agency. The NAACP alleged that the school board had maintained a system of *de jure* segregation. Specifically, the complaint alleged "that the Seattle School Board had created or perpetuated unlawful racial segregation through, *e.g.,* certain school-transfer criteria, a construction program that needlessly built new schools in white areas, district line-drawing criteria, the maintenance of inferior facilities at black schools, the use of explicit racial criteria in the assignment of teachers and other staff, and a general pattern of delay in respect to the implementation of promised desegregation efforts." *Id.,* at 810. As part of a settlement with the Office for Civil Rights, the school board implemented the "Seattle Plan," which used busing and mandatory reassignments between elementary schools to reduce racial imbalance and which was the subject of the state initiative at issue in *Seattle.* . . .

The broad language used in *Seattle,* however, went well beyond the analysis needed to resolve the case. The Court there seized upon the statement in Justice Harlan's concurrence in *Hunter* that the procedural change in that case had "the clear purpose of making it more difficult for certain racial and religious minorities to achieve legislation that is in their interest." 385 U. S., at 395. That language, taken in the context of the facts in *Hunter,* is best read simply to describe the necessity for finding an equal protection violation where specific injuries from hostile discrimination were at issue. The *Seattle* Court, however, used the language from the *Hunter* concurrence to establish a new and far-reaching rationale. *Seattle* stated that where a government policy "inures primarily to the benefit of the minority" and "minorities . . . consider" the policy to be "'in their interest,'" then any state action that "place[s] effective decisionmaking authority over" that policy "at a different level of government" be reviewed under strict scrutiny. 458 U. S., at 472, 474. In essence, according to the broad reading of *Seattle,* any state action with a "racial focus" that makes it "more difficult for certain racial minorities than for other groups" to "achieve legislation that is in their interest" is subject to strict scrutiny. It is this reading of *Seattle* that the Court of Appeals found to be controlling here. And that reading must be rejected.

The broad rationale that the Court of Appeals adopted goes beyond the necessary holding and the meaning of the precedents said to support it; and in the instant case neither the formulation of the general rule just set forth nor the precedents cited to authenticate it suffice to invalidate Proposal 2. The expansive reading of *Seattle* has no principled limitation and raises serious questions of compatibility with the Court's settled equal protection jurisprudence. To the extent *Seattle* is read to require the Court to determine and declare which political policies serve the "interest" of a group defined in racial terms, that rationale was unnecessary to the decision in *Seattle*; it has no support in precedent; and it raises serious constitutional concerns. That expansive language does not provide proper guide for decisions and should not be deemed authoritative or controlling. The rule that the Court of Appeals elaborated and respondents seek to establish here would contradict central equal protection principles.

In cautioning against "impermissible racial stereotypes," this Court has rejected the assumption that "members of the same racial group—regardless of their age, education, economic status, or the community in which they live—think alike, share the same political interests, and will prefer the same candidates at the polls." *Shaw* v. *Reno,* 509 U. S. 630, 647 (1993); see also *Metro Broadcasting, Inc.* v. *FCC,* 497 U. S. 547, 636 (1990) (KENNEDY, J., dissenting) (rejecting the "demeaning notion that members of . . . defined racial groups ascribe to certain 'minority views' that must be different from those of other citizens"). It cannot be entertained as a serious proposition that all individuals of the same race think alike. Yet that proposition would be a necessary beginning point were the *Seattle* formulation to control, as the Court of Appeals held it did in this case. And if it were deemed necessary to probe how some races define their own interest in political matters, still another beginning point would be to define individuals according to race. But in a society in which those lines are becoming more blurred, the attempt to define race based categories also raises serious questions of its own. Government action that classifies individuals on the basis of race is inherently suspect and carries the danger of perpetuating the very racial divisions the polity seeks to transcend. Were courts to embark upon this venture not only would it be undertaken with no clear legal standards or accepted sources to guide judicial decision but also it would result in, or at least impose a high risk of, inquiries and categories dependent upon demeaning stereotypes, classifications of questionable constitutionality on their own terms.

Even assuming these initial steps could be taken in a manner consistent with a sound analytic and judicial framework, the court would next be required to determine the policy realms in which certain groups—groups defined by race—have a political interest. That undertaking, again without guidance from any accepted legal standards, would risk, in turn, the creation of incentives for those who support or oppose certain policies to cast the debate in terms of racial advantage or disadvantage. Thus could racial antagonisms and conflict tend to arise in the context of judicial decisions as courts undertook to announce what particular issues of public policy should be classified as advantageous to some group defined by race. This risk is inherent in adopting the *Seattle* formulation.

There would be no apparent limiting standards defining what public policies should be included in what *Seattle* called policies that "inur[e] primarily to the benefit of the minority" and that "minorities . . . consider" to be "'in their interest.'" 458 U. S., at 472, 474. Those who seek to represent the interests of particular racial groups could attempt to advance those aims by demanding an equal protection ruling that any number of matters be foreclosed from voter review or participation. In a nation in which governmental policies are wide ranging, those who seek to limit voter participation might be tempted, were this Court to adopt the *Seattle* formulation, to urge that a group they choose to define by race or racial stereotypes are advantaged or disadvantaged by any number of laws or decisions. Tax policy, housing subsidies, wage regulations, and even the naming of public schools, highways, and monuments are just a few examples of what could become a list of subjects that some organizations could insist should be beyond the power of voters to decide, or beyond the power of a legislature to decide when enacting limits on the power of local authorities or other governmental entities to address certain subjects. Racial division would be validated, not discouraged, were the *Seattle* formulation, and the reasoning of the Court of Appeals in this case, to remain in force.

Perhaps, when enacting policies as an exercise of democratic self-government, voters will determine that race based preferences should be adopted. The constitutional validity of some of those choices regarding racial preferences is not at issue here. The holding in the instant case is simply that the courts may not disempower the voters from choosing which path to follow. In the realm of policy discussions the regular give-and-take of debate ought to be a context in which rancor or discord based on race are avoided, not invited. And if these factors are to be interjected, surely it ought not to be at the invitation or insistence of the courts. . . .

By approving Proposal 2 and thereby adding §26 to their State Constitution, the Michigan voters exercised their privilege to enact laws as a basic exercise of their democratic power. . . .

. . .Our constitutional system embraces, too, the right of citizens to debate so they can learn and decide and then, through the political process, act in concert to try to shape the course of their own times and the course of a nation that must strive always to make freedom ever greater and more secure. Here Michigan voters acted in concert and statewide to seek consensus and adopt a policy on a difficult subject against a historical background of race in America that has been a source of tragedy and persisting injustice. That history demands that we continue to learn, to listen, and to remain open to new approaches if we are to aspire always to a constitutional order in which all persons are treated with fairness and equal dignity. Were the Court to rule that the question addressed by Michigan voters is too sensitive or complex to be within the grasp of the electorate; or that the policies at issue remain too delicate to be resolved save by university officials or faculties, acting at some remove from immediate public scrutiny and control; or that these matters are so arcane that the electorate's power must be limited because the people cannot prudently exercise that power even after a full debate, that holding would be an unprecedented restriction on the exercise of a fundamental right held not just by one person but by all in common. It is the right to speak and debate and learn and then, as a matter of political will, to act through a lawful electoral process.

. . .It is demeaning to the democratic process to presume that the voters are not capable of deciding an issue of this sensitivity on decent and rational grounds. The process of public discourse and political debate should not be foreclosed even if there is a risk that during a public campaign there will be those, on both sides, who seek to use racial division and discord to their own political advantage. An informed public can, and must, rise above this. The idea of democracy is that it can, and must, mature. Freedom embraces the right, indeed the duty, to engage in a rational, civic discourse in order to determine how best to form a consensus to shape the destiny of the Nation and its people. These First Amendment dynamics would be disserved if this Court were to say that the question here at issue is beyond the capacity of the voters to debate and then to determine.

These precepts are not inconsistent with the well-established principle that when hurt or injury is inflicted on racial minorities by the encouragement or command of laws or other state action, the Constitution requires redress by the courts. Cf. *Johnson* v. *California*, 543 U. S. 499, 511–512 (2005). As already noted, those were the circumstances that the Court found present in *Mulkey*, *Hunter*, and *Seattle*. But those circumstances are not present here.

For reasons already discussed, *Mulkey*, *Hunter*, and *Seattle* are not precedents that stand for the conclusion that Michigan's voters must be disempowered from acting. Those cases were ones in which the political restriction in question was designed to be used, or was likely to be used, to encourage infliction of injury by reason of race. What is at stake here is not whether injury will be inflicted but whether government can be instructed not to follow a course that entails, first, the definition of racial categories and, second, the grant of favored status to persons in some racial categories and not others. The electorate's instruction to governmental entities not to embark upon the course of race-defined and race-based preferences was adopted, we must assume, because the voters deemed a preference system to be unwise, on account of what voters may deem its latent potential to become itself a source of the very resentments and hostilities based on race that this Nation seeks to put behind it. Whether those adverse results would follow is, and should be, the subject of debate. Voters might likewise consider, after debate and reflection, that programs designed to increase diversity—consistent with the Constitution—are a necessary part of progress to transcend the stigma of past racism.

This case is not about how the debate about racial preferences should be resolved. It is about who may resolve it. There is no authority in the Constitution of the United States or in this Court's precedents for the Judiciary to set aside Michigan laws that commit this policy determination to the voters . . . . Deliberative debate on sensitive issues such as racial preferences all too often may shade into rancor. But that does not justify removing certain court-determined issues from the voters' reach. Democracy does not presume that some subjects are either too divisive or too profound for public debate.

The judgment of the Court of Appeals for the Sixth Circuit is reversed.

It is so ordered.

JUSTICE KAGAN took no part in the consideration or decision of this case.

[The concurring opinion of Justice Roberts, the concurring opinion of Justice Breyer, and the concurring opinion of Justices Scalia and Thomas, have been omitted.]

JUSTICE SOTOMAYOR, with whom JUSTICE GINSBURG joins, dissenting.

[A majority of the dissent, including background on the case, earlier decisions, and response to each of the concurring opinions, has been omitted.]

. . . The Constitution does not protect racial minorities from political defeat. But neither does it give the majority free rein to erect selective barriers against racial minorities. The political-process doctrine polices the channels of change to ensure that the majority, when it wins, does so without rigging the rules of the game to ensure its success. Today, the Court discards that doctrine without good reason.

In doing so, it permits the decision of a majority of the voters in Michigan to strip Michigan's elected university boards of their authority to make decisions with respect to constitutionally permissible race-sensitive admissions policies, while preserving the boards' plenary authority to make all other educational decisions. "In a most direct sense, this implicates the judiciary's special role in safeguarding the interests of those groups that are relegated to such a position of political powerlessness as to command extraordinary protection from the majoritarian political process." *Seattle*, 458 U. S., at 486 (internal quotation marks omitted). The Court abdicates that role, permitting the majority to use its numerical advantage to change the rules mid-contest and forever stack the deck against racial minorities in Michigan. The result is that Michigan's public colleges and universities are less equipped to do their part in ensuring that students of all races are "better prepare[d] . . . for an increasingly diverse workforce and society . . ." *Grutter*, 539 U. S., at 330 (internal quotation marks omitted).

Today's decision eviscerates an important strand of our equal protection jurisprudence. For members of historically marginalized groups, which rely on the federal courts to protect their constitutional rights, the decision can hardly bolster hope for a vision of democracy that preserves for all the right to participate meaningfully and equally in self-government.

I respectfully dissent.

SOURCE: U.S. Supreme Court. *Schuette v. BAMN.* 572 U.S.__(2014). www.supremecourt.gov/opinions/13pdf/12-682_8759.pdf.

OTHER HISTORIC DOCUMENTS OF INTEREST

FROM PREVIOUS *HISTORIC DOCUMENTS*

First Affordable Care Act Deadline Passes

MAY 1, 2014

In late 2013, the launch of the online signup for the federal health exchange, a key tenet of the Affordable Care Act of 2010 (ACA), was rife with problems. Individuals seeking health insurance were unable to sign up after the system crashed due to the overload of users. It was more than two months before full functionality was restored and individuals could find and choose a new health insurance plan. The failings of the website drew instant criticism from Republicans, who likened the inability to run a website to the failings of the ACA itself. President Barack Obama continued to stand by his landmark piece of legislation, urging patience as the federal exchange was implemented. By the end of the first ACA enrollment period, more than eight million individuals were able to enroll for health insurance coverage through the federal exchange or one of thirteen state-based exchanges.

2014 CHANGES TO THE AFFORDABLE CARE ACT

As written, the ACA was enacted in rolling phases. In 2014, new segments included eliminating the ability of insurance companies to charge higher rates based on gender or refuse coverage to those with pre-existing conditions. Insurance companies were also prohibited from capping the amount of coverage a person can receive each year; and insurers could no longer drop or limit coverage for individuals who choose to participate in clinical trials treating cancer or other life threatening diseases.

More important, starting in 2014 the law would make it easier for millions of Americans to afford coverage. Tax credits for those between 100 percent and 400 percent of the poverty line (who would not otherwise receive affordable coverage) would help lower premium rates on a monthly, advanced basis, rather than forcing the insured to wait until filing their taxes. Cost sharing was also available to those qualified to help pay for copayments, deductibles, and coinsurance. Families earning less than 133 percent of the poverty line (approximately $29,000 for a family of four) would be eligible for Medicaid under new expanded guidelines. To help states afford this increase in Medicaid enrollment, the federal government was paying 100 percent of the cost for the first three years, and 90 percent thereafter. The small business tax credit was also increased in 2014 to help make providing coverage to employees more affordable; qualified employers could receive up to 50 percent of their own contribution.

To encourage all Americans to find and enroll in affordable health care plans, starting in 2014, those who did not receive coverage from their employer, Medicaid, Medicare, or through the exchange would be required to pay a fee at tax filing. That fee was intended to help offset the cost of providing health care to the uninsured. Exemptions were made available for individuals unable to find affordable coverage.

Successful First Enrollment Period

After a litany of delays, the first enrollment period for insurance under the federal exchange ended on March 31, 2014 (a special enrollment period was opened through April 19, 2014, for those with waivers who started but were unable to complete an application before the March 31 deadline). Less than two months later, on May 1, the Department of Health and Human Services (HHS) reported the final enrollment statistics: 8 million individuals signed up for a health insurance plan through the federal and state marketplaces, a total of 5.4 million signed up under the federal exchange, and 2.6 million went through a state-based exchange. Medicaid and the Children's Health Insurance Program (CHIP) also saw their enrollments grow by a total of 4.8 million individuals. Approximately 47 percent of enrollments in the state and federal exchanges occurred in March and April.

In its report, HHS also detailed the demographic distribution of those enrolling in the exchanges. As anticipated, young adults (those aged eighteen to thirty-four) accounted for only 28 percent of total enrollees, despite the high number of uninsured individuals in this age bracket. Some of those uninsured young adults likely chose to seek coverage off of the exchange, potentially through an employer. The smallest enrollment group was those aged fifty-five to sixty-four, making up only 25 percent of enrollments, while the largest was individuals between the ages of thirty-five and fifty-five, at 40 percent.

Women enrolled in greater numbers than men, accounting for 54 percent of enrollees, and they tended to be somewhat older. The report detailed the race/ethnicity of those enrolling only in the federal exchange. More than 30 percent opted not to answer the race and ethnicity question or chose "other" when enrolling in a federal exchange plan, but of those who did respond nearly 63 percent were white, 10.7 percent were Latino, 16.7 percent were African American, 7.9 percent were Asian, 0.3 percent were American Indian/Alaskan Native, 1.3 percent identified as multiracial, and 0.1 percent were Hawaiian or Pacific Islander. Analysts have noted that the portion of Hispanics who registered is likely far lower than those who require coverage, partly because Spanish-language enrollment materials were not released at the same time as the exchange went live.

During the open enrollment period, 8.7 million of the 13.5 million who went to the exchange websites and were deemed eligible for a plan were also determined to be eligible for financial assistance. This is in addition to another 6.7 million individuals who were considered to be eligible for Medicaid. Of those who qualified for assistance, 2 million did not select or enroll in an insurance plan. According to Timothy Jost, a professor at Washington and Lee University School of Law, there are a variety of factors why this number might be high: the individual may have chosen an off-market plan, found employer insurance, or ultimately chosen to remain uninsured.

Questions about Whether the Program is Working

A key argument raised by those in support of the ACA as it made its way through Congress was that it would significantly reduce the number of uninsured Americans. The HHS report on the first enrollment period did not include data on how many enrollees in the federal or state marketplaces were previously uninsured. However, in an October report, HHS noted that based on Gallup-Healthways Well-Being Index data, approximately 10.3 million individuals aged eighteen to sixty-four who were previously uninsured gained coverage under the ACA by June 2014.

Some ACA opponents questioned whether marketplace enrollees will actually pay their premiums; individuals are not considered to be officially covered by a plan until the first premium is paid. The May HHS report did not include data on this factor; however, the Republican leadership of the House Energy and Commerce Committee released its own report on April 30, which found that only 67 percent of enrollees had paid their first month's premium by April 15. The data contained in the Republican report was based on information collected from 160 separate insurers who were offering their plans on the federal exchange.

In a response from Democrats on the committee in a memo titled "Misleading Republican Report on ACA Enrollment," they argue that the timeframe from which the data is pulled makes the claims inherently flawed. By April 15, eight million individuals had enrolled in plans. However, less than five million of those individuals were required to pay their premiums by that time. In fact, three million individuals did not need to make their initial premium payment until April or later. According to the Democratic response, only those who signed up for coverage by March 15 needed to make the initial premium payment by April 15. However, almost 40 percent of all exchange enrollees signed up between March 15 and April 15, pushing their initial premium payment dates beyond April 15.

Enrollment Data Overstated

In November, it was announced that the original data about the number of plans purchased during the first enrollment year had been overstated by more than 5 percent. That error was discovered by the House Oversight and Government Reform Committee, where investigators found that 400,000 of the individual enrollments counted in the May HHS data were for dental plans only and not medical options. HHS secretary Sylvia Matthews Burwell called the error an oversight and the mistake "unacceptable." House Oversight Committee chairman Darrell Issa, R-Calif., was unwilling to accept the department's apology. "The claim that this was only [an] accident stretches credulity," he said. HHS promised that any future releases of data would not include dental-only enrollees. The overstated data was repeated in an October report, which was then adjusted in November.

Not only has HHS been under fire for overstating its data, it has also faced criticism for its failure to consistently release data. Some of the thirteen state exchanges have provided constant updates, with Massachusetts providing daily traffic figures from its exchange website. By contrast, HHS has released data in piecemeal fashion. Consumer advocacy and health care groups have urged the department to be more transparent in reporting enrollment data. "Everybody needs the data," said Betsy Imholz, special projects director at Consumers Union. "What we want is regular, transparent data so we can make good policy choices going forward." According to the Centers for Medicare and Medicaid Services administrator Marilyn Tavenner, the site still needs to complete some back-end technology work before it can easily pull and report enrollment statistics.

Uncertainty Ahead

The second ACA enrollment period began in October 2014 and would run through February 15, 2015. HHS hoped to enroll or re-enroll between nine million and 9.9 million individuals during this period. According to HHS, on the first day of open enrollment, half a million people logged into www.healthcare.gov, with 100,000 signing up for coverage. It was expected that many of the insurance options offered on the exchange would raise their premiums during the second enrollment period, and questions remain about whether those who signed up during the first enrollment period would choose different, cheaper options, or opt to find health insurance coverage elsewhere. There was also the remaining question about whether the millions of uninsured Americans who did not choose a plan during the first enrollment period would seek health insurance during the new open enrollment period.

Like the federal government, the thirteen states that chose to offer their own exchanges had greater success at the start of the second enrollment period than they had experienced in 2013. States like Maryland and Massachusetts, which experienced rollout issues similar to that of the federal exchange, reported no major problems. Only Washington State's exchange website was temporarily shut down to correct a glitch that was giving users incorrect subsidy information.

Even though the state and federal exchanges have overcome a majority of their initial problems, uncertainties still abound for the ACA. Republicans, who have fought against the law since its inception, took control of Congress during the November midterm elections. One Republican, Sen. Marco Rubio of Florida, noted that one of the first things Republicans would do after taking office in January 2015 would be to review the ACA and dismantle certain portions of it. "One of the biggest threats to the American dream is the rising cost of living, which Obamacare is making worse through rising health care costs and loss of coverage," Rubio said in January 2015. Echoing his remarks, Rep. Andy Harris, R-Md., added, "The American people should not have to shoulder the burden of the president's failed health-care plan." Both Rubio and Harris have sponsored bills in their respective chambers to ensure that the federal government does not use the ACA to bail out health insurance providers.

—Heather Kerrigan

Following are excerpts from the Department of Health and Human Services' May 1, 2014, report on Affordable Care Act insurance coverage during the first enrollment period.

DOCUMENT   *HHS Report Details ACA Enrollment*

May 1, 2014

[Footnotes and figures have been omitted.]

This is the sixth in a series of issue briefs highlighting national and state-level enrollment-related information for the Health Insurance Marketplace (Marketplace). This brief includes data for states that are implementing their own Marketplaces (also known as State-Based Marketplaces or SBMs), and states with Marketplaces that are supported by or fully run by the Department of Health and Human Services (including those run in partnership with states, also known as the Federally-facilitated Marketplace or FFM).

This brief also includes updated data on the characteristics of persons who have selected a Marketplace plan (by gender, age, and financial assistance status) and the plans that they have selected (by metal level). Additionally, for the first time, Appendix C of this report includes self-reported race/ethnicity data on persons who have selected a Marketplace plan through the FFM. This report also includes data on other characteristics of people who have selected plans in the FFM and the plans they have selected. (Detailed state-level tables can be found in Appendix E, and in the Addendum to the Report).

KEY MARKETPLACE ENROLLMENT STATISTICS

- **Over 8 million** people have selected a plan through the Health Insurance Marketplace (SBMs and FFM) through March 31st (including additional special enrollment period (SEP) activity reported through Saturday, April 19th).
- **2.2 million (28 percent)** of the people who selected a Marketplace plan during the initial open enrollment period were young adults between the ages of 18 and 34. A total of 2.7 million (34 percent) were between the ages of 0 and 34 (including additional SEP activity reported through Saturday, April 19th).
- **Nearly 3.8 million** people selected a Marketplace plan during the March enrollment surge at the end of the initial open enrollment period, including nearly **1.2 million** young adults (ages 18-34), or 31 percent of the total surge, who selected a Marketplace plan during March (including additional SEP activity reported through Saturday, April 19th).
- **47 percent** of the total number of people who selected a Marketplace plan and **52 percent** of the young adults (ages 18-34) who selected a Marketplace plan did so during the last month of the initial open enrollment period (including additional SEP activity reported through Saturday, April 19th).
- The number of young adults who selected Marketplace plans doubled during the last month of the initial open enrollment period, from nearly 1.1 million (during the first 5 months) to more than 2.2 million (including additional SEP activity reported through Saturday, April 19th).
- Over the course of the initial open enrollment period, consumer interest in the Marketplace was high, as measured by 98 million website visits and 33 million calls to the call centers (FFM and SBMs combined, including additional SEP activity reported through Saturday, April 19th).

This report captures cumulative enrollment-related activity during the initial open enrollment period (10-1-13 to 3-31-14), including activity associated with individuals who qualified for a Special Enrollment Period (SEP) that was reported through 4-19-14. The data on SEP activity include information for those who qualified for an SEP because they were "in line" on 3-31-14, as well as those who qualified for an SEP for other reasons. Several metrics are reported, including: the number of visits to the Marketplace websites, the number of calls to the Marketplace call centers, the number of persons who have been determined or assessed eligible by the Marketplaces for Medicaid or the Children's Health Insurance Program (CHIP), and the number of persons who have selected a plan through the Marketplace.

The cumulative number of individuals that have selected a Marketplace plan between 10-1-13 and 3-31-14, including additional SEP activity reported through April 19th is over 8 million (including those who have paid a premium and those who have not yet paid a premium).

. . . consistent with expectations, the proportion of young adults (ages 18 to 34) who have selected a Marketplace plan through the SBMs and FFM has remained strong. Young adults accounted for 31 percent of the Marketplace plan selections after March 1st, which was 4 percentage points higher than their share of plan selections between 12-29-13 and

3-1-14 (27 percent) and 7 percentage points higher than their share of plan selections between 10-1-13 and 12-28-13 (24 percent). Meanwhile, the proportion of older adults (ages 35 and over) selecting a Marketplace plan has continued to decrease (from 70 percent between 10-1-13 and 12-28-13 to 62 percent after March 1st).

There was an 89 percent increase in the cumulative number of individuals who selected a Marketplace plan after March 1st (including SEP activity through 4-19-14).

The total number of new Marketplace plan selections was significantly higher after March 1st (including SEP activity through 4-19-14) when compared with comparable data for February (nearly 3.8 million versus 0.9 million, respectively), consistent with expectations that the rate of Marketplace plan selections would increase as the March 31, 2014 end of the initial open enrollment period approached.

Enrollment Growth in March

As expected, an enrollment surge occurred in March as the close of the open enrollment period approached for the Marketplace. This is consistent with the experience of private employers, the Federal Employees Health Benefits Program (FEHBP), and Medicare Part D.

. . . approximately 0.9 million (12 percent) of the more than 8 million total Marketplace plan selections during the initial open enrollment period (including SEP activity through 4-19-14) were selected after 3-31-14.

As discussed earlier, the total number of Marketplace plan selections at the end of the initial open enrollment period was over 8 million (including SEP activity through 4-19-14). We note that the Congressional Budget Office (CBO) Marketplace enrollment projection of 6 million for 2014 is estimated based on average enrollment for the calendar year (full-year equivalents from CMS enrollment data will not be available until sometime in 2015). It is important to note that the Marketplace plan selection data as of the end of the open enrollment period do not represent effectuated enrollment (e.g., those who have paid their premium), and does not include the additional persons who will experience a qualifying life event (also known as a change in life circumstances, such as having a baby, getting married, getting divorced, or losing other coverage) that enables them to qualify for an SEP and enroll in Marketplace coverage for 2014 through the end of the year.

Effectuated Enrollment

CMS does not yet have comprehensive and accurate data about effectuated enrollment (that is, the number of individuals who have effectuated their enrollment and gained coverage through payment of the first premium). However, some issuers have made public statements indicating that 80 percent to 90 percent of the people who have selected a Marketplace plan have made premium payments. Issuers have the flexibility to determine when premium payments are due.

Increase in Health Insurance Coverage

In addition to the more than 8 million people who have selected plans through the Marketplace during the initial open enrollment period (including SEP activity through 4-19-14), CBO recently estimated that an additional 5 million people have purchased coverage outside of the Marketplace in Affordable Care Act-compliant plans. Meanwhile, the Blue Cross Blue

Shield Association estimates that its plans have enrolled 1.7 million in Affordable Care Act-compliant, off-Marketplace plans. Additionally, E-Health reports that 45 percent of its off-Marketplace enrollees from January through early March of 2014 were ages 18 to 34.

Moreover, recent national surveys indicate that the number of Americans with health insurance coverage is growing, and the number of 18 to 64 year olds who are uninsured is declining. For example, Gallup has found a 3 percentage point decrease in the uninsured rate for adults (18 to 64) from the third quarter of 2014 to March 2014 (18 percent versus 15 percent, respectively, corresponding to a 7.26 million decline in the number of uninsured adults). Similarly, the Urban Institute estimates a 2.7 percentage point decrease in the uninsured rate for adults (18 to 64) from October 1, 2013 to March 31, 2014 (corresponding to a 5.4 million decline in the number of uninsured adults). Meanwhile, the RAND Corporation estimates a 4.7 percentage point decrease in the uninsured rate (corresponding to a net decrease of 9.3 million uninsured adults, ages of 18 to 64) from the last week of September 2013 through March 2014.

Single Risk Pool in Each State

To increase stability and comparability in health plan rating, the Affordable Care Act requires a single risk pool in each state, encompassing both plans that were purchased inside of the Marketplace ("Marketplace plans") and Affordable Care Act-compliant plans that were purchased outside of the Marketplace. Risk-adjustment occurs across all plans in each state's single risk pool. The Department will have more complete data on the size of the single risk pool in each state as issuers report their enrollment for medical loss ratio, rate review, and risk adjustment purposes over the course of the next year.

Enrollment Growth at the End of the Open Enrollment Period

There was continued growth in total Marketplace plan selections after March 1st (including SEP activity through 4-19-14), compared to the October-February period:

- **Marketplace Total (SBMs and FFM)** – there was an 89 percent increase in plan selections after March 1st (including SEP activity through 4-19-14)
  - o the 4.2 million cumulative number in October-February rose by nearly 3.8 million after March 1st to a cumulative total of more than 8 million (including SEP activity through 4-19-14)

- **SBMs** – there was a 59 percent increase in plan selections after March 1st (including SEP activity through 4-19-14)
  - o the 1.6 million cumulative number for October-February rose by more than 0.9 million after March 1st to a cumulative total of nearly 2.6 million (including SEP activity through 4-19-14)

- **FFM** – there was a 108 percent increase in plan selections after March 1st (including SEP activity through 4-19-14)
  - o the 2.6 million cumulative number in October-February rose by 2.8 million after March 1st to a cumulative total of 5.4 million (including SEP activity through 4-19-14)

The following are highlights of Marketplace enrollment-related information for the initial open enrollment period, including additional SEP activity through 4-19-14. . . .

Cumulative Highlights for the period: October 1, 2013 – March 31, 2014 (including Additional Special Enrollment Period Activity through 4-19-14)

Marketplace Eligibility Determinations and Plan Selection

- Number of Eligible Persons who have Selected a Plan through the SBMs and FFM: 8 million
- Number of Persons who have had a Medicaid/CHIP Determination or Assessment through the Marketplaces: 6.7 million (does not include individuals applying through State Medicaid/CHIP agencies.)

Marketplace Plan Selection by Gender

- 46 percent of the persons who have selected a Marketplace plan are male
- 54 percent of the persons who have selected a Marketplace plan are female Marketplace Plan Selection by Age
- 28 percent of the persons who have selected a Marketplace plan are between the ages of 18 and 34

    o The percentage of young adults among persons who selected a Marketplace plan after March 1st (31 percent) was 4 percentage points higher than it was in January and February, and 7 percentage points higher than it was from October through December (27 percent and 24 percent, respectively)

- 34 percent of the persons who have selected a Marketplace plan are between the ages of 0 and 34

Marketplace Plan Selection by Metal Level

- 20 percent of the persons who have selected a Marketplace plan have selected a Bronze plan
- 65 percent of the persons who have selected a Marketplace plan have selected a Silver plan
- 9 percent of the persons who have selected a Marketplace plan have selected a Gold plan
- 5 percent of the persons who have selected a Marketplace plan have selected a Platinum plan
- 2 percent of the persons who have selected a Marketplace plan have selected a Catastrophic plan

Marketplace Plan Selection by Financial Assistance Status

- 85 percent of the persons who have selected a Marketplace plan have selected a Marketplace Plan with Financial Assistance

FFM Marketplace Plan Selection by Gender and Age

- 29 percent of the males who have selected a Marketplace plan through the FFM are between 18 and 34

- 28 percent of the females who have selected a Marketplace plan through the FFM are between 18 and 34

FFM Marketplace Plan Selection by Gender and Metal Level

- 71 percent of the females who have selected a Marketplace plan through the FFM have selected a Silver plan
- 67 percent of the males who have selected a Marketplace plan through the FFM have selected a Silver plan

FFM Marketplace Plan Selection by Financial Assistance Status and Metal Level

- 76 percent of the persons who have selected a Marketplace plan with Financial Assistance through the FFM have selected a Silver plan
- 95 percent of the persons selecting a Silver plan in the FFM will be receiving Federal financial assistance in paying their premiums
- 25 percent of the persons who have selected a Marketplace plan without Financial Assistance through the FFM have selected a Silver plan
- 33 percent of the persons who have selected a Marketplace plan without Financial Assistance through the FFM have selected a Bronze plan

FFM Marketplace Plan Selection by Metal Level and Age

- 68 percent of the young adults between the ages of 18 and 34 who selected a Marketplace plan through the FFM selected a Silver plan
- 17 percent of the young adults between the ages of 18 and 34 who selected a Marketplace plan through the FFM selected a Bronze plan
- 7 percent of the young adults between the ages of 18 and 34 who selected a Marketplace plan through the FFM selected a Gold plan
- 4 percent of the young adults between the ages of 18 and 34 who selected a Marketplace plan through the FFM selected a Platinum plan
- 5 percent of the young adults between the ages of 18 and 34 who selected a Marketplace plan through the FFM selected a Catastrophic plan

    o Young adults account for 83 percent of all catastrophic plan selections through the FFM. . . .

OVERVIEW OF ENROLLMENT-RELATED ACTIVITY TO DATE

Selected a Marketplace Plan – Over 8 million persons selected a Marketplace plan during the initial open enrollment period (including additional SEP activity through 4-19-14), including nearly 2.6 million in SBMs and 5.4 million in the FFM (these numbers include those who have paid a premium and those who have not yet paid a premium, regardless of when their coverage begins).

The following are additional highlights of the data on the characteristics of Marketplace plan selections during the initial open enrollment period, including SEP activity through 4-19-14. . . .

- *Marketplace Plan Selections by Gender* – The gender distribution of Marketplace plan selections has remained constant. More than half of the people who have selected a Marketplace plan through the SBMs and FFM between 10-1-13 and 3-31-14 (including additional SEP activity through 4-19-14) are female (54 percent of the total for the Marketplace as a whole, excluding plan selections where gender is unknown), while the remaining 46 percent are male. The comparable proportions for the first five months of the initial open enrollment period were 55 percent and 45 percent, respectively.

o SBMs: 53 percent female, 47 percent male (10-1-13 to 3-31-14, including SEP activity through 4-19-14).

o FFM: 55 percent female, 45 percent male (10-1-13 to 3-31-14, including SEP activity through 4-19-14).

By comparison, males account for half (50 percent) of the total non-elderly population in the United States (ages 0 to 64).

- *Marketplace Plan Selections by Metal Level* – The proportion of Silver Marketplace plan selections has continued to increase. Silver plans account for nearly two-thirds (65 percent) of the Marketplace plan selections in the SBMs and FFM between 10-1-13 and 3-31-14, including additional SEP activity through 4-19-14 (compared with 63 percent during the first five months of the initial enrollment period).

o SBMs: 58 percent Silver (10-1-13 to 3-31-14, including SEP activity through 4-19-14).

o FFM: 69 percent Silver (10-1-13 to 3-31-14, including SEP activity through 4-19-14).

The metal level distribution of the remaining Marketplace plan selections (SBMs and FFM combined) are as follows: bronze (20 percent), gold (9 percent), platinum (5 percent), and catastrophic (2 percent).

- *Marketplace Plan Selections by Financial Assistance Status* – The proportion of Marketplace plan selections with financial assistance (i.e., Marketplace plan selections by individuals who are eligible to receive financial assistance) has also continued to increase. More than eight out of ten (85 percent) of the people who selected a Marketplace plan through the SBMs and FFM between 10-1-13 and 3-31-14 (including additional SEP activity through 4-19-14) are eligible to receive Federal financial assistance in paying their premiums. The comparable proportion for the first five months of the initial open enrollment period was 83 percent.

o SBMs: 82 percent in Marketplace plans with financial assistance (10-1-13 to 3-31-14, including SEP activity through 4-19-14).

o FFM: 86 percent in Marketplace plans with financial assistance (10-1-13 to 3-31-14, including SEP activity through 4-19-14).

Tax credits for premium assistance may be available to individuals with family incomes between 100 and 400 percent of the Federal Poverty Level (138 to 400 percent of FPL in states taking the Federally-funded option to expand Medicaid). These percentages are consistent with previous estimates. It is also important to note that people who are not eligible for advance premium tax credits may have chosen to enroll in an Affordable Care Act-compliant, off-Marketplace plan instead; including them in the denominator would lower the percentages of people in Affordable Care Act-compliant plans in the individual market who are receiving premium assistance.

Additional Characteristics of FFM Marketplace Plan Selections – The following are highlights of data on additional characteristics of FFM Marketplace plan selections between 10-1-13 and 3- 31-14 (including additional SEP activity through 4-19-14), based on cross-tabulations of the above mentioned metrics. . . .

- *FFM Marketplace Plan Selections by Gender and Age*

  o Young adults (ages 18-34) accounted for 29 percent of all males selecting Marketplace plans through the FFM, compared with 28 percent of all females selecting Marketplace plans through the FFM, and 28 percent of all FFM Marketplace plan selections as a whole.

  o Meanwhile, adding children ages 0 to 17 results in males between the ages of 0 and 34 accounting for over a third (36 percent) of all males selecting Marketplace plans through the FFM, compared with 33 percent for females, and 35 percent for all persons who selected a Marketplace plan through the FFM.

- *FFM Marketplace Plan Selections by Gender and Metal Level*

  o Females were more likely to select Silver plans in the FFM (71 percent versus 67 percent for males).

  o Males were more likely to select Bronze plans in the FFM (19 percent versus 16 percent for females).

- *FFM Marketplace Plan Selections by Financial Assistance Status and Metal Level*

  o Persons selecting a Marketplace plan who are eligible to receive financial assistance were more likely to select Silver plans in the FFM (76 percent versus 25 percent for persons selecting a Silver Marketplace plan without financial assistance).

  o Persons selecting a Marketplace plan without financial assistance were more likely to select Bronze plans in the FFM than other metal levels (33 percent versus 15 percent for persons selecting a Marketplace plan with financial assistance). They were also more likely to select gold, platinum and catastrophic plans than were persons who are eligible to receive financial assistance.

  o More than nine out of ten (95 percent) of the persons selecting a Silver plan in the FFM are eligible to receive Federal financial assistance in paying their premiums.

- *FFM Marketplace Plan Selections by Metal Level and Age*

  o Among young adults (ages 18 to 34), 68 percent selected a Silver plan, while 17 percent selected a Bronze plan, 7 percent selected a Gold plan, 4 percent selected a Platinum plan, and 5 percent selected a Catastrophic plan.

  o One out of three (34 percent) of the 1.1 million persons who selected a stand-alone dental plan through the FFM are young adults (ages 18-34).

Web Site and Call Center Volume – There were 98 million visits to the SBM and FFM websites, and 33 million calls to the SBM and FFM call centers between 10-1-13 and 3-31-14 (including additional SEP activity through 4-19-14).

[The remainder of the report, containing the appendices, has been omitted.]

Source: U.S. Department of Health and Human Services. "Health Insurance Marketplace: Summary Enrollment Report for the Initial Annual Open Enrollment Period." May 1, 2014. http://aspe.hhs.gov/health/reports/2014/MarketPlaceEnrollment/Apr2014/ib_2014Apr_enrollment.pdf.

OTHER HISTORIC DOCUMENTS OF INTEREST

FROM PREVIOUS *HISTORIC DOCUMENTS*

Nigerian Government and African Union Respond to Kidnapping by Boko Haram

MAY 2 AND 8, 2014

On an April evening in Nigeria's northeastern Borno State, Islamic extremists kidnapped more than 200 teenage girls from a school in the region. The girls' abduction was the latest incident in a growing Islamic insurgency led by the jihadist group Boko Haram that has racked the country, resulting in thousands of deaths and forcing more than one million Nigerians from their homes. The Nigerian government's slow response to the kidnapping and seeming inability to locate and rescue the girls sparked protests by the girls' family members and their supporters—including those in major international cities—who criticized President Goodluck Jonathan and called for him to act more aggressively to bring the girls home.

Students Seized

In mid-April, hundreds of students from across the Borno State were called to the Government Girls Secondary School, an elite academy for Muslim and Christian girls in the town of Chibok. Schools in the region had been closed for four weeks because of recent attacks by Boko Haram on nearby villages and schools, but the students were now being called in for exams. On the evening of April 14, Islamic militants kidnapped more than 200 girls between sixteen and eighteen years old, loading them into the backs of pickup trucks before setting the school on fire.

Initially, the Nigerian government was unable to provide an accurate count of how many students had been taken and how many had managed to escape. Education officials first reported that eighty-five girls had been kidnapped. On April 16, Major General Chris Olukolade, a spokesperson for Nigeria's Ministry of Defense, claimed that the military had returned more than eighty girls to their families and that only eight were still missing. Yet two days later, it became clear that report had been fabricated, as officials reported that 129 girls had been kidnapped and eighty-five were still missing; the other twenty-four had managed to escape, they said, by either jumping off the back of their abductors' trucks or running into the neighboring Sambisa Forest. On April 21, Borno State governor Kashim Settima visited the school, where the girls' parents gave him a list of 234 students who were missing. Around the same time, the Chibok school's principal, Asabe Kwambura, told the Associated Press that forty-three students had been accounted for and that 230 were still missing.

The conflicting reports and misinformation from the government spurred early criticisms and frustrations from the girls' parents, their supporters, and foreign officials. "The failure of the government to even get a clear count further reinforces a perception of systemic governmental failure that plays into the narrative not only of Boko Haram, but also other dissident groups opposing Nigeria's constitutional order," said J. Peter Pham, director of the Atlantic Council's Africa Center.

On May 1, Borno State police commissioner Tanko Lawan reported that 276 girls were missing and that fifty-three had escaped their kidnappers. Lawan explained that it had been difficult for officials to determine the final numbers because students from around the state had been brought to the Chibok school. "The students were drawn from schools in Izge, Lassa, Ashigashiya and Warabe A. and that is why, after the unfortunate incident, there were various numbers flying around as to the actual number of girls that were taken away," Lawan said.

Boko Haram Claims Responsibility

On May 5, the Islamic jihadist and terrorist organization Boko Haram claimed responsibility for the kidnapping. In a video, the group's leader, Abubakar Shekau, threatened to sell the girls into slavery; he would later release another video calling for the government to exchange imprisoned Boko Haram militants for the girls.

Based in northeast Nigeria, Boko Haram seeks to institute an Islamic caliphate in the country, but a particularly radical version of one. Many Muslims in Nigeria who support Sharia law do not agree with Boko Haram's views because of their extremism. The group is particularly opposed to Western-style modern education, claiming it diverts people from following true Islam. In fact, the name Boko Haram means "Western education is sinful." The group has killed thousands of Nigerians across dozens of attacks and has targeted schools since 2010, promising to continue such acts for as long as the government interferes with traditional Islamic education. In the months before the Chibok school kidnapping, Boko Haram invaded two villages in Borno State, rounding up approximately 100 Christian men before brutally killing them; overtaken more than a dozen villages in eastern Nigeria, causing thousands of people to flee; attacked the Giwa military barracks in an effort to free imprisoned comrades; and set off a bomb at a bus station in Abuja, killing seventy-five. They also abducted another eight schoolgirls on May 5.

Nigeria has primarily relied on its poorly trained and ill-equipped military to fight back against Boko Haram, rather than a more comprehensive counterinsurgency effort—a strategy that has been largely unsuccessful. Nigeria has also contended with a lack of cooperation from neighboring Cameroon, Niger, and Chad, which have allowed Boko Haram militants to take refuge in those countries when facing attack. Shortly before the kidnapping in Chibok, the Nigerian government conducted air raids in the Sambisa Forest, a known refuge of the terrorists, and around the mountain caves along the border with Chad.

Local and Global Outcry over Attack, Government Inaction

The international community immediately condemned the kidnapping and called for the girls' release. The African Union Commission Chairperson's Special Envoy for Women, Peace and Security issued a particularly strong statement condemning the "horrific abduction of young girls," stating that "attacks against the liberty of children and targeting schools are prohibited under international law and cannot be justified under any circumstance." The envoy added, "Schools are and must remain places of safety and security, where children can learn and grow in peace. Girls and young women must be allowed to go to school without fear of violence and unjust treatment and exercise their rightful role as equal citizens of the world."

Leaders from countries including the United Kingdom, France, China, Israel, and the United States pledged to provide assistance to Nigeria, particularly in the form of intelligence experts and reconnaissance aircraft, to help the government find and rescue the girls. In some cases, the Nigerian government was slow to respond. U.S. secretary of state John Kerry noted that the United States had been offering to help "from day one," but the offers were ignored until early May.

Indeed, President Jonathan did not publicly acknowledge the kidnapping until a rally held in support of the girls' families on May 1. "The cruel abduction of some innocent girls, our future mothers and leaders, in a very horrific and despicable situation in Borno state is quite regrettable," he said, adding that Nigeria would "triumph over all this evil that wants to debase our humanity." The president's slow response and the lack of progress in finding the girls frustrated their parents, prompting some to search the Sambisa Forest on their own. People across Nigeria protested in the country's major cities, accusing the government of acting too slowly and inefficiently. Their anger gave rise to an international social media campaign, #BringBackOurGirls, that went viral and even extended offline as the group behind the campaign organized rallies in cities across the United States and in London. Nigerian officials claimed they were doing all they could to find the girls. "Every information relayed to security agencies has so far been investigated, including the search of all places suspected as a possible hide-away of the kidnapped girls," said Information Minister Labaran Maku.

A report released in May by Amnesty International created new challenges for the government. According to the report, Nigerian authorities received an alert about a potential attack in Chibok hours before the kidnapping occurred. Civilian patrols in a neighboring village began a chain of warning calls the night of April 14 after they saw unidentified armed men on motorcycles in town. Two senior military officials had confirmed to Amnesty International that the military had indeed known about the planned attack. "The fact that Nigerian security forces knew about Boko Haram's impending raid, but failed to take the immediate action needed to stop it, will only amplify the national and international outcry at this horrific crime," said Netsanet Belay, Amnesty International's Africa director for research and advocacy.

Amid these criticisms, President Jonathan convened a meeting on May 2 with Vice President Namadi Sambo, Defense Minister General Aliyu Gusau, and various service chiefs and heads of security agencies to discuss the country's security situation, including the Chibok kidnapping. The security chiefs briefed the other officials on their efforts to find the girls, noting that the Air Force had conducted extensive air surveillance of all routes leading into and out of Chibok all the way to the borders of Chad and Cameroon, and that they had also been searching other parts of Borno and Adamawa States. They added that they had been investigating any and all leads on suspected hiding places and would continue to search possible locations. The president instructed the security agencies to take additional measures to enhance public safety and called for intensified efforts to find the girls, including increased cooperation from the public to share information. "Wherever the girls are in the world, we will get them back, apprehend and punish the culprits," Jonathan said.

As the weeks passed, new developments were few and far between. Protests continued throughout Nigeria, with #BringBackOurGirls at one point threatening to sue the Nigerian government over demonstrators' arrests. On June 2, Police Commissioner Joseph Mbu announced a ban on protests surrounding the kidnapping, claiming they posed "a serious security threat." However, his office released a statement the following day saying that the ban did not in fact exist. "The Police High Command wishes to inform the general public that the Force has not issued any order banning peaceful assemblies/protests anywhere in Nigeria," the statement read. "The Police only issued advisory notice, enjoining citizens to apply caution in the said rallies, particularly in the Federal Capital Territory and its environs." Doyin Okupe, an adviser to the president, defended the commissioner in an interview with CNN, saying it was "like asking people, look, before you go on a protest, you have to come to the police, to come and clear with the police and let us work together to ensure that nobody's life is in danger." Okupe also told CNN that the military knew where the girls were, "but as you will understand, you just cannot storm a place like that." Officials had reportedly ruled out the possibility of a military effort to try to free the girls due to fears they could be killed. Several analysts suggested that the only way to resolve the situation was to negotiate with Boko Haram, but President Jonathan refused to do so.

In October, Human Rights Watch released a report, based on witness accounts and escapees, that described the abuses suffered by Boko Haram's female captives, including forced marriages and religious conversions, rape, and slave labor. Borno-Yobe People's Forum also reported that some of the kidnapped girls were being sold into marriage to militants for roughly $12 and that some had been taken across Nigeria's borders into Cameroon and Chad.

Girls Still Missing

In mid-October, roughly six months after the kidnapping, the Nigerian army announced that the girls would be released as part of a truce between the government and Boko Haram. The truce was reportedly reached after a month of negotiations that had taken place in Saudi Arabia. The news was met with skepticism, however, since the military had to retract a similar announcement in September. As of the end of 2014, the kidnapped girls have not been released.

—Linda Fecteau Grimm

Following is a press statement by the Nigerian minister of information on May 2, 2014, regarding the kidnapping of more than 200 schoolgirls; and a statement by the African Union on May 8, 2014, condemning Boko Haram for the kidnapping and calling for a return of the schoolgirls.

Nigerian Government Remarks on Kidnapping by Boko Haram

May 2, 2014

President Goodluck Jonathan today called a high-level meeting at Aso Villa to review the security situation in the country, particularly the bombing at Nyanya yesterday, and the unfortunate kidnapping by suspected terrorists of girls of Government Secondary School, Chibok, Borno State, on 15th April, 2014. The meeting was attended by Vice President Namadi Sambo, Defence Minister General Aliyu Gusau (rtd), Service Chiefs and heads of security agencies.

The meeting received updates on the second Nyanya bombing, the ongoing search for the Chibok girls, and efforts made so far to deal with related incidents of insecurity and terrorism in the country. On the latest bomb explosion in Nyanya, the President directed security chiefs to increase surveillance and expedite investigation into the explosion to ensure that those behind the heinous act are arrested and brought to justice. The President also gave instructions for additional proactive measures by security agencies to enhance public safety, including increased public awareness for citizens to step up their cooperation with security agencies by reporting suspected activities and persons likely to cause a breach of public peace, safety and security.

On the unfortunate kidnap of the Chibok girls, the security chiefs briefed the meeting on efforts so far made to locate and rescue the girls, and bring the perpetrators to justice. Extensive and intensive aerial surveillance by the Air Force has been carried out in all the routes leading into and out of Chibok up to the Chad and Cameroun borders. Other parts of Borno and Adamawa states are also under the searchlight. Every information relayed to security agencies has so far been investigated, including the search of all places suspected as a possible hide-away of the kidnapped girls. The police, backed up by the military and DSS, have combed and are still combing all reported places that the girls might have been taken to. In view of the inconsistent and contradictory information available to government on the Chibok abduction, the President has set up a fact-finding committee comprising security agencies, civil society, international organisations and other stakeholders.

The President commiserates with the families of the deceased in the latest bombing at Nyanya, and empathises with all those who were injured in the incident. He has also directed full medical treatment for the victims at government expense. The President also shares in the pain and anguish of the parents and guardians of the Chibok girls abducted by the terrorists. The President's heart goes out to these our unfortunate daughters who have had to endure the trauma of abduction and separation from their loved ones. The government and people of Nigeria stand solidly by them. The President further appeals to the parents, guardians, relations and members of the public to furnish security agencies with all the information that will assist in the rescue of the girls.

Government also appreciates the public outpouring of support and the sentiment expressed so far by all Nigerians, including civil society groups who have come out to condemn the abduction of the girls and terrorism in the country. Government strongly believes that the people of Nigeria, standing together, will overcome the current security challenges. The President has directed that the security agencies should intensify efforts to rescue the Chibok girls. The President assures Nigerians that "wherever the girls are in the world, we will get them back, apprehend and punish the culprits".

SOURCE: Federal Republic of Nigeria. "Press Statement by the Hon. Minister of Information, Labaran Maku, on the Current Security Situation in the Country." May 2, 2014. http://fmi.gov.ng/latest/50237.

African Union Remarks on Kidnapping in Nigeria

May 8, 2014

We strongly condemn the horrific abduction of young girls from the Chibok Government Girls Secondary School in Borno State in Nigeria.

We are extremely concerned that about 230 young girls aged between 16-18 were taken from their school on the night of 14th April, 2014, and horrified that Eight more girls were abducted on Monday, May 5, 2014 in the same province of Borno.

We send our sympathy to the families of the children, and urge those who are responsible for their abduction to release them unharmed, and return them to their families, where they rightfully belong.

Attacks against the liberty of children and targeting schools are prohibited under international law and cannot be justified under any circumstance. Not on our watch.

Schools are and must remain places of safety and security, where children can learn and grow in peace. Girls and young women must be allowed to go to school without fear of violence and unjust treatment and exercise their rightful role as equal citizens of the world.

The Protocol to the African Charter on Human and on the Rights of Women in Africa states, "Every woman shall have the right to respect as a person and to the free development of her personality". Women and girls have the right to live free from intimidation, persecution and all other forms of discrimination.

The Charter further stipulates that "States Parties shall adopt and implement appropriate measures to ensure the protection of every woman's right to respect for her dignity and protection of women from all forms of violence, particularly sexual and verbal violence".

We call on the Nigerian Government, regional organizations, the AU and the international community to join forces to urgently and decisively act to bring the children home to their families and protect them from further danger.

We stand with the Nigerian people, especially the parents and families of the abducted girls.

SOURCE: African Union. "Statement on the Kidnapping of the Nigerian School Girls from the Office of the African Union Commission (AUC) Chairperson's Special Envoy for Women, Peace and Security." May 8, 2014. www.au.int/en/sites/default/files/Statement%20on%20the%20Kidnapping%20of%20the%20 Nigerian%20School%20Girls%20office%20of%20the%20AUC%20Chairperson.pdf.

OTHER HISTORIC DOCUMENTS OF INTEREST

Supreme Court Rules on
Prayer in Council Meetings

MAY 5, 2014

In *Town of Greece v. Galloway*, the Supreme Court ruled on whether a small upstate New York town's practice of opening its town board meetings with a prayer led by a local clergy violated the Establishment Clause of the First Amendment when, over the course of eight years, all the participating ministers were Christian and gave overtly Christian prayers. In a narrowly divided opinion that split the Court 5–4, Justice Anthony M. Kennedy, writing for the majority, found no constitutional violation. His opinion emphasized the history and tradition of legislative prayer in our country because it has been practiced continuously since the very framing of the Constitution. He concluded that nothing in this case distinguished it from a line of cases that found such ceremonies to be "deeply embedded in the history and tradition of this country." The dissent, written by Justice Elena Kagan, emphasized her agreement with the precedents and the idea that government need not be a "religion-free zone." But in this case, she thought, as did the other dissenters, there were some important differences that should have led to a different result. Although the Court split along its ideological divide with the Court's conservative members in the majority, the administration of President Barack Obama had supported the Town of Greece, the winning party.

THE COURT AND PRAYER IN LEGISLATIVE SESSIONS

The First Amendment to the Constitution contains what is known as the "Establishment Clause," which reads: "Congress shall make no law respecting an establishment of religion." In 1983, the Supreme Court, in *Marsh v. Chambers*, delivered the definitive precedent regarding the application of this constitutional prohibition to the practice of opening state legislative sessions with a prayer. In that case, the Court ruled that Nebraska's long tradition of opening its legislature with a prayer delivered by a chaplain paid with state funds was in the same tradition as the opening of the U.S. Congress with prayer, a practice that goes back to the very start of the country. In fact, one of the first acts of the First Congress, shortly after passing the First Amendment, was to appoint and pay official chaplains. After exploring this tradition, the Court concluded that "in light of the unambiguous and unbroken history of more than 200 years, there can be no doubt that the practice of opening legislative sessions with prayer has become part of the fabric of our society." Because the *Marsh* precedent is so clear, the issue that the Supreme Court in *Town of Greece v. Galloway* had to decide was whether the facts differed in any appreciable way so as to lead to a different result.

The town of Greece, New York, has a population of 94,000 and holds monthly town board meetings that, since 1999, have started with a roll call, a recitation of the Pledge of Allegiance, and a prayer given by a clergy who is selected on a rotating basis from local congregations listed in the town directory. The majority of congregations in town are Christian and, although the prayer program is open to all, the participating ministers as of 2007 had been exclusively Christian. Guest clergy were free to compose their own prayers and many used a very distinctly Christian idiom, some inviting all present to stand and bow their heads and pray. Susan Galloway and Linda Stephens attended the board meeting to speak about issues of local concern and objected to the prayers. They filed suit alleging that the town violated the First Amendment's Establishment Clause by preferring Christians over other prayer givers and by sponsoring sectarian prayers, such as those given "in Jesus' name." The District Court found that the town's practices were consistent with the First Amendment but was overturned on appeal by the Second Circuit Court of Appeals, which held that some aspects of the prayer program, "viewed in their totality by a reasonable observer, conveyed the message that Greece was endorsing Christianity."

The Supreme Court granted certiorari to decide whether the town's practices violated the Establishment Clause and reversed the Second Circuit.

MAJORITY FINDS NO CONSTITUTIONAL VIOLATION

The Court examined the town of Greece's prayer practice to determine whether it fit within the history and tradition long followed by Congress and the state legislatures. The respondents argued that the town's practice varied from those approved by the Court in earlier precedents both in the content of the prayer and in the context. Justice Kennedy wrote the opinion that rejected both of these arguments. He was joined in his full opinion by Chief Justice John G. Roberts Jr. and Justice Samuel A. Alito, while Justices Antonin Scalia and Clarence Thomas joined most of the opinion and concurred with the judgment.

Unlike the prayers at issue in the *Marsh* case, which were predominantly nonsectarian, those at issue in this case were described as "overtly Christian" in content. Those challenging the prayers argued that the First Amendment should require legislative prayer to be "nonsectarian, or not identifiable with any one religion." After discussing the explicitly religious themes of our earliest congressional invocations, the majority held that the prayers here were consistent with the nation's traditions. Legislative prayers do not need to be scrubbed of any reference to a specific religion to satisfy the Establishment Clause, which, according to the Court, does not require that the prayers mention only generic religious references. On the contrary, judges should not play the role of censors of religious speech, evaluating the content of prayers. To do so, Justice Kennedy wrote, "would involve government in religious matters to a far greater degree than is the case under the town's current practice of neither editing or approving prayers in advance nor criticizing their content after the fact." He did suggest that the content of some prayers would potentially cross the line into a constitutional violation, but he found this unlikely "absent a pattern of prayers that over time denigrate, proselytize, or betray an impermissible government purpose."

The second strand of arguments marshaled against the town of Greece's prayers involved the context in which the prayers occur. In Congress and state legislatures, the opening prayer is delivered before the congressional members, where the public is segregated from the legislative activity. In town meetings, by contrast, citizens attend to speak directly on matters of local importance or to petition the board for actions that may impact them personally, such as those involving permits, licenses, and zoning. The respondents argued that sectarian prayer in this context coerces participation by nonadherents, subtly pressuring them to participate in prayers that may violate their beliefs in order to please the town councilmembers that they have come to petition. This would violate the First Amendment principle that government may not coerce its citizens "to support or participate in any religion or its exercise." Even so, Justice Kennedy was not convinced that "the act of offering a brief, solemn, and respectful prayer to open its monthly meetings, compelled its citizens to engage in a religious observance." He did, however, keep open the possibility that prayers could, on different facts, amount to coercion of nonbelievers. He wrote: "The analysis would be different if town board members directed the public to participate in the prayers, singled out dissidents for opprobrium, or indicated that their decisions might be influenced by a person's acquiescence in the prayer opportunity." This is where he lost the support of Justices Scalia and Thomas, who did not join this part of the opinion, but wrote separately that, in their view, only "actual legal coercion" could ever form the basis for an Establishment Clause violation. Justice Thomas went still further, writing for only himself, questioning whether the Establishment Clause has any application to state and local governments at all.

THE DISSENTERS

Justice Kagan wrote the main dissent, joined by Justices Ruth Bader Ginsburg, Stephen G. Breyer, and Sonia Sotomayor. In some ways, there was not a huge divide between the dissent and the majority opinions. All the justices accepted the notion that legislative prayer does not necessarily run up against First Amendment prohibitions and that, as the dissent pointed out, the public forum need not be protected by "a bright separationist line." But the agreement ended there.

Justice Kagan's dissent found that the facts of this case ran afoul of "the First Amendment's promise that every citizen, irrespective of her religion, owns an equal share in her government." Raising the perspective of religious minorities, she focused on the principle of religious equality embedded in the Establishment Clause, describing it as "the breathtakingly generous constitutional idea that our public institutions belong no less to the Buddhist or Hindu than to the Methodist or Episcopalian." She agreed with the respondents that the context of a town hall meeting populated with ordinary citizens who have come to petition their government requires more sensitivity to the prayers offered than do the prayers opening sessions of legislatures or Congress. But Greece, the dissent emphasized, showed no such sensitivity. The town made no effort to foster religious diversity or to reach out to adherents of non-Christian religions, instead "month in and month out for over a decade, prayers steeped in only one faith, addressed toward members of the public, commenced meetings to discuss local affairs and distribute government benefits." The prayers "put some residents to the unenviable choice of either pretending to pray like the majority or declining to join its communal activity, at the very moment of petitioning their elected leaders." This, Justice Kagan wrote, "crossed a constitutional line."

In a separate concurring opinion, Justice Alito characterized the dissenters' concerns as "really quite niggling" because all that the town would need to do to avoid constitutional problems would be to either request less sectarian language from those giving the prayers or invite clergy of diverse faiths to participate. The fact that he found her objections "really quite niggling," Justice Kagan responded in a footnote, "says all there is to say about the difference between our respective views."

IMPACT OF THE DECISION

The result of this case was not unexpected by most court watchers, and many now predict that it will clear the way for more local governments to begin meetings with prayer, even if that prayer reflects only the views of the majority religions, with very little fear of judicial interference.

As expected, the reactions to the decision were varied. Lead counsel for the Alliance Defending Freedom, the organization that represented the town of Greece, Thomas G. Hungar, praised the decision. "The Supreme Court has reaffirmed that the practice of prayer before legislative bodies is firmly embedded in the history and traditions of this nation," Hungar said. "In so doing, they have simply reinforced what has been true about America since its founding: Americans should be free to speak and act consistently with their own beliefs."

David L. Barkey, of the Anti-Defamation League, had a different view. "Regrettably, the plurality opinion opens the door wide to overtly sectarian prayers before public meetings of government bodies," Barkley said. While the majority opinion did say that such prayers would not be without any constraints, he called these limitations "tepid," and predicted that they will "not adequately protect those who are in religious minorities from feeling isolated, vulnerable, or like second-class citizens in their own communities."

—Melissa Feinberg

Following is the edited text of the Supreme Court's decision in Town of Greece v. Galloway *in which the Court ruled on May 5, 2014, to uphold the right of council members to pray during their meetings.*

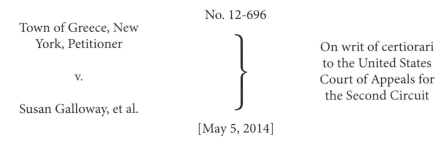

Town of Greece v. Galloway

May 5, 2014

[Footnotes have been omitted.]

No. 12-696

Town of Greece, New
York, Petitioner

v.

Susan Galloway, et al.

On writ of certiorari
to the United States
Court of Appeals for
the Second Circuit

[May 5, 2014]

JUSTICE KENNEDY delivered the opinion of the Court, except as to Part II–B.*

The Court must decide whether the town of Greece, New York, imposes an impermissible establishment of religion by opening its monthly board meetings with a prayer. It must be concluded, consistent with the Court's opinion in *Marsh* v. *Chambers*, 463 U. S. 783 (1983), that no violation of the Constitution has been shown.

[Section I, containing background on the case, has been omitted.]

II

In *Marsh* v. *Chambers*, 463 U. S. 783, the Court found no First Amendment violation in the Nebraska Legislature's practice of opening its sessions with a prayer delivered by a chaplain paid from state funds. The decision concluded that legislative prayer, while religious in nature, has long been understood as compatible with the Establishment Clause. As practiced by Congress since the framing of the Constitution, legislative prayer lends gravity to public business, reminds lawmakers to transcend petty differences in pursuit of a higher purpose, and expresses a common aspiration to a just and peaceful society. The Court has considered this symbolic expression to be a "tolerable acknowledgement of beliefs widely held," *Marsh*, 463 U. S., at 792, rather than a first, treacherous step towards establishment of a state church. . . .

A

Respondents maintain that prayer must be nonsectarian, or not identifiable with any one religion; and they fault the town for permitting guest chaplains to deliver prayers that "use overtly Christian terms" or "invoke specifics of Christian theology." A prayer is fitting for the public sphere, in their view, only if it contains the "'most general, nonsectarian reference to God,'" *id.*, at 33 (quoting M. Meyerson, Endowed by Our Creator: The Birth of Religious Freedom in America 11–12 (2012)), and eschews mention of doctrines associated with any one faith. They argue that prayer which contemplates "the workings of the Holy Spirit, the events of Pentecost, and the belief that God 'has raised up the Lord Jesus' and 'will raise us, in our turn, and put us by His side'" would be impermissible, as would any prayer that reflects dogma particular to a single faith tradition. *Id.*, at 34 (quoting App. 89a and citing *id.*, at 56a, 123a, 134a).

An insistence on nonsectarian or ecumenical prayer as a single, fixed standard is not consistent with the tradition of legislative prayer outlined in the Court's cases. The Court found the prayers in *Marsh* consistent with the First Amendment not because they espoused only a generic theism but because our history and tradition have shown that prayer in this limited context could "coexis[t] with the principles of disestablishment and religious freedom." 463 U. S., at 786. The Congress that drafted the First Amendment would have been accustomed to invocations containing explicitly religious themes of the sort respondents find objectionable. . . .

To hold that invocations must be nonsectarian would force the legislatures that sponsor prayers and the courts that are asked to decide these cases to act as supervisors and censors of religious speech, a rule that would involve government in religious matters to a far greater degree than is the case under the town's current practice of neither editing or approving prayers in advance nor criticizing their content after the fact. Cf. *Hosanna-Tabor Evangelical Lutheran Church and School* v. *EEOC*, 565 U. S. ___, ___ (2012). Our Government is prohibited from prescribing prayers to be recited in our public institutions in order to promote a preferred system of belief or code of moral behavior. *Engel* v. *Vitale*, 370 U. S. 421, 430 (1962). It would be but a few steps removed from that prohibition for legislatures to require chaplains to redact the religious content from their message in order to make it acceptable for the public sphere. Government may not mandate a civic religion that stifles any but the most generic reference to the sacred any more than it may prescribe a religious orthodoxy. . . .

Respondents argue, in effect, that legislative prayer may be addressed only to a generic God. The law and the Court could not draw this line for each specific prayer or seek to require ministers to set aside their nuanced and deeply personal beliefs for vague and artificial ones . . . . Once it invites prayer into the public sphere, government must permit a prayer giver to address his or her own God or gods as conscience dictates, unfettered by what an administrator or judge considers to be nonsectarian.

In rejecting the suggestion that legislative prayer must be nonsectarian, the Court does not imply that no constraints remain on its content. The relevant constraint derives from its place at the opening of legislative sessions, where it is meant to lend gravity to the occasion and reflect values long part of the Nation's heritage. Prayer that is solemn and respectful in tone, that invites lawmakers to reflect upon shared ideals and common ends before they embark on the fractious business of governing, serves that legitimate function. If the course and practice over time shows that the invocations denigrate nonbelievers or religious minorities, threaten damnation, or preach conversion, many present may consider the prayer to fall short of the desire to elevate the purpose of the occasion and to unite lawmakers in their common effort. That circumstance would present a different case than the one presently before the Court. . . .

Finally, the Court disagrees with the view taken by the Court of Appeals that the town of Greece contravened the Establishment Clause by inviting a predominantly Christian set of ministers to lead the prayer. The town made reasonable efforts to identify all of the congregations located within its borders and represented that it would welcome a prayer by any minister or layman who wished to give one. That nearly all of the congregations in town turned out to be Christian does not reflect an aversion or bias on the part of town leaders against minority faiths. So long as the town maintains a policy of nondiscrimination, the Constitution does not require it to search beyond its borders for non-Christian prayer givers in an effort to achieve religious balancing. The quest to promote "a 'diversity' of religious views" would require the town "to make wholly inappropriate judgments about the number of religions [it] should sponsor and the relative frequency with which it should sponsor each," *Lee*, 505 U. S., at 617 (Souter, J., concurring), a form of government entanglement with religion that is far more troublesome than the current approach.

B

Respondents further seek to distinguish the town's prayer practice from the tradition upheld in *Marsh* on the ground that it coerces participation by nonadherents. They and some *amici* contend that prayer conducted in the intimate setting of a town board meeting differs in fundamental ways from the invocations delivered in Congress and state legislatures, where the public remains segregated from legislative activity and may not address the body except by occasional invitation. Citizens attend town meetings, on the other hand, to accept awards; speak on matters of local importance; and petition the board for action that may affect their economic interests, such as the granting of permits, business licenses, and zoning variances. Respondents argue that the public may feel subtle pressure to participate in prayers that violate their beliefs in order to please the board members from whom they are about to seek a favorable ruling. In their view the fact that board members in small towns know many of their constituents by name only increases the pressure to conform.

It is an elemental First Amendment principle that government may not coerce its citizens "to support or participate in any religion or its exercise." On the record in this case the Court is not persuaded that the town of Greece, through the act of offering a brief, solemn, and respectful prayer to open its monthly meetings, compelled its citizens to engage in a religious observance. The inquiry remains a fact-sensitive one that considers both the setting in which the prayer arises and the audience to whom it is directed. . . .

The analysis would be different if town board members directed the public to participate in the prayers, singled out dissidents for opprobrium, or indicated that their decisions might be influenced by a person's acquiescence in the prayer opportunity. No such thing occurred in the town of Greece. Although board members themselves stood, bowed their heads, or made the sign of the cross during the prayer, they at no point solicited similar gestures by the public. Respondents point to several occasions where audience members were asked to rise for the prayer. These requests, however, came not from town leaders but from the guest ministers, who presumably are accustomed to directing their congregations in this way and might have done so thinking the action was inclusive, not coercive. . . . Respondents suggest that constituents might feel pressure to join the prayers to avoid irritating the officials who would be ruling on their petitions, but this argument has no evidentiary support. Nothing in the record indicates that town leaders allocated benefits and burdens based on participation in the prayer, or that citizens were received differently depending on whether they joined the invocation or quietly declined. In no instance did town leaders signal disfavor toward non-participants or suggest that their stature in the community was in any way diminished. A practice that classified citizens based on their religious views would violate the Constitution, but that is not the case before this Court.

In their declarations in the trial court, respondents stated that the prayers gave them offense and made them feel excluded and disrespected. Offense, however, does not equate to coercion. Adults often encounter speech they find disagreeable; and an Establishment Clause violation is not made out any time a person experiences a sense of affront from the expression of contrary religious views in a legislative forum, especially where, as here, any member of the public is welcome in turn to offer an invocation reflecting his or her own convictions. . . . If circumstances arise in which the pattern and practice of ceremonial, legislative prayer is alleged to be a means to coerce or intimidate others, the objection can be addressed in the regular course. But the showing has not been made here, where the prayers neither chastised dissenters nor attempted lengthy disquisition on religious dogma. Courts remain free to review the pattern of prayers over time to determine whether they comport with the tradition of solemn, respectful prayer approved in *Marsh*, or whether coercion is a real and substantial likelihood. But in the general course legislative bodies do not engage in impermissible coercion merely by exposing constituents to prayer they would rather not hear and in which they need not participate. . . .

In the town of Greece, the prayer is delivered during the ceremonial portion of the town's meeting. Board members are not engaged in policymaking at this time, but in more general functions, such as swearing in new police officers, inducting high school athletes into the town hall of fame, and presenting proclamations to volunteers, civic groups, and senior citizens. It is a moment for town leaders to recognize the achievements of their constituents and the aspects of community life that are worth celebrating. By inviting ministers to serve as chaplain for the month, and welcoming them to the front of the room alongside civic leaders, the town is acknowledging the central place that religion, and religious institutions, hold in the lives of those present. Indeed, some congregations are not simply spiritual homes for town residents but also the provider of social services for citizens regardless of their beliefs. . . . The inclusion of a brief, ceremonial prayer as part of a larger exercise in civic recognition suggests that its purpose and effect are to acknowledge religious leaders and the institutions they represent rather than to exclude or coerce nonbelievers.

Ceremonial prayer is but a recognition that, since this Nation was founded and until the present day, many Americans deem that their own existence must be understood by precepts far beyond the authority of government to alter or define and that willing participation in civic affairs can be consistent with a brief acknowledgment of their belief in a higher power, always with due respect for those who adhere to other beliefs. The prayer in this case has a permissible ceremonial purpose. It is not an unconstitutional establishment of religion.

* * *

The town of Greece does not violate the First Amendment by opening its meetings with prayer that comports with our tradition and does not coerce participation by nonadherents. The judgment of the U. S. Court of Appeals for the Second Circuit is reversed.

It is so ordered.

[The concurring opinion of Justices Alito and Scalia, the concurring opinion of Justices Thomas and Scalia, and the dissenting opinion of Justice Breyer have been omitted.]

JUSTICE KAGAN, with whom JUSTICE GINSBURG, JUSTICE BREYER, and JUSTICE SOTOMAYOR join, dissenting.

For centuries now, people have come to this country from every corner of the world to share in the blessing of religious freedom. Our Constitution promises that they may worship in their own way, without fear of penalty or danger, and that in itself is a momentous offering. Yet our Constitution makes a commitment still more remarkable—that however those individuals worship, they will count as full and equal American citizens. A Christian, a Jew, a Muslim (and so forth)—each stands in the same relationship with her country, with her state and local communities, and with every level and body of government. So that when each person performs the duties or seeks the benefits of citizenship, she does so not as an adherent to one or another religion, but simply as an American.

I respectfully dissent from the Court's opinion because I think the Town of Greece's prayer practices violate that norm of religious equality—the breathtakingly generous constitutional idea that our public institutions belong no less to the Buddhist or Hindu than to the Methodist or Episcopalian. I do not contend that principle translates here into a bright separationist line. To the contrary, I agree with the Court's decision in *Marsh* v. *Chambers*, 463 U. S. 783 (1983), upholding the Nebraska Legislature's tradition of beginning each session with a chaplain's prayer. And I believe that pluralism and inclusion in a town hall can satisfy the constitutional requirement of neutrality; such a forum need not become a religion-free zone. But still, the Town of Greece should lose this case. The practice at issue here differs from the one sustained in *Marsh* because Greece's town meetings involve participation by ordinary citizens, and the invocations given—directly to those citizens—were predominantly sectarian in content. Still more, Greece's Board did nothing to recognize religious diversity: In arranging for clergy members to open each meeting, the Town never sought (except briefly when this suit was filed) to involve, accommodate, or in any way reach out to adherents of non-Christian religions. So month in and month out for over a decade, prayers steeped in only one faith, addressed toward members of the public, commenced meetings to discuss local affairs and distribute government benefits. In my view, that practice does not square with the First Amendment's promise that every citizen, irrespective of her religion, owns an equal share in her government.

[Sections I, II A, and II B of the dissent, outlining the majority's opinion and previous rulings, have been omitted.]

C

. . . To recap: *Marsh* upheld prayer addressed to legislators alone, in a proceeding in which citizens had no role—and even then, only when it did not "proselytize or advance" any single religion. 463 U. S., at 794. It was that legislative prayer practice (not every prayer in a body exercising any legislative function) that the Court found constitutional given its "unambiguous and unbroken history." *Id.*, at 792. But that approved practice, as I have shown, is not Greece's. None of the history *Marsh* cited—and none the majority details today—supports calling on citizens to pray, in a manner consonant with only a single religion's beliefs, at a participatory public proceeding, having both legislative and adjudicative components. And so, contra the majority, Greece's prayers cannot simply ride on the constitutional coattails of the legislative tradition *Marsh* described. The Board's practice must, in its own particulars, meet constitutional requirements. . . .

To decide how Greece fares on that score, think again about how its prayer practice works, meeting after meeting. . . . Let's say that a Muslim citizen of Greece goes before the Board to share her views on policy or request some permit. Maybe she wants the Board to put up a traffic light at a dangerous intersection; or maybe she needs a zoning variance to build an addition on her home. But just before she gets to say her piece, a minister deputized by the Town asks her to pray "in the name of God's only son Jesus Christ." . . . She must think—it is hardly paranoia, but only the truth—that Christian worship has become entwined with local governance. And now she faces a choice—to pray alongside the majority as one of that group or somehow to register her deeply felt difference. She is a strong person, but that is no easy call—especially given that the room is small and her every action (or inaction) will be noticed. She does not wish to be rude to her neighbors, nor does she wish to aggravate the Board members whom she will soon be trying to persuade. And yet she does not want to acknowledge Christ's divinity, any more than many of her neighbors would want to deny that tenet. So assume she declines to participate with the others in the first act of the meeting—or even, as the majority proposes, that she stands up and leaves the room altogether. At the least, she becomes a different kind of citizen, one who will not join in the religious practice that the Town Board has chosen as reflecting its own and the community's most cherished beliefs. And she thus stands at a remove, based solely on religion, from her fellow citizens and her elected representatives.

Everything about that situation, I think, infringes the First Amendment . . . .

None of this means that Greece's town hall must be religion- or prayer-free. "[W]e are a religious people," *Marsh* observed, 463 U. S., at 792, and prayer draws some warrant from tradition in a town hall, as well as in Congress or a state legislature, see *supra*, at 8–9. What the circumstances here demand is the recognition that we are a pluralistic people too. When citizens of all faiths come to speak to each other and their elected representatives in a legislative session, the government must take especial care to ensure that the prayers they hear will seek to include, rather than serve to divide. No more is required—but that much is crucial—to treat every citizen, of whatever religion, as an equal participant in her government.

And contrary to the majority's (and JUSTICE ALITO's) view, see *ante*, at 13–14; *ante*, at 4–7, that is not difficult to do. If the Town Board had let its chaplains know that they should speak in nonsectarian terms, common to diverse religious groups, then no one would have valid grounds for complaint. . . . Or if the Board preferred, it might have invited clergy of many faiths to serve as chaplains, as the majority notes that Congress does. When one month a clergy member refers to Jesus, and the next to Allah or Jehovah—as the majority hopefully though counterfactually suggests happened here,—the government does not identify itself with one religion or align itself with that faith's citizens, and the effect of even sectarian prayer is transformed. So Greece had multiple ways of incorporating prayer into its town meetings—reflecting all the ways that prayer (as most of us know from daily life) can forge common bonds, rather than divide.

But Greece could not do what it did: infuse a participatory government body with one (and only one) faith, so that month in and month out, the citizens appearing before it become partly defined by their creed—as those who share, and those who do not, the community's majority religious belief. In this country, when citizens go before the government, they go not as Christians or Muslims or Jews (or what have you), but just as Americans (or here, as Grecians). That is what it means to be an equal citizen, irrespective of religion. And that is what the Town of Greece precluded by so identifying itself with a single faith. . . .

[Sections III and IV, further refuting the majority's key arguments, have been omitted.]

For me, that remarkable guarantee means at least this much: When the citizens of this country approach their government, they do so only as Americans, not as members of one faith or another. And that means that even in a partly legislative body, they should not confront government-sponsored worship that divides them along religious lines. I believe, for all the reasons I have given, that the Town of Greece betrayed that promise. I therefore respectfully dissent from the Court's decision.

SOURCE: U.S. Supreme Court. *Town of Greece v. Galloway.* 572 U.S.__(2014). www.supremecourt.gov/opinions/13pdf/12-696_bpm1.pdf.

OTHER HISTORIC DOCUMENTS OF INTEREST

FROM PREVIOUS *HISTORIC DOCUMENTS*

■ Supreme Court on Prayer at Public School Graduation, *1992*, p. 553

European Union Court Backs Right to Be Forgotten in Google Case

MAY 13, 2014

U.S. Internet giant Google suffered a setback when the European Union Court of Justice (ECJ) on May 13, 2014, ruled that companies like Google that operate search engines may be forced to delete certain links to online data if the data subject asks them. The case concerned a Spanish man who had asked Google to remove links to two newspaper articles that reported on a real-estate auction that was held to recover social security debts the man owed. His complaint against Google went all the way to the EU's highest court after Google appealed a decision taken by Spain's data protection authority, which ordered the company to delete the links. With Internet search engines having become so ubiquitous, the judgment was considered a landmark one. The EU court confirmed for the first time that search engine operators are required to comply with European data privacy legislation. The ruling came as the EU's legislators continued to work on a draft law to update the existing data privacy regulations. One of the most contentious issues in this legislative reform process is whether to create a new "right to be forgotten" in the digital world.

Spanish Plaintiff and Case Background

In 2010, Mario Costeja González, a Spanish man, filed a complaint both against the publisher of the articles, a Catalonia-based newspaper, *La Vanguardia*, and Google Spain, a subsidiary of the California-headquartered parent company. The plaintiff argued that his debt issues were now resolved and so the articles about the auction were no longer relevant. After assessing his claims, Spain's Data Protection Agency came to the conclusion that *La Vanguardia* did not have to take down the information because it had legally published it. However, it found that Google should withdraw the links from its search engine index. Google appealed that decision to Spain's High Court, which in turn referred to the Luxembourg-based ECJ for a preliminary ruling or guidance on how to interpret European law.

The EU enacted its original data protection Directive in 1995 just as the Internet—and Internet search engines—were starting to be used by the wider public. While the EU is overhauling that 1995 Directive to make it relevant to today's digital environment, the ECJ focused its ruling on the law as it stands. Under the Court's procedures, before issuing the preliminary ruling—which cannot be appealed—an Advocate General issues a nonbinding set of conclusions. The Advocate General for this case, Niilo Jääskinen, published his conclusions on June 25, 2013. He argued that Google was not a data "controller" within the meaning of the 1995 Directive and so its responsibilities to protect personal data were somewhat limited. While Google could theoretically be required to remove illegal or inappropriate content, in this instance the information was legally published and accurate at the time, so removing it would be tantamount to censorship, he argued.

It came as a bit of a surprise, then, when the ECJ judges, in their ruling, diverged so markedly from the Advocate General's opinion. They ruled that Google's search engine was indeed fully bound by the EU Data Protection Directive because Google collects and processes data, even though it may not have been the original publisher of that data. In addition, even though the company is headquartered in the United States, it is obliged to comply with EU privacy law because it has a subsidiary established in Spain that promotes and sell advertisements there. The ECJ said that "in certain circumstances" Google could be obliged to remove links to webpages that are published by third parties, which mention a person's name.

When deciding whether or not to delete links to information, a "fair balance" should be struck between the data subject's right to privacy on the one hand and the Internet user's interest in accessing information on the other, the Court found. A data subject's right of privacy should generally override an Internet user's right to information, but there are exceptions to this principle—in other words, there are circumstances in which an Internet user should have the right to the information. An example the Court gave of such an exception would be where the data subject is a public figure. The Court ruled that it should be possible to remove data that is inadequate, irrelevant, or no longer relevant or excessive. Moreover, a data subject should be able to petition a search engine company directly rather than having to go to the original publisher of the information or appeal to their national data protection authority.

RULING REVEALS DEEP DIVISIONS

The ECJ ruling generated a broader discussion on the right to be forgotten, a nascent concept that the EU is pioneering, which seeks to empower a data subject to have certain publicly accessible online data about them deleted. The judgment was essentially a boost for the supporters of the right to be forgotten and a blow for its critics. The plaintiff, González, said in a newspaper interview after the ruling, "I was fighting for the elimination of data that adversely affects people's honor, dignity and exposes their private lives. Everything that undermines human beings, that's not freedom of expression." By contrast, Google said that it was "a disappointing ruling for search engines and online publishers in general. We are very surprised that it differs so dramatically from the Advocate General's opinion and the warnings and consequences that he spelled out."

Politicians were quick to weigh in on the ruling. There was a notable divide between reactions from the United Kingdom, which were mostly sympathetic to Google's arguments about the need to avoid censorship, and Germany, where there was greater sympathy for the plaintiff's pro-privacy argument. German vice-chancellor and finance minister Sigmar Gabriel said, "Europe stands for the opposite of this totalitarian idea of making every detail of human behavior, human emotion, and human thought an object of capitalistic commercial exploitation." A German member of the European Parliament, Jan Philipp Albrecht, who is an expert on this policy area, said that the ruling "clarifies that search engine operators are responsible for the processing of personal data even if it comes from public sources." The British-based advocacy group, Index on Censorship, said that the judgment "violates the fundamental principles of freedom of expression." The group, which defends the right of freedom of expression, said that the new obligation being imposed on Google operator was "akin to marching into a library and forcing it to pulp books." The British justice secretary, Chris Grayling, voiced his concern about the precedent that was being set in favor of the right to be forgotten in the digital world, calling it "a regime that no one will pay for."

Underscoring how wide-reaching the issue is, much of the media coverage gave multiple concrete examples of compromising or unflattering online information that has proven to be a thorn in the side of the data subjects. They included a campground owner who claimed that he had lost business because when people did a Google search on his site, the highest-ranked result was a horrific industrial accident that occurred there decades earlier. Another case involved Max Mosley, the former president of the Formula One racing company, who successfully sued in French and German courts to have online images of him attending a sex orgy deleted. Mosley's lawyer, Tanja Irion, said of the ruling, "It is clear that Google's standard argument that the company isn't responsible for the content of its search results has broken down."

While the ECJ established a limited right to be forgotten, it left a lot of questions unanswered, too. For instance, it did not say whether, when data is deleted, it should be made inaccessible only in the data subject's home country, or from anywhere in the world. Whereas Google's having a subsidiary in Spain made it bound by the EU's data privacy rules, the Court did not clarify whether an online search engine company that has no corporate seat in the EU would be similarly bound. It also remained unclear to what extent a company like Google can unilaterally decide to remove links to information and to what extent it needs to discuss with the relevant data protection authority how to handle requests. Many of the academic experts who commented on the ruling predicted that in practice, companies such as Google would need to learn to work in closer collaboration with data protection authorities to deal with this complex issue.

WIDER REVAMP OF DATA POLICY RULES

The right to be forgotten, which the ECJ ruling focused on, is just one of numerous privacy-related issues that the EU is broaching as it overhauls the 1995 directive. The European Commission, the EU's executive arm, proposed a regulation in January 2012 that would further strengthen an already-strict data privacy regime. The EU's two lawmaking arms, the European Parliament and Council of Ministers, are in the process of considering this draft legislation, with the Commission urging them to agree on the final text in 2015. The proposed legislation empowers data protection authorities to impose fines of up to 5 percent of a company's annual turnover on those who breach the new regulation. The draft legislation also spells out what companies need to do to notify data subjects if a security breach causes unauthorized persons to get access to their personal data.

The economic stakes are enormous, which is why the United States is paying close attention to the European debate. Most of the big Internet-centered companies—Google, Apple, Facebook, Twitter, Amazon, and Microsoft—are U.S.-owned. With this in mind, U.S. administration officials have been demanding that the new EU rules not impede the free flow of online data because this is critical to these companies being able to turn a profit. At the same time, the administration of President Barack Obama is negotiating with the EU Commission an update of the Safe Harbor agreement that the two signed back in 2000, which allows U.S. companies to export data from Europe to the United States if they pledge to abide by EU data protection norms. The political climate on the data privacy issue has become more fraught ever since the revelations of former National Security Agency (NSA) contractor Edward Snowden in summer 2013 of mass NSA surveillance of Internet users' communications.

In a related development, in November 2014 the European Parliament passed a nonbinding resolution that urged the EU Commission to "consider proposals with the aim of unbundling search engines from other commercial services." The Commission had launched an antitrust probe against Google in 2010 to determine whether the latter had abused its dominant position in Europe's online search engine market, given that it controls 90 percent of this market. Meanwhile, by the end of 2014 Google received more than 175,000 requests from users since the ruling and had accepted about half of them, the company said.

—Brian Beary

Following is the text of a press release from the European Commission on May 13, 2014, on the preliminary ruling in the case of Google Spain SL, Google Inc. v. Agencia Espanola de Protección de Datos, Mario Costeja González, *upholding a lower court ruling that Google must delete specific results from its search engine when requested.*

European Court Backs Right to Be Forgotten

May 13, 2014

[Footnote omitted.]

An internet search engine operator is responsible for the processing that it carries out of personal data which appear on web pages published by third parties

Thus, if, following a search made on the basis of a person's name, the list of results displays a link to a web page which contains information on the person in question, that data subject may approach the operator directly and, where the operator does not grant his request, bring the matter before the competent authorities in order to obtain, under certain conditions, the removal of that link from the list of results

An EU directive has the objective of protecting the fundamental rights and freedoms of natural persons (in particular the right to privacy) when personal data are processed, while removing obstacles to the free flow of such data.

In 2010 Mario Costeja González, a Spanish national, lodged with the Agencia Española de Protección de Datos (Spanish Data Protection Agency, the AEPD) a complaint against La Vanguardia Ediciones SL (the publisher of a daily newspaper with a large circulation in Spain, in particular in Catalonia) and against Google Spain and Google Inc. Mr Costeja González contended that, when an internet user entered his name in the search engine of the Google group ('Google Search'), the list of results would display links to two pages of La Vanguardia's newspaper, of January and March 1998. Those pages in particular contained an announcement for a real-estate auction organised following attachment proceedings for the recovery of social security debts owed by Mr Costeja González.

With that complaint, Mr Costeja González requested, first, that La Vanguardia be required either to remove or alter the pages in question (so that the personal data relating to him no longer appeared) or to use certain tools made available by search engines in order to protect the data. Second, he requested that Google Spain or Google Inc. be required to remove or conceal the personal data relating to him so that the data no longer appeared in the search results and in the links to La Vanguardia. In this context, Mr Costeja González stated that the attachment proceedings concerning him had been fully resolved for a number of years and that reference to them was now entirely irrelevant.

The AEPD rejected the complaint against La Vanguardia, taking the view that the information in question had been lawfully published by it. On the other hand, the complaint was upheld as regards Google Spain and Google Inc. The AEPD requested those two companies to take the necessary measures to withdraw the data from their index and to render access to the data impossible in the future. Google Spain and Google Inc. brought two actions before the Audiencia Nacional (National High Court, Spain), claiming that the AEPD's decision should be annulled. It is in this context that the Spanish court referred a series of questions to the Court of Justice.

In today's judgment, the Court of Justice finds, first of all, that by searching automatically, constantly and systematically for information published on the internet, the operator of a search engine 'collects' data within the meaning of the directive. The Court considers, furthermore, that the operator, within the framework of its indexing programmes, 'retrieves', 'records' and 'organises' the data in question, which it then 'stores' on its servers and, as the case may be, 'discloses' and 'makes available' to its users in the form of lists of results. Those operations, which are referred to expressly and unconditionally in the directive, must be classified as 'processing', regardless of the fact that the operator of the search engine carries them out without distinction in respect of information other than the personal data. The Court also points out that the operations referred to by the directive must be classified as processing even where they exclusively concern material that has already been published as it stands in the media. A general derogation from the application of the directive in such a case would have the consequence of largely depriving the directive of its effect.

The Court further holds that the operator of the search engine is the 'controller' in respect of that processing, within the meaning of the directive, given that it is the operator which determines the purposes and means of the processing. The Court observes in this regard that, inasmuch as the activity of a search engine is additional to that of publishers of websites and is liable to affect significantly the fundamental rights to privacy and to the protection of personal data, the operator of the search engine must ensure, within the framework of its responsibilities, powers and capabilities, that its activity complies with the directive's requirements. This is the only way that the guarantees laid down by the directive will be able to have full effect and that effective and complete protection of data subjects (in particular of their privacy) may actually be achieved.

As regards the directive's territorial scope, the Court observes that Google Spain is a subsidiary of Google Inc. on Spanish territory and, therefore, an 'establishment' within the meaning of the directive. The Court rejects the argument that the processing of personal data by Google Search is not carried out in the context of the activities of that establishment in Spain. The Court holds, in this regard, that where such data are processed for the purposes of a search engine operated by an undertaking which, although it has its seat in a non-member State, has an establishment in a Member State, the processing is carried out 'in the context of the activities' of that establishment, within the meaning of the directive, if the establishment is intended to promote and sell, in the Member State in question, advertising space offered by the search engine in order to make the service offered by the engine profitable.

So far as concerns, next, the extent of the responsibility of the operator of the search engine, the Court holds that the operator is, in certain circumstances, obliged to remove links to web pages that are published by third parties and contain information relating to a person from the list of results displayed following a search made on the basis of that person's name. The Court makes it clear that such an obligation may also exist in a case where that name or information is not erased beforehand or simultaneously from those web pages, and even, as the case may be, when its publication in itself on those pages is lawful.

The Court points out in this context that processing of personal data carried out by such an operator enables any internet user, when he makes a search on the basis of an individual's name, to obtain, through the list of results, a structured overview of the information relating to that individual on the internet. The Court observes, furthermore, that this information potentially concerns a vast number of aspects of his private life and that, without the search engine, the information could not have been interconnected or could have been only with great difficulty. Internet users may thereby establish a more or less detailed profile of the person searched against. Furthermore, the effect of the interference with the person's rights is heightened on account of the important role played by the internet and search engines in modern society, which render the information contained in such lists of results ubiquitous. In the light of its potential seriousness, such interference cannot, according to the Court, be justified by merely the economic interest which the operator of the engine has in the data processing.

However, inasmuch as the removal of links from the list of results could, depending on the information at issue, have effects upon the legitimate interest of internet users potentially interested in having access to that information, the Court holds that a fair balance should be sought in particular between that interest and the data subject's fundamental rights, in particular the right to privacy and the right to protection of personal data. The Court observes in this regard that, whilst it is true that the data subject's rights also override, as a general rule, that interest of internet users, this balance may however depend, in specific cases, on the nature of the information in question and its sensitivity for the data subject's private life and on the interest of the public in having that information, an interest which may vary, in particular, according to the role played by the data subject in public life.

Finally, in response to the question whether the directive enables the data subject to request that links to web pages be removed from such a list of results on the grounds that he wishes the information appearing on those pages relating to him personally to be 'forgotten' after a certain time, the Court holds that, if it is found, following a request by the data subject, that the inclusion of those links in the list is, at this point in time, incompatible with the directive, the links and information in the list of results must be erased. The Court observes in this regard that even initially lawful processing of accurate data may, in the course of time, become incompatible with the directive where, having regard to all the circumstances of the case, the data appear to be inadequate, irrelevant or no longer relevant, or excessive in relation to the purposes for which they were processed and in the light of the time that has elapsed. The Court adds that, when appraising such a request made by the data subject in order to oppose the processing carried out by the operator of a search engine, it should in particular be examined whether the data subject has a right that the information in question relating to him personally should, at this point in time, no longer be linked to his name by a list of results that is displayed following a search made on the basis of his name. If that is the case, the links to web pages containing that information must be removed from that list of results, unless there are particular reasons, such as the role played by the data subject in public life, justifying a preponderant interest of the public in having access to the information when such a search is made.

The Court points out that the data subject may address such a request directly to the operator of the search engine (the controller) which must then duly examine its merits. Where the controller does not grant the request, the data subject may bring the matter before the supervisory authority or the judicial authority so that it carries out the necessary checks and orders the controller to take specific measures accordingly.

SOURCE: European Commission. Court of Justice of the European Union. "An Internet search engine operator is responsible for the processing that it carries out of personal data which appear on web pages published by third parties." May 13, 2014. http://europa.eu/rapid/press-release_CJE-14-70_en.htm. © European Union

OTHER HISTORIC DOCUMENTS OF INTEREST

FROM PREVIOUS *HISTORIC DOCUMENTS*

- European Union Begins Google Antitrust Investigation, *2010*, p. 605

Federal Communications Commission Proposes Net Neutrality Rules

MAY 18, 2014

In January 2014, the U.S. Court of Appeals for the District of Columbia Circuit issued a key ruling in a case surrounding "network neutrality," the concept that Internet providers should not block or slow access to certain websites or content, even if that content slows down their network. At issue was the Federal Communications Commission's (FCC) concern that broadband providers had both the ability and the incentive to limit the open nature of the Internet for business gains following an assertion by Comcast that it had the right to slow its customers' access to a file-sharing website. In December 2010, the FCC issued the Open Internet Order 2010, which prevented broadband providers from blocking lawful content and services, prohibited unreasonable discrimination against lawful network traffic, and required providers to disclose their network management practices, performance characteristics, and terms of use to the FCC. Verizon sued the FCC in January 2011, claiming the agency did not have the authority to issue such orders. The Court of Appeals for the D.C. Circuit ruled in Verizon's favor in *Verizon v. FCC* in 2014, finding that portions of the FCC's net neutrality rules contradicted the agency's earlier decision that broadband was an "information service" and therefore largely outside its regulatory authority. However, the court did uphold the FCC's authority in other areas and the agency's determination that rules protecting an open Internet were needed. This in turn prompted the agency to reexamine its order and consider alternative regulations in line with the legal framework set forth by the court—a process that went on to spark a major, highly charged policy debate that continued throughout 2014.

FCC Revises Its Approach to Open Internet Rules

Following the court's decision, FCC chairman Tom Wheeler announced that the agency would not appeal the ruling. Instead, it would seek to reinstate open Internet rules that could achieve the goals of the 2010 order but would follow the legal roadmap laid out by the court. Specifically, the court upheld the FCC's authority under Section 706 of the Telecommunications Act of 1996, which requires the agency to determine whether "advanced telecommunications capability [i.e., broadband or high-speed access] is being deployed to all Americans in a reasonable and timely fashion." If it is not, the FCC can "take immediate action to accelerate deployment of such capability by removing barriers to infrastructure investment and by promoting competition in the telecommunications market."

On May 15—after an intense period of lobbying by companies, interest groups, members of Congress, and consumers—the FCC voted to approve and issued a Notice of Proposed Rulemaking (NPRM) to seek public comments on how best to protect and promote an open

Internet. The NPRM included several initial proposed rules as well as a series of questions for the public. One of the most controversial items within the NPRM was a question of whether "paid prioritization," in which Internet service providers (ISPs) can charge companies more if they wanted faster connection speeds, should be banned. This caused many to question whether the FCC would ultimately allow so-called "fast lanes" and raised concerns that the agency would create a regulatory system that would separate Internet users into "haves" and "have nots," though Wheeler stated publicly that he would "work to see that that does not happen." Another controversial item was a proposal to reclassify broadband providers as "common carriers" like utility companies, which would give the FCC much greater authority to regulate them under Title II of the Communications Act of 1934.

Other items in the NPRM included a proposal to enhance the FCC's initial transparency rule—the only component of the 2010 order not vacated by the court—to require tailored disclosures from broadband providers. The disclosures would need to include information about the nature of network congestion that impacts consumers' use of online services as well as timely notification of any new practices that could change a consumer's or a content provider's relationship with the network. The NPRM also proposed reviving the FCC's "no-blocking" rule and requested input on developing a set of criteria that could be used to determine whether a provider's conduct is hurting consumers, competition, free expression, or civic engagement. Yet another proposal suggested creating a new process for resolving Internet access-related disputes, to involve an ombudsman who would field complaints and investigate them as needed.

The FCC argued that consumers were paying ISPs for a service—a path to the Internet—therefore it would be unlawful for the ISPs to not provide said service, particularly if the network operator deliberately slowed the speed below what a customer paid for; blocked access to lawful content; charged more for bandwidth to support streaming content when a customer had already paid for it; or prioritized network capacity in a way that deprived the customer of what they paid for.

"There is ONE Internet. Not a fast Internet, not a slow Internet; ONE Internet," said Wheeler in a statement. "It must be fast, robust and open. The speed and quality of the connection the consumer purchases must be unaffected by what content he or she is using." This was also important, Wheeler said, for maintaining a level playing field for all businesses. "Small companies and startups must be able to effectively reach consumers with innovative products and services and they must be protected against harmful conduct by broadband providers," he said. "The prospect of a gatekeeper choosing winners and losers on the Internet is unacceptable."

FCC commissioner Mignon Clyburn, who voted with Wheeler and Commissioner Jessica Rosenworcel to approve the NPRM, sought to reassure critics of government-based Internet regulation. "At its core, an open Internet means that consumers, not a company, not the government, determine winners and losers," Clyburn said. "All of this, however, does not nor will it ever, occur organically. Without rules governing a free and open Internet it is possible that companies . . . could independently determine whether they want to discriminate or block content, pick favorites, charge higher fees or distort the market."

Yet Commissioner Michael O'Rielly dissented, voting against the NPRM with Commissioner Ajit Pai. "The premise for imposing net neutrality rules is fundamentally flawed and rests on a faulty foundation of make-believe statutory authority," O'Rielly said. "I have serious concerns that this ill-advised item will create damaging uncertainty and head the Commission down a slippery slope of regulation."

A FLOOD OF FEEDBACK

The NPRM's approval began a four-month comment period that lasted through September 15. The FCC quickly faced a strong and largely critical reaction from a broad swath of groups, some of which echoed concerns raised earlier in the spring. Large telecommunications providers claimed that reclassifying broadband as a utility would lead to burdensome regulations that could hurt their business and ability to serve customers. "For the FCC to impose 1930s utility regulation on the Internet would lead to years of legal and regulatory uncertainty and would jeopardize investment and innovation in broadband," said Randal Milch, Verizon's executive vice president for public policy. CEOs from twenty-eight such companies had previously written to the FCC, warning that a reclassification "would impose great costs, allowing unprecedented government micromanagement of all aspects of the Internet economy." The letter went on to argue that "new service offerings, options, and features would be delayed or altogether foregone" and that "[c]onsumers would face less choice, and a less adaptive and responsive Internet."

Many Republican lawmakers argued that new regulations would be unnecessary and could be a slippery slope to government control over the Internet. "We have said repeatedly that the Obama administration's net neutrality rules are a solution in search of a problem," said Reps. Fred Upton, R-Mich., and Greg Walden, R-Ore., in a statement. "The marketplace has thrived and will continue to serve customers and invest billions annually to meet Americans' broadband needs without these rules." Other lawmakers balked at the FCC's seeming consideration of paid prioritization. "Pay-to-play arrangements are inherently discriminatory and anticompetitive, and therefore should be prohibited as a matter of public policy," wrote Sen. Al Franken, D-Minn., in a letter to Wheeler. Sen. Patrick Leahy, D-Vt., echoed these concerns: "The very essence of net neutrality is that a better idea or service should be allowed to succeed on its merits and not have to pay tolls to reach potential customers."

More than 100 Internet companies also cautioned that paid prioritization "represents a grave threat to the Internet." Open Internet advocates noted that under such a structure, new start-ups would be at a disadvantage to bigger, established companies that could afford to pay for faster network speeds. These advocates did, however, strongly support the FCC's reclassification proposal because it would enable the agency to more clearly define, impose, and legally support net neutrality rules. "Recognizing our nation's communications providers as common carriers under the law is common sense," read a letter to the FCC from thirty-six lawmakers. Still, many other open Internet supporters argued the FCC's rules did not go far enough.

Between May 15 and July 18, the first half of the comment period, nearly 800,000 comments were filed with the FCC. In fact, this first period was extended after the FCC's website crashed due to traffic. Analyses by the Pew Research Center and the Sunlight Foundation revealed that grassroots efforts played an important role in driving comment volume. According to Pew, 45 percent of the comments submitted in the last week of the comment period matched templates provided by Battle for the Net and DearFCC.org, two pro-net neutrality organizations. The Sunlight Foundation also identified about twenty different pro-net neutrality templates among the comments, which collectively accounted for approximately 60 percent of the FCC's total comments. In all, the FCC received nearly four million comments, underscoring the controversial and polarizing nature of the agency's proposals.

A Presidential Proposal

Complicating matters for the FCC, President Barack Obama unveiled his own net neutrality plan on November 10, calling for the FCC to reclassify all elements of broadband services as utilities under Title II. Obama said "the FCC should create a new set of rules protecting net neutrality and ensuring that neither the cable company nor the phone company will be able to act as a gatekeeper, restricting what you can do or see online." The president's plan not only echoed several elements of the FCC's NPRM, such as no content blocking and increased transparency, but also called for "an explicit ban on paid prioritization and any other restriction that has a similar effect." He also argued that the same rules should be fully applicable to mobile broadband as well. "The Internet has been one of the greatest gifts our economy—and our society—has ever known," he said. "The FCC was chartered to promote competition, innovation, and investment in our networks. In service of that mission, there is no higher calling than protecting an open, accessible, and free Internet."

Although the FCC is an independent agency, Obama's proposal did impact its rulemaking process. Prior to the president's announcement, Wheeler had considered something of a hybrid approach to rulemaking—one in which the relationship between ISPs and content companies would be reclassified under the stronger Title II, while the FCC would take a lighter regulatory stance on the relationship between consumers and the broadband providers. Yet this approach was not aligned with Obama's plan.

In a statement, Wheeler thanked the president for his input and said the FCC "would incorporate the President's submission into the record of the Open Internet proceeding," while noting the length and extent of the public comment process the FCC had just undergone. Wheeler also suggested that the FCC would need more time, at least several months, to finish its work gathering and analyzing comments and writing rules that could stand up to legal scrutiny. Indeed, the agency had not finished writing new rules, let alone voted on them, at the end of the year.

—Linda Fecteau Grimm

Following is a May 18, 2014, press release from the Federal Communications Commission (FCC) announcing its intent to seek public input on proposed net neutrality rules; and statements from FCC chair Tom Wheeler and Commissioner Mignon Clyburn, also from May 18, 2014, on net neutrality and the rulemaking process.

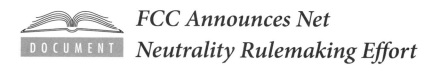

FCC Announces Net Neutrality Rulemaking Effort

May 18, 2014

The Federal Communications Commission today launched a rulemaking seeking public comment on how best to protect and promote an open Internet. The Notice of Proposed Rulemaking adopted today poses a broad range of questions to elicit the broadest range of input from everyone impacted by the Internet, from consumers and small businesses to providers and start-ups. The Internet is America's most important platform for economic growth, innovation, competition, free expression, and broadband investment and deployment. The Internet has become an essential tool for Americans and for the growth of American businesses. That's because the Internet has been open to new content, new products and new services, enabling consumers to choose whatever legal content, services and applications they desire.

The FCC has previously concluded that broadband providers have the incentive and ability to act in ways that threaten Internet openness. But today, there are no rules that stop broadband providers from trying to limit Internet openness. That is why the Notice adopted by the FCC today starts with a fundamental question: "What is the right public policy to ensure that the Internet remains open?"

The FCC proposes to rely on a legal blueprint set out by the United States Court of Appeals for the District of Columbia Circuit in its January decision in *Verizon v. FCC*, using the FCC's authority to promote broadband deployment to all Americans under Section 706 of the Telecommunications Act of 1996. At the same time, the Commission will seriously consider using its authority under the telecommunications regulation found in Title II of the Communications Act. In addition, the Notice:

- Proposes to retain the definitions and scope of the 2010 rules, which governed broadband Internet access service providers, but not services like enterprise services, Internet traffic exchange and specialized services.
- Proposes to enhance the existing transparency rule, which was upheld by the D.C. Circuit. The proposed enhancements would provide consumers, edge providers, and the Commission with tailored disclosures, including information on the nature of congestion that impacts consumers' use of online services and timely notice of new practices.
- As part of the revived "no-blocking" rule, proposes ensuring that all who use the Internet can enjoy robust, fast and dynamic Internet access.
- Tentatively concludes that priority service offered exclusively by a broadband provider to an affiliate should be considered illegal until proven otherwise.
- Asks how to devise a rigorous, multi-factor "screen" to analyze whether any conduct hurts consumers, competition, free expression and civic engagement, and other criteria under a legal standard termed "commercial reasonableness."
- Asks a series of detailed questions about what legal authority provides the most effective means of keeping the Internet open: Section 706 or Title II.
- Proposes a multi-faceted process to promptly resolve and head off disputes, including an ombudsperson to act as a watchdog on behalf of consumers and start-ups and small businesses.

Action by the Commission May 15, 2014, by Notice of Proposed Rulemaking (FCC 14-61). Chairman Wheeler and Commissioner Clyburn with Commissioner Rosenworcel concurring and Commissioners Pai and O'Rielly dissenting. Chairman Wheeler, Commissioners Clyburn, Rosenworcel, Pai and O'Rielly issuing statements.

SOURCE: Federal Communications Commission. "FCC Launches Broad Rulemaking on How Best to Protect and Promote the Open Internet." May 18, 2014. www.fcc.gov/document/fcc-launches-broad-rulemaking-protect-and-promote-open-internet.

FCC Chair Tom Wheeler Remarks on Net Neutrality

May 18, 2014

I strongly support an open, fast and robust Internet. This agency supports an Open Internet.

There is ONE Internet. Not a fast internet, not a slow internet; ONE Internet.

The attention being paid to this topic is proof of why the open and free exchange of information must be protected. Thank you to the thousands who have emailed me personally. Thank you to those who felt so strongly about the issue that they camped outside. The Founding Fathers must be looking down and smiling at how the republic they created is practicing the ideals they established.

By releasing this Item today those who have been expressing themselves will now be able to see what we are actually proposing. They have been heard, we look forward to further input, and we say thank you.

Today we take another step in what has been a decade-long effort to preserve and protect the Open Internet. Unfortunately, those previous efforts were blocked twice by court challenges by those who sell Internet connections to consumers. Today this agency moves to surmount that opposition and to stand up for consumers and the Open Internet.

This *Notice of Proposed Rulemaking* starts an important process. Where it ends depends on what we learn during this process. That is why I am grateful for all the attention this topic has received. We start with the simple, obvious premise: Protecting the Open Internet is important both to consumers and to economic growth. We are dedicated to protecting and preserving an Open Internet. What we are dealing with today is a proposal, not a final rule. With this *Notice* we are specifically asking for input on different approaches to accomplish the same goal: an Open Internet.

The potential for there to be some kind of "fast lane" available to only a few has many people concerned. Personally, I don't like the idea that the Internet could become divided into "haves" and "have nots." I will work to see that does not happen. In this Item we specifically ask whether and how to prevent the kind of paid prioritization that could result in "fast lanes."

Two weeks ago I told the convention of America's cable broadband providers something that is worth repeating here, "If someone acts to divide the Internet between 'haves' and 'have nots,'" I told the cable industry, "we will use every power at our disposal to stop it." I will take a backseat to no one that privileging some network users in a manner that squeezes out smaller voices is unacceptable. Today, we have proposed how to stop that from happening, including consideration of the applicability of Title II.

There is only ONE Internet. It must be fast, robust and open. The speed and quality of the connection the consumer purchases must be unaffected by what content he or she is using. And there has to be a level playing field of opportunity for new ideas. Small companies and startups must be able to effectively reach consumers with innovative products and services and they must be protected against harmful conduct by broadband providers. The prospect of a gatekeeper choosing winners and losers on the Internet is unacceptable.

Let's look at how the Internet works at the retail level. The consumer accesses the Internet using connectivity provided by an Internet Service Provider (ISP). That connectivity should be open and inviolate; it is the simple purchase of a pathway. I believe it would be commercially unreasonable—and therefore not permitted—for the ISP not to deliver the contracted-for open pathway.

Let's consider specifically what that means. I want to get to rules that work like this:

- If the network operator slowed the speed below that which the consumer bought (for reasons other than reasonable network management), it would be a commercially unreasonable practice and therefore **prohibited,**
- If the network operator blocked access to lawful content, it would violate our no blocking rule and be commercially unreasonable and therefore doubly **prohibited,**
- When content provided by a firm such as Netflix reaches the consumer's network provider it would be commercially unreasonable to charge the content provider to use the bandwidth for which the consumer had already paid and therefore **prohibited,**
- When a consumer buys specified capacity from a network provider he or she is buying open capacity, not capacity the network can prioritize for its own profit purposes. Prioritization that deprives the consumer of what the consumer has paid for would be commercially unreasonable and therefore **prohibited.**

Simply put, when a consumer buys a specified bandwidth, it is commercially unreasonable – and thus a violation of this proposal—to deny them the full connectivity and the full benefits that connection enables.

Also included in this proposal are two new powers for those who use the Internet and for the Commission:

- **Expanded transparency will require networks to inform on themselves:** The proposal expands the existing transparency rules to require that networks disclose any practices that could change a consumer's or a content provider's relationship with the network. I thus anticipate that, if a network ever planned to take an action that would affect a content provider's access there would be time for the FCC to consider petitions to review such an action.
- **Voice for the Average American:** Recognizing that Internet entrepreneurs and consumers shouldn't have to hire a lawyer to call the Commission's attention to a grievance, an Ombudsperson would be created within the FCC to receive their complaints and, where warranted, investigate and represent their case.

Separate and apart from this connectivity is the question of interconnection ("peering") between the consumer's network provider and the various networks that deliver to that ISP. That is a different matter that is better addressed separately. Today's proposal is all about what happens on the broadband provider's network and how the consumer's connection to the Internet may not be interfered with or otherwise compromised.

The situation in which this Commission finds itself is inherited from the actions of previous Commissions over the last decade. The D.C. Circuit's ruling in January of this year upheld our determination that we need rules to protect Internet openness, and upheld our authority under Section 706 to adopt such rules, even while it found that portions of the *2010 Open Internet Order* were beyond the scope of our authority. In response, I promptly stated that we would reinstate rules that achieve the goals of the 2010 *Order* using the Section 706-based roadmap laid out by the court. That is what we are proposing today. Section 706 is one of the two principal methods proposed to accomplish the goals of an Open Internet. Today we are seeking input on both Section 706 and Title II of the Communications Act.

We are specifically asking for input as to the benefits of each and why one might be preferable to another. We have established a lengthy comment and reply period sufficient to allow everyone an opportunity to participate. As a former entrepreneur and venture capitalist, I know the importance of openness first hand. As an entrepreneur, I have had products and services shut out of closed cable networks. As a VC, I invested in companies that wouldn't have been able to innovate if the Internet weren't open. I have hands-on experience with the importance of network openness.

I will not allow the national asset of an Open Internet to be compromised. I understand this issue in my bones. I can show you the scars from when my companies were denied open access in the pre-Internet days.

The consideration we are beginning today is not about whether the Internet must be open, but about <u>how</u> and <u>when</u> we will have rules in place to assure an Open Internet. My preference has been to follow the roadmap laid out by the D.C. Circuit in the belief that it was the fastest and best way to get protections in place. I have also indicated repeatedly that I am open to using Title II.

This rulemaking begins the process by putting forth a proposal, asking important and specific questions, and opening the discussion to all Americans. We look forward to hearing feedback on all these approaches.

Source: Federal Communications Commission. "Statement of Chairman Tom Wheeler Re: Protecting and Promoting the Open Internet, GN Docket No. 14-28." May 18, 2014. https://apps.fcc.gov/edocs_public/attachmatch/DOC-327104A2.pdf.

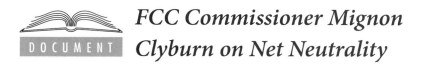

FCC Commissioner Mignon Clyburn on Net Neutrality

May 18, 2014

When my mother calls, with public policy concerns, I know there is a problem.

In my 16 years as a public servant, Emily Clyburn has never called me about a substantive issue under consideration. Not during my time serving on the South Carolina Public Service Commission. Not during my tenure here as a Commissioner nor as Acting Chairwoman. Never. But all of that changed on Monday, April 28th.

Please indulge me for a moment. My mother is a very organized, intuitive and intelligent woman. She was a medical librarian and earned a master's degree while she raised three girls. She is smart, thoughtful and engaged. She is a natural researcher. So when she picked up the phone to call me about this issue, I knew for sure something was just not right.

She gave voice to three basic questions which, and as of today's date, her message remains on my telephone and in personal memory banks: (1) "what is this net neutrality issue?" (2) "can providers do what they want to do?" and (3) "did it already pass?"

So, like any good daughter with an independent streak, I will directly answer my mother's questions in my own time and in my own way. But her inquiry truly echoes the calls, emails and letters I have received from thousands of consumers, investors, startups, healthcare providers, educators and others across the country who are equally concerned and confused. All of this demonstrates, (no pun intended) how fundamental the Internet has become for all of us.

So, why are we here, and exactly what is net neutrality or Open Internet? First, let me start from a place where I believe most of us can agree that a free and open exchange of ideas is critical to a democratic society. Consumers with the ability to visit whatever website and access any lawful content of their choice, interact with their government, apply for a job, even monitor their household devices. Educators have the capacity to leverage the best digital learning tools for their students. Healthcare providers treating their patients with the latest technologies—all of this occurring without those services or content being discriminated against or blocked.

All content, all "bits," being treated equally. Small startups on a shoestring budget with novel ideas have the ability to reach millions of people and compete on equal footing with those established players and their considerable budgets. Innovation abounds with new applications, technologies and services.

At its core, an open Internet means that consumers, not a company, not the government, determine winners and losers. It is the free market at its best. All of this, however, does not nor will it ever, occur organically. Without rules governing a free and open Internet it is possible that companies—fixed and wireless broadband providers—could independently determine whether they want to discriminate or block content, pick favorites, charge higher fees or distort the market.

I have been listening to concerns not just from my mother, but from thousands of consumers and interested parties. Startups that fear, they "won't even get a chance to succeed," if access to consumers is controlled by corporations, rather than a competitive level playing field. Investors who say they will be reticent to commit money to new companies because they are concerned that their new service will not be able to reach consumers in the marketplace because of high costs or differential treatment.

Educators, even where there is a high capacity connection at the school, feel that their students may not be able to take advantage of the best in digital learning if the quality of the content is poor. Healthcare professionals worrying that the images they need to view will load too slowly and that patients will be unable to benefit from the latest technologies and specialized care made possible through remote monitoring. And, I am hearing from everyday people, who say that we need to maintain the openness of the Internet and that this openness enables today's discourse to be viewed by thousands, and offers them the ability to interact directly with policy makers and engage in robust exchanges like we are experiencing today.

In fact, let me say how impressed I was when I spoke with some of you on Maine Street earlier this week. You came to Washington from North Carolina, New York, Pennsylvania, and Virginia at your own expense to affirm just how important this issue is to you. You made it clear that the Internet is a great equalizer in our society and that average consumers should have the same access to the Internet as those with deep pockets.

There are dozens of examples across the globe where we have seen firsthand the dangers to society when people are not allowed to choose. Governments blocking access to content and stifling free speech and public discourse.

Countries, including some in Europe, where providers have congested or degraded content, and apps are being blocked from certain mobile devices. Hints of problems have occurred even here at home, particularly with regard to apps on mobile devices, even though providers in the United State [sic], have been subject to net neutrality principles and rules with the threat of enforcement for over a decade.

So, to Mom and to all of you, this is an issue about promoting our democratic values of free speech, competition, economic growth, and civic engagement.

The second she posed was, can providers just do what they want? The short answer, is yes. As of January we have no rules to prevent discrimination or blocking.

This is actually a significant change because the FCC has had policies in place dating back to 2004, when the Commission under former Chairman, and my friend Michael Powell, unanimously adopted four principles of an open Internet in the Internet Policy Statement. These principles became the rules of the road with the potential for enforcement. Then, in 2010, the Commission formally adopted rules to promote an open Internet by preventing blocking, and unreasonable discrimination.

When the Commission approved these rules, I explained why I would have done some things differently. For instance, I would have applied the same rules to both fixed and mobile broadband; prohibited paid priority agreements; limited any exceptions to the rule; and I am on record as preferring a different legal structure. The 2010 rules reflect a compromise . . . yes, Mom, I do compromise at times. But in January 2014, the D.C. Circuit disagreed with our legal framework . . . so here we are, again.

And I say again, that the court decision means that today we have no unreasonable discrimination or no blocking rules on the books. Nothing prevents providers from acting in small ways that largely may go undetected. And, nothing prevents them from acting in larger ways to discriminate against or even block certain content. To be fair, providers have stated that they intend, for the time being, not to do so and have publicly committed to retain their current policies of openness. But, for me, the issue comes down to whether broadband providers should have the ability to determine, on their own, whether the Internet is free and open OR whether we should have basic and clear rules of the road in place to ensure that this occurs as we have had for the last decade.

And, this may be surprising to some but I have chosen to view the court decision in a positive light for it has given us a unique opportunity to take a fresh look and evaluate our policy in light of the developments that have occurred in the market over the last four years, including the increased use of WiFi, deployment of LTE, faster speeds and connections to homes, schools, libraries, and the increased use of broadband on mobile devices, to name a few. The remand enables us to issue this clarion call to the public where they can once again help us answer that most important question of how to protect and maintain a free and open Internet. That ability officially begins for everyone today.

The third question, and, judging by the headlines and subsequent reactions, my Mother is in good company here, was "has, it, passed?" No, it has not, but let me explain. Some press accounts have reported that the Chairman's initial proposal is what we are voting on, and have conflated proposed rules with, final rules. Neither is accurate.

For those who practice in this space, I ask that you bear with me for a moment. When the Chairman circulates an item, it is indeed a reflection of his vision. My office then evaluates the proposal, listens to any concerns voiced by interested parties, including consumers, then considers whether we have concerns and, if so, what changes we want to request so that we could move to a position of support.

This item was no different. It is true. I too had significant concerns about the initial proposal but after interactions among the staff, my office, and the Chairman's office, this item has changed considerably over the last few weeks and I greatly appreciate the Chairman incorporating my many requests to do so. Though I still may have preferred to make portions of the draft more neutral, what we are voting on today asks about a number of alternatives, which will allow for a well-rounded record to develop, on how best to protect the public interest.

Second, today, we are voting only on proposed rules—not final rules. Again, this item is an official call inviting interested parties to comment, to discuss the pros and cons of various approaches, and to have a robust dialogue about the best path forward. When the Chairman hits the gavel after votes are cast on this item this morning, it will signal the start of 120 unique days of opportunity each of you has in shaping and influencing the direction of one of the world's most incredible platforms. The feedback up until now has been nothing short of astounding but the real call to action begins after this vote is taken. Comments are due on July 15th, and there is ample time to evaluate any of the proposals and provide meaningful feedback.

You have spoken and I am listening. Your power will never be underestimated, and I sincerely hope that your passion continues. As I said to those I met with outside of FCC headquarters, this is your opportunity to formally make your point on the record. You have the ear of the entire FCC. The eyes of the world are on all of us. Use your voice and this platform to continue to be heard.

I will do all that I can independently, and with the Chairman, to identify ways to encourage a more interactive dialogue with all stakeholders whether through town halls, workshops, webinars, or social media because I know with a robust record this Commission will be able [to] move quickly and get to the finish line with the adoption of permanent rules that provide certainty, and which are clear and enforceable.

So, mom, I hope that answers most of your questions and I sincerely hope that you won't feel compelled to ask me any more significant policy questions for another 16 years.

In all seriousness, I want to thank the dedicated staff from the Office of General Counsel, including Jonathan Sallet and Stephanie Weiner, as well as the Wireline Competition and Wireless Telecommunications Bureaus, for their work on this significant item. And I want to especially thank my Wireline Legal Advisor, Rebekah Goodheart, for her expert work on this item.

SOURCE: Federal Communications Commission. "Statement of Commissioner Mignon L. Clyburn Re: Protecting and Promoting the Open Internet, GN Docket No. 14-28." May 18, 2014. https://apps.fcc.gov/edocs_public/attachmatch/DOC-327104A3.pdf.

OTHER HISTORIC DOCUMENTS OF INTEREST

FROM PREVIOUS *HISTORIC DOCUMENTS*

Secretary Kerry and Prime Minister Modi Remark on Historic Indian Election

MAY 20, 26, AND 27, 2014

In May 2014, India was the site of the world's largest election where more than 530 million citizens turned out to choose representatives for their lower house of parliament, the Lok Sabha. Indian citizens who came to the polls were focused on key issues such as inflation, corruption, security, and unemployment. When the results were announced, the National Democratic Alliance (NDA) had proven its dominance by winning a majority of the seats. As leader of the majority party, Narendra Modi was invited to form a government and lead the nation as prime minister. Modi now faces the challenge of expanding India's role on the global stage while also tackling domestic issues.

THE LONG INDIAN ELECTION

The Indian government is comprised of a bicameral parliament led by a prime minister. The lower house, the Lok Sabha, consists of 545 seats, of which 543 are elected and two are appointed by the president of India. Elections for the lower house take place every five years, or when the president decides to dissolve parliament. Members of the upper house, the Rajya Sabha, are elected by state legislatures. The Lok Sabha is considered the more powerful of the two houses despite being deemed the "lower house" because it has the power to pass financial legislation.

In April and May 2014, voters were set to choose members of the Lok Sabha. Indian elections are broken up into nine phases over the course of six weeks. Each state votes in a separate phase, with multiple states voting on the same day. The 2014 election ran from April 7 to May 12. The largest voting day of this election was Phase 5 on April 17, when 200 million eligible voters went to the polls.

The April-May 2014 election was the first in the nation's history to feature an option of "none of the above" on the ballot, a nod to citizen's discontent with their leaders, many of whom had been found guilty in a series of corruption scandals in 2013. The election was also the first that allowed nonresident Indians, those who are citizens of the country but have chosen to live outside its borders, to vote. The lengthy election cost the government nearly $600 million and required the assistance of 6.6 million civil servants and employees.

KEY CAMPAIGN ISSUES

There were two primary issues during the 2014 Lok Sabha campaigns: the economy and government corruption. India has traditionally had a higher-than-average inflation rate. Heading into the election, inflation was at 10.9 percent, slightly higher than previous years, but still a relatively average rate for India. Even so, common goods were difficult for the average Indian family to afford. The NDA stated during the campaign that it intended to put new policies in place, such as the creation of a Price Stabilisation Fund and National Agriculture Market, which would make common goods more accessible. The United Progressive Alliance (UPA), the NDA's main competitor, repeatedly indicated that it wanted economic equality for all Indians but failed to provide a clear strategy for how this would be achieved.

Unemployment was also a focal point for voters. The estimated 3 percent urban and 2 percent rural unemployment rate was expected to rise in the upcoming year. The NDA proposed more self-employment opportunities, a focus on agriculture jobs, and greater government investment in infrastructure projects as a way to reduce the unemployment rate and help more Indians participate in the economy. In contrast, the UPA proposed using an old military strategy known as "one rank, one pension," which would allow the pension payments of past retirees to grow as newer employees leave the workforce, thus increasing the spending power of older Indians. Neither party offered a specific agenda for how it might aid the largest group of unemployed citizens: highly educated young people.

After two high-profile corruption scandals in recent years, Indian voters were also concerned about the morality of their leaders. Starting in 2007, political officials undercharged cell phone companies for their radio frequency band licenses while simultaneously creating second-generation (2G) allowances for cell phones. The Indian officials involved in the scandal made millions of dollars in the process, none of which went back into the nation's economy (the leaders of the scandal were eventually arrested in 2011). In 2010, a new corruption scheme came to light when political figures were highly criticized for the exorbitant amount of money spent to encourage the Commonwealth Games organizers to hold the event in New Delhi. Not only was the government wasting millions while the nation's poorest languished, it was also committing labor violations in its treatment of the workers tasked with creating facilities for the games. Both these scandals had an impact on foreign investment, according to India's Communications and IT minister Kapil Sibal. "It . . . has slowed down foreign equity coming into India. All that has certainly happened, and I think we ourselves are responsible for that," he said.

RESULTS OF THE ELECTION

On May 16, the Election Commission of India released the results of the 2014 Lok Sabha election. The NDA secured the majority of the seats, winning 336. The Bharatiya Janata Party (BJP), the largest faction in the NDA, led by Modi, secured 282 of those seats. The BJP's victory marked an increase of 166 seats from the 2009 parliamentary election. The UPA was the second highest vote-getting coalition, winning sixty seats, a decline of 162 from the previous election in 2009. The Indian National Congress (INC), the UPA's largest member, won only forty-four seats, its worst showing in a Lok Sabha general election to date.

After Prime Minister Manmohan Singh announced that he would not stand for reelection, Modi, the former minister of Gujarat state, was asked by the president to form a government. Although Modi was instrumental in bringing the NDA to victory, his record was tarnished. Modi has been criticized for decisions he made during the 2002

Gujarat riots to crack down on protests and his perceived failure to stop the murders of Muslims during the riots. But Modi has also been praised for his domestic and international work, most important for the economic growth he brought to Gujarat.

Modi was largely popular with a segment of Indians who have traditionally shied away from involvement in politics: young people. During his campaign, Modi was one of the first Indian politicians to heavily incorporate social media into his campaign. When the BJP was victorious, Modi tweeted "India has won!," which became the most retweeted item in India in 2014. In his victory speech, Modi promised to bring the country a sense of social togetherness. "India's social differences will come together and make a flag, just like different threads come together to weave a cloth," he said. In forming his government, Modi sought to reduce the scope of his cabinet in an effort to cut both costs and bureaucracy. Through his guiding principle of "Minimum Government and Maximum Governance," instead of the traditional seventy cabinet ministers, Modi chose to appoint only forty-five.

India's Post-Election Future

High turnout in the 2014 Lok Sabha election will serve as a call to action for the new governing coalition. Domestically, the government's focus will be on lowering unemployment and reducing inflation with the aim of helping India's poorest citizens. Modi promised to create a government that "thinks about the poor, listens to the poor, and which exists for the poor," adding that "our dream is to fulfill their dreams." Foreign investment will be of utmost importance in achieving these goals.

Modi, a pro-business politician, and the NDA are leading a movement toward greater interaction with international allies in an effort to improve India's status on the global stage. India is looking to open up trade talks with neighboring Asian nations with whom it has not previously had close trade ties. Specifically, Modi has expressed a keen interest in forging a closer trading relationship with China. Modi met with Chinese leaders in September, during which the two nations signed a number of Memorandums of Understanding in areas of agreed upon cooperation such as economic development, customs, and infrastructure.

Modi also intended to continue his nation's strong military and strategic alliance with Russia. "The steadfast support of the people of Russia for India has been there even at difficult moments in our history," said Modi in December. In a nod to the conflict between Russia and Ukraine, Modi added, "India, too, has always stood with Russia through its own challenges." This enduring relationship was vital for Russian president Vladimir Putin, who could count on revenue from Indian military purchases to help shore up its weak economy. The two nations signed an agreement in December for a $5 billion fixed-price oil contract, as well as the purchase of twenty nuclear reactors.

The United States, one of India's key allies, celebrated Modi's victory and the nation's successful election and promised to continue working with the government on issues of mutual interest. "The United States stands ready to work closely with Prime Minister Modi and the new government to promote shared prosperity and strengthen our security," said U.S. secretary of state John Kerry. "The friendship between the world's oldest democracy and the world's largest democracy is absolutely vital, and the United States is deeply invested in our strategic relationship. We look forward to strengthening our partnership based on common values, shared democratic traditions, and the binding ties between our peoples." In August, Kerry met with Prime Minister Modi to encourage him to sign the World Trade Organization's Trade Facilitation Agreement Protocol. India had chosen not to sign the document because it did not feel that its concerns about food security and public stockholding were properly addressed; however, Kerry said that if the nation intended to increase its trade alliances across Asia and expand trade with the United States, failure to sign the protocol sent a confusing message. In September, Modi traveled to the United States where he held meetings with President Barack Obama that the National Security Council deemed "extraordinarily successful" and "a boost in terms of the vision and focus that we have for our bilateral relations."

—Alexis Atwater

Following is a statement by U.S. secretary of state John Kerry on May 20, 2014, congratulating India on a successful and historic election; and two press releases issued by Prime Minister Narendra Modi's office on May 26 and 27, 2014, on the formation of his government and assent to the prime ministerial position.

DOCUMENT

Secretary Kerry Offers Congratulations to New Indian Leaders

May 20, 2014

I offer my congratulations to the Bharatiya Janata Party on their resounding victory in India's historic national election, and to Narendra Modi on his election as Prime Minister of India. I also extend warm congratulations to all the newly elected parliamentarians.

When the people of India hold the biggest democratic election in human history, all the world tunes in to watch. And what we saw has been nothing short of remarkable: more voters cast their ballots freely and fairly than any other in world history, with over 530 million Indians going to the polls. The voice of the Indian electorate is clear and unequivocal in its call for economic opportunity and effective governance for all.

The United States stands ready to work closely with Prime Minister Modi and the new government to promote shared prosperity and strengthen our security. The friendship between the world's oldest democracy and the world's largest democracy is absolutely vital, and the United States is deeply invested in our strategic relationship. We look forward to strengthening our partnership based on common values, shared democratic traditions, and the binding ties between our peoples.

Every time I visit India, I'm struck by the vibrancy of your culture, the energy of your youth, and the strength of your democratic institutions. I look forward to returning to India soon and echo President Obama's invitation to Prime Minister Modi to visit the United States at the earliest opportunity.

SOURCE: U.S. Department of State. "Indian Elections and Formation of New Government." May 20, 2014. www.state.gov/secretary/remarks/2014/05/226344.htm.

Prime Minister Modi
Forms Government

May 26, 2014

Prime Minister designate Shri Narendra Modi shared a press release on Twitter which stated that the PM-designate had made a historic change in the formation of Ministries.

The Press Release stated:

The Prime Minister-designate Shri Narendra Modi has made a historic change in the formation of Ministries. For the first time, he adopted guiding principle of "Minimum Government and Maximum Governance" and also rationalization with a commitment to bring a change in the work culture and style of governance.

It is a good beginning in transforming entity of assembled ministries to Organic Ministries. It will bring more coordination between different departments, will be more effective and bring a speed in process.

The focus is on convergence in the activities of various Ministries where one cabinet Minister will be heading a cluster of Ministries who are working in complimentary sectors.

Mr. Modi is eventually aiming at Smart Governance where the top layers of Government will be downsized and there would be expansion at the grass root level.

Shri Narendra Modi is aware of the high expectations of the people. For whole four days, he was busy with the formation of Ministry and discussing various alternatives to effective governance, convergence and coordination between various ministries.

Earlier, there was political instability and multi-party governments, the ministry formation was almost done in a bifurcated manner.

Shri Narendra Modi tried in a rational manner to club like-minded departments in the ministry formation in such way to convert entity of assembled ministry to organic entity.

He formed ministry using as an instrument to deal with challenges and expectation of people.

Integrated and inter-connected nature of Governance is being focused in this positive change.

He emphasized that the ministry can deliver, can govern and can bring change in style of functioning.

In the ministry formation, the process of development will be more inclusive than it has been.

SOURCE: Prime Minister of India. "Narendra Modi shares press release stating the new Ministry Formation as a step towards Smart Governance." May 26, 2014. http://pmindia.gov.in/en/news_updates/narendra-modi-shares-press-release-stating-the-new-ministry-formation-as-a-step-towards-smart-governance/.

Shri Narendra Modi Assumes
Office as 15th Prime Minister of India

May 27, 2014

Shri Narendra Modi today assumed office as the Fifteenth Prime Minister of India.

Shri Narendra Modi offered floral tributes to Mahatma Gandhi in his office at South Block, and assumed charge of the office of Prime Minister.

Shri Narendra Modi as an able administrator, has focused on good governance initiatives as well as development to bring about qualitative change in the lives of the people. He has adopted the guiding principle of "Minimum Government and Maximum Governance" and also rationalization with a commitment to bring a change in the work culture and style of governance.

He held a short briefing with the Principal Secretary to PM Shri Nripendra Mishra and senior officers in PMO.

Senior PMO officials welcomed and received Shri Narendra Modi, when he arrived at the Prime Minister's Office in South Block.

Source: Prime Minister of India. "Shri Narendra Modi assumes office as 15th Prime Minister of India." May 27, 2014. http://pmindia.gov.in/en/news_updates/shri-narendra-modi-assumes-office-as-15th-prime-minister-of-india/.

OTHER HISTORIC DOCUMENTS OF INTEREST

FROM PREVIOUS *HISTORIC DOCUMENTS*

- President Bush and Prime Minister Singh on U.S.-Indian Relations, *2006*, p. 95

Thai Military Seizes Power in Coup

MAY 22 AND 24, AND JUNE 6, 2014

Following months of unrest, on May 22, 2014, Thailand's military overthrew the government and suspended the constitution in a coup. The government takeover marked the twelfth coup in Thailand's history since 1932. The new military government has heavily suppressed personal freedoms, banned protests, and controlled the media. The military leaders argue that such strict control of the population is necessary to restore order after months of unrest in the lead up to the coup. The nation's fate remains uncertain as countries around the globe push for a return to civilian government.

Opposing Political Factions

The junta decision to overthrow the government surprised many, as General Prayut Chan-o-cha, commander of the Royal Thai Army, had dismissed earlier calls to intervene militarily during the political upheaval. Military control was announced just after the opposing government factions met to resume negotiations, a step toward developing a unity government that would distribute power among the various parties in Thailand. General Prayut announced in a broadcast on all television channels: "In the interest of rule and order, we are taking over powers. Please do not panic and carry on with your daily activities." With the general's announcement of takeover, the negotiations abruptly stopped, leaving the two factions as divided as ever.

The United Front for Democracy Against Dictatorship (UDD), commonly called "red shirts" because its supporters wear the color red, is comprised of mostly rural citizens from Northern Thailand. This populist political group formed in opposition to a military coup that took place in 2006. The group seeks to reform a system that they claim unfairly places members of the aristocracy in places of power, disenfranchising the majority of poorer Thai citizens. The majority of UDD members support deposed Prime Minister Thaksin Shinawatra who remains in self-imposed exile following the military takeover.

The UDD has been characterized by its rival group, the People's Alliance for Democracy (PAD), or "yellow shirts," as antimonarchy. This charge is highly inflammatory in Thai politics due to the great reverence for the monarch and strict laws prohibiting speaking ill of the monarchy or speculating about affairs inside the palace. Such offences are punishable with jail time. Thailand's most recent prime minister, Yingluck Shinawatra (sister of deposed prime minister Thaksin Shinawatra), was removed from office on May 7, 2014, as a result of tenuous corruption charges leading to further unrest in the lead up to the declaration of martial law by the Thai military. The red shirts hope to draft a new constitution that includes provisions to overturn the charges against many UDD leaders in criminal cases, including former prime minister Thaksin Shinawatra.

This provision is not popular with the PAD, as the group originated as an alliance of protesters in direct opposition to Thaksin Shinawatra's rule. The PAD is mostly composed of upper to middle class Thai people, mainly from the south. The yellow shirts are closely aligned with the Thai Army and with the monarchy. In 2006, the PAD overthrew the popularly elected government supported by the UDD (led by Thaksin) and dissolved soon thereafter, having achieved the group's primary aim. When entities affiliated with Thaksin won the 2007 general election, the PAD re-formed. Both groups organized protests in the power struggle that followed with devastating and bloody ends. In much the same way, the current political crisis and related violent protests have claimed upward of twenty-five lives.

When the military took over on May 22, 2014, forming the National Council for Peace and Order (NCPO) led by General Prayut, the commander of the Royal Thai Army dissolved the Senate and issued an interim constitution granting the NCPO amnesty and sweeping power.

U.S. Response to the Takeover

The United States and Thailand have a long-standing bilateral relationship dating back to 1832, with the signing of the Treaty of Amity and Commerce the following year. Throughout the years, diplomatic ties between the United States and Thailand have remained strong, even as modern Thailand continues to be plagued by government instability punctuated by multiple military insurrections. Thailand remains the oldest treaty ally of the United States in Asia, though the May 2014 coup has produced, arguably limited, negative implications for the friendship between the two nations.

Shortly after the Thai military suspended the constitution and took control of the government—an act that General Prayut said would be temporary—the United States canceled several events, including the 2014 Exercise Cooperation Afloat Readiness and Training, a visit to Thailand by the U.S. Pacific Fleet Commander, and an invitation for the Royal Thai Armed Forces commanding general to visit U.S. Pacific Command.

In a press briefing the weekend following the military takeover in Thailand, State Department deputy spokesperson Marie Harf said the United States would also cancel a U.S. government-sponsored firearms training program in Thailand for the Royal Thai Police that was scheduled to begin later in May. In a similar statement, Pentagon press secretary Rear Admiral John Kirby stated, "While we have enjoyed a long and productive military-to-military relationship with Thailand, our own democratic principles and U.S. law require us to reconsider U.S. military assistance and engagements." Though the administration did not announce plans to freeze military relations, the overwhelming theme from both agency spokespeople is the desire for a swift return to democratic rule with a speedy path forward to free elections.

The level of monetary involvement from the United States in those exercises was reportedly limited. It is unlikely that this relatively small amount, approximately $4.5 million in financial support, will greatly impact the Thai military. This amount is a drop in the bucket when contrasted with the level of U.S. aid to Egypt, in excess of $1 billion, which would have been suspended had the United States declared the 2013 uprising in Egypt to be a coup. By U.S. law, the declaration of a coup requires the suspension of financial assistance.

Markets initially stabilized with the announcement of martial law due to optimism regarding a swift resolution to the persistent political turmoil, but trade and tourism have declined significantly as military rule and uncertainty persist. According to data from the U.S. Department of State, the United States is Thailand's third-largest bilateral trading partner and one of the largest contributors to the country's foreign direct investment. Following the statement on May 22, 2014, the United States reviewed assistance and engagement and issued travel warnings for American citizens.

The Department of State continues to reiterate that U.S. officials remain concerned by the actions of the Thai military and call for the release of political detainees. Leaders of the Thai military maintain their intention to hold political activists, including former prime minister Shinawatra, in custody as they deem necessary. In his press statement on May 22, Secretary of State John Kerry called for a restoration of the press and a return to "respect for human rights and fundamental freedoms." Initially, the press was shut down, schools temporarily closed, and a nationwide curfew instituted in the name of public safety—all of these actions at odds with American ideals and those of her allies.

Continuing Protests

As military rule continues in Thailand and the date of the next election is delayed, protests continue. In November 2014, during an appearance by General Prayut, students at a university in northeastern Thailand stood up wearing T-shirts bearing anticoup slogans. The students also raised their hands, giving the three-fingered salute from the well-known U.S. book series *The Hunger Games*. The symbol has been adopted by protesters in Thailand to signify opposition to the coup. The students were immediately arrested. According to a report by CNN, the five protesters in this particular incident were charged with violating martial law and face the threat of expulsion from their university. The five, like many other protesters, were also required to sign an agreement that they would not participate in any further "political activity."

The NCPO has banned unauthorized meetings with more than five people and those who violate this regulation risk trials in military courts. Civilian courts have been suspended until new elections are held and a civilian government is selected. In such military tribunals, there are no appeals and all decisions are final. The NCPO claims that these strict measures are necessary to restore order following the extended period of contentious protests. Other forms of protests that are now banned include "democracy picnics," where citizens distribute sandwiches and eat together in a group to show their common bond, as well as publicly reading the book *1984* by George Orwell.

National Public Radio (NPR) reports that the current military rulers of Thailand have blocked domestic access to a report from Human Rights Watch (HRW) on the current state of citizens in Thailand. When one attempts to access the report from locations inside the country, browsers display a message from the Ministry of Information and Communications Technology that the website has "inappropriate content and has been suspended." Representatives from HRW see the need to block the report as an indication of the situation in Thailand. All media outlets remain under strict control. Advertisements on billboards warn that "liking" negative messages about the monarchy or the government on social media sites such as Facebook are punishable by jail or fine. According to Reuters, General Prayut defends such actions saying, "I did not seize power for my benefit. We do not want to abuse power and we do not want to use force." The NCPO insists that the strict rules are working, but critics such as Amnesty International and HRW contend that the appearance that the measures are working is simply a mask of fear rather than an easing of tensions.

—Sarah Gall

Following is the text of a press statement delivered by U.S. secretary of state John Kerry on May 22, 2014, expressing concern about the military's overthrow of Thailand's government; the text of an article from the U.S. Department of Defense on May 24, 2014, regarding the U.S. decision to halt military engagements with Thailand; and excerpts from a June 6, 2014, speech by General Prayut Chan-o-cha, with regard to the military takeover of the Thai government.

Secretary Kerry Responds to Thailand Coup

May 22, 2014

I am disappointed by the decision of the Thai military to suspend the constitution and take control of the government after a long period of political turmoil, and there is no justification for this military coup. I am concerned by reports that senior political leaders of Thailand's major parties have been detained and call for their release. I am also concerned that media outlets have been shut down. I urge the restoration of civilian government immediately, a return to democracy, and respect for human rights and fundamental freedoms, such as press freedoms. The path forward for Thailand must include early elections that reflect the will of the people.

While we value our long friendship with the Thai people, this act will have negative implications for the U.S.–Thai relationship, especially for our relationship with the Thai military. We are reviewing our military and other assistance and engagements, consistent with U.S. law.

SOURCE: U.S. Department of State. "Coup in Thailand." May 22, 2014. www.state.gov/secretary/remarks /2014/05/226446.htm.

Department of Defense Curbs Thai Military Engagements

May 24, 2014

Following a coup by the Thai military, the United States has curtailed military-to-military engagement with the Kingdom of Thailand in accordance with U.S. law, Pentagon press secretary Navy Rear Adm. John Kirby said in a written statement today.

The Royal Thai Armed Forces took over the country Thursday after earlier imposing martial law. Kirby called on Thai military leaders to "end this coup and restore to the people of Thailand both the principles and the process of democratic rule, including a clear path forward to elections."

Thailand is one of America's oldest allies. The first treaty between the nations was ratified in 1837, and today Thailand is a "major non-NATO military ally."

Kirby referenced this long association in his statement. "While we have enjoyed a long and productive military-to-military relationship with Thailand, our own democratic principles and U.S. law require us to reconsider U.S. military assistance and engagements," he said.

In response to the coup, the United States has canceled the ongoing exercise Cooperation Afloat Readiness and Training 2014. The visit of U.S. Pacific Fleet commander Navy Adm. Harry Harris, which was set for next month, has also now been canceled.

In addition, the United States has rescinded an invitation to Royal Thai Armed Forces Commander General Thanasak Patimaprakorn to visit U.S. Pacific Command in June.

"We will continue to review additional engagements as necessary until such time that events in Thailand no longer demand it," Kirby said. "We urge the Royal Thai Armed Forces to act in the best interests of their fellow citizens by ending this coup and restoring the rule of law and the freedoms assured those citizens through democratic principles."

Thailand is one of 23 nations scheduled to participate in the Rim of the Pacific Exercises that begin June 26 and last through August. Thailand also hosts the annual Cobra Gold exercises, one of the largest exercises in Southeast Asia. The 2014 iteration of Cobra Gold ended in February.

SOURCE: U.S. Department of Defense. "Coup Leads U.S. to Curtail Thai Military Engagements." May 24, 2014. www.defense.gov/news/newsarticle.aspx?id=122328.

General Prayut Remarks on the Situation in Thailand Following Coup

June 6, 2014

Good evening to all Thai people in all sectors—be they government officials, the police and military, the private sector and the general public—that have given support and cooperation in moving our country forward together with the National Council for Peace and Order (NCPO) since 22 May 2014.

Let me reiterate that there were many reasons why it was necessary for the NCPO to take control of national administration. The most important was because we respect the democratic process.

Our decision was based on the fact that the three main branches of national administration—executive, legislative, and judiciary—were being undermined. We therefore have had to safeguard democracy. We came in to make our country stronger, laying firmer foundations to prevent the structure from collapsing so that our country will be ready to move towards becoming a fully functioning democracy.

The undermining structure which I mentioned involves the conflicting and overlapping working relationship between the public sector (civil service and political appointees), the private and business sectors and the civil society. It was problematic and led to a situation where respect for the laws was scant. General laws were ineffective. Special laws such as the Internal Security Act, Emergency Decree, and Martial Law had to be invoked.

Independent agencies were unable to fully perform their duties. The judicial system was not working effectively. People started to lose trust and faith in the whole system. Laws and law enforcement officers were not being respected, making it impossible to solve the issues. We were thus becoming an immoral society. I will not mention about the existing good things but will only mention things that are damaging.

Therefore a society without morality, without virtue, without good governance, could not move the country forward. The country must be ruled with good governance as His Majesty the King has clearly and continuously shown us.

State officials and other systems were being controlled and manipulated in every way by corrupt individuals, political parties and populist schemes. There were even problems with the passing or drafting of the laws due to interference in the interconnected administrative systems. There were some good things, but I shall refer only to the problems. As a result, there were widespread conflicts at many levels from the civil society to socio-economic. On international relations, we were losing trust and confidence and our dignity was not duly honoured by the international community.

We understand that we are living in a democratic world, but is Thailand ready in terms of people, form and method? We need to solve many issues; from administration to budget system, corruption, and even the starting point of democracy itself—the election. Parliamentary dictatorship has to be removed. All these have caused conflict and unhappiness among Thai people. Government officials could not work. So I had to ask myself "Can we let this continue?". We tried everything to resolve the problem through peaceful dialogue and legal means.

This situation has been going on for more than 9 years, and the past 6 months have been the most intense period. There were many deaths, injuries, losses, and resulting legal cases, many of which are still unresolved. What we are doing today is to try and bring everything back to normal. We intend to return happiness to everyone living in Thailand, both Thais and foreigners; expand economic and social cooperation with our partners, and prepare ourselves for the ASEAN Community and AEC in the near future.

Today, we have received both praise and criticisms. It is normal that there are people who agree with us as well as people who do not. But in the interest of national administration, I will mainly consider the criticisms. These will be carefully considered and analyzed. If they come from good intention and are for the benefit of the nation, I will turn them into actions. It is normal to have people who disagree with you when you take on such an important task. But please be assured that we are doing the best we can in order to achieve our goal of a fully functioning democracy which is accepted by all sides.

In exercising state power at present time, general laws and martial law are still concomitantly necessary. In the past, people were not respecting the general laws. Although today we are using the highest security law, not all components are being exercised but only those that we deemed necessary. There may be some disruptions or inconveniencies for some groups or foreigners, but we are asking for your understanding of our intentions. If we cannot keep the situation under control after we invoked the martial law, then no other laws in the world will work in Thailand. We will try to return to the use of normal laws as soon as possible, but people have to respect the law. I do not want the international community to view us as lawless people who use violence as a means to get what we want. We have to change this perception.

If these conflicts and violence or incitements continue, a successful and peaceful election is impossible. If the elections were to take place and a government was formed amidst conflict, violence, and protests, and was not accepted by the people, will the problem ever be resolved? There may be new protests and we will have to use force to suppress them. We have gone that way many times unsuccessfully. . . .

As for the international community, we are asking for your patience to give us time as we build our country and a democracy in which the Thai people possess discipline and a true understanding of democracy with good governance in accordance with the philosophy of sufficiency economy of His Majesty the King. Everybody is equal, in a society with morals, compassion, and unity. We have to look ahead to the people and the problems that we need to overcome. We have to look beyond ourselves or our own benefits.

The NCPO has been working for only 2 weeks. We have given our priority to solving the economic problems concerning people with low income. We have continued with the operations of all 21 ministries in accordance with the NCPO's policies. We listened to all stakeholders, be it public or private sectors dealing with economic and social affairs as well as the general public—and consider all suggestions and use them as guidance. Existing procedures are reviewed, adjusted, and improved upon through brainstorming and discussions between government officials and the NCPO. . . .

Please be confident of our work commitment. We put people's need first. Problems such as rice, agricultural products, tax, and energy price will be thoroughly checked, or delayed, in order to find the best approach. All solutions must be based on principle and rationale. People do not consider facts and tend to believe what we like, what we want to believe, but sometimes we must listen to the other side, or look at the whole picture. This is why I need to receive explanations and clarifications from all agencies that are facing obstacles in order for me to see the whole picture.

Today we do not yet have the facts on many issues which require legal and procedural considerations. For example, the issues of energy and state enterprises are complex and need to be considered carefully. They are also connected to other issues such as tax reduction and oil prices, which will be affected. Therefore we have to start by looking at the whole structure. This issue may be delayed for a while, but will continue as planned once the root problems have been located and tackled. If we reduce prices as requested without having resolved the fundamental problems, other problems concerning transportation and utilities will surely follow. We will have to carefully look at all aspects, including details of investors, their profit expectations, and most importantly the real benefits they bring to the Thai people.

I can assure you that the NCPO does not gain anything from this. We are here to resolve the problems, not to create more. I urge you all to be vigilant and help us stop all corruption through the use of law, and to avoid further conflict and confrontations. The NCPO will look into the problems brought to its attention and try to solve our shared problem.

I understand it is very dangerous to use absolute power to resolve national economic and financial problems, especially in the long run. But the most important problems we are facing today concern energy, taxation, prices of goods, and unchecked creditor networks. All these must be dealt with as soon as possible, but with careful consideration. If we rush into things and create more problems later, we will be held accountable and criticized.

We will expedite the approval of various projects to stimulate the market. Next week we will have a meeting to discuss projects which need executive approval at the ministerial level. Foreign investments, especially those with high budgets and long-term contracts will also be reviewed. All agreements must be legal, honourable, and accepted by the Thai people.

My intention is to create unity among Thai people. People should feel that they and their properties are safe and secure; that they live in a social order that is just and moral—a society that does not tolerate corruption.

As for the justice system, I think all agencies involved already know their duties and the scope of their powers. However, they have to be able to perform their duties without outside pressure and influence. In the past, this was not the case and people started to lose respect for the laws and the system. The NCPO has removed these external influences for you so it is time to regain people's trust and confidence.

I have touched on many issues involving many people. The curfew has been shortened, or lifted, in certain tourist areas. We will continue to reduce the restrictions imposed by martial law as the situation improves.

Some media such as television and radio satellite stations have been known to cause and promote conflict. These are being investigated and will be closed if found to be the cause of the problems. Contracts and agreements will have to be reconsidered. I am asking for the cooperation from all media to stop inciting conflict and support us in our efforts to resolve national problems.

We have seized a large number of war-grade weapons during the past weeks. We are investigating the sources and networks of these weapons. These people were given the chance to turn themselves and their weapons in to the authorities. They have not, so now we are doing our duty. War weapons have been smuggled into Thailand through our borders. Military and police personnel can only observe certain border areas while the smugglers keep changing their routes. I take full responsibility for this matter. We need to find new measures to support and enhance these military operations, such as procuring modern techonology [sic] equipment which is used in other countries. But we have budget contraints [sic]. Therefore we need to enlist the help of the local people to keep a watchful eye over the border areas. . . .

There are many other issues I would like to talk about but I shall find time to do so at a later date. I appeal to the university students and human rights groups and activists to refrain from instigating abrasive protest movements. If these movements persist, we may pursue legal proceedings. To our younger generation, you should understand that the nation needs time to improve and heal. When it comes to a point when we cannot move forward, we have to pause and fix our problems and push forward with hard work.

These are the main areas I wanted to convey to you today.

Delays in taxation and other fiscal rates, SME reform, and other commercial undertakings are in the process of being improved. All the issues that have been proposed to me, I am aware of the obstacles thanks to consultations with civil servants and information received from the general public and the media. We have been able to organize our priorities accordingly and will start to improve pending issues such as national revenue, and national spending, in particular large-scale investments in infrastructure. What is most important is who benefits from these projects. It must be the general public and not just big industry. We will need to see how industry can help improve our handling of social issues such as public utilities, air pollution and waste disposal, especially building refuse management facilities and recycling centres. I have already given instructions so that these measures will lead to sustainable solutions and a stronger Thailand. Therefore let us come together to reform our country. I appeal to you all to join together and rebuild our nation. I urge all sectors to support me, the NCPO and the civil servants in a spirit of nonpartisan cooperation.

There have been gestures of holding 3 fingers in protest—that is fine. I have no conflict with you. But perhaps it would [be] more appropriate if you can do this within your homes rather than in public. But how about if we all raise 5 fingers instead—2 for the country, and the other 3 to signify religion, monarchy and the people. Raising 3 fingers is copying foreign films, but we should be proud of own identity. We can all live together regardless of our differences. All major reforms take time, but we can all work together to make this process quicker.

Thank you all for sparing your precious time to listen to me. I am doing my best to ease tensions. I do not wish for anyone to fear the use of full administrative power. Those who have not committed any wrongdoings have nothing to fear, because our aim is to bring back righteousness and fairness to all people. The judicial process will determine that in the end.

Once again, thank you very much and I ask for your cooperation and continued support. I believe that all Thai people understand my intentions.

Thank you very much.

SOURCE: Ministry of Foreign Affairs of The Kingdom of Thailand. "Unofficial translation National Broadcast by General Prayut Chan-o-cha Head of the National Council for Peace and Order 6 June 2014." June 6, 2014. www.mfa.go.th/main/th/media-center/3756/46368-Unofficial-translation-National-Broadcast-by-Gener.html.

OTHER HISTORIC DOCUMENTS OF INTEREST

FROM PREVIOUS *HISTORIC DOCUMENTS*

Veterans Affairs Secretary Resigns Amid Scathing Report

MAY 30 AND JUNE 3, 2014

In April 2014, a whistleblower brought to light a scheduling scandal at the Phoenix Veterans Affairs hospital that was leaving hundreds of patients on wait lists, causing serious delays in medical assistance, and even leading to some deaths. According to reports, the hospital kept two sets of records with wait time data: an "official" record that was reported to the U.S. Department of Veterans Affairs (VA) and an internal list that reflected the actual wait times, which at times were months longer than reported. As the scandal unraveled, key leaders at the VA stepped down, including Secretary Eric Shinseki, who had held his position since 2009.

Report Reveals VA Failings

In late 2012, the VA rolled out an electronic wait time tracking system in its medical centers to determine how long veterans were waiting for care, all in an effort to improve timely service. By 2013, both the VA's own inspector general and the U.S. Government Accountability Office told Congress that wait times were still unacceptably high and scheduling practices across VA medical centers were inconsistent and problematic. The Carl T. Hayden VA Medical Center in Phoenix, Arizona, however, touted its dramatic reduction in patient wait times, ignoring the fact that veterans were waiting up to twenty weeks to have an appointment created. In response, Dr. Sam Foote, a doctor at the Phoenix VA hospital filed a complaint with the agency's inspector general, noting that wait time data only appeared positive because it was being manipulated behind the scenes, and that, in turn, veterans were dying while waiting for assistance. Foote also took this information to the *Arizona Republic*, which wrote a series of articles detailing the medical center's failings.

In response to Foote's claim and growing public calls for an investigation, in April 2014, the VA inspector general launched an audit study of the medical center. The next month, Secretary Shinseki ordered a review of all VA hospitals and Congress launched a series of hearings into the VA's purported failings. On May 28, 2014, the VA's inspector general released an interim report detailing the findings of his investigation into the Phoenix VA hospital. In his report, he noted that 1,700 patients were placed on unofficial wait lists outside the new electronic tracking system, which left some without necessary treatments for up to 115 days.

Unfortunately, these problems were not confined to Phoenix. According to the nationwide audit ordered by Shinseki, details of which were released on June 9, 70 percent of medical facilities had secret waiting lists for veterans facing delayed care, and more than 100,000 veterans around the country faced long wait times when seeking care. The audit concluded that the VA facilities had allowed a culture to develop that shied away from confronting the serious problems it faced in providing adequate care to veterans.

The VA reports were not the first to reveal serious failings at VA health facilities. In 2008, a report by technology consulting firm Booz Allen Hamilton found severe care delays caused by "the current shortage of nurses, nurse practitioners, primary care providers, and specialty physicians." In response to the findings in the Booz Allen report, the VA put in place new standards, including setting a goal in 2011 of fourteen-day wait times. Such standards, according to the VA inspector general's report, were "simply not attainable."

SECRETARY SHINSEKI RESIGNS

Secretary Shinseki was called before Congress to testify when the whistleblower's accusations came to light, and then again following the VA inspector general's report release. During testimony on May 15, Shinseki told a Senate panel that he was "mad as hell" about the findings. Shinseki promised to work with his key staff to find ways to resolve the problems revealed in the reports, but, in response to heavy questioning from senators, said that he would not immediately fire any members of his senior staff or step down himself. One day after his testimony, Shinseki accepted the resignation of Dr. Robert Petzel, the head of VA Health Care. Petzel had already announced plans to retire, but according to sources close to the secretary, Sen. Mark Begich, D-Alaska, was working behind the scenes to force a high-level leadership change. "Sometimes you've got to have some heads roll to get the system to shape up," Begich said.

Throughout his time in office, and even during his initial appearance before Congress on the VA scandal in April, Shinseki enjoyed heavy support. However, once the inspector general's report was released, more than 100 members of Congress signed a letter calling on the secretary to step down. On May 30, 2014, the VA chief spoke to a group about housing for homeless veterans, and at the conclusion of his speech said, "Given the facts I now know, I apologize as the senior leader of the Department of Veterans Affairs. I extend that apology to the people whom I care about most deeply—the Veterans of this great country—and to their families and loved ones, whom I have been honored to serve for over five years now—the call of a lifetime." He continued, "I also offer that apology to Members of Congress who have supported me, to Veterans Service Organizations, and to the American people. All of them deserve better from their VA."

Shinseki did not announce his plans for resignation during that speech; however, later that afternoon he presented his official resignation to President Barack Obama. Shinseki's resignation was announced by President Obama following a meeting between the two. The president noted that the secretary cared deeply for America's veterans, but that he could not effectively run the department when faced with so much political backlash. "We don't have time for distractions," the president said. "We need to fix the problem." Shinseki was replaced on an interim basis by his deputy, Sloan Gibson, a West Point graduate who had been with the department since February. In June, it was Gibson who brought to light the fact that at least eighteen veterans died while waiting for care at the Carl T. Hayden Medical Center.

Robert A. McDonald, a veteran and former CEO of Procter and Gamble, was nominated by President Obama in June to take on the role of secretary. His confirmation process was relatively easy in Congress, and he was sworn in on July 30, 2014. McDonald was considered by many in Congress to be the strong leader the VA needed to turn around its failing system. Congressional leaders urged the president to work with them to make the VA a priority and give McDonald all the support he needed to make any necessary changes.

Overrun VA System

The VA health care system has long struggled to maintain quality of care while providing services for an ever-growing number of clients. Over the past five years, the number of those seeking treatment with the VA has increased 26 percent; the health care facilities themselves have not been able to keep pace with their own staffing. Today, many of those seeking treatment are Vietnam veterans with chronic conditions like diabetes or cancer, or veterans returning from Iraq and Afghanistan with PTSD, brain injuries, and loss of limb. Both sets of veterans require expensive, often long-term care.

Republicans and Democrats disagree about what the primary problem is for the VA and how to fix it. Republicans believe that the problem is an inefficient delivery system, while Democrats argue that, even with an annual budget of $154 billion, the system suffers from a shortage of qualified doctors and adequate facilities.

To address some of the concerns presented by the VA audits, bipartisan legislation was introduced in the Senate on June 3, 2014, which would create a two-year pilot program that would allow veterans to find private, non-VA care if they live more than forty miles from a VA facility or have been waiting more than thirty days for treatment. The legislation would also provide funds for hiring additional doctors and nurses and for building twenty-six new medical facilities in eighteen states. The bill would give the VA more authority to fire those found incompetent of management. "Does it solve all of the problems facing our veterans? Absolutely not. Should we come back and deal with this issue? Absolutely," said Sen. Bernie Sanders, I-Vt., who cosponsored the legislation with Sen. John McCain, R-Ariz. The bill was reconciled with similar legislation circulating in the House and was signed into law in August as the Veterans Access, Choice and Accountability Act of 2014.

While testifying before Congress in July, interim secretary Gibson said that entirely fixing the problem would cost approximately $17.6 billion over the next three years and require hiring 1,500 new doctors and 8,500 new nurses and clinicians, the latter of which could prove a difficult undertaking given the national shortage of qualified nurses. According to Gibson, this would only address current demand and shortfalls and additional investment would be necessary to meet future needs. Gibson faced criticism for his assertions that so much would be required. "Given that this figure seems to have magically fallen out of the sky today—after years of assertions from VA leaders at all levels that they had nearly every dollar and every person necessary to accomplish VA's mission—it would be an act of budgetary malpractice to blindly sign off on this request," said Rep. Jeff Miller, R-Fla. Rep. Sanders agreed that taking a critical look at the figures proposed by Gibson was sound; however, he said it would "deny reality" to ignore the VA's immediate request for more medical staff.

VA Scandal Deepens

As Congress debated how to move forward to address the scandal, Florida's Gov. Rick Scott announced that he would file a lawsuit against the VA to give him more autonomy to regulate the facilities in his state. There, the governor said that a hospital in Gainesville found a secret handwritten waiting list and that state inspectors had been denied access to multiple VA facilities. The lawsuit was filed by the state on June 5, 2014, and accuses the VA of providing inadequate care to veterans in Florida. According to the suit, "The VA's refusal to permit any such inspection or respond to (the state's) public records requests, in the face of an ever-growing body of consumer complaint evidence, has led [us] to be reasonably concerned that the VA is failing the very population it is charged by Congress with protecting—America's veterans and their families." The VA has refused to comment publicly on the suit.

In nearby North Carolina, top officials were put on leave and stripped of their command at the Army's Fort Bragg hospital, where two patients in their twenties died and complications from infection were rampant. There, the problem became a key issue in the November Senate election.

—Heather Kerrigan

Following is the text of a speech delivered by former Veterans Affairs secretary Eric Shinseki on May 30, 2014, prior to submitting his resignation; a statement by President Barack Obama, also on May 30, 2014, accepting Shinseki's resignation; and excerpts from the VA's investigation into secret waiting lists, released on June 3, 2014.

DOCUMENT

Secretary Shinseki Remarks on Veterans Affairs Crisis

May 30, 2014

[The portion of Secretary Shinseki's remarks that do not apply to the wait list scandal have been omitted.]

After Wednesday's release of an interim Inspector General report, we now know that VA has a systemic, totally unacceptable lack of integrity within some of our Veterans Health Administration facilities. That breach of trust involved the tracking of patient wait times for appointments.

The initial findings of our ongoing internal review of other large VA healthcare facilities also show that to be true. That breach of integrity is irresponsible, it is indefensible, and unacceptable to me.

I said when this situation began that the problem was limited and isolated because I believed that. I no longer believe it. It is systemic. I was too trusting of some, and I accepted, as accurate, reports that I now know to have been misleading with regard to patient wait times.

I can't explain the lack of integrity amongst some of the leaders of our healthcare facilities. This is something I very rarely encountered during 38 years in uniform. I will not defend it because it is indefensible. But I can take responsibility for it, and I do.

Given the facts I now know, I apologize as the senior leader of the Department of Veterans Affairs. I extend that apology to the people whom I care about most deeply—the Veterans of this great country—and to their families and loved ones, whom I have been honored to serve for over five years now—the call of a lifetime.

I also offer that apology to Members of Congress who have supported me, to Veterans Service Organizations, and to the American people. All of them deserve better from their VA.

But I know this leadership and integrity problem can and must be fixed—now. So I am taking the following actions:

- I've initiated the process for the removal of the senior leaders at the Phoenix VA Medical Center.
- We will use all authority at our disposal to enforce accountability among senior leaders who are found to have instigated or tolerated dishonorable or irresponsible scheduling practices at VA healthcare facilities.
- I have also directed that no VHA senior executive will receive any type of performance award this year.
- I've directed that patient wait times be deleted from VHA employees' evaluation reports as a measure of their success.
- We are contacting each of the 1,700 Veterans in Phoenix waiting for appointments to bring them the care they need and deserve—and we will continue to accelerate access to care for Veterans nationwide who need it, utilizing care both in and outside the VA system.
- We'll announce the results of our nationwide audit of all VA healthcare facilities in the coming days.
- I now ask Congress to support Senator Sanders' proposed bill giving VA's Secretary greater authority to remove senior leaders.
- I ask the support of Congress to fill existing VA leadership positions that are vacant.

Again, this situation can be fixed—with VA, VSOs, Congress, and all VA stakeholders working together, with the best interests of Veterans at heart, in the days ahead—just as we have done over the past five years on Veterans' homelessness.

God bless our Veterans, especially those in greatest need of our prayers and our help. And may God continue to bless this great country of ours. Thank you.

Source: U.S. Department of Veterans Affairs. "Remarks by Secretary Eric K. Shinseki." May 30, 2014. www.va.gov/opa/speeches/2014/05_30_2014.asp.

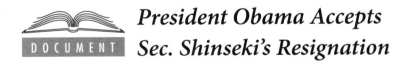

President Obama Accepts Sec. Shinseki's Resignation

May 30, 2014

The President. Good morning, everybody. A few minutes ago, Secretary Shinseki and Rob Nabors, who I've temporarily assigned to work with the VA, presented me with the department's initial review of VA facilities nationwide. And what they've found is that the misconduct has not been limited to a few VA facilities, but many across the country. It's totally unacceptable. Our veterans deserve the best. They've earned it. Last week, I said that if we found misconduct, it would be punished. And I meant it.

Secretary Shinseki has now begun the process of firing many of the people responsible, including senior leaders at the Phoenix VA. He's canceled any possible performance bonuses this year for VHA senior executives. And he has ordered the VA to personally contact every veteran in Phoenix waiting for appointments to get them the care that they need and that they deserve.

This morning I think some of you also heard Ric take a truly remarkable action. In public remarks, he took responsibility for the conduct of those facilities and apologized to his fellow veterans and to the American people. And a few minutes ago, Secretary Shinseki offered me his own resignation. With considerable regret, I accepted.

Ric Shinseki has served his country with honor for nearly 50 years. He did two tours of combat in Vietnam. He's a veteran who left a part of himself on the battlefield. He rose to command the First Cavalry Division, served as Army Chief of Staff, and has never been afraid to speak truth to power.

As Secretary of the VA, he presided over record investments in our veterans: enrolling 2 million new veterans in health care; delivering disability pay to more Vietnam veterans exposed to agent orange; making it easier for veterans with posttraumatic stress, mental health issues, and traumatic brain injury to get treatment; improving care for our women veterans. At the same time, he helped reduce veteran homelessness and helped more than 1 million veterans, servicemembers, and their families pursue their education under the post-9/11 GI bill.

So Ric's commitment to our veterans is unquestioned. His service to our country is exemplary. I am grateful for his service, as are many veterans across the country. He has worked hard to investigate and identify the problems with access to care, but as he told me this morning, the VA needs new leadership to address them. He does not want to be a distraction, because his priority is to fix the problem and make sure our vets are getting the care that they need. That was Ric's judgment on behalf of his fellow veterans. And I agree. We don't have time for distractions. We need to fix the problem.

For now, the leader that will help move us forward is Sloan Gibson, who will take on the reins as Acting Secretary. Sloan became Deputy Secretary at the VA just 3 months ago, but he too has devoted his life to serving our country and our veterans. His grandfather fought on the front lines of World War I. His father was a tail-gunner in World War II. Sloan graduated from West Point, earned his Airborne and Ranger qualifications, and served in the infantry. And most recently, he was president and CEO of the USO, which does a remarkable job supporting our men and women at war, their families, our wounded warriors, and families of the fallen.

So all told, Sloan has 20 years of private sector and nonprofit experience that he brings to bear on our ongoing work to build a 21st-century VA. And I'm grateful that he is willing to take on this task.

I met with Sloan after I met with Ric this morning and made it clear that reforms should not wait. They need to proceed immediately. I've also asked Rob Nabors to stay at the VA temporarily to help Sloan and the department through this transition and to complete his own review of the VHA. In the meantime, we're going to look diligently for a new permanent VA Secretary, and we hope to confirm that successor and fill that post as soon as possible.

Now, we're going to do right by our veterans across the board, as long as it takes. We're not going to stop working to make sure that they get the care, the benefits, and the opportunities that they've earned and they deserve. I said we wouldn't tolerate misconduct, and we will not. I said that we have to do better, and we will. There are too many veterans receiving care right now who deserve all of our best efforts and an honest assessment if something is not working.

This week, I visited some of our men and women in uniform at different stages of their service: our newest Army officers who graduated from West Point, our troops currently serving in Afghanistan, our veterans and our military families at Arlington. And what I saw is what I've seen in every single servicemember, veteran, and military spouse that I have had the privilege to meet: a selfless, clear-eyed commitment to serving their country the best way that they know how. They're the best that our country has to offer. They do their duty. They expect us to do ours.

So today I want every man and woman who's served under our flag to know, whether your tour has been over for decades or it's just about to end, we will never stop working to do right by you and your families.

Let me take a couple questions. All right? Leo Shane from *Military Times.*

Former Secretary of Veterans Affairs Eric K. Shinseki/Veterans Health Administration System

Q. Mr. President, what changed in your opinion of Secretary Shinseki in the last few days? You had said you had confidence in him—even him coming in today and saying it was time for him to resign—what made the difference in your mind?

The President. Ric's judgment. I think his belief that he would be a distraction from the task at hand, which is to make sure that what's broken gets fixed so that his fellow veterans are getting the services that they need.

I want to reiterate, he is a very good man. I don't just mean he's an accomplished man. I don't just mean that he's been an outstanding soldier. He's a good person who's done exemplary work on our behalf. And under his leadership, we have seen more progress on more fronts at the VA and a bigger investment in the VA than just about any other VA Secretary: cut veterans homelessness by 24 percent; brought in folks who had been exposed to agent orange who had been waiting for decades to get the services and benefits that they had earned; making sure that posttraumatic stress disorder and traumatic brain injury was dealt with in a serious way; making sure we had facilities for our women vets, who all too often weren't receiving the kind of specialized services that they needed. So he's been a champion of our veterans. And where there's problems, he has been ready and willing to get in there and fix them. So with the disability backlog that had shot up as a consequence of the admission of the agent orange veterans, as well as making it easier to apply for posttraumatic stress disorder disability claims, when it spiked, he went at it in a systematic way, and we've now cut it by 50 percent over the course of the last year or so.

He's not adverse to admitting where there's a problem and going after it. But we occupy a—not just an environment that calls for management fixes, we've also got to deal with Congress and you guys. And I think it—Ric's judgment that he could not carry out the next stages of reform without being a distraction himself.

And so my assessment was, unfortunately, that he was right. I regret that he has to resign under these circumstances, but I also have confidence in Sloan, and I share Ric Shinseki's assessment that the number-one priority is making sure that problems get fixed so that if there's a veteran out there who needs help that they're getting a schedule and they're able to come in and see a doctor, and that if there are facilities that don't have enough doctors or do not have enough nurses or do not have enough space, that that information immediately gets in the hands of decisionmakers, all the way up to me and all the way to Congress, so that we can get more resources in there to help folks.

And that seems to be the biggest problem. I think that's the thing that offended Secretary Shinseki the most during the course of this process. He described to me the fact that when he was in theater, he might have to order an attack just based on a phone call from some

20-something-year-old corporal, and he's got to trust that he's getting good information. And it's life or death. And I think he is deeply disappointed in the fact that bad news did not get to him and that the structures weren't in place for him to identify this problem quickly and fix it. His priority now is to make sure that happens, and he felt like new leadership would be—would serve our veterans best. And I agree with him.

Phil Mattingly [Bloomberg Television].

Department of Veterans Affairs/Veterans Health Administration System

Q. Thank you, Mr. President. Based on the audit, at least the early-stage audit the Secretary presented to you——

The President. Yes.

Q. ——is there a sense that there was criminal wrongdoing? And I guess, more broadly, how much responsibility do you personally bear, as this being an issue you campaigned on and cared about deeply—you said cared about deeply during your administration—now that we're at this point?

The President. Well, I will leave it up to the Justice Department to make determinations in terms of whether there's been criminal wrongdoing. In terms of responsibility, as I've said before, this is my administration; I always take responsibility for whatever happens. And this is an area that I have a particular concern with. This predates my Presidency. When I was in the Senate, I was on the Veterans Affairs Committee. I heard firsthand veterans who were not getting the kinds of services and benefits that they had earned. And I pledged that if I had the privilege of serving as Commander in Chief and President, that we would fix it.

The VA is a big organization that has had problems for a very long time: in some cases, management problems; in some cases, funding problems. And so what we've tried to do is to systematically go after the problems that we were aware of and fix them. And where we have seen our veterans not being properly served—whether it was too many homeless veterans or a disability claims process that was taking too long—we would go at it and chip away at it and fix it.

When it came to funding, we've increased funding for VA services in an unprecedented fashion, because we understood that it's not enough just to give lip service to our veterans, but not being willing to put our money where our mouth is.

And so what I can say confidently is that this has been a priority, it's been a priority reflected in my budget, and that in terms of managing the VA—where we have seen a problem, where we have been aware of a problem—we have gone after it and fixed it and have been able to make significant progress.

But what is absolutely clear is, this one, this issue of scheduling, is one that the reporting systems inside of the VHA did not surface to the level where Ric was aware of it or we were able to see it. This was not something that we were hearing when I was traveling around the country: the particular issue of scheduling. And what we're going to have to do—part of the review is going to have to be to see how do we make sure that we get information about systems that aren't working.

I just was talking to Rob Nabors, and he described to me, for example, just in very specific detail, how in some of these facilities, you've got computer systems for scheduling that date back to the nineties; situations in which one scheduler might have to look at four or five different screens to figure out where there's a slot and where there might be a doctor available; situations in which they're manually passing requests for an appointment over to somebody else, who's then inputting them. Right? So you have, in many cases, old systems, broken-down systems.

This is stuff that is eminently fixable, but we've got to know about it. And the big concern that I've got, and what I'm going to be interested in finding out, is how is it that in a number of these facilities, if in fact you have veterans who are waiting too long for an appointment, that that information didn't surface sooner so that we could go ahead and fix it.

One last point I want to make on this: When veterans have gotten access to the system, the health care itself that they are receiving has gotten high marks from our veterans service organizations and the veterans themselves. So I think it's important to keep in mind that what the review indicates so far, at least, is that there have been great strides made in the actual care provided to veterans. The challenge is getting veterans into the door, particularly for their first appointment, in some cases, and where they don't have an established relationship with a doctor and they're not in the system.

Part of that is going to be technology. Part of that is management. But as Ric Shinseki himself indicated, there is a need for a change in culture within the VHA and perhaps the VHA as a whole—or the VA as a whole, that makes sure that bad news gets surfaced quickly so that things can be fixed. And I know that was the attitude of Secretary Shinseki and that was what he communicated to folks under him, but they didn't execute. And that's a problem.

Christi Parsons [*Chicago Tribune*], last question.

Former Secretary of Veterans Affairs Eric K. Shinseki/Secretary of Health and Human Services Kathleen Sebelius/Veterans Health Administration System/Acting Secretary of Veterans Affairs Sloan D. Gibson

Q. Thank you, Mr. President. You said that it was the General's own judgment that made the decision for you here. If I remember correctly, Secretary Sebelius offered you her resignation after healthcare.gov failed.

The President. Right.

Q. ——and you declined to take it.

The President. Yes.

Q. So I wonder if there's a little bit of scapegoating taking place here.

The President. Meaning?

Q. Meaning, is—I mean—the dysfunction within the department seems to have been very deep and very widespread.

The President. Yes.

Q. So is lopping off the head of it really the best step to take going forward here? Is there—what I'm asking is, is there a political reason for removing him other than going straight to the problem of the bureaucracy?

The President. Well, the distractions that Ric refers to in part are political. He needs to be—at this stage, what I want is somebody at the VA who is not spending time outside of solving problems for the veterans. I want somebody who's spending every minute of every day figuring out have we called every single veteran that's waiting; have they gotten a schedule; are we fixing the system; what kind of new technology do we need; have we made a realistic assessment of how long the wait times are right now and how are we going to bring those wait times down in certain facilities where the wait times are too long; if we need more money, how much more money do we need to ask from Congress and how am I going to make sure Congress delivers on that additional funding.

That's what I want somebody at the VA focused on, not how are they getting second-guessed and speculation about their futures and so forth and so on. And that was what Ric agreed to as well.

With respect to Secretary Sebelius, at the time I thought it would be a distraction to replace somebody at HHS at a time when we were trying to fix that system. And I wanted to just stay focused because I knew that if we beared down on it and we got folks enrolled that it would work.

So in each instance, my primary decision is based on: How can I deliver service to the American people, and in this case, how can I deliver for our veterans? And because they are people of integrity, I think in both the cases of Secretary Sebelius, but certainly, in the case here of Ric Shinseki, they've got the same priority. They're view is, what is it that is going to best deliver on behalf of folks who, as Ric said this morning, have been let down?

Q. Well, I remember at the time that you felt she had so much knowledge about what had gone wrong that you couldn't afford to lose that.

The President. Right.

Q. Does somebody with 3 months in leadership at the Department have the capacity to attack the problem quickly now?

The President. Well, we're going to need a new VA Secretary. So Sloan is Acting. Sloan, I think, would be the first to acknowledge that he's going to have a learning curve that he's got to deal with.

But the nature of the problem that has surfaced and has been the cause of this attention is one that we can start tackling right away, and without completely transforming the system we can immediately make some progress. We're going to have some longer term issues that we're going to have to take care of.

So my first step is everybody who's out there waiting, get them an appointment. If we need more doctors, let's figure out how we can surge some doctors in there to make sure that they're getting the help that they need. What I wanted to make sure of then is that even if it's still patchwork, how do we make sure that there is no slippage between somebody making a phone call and them getting an appointment scheduled? And let's have a realistic time for how soon they're going to get an appointment. Those are things that don't require rocket science. It requires execution, it requires discipline, it requires focus. Those are things that Sloan has.

There are then going to be some broader issues that we're going to have to tackle. The information systems inside the VHA, those are probably going to have to be changed. That will cost some money, that will take some time, and it will have to be implemented. I think there are going to have to be some changes in the culture within the VHA, because as I said, they're providing very good service, medical treatment to our veterans when they get in the system, but they don't have, apparently, the state-of-the-art operations that you would want to see, for example, in a major medical center or hospital.

Now, keep in mind, those of us who are outside of the VA system and try to get an appointment with the doctor in the private sector and try to get an appointment for—a schedule for a hospital visit, there are probably some wait times as well. So part of what we have to do is figure out what are realistic benchmarks for the system.

And my suspicion is that with not only all the veterans from Iraq and Afghanistan coming back, but also the aging of our Vietnam vets who may have more chronic illnesses, may need more visits, we may need to get more doctors, and we may need to get more nurses. And that's going to cost some money, which means that's going to have to be reflected in a Veteran Affairs budget, which I have consistently increased. Even during fiscally tight times, there's been no area where I've put more priority than making sure that we're delivering the kind of budget that's necessary to make sure our veterans are being served, but it may still not be enough.

And we're going to—but before we start spending more money, our first job is let's take care of some basic management issues that I think can be fixed.

All right? Thank you.

SOURCE: Executive Office of the President. "Remarks on the Resignation of Eric K. Shinseki as Secretary of Veterans Affairs and the Appointment of Sloan D. Gibson as Acting Secretary of Veterans Affairs and an Exchange With Reporters." May 30, 2014. *Compilation of Presidential Documents* 2014, no. 00408 (May 30, 2014). www.gpo.gov/fdsys/pkg/DCPD-201400408/pdf/DCPD-201400408.pdf.

Department of Veterans Affairs Releases Audit Results

June 3, 2014

[All footnotes and graphics have been omitted.]

ACCESS AUDIT RESULTS

At the direction of the Secretary of the Department of Veterans Affairs (VA), the Veterans Health Administration (VHA) conducted an Access Audit to determine if allegations about inappropriate scheduling practices are isolated instances of improper practices or if broader, more systemic problems exist. The audit was designed to:

1. Gauge front-line staff understanding of proper scheduling processes;

2. Assess the frequency and pervasiveness of both desired and undesirable practices employed to record Veteran preferences for appointment dates, manage waiting lists, and process requests for specialty consultation; and

3. Identify factors that interfere with schedulers' ability to facilitate timely care for veterans.

The Access Audit was by necessity a rapidly deployed, system-wide assessment of scheduling practices across VA, and was not intended as a formal investigation of individual staff or managers. Site survey teams were not able to interview all employees, and time did not allow assessment of intent or potential culpability. All of the information collected from audit site visits has been shared with VA's Office of Inspector General (OIG).

Audit Scope

The audit was conducted in two phases. Phase One covered VA medical centers (VAMC) and large Community-Based Outpatient Clinics (CBOC) serving at least 10,000

Veterans. Phase Two covered additional VA facilities, including Hawaii VA and Phoenix VA Health Care Systems. Combined, the two phases covered 731 total facilities, including 140 parent facilities and all VAMCs. During the course of the audit, over 3,772 staff were interviewed.

Audit Findings

The Phase One findings were a strong basis to commence immediate action, even while Phase Two data were being collected. Ultimately, VA chose to limit Phase Two data collection after initial assessments restated high consistency with the findings of Phase One.

The Access Audit was subject to certain limitations (emphasized in later sections of this report) that were unavoidable given the scope and accelerated timeframe. Notwithstanding these limitations, findings include:

1. Efforts to meet needs of Veterans (and clinicians) led to an overly complicated scheduling process that resulted in high potential to create confusion among scheduling clerks and front-line supervisors.

2. Meeting a 14-day wait-time performance target for new appointments was simply not attainable given the ongoing challenge of finding sufficient provider slots to accommodate a growing demand for services. Imposing this expectation on the field before ascertaining the resources required and its ensuing broad promulgation represent an organizational leadership failure.

3. The concept of "desired date" is a scheduling practice unique to VA, and difficult to reconcile against more accepted practices such as negotiating a specific appointment date based on provider availability, or using a "return to clinic" interval requested by providers.

4. Overall, 13 percent of scheduling staff interviewed indicated they received instruction (from supervisors or others) to enter in the "desired date" field a date different from the date the Veteran had requested. At least one instance of such practices was identified in 76 percent of VA facilities. In certain instances this may be appropriate (e.g., a provider-directed date can, under VA policy, override a date specified by a patient), but the survey did not distinguish this, nor did it determine whether this was done through lack of understanding or malintent unless it was clearly apparent.

5. Eight percent of scheduling staff indicated they used alternatives to the Electronic Wait List (EWL) or Veterans Health Information Systems and Technology Architecture (VistA) package. At least one of such instance was identified in 70 percent of facilities. As with desired date practices, we did not probe the extent to which some of these alternatives might have been justified under VA policy. The questionnaire employed did not isolate appropriate uses of external lists.

6. Findings indicate that in some cases, pressures were placed on schedulers to utilize inappropriate practices in order to make waiting times (based on desired date, and the waiting lists), appear more favorable. Such practices are sufficiently pervasive to require VA re-examine its entire performance management system and, in particular, whether current measures and targets for access are realistic or sufficient.

7. Staffing challenges were identified in small CBOCs, especially where there were small counts of providers or administrative support.

Obstacles to Timely Access

Critical insights came from asking front-line staff members to rate the degree to which certain factors interfered with timely access to care. The highest scored single barrier or challenge was lack of provider slots, closely followed by the peculiarities of the fourteen day goal. Limited clerical staffing was also deemed a significant obstacle.

Obstacles that have been posited as significant inhibitors to scheduling timely appointments, such as inadequate training of schedulers, or the inflexibility of the legacy 2.0 VistA scheduling software system, were cited much less often during this audit.

We also highlight that there were many potential opportunities identified that could improve the consistency of desirable practices among schedulers, such as calling Veterans about upcoming appointments, addressing other obstacles, making performance improvement activities more routine, and ensuring that clinic operations data are regularly reviewed at team and management meetings.

Further Actions

VA will establish follow-up accountability actions based on the results of the audit. Senior leaders will be held accountable to implement policy, process, and performance management recommendations stemming from this audit and other reviews. Where audited sites identify concerns within the parent facility or its affiliated clinics, the VA will trigger administrative procedures to ascertain the appropriate follow-on actions for specific individuals.

Based on the findings of the audit, VA will critically review its performance management, education, and communication systems to determine how performance goals were conveyed across the chain of command such that some front-line, middle, and senior managers felt compelled to manipulate VA's scheduling processes. This behavior runs counter to VA's core values; the overarching environment and culture which allowed this state of practice to take root must be confronted head-on if VA is to evolve to be more capable of adjusting systems, leadership, and resources to meet the needs of Veterans and families. It must also be confronted in order to regain the trust of the Veterans that VA serves.

[The remainder of the report, detailing the findings, has been omitted.]

Source: U.S. Department of Veterans Affairs. "Department of Veterans Affairs Access Audit System-Wide Review of Access." June 3, 2014. www.va.gov/health/docs/VAAccessAuditFindingsReport.pdf.

OTHER HISTORIC DOCUMENTS OF INTEREST

FROM PREVIOUS *HISTORIC DOCUMENTS*

President Obama Remarks on Release of Sergeant Bowe Bergdahl

MAY 31, 2014

On May 31, 2014, President Barack Obama announced that the United States had secured the release of Sergeant Bowe Bergdahl, who had been held captive by the Taliban for five years. In exchange for Bergdahl, the United States freed five Taliban-affiliated detainees from Guantánamo Bay. Congressional leaders raised concern that the United States had released dangerous terrorists who would likely rejoin the fight and expressed outrage that the president had not given them the requisite thirty days' notice before completing such an exchange. Army officials, while happy to have a U.S. soldier safely back in his own country, began their own investigation into Bergdahl's disappearance and capture by the Taliban, ultimately determining that he voluntarily walked away from his unit. Sgt. Bergdahl will likely face court-martial on desertion charges.

DEBATE OVER SWAP

Sgt. Bergdahl was captured by the Taliban in 2009 after he left his unit in Afghanistan. In July of that year, the Taliban released a video showing their captive and the military began developing plans to find and rescue Bergdahl. To secure his release, the Taliban demanded that the United States pay a ransom of $1 million and release twenty-one prisoners from Guantánamo Bay; when met with U.S. resistance, this demand was later amended to six detainees, and later five after one of the desired detainees died. The plan to exchange Bergdahl for five Taliban-affiliated Guantánamo detainees was first proposed in November 2011, when it was presented to House Speaker John Boehner, R-Ohio, and other top Republicans and Democrats. During the briefing on the swap, intelligence agencies and the State Department outlined the plan, which they felt might act as a first step toward reconciliation talks with the Taliban, an issue thought to be key to bringing stability to Afghanistan. On December 12 and 19, 2011, House and Senate members responded with questions about whether such a swap would put soldiers at greater risk and how the administration could be confident that those released would not return to fighting. A follow-up briefing was held in late January 2012, but there was no resolution regarding the swap. Shortly thereafter, the administration indicated that there was no longer an opportunity to complete the exchange and free Bergdahl. According to Republicans, they were assured by the White House that should the opportunity present itself in the future, they would be informed and consulted. That did not happen, and members of Congress received little to no notice about the impending May swap.

Ultimately, on May 31, the U.S. Delta Force unit operating in eastern Afghanistan completed Bergdahl's release in what was described as a peaceful handover. President Obama's administration came under fire immediately after the swap was complete, because the Pentagon did not give Congress the requisite thirty days' notice before completing such a transaction. The White House argued that Bergdahl was in imminent danger and any discussion of his release could have jeopardized the mission. The Government Accountability Office (GAO) completed its own investigation into the matter and found that the Pentagon broke the law by failing to inform Congress. While stressing that it was not commenting on the merits of the prisoner swap, the GAO also noted that the Defense Department broke the law when it "appropriated funds to carry out the transfer when no money was available for that purpose." Pentagon spokesperson Rear Adm. John Kirby said that the White House, Pentagon, and Defense Department all agreed that the swap needed to be carried out swiftly if Bergdahl was to be brought home safely. They felt "it was necessary and appropriate to forgo 30 days' notice," he said.

Congressional Republicans went on the attack following the GAO's investigation, using it as an indication that the president was overstepping his executive power. "While the President has a habit of ignoring laws relating to domestic policy, such as health care and immigration, the latest overreach regarding our national security has dangerous implications," said Sen. Saxby Chambliss, R-Ga. "The United States has a long-standing policy of not negotiating with terrorists for good reason, and these senior Taliban leaders will soon rejoin the fight."

Top military officials continued to support the exchange. The deal was unanimously backed by the Joint Chiefs of Staff. "I balanced the risk of transferring the detainees with the importance of returning a U.S. soldier from enemy captivity," wrote Joint Chiefs chairman Gen. Martin Dempsey in a letter to the Senate Armed Services Committee. "I concluded the risk posed by the detainees' future activity would be less grave than breaking faith with our forces in combat." Army chief of staff Gen. Ray Odierno also noted that he supported the decision.

Americans did not similarly agree with the deal. According to a June CBS News Poll, 45 percent of those surveyed disapproved of the exchange, while only 37 percent approved of it. Republicans were more likely than Democrats to oppose the exchange, as were current or former military members. Fifty-six percent of Americans agreed that the United States gave up too much to get Bergdahl back.

President Obama refused to apologize for his decision to conduct the swap in exchange for Bergdahl. During a press conference with British prime minister David Cameron, the president said, "We have a basic principle: we do not leave anybody wearing the American uniform behind," adding that "we had a prisoner of war whose health had deteriorated, and . . . we saw an opportunity, and we seized it. I make no apologies for that."

DETAINEES RELEASED

Five prisoners from Guantánamo were released to Qatar in exchange for Bergdahl. It will be the responsibility of the Qatari government to ensure that the former detainees do not leave the country or find their way back into terrorist cells. These detainees included Khairullah Khairkhwa, who most notably was a key player in launching the Taliban movement and had direct ties to Osama bin Laden. Mullah Norullah Noori was a senior Taliban commander. Mohammad Fazl was also a senior Taliban leader and is under consideration for prosecution for war crimes for the mass killing of Shiite Muslims in 2000 and 2001. Abdul Haq Wasiq was deputy chief of the Taliban intelligence service, while Mohammed Nabi was chief of security for the Taliban in Qalat. Following the release of the five detainees, the Taliban released a statement saying it "has been for a long time attempting to free all the imprisoned Afghan prisoners inside and outside the country" and restore "the right of freedom to them quickly."

Those opposed to the swap expressed concern that the released would find a way to become actively involved in fighting for the Taliban again. "We have made a serious, serious geopolitical mistake. We've empowered the Taliban," said House Intelligence Committee chairman Mike Rogers, R-Mich. Sen. John McCain, R-Ariz., himself a former prisoner of war, agreed with the swap, but felt that other detainees should have been released instead of the five who had been chosen. "I think we should do everything we can in our power to win the release of any American being held, but not at the expense of the lives and well-being of their fellow service men and women," said McCain.

QUESTIONS ABOUT BERGDAHL'S DISAPPEARANCE

Following Bergdahl's release, the Army said that it would continue to review the situation surrounding his disappearance and captivity. From the moment Bergdahl was reported missing, questions began swirling about the circumstances of his disappearance. Some who were in his unit say that on June 30, 2009, Bergdahl voluntarily left his base in the eastern Afghan province of Paktika. (An Army fact-finding mission conducted in 2010 reached the same conclusion.) It was not the first time he had left without permission. However, in all of the instances in which Bergdahl disappeared from his unit, no one reported the soldier missing. In interviews following his disappearance, unit members said that he had been acting strange and kept mentioning that he wanted to explore Afghanistan and walk to India. Many were outraged at Bergdahl's disregard for those he was working with. "He knowingly deserted and put thousands of people in danger because he did. We swore to an oath and we upheld ours. He did not," said Bergdahl's platoon member Cody Full.

E-mail published by *Rolling Stone* that Bergdahl sent to his parents indicated he was considering desertion and was "ashamed to even be American." In the e-mail, he wrote, "The future is too good to waste on lies. And life is way too short to care for the damnation of others, as well as to spend it helping fools with their ideas that are wrong." In addition to the e-mail, Bergdahl also mailed his uniform home to his parents.

BERGDAHL REINTEGRATION

After arriving back in the United States on June 13, the twenty-eight-year-old soldier was taken to San Antonio for additional treatment and reintegration into society. The reintegration process, which doctors rehearsed every six months since Bergdahl was taken hostage, included allowing him to begin making decisions for himself and traveling into public for short periods of time. The process will also include a reintroduction to his family members. According to military leaders, it is up to Bergdahl to decide when he wants to contact his friends and family. As his health improved, Bergdahl was released back into active military duty and was given a desk job at Fort Sam Houston. Bergdahl said through his lawyer that his ultimate goal is to leave military service and pursue a college degree.

The initial investigation launched by the Army in June found that there was no evidence of misconduct on the part of Bergdahl during his captivity. However, in December, the case was referred to a four-star general who would review whether Bergdahl's disappearance warranted a court-martial for desertion. In January 2015, media outlets reported that Bergdahl would face trial for desertion, which during a time of war can carry a maximum penalty of death. However, senior military officials denied that a decision had been reached on the Bergdahl case. If he is court-martialed, it is unlikely that Bergdahl would face a death sentence because there was never an official declaration of war in Afghanistan. Instead, he would likely face a maximum sentence of dishonorable discharge from military service and up to five years in prison. In late March 2015, the Army announced desertion charges against Bergdahl. A July 2015 hearing will determine whether there is enough evidence for a court-martial.

—Heather Kerrigan

Following is the transcript of a statement by President Barack Obama on May 31, 2014, upon the release of Sgt. Bowe Bergdahl; and the text of a speech by President Obama, also on May 31, 2014.

President Obama Issues Statement on Sgt. Bergdahl's Release

May 31, 2014

Today the American people are pleased that we will be able to welcome home Sergeant Bowe Bergdahl, held captive for nearly 5 years. On behalf of the American people, I was honored to call his parents to express our joy that they can expect his safe return, mindful of their courage and sacrifice throughout this ordeal. Today we also remember the many troops held captive and whom remain missing or unaccounted for in America's past wars. Sergeant Bergdahl's recovery is a reminder of America's unwavering commitment to leave no man or woman in uniform behind on the battlefield. And as we find relief in Bowe's recovery, our thoughts and prayers are with those other Americans whose release we continue to pursue.

For his assistance in helping to secure our soldier's return, I extend my deepest appreciation to the Amir of Qatar. The Amir's personal commitment to this effort is a testament to the partnership between our two countries. The United States is also grateful for the support of the Government of Afghanistan throughout our efforts to secure Sergeant Bergdahl's release.

This week, the United States renewed its commitment to the Afghan people and made clear that we will continue to support them as [they] chart their own future. The United States also remains committed to supporting an Afghan-led reconciliation process as the surest way to achieve a stable, secure, sovereign, and unified Afghanistan. While we are mindful of the challenges, it is our hope Sergeant Bergdahl's recovery could potentially open the door for broader discussions among Afghans about the future of their country by building confidence that it is possible for all sides to find common ground.

SOURCE: Executive Office of the President. "Statement on the Release of Sergeant Bowe R. Bergdahl, USA, From Captivity by Taliban Forces in Afghanistan." May 31, 2014. *Compilation of Presidential Documents* 2014, no. 00419 (May 31, 2014). www.gpo.gov/fdsys/pkg/DCPD-201400419/pdf/DCPD-201400419.pdf.

President Obama and Sgt. Bergdahl's Parents Welcome Release

May 31, 2014

The President. Good afternoon, everybody. This morning I called Bob and Jani Bergdahl and told them that after nearly 5 years in captivity, their son Bowe is coming home.

Sergeant Bergdahl has missed birthdays and holidays and the simple moments with family and friends, which all of us take for granted. But while Bowe was gone, he was never forgotten. His parents thought about him and prayed for him every single day, as did his sister Sky, who prayed for his safe return.

He wasn't forgotten by his community in Idaho or the military, which rallied to support the Bergdahls through thick and thin. And he wasn't forgotten by his country, because the United States of America does not ever leave our men and women in uniform behind.

As Commander in Chief, I am proud of the servicemembers who recovered Sergeant Bergdahl and brought him safely out of harm's way. As usual, they performed with extraordinary courage and professionalism, and they have made their Nation proud.

Right now our top priority is making sure that Bowe gets the care and support that he needs and that he can be reunited with his family as soon as possible.

I'm also grateful for the tireless work of our diplomats and for the cooperation of the government of Qatar in helping to secure Bowe's release. We've worked for several years to achieve this goal, and earlier this week I was able to personally thank the Amir of Qatar for his leadership in helping us get it done. As part of this effort, the United States is transferring five detainees from the prison in Guantanamo Bay to Qatar. The Qatari Government has given us assurances that it will put in place measures to protect our national security.

I also want to express gratitude to the Afghan Government, which has always supported our efforts to secure Bowe's release. Going forward, the United States will continue to support an Afghan-led process of reconciliation, which could help secure a hard-earned peace within a sovereign and unified Afghanistan.

As I said earlier this week, we're committed to winding down the war in Afghanistan, and we are committed to closing Gitmo. But we also made an ironclad commitment to bring our prisoners of war home. That's who we are as Americans. It's a profound obligation within our military, and today, at least in this instance, it's a promise we've been able to keep.

I am mindful, though, that there are many troops who remained missing in the past. That's why we're never going to forget; we're never going to give up our search for servicemembers who remain unaccounted for. We also remain deeply committed to securing the release of American citizens who are unjustly detained abroad and deserve to be reunited with their families, just like the Bergdahls soon will be.

Bob and Jani, today families across America share in the joy that I know you feel. As a parent, I can't imagine the hardship that you guys have gone through. As President, I know that I speak for all Americans when I say we cannot wait for the moment when you are reunited and your son Bowe is back in your arms. So with that, I'd like Bob to have an opportunity to say something, and Jani, if she'd like, as well. Please.

[Comments by Sgt. Bergdahl's parents have been omitted.]

SOURCE: Executive Office of the President. "Remarks on the Release of Sergeant Bowe R. Bergdahl, USA, From Captivity by Taliban Forces in Afghanistan." May 31, 2014. *Compilation of Presidential Documents* 2014, no. 00420 (May 31, 2014). www.gpo.gov/fdsys/pkg/DCPD-201400420/pdf/DCPD-201400420.pdf.

OTHER HISTORIC DOCUMENTS OF INTEREST

FROM PREVIOUS *HISTORIC DOCUMENTS*

June

U.S., United Nations, and Swedish Leaders on Installation of Palestinian Unity Government

JUNE 2 AND 3, AND OCTOBER 12, 2014

Amid heavy international criticism, on April 23, 2014, Palestinian factions Hamas and Fatah announced an historic reconciliation agreement. U.S. leaders considered the agreement a blow to ongoing Israeli-Palestinian peace talks, and Israel ended up canceling the discussions. Israel has continued to demand that until Hamas disarms, it will not come back to the bargaining table. The new Palestinian government has shifted its focus away from the talks and is instead working on legitimizing itself on the international stage.

THE CONFLICT BETWEEN HAMAS AND FATAH

Over the past half century, coverage of the Israeli-Palestinian conflict has highlighted the difficulty of reconciling two historically estranged peoples. Apart from emotive concerns regarding custody of ancestral lands as well as sacred sites within contested East Jerusalem, internal divisions on both sides have also presented practical obstacles to a comprehensive peace deal. The Palestinian statehood project has been thwarted through a series of failed negotiations. With each setback, observers have blamed the rivalry between the Palestinian Liberation Organization (PLO), led by the moderate Fatah group, and the radical Hamas movement. Hamas rejected the PLO's acceptance of the 1993 Oslo Accords, in which Israel granted the PLO autonomy in the West Bank and Gaza in exchange for the PLO's recognition of Israel. This stance has contributed to present divisions within Palestinian politics.

The Israeli government has frequently demanded that Hamas either be excluded from any final agreement or relinquish its long-held ambition to reclaim all territory ceded to Israel at its founding in 1948. Hamas has claimed responsibility for attacks on civilians and remains on international lists of terrorist groups, including the Foreign Terrorist Organizations List published by the U.S. State Department. Nevertheless, it enjoys strong popular support due to its dual mission of welfare programs combined with armed struggle for Palestinian statehood.

The most recent breach between Fatah and Hamas followed Hamas's victory in legislative elections in January 2006, which granted the latter control of the domestic agenda, resulting in the suspension of most international aid. Fatah's Mahmood Abbas remained president but his calls for greater flexibility toward Israel to secure an independent state were largely unheeded, contributing to growing tensions. Meanwhile, Israel stopped transferring tax revenues to the Palestinian government, intensifying political discord as civil servants went unpaid. The parties struggled to form a government acceptable to external interests, prompting Abbas to increase the powers of the presidency to undercut his rivals. The two groups also established competing security organizations, culminating in a brief war in July 2007 in the eastern Gaza Strip, the host of Palestinian governing institutions. Jewish settlers had withdrawn from the area in 2005. Hamas gained control of Gaza in July 2007 and Fatah established a rival government in the West Bank. This division endured until the announcement of a unity government for all Palestinian territories in April 2014.

During Hamas's tenure in control of Gaza, civilians often lacked access to basic supplies due to a joint Israeli-Egyptian blockade of the area to prevent weapons from reaching the militant group. Hamas responded by building tunnels to reinforce civilian and military supplies, provoking sporadic Israeli raids targeting the underground network. The tunnels were also used to stage cross-border attacks, which preceded two campaigns against the territory. In December 2008, the Israeli government launched Operation Cast Lead, causing a collective more than 1,400 casualties prior to a unilateral Israeli ceasefire in January 2012. Later in November 2012, the government began Operation Pillar of Defense, which resulted in further loss of life. Both operations caused significant damage to services and infrastructure, deepening public support for Hamas, even as Israel and international allies presented Israel's actions as a justified response to repeated attacks on its own civilians.

The blockade, however, wore on Hamas's resolve to govern independently of Fatah, especially amid setbacks for Islamist allies pitted against establishment alternatives elsewhere in the region following the Arab Spring. Egypt, a traditional mediator in Israeli and Palestinian controversies, had been briefly controlled by the sympathetic Muslim Brotherhood. However, the group was removed from power by a military interim government in July 2013, just before the new peace talks resumed between Fatah and Israel in that same month. Meanwhile, Fatah became more receptive toward the idea of reconciliation as peace talks progressed slowly, although the two parties remained poles apart on issues like Israeli settlements, right-of-return for descendants of Palestinians evicted from their homes, and claims to Jerusalem.

HAMAS AND FATAH ANNOUNCE UNITY GOVERNMENT

On April 23, 2014, Fatah and Hamas announced a reconciliation agreement, which called for the formation of a unity government within five weeks and new elections within six months. Israel responded by ending peace talks scheduled to extend until June that year, while threatening punitive measures. The United States described the development as "unhelpful." Nevertheless, Palestinian parties consulted U.S. law prior to the formation of a technocratic interim government on June 2 that year to confirm that Hamas representation within the cabinet would not be sufficient to trigger restrictions on American aid to the territory. The Obama government views continued financial support as a stabilizing factor that also affords it leverage in any future negotiations.

Israel, for its part, pledged to introduce economic sanctions and consider the reconstituted Palestinian Authority (PA) responsible for any attacks originating in the Gaza Strip, although President Abbas pledged support for continued security coordination between the PA and the Israeli state. Bilateral ties were deeply strained by the kidnapping and murder of three Israeli teenagers in June 2014, provoking the initiation of Israel's campaign, Operation Protective Edge on July 8, which in turn elicited rocket responses from militants. An Egyptian-brokered ceasefire was announced on August 26. The conflict resulted in 2,177 casualties, the majority of whom were Palestinian.

The broader international response to the reconstituted PA has been cautiously positive, with the European Union and members of the non-aligned movement signaling their
support for Palestinian unity and their willingness to work with the government for the
time being. The PA received these messages as a collective endorsement of its bid for statehood. It struggled, however, to meet its own benchmarks in 2014. In October that year,
news reports indicated that elections had been postponed indefinitely despite the reconciliation agreement's stipulation that they be held within six months. All sitting legislators
and President Abbas hold expired mandates, but pressing logistical concerns appeared to
take precedence over electoral planning that year. Hamas blamed Fatah's organizational
competence for the delay in a meeting in November, stating that the interim government's
term had expired and that new national negotiations regarding representation, services,
and security were necessary. Controversy persisted regarding responsibility for security in
the Gaza Strip and whether Hamas would be permitted to operate welfare and political
programs in the West Bank.

The impact of Israeli economic sanctions is uncertain. Israel has largely devolved
responsibility for local policing to the PA, and severe restrictions on tax revenue transfers
could impede its ability to govern, strengthening the local credibility of Islamist factions.
A suspension in services would also impact living standards, supporting accusations of
Israeli indifference toward Palestinian people. Sanctions were expected to continue until
at least the conclusion of snap elections in Israel in March 2015, however, reflecting the
influence of nationalist voters.

PROSPECTS FOR PALESTINIAN UNITY, GOVERNANCE, AND INTERNATIONAL RECOGNITION

Following Israel's early exit from peace talks in April 2014, Palestinian authorities
increasingly shifted toward building legitimacy through international law and diplomacy rather than through mediated bilateral negotiations. After Sweden's recognition
of Palestine in November 2014, 135 countries have now acknowledged the Palestinian
state. Palestine also joined the International Criminal Court (ICC) in January 2015 and
was expected to lobby the court to review violence during Operation Protective Edge in
2014. The accession was criticized by the United States as a unilateral move that would
undermine future peace talks. Israel responded by freezing access to $127 million in
withheld taxes, forcing the PA to take out a loan to pay civil servants 60 percent of their
salaries for the preceding month.

Although Palestine is building a legal and diplomatic profile abroad, Hamas may find
its struggle for acceptance more challenging, because it remains listed as an international
terrorist organization by the United States and the Israel. However, it was removed from
the EU list of terrorist groups in December 2014, reflecting antipathy toward Israeli policies in Europe following the last Gazan conflict.

Israel continues to insist that Hamas disarm as a precondition for lifting its blockade
on Gaza, the source of most attacks, with implications for business and daily life. Checkpoints remain in place along the borders of Palestinian territories, with residents often
required to pass through two sets of barriers operated separately by Hamas and Fatah,
reflecting ongoing conflict regarding the division of governing responsibilities. Workers'
unions have resisted efforts to streamline civil services by merging staff employed by Fatah
and Hamas. The credibility of the government is also undermined by outstanding humanitarian needs, including inadequate shelter in areas decimated by fighting in July and

August 2014. Public frustration with slow progress by the interim government could grow as elections are postponed, calling into question the future of a united PA. It is also unlikely to collect a peace dividend from a deal with Israel in the near term, slowing reconstruction and development.

—Anastazia Clouting

Following is the text of a statement from House Foreign Affairs Committee chairman Ed Royce, R-Calif., on June 2, 2014, and a press release from the United Nations on June 3, 2014, both remarking on the installation of the new Palestinian unity government; and the edited text of a speech by Swedish Foreign Affairs minister Margot Wallström on October 12, 2014, regarding Sweden's recognition of Palestinian statehood.

Rep. Royce Expresses Concern about Unity Government

June 2, 2014

Today, U.S. Rep. Ed Royce (R-CA), Chairman of the House Foreign Affairs Committee, issued the following statement in response to the establishment of a new Palestinian government between the Palestine Liberation Organization and Hamas:

"It's hard to see a government that embraces Hamas getting us closer to peace, much less helping its people. While the 'unity government' hides behind the facade of nonpartisan bureaucrats, it was only born out of support from Hamas—a terrorist organization that continues to call for Israel's annihilation. Hamas is no partner for peace; nor a legitimate recipient of aid."

SOURCE: House Foreign Affairs Committee. "Chairman Royce Statement on Establishment of New Palestinian Government." June 2, 2014. http://foreignaffairs.house.gov/press-release/chairman-royce-statement-establishment-new-palestinian-government.

UN Secretary Ban on Palestinian Unity Government

June 3, 2014

Secretary-General Ban Ki-moon today welcomed the announcement of the formation of a Palestinian unity government headed by Prime Minister Rami Hamdallah, and hoped that new opportunities for progress towards a two-State solution with Israel will emerge soon.

The formation of the government of national consensus was announced yesterday by Palestinian President Mahmoud Abbas, and follows the reconciliation deal reached in April by rival factions Fatah and Hamas. The UN had received assurances that the deal would be implemented on the basis of previous commitments such as the recognition of Israel and non-violence.

"The United Nations has long underscored the need for progress towards Palestinian unity in line with existing resolutions, within the framework of the Palestinian Authority and the commitments of the Palestine Liberation Organization," said a statement issued by the Secretary-General's spokesperson.

"The Secretary-General takes note of the renewed assurances yesterday by President Abbas that the Government will continue to abide by those commitments of recognition of Israel, non-violence and adherence to previous agreements.

"The Secretary-General also notes that the Palestine Liberation Organization will remain responsible for holding peace negotiations with the State of Israel, a commitment President Abbas has reaffirmed, and hopes that new opportunities for progress toward a two-State solution will emerge soon."

The statement added that the UN stands ready to lend its full support to the new government in its effort to reunite the West Bank and Gaza, in line with the unity deal, under one legitimate Palestinian authority, including by addressing the serious political, security, humanitarian and economic challenges in Gaza, and holding long overdue elections.

These issues were discussed today by the UN Special Coordinator for the Middle East Peace Process, Robert Serry, in his meeting with Prime Minister Hamdallah, the statement noted.

SOURCE: United Nations. News Centre. "UN chief welcomes formation of Palestinian unity government." June 3, 2014. www.un.org/apps/news/story.asp?NewsID=47947#.VM75C4unHKA.

 ## *Swedish Foreign Affairs Minister Remarks on Palestinian Statehood*

October 12, 2014

Excellencies, friends,

A six year-old girl in Gaza has experienced three wars during her lifetime. During the course of a few short weeks this past summer, more than 500 children died. Families were torn apart. Schools were destroyed. The hopes and aspirations of young Palestinians—the generation of the future—were once again crushed.

Now, arms seem to have come to rest again.

We need to keep it that way, through determined diplomatic and political efforts, and through substantial economic support. My country is trying to do both.

The Government of Sweden will recognise the State of Palestine.

Some say this announcement is premature—that it will make the peace process more difficult. Our own worry is rather the opposite—that it might be too late.

The peace process is stalled. Facts on the ground are rapidly changing and will soon render a two-state solution not only more difficult, but almost impossible.

There really is no time to waste. Our recognition aims at making the parties to the conflict less unequal. It aims at supporting moderate Palestinians, providing a positive injection into the dynamics of the Middle East Peace Process, and sending a clear and convincing signal to younger generations that there is an alternative to violence and an alternative to the status quo.

Sweden firmly believes that a negotiated two-state solution that guarantees the legitimate aspirations of both peoples in terms of security and national self-determination remains the solution.

We commend the impressive state-building efforts and reforms undertaken by the Palestinian Authority—often under very difficult circumstances. The Palestinian Authority has state-readiness. This has been recognised by the international community.

But recognition also means responsibility. Just as we have expectations on Israel—and they have been clearly voiced, including by the EU—we also have expectations on Palestine, not least since there is a willingness to continue reforms, and to have a strong and well-functioning consensus government in place. We expect the Palestinian government to fight corruption and nepotism, to guarantee respect for civil and political rights, to create opportunities for public participation and accountability, and to increase the political influence of women.

And we expect it—as well as the Government of Israel—to do everything to ensure that both peoples can live in peace and security. This cannot be done through bombs or rockets, war or violence, humiliation or threats. Genuine security can only be achieved through peace.

The consensus government in itself is a confirmation of the unity of the whole of Palestine: the West Bank, including East Jerusalem, and Gaza. They belong together, and they should be physically linked to each other, with Gaza as a window to the sea. This fact should be a guiding star for the international community in our aid to Palestine.

The focus today is on the people of Gaza.

The war made an already critical situation worse, generating immense needs: housing, infrastructure, schools and medical relief. To meet these needs, and to facilitate the development of a sustainable economy, the policy of the closure of Gaza must come to an end. Restrictions must be lifted. Mechanisms for import and—perhaps even more importantly—export are crucial conditions for economic development, state-building and basic services delivery. I welcome the constructive engagement of Israel in the establishment of the tripartite agreement to allow imports of construction material to Gaza. It is a small but important first step towards opening the borders.

The Swedish Government will soon adopt a new five-year plan for its development assistance to Palestine. It will focus on state-building, environment, climate and sanitation as well as private sector development. It will aim at creating conditions for women to enjoy their rights, shape political decisions and participate fully in the economy. And it will increase already the significant Swedish support to Palestine. Swedish annual assistance to the Palestinians amounts to over USD 100 million, including USD 40 million in core funding of UNRWA. This year USD 20 million has been assigned to humanitarian aid to Gaza. Today, I can announce that Sweden has decided to contribute an additional USD 10 million to Gaza in humanitarian and development support.

Palestinians need our solidarity and our long-term support to live on their land in dignity and peace.

We must not lose track of the real goal: a negotiated two-state solution and an end to the occupation.

We should all realise that giving people hope for a better life is a strategic way to obtain sustainable peace.

We owe this to the children of Gaza.

Thank you.

SOURCE: Government of Sweden. "Address at The Cairo Conference on Palestine—Reconstructing Gaza." October 12, 2014. www.government.se/sb/d/3211/a/247911.

OTHER HISTORIC DOCUMENTS OF INTEREST

FROM THIS VOLUME

- U.S., Palestinian, and Israeli Leaders Remark on Peace Process, p. 118
- United Nations Accuses Hamas of War Crimes, p. 398

FROM PREVIOUS *HISTORIC DOCUMENTS*

Egyptian President
Sisi on His Inauguration

JUNE 8, 2014

In July 2013, after approximately one year in office, Egyptian president Mohamed Morsi was deposed by the nation's military following weeks of violent protests. The fate of the fledgling democracy, which in 2011 overthrew its long-time dictatorial ruler Hosni Mubarak, was put in question when the military seized power and suspended the constitution. World leaders urged the military chief, Abdel Fattah el-Sisi, to hold elections as soon as possible to choose a new government. Sisi did so in May 2014, and he was elected president with 93 percent of the vote. Election observers expressed skepticism at the overwhelming victory, and questions remain regarding how Sisi will be able to continue the progress made in Egypt since the 2011 Arab Spring uprising.

Morsi's Government Crumbles

After coming to office in June 2012, Morsi worked to follow through on his election promise of installing a truly democratic and inclusive government in Egypt. He started his term by calling parliament back into session, appointing a prime minister, and forcing the resignation of senior military leaders. Morsi also established a constitutional committee to draft a new governing document and proclaimed that the group would be free from legal recourse. That announcement drew instant criticism from Egyptians, who took to the streets to protest what they saw as an attempt at authoritarian rule. Morsi relented, and voters ultimately passed the draft constitution with 64 percent of the vote.

In early 2013, demonstrators gathered to mark the fall of Mubarak. Those protests quickly turned into a movement against Morsi and his handling of the constitutional process. Morsi ordered troops into the streets and declared emergency law in various cities throughout the country. The protests increased in momentum through the spring and into the summer and called for the president to resign. On July 3, Morsi reached out to the military to try to form a consensus government that would leave him in power. The Armed Forces Supreme Council (SCAF) rejected any such negotiations and instead arrested the president, suspended the constitution, and called for new elections. Following the president's ouster, Chief Justice Adly Mansour was appointed interim president and was expected to oversee the government until a new round of elections could be held. In an attempt to allay the fears of the public, General Sisi said that the military had no intention of taking over the government or involving itself in politics. Instead, Sisi said in a televised address that removing Morsi was done in hopes of bringing "national reconciliation."

The response to Morsi's overthrow was swift. Leaders around the world called on the military to follow through on its promise and hold new elections as soon as possible to avoid a fall back into violence. "We are deeply concerned by the decision of the Egyptian Armed Forces to remove President Morsi and suspend the Egyptian Constitution," said

U.S. president Barack Obama. Morsi supporters condemned what they called a coup d'état, a term President Obama refused to use.

Now in power, the military began cracking down on daily protests and camps set up by Morsi supporters. On August 14, the military entered two of the largest camps and forcibly expelled protesters, burning down tents and a mosque. The Egyptian Health Ministry estimated that nearly 600 civilians were killed during the raid. Human rights groups around the world called for an immediate investigation into the raid and called for those responsible for the deaths to be brought to justice.

As a further blow to opposition groups, the Muslim Brotherhood was disbanded by court order in September 2013, forcing the group back underground and out of public life. More than 1,000 members of the party have been sentenced to death in Egyptian courts since Morsi was overthrown. Morsi was put on trial in November for inciting murder, espionage, deception, and treason, but his trial has been held up until a date to be determined in 2015.

MILITARY LEADER CHARGED WITH RUNNING GOVERNMENT

In January 2014, a referendum was called on a new draft of the constitution, which was largely written by the military and its supporters. In the days leading up to the vote, the military sought out and arrested opponents of the new governing document. In the end, approximately 35 percent of the electorate went to the polls but those voters overwhelmingly approved the new constitution with 98 percent of the vote.

With a governing document in place, Sisi adhered to his promise after Morsi was overthrown and set a date for presidential elections. After a short election season during which Sisi campaigned against only one other opponent, Hamdeen Sabahi, Sisi was elected on May 30, 2014, with 93 percent of the vote. Sabahi garnered less than 4 percent. Sisi's supporters had hoped that the overwhelming victory would put to rest any question of the new leader's legitimacy. However, the immediate concern voiced by election observers brought even more uncertainty to Sisi's government.

International election observers and Sisi's opponent found that the vote was less than credible. Sisi's opponent Sabahi said that he "cannot give any credibility or ratification to the announced numbers of turnout or results" and called the election "an insult to the intelligence of Egyptians." Eric Bjornlund, president of Democracy International, an election-monitoring group funded by the United States, called the election "hugely troubling" and said that a "repressive political environment made a genuinely democratic presidential election impossible." The European Union's observers called the election "free but not always very fair" and noted that there were a number of areas that did not appear to follow Egypt's constitutional principles.

One of the biggest points of concern raised by election observers was the last-minute addition of a third day of voting. Observers had noted during the first two days that polling locations were relatively empty. Because of this, Sisi's interim government chose to add a third day of balloting in an effort to strengthen turnout. Most election observers saw this as an attempt to ensure Sisi's victory and a serious threat to the credibility of the election. By the close of the third and final day of voting, 47 percent of eligible voters cast a ballot, lower than the 52 percent who turned out to vote in Morsi's election.

The Egyptian government's independent election commission certified the vote, but one judge voiced his concern about whether the election was truly a democratic process. "I argue for canceling elections," said Nabil Salib, until "illiteracy vanishes, citizens' living conditions are secured at least to a minimum standard, their will is liberated and their culture is sophisticated." He instead called on Sisi to appoint a group of judges and intellectuals to choose an interim government to begin instilling reforms.

PRESIDENT SISI'S POLICIES AND GOVERNANCE

During his campaign, Sisi rarely addressed his policy priorities, which according to one aide was an attempt to avoid debate and controversy. One major policy that Sisi has been clear on, however, is the importance of individual contributions toward solving Egypt's most pressing problems. In his inaugural address, Sisi remarked, "We should work together so that the fruits of our economic development reach all the sons of Egypt." Sisi himself has said that he will donate half his salary and personal assets to programs that support the nation's economy. He has even asked citizens to make sacrifices, like riding bikes rather than driving to save on the nation's oil imports.

Sisi, who is deeply devoted to Islam, has also spoken publicly about the importance of his faith. This raised some concern in different pockets of Egypt where people worry that the role of religion in government will become too large. When he took office, Sisi surrounded himself with advisors who share his religious beliefs. But, in an effort to reduce some concern, Sisi asked his interior ministry to ban religious slogans from appearing on vehicles. At the same time, however, he called on the Ministry of Youth and Sports to combat atheism among young people and also announced that only preachers with specific licenses from the government would be permitted to deliver sermons.

To govern without clearly stated objectives, Sisi has used the Egyptian media to help create a cult of personality around his office. Not only has the media picked up Sisi's message that he has kept Egypt from falling into extremism seen around the Middle East, they have also reported that he is making strides on the global stage. Media outlets have indicated that international leaders have welcomed Sisi as the nation's legitimate ruler rather than a military dictator who overthrew a democratically elected president. When Sisi made a speech at the United Nations in October, he closed with the phrase "Long Live Egypt!" Television viewers in Egypt then heard thundering applause, which led them to believe that such a call to action was well received and supported by the other delegates. In reality, it was Sisi's own entourage who was clapping, while delegates sat silently.

All these stories have given Sisi an unprecedented amount of power that faces little resistance. According to Khaled Fahmy, a history professor at the American University in Cairo, "What we are witnessing now breaks all previous precedents, and I don't think we have seen the end of it." Such power allowed the president to begin slashing fuel subsidies, which make up a third of the government's budget, without strong opposition. Politicians have generally shied away from this issue because it is unpopular with citizens.

Sisi has been able to structure his government in a way that places utmost power in the executive. The initial roadmap presented by Sisi after he took power following Morsi's ouster was to hold parliamentary elections prior to the presidential election. In consolidating his own power, Sisi revised that roadmap, and once he was elected instilled in himself both executive and legislative authority. He has also passed a law that ensures that no single party can gain more power than the president. After a series of delays, Sisi said that he would hold parliamentary elections in March 2015; however, on March 1, 2015, the vote was delayed indefinitely.

Pressing Challenges

Perhaps Sisi's greatest challenge as president will be invigorating a stalled economy where nearly half the population lives below or just above the poverty line. He believes strongly in the importance of shared government and private investment and has been working to round up investors for much needed infrastructure projects, such as housing developments. The nation relies heavily on foreign investment, a majority of which comes from Middle Eastern allies such as Saudi Arabia and Kuwait. Behind the scenes, these countries have pushed Sisi to develop a well-defined economic policy that could help them justify their investments.

The United States has also been a key investor in Egypt. After Sisi's crackdown on opposition to his government, the United States chose to suspend a portion of its more than $1 billion in annual aid to the country. President Barack Obama has said that the country will restore the funds if Sisi moves to create a more inclusive democracy. However, it appears that Sisi has not been affected by the decision, and the United States even decided to restart military aid that it had been withholding. The two nations will be involved in a delicate balancing act for some time, because the United States is keen to have Egypt's strong support in the fight against the Islamic State of Iraq and the Levant (ISIL).

—Heather Kerrigan

Following are excerpts from Abdel Fattah el-Sisi's speech on June 8, 2014, during his inauguration as president of Egypt.

New Egyptian President Gives Inaugural Address

June 8, 2014

. . . Dear citizens,

I address you today after taking the constitutional oath as president of the Arab Republic of Egypt. I was sworn in to maintain the republican system that was established by the glorious July revolution to preserve justice and equality and to protect the dignity of the Egyptian citizen. I was also sworn in to respect the constitution and the law; our new constitution; the constitution of our civil State and its civil ruling; the constitution of hard work and strong will that encompasses all segments of our Egyptian society and regulates relations among the authorities; the constitution that protects rights and freedoms for all. I was sworn in also to take care to the full of the interests of the people; all the people as I am the president of all Egyptians, with no discrimination between one citizen and another, with no exclusion to anybody as every Egyptian has his national role to undertake. I was also sworn in to maintain the independence of the homeland and its unity and territorial integrity.

This nation has come under a real threat that would have harmed the unity of its people and its territorial integrity but our popular revolution on June 30 has restored January 25 revolution and rectified its course in a bid to protect the homeland and maintain its unity.

Brothers and sisters the sons of the great Egyptian people, I have no words to express my pleasure of you and my good faith in you. My real pleasure today emanates from the immense unity and solidarity among the Egyptian people that was based on your political awareness and democratic struggle. You have given to the whole world a model example to be followed in civilized behavior and undertaking responsibility. You have also proven your ability that did not stop at toppling failed or despotic regimes but also translating it by your minds and hands into a real democratic will that was manifested at ballot boxes for the second time in less than five months.

At this critical juncture of the history and fate of our nation, I found my feelings mixed between happiness because of your confidence, hope to be able to stand up to challenges and proving that this confidence was deserved and fear from Allah and hope in His mercy and help. I pray to Him in every prayer relying on Him to guide me to the right path and assist me in my duty to undertake it to the full.

The social contract between the State, represented in its president and institutions, and the people could not stand properly relying on one party alone. Rather, it should be undertaken through commitment by the two parties. We will depend on frankness and honesty as a method of applying our social contract. We will also share getting knowledge of the truth and we will also share efforts and hard work. This way, we will reap together the fruits of our cooperation embodied in political stability, security and diversified economic growth along with social justice and guaranteed rights and freedoms for all.

The honorable sons of Egypt, two glorious revolutions on January 25 and June 30 have paved the way for a beginning of a new performance in the history of the Egyptian State that seeks establishing power not oppression and seeks protecting peace not aggression; defending the State of law, justice and right and seeks uprooting terrorism and spreading instead security in all parts of the country at a time when it protects the rights and freedoms.

A new performance in the history of the Egyptian State that supports a giant economy and national projects by the State and the private sector along with direct investments at a time when it protects the rights of the poor and low-income brackets and develop the marginalized areas while maintaining and enhancing the system of values and moralities and guarantees freedom of thought and creativity for arts and literature and believes in and welcomes openness while maintaining the Egyptian identity and our cultural values.

The new Egypt will work for the future while interacting with the requirements of the present and benefiting from the experiences of the past. . . .

The great Egyptian people;

You have come to know a man from the Armed Forces and the confidence and appreciation you have shown through entrusting him to undertake that post is mainly based on the stance of this great and patriotic military institution on your hopes and aspirations.

At the moment when I was honored with taking over the presidential post, this was the Armed Forces; the factory of men and symbol of discipline and commitment and the edifice of Egyptian patriotism throughout ages. We all believe that all the good is in the hands of Allah but also Allah has created the means and ways and Allah has willed that this patriotic institution play a basic role in the victory of the people's will in the January 25 and June 30 revolutions.

The Egyptian Armed Forces have sided with the will of the people and managed with patriotism and sincerity of its men to stand up to all plots that were hatched up to undermine the safety and stability of the homeland. If we consider closely our regional context, we will realize the meaning that the State's army be a patriotic and united and does not believe in anything but in the homeland steering away from any biased stances or orientations. The

Egyptian army will remain from the people and for the people believing that its contribution is maintained at times of war and peace and the history will attest that our Armed Forces have undertaken a great patriotic role in maintaining this homeland safe and sound and keeping its people unified.

. . . We will build Egypt through the will of Allah to be a nation that is based on social justice and human dignity guaranteeing freedom and decent life. You should be aware that if Egypt has proven once again that it is hard to break, that was through the providence of Allah and the unity of its State including the people and institutions. . . .

The sons of Egypt;

I am looking forward to a new era that is based on reconciliation and tolerance for the sake of the homeland; reconciliation with the past and reconciliation with those who differ for the homeland and not over the homeland; reconciliation among all sons of the homeland except those who committed crimes against it or adopted violence as a method.

I am looking forward that all the sons of the homeland, who see Egypt as their homeland, would square up for building together a future where no Egyptian is excluded and where freedom, national dignity, social justice and decent life prevail. But those who shed the blood of innocent people and killed sincere sons of Egypt have no place in this march. I say it loud and clear that there will be no leniency or reconciliation with those who resorted to violence or would try block our march towards the future that we seek for our sons. No leniency or reconciliation with those who seek a State without prestige. . . .

Brothers and sisters;

I would like on this score to point out that economic development will not bear fruit or attain comprehensive progress of the nation without going side by side with social development. We should work together so that the fruits of our economic development reach all the sons of Egypt atop of whom come the simple people and the most needy.

We should work to achieve a real progress in the services extended by the State to the public. But the State will not be able to do this actually unless our work and production would increase. Economic and social development should go side by side with cultural development that could be attained through the contribution of men of culture and creativity along with media people and artists of Egypt. They have a major role to play through addressing the minds and souls of people in an effort to rectify the erroneous thought and elevate their ethical sense and encourage them to work hard. They would also contribute to putting right the common sense of the Egyptian people that restores to the Egyptian arts and literature their brightness and help document for this era of the history of our nation.

In as much as I felt satisfied with the artistic contribution to awakening the national feelings of Egyptians and encouraging them to participate in political life, I regretted that there is no an great national work of art that documents for two glorious revolutions that would be considered an artistic icon displayed in every part of the world to immortalize the memory of our martyrs in line with several other major works of art that have an international nature.

As for renewing the religious discourse, its importance lies in boosting the aspect of moral values that includes also maintaining the real moderate image of our Islamic religion and molding minds and consciences of Muslims so that they would be preachers of this religion in the world. If the enlightened Imam Mohamed Abdu had said after a European tour "I have seen in Europe Islam without Muslims and I have seen in our country Muslims without Islam", although the moralistic state of affairs at that time was much better than that of today, then what could we say about what is taking place in our societies these days.

Mistaken he who would confine the role of religion in life to that of rites and rituals barring daily treatment with people given the fact that the core of religion is practical treatment with people as our prophet Muhammad, peace be upon him, said that "he whose prayers would not prevent him from doing wrong, then his prayers are useless".

Then where is the impact of our religious rituals on our daily treatments? Work is some sort of worship. Also worship includes respecting the elderly and being merciful to the younger, being committed to civilized behavior on the Egyptian street and being honest regarding rights and responsibilities. Is this Egypt which we would like to see? Is it Egypt that we launched two revolutions for the future of its people?

I fervently urge every Egyptian family, every school, every mosque and every church to work for entrenching good morals and noble values and high principles in the minds and hearts of young people. Make this method the base of upbringing the children and upgrading their souls as nations are based on morals and if morals have been undermined then everything is lost.

We cannot speak about renewing the religious discourse without mentioning the role of Al-Azhar in this respect given the fact that the 1,000-year-old Al-Azhar is the beacon of religious knowledge that spread Islam and disseminated its true teachings in all Islamic countries including the non-Arab nations in Asia and Africa. . . .

I urge all officials in the Egyptian State institutions to upgrade and reform their institutions. Let fighting corruption be their motto and our motto in the coming period. I confirm that fighting corruption in all its forms will be comprehensive. I would not say that there will be no leniency with the corrupt; but rather there will be no mercy with anybody who is proved involved in any case of corruption whatsoever this case is.

Our coming phase requires sincere efforts that keep in mind preserving public funds and fearing Allah while dealing with this nation and this people. . . .

Brothers and sisters;

Your role in the coming stage of building is not less important than that of the State institutions. We are all required to hold high the value of altruism and self-effacing. No voice could be higher than the voice of the higher interest of the nation. We should pool our efforts together. The Egyptian woman is urged more than any other time to contribute, as it is common with her, to the coming stage of building even if she was not a working woman. For those who downplay the role of the working woman, I tell them you are not aware of the wisdom of the Creator or of the role of women in our life. She is the reason of the existence of the society and it is behind its continuation. The Egyptian woman has proven her political awareness and her basic role in the society and was inspired by her active participation in the 1919 revolution, so she participated in the two great revolutions and then took part massively in the referendum on the constitution and then in the presidential elections.

All appreciation and admiration are to the role of women. I have full confidence that she will maintain her contribution and preserve her role as a mother, sister, wife and daughter. She will continue her efforts in the coming phase of building. I promise her that, out of my appreciation for her active role in the society and her remarkable stance regarding the recent national moves, I will exert all efforts so that she gets a fair representation in the coming parliament and in the various executive posts.

For Egypt's young men and women; the hope of the future, the holders of the torches of knowledge and enlightenment, I tell them: this nation is for you and by you, you are who will reconstruct and build it. It will only stand up on its feet in all fields of life through your active contribution. Your role is appreciated and commended but it is not yet complete. You are who ignited the spark of the revolution and completed its march in cooperation with all segments of the people. But the homeland is still badly in need of your sincere work and your spirit which is full of hope and life; the spirit of continuation and renewal. You are approaching a phase of building and empowerment; so you should contribute through the legitimate channels to enriching the political, economic and social life of your nation.

From my position here, I say you the young people of Egypt; you are the hope and the future; you are who will build the new Egypt with your hands and minds; the new Egypt with its new constitution and what it contains of rights, duties, freedoms and responsibilities. For my part, I will work, through your cooperation, to achieve a better future for you and your sons. I will be a president of Egypt and of all Egyptians; young and elderly people, men and women.

As for the simple people of this nation, I tell them you have suffered a lot over several decades and instead of achieving your dreams for a decent life, your suffering have been doubled over the past years and your dreams have been dashed by several obstacles that prevented their realization.

I promise you that I will exert all what I can and spare no effort, I will work relentlessly for long hours for you and I am sure that you will work like me and more. Also, I promise you and all Egyptians that we will reap the fruits during this term of presidency and that the State and its institutions will be keen on attaining higher rates of unprecedented achievements as long as you are supporting it with your minds and hands. Actually, with the will of Allah, I promise the simple people and low-income brackets of the Egyptian people to provide for them a better life over the coming four years.

The sons of the honorable Egyptian people, with the providence of Allah, and through serious cooperation and goodwill, we have managed to achieve the first two steps of the future road map. We will work with the same patriotic spirit to complete and achieve the third step of the road map which is the parliamentary election. Be sure that your vote is a responsibility and that several things will depend on your choice of the people's representatives. We are badly in need of a new house of representatives that effectively contribute to transferring the texts of the new constitution into mandatory laws translating rights and freedoms mentioned in the constitution into a tangible reality in word and action. The parliament will be different in its powers in accordance with the new constitution. This is why your vote will be a testimony so do not withhold it and give it to those who deserve. Be careful and choose properly who will represent you and take care of your interests and convey your voice honestly. Choose those who are fair and honest actually and those who will support you and work for achieving your hopes and preserving your homeland.

Sons of Egypt;

The benefits of a homeland as much as being a blessing to its people require exerting doubled efforts for maintaining, increasing and defending them. Egypt the cradle of civilization has been endowed by Allah with great bounties and immense advantages. This is why its geographical location became a moving history and its history became a static geography. The pharaonic Egypt by virtue of birth and civilization, the Arab Egypt by virtue of language and culture, the African Egypt by virtue of roots and existence and the Mediterranean Egypt by virtue of nature and spirit is a unique mixture that rarely occurs twice in the four corners of the globe. This state of affairs requires us all to work to be up to the level of responsibility to preserve the major role of the homeland in all circles of the Egyptian foreign policy that will never be realized except through hard work and building at the internal level.

Egypt at the internal level possesses potentials and determiners that will actually steer our foreign policy and will determine our position at the international level. The more our internal front is strong and united, the more our economy will be strong, the more our decision will be independent, the more our voice will be heard and our will be free. . . .

As for our coming international relations, they will be democratic, balanced and diversified with no party being an alternative to another. Egypt could now see all parts of the world. The new Egypt will be open to everybody and will not confine itself to a certain direction and will not stop at certain orientation.

We are looking forward to activating and promoting our relations with every party who supported or will support the will of the Egyptian people. We promise them cooperation in all fields. This cooperation will not stop at taking pride of it at the official levels but will be extended to be established in the conscience of our peoples and be associated in their minds with giant national projects and base for receiving heavy industries.

Egypt with all its potentials should be open in its international relations. The age of tutelage in these relations is now over. These relations as of now will be determined according to how far our friends are willing to cooperate and help attain the interests of the Egyptian people. Egypt is the point of balance and stability in the Middle East and a passage way of the world's international trade. Egypt is the center of religious enlightenment in the Islamic world, with its Al-Azhar Al-Sherif and its honorable scholars, adopting the method of parity, commitment and mutual respect and non-interference in the internal affairs as basic principles for its foreign policy in the coming phase. . . .

Dear citizens;

I salute the souls of our martyrs; the martyrs of our two revolutions and the martyrs of the Armed Forces and the police. I appreciate their sacrifices for the sake of the nation and I am fully aware of the magnitude of the suffering and psychological pain of their families. Their souls that are now happy in paradise will remain asking us to love this country and extend sacrifices for it and work together to carve out its future.

I tell their clean souls that you have defended with us not only Egypt but also the whole region at large. You have defended not only our identity but also our true Islamic religion with its moderate nature. So we should appreciate the sacrifices of our martyrs and take care of our nation. We should unify our ranks and word and should not be divided and enough for our country shouldering problems that if we could not address and handle immediately, heavy consequences will take place.

I tell you all help me strongly to build our nation of which we dream and live in it protected by the umbrella of right, justice and decent life and where we can breathe the winds of freedom and commitment and feel in it equality and fair opportunities as a reality and life style. Be sure that the ship of the nation is one if it is rescued then we are all rescued.

The sons of Egypt;

I am full of optimism over this nation. But Allah, who commanded us to be optimistic, ordered us to work hard and adopt scientific methods and urged us to be united and just rely on Him but not depend on Him without exerting any effort. Glory could not be built on the basis of ignorance, and the methods of accusing others of disloyalty will only lead to failure. I urge you all to prove to everybody who sought to divide us or break our will that he was mistaken in his understanding and reading of history. We are the pulse of one heart and our unity could never be changed.

I pray to Allah the Almighty to guide us to all the good for our country and I appeal to Him to maintain His mercy and love for us and to keep Egypt and its people safe, stable and secure as it has always been as He said in His Holy Quran: "With the will of Allah you enter Egypt safely". Long live Egypt safe and stable. Long live Egypt dignified and honored. Long live Egypt with the providence and care of Allah.

SOURCE: Egyptian State Information Service. "Statement by President Abdel Fattah El Sisi at the ceremony marking his inauguration at Qasr el-Qubba Palace." June 8, 2014. www.sis.gov.eg/En/Templates/Articles/tmpArticles.aspx?ArtID=78278#.VMmvEIunHKB.

OTHER HISTORIC DOCUMENTS OF INTEREST

FROM PREVIOUS *HISTORIC DOCUMENTS*

United Nations and U.S. Respond to Increasing Violence in Mosul

JUNE 10 AND 24, 2014

Continuing its land grab in Iraq, on June 10, 2014, militants known as the Islamic State of Iraq and the Levant (ISIL) captured the Iraqi city of Mosul and continued their drive toward Baghdad. The Iraqi army was unable to stop ISIL's movement, and many troops deserted their posts in the wake of brutal murders of soldiers. Prime Minister Nouri al-Maliki struggled to determine how best to respond to the growing threat, while at the same time attempting to form a government following parliamentary elections. Without strong and cohesive leadership, many international analysts said that the nation appeared to be on the brink of collapse.

The Battle for Mosul

With sectarian violence on the rise in Iraq since U.S. troop withdrawal in 2011, militants seized the opportunity of a weakened state to establish a caliphate, an Islamic government controlled by a leader considered to be a descendent of the Prophet Mohammed. The ISIL militants, known alternatively as ISIS and the Islamic State, started their push to claim areas of Iraq in December 2013. ISIL was able to bolster its numbers by recruiting local militia who felt that the Shia-dominated government, led by Prime Minister Maliki, had discriminated against Sunnis in an effort to consolidate power. By January 2014, with the help of the local militias, ISIL had taken control of Fallujah, a strategically significant city given its close proximity to Baghdad.

Emboldened by its victory, ISIL continued its efforts to claim Iraqi territory for its caliphate, setting Mosul, the country's second largest city, in its sights. On June 6, ISIL entered Mosul, shooting its way through checkpoints and advancing into the city. Suicide bombers spread out around Mosul, targeting Iraqi military positions. Over two days of fighting, an estimated sixty-one ISIL fighters and forty-one Iraqi troops were killed. Reports out of Iraq at the time indicated that the ISIL fighters who initially entered Mosul were joined by sleeper cells that helped take control of government installations, including the city's airport. As the insurgents worked their way through the city, they murdered soldiers and took weapons, helicopters, and other large pieces of military equipment into their control.

In response to ISIL's movements, the Iraqi government sent 30,000 troops to Mosul. The troops, who were trained and equipped by U.S. forces, are largely said to have become disillusioned with their role in the security of Iraq as ISIL has ramped up its violent tactics. Many troops have fled the daily bombings and brutal murders, thus weakening the Iraqi government's ability to halt ISIL's movements. Even though ISIL itself is only thought to have somewhere between 3,000 and 5,000 total fighters across Iraq, its ability to win support of local militias helped it easily overrun the 30,000 troops in Mosul. On June 10, ISIL seized control of the city and nearly its entire province of Nineveh.

Following their success in Mosul, ISIL fighters pushed toward the capital city of Baghdad, on the way taking control of an oil refinery in Baiji, which experienced days of fighting in which both the Iraqi army and ISIL claimed control of the area. In the end, ISIL fighters maintained control of the oil refinery and then moved into Tikrit, former Iraqi president Saddam Hussein's hometown. By June 12, ISIL fighters were within an hour of Baghdad.

The Iraqi army offered some weak resistance in Tikrit. On June 26, the government attempted to recapture the city by launching an airborne assault and ground attack; however, within a few days the Iraqi forces pulled back, unable to secure a victory. Less than three weeks later, in mid-July, the forces launched another attempt to regain Tikrit, but this time retreated within a day.

State of Emergency Declared; Refugees Flee

On June 10, 2014, following a heavy onslaught of force from ISIL fighters, Prime Minister Maliki asked parliament to declare a state of emergency, which would give the government greater arrest and curfew power. Parliament refused, and Sunni legislators opposed to Maliki decried the request as a power grab. Without support from parliament, Maliki traveled to Samarra, which had not yet fallen to ISIL, and called on all Iraqis to use that area as a starting point to take up arms against ISIL and retake their land.

Following the ISIL onslaught, upwards of 150,000 Iraqis fled Nineveh province. Tens of thousands of these refugees ended up in the Iraqi Kurdistan region, where Kurdish president Masoud Barzani requested assistance from the United Nations. "I . . . urge the United Nations High Commissioner for Refugees (UNHCR) to provide relief and support for the displaced people fleeing the violence in Mosul," Barzani said in a statement, adding that his own security forces would ensure the safety of the refugees. He further called on Iraq's central government to consider his request to work together to fight ISIL.

Many of the refugees fleeing the fighting were religious minorities. Although the conflict in Iraq has largely been painted as a struggle between Shias and Sunnis, there are a number of other Iraqis who have found themselves as the targets of ISIL aggression, including Christians, Yazidis, Bahais, Kakais, Faili Kurds, Turkmen, Sabian Mandaeans, and Shabaks. Due to persecution suffered for hundreds of years, many of these groups have operated in secrecy, and after the fall of Mosul these groups fled into Kurdish-controlled cities where some sought refuge and others took up arms.

Both those who fled and those who remained behind have come under attack by ISIL fighters. On August 7, minorities fleeing the newly captured city of Qaraqosh, which has a large Christian population, were massacred. Men were shot or burned alive, and women were taken prisoner and sold to ISIL fighters as brides. ISIL militants razed places of worship, artifacts, and documents in all the cities they captured. This included destroying a sacred Christian and Jewish site, the tomb of Jonah.

Global Response to ISIL Takeover

The U.S. State Department called the situation in Mosul "extremely serious," and spokesperson Jen Psaki said that the United States would support "a strong, coordinated response to push back against this aggression." For the first half of 2014, the United States worked with its allies and the Iraqi government to attempt to bring more stability to the region through diplomatic and humanitarian efforts. Even given the failure of such efforts, the United States has stopped short of sending troops and entering another ground war because it had just wound down its involvement in both Iraq and Afghanistan, and a war-weary public would not support additional ground action.

The U.S. position on security aid for Iraq must also take into consideration Iran's involvement in the response. Iranian president Hassan Rouhani has promised Maliki that he will send aid to protect Shia holy sites and to fight the ISIL militants who he has deemed "barbaric." Claims by both Iranian and Iraqi security forces indicate that Iran has already sent members of its Revolutionary Guard to Iraq to help Iraqi troops.

Turkey's government, which has been more heavily focused on ISIL's rise in Syria, has also been cautious in its response but said that it would retaliate against ISIL if it killed any of the Turkish citizens who were kidnapped from the Turkish consulate in Mosul by the group on June 11. The hostages were ultimately released on September 20. Of particular concern in Turkey is the number of Iraqi refugees crossing into its territory when its relief programs are already severely underfunded and hampered by Syrian refugees.

Turkey has joined Iraq's Kurdish region in calling on the United Nations and its members to send humanitarian aid. Leaders at the United Nations have expressed grave concern about the ongoing refugee situation, which by early August had seen upwards of 300,000 Iraqis flee their homes. Gyorgy Busztin, the UN deputy special representative of the United Nations Secretary-General (DSRSG) for Iraq, issued a statement calling for Iraq and the Kurdistan region to work together on ensuring vital resources reach those who have been displaced. Further, he stated, "I also urgently call on the members of the international community to provide assistance to the Governments of Iraq and the Kurdistan Region to combat the threat posed by ISIL and associated armed groups and to ensure the protection of civilians from the effects of violence, particularly members of Iraq's ethnic and religious minorities who are now at serious risk."

Iraq's Future

ISIL's rise in Iraq has led to a further fractioning of its society, and questions have been raised around the international community about whether it will become a failed state. "Iraq is facing a mortal threat to its existence as a nation and as a political system. These forces of terrorism and extremism are trying to establish themselves. Should ISIS ever control the west of our country and the east of Syria with all the region's resources—who would then be safe in this region?" Foreign Minister Hoshyar Zebari said in an interview with Germany's *Der Spiegel*.

Part of the fear in the international community is whether Maliki will be able to keep Iraq on its path to democracy. The prime minister struggled to form a government following the April 30 parliamentary elections, but Zebari said the problem in Iraq is not simply one of political strength: "A political majority is not enough in Iraq. You can win but you cannot govern with it. It is not 'winner take all' in Iraq. There has to be a compromise."

Maliki's State of Law party led at the April 30 polls; however, when the new parliament met for the third time in July to select a new speaker, president, and prime minister, its session was almost immediately adjourned because any attempts to reach a compromise stalled. The prime minister has rejected calls from international leaders and members of parliament for a more inclusive coalition, saying that he would not form a "national salvation government," which he deemed a coup.

—Heather Kerrigan

Following is a press statement from the U.S. State Department on June 10, 2014; a statement from the United Nations Secretary-General's office, also on June 10, 2014; and a statement from the UN Office of the Coordination of Humanitarian affairs on June 24, 2014, all condemning the ISIL attacks on Mosul.

State Department Condemns ISIL Attack on Mosul

June 10, 2014

The United States is deeply concerned about the events that have transpired in Mosul over the last 48 hours where elements of the Islamic State of Iraq (ISIL) have taken over significant parts of the city. The situation remains extremely serious. Senior U.S. officials in both Washington and Baghdad are tracking events closely in coordination with the Government of Iraq, as well as Iraqi leaders from across the political spectrum including the Kurdistan Regional Government (KRG), and support a strong, coordinated response to push back against this aggression. We also commend efforts by the KRG to respond to the ongoing humanitarian crisis. The United States will provide all appropriate assistance to the Government of Iraq under the Strategic Framework Agreement to help ensure that these efforts succeed.

ISIL continues to gain strength from the situation in Syria, from which it transfers recruits, sophisticated munitions, and resources to the fight in Iraq. It should be clear that ISIL is not only a threat to the stability of Iraq, but a threat to the entire region. This growing threat exemplifies the need for Iraqis from all communities to work together to confront this common enemy and isolate these militant groups from the broader population.

The United States stands with the Iraqi people and the people of Ninewa and Anbar now confronting this urgent threat. We will continue to work closely with Iraqi political and security leaders on a holistic approach to diminish ISIL's capacity and ability to operate within Iraq's borders. Our assistance enables Iraq to combat ISIL on the front lines, where hundreds of Iraqi security force personnel have been killed and injured in that fight this year.

Source: U.S. Department of State. "U.S. Condemns ISIL Assault on Mosul." June 10, 2014. www.state.gov/r/pa/prs/ps/2014/06/227378.htm.

UN Expresses Concern about ISIL Threat in Iraq

June 10, 2014

The Secretary-General is gravely concerned by the serious deterioration of the security situation in Mosul, where thousands of civilians have been displaced in the recent violence. He strongly condemns the terrorist attacks in Anbar, Baghdad, Diyala, Ninewa, and Salah al-Din provinces that have killed and wounded scores of civilians over the past several days. The Secretary-General extends his profound condolences to the families of the victims and to the Government of Iraq.

The Secretary-General urges all political leaders to show national unity against the threats facing Iraq, which can only be addressed on the basis of the Constitution and within the democratic political process. He encourages the Government of Iraq and the Kurdish Regional Government to cooperate in restoring security to Ninewa Province and in delivering urgently needed humanitarian aid. The United Nations Assistance Mission for Iraq (UNAMI) stands ready to support these efforts.

The Secretary-General remains deeply concerned about the situation in Anbar. He welcomes the convening of an Anbar reconciliation conference and strongly encourages all local tribal, political and religious leaders to participate constructively in order to put an end to the fighting.

The Secretary-General recalls that all Member States have an obligation to implement and enforce the targeted financial sanctions, arms embargo and travel ban imposed on the Islamic State of Iraq and the Levant (ISIL) under the sanctions regime pursuant to Security Council resolutions 1267 and 1989.

The United Nations, including UNAMI, will continue to support the Government and people of Iraq in building a peaceful, democratic and prosperous country.

SOURCE: United Nations. "Statement Attributable to the Spokesman for the Secretary-General on Iraq." June 10, 2014. www.un.org/sg/statements/index.asp?nid=7765.

UN Urges for Humanitarian Aid in Iraq

June 24, 2014

The UN and its humanitarian partners have revised their strategic response plan for Iraq and are now calling for US$312 million to support 1 million people through the end of 2014. The original plan, issued in February, sought $105 million.

This revision comes on the heels of the displacement of 650,000 people following the fall of the city of Mosul earlier this month. In all, some 1.2 million Iraqis have been displaced by violence since the start of the year.

PEOPLE NEED WATER, FOOD, SHELTER AND PROTECTION

In a statement released at the end of last week, the Humanitarian Coordinator for Iraq, Jacqueline Badcock, said that hundreds of thousands of people were in need of basic support.

"Many are staying in the open and urgently need water, food, shelter and latrines," she said.

"There are concerns for their protection and reports of an increase in gender-based violence among the displaced.

Other pressing needs include healthcare, education and protection.

HUMANITARIAN ACCESS LIMITED, FUNDING INADEQUATE

"Humanitarian agencies are rapidly scaling up," said Ms. Badcock. "Food, water, tents and other essential supplies are reaching families in need, additional staff are being mobilized, and emergency funds are being released."

However, Ms. Badcock warned that ongoing conflict and an extremely volatile environment meant that humanitarian access to displaced people could be limited.

"I remind all parties to the conflict that they must allow unfettered and sustained humanitarian access to all people in need," she said.

Aid efforts are further thwarted by a slow donor response. Only $19 million – six per cent of the revised response plan—has been received.

SOURCE: United Nations. Office for the Coordination of Humanitarian Aid. "Iraq: Mass displacements prompt urgent plea." June 24, 2014. www.unocha.org/top-stories/all-stories/iraq-mass-displacements-prompt-urgent-plea.

OTHER HISTORIC DOCUMENTS OF INTEREST

FROM THIS VOLUME

FROM PREVIOUS *HISTORIC DOCUMENTS*

House Subcommittee Holds Hearing on General Motors Ignition Switch Recall

JUNE 18, 2014

On June 18, 2014, in the second of a series of hearings held by the U.S. House of Representatives Subcommittee on Oversight and Investigations (a division of the House Committee on Energy and Commerce), General Motors Company (GM) CEO Mary Barra delivered testimony regarding the company's handling of a safety recall initiated in February 2014. The recall was issued on February 7, 2014, as a result of problems relating to the ignition switch in multiple GM-produced vehicles. Additional defects discovered after the initial recall prompted the automaker to issue several subsequent recalls, bringing the number of vehicles recalled to more than 29 million.

EVENTS LEADING TO THE RECALL

On February 7, 2014, GM initiated a recall of the Chevrolet Cobalt and Pontiac G5 vehicles. The problem: a faulty ignition switch. It was discovered that ignition switches in these models could be inadvertently jostled out of the "run" position, resulting in a loss of electrical power or engine shut-off. Without power, the air bags may not deploy during a crash. According to GM, "This risk increases if your key ring is carrying added weight . . . or your vehicle experiences rough road conditions or other jarring or impact related events. If the ignition switch is not in the run position . . . the risk of injury or fatality [increases]."

A report commissioned by GM traces the ignition switch problem back to 2001, when GM engineers noticed problems during preproduction testing of the Saturn Ion. Similar problems were noted again with the Ion several years later and with the Chevrolet Cobalt in 2004 when a GM engineer reported that he bumped the key in a Cobalt during testing, causing it to lose power without warning. Continued reports of Chevrolet Cobalts losing power when the keys were bumped led GM engineers to propose a redesign to correct the problem, but the fix was canceled due to its cost.

The ignition switch was modified in 2006 due to continued problems, but contrary to industry practice, the part number was not changed on the redesigned switch. As a result, few were aware of the fix and the information about the change was not circulated. The new ignition switches were installed starting with 2007 Cobalts, but GM continued to use the same part number as that of the faulty switch.

As a result of an increasing number of reported fatal accidents in Cobalts during which the airbags failed to deploy, an official with the National Highway Traffic Safety Administration (NHTSA) suggested opening an investigation into a pattern of airbag nondeployment involving Chevrolet Cobalts and Saturn Ions. The NHTSA investigation was blocked internally, because the move was seen as unwarranted by many within the organization. During this same time, GM ordered an internal investigation to identify common characteristics of Cobalt front crashes. Former U.S. attorney Anton R. Valukas led the GM investigation. According to the Valukas report, the internal testing at GM concluded that in several of the crashes in which the airbags did not deploy, the ignition switch was not in the "run" position. In addition to these earlier tests, GM ordered a new investigation in 2011 into the same issue. During this series of tests, ignition switches were removed from vehicles in salvage yards from various years and tested. Engineers concluded that crashes in which the ignition was switched out of the "run" position were confined to 2007 models and earlier. GM ordered yet another internal investigation in 2013, and investigators concluded that changes must have been made to the ignition switch sometime after the cars first went into production. After the 2013 investigation, a GM committee recommended a recall, which led to the recall of approximately 800,000 vehicles in February of 2014. This early number later ballooned to almost 30 million recalled vehicles. The switch problem led to the death of at least thirteen people and hundreds of injuries.

"The New GM"

Barra became GM's CEO in January 2014 just prior to the beginning of the recalls, leading some to question her ability to weather such heavy scrutiny. In her first appearance before Congress in early April 2014, GM CEO Barra was accused of deflecting questions. In her testimony to Congress on April 1, 2014, and again on June 18, 2014, Barra was sure to note the distinction between "the new GM" and "the old GM." This reference is in regard to the emergence of a new General Motors following filing for Chapter 11 bankruptcy as part of a bailout deal with the U.S. government. Barra's repetitive testimony spawned jokes and was featured in a *Saturday Night Live* skit—the refrain: "The first rule in new GM is you never talk about old GM."

During the April 8, 2014, broadcast of NPR's *Morning Edition*, Sonari Glinton posed a question very similar to inquiries by the subcommittee just a few days earlier: "Exactly how new is the new GM?" Barra insisted in her April 1, 2014, testimony that the contrast is stark. Others, including members of the subcommittee, would disagree. During the NPR broadcast, Glinton spoke with experts from *Consumer Reports* and from Morningstar investment research firm. The consensus was that the actual products—the cars—seemed to be rated better and, in some cases, "the best." The failings of the new GM seemed to be more closely linked to its corporate culture. It is this culture that is ultimately said to be to blame for the decade-long delay in the recall of a product with a known safety defect.

Barra's second testimony relied more heavily on facts than rhetoric. In opening statements of the subcommittee hearing held on June 18, 2014, Rep. Tim Murphy, R-Pa., and Rep. Fred Upton, R-Mich., referred consistently to the Valukas report. Portions of this report were shared with members of Congress and with the general public. Specific questions regarding this report are the basis for the June 18, 2014, hearing.

As chairman of the House Subcommittee on Oversight and Investigations, Rep. Murphy expressed his alarm regarding GM's failure to recall faulty vehicles in a timely manner and concern regarding the general "incompetence and neglect" uncovered by the report. Rep. Upton, chairman of House Committee on Energy and Commerce, expressed a similar concern and made note of the "fatal consequences for unsuspecting drivers— including two teenagers from [his] own community."

The Valukas report points to a systemic failure at GM—a culture of bureaucracy, where responsibility is shirked with "the GM nod." Barra noted in her opening statement that a number of actions had been taken to reshape the culture of the company as a result of the findings of the report.

THE ROAD AHEAD

The NHTSA has faced criticism for its own delay in handling the ignition switch recall. In testimony given before the House Subcommittee on Oversight and Investigations in the course of the GM recall hearings, acting NHTSA administrator David Friedman testified that GM did not provide NHTSA with the proper documents for the body to have conducted an investigation. He maintained that had GM properly complied with the Transportation Recall Enhancement, Accountability, and Documentation (TREAD) Act of 2000, NHTSA would have been able to act more decisively. The TREAD Act requires manufacturers to report periodically in good faith to NHTSA. This law, referenced in Rep. Murphy's opening statement on June 18, 2014, contains provisions requiring vehicle and equipment manufacturers to advise NHTSA of foreign safety recalls and other safety campaigns. TREAD outlines civil penalties for violations of vehicle safety laws and criminal penalties for misleading the secretary of Transportation about safety defects that have caused death or injury.

According to Friedman, "GM had critical information that would have helped identify this defect." Had the primary items that GM failed to share with NHTSA—that a new ignition switch was designed and installed in 2006 without assigning a new part number and that GM had conducted internal investigations concluding that defective ignition switches were the cause of the pattern of nondeployment of the airbags in fatal crashes—been reported, NHTSA would have acted differently. The agency said it plans to review its communication agreement with GM to ensure that all pertinent documents regarding the GM recall are provided to NHTSA in a timely manner.

In May 2014, GM was ordered to pay $35 million to the U.S. Treasury to settle a federal civil investigation into the timeliness of the ignition switch recall. This settlement is the largest of its kind and the maximum penalty enacted by TREAD. In a statement to the press following the settlement, Transportation secretary Anthony Foxx pushed Congress to pass legislation to increase such fines. "Safety is our top priority, and today's announcement puts all manufacturers on notice that they will be held accountable if they fail to quickly report and address safety-related defects," said Foxx. "While we will continue to aggressively monitor GM's efforts in this case, we also urge Congress to . . . increase the penalties we could levy in cases like this from $35 million to $300 million, sending an even stronger message that delays [in reporting] will not be tolerated."

The settlement mandated internal changes at GM to help detect safety problems and streamline reporting to NHTSA. Barra outlined steps taken as a result of the settlement in her June statement before Congress, including the creation of a new position to oversee global safety and the hiring of thirty-five in-house safety investigators. Crash victims will be compensated through a fund established by GM. The fund will be administered by Ken Feinberg, known for his expertise in victim compensation for large-scale tragedies such as the September 11, 2001, terrorist attacks and the April 15, 2013, Boston Marathon bombing.

—Sarah Gall

Following are the opening remarks of Representatives Tim Murphy, R-Pa., and Fred Upton, R-Mich., on June 18, 2014, at a House Energy and Commerce committee hearing; and the testimony of GM CEO Mary Barra, delivered during that hearing.

Rep. Murphy Opens
General Motors Hearing

June 18, 2014

(As Prepared for Delivery)

Ms. Barra, when you were before this committee almost three months ago, you could not answer many of this subcommittee's questions about why it took General Motors years to figure out why the airbags in its Cobalts, Ions, HHRs were not deploying when they should have. It took GM years before finally issuing a safety recall.

And now, Mr. Valukas has made public his report on the GM fiasco in which he concludes there doesn't appear to be a case of a cover-up or a conspiracy. Instead, according to Mr. Valukas' report, GM's failure to recall faulty vehicles was a case of "incompetence and neglect."

I still have questions about whether GM employees knowingly withheld information during previous liability lawsuits—information that could have led to an earlier recall and prevented some of these tragedies from occurring.

In many ways the facts surrounding what finally resulted in the GM recall are far more troubling than a cover-up. GM engineers and attorneys who were given the facts—including reports on stalls and airbag malfunctions—and who were tasked with figuring out what went wrong—didn't connect the dots. That's because they were either incompetent or intentionally indifferent.

Today, I want to know from both Ms. Barra and Mr. Valukas not just how it happened but why did this happen.

Even when a good law like the TREAD Act of 2000 is in place it requires people to use common sense, value a moral code, and have a motivation driven by compassion for it to be effective. Here the key people at GM seemed to lack all of these in a way that underscores that we cannot legislate common sense, mandate morality, nor litigate compassion. At some point, it's up to the culture of the company that has to go beyond paperwork and rules.

The failures at GM were ones of accountability and culture. If employees do not have the moral fiber to do the right thing, and do not have the awareness to recognize when mistakes are being made, then the answer must be to change the people or change the culture.

That's a lesson another large organization under congressional scrutiny should also take to heart; I hope officials from the Department of Veterans Affairs are watching.

What is particularly frustrating about GM is that the company appeared in no great hurry to figure out the problems with its vehicles. Despite customer complaints, reports from GM's own engineers that they were able to turn off the ignition switch with their knees during test drives, and finally reports of deaths—it wasn't until 2009 that GM figured out the airbags had any connection to the power mode status of the car.

Then, it took another four years to link that finding to one of the components that determines the power mode—the ignition switch. And that discovery was not a result of GM's own investigative work, but raised in the course of a lawsuit brought by the family of a young woman who died behind the wheel of a Cobalt.

How was this discovered?

An investigator for the family simply took two ignition switches apart and compared them—something GM failed to do during the over seven years of investigations into the mystery of Cobalt airbag nondeployments.

Ms. Barra—you sought this internal investigation of the ignition switch recall and you have publicly acknowledged how troubling its findings are. Your company has cooperated with this committee's investigation. You have taken corrective action by changing procedures and trying to remove roadblocks to make sure safety concerns come to light. Based on this report, though, there are no easy fixes for the kinds of systemic, cultural breakdowns and fundamental misunderstandings that permitted GM engineers not to suspect a safety problem when Cobalts were stalling due to a faulty ignition switch.

The possibility that these problems are pervasive and cultural deeply concerns me. We learned Monday that GM has announced yet another recall—it's [sic] thirty-ninth since January. This one is hauntingly similar to the Cobalt ignition switch recall. The ignition switch in certain Buicks, Chevys, and Cadillacs inadvertently moves out [of] the "Run" position if the key has too much weight on it, causing the car to lose power and stall. The model years for the recalled vehicles goes back to the year 2000.

Mr. Valukas—your report tells us about the engineering and legal failings with GM, but what it doesn't divulge is whether GM attorneys made conscious decisions during discovery in other product liability lawsuits that prevented the truth from coming out sooner and potentially saving lives. That kind of malfeasance would be the crux of a cover-up. I want to delve deeper into that issue today.

A harder question to answer—and for you, Ms. Barra to solve—is why did this happen. We know engineers approved a part that did not meet specifications. Why? Was it a cost concern? Was it a rush to get a car on the road? Was it just sloppy? When complaints were raised about the Cobalt's ignition switch almost as soon as the car was on the road, why did engineers not diagnose stalling as a safety problem? Again, was this a lack of basic education about how the car worked—or is it something less specific, but more difficult to address: a culture that does not respect accountability and that does not take responsibility for problems. When investigations drifted for years, there seems to be little to no evidence to suggest that this troubled anyone. Some of this is undoubtedly poor information sharing and silos—and a failure to properly document change orders. But why didn't anyone at GM ask: we have known for years we have an airbag system that isn't working when it should—when are we going to do something about it?

Ms. Barra and Mr. Valukas, I thank you for being here today and I look forward to your testimony.

Source: House Committee on Energy and Commerce. "Opening Statement of the Honorable Tim Murphy, Subcommittee on Oversight and Investigations, Hearing on 'The GM Ignition Switch Recall: Investigation Update.'" June 18, 2014. http://energycommerce.house.gov/sites/republicans.energycommerce.house.gov/files/Hearings/OI/20140618/HHRG-113-IF02-MState-M001151-20140618.pdf.

Rep. Upton Remarks on General Motors Recall

June 18, 2014

(As Prepared for Delivery)

Ms. Barra, thank you for returning back to the committee today. Three months ago we held our first hearing on the GM ignition switch recall. We asked a lot of questions, but we got few answers. I expect things to go differently today.

We have the Valukas report in hand, and we have its words seared in our minds. Our investigation tracks with the findings of the report: a maddening and deadly breakdown over a decade plagued by missed opportunities and disconnects. Engineers didn't comprehend how their cars operated or how vehicle systems were linked together. The company believed a car that stalled while driving wasn't necessarily a safety concern. Investigators let investigations drift for years despite having proof right before their eyes that an airbag system wasn't deploying when it should have. And all of this existed in a bureaucratic culture where employees avoided taking responsibility with a nod of the head.

Ms. Barra, you have said you found this report deeply troubling. I find it deplorable, disturbing, and downright devastating—to you, to GM, to folks in Michigan who live and breathe pride in our auto industry, but most of all, to the families of the victims.

The recall announced on Monday makes it painfully clear this is not just a Cobalt problem. A new set of vehicles—including multiple Chevrolet, Cadillac, and Buick models—are facing an ignition switch recall for the very same kind of torque problem that lurked for over a decade in the Cobalt and similar small vehicles, with fatal consequences for unsuspecting drivers—including two teenagers from my own community.

Ms. Barra and Mr. Valukas, many questions today will focus on how and why this happened. I intend to focus on how we can make sure it never happens again. A culture that allowed safety problems to fester for years will be hard to change. But if GM is going to recover and regain the public's trust, it must learn from this report and break the patterns that led to this unimaginable systemic breakdown. I want specifics on whether the changes you have already put in place have made a difference.

With the Valukas report, GM has provided its assessment of what went wrong. I want to be clear today that our investigation continues. This committee has reviewed over one million pages of documents and interviewed key personnel from GM and NHTSA. While we are addressing GM's actions and response today, we will address NHTSA's part of this story in the near future. We don't yet have all the answers about what changes in our laws, the regulator's practices, or the company's culture would have prevented this safety defect from lingering so long or harming so many. But we will find out. The system failed and people died, and it could have been prevented.

SOURCE: House Committee on Energy and Commerce. "Opening Statement of the Honorable Fred Upton, Subcommittee on Oversight and Investigations, Hearing on 'The GM Ignition Switch Recall: Investigation Update.'" June 18, 2014. http://energycommerce.house.gov/sites/republicans.energycommerce.house.gov/files/Hearings/OI/20140618/HHRG-113-IF02-MState-U000031-20140618.pdf.

GM CEO Barra Testifies Before Congress on Recall

June 18, 2014

Thank you, Mr. Chairman.

I appreciate the chance to appear before you again today on the ignition switch recall issue.

When I was here 11 weeks ago, I told you how we intended to proceed with this matter. I promised that we would conduct a comprehensive and transparent investigation into the causes of the ignition switch problem. I promised we would share the findings of the report with Congress, our regulators, NHTSA, and the Courts. I promised we would hold people accountable and make substantive and rapid changes in our approach to recalls. Finally, I promised we would engage Ken Feinberg to develop a just and timely program for compensating the families who lost loved ones and those who suffered serious physical injury.

We have done each of these things and more. And I welcome the opportunity to discuss them with you further.

The Valukas report, as you now know, is extremely thorough, brutally tough and deeply troubling. It paints a picture of an organization that failed to handle a complex safety issue in a responsible way. I was deeply saddened and disturbed as I read the report. For those of us who have dedicated our lives to this company, it is enormously painful to have our shortcomings laid out so vividly. There is no way to minimize the seriousness of what Mr. Valukas and his investigators uncovered.

On June 2, Mr. Valukas presented the findings of his investigation to the Board of Directors of General Motors. I will leave it to Mr. Valukas to comment on his report. For my part, I want you to know my reaction to the report and some of the actions I have taken since receiving it.

1. After reviewing the Valukas report, we made a number of personnel decisions. Fifteen individuals identified in the report are no longer with the company.

2. We have restructured our safety decision-making process to raise it to the highest levels of the company, addressing a key point in the Valukas report that critical information was kept from senior management. Under the new system, that problem should never be repeated.

3. We announced the creation of, and have implemented, a new Global Product Integrity organization that will enhance our overall safety and quality. And, we are taking an aggressive approach on recalls as we are bringing greater rigor and discipline to our analysis and decisionmaking process regarding recalls and other potential safety-related matters. This is difficult, but it is absolutely the right thing to do. As I have told our employees, this is the new norm.

4. As we discussed last time, we engaged Ken Feinberg to review options for establishing a compensation fund, and that process is moving forward rapidly. Mr. Feinberg has full authority to establish eligibility criteria for victims and determine compensation levels. He has indicated he will share the final criteria with us by the end of the month. We also expect to begin processing claims by August 1.

5. We created a new position of VP of Global Safety and appointed Jeff Boyer, a highly respected expert in the field, to the position. I have personally told Jeff he will have whatever resources he needs to do this job. In fact, we have named a senior attorney to serve as his chief legal adviser.

6. We added 35 safety investigators that will allow us to identify and address issues much more quickly.

7. We instituted a Speak Up For Safety program encouraging employees to report potential safety issues quickly. And we are going to recognize employees when they do so. More than a campaign or program, it's the start of changing the way we think at GM.

Two weeks ago, I purposefully addressed an audience of 1,200 employees at our Vehicle Engineering Center about the report. This address was simultaneously broadcast to all GM facilities around the world. I told our team as bluntly as I knew how, that the series of questionable actions and inactions uncovered in the investigation were inexcusable.

I also told them that while I want to solve the problems as quickly as possible, I never want anyone associated with GM to forget what happened. I want this terrible experience permanently etched in our collective memories. This isn't just another business challenge. This is a tragic problem that never should have happened. And it must never happen again.

This report makes a series of recommendations in eight main areas. I have committed the company to act on all of the recommendations, and we are moving forward on many of them already.

Finally, Mr. Chairman and Members of the Committee, I know some of you are wondering about my commitment to solve the deep underlying cultural problems uncovered in this report. The answer is I will not rest until these problems are resolved. As I told our employees, I am not afraid of the truth.

And I am not going to accept business as usual at GM. It's time—in fact, it's past time—to debunk the myths in our company so we can unleash the full power of our 200,000 employees, our 21,000 dealers and our 23,000 suppliers.

We are a good company, but we can and must be much better. That's my focus and that's my promise to you, our employees, our customers, our shareholders and the American people.

Thank you again for having me here today.

I am pleased to take your questions.

SOURCE: House Committee on Energy and Commerce. "Testimony of Mary T. Barra Before the Subcommittee on Oversight and Investigations House Committee on Energy and Commerce." June 18, 2014. http://docs.house.gov/meetings/IF/IF02/20140618/102345/HHRG-113-IF02-Wstate-BarraM-20140618.pdf.

OTHER HISTORIC DOCUMENTS OF INTEREST

FROM PREVIOUS *HISTORIC DOCUMENTS*

Supreme Court Rules on Aereo Television Service

JUNE 24, 2014

In early 2014, the U.S. Supreme Court heard a copyright case related to a new television transmission service known as Aereo. Aereo's business model was based on grabbing television signals and pulling them into individual antennas. Users could pay for access to a personal antenna and from there could watch a variety of network and cable television shows. In the end, the Court ruled 6–3 that this was a clear violation of copyright law because Aereo was publicly performing copyrighted works without paying the appropriate fees to the copyright holder.

AEREO'S BUSINESS MODEL

The Aereo business model is simple. Anyone could pay the company a fee to receive network television over the Internet. This would give the subscriber access to an individual antenna housed at one of Aereo's many facilities in its twelve markets. The subscriber then turns on his or her Internet-connected device and tunes to a particular channel. Aereo uses the personal antenna to save the program in a file and then send the program's data over the Internet to the user, causing an almost imperceptible seconds-long delay in playback for live shows. Subscribers could also opt to use Aereo as a DVR and record programs for later viewing. Aereo was able to charge subscribers minimal fees—around $8 to $12 per month—because its own costs were low, primarily because it did not pay the networks for access to their television shows. According to Aereo, it is no different than a middleman, like a VCR, because the programs its subscribers watch are being recorded and watched later, even though it may be only seconds after a program starts.

The problem, according to ABC, CBS, NBC, Fox, and other broadcasters who filed a lawsuit against the startup, is that this is a clear violation of copyright law. Networks and cable companies spend millions of dollars each year to develop programs and recoup those costs through licensing fees. Without payment from those who rebroadcast the material, the network business model could fall apart. For its part, Aereo counters that a majority of revenue brought into the networks is through advertising, not licensing fees. These fees, however, have increased while advertising revenue has decreased. In 2013, licensing fees totaled $3.3 billion and are expected to more than double by 2019 to $7.6 billion.

The question before the courts was hinged on how "public" and "performance" are interpreted in U.S. copyright law. Initially, the court of appeals ruled in Aereo's favor, saying that the company was not sending the performances to the "public" because each subscriber had a personal antenna. Therefore, all the transmissions were private performances and outside the bounds of copyright law. Unsatisfied by the ruling, the networks asked the Supreme Court to hear the case, which it agreed to do in January 2014.

During oral arguments before the Supreme Court, former solicitor general Paul Clement, who argued on behalf of the networks, sought to alleviate the concerns of the justices that a ruling against Aereo would ultimately impact many businesses, including those that stream content or offer cloud computing services. There is "a fundamental difference between a service that . . . provides new content to all sorts of end-users, essentially any paying stranger," he argued, and "a service that provides a locker, a storage device." Representing the defendant, David Frederick attempted to promote the idea that a ruling against Aereo would ultimately impact these other companies, saying it would "absolutely threaten cloud computing." He also added that broadening the interpretation of copyright laws could be a "potentially ruinous liability" for many companies.

Copyright Infringement

In their ruling, the justices focused specifically on the Copyright Act's Transmit Clause, which reads that preforming a work publicly means "to transmit or otherwise communicate a performance or display of the work . . . to the public, by means of any device or process, whether the members of the public capable of receiving the performance or display receive it in the same place or in separate places and at the same time or at different times."

In the 6–3 decision written by Justice Stephen G. Breyer, the Court ruled that Aereo was in direct violation of the Copyright Act's Transmit Clause, because it was performing copyrighted works without permission from, or making payment to, the copyright holders, here, the networks. Justice Breyer was joined in his opinion by Chief Justice John G. Roberts Jr. and Justices Ruth Bader Ginsburg, Elena Kagan, Anthony Kennedy, and Sonia Sotomayor.

The problem, as the Court saw it, was that television shows are all copyrighted works, which prevents any other entity from publicly performing that work unless the copyright holder is compensated. In making this ruling, the Court leaned on the 1976 revision of the Copyright Act, in which Congress sought to stop cable networks from grabbing television broadcasts and redelivering them to customers at a fee, without paying copyright fees to the original network. In its 1976 revision, Congress defined public performance as "to transmit . . . a performance . . . to the public, by means of any device or process, whether the members of the public . . . receive it in the same place or in separate places and at the same time or at different times." Transmit was also defined as "to communicate . . . by any device or process whereby images or sounds are received beyond the place from which they are sent."

According to the Court, Aereo was doing exactly what cable providers did prior to 1976: publicly rebroadcasting copyrighted works without the appropriate permissions or paying the required fees. Aereo argued that it could not be found in violation of the Copyright Act because it was not truly redistributing the programs but was instead providing the hardware (here, an antenna) to enable customers to access these programs. Essentially, Aereo said, it was providing something akin to a DVD recorder. The Court rejected this claim, writing, "Aereo is not simply an equipment provider." Instead, it bears an "overwhelming likeness" to cable companies. The majority rejected the idea that Aereo is inherently different from the cable providers because it provides network shows for single viewing, rather than sending out a show in a stream to multiple subscribers.

Justice Antonin Scalia wrote a dissenting opinion, in which he was joined by Justices Clarence Thomas and Samuel A. Alito. Scalia argued specifically that Aereo had found a loophole in copyright law, noting that the Court could not construe Aereo's distribution method as a public performance because each individual user was able to choose his or her own program. Scalia wrote that the majority opinion "will sow confusion for years to come" that would be difficult to apply in lower court cases.

CHANGING TELEVISION SERVICES

In its arguments before the Court, Aereo indicated that if its own activities were found illegal, it would call into question plenty of other technologies, like cloud computing. In *American Broadcasting Cos. v. Aereo*, however, the Court decided to make a narrow ruling as it relates only to Aereo rather than expanding the scope to cover these other growing technologies. According to the Court, things like cloud computing did not fall under the ruling because, in those instances, people have the right to the materials and are simply storing them remotely.

With changing distribution methods for television shows, it is likely that the issue of how copyright applies to various technology services will be called into question again. Already, other companies are stepping up to take Aereo's place, hoping to scoot around the Supreme Court's copyright ruling. One such company is Simple.TV, owned by Mark Ely, who was promoting his company on social media following the Court's ruling. "We're telling Aereo customers: 'Your favorite service is going away. Here's an idea that isn't,'" said Ely. Simple.TV, like other similar companies, are trying to appeal to the increasing number of television viewers who are canceling cable subscriptions and instead turning to services like Amazon, Netflix, and Hulu. Many of these companies differ from Aereo in that they do provide physical equipment that users need to capture television signals in their own homes—companies like TiVo, Roku, and Simple.TV sell hardware that users need to stream content onto their televisions or other Internet-connected devices.

Industry analysts believe that these companies will never truly disrupt the $167 billion U.S. television market at once but will instead have to chip away at their stronghold. "I don't think you are going to find a silver bullet to disrupt the broadcast industry," said venture capitalist Kenneth Lerer. "I think you are going to find a lot of little bullets."

Broadcast networks and cable providers are well aware of the decline in traditional viewing and the growth of individuals watching programming over the Internet. In response, they are slowly making changes to their own business models to meet public demand. Comcast, the nation's largest cable provider, now offers a bundle that includes cloud-based television streaming, among other services. No one, it seems, plans to ignore the changing times. "We are not against people moving forward and offering our content online and all sorts of places, as long as it is appropriately licensed," said Leslie Moonves, the chief executive at CBS. "Innovation is still alive and well and thriving."

AUGUST INJUNCTION

Three days after the Supreme Court's ruling, Aereo closed its business and began seeking a cable license. In August, the company filed a dissent against an injunction to stop it from "streaming, transmitting, retransmitting, or otherwise publicly performing any Copyrighted Programming over the Internet . . . or by means of any device or process throughout the United States of America, while the Copyrighted Programming is still being broadcast." According to the broadcasters who filed the injunction motion, this was in line with the U.S. Supreme Court's June ruling. In response, Aereo continued to contend that it is a "cable system" and therefore should receive a statutory license under

Section 111 of the Copyright Act: "At oral argument, the Court made clear its understanding that its ruling would entitle Aereo to a Section 111 license when Justice Sotomayor specifically stated, 'We say they're a cable company, they get the compulsory license.'" If Aereo is unable to receive such a license, it wants to narrow the injunction to apply only to its live service and not to the recorded portions of its service. A preliminary injunction was granted in October, but it only covered the streaming of live shows and did not cover delayed programs.

—Heather Kerrigan

Following are excerpts from the Supreme Court's decision in American Broadcast Cos. v. Aereo *in which the Court ruled 6–3 on June 24, 2014, that Aereo was in violation of U.S. copyright law when it rebroadcast television shows to its subscribers without paying redistribution fees.*

DOCUMENT *American Broadcast Cos. v. Aereo*

June 24, 2014

[All footnotes have been omitted.]

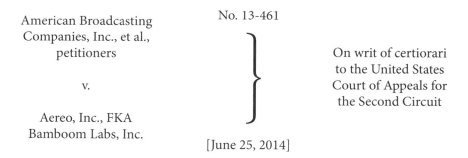

American Broadcasting Companies, Inc., et al., petitioners

v.

Aereo, Inc., FKA Bamboom Labs, Inc.

No. 13-461

On writ of certiorari to the United States Court of Appeals for the Second Circuit

[June 25, 2014]

JUSTICE BREYER delivered the opinion of the Court.

The Copyright Act of 1976 gives a copyright owner the "exclusive righ[t]" to "perform the copyrighted work publicly." 17 U. S. C. §106(4). The Act's Transmit Clause defines that exclusive right as including the right to

"transmit or otherwise communicate a performance ... of the [copyrighted] work ... to the public, by means of any device or process, whether the members of the public capable of receiving the performance ... receive it in the same place or in separate places and at the same time or at different times." §101.

We must decide whether respondent Aereo, Inc., infringes this exclusive right by selling its subscribers a technologically complex service that allows them to watch television programs over the Internet at about the same time as the programs are broadcast over the air. We conclude that it does.

[Section I, offering background on Aereo's business model, has been omitted.]

II

This case requires us to answer two questions: First, in operating in the manner described above, does Aereo "perform" at all? And second, if so, does Aereo do so "publicly"? We address these distinct questions in turn.

Does Aereo "perform"? See §106(4) ("[T]he owner of [a] copyright . . . has the exclusive righ[t] . . . to perform the copyrighted work publicly" (emphasis added)); §101 ("To *perform* . . . a work 'publicly' means [among other things] to transmit . . . a performance . . . of the work . . . to the public . . . " (emphasis added)). Phrased another way, does Aereo "transmit . . . a performance" when a subscriber watches a show using Aereo's system, or is it only the subscriber who transmits? In Aereo's view, it does not perform. It does no more than supply equipment that "emulate[s] the operation of a home antenna and [digital video recorder (DVR)]." Brief for Respondent 41. Like a home antenna and DVR, Aereo's equipment simply responds to its subscribers' directives. So it is only the subscribers who "perform" when they use Aereo's equipment to stream television programs to themselves.

Considered alone, the language of the Act does not clearly indicate when an entity "perform[s]" (or "transmit[s]") and when it merely supplies equipment that allows others to do so. But when read in light of its purpose, the Act is unmistakable: An entity that engages in activities like Aereo's performs.

A

History makes plain that one of Congress' primary purposes in amending the Copyright Act in 1976 was to overturn this Court's determination that community antenna television (CATV) systems (the precursors of modern cable systems) fell outside the Act's scope. In *Fortnightly Corp. v. United Artists Television, Inc.,* 392 U. S. 390 (1968), the Court considered a CATV system that carried local television broadcasting, much of which was copyrighted, to its subscribers in two cities. The CATV provider placed antennas on hills above the cities and used coaxial cables to carry the signals received by the antennas to the home television sets of its subscribers. The system amplified and modulated the signals in order to improve their strength and efficiently transmit them to subscribers. A subscriber "could choose any of the . . . programs he wished to view by simply turning the knob on his own television set." *Id.,* at 392. The CATV provider "neither edited the programs received nor originated any programs of its own." *Ibid.*

Asked to decide whether the CATV provider infringed copyright holders' exclusive right to perform their works publicly, the Court held that the provider did not "perform" at all. See 17 U. S. C. §1(c) (1964 ed.) (granting copyright holder the exclusive right to "perform . . . in public for profit" a nondramatic literary work), §1(d) (granting copyright holder the exclusive right to "perform . . . publicly" a dramatic work). The Court drew a line: "Broadcasters perform. Viewers do not perform." 392 U. S., at 398 (footnote omitted). And a CATV provider "falls on the viewer's side of the line." Id., at 399.

The Court reasoned that CATV providers were unlike broadcasters. . . . Instead, CATV providers were more like viewers, for "the basic function [their] equipment serves is little different from that served by the equipment generally furnished by" viewers. Id., at 399. "Essentially," the Court said, "a CATV system no more than enhances the viewer's capacity to receive the broadcaster's signals [by] provid[ing] a well-located antenna with an efficient connection to the viewer's television set." Ibid. Viewers do not become performers by using "amplifying equipment," and a CATV provider should not be treated differently for providing viewers the same equipment. . . .

B

In 1976 Congress amended the Copyright Act in large part to reject the Court's holdings in *Fortnightly* and *Teleprompter*. See H. R. Rep. No. 94–1476, pp. 86–87 (1976) (hereinafter H. R. Rep.) (The 1976 amendments "completely overturned" this Court's narrow construction of the Act in *Fortnightly* and *Teleprompter*). Congress enacted new language that erased the Court's line between broadcaster and viewer, in respect to "perform[ing]" a work. The amended statute clarifies that to "perform" an audiovisual work means "to show its images in any sequence or to make the sounds accompanying it audible." §101; see *ibid*. (defining "[a]udiovisual works" as "works that consist of a series of related images which are intrinsically intended to be shown by the use of machines . . . , together with accompanying sounds"). Under this new language, *both* the broadcaster *and* the viewer of a television program "perform," because they both show the program's images and make audible the program's sounds. See H. R. Rep., at 63 ("[A] broadcasting network is performing when it transmits [a singer's performance of a song] . . . and any individual is performing whenever he or she . . . communicates the performance by turning on a receiving set").

Congress also enacted the Transmit Clause, which specifies that an entity performs publicly when it "transmit[s] . . . a performance . . . to the public." §101; see *ibid*. (defining "[t]o 'transmit' a performance" as "to communicate it by any device or process whereby images or sounds are received beyond the place from which they are sent"). Cable system activities, like those of the CATV systems in *Fortnightly* and *Teleprompter*, lie at the heart of the activities that Congress intended this language to cover. See H. R. Rep., at 63 ("[A] cable television system is performing when it retransmits [a network] broadcast to its subscribers"); see also *ibid*. ("[T]he concep[t] of public performance . . . cover[s] not only the initial rendition or showing, but also any further act by which that rendition or showing is transmitted or communicated to the public"). The Clause thus makes clear that an entity that acts like a CATV system itself performs, even if when doing so, it simply enhances viewers' ability to receive broadcast television signals.

Congress further created a new section of the Act to regulate cable companies' public performances of copyrighted works. See §111. Section 111 creates a complex, highly detailed compulsory licensing scheme that sets out the conditions, including the payment of compulsory fees, under which cable systems may retransmit broadcasts. H. R. Rep., at 88 (Section 111 is primarily "directed at the operation of cable television systems and the terms and conditions of their liability for the retransmission of copyrighted works").

Congress made these three changes to achieve a similar end: to bring the activities of cable systems within the scope of the Copyright Act.

C

This history makes clear that Aereo is not simply an equipment provider. Rather, Aereo, and not just its subscribers, "perform[s]" (or "transmit[s]"). Aereo's activities are substantially similar to those of the CATV companies that Congress amended the Act to reach. . . .

We recognize, and Aereo and the dissent emphasize, one particular difference between Aereo's system and the cable systems at issue in *Fortnightly* and *Teleprompter*. The systems in those cases transmitted constantly; they sent continuous programming to each subscriber's television set. In contrast, Aereo's system remains inert until a subscriber indicates that she wants to watch a program. Only at that moment, in automatic response to the subscriber's request, does Aereo's system activate an antenna and begin to transmit the requested program.

This is a critical difference, says the dissent. It means that Aereo's subscribers, not Aereo, "selec[t] the copyrighted content" that is "perform[ed]," *post*, at 4 (opinion of SCALIA, J.), and for that reason they, not Aereo, "transmit" the performance. Aereo is thus like "a copy shop that provides its patrons with a library card." *Post*, at 5. A copy shop is not directly liable whenever a patron uses the shop's machines to "reproduce" copyrighted materials found in that library. See §106(1) ("exclusive righ[t] . . . to reproduce the copyrighted work"). And by the same token, Aereo should not be directly liable whenever its patrons use its equipment to "transmit" copyrighted television programs to their screens.

In our view, however, the dissent's copy shop argument, in whatever form, makes too much out of too little. Given Aereo's overwhelming likeness to the cable companies targeted by the 1976 amendments, this sole technological difference between Aereo and traditional cable companies does not make a critical difference here. . . .

III

Next, we must consider whether Aereo performs petitioners' works "publicly," within the meaning of the Transmit Clause. Under the Clause, an entity performs a work publicly when it "transmit[s] . . . a performance . . . of the work . . . to the public." §101. Aereo denies that it satisfies this definition. It reasons as follows: First, the "performance" it "transmit[s]" is the performance created by its act of transmitting. And second, because each of these performances is capable of being received by one and only one subscriber, Aereo transmits privately, not publicly. Even assuming Aereo's first argument is correct, its second does not follow.

We begin with Aereo's first argument. What performance does Aereo transmit? Under the Act, "[t]o 'transmit' a performance . . . is to communicate it by any device or process whereby images or sounds are received beyond the place from which they are sent." *Ibid*. And "[t]o 'perform '"an audiovisual work means "to show its images in any sequence or to make the sounds accompanying it audible." *Ibid*.

Petitioners say Aereo transmits a *prior* performance of their works. Thus when Aereo retransmits a network's prior broadcast, the underlying broadcast (itself a performance) is the performance that Aereo transmits. Aereo, as discussed above, says the performance it transmits is the *new* performance created by its act of transmitting. That performance comes into existence when Aereo streams the sounds and images of a broadcast program to a subscriber's screen. . . .

But what about the Clause's further requirement that Aereo transmit a performance "to the public"? As we have said, an Aereo subscriber receives broadcast television signals with an antenna dedicated to him alone. Aereo's system makes from those signals a personal copy of the selected program. It streams the content of the copy to the same subscriber and to no one else. One and only one subscriber has the ability to see and hear each Aereo transmission. The fact that each transmission is to only one subscriber, in Aereo's view, means that it does not transmit a performance "to the public."

In terms of the Act's purposes, these differences do not distinguish Aereo's system from cable systems, which do perform "publicly." Viewed in terms of Congress' regulatory objectives, why should any of these technological differences matter? They concern the behind-the-scenes way in which Aereo delivers television programming to its viewers' screens. They do not render Aereo's commercial objective any different from that of cable companies. Nor do they significantly alter the viewing experience of Aereo's subscribers. . . .

Moreover, the subscribers to whom Aereo transmits television programs constitute "the public." Aereo communicates the same contemporaneously perceptible images and sounds to a large number of people who are unrelated and unknown to each other. This matters because, although the Act does not define "the public," it specifies that an entity performs publicly when it performs at "any place where a substantial number of persons outside of a normal circle of a family and its social acquaintances is gathered." . . .

IV

Aereo and many of its supporting *amici* argue that to apply the Transmit Clause to Aereo's conduct will impose copyright liability on other technologies, including new technologies, that Congress could not possibly have wanted to reach. We agree that Congress, while intending the Transmit Clause to apply broadly to cable companies and their equivalents, did not intend to discourage or to control the emergence or use of different kinds of technologies. But we do not believe that our limited holding today will have that effect.

For one thing, the history of cable broadcast transmissions that led to the enactment of the Transmit Clause informs our conclusion that Aereo "perform[s]," but it does not determine whether different kinds of providers in different contexts also "perform." For another, an entity only transmits a performance when it communicates contemporaneously perceptible images and sounds of a work. See Brief for Respondent 31 ("[I]f a distributor . . . sells [multiple copies of a digital video disc] by mail to consumers, . . . [its] distribution of the DVDs merely makes it possible for the recipients to perform the work themselves—it is not a 'device or process' by which the *distributor* publicly performs the work" (emphasis in original)).

Further, we have interpreted the term "the public" to apply to a group of individuals acting as ordinary members of the public who pay primarily to watch broadcast television programs, many of which are copyrighted. We have said that it does not extend to those who act as owners or possessors of the relevant product. And we have not considered whether the public performance right is infringed when the user of a service pays primarily for something other than the transmission of copyrighted works, such as the remote storage of content. See Brief for United States as *Amicus Curiae* 31 (distinguishing cloud-based storage services because they "offer consumers more numerous and convenient means of playing back copies that the consumers have *already* lawfully acquired" (emphasis in original)). In addition, an entity does not transmit to the public if it does not transmit to a substantial number of people outside of a family and its social circle.

We also note that courts often apply a statute's highly general language in light of the statute's basic purposes. Finally, the doctrine of "fair use" can help to prevent inappropriate or inequitable applications of the Clause. See *Sony Corp. of America v. Universal City Studios, Inc.*, 464 U. S. 417 (1984).

We cannot now answer more precisely how the Transmit Clause or other provisions of the Copyright Act will apply to technologies not before us. We agree with the Solicitor General that "[q]uestions involving cloud computing, [remote storage] DVRs, and other novel issues not before the Court, as to which 'Congress has not plainly marked [the] course,' should await a case in which they are squarely presented." Brief for United States as *Amicus Curiae* 34 (quoting *Sony, supra*, at 431 (alteration in original)). And we note that, to the extent commercial actors or other interested entities may be concerned with the relationship between the development and use of such technologies and the Copyright Act, they are of course free to seek action from Congress. Cf. Digital Millennium Copyright Act, 17 U. S. C. §512.

***

In sum, having considered the details of Aereo's practices, we find them highly similar to those of the CATV systems in *Fortnightly* and *Teleprompter*. And those are activities that the 1976 amendments sought to bring within the scope of the Copyright Act. Insofar as there are differences, those differences concern not the nature of the service that Aereo provides so much as the technological manner in which it provides the service. We conclude that those differences are not adequate to place Aereo's activities outside the scope of the Act.

For these reasons, we conclude that Aereo "perform[s]" petitioners' copyrighted works "publicly," as those terms are defined by the Transmit Clause. We therefore reverse the contrary judgment of the Court of Appeals, and we remand the case for further proceedings consistent with this opinion.

It is so ordered.

JUSTICE SCALIA, with whom JUSTICE THOMAS and JUSTICE ALITO join, dissenting.

This case is the latest skirmish in the long-running copyright battle over the delivery of television programming. Petitioners, a collection of television networks and affiliates (Networks), broadcast copyrighted programs on the public airwaves for all to see. Aereo, respondent, operates an automated system that allows subscribers to receive, on Internet-connected devices, programs that they select, including the Networks' copyrighted programs. The Networks sued Aereo for several forms of copyright infringement, but we are here concerned with a single claim: that Aereo violates the Networks' "exclusive righ[t]" to "perform" their programs "publicly." 17 U. S. C. §106(4). That claim fails at the very outset because Aereo does not "perform" at all. The Court manages to reach the opposite conclusion only by disregarding widely accepted rules for service-provider liability and adopting in their place an improvised standard ("looks-like-cable-TV") that will sow confusion for years to come.

[The body of the dissent has been omitted.]

✳✳✳

I share the Court's evident feeling that what Aereo is doing (or enabling to be done) to the Networks' copyrighted programming ought not to be allowed. But perhaps we need not distort the Copyright Act to forbid it. As discussed at the outset, Aereo's secondary liability for performance infringement is yet to be determined, as is its primary and secondary liability for reproduction infringement. If that does not suffice, then (assuming one shares the majority's estimation of right and wrong) what we have before us must be considered a "loophole" in the law. It is not the role of this Court to identify and plug loopholes. It is the role of good lawyers to identify and exploit them, and the role of Congress to eliminate them if it wishes. Congress can do that, I may add, in a much more targeted, better informed, and less disruptive fashion than the crude "looks-like-cable-TV" solution the Court invents today.

We came within one vote of declaring the VCR contraband 30 years ago in *Sony*. See 464 U. S., at 441, n. 21. The dissent in that case was driven in part by the plaintiffs' prediction that VCR technology would wreak all manner of havoc in the television and movie industries. See *id.*, at 483 (opinion of Blackmun, J.); see also Brief for CBS, Inc., as *Amicus Curiae*, O. T. 1982, No. 81–1687, p. 2 (arguing that VCRs "directly threatened" the bottom line of "[e]very broadcaster").

The Networks make similarly dire predictions about Aereo. We are told that nothing less than "the very existence of broadcast television as we know it" is at stake. Brief for Petitioners 39. Aereo and its *amici* dispute those forecasts and make a few of their own, suggesting that a decision in the Networks' favor will stifle technological innovation and imperil billions of dollars of investments in cloud-storage services. See Brief for Respondents 48–51; Brief for BSA, The Software Alliance as *Amicus Curiae* 5–13. We are in no position to judge the validity of those self-interested claims or to foresee the path of future technological development. See *Sony, supra*, at 430–431; see also *Grokster*, 545 U. S., at 958 (BREYER, J., concurring). Hence, the proper course is not to bend and twist the Act's terms in an effort to produce a just outcome, but to apply the law as it stands and leave to Congress the task of deciding whether the Copyright Act needs an upgrade. I conclude, as the Court concluded in *Sony*: "It may well be that Congress will take a fresh look at this new technology, just as it so often has examined other innovations in the past. But it is not our job to apply laws that have not yet been written. Applying the copyright statute, as it now reads, to the facts as they have been developed in this case, the judgment of the Court of Appeals must be [affirmed]." 464 U. S., at 456.

I respectfully dissent.

SOURCE: U.S. Supreme Court. *American Broadcast Cos. v. Aereo.* 573 U.S.__(2014). www.supremecourt .gov/opinions/13pdf/13-461_l537.pdf.

OTHER HISTORIC DOCUMENTS OF INTEREST

FROM PREVIOUS *HISTORIC DOCUMENTS*

Supreme Court Rules on Cell Phone Privacy

JUNE 25, 2014

In *Riley v. California*, the U.S. Supreme Court was challenged with bringing the Fourth Amendment into the digital age, addressing whether the police may search an arrested individual's cell phone and accompanying data without a warrant. The Court relied on three legal precedents, deemed the "trilogy," to establish the parameters for the lawful search of an arrested individual before debating whether the digital data found on a cell phone applied to each of the three principles. The defense argued that cell phones, filled with extensive data specific to an individual, present a different situation than physical objects, a distinction worthy of protections under the Fourth Amendment. In a landmark case for privacy rights in the digital age, the Court unanimously agreed, ruling that police must obtain a warrant before searching an arrested individual's cell phone, except in "exigent circumstances." Chief Justice John G. Roberts Jr. authored the opinion, which addressed two separate but similar cases, the first involving a smartphone and the second involving a flip phone. While the future applications of the Court's landmark decision are still to be seen, legal scholars agree that, with its ruling in *Riley*, the Court has officially recognized the tremendous potential for privacy invasion that accompanies searches of digital data.

TWO LINKED CASES

On August 22, 2009, David Leon Riley, a San Diego college student, was pulled over for having an expired auto registration. During the routine traffic stop, police discovered that Riley's license was suspended, and his car was subsequently impounded. At the impound lot, police lawfully searched the car, during which they found two loaded handguns. Police arrested Riley for possession of concealed and loaded firearms and confiscated all items on his person, including his smartphone. Upon searching the contents of the recovered phone, police found images associated with a local street gang and information that linked Riley to an earlier shooting.

Leaning heavily on the information found on the suspect's phone, the State prosecuted and convicted Riley of various crimes in connection with the gang shooting, including attempted murder. The defendant's lawyers moved to suppress the information found on Riley's cell phone, citing protections under the Fourth Amendment, which reads: "The right of the people to be secure in their persons, houses, papers, and effects, against unreasonable searches and seizures, shall not be violated." The motion was unsuccessful.

On appeal, the ruling was upheld based on the legal precedent set by the California Supreme Court decision *People v. Diaz*. In *Diaz*, the court held that the Fourth Amendment allows police to search a suspect's cell phone without a warrant, even if the search is conducted at a later date and a different location, if the phone is found near or on the suspect at the time of arrest. Riley was sentenced to fifteen years to life in prison.

Two years earlier, Boston-area police arrested Brima Wurie and seized two cell phones after they observed him making an alleged drug deal from his car. The call history of one of the phones, a flip phone without Internet access, revealed repeated calls to a specific residence. After tracing the number to a local apartment building, police obtained a warrant to search the premises where they found drugs, drug paraphernalia, weapons, and ammunition. Wurie was charged and convicted in *United States v. Wurie*.

Like Riley, Wurie attempted to suppress the evidence found on his cell phone and lost the motion. However, unlike Riley, on appeal, the U.S. Court of Appeals for the First Circuit reversed the denial of the suppression motion and threw out all information obtained through the search of Wurie's flip phone.

On July 30, 2013, Riley filed a petition for a writ of certiorari, requesting the U.S. Supreme Court to review the decision. The Court agreed to hear the case.

A "Trilogy" of Legal Precedents

In deciding *Riley v. California*, the Court relied on three legal precedents to establish the proper scope of a search leading to arrest: *Chimel v. California*, *United States v. Robinson*, and *Arizona v. Gant*.

The first, the 1969 decision *Chimel v. California*, established the overarching rationales for a search during an arrest. In *Chimel*, the Court established that police may search an arrested suspect's immediate area as the suspect may pose an immediate threat to police and their investigation by using a weapon or destroying evidence within their reach. The second precedent, grounded in *United States v. Robinson*, determined that a search of an arrested suspect is reasonable under the Fourth Amendment. Finally, the third principle, articulated in the 2009 case *Arizona v. Gant*, established that police must demonstrate an actual and continuing threat to their safety, or a need to prevent the suspect from tampering with evidence related to the crime, to justify a warrantless search of a vehicle after the driver and passengers have been subdued. Taken together, each principle, which the Court described as "the trilogy," established the pillars for the search incident to arrest doctrine.

The challenge for the Court, one that had been inconclusively debated and dissected by lower circuit courts and state Supreme Courts across the country, was whether searches of cell phone data fell under this trilogy of legal precedents, thus affirming that it is constitutional for police to search a suspect's cell phone and accompanying data without first obtaining a warrant.

Unanimous Decision Upholding Individuals' Digital Privacy

In writing the unanimous majority opinion, Chief Justice Roberts reversed the original decision, establishing that police must obtain warrants before searching the cell phones of arrested suspects. For Roberts, cell phones and the data within present a different situation than that found under prior legal precedents. "The fact that technology now allows an individual to carry such information in his hand does not make the information any less worthy of the protection for which the Founders fought," he wrote in the majority ruling. He also noted the fundamental role cell phones play in modern American life, describing them as "such a pervasive and insistent part of daily life that the proverbial visitor from Mars might conclude they were an important feature of human anatomy." According to Roberts, modern cell phones "are not just another technological convenience," but instead hold the many "privacies of life" worthy of protection.

The chief justice further outlined the majority's position by offering specific rebukes of the government's use of the search incident to arrest trilogy in the context of modern cell phones. With an eye toward the Court's rulings in *Chimel* and *Gant*, Roberts wrote that while the police may examine, for example, whether a cell phone contains a razor blade between the phone and the case, "[o]nce an officer has secured a phone and eliminated any potential physical threats, however, data on the phone can endanger no one." He also dismissed the possibility of a suspect destroying evidence by "remote wiping and data encryption," noting that the Court has been given "little reason to believe that either problem is prevalent." The opinion added that, regarding remote wiping, "law enforcement is not without specific means to address the threat," suggesting, for example, that officers disconnect the phone from the network by removing the battery or by placing it in an enclosure that prevents radio waves.

In perhaps the clearest critique of the government's position, Roberts argued that while the rule established under *Robinson* strikes "the appropriate balance in the context of physical objects," it is not applicable to digital contents and data, such as those found on cell phones. According to the Court, "[m]odern cell phones, as a category, implicate privacy concerns far beyond those implicated by the search of a cigarette pack, a wallet, or a purse," objects that the government argued were analogous to cell phones. Even the term "cell phone" was characterized as a misnomer by the Court. "[M]any of these devices are in fact minicomputers that also happen to have the capacity to be used as a telephone. They could just as easily be called cameras, video players, rolodexes, calendars, tape recorders, libraries, diaries, albums, televisions, maps, or newspapers." These applications, coupled with cell phones' immense storage capacity, are able to paint a more detailed and clearer picture of an individual's private life than physical objects.

Last, the Court outlined how privacy has changed in the digital age. With the advent of flip-phones and now smartphones, people now have with them at all times a detailed record of their digital lives, a stark distinction from a decade ago. "Today, by contrast, it is no exaggeration to say that many of the more than 90% of American adults who own a cell phone keep on their person a digital record of nearly every aspect of their lives—from the mundane to the intimate," the majority found. According to the Court, this amount of readily available data presents a unique privacy challenge in the event of an arrest. According to the Court, "[a]llowing the police to scrutinize such records on a routine basis is quite different from allowing them to search a personal item or two in the occasional case."

Given the innate differences between digital data and physical items, the justices "decline[d] to extend *Robinson* to searches of data on cell phones, and hold instead that officers must generally secure a warrant before conducting such a search."

IMPACT GOING FORWARD

Legal experts rushed to describe the decision as a landmark victory for digital privacy rights. "The decision brings the Fourth Amendment into the 21st century," Jeffrey L. Fisher, a lawyer for Riley, remarked, adding, "The core of the decision is that digital information is different. It triggers privacy concerns far more profound than ordinary physical objects." Yet despite offering immediate protection for the more than 12 million people arrested every year, the impact of *Riley v. California* will undoubtedly be much broader. Legal scholars believe that future applications will govern searches of tablets, laptop computers, and other handheld electronic devices, and may one day even be broadened to cover homes and businesses.

Others believe the reasoning behind *Riley* may apply to searches of information held by third parties like phone companies. Specifically, Roberts's approving citation of a concurring opinion by Justice Sonia Sotomayor in *United States v. Jones*, a 2012 case requiring police to obtain a warrant to attach a GPS device to monitor a suspect's car, may foreshadow future debates in modern privacy. Traditionally, the Court has held that police do not need a warrant to obtain information given to third parties. However, according to Sotomayor in *Jones*, "This approach is ill suited to the digital age, in which people reveal a great deal of information about themselves to third parties in the course of carrying out mundane tasks," such as visiting websites and purchasing goods online. When read in conjunction with the unanimous ruling in *Riley*, Sotomayor's opinion hints at a change that legal scholars believe may one day transform Fourth Amendment privacy rights in the context of today's digital age.

While the future legal applications of *Riley* are still to be determined, the Court's decision is refreshingly clear: "Our answer to the question of what police must do before searching a cell phone seized incident to an arrest is accordingly simple—get a warrant."

—Robert Howard

The following are excerpts from the U.S. Supreme Court ruling in Riley v. California, *in which the Court ruled unanimously that police must obtain a warrant before searching the digital information on a cell phone of an arrested suspect.*

DOCUMENT   *Riley v. California*

June 25, 2014

[Footnotes have been omitted.]

Nos. 13-132, 13-212

David Leon Riley, Petitioner

v.

California, Petitioner

United States, Petitioner

v.

Brima Wurie

On writ of certiorari to the Court of Appeals of California

On writ of certiorari to the United States Court of Appeals for the Second Circuit

[June 25, 2014]

CHIEF JUSTICE ROBERTS delivered the opinion of the Court.

These two cases raise a common question: whether the police may, without a warrant, search digital information on a cell phone seized from an individual who has been arrested.

[Sections I and II, containing background information on the case, have been omitted.]

III

These cases require us to decide how the search incident to arrest doctrine applies to modern cell phones, which are now such a pervasive and insistent part of daily life that the proverbial visitor from Mars might conclude they were an important feature of human anatomy. A smart phone of the sort taken from Riley was unheard of ten years ago; a significant majority of American adults now own such phones. See A. Smith, Pew Research Center, Smartphone Ownership—2013 Update (June 5, 2013). Even less sophisticated phones like Wurie's, which have already faded in popularity since Wurie was arrested in 2007, have been around for less than 15 years. Both phones are based on technology nearly inconceivable just a few decades ago, when *Chimel* and *Robinson* were decided.

Absent more precise guidance from the founding era, we generally determine whether to exempt a given type of search from the warrant requirement "by assessing, on the one hand, the degree to which it intrudes upon an individual's privacy and, on the other, the degree to which it is needed for the promotion of legitimate governmental interests." *Wyoming v. Houghton*, 526 U.S. 295, 300 (1999). Such a balancing of interests supported the search incident to arrest exception in *Robinson*, and a mechanical application of *Robinson* might well support the warrantless searches at issue here.

But while *Robinson*'s categorical rule strikes the appropriate balance in the context of physical objects, neither of its rationales has much force with respect to digital content on cell phones. On the government interest side, *Robinson* concluded that the two risks identified in *Chimel*—harm to officers and destruction of evidence—are present in all custodial arrests. There are no comparable risks when the search is of digital data. In addition, *Robinson* regarded any privacy interests retained by an individual after arrest as significantly diminished by the fact of the arrest itself. Cell phones, however, place vast quantities of personal information literally in the hands of individuals. A search of the information on a cell phone bears little resemblance to the type of brief physical search considered in *Robinson*.

We therefore decline to extend *Robinson* to searches of data on cell phones, and hold instead that officers must generally secure a warrant before conducting such a search.

A

We first consider each *Chimel* concern in turn. In doing so, we do not overlook *Robinson*'s admonition that searches of a person incident to arrest, "while based upon the need to disarm and to discover evidence," are reasonable regardless of "the probability in a particular arrest situation that weapons or evidence would in fact be found." 414 U.S., at 235. Rather than requiring the "case-by-case adjudication" that *Robinson* rejected, *ibid.*, we ask instead whether application of the search incident to arrest doctrine to this particular category of effects would "untether the rule from the justifications underlying the *Chimel* exception," *Gant, supra*, at 343, 129 S.Ct. 1710. See also *Knowles v. Iowa*, 525 U.S. 113, 119 (1998) (declining to extend *Robinson* to the issuance of citations, "a situation where the concern for officer safety is not present to the same extent and the concern for destruction or loss of evidence is not present at all").

1

Digital data stored on a cell phone cannot itself be used as a weapon to harm an arresting officer or to effectuate the arrestee's escape. Law enforcement officers remain free to examine the physical aspects of a phone to ensure that it will not be used as a weapon—say, to determine whether there is a razor blade hidden between the phone and its case. Once an officer has secured a phone and eliminated any potential physical threats, however, data on the phone can endanger no one.

Perhaps the same might have been said of the cigarette pack seized from Robinson's pocket. Once an officer gained control of the pack, it was unlikely that Robinson could have accessed the pack's contents. But unknown physical objects may always pose risks, no matter how slight, during the tense atmosphere of a custodial arrest. The officer in *Robinson* testified that he could not identify the objects in the cigarette pack but knew they were not cigarettes. See 414 U.S., at 223, 236, n. 7. Given that, a further search was a reasonable protective measure. No such unknowns exist with respect to digital data. As the First Circuit explained, the officers who searched Wurie's cell phone "knew exactly what they would find therein: data. They also knew that the data could not harm them." 728 F.3d, at 10.

The United States and California both suggest that a search of cell phone data might help ensure officer safety in more indirect ways, for example by alerting officers that confederates of the arrestee are headed to the scene. There is undoubtedly a strong government interest in warning officers about such possibilities, but neither the United States nor California offers evidence to suggest that their concerns are based on actual experience. The proposed consideration would also represent a broadening of *Chimel*'s concern that an *arrestee himself* might grab a weapon and use it against an officer "to resist arrest or effect his escape." 395 U.S., at 763. And any such threats from outside the arrest scene do not "lurk[ ] in all custodial arrests." *Chadwick*, 433 U.S., at 14–15. Accordingly, the interest in protecting officer safety does not justify dispensing with the warrant requirement across the board. To the extent dangers to arresting officers may be implicated in a particular way in a particular case, they are better addressed through consideration of case-specific exceptions to the warrant requirement, such as the one for exigent circumstances. See, *e.g., Warden, Md. Penitentiary v. Hayden*, 387 U.S. 294, 298–299 (1967) ("The Fourth Amendment does not require police officers to delay in the course of an investigation if to do so would gravely endanger their lives or the lives of others.").

2

The United States and California focus primarily on the second *Chimel* rationale: preventing the destruction of evidence.

Both Riley and Wurie concede that officers could have seized and secured their cell phones to prevent destruction of evidence while seeking a warrant. See Brief for Petitioner in No. 13–132, p. 20; Brief for Respondent in No. 13–212, p. 41. That is a sensible concession. See *Illinois v. McArthur*, 531 U.S. 326, 331–333, (2001); *Chadwick, supra*, at 13, and n. 8. And once law enforcement officers have secured a cell phone, there is no longer any risk that the arrestee himself will be able to delete incriminating data from the phone.

The United States and California argue that information on a cell phone may nevertheless be vulnerable to two types of evidence destruction unique to digital data—remote wiping and data encryption. Remote wiping occurs when a phone, connected to a wireless network, receives a signal that erases stored data. This can happen when a third party sends a remote signal or when a phone is preprogrammed to delete data upon entering or leaving certain geographic areas (so-called "geofencing"). See Dept. of Commerce, National Institute of Standards and Technology, R. Ayers, S. Brothers, & W. Jansen, Guidelines on Mobile Device Forensics (Draft) 29, 31 (SP 800–101 Rev. 1, Sept. 2013) (hereinafter Ayers). Encryption is a security feature that some modern cell phones use in addition to password protection. When such phones lock, data becomes protected by sophisticated encryption that renders a phone all but "unbreakable" unless police know the password. Brief for United States as *Amicus Curiae* in No. 13–132, p. 11.

As an initial matter, these broader concerns about the loss of evidence are distinct from *Chimel*'s focus on a defendant who responds to arrest by trying to conceal or destroy evidence within his reach. See 395 U.S., at 763–764. With respect to remote wiping, the Government's primary concern turns on the actions of third parties who are not present at the scene of arrest. And data encryption is even further afield. There, the Government focuses on the ordinary operation of a phone's security features, apart from any active attempt by a defendant or his associates to conceal or destroy evidence upon arrest.

We have also been given little reason to believe that either problem is prevalent. The briefing reveals only a couple of anecdotal examples of remote wiping triggered by an arrest. See Brief for Association of State Criminal Investigative Agencies et al. as *Amici Curiae* in No. 13–132, pp. 9–10; see also Tr. of Oral Arg. in No. 13–132, p. 48. Similarly, the opportunities for officers to search a password-protected phone before data becomes encrypted are quite limited. Law enforcement officers are very unlikely to come upon such a phone in an unlocked state because most phones lock at the touch of a button or, as a default, after some very short period of inactivity. See, e.g., iPhone User Guide for iOS 7.1 Software 10 (2014) (default lock after about one minute). This may explain why the encryption argument was not made until the merits stage in this Court, and has never been considered by the Courts of Appeals.

Moreover, in situations in which an arrest might trigger a remote-wipe attempt or an officer discovers an unlocked phone, it is not clear that the ability to conduct a warrantless search would make much of a difference. The need to effect the arrest, secure the scene, and tend to other pressing matters means that law enforcement officers may well not be able to turn their attention to a cell phone right away. See Tr. of Oral Arg. in No. 13–132, at 50; see also Brief for United States as *Amicus Curiae* in No. 13–132, at 19. Cell phone data would be vulnerable to remote wiping from the time an individual anticipates arrest to the time any eventual search of the phone is completed, which might be at the station house hours later. Likewise, an officer who seizes a phone in an unlocked state might not be able to begin his search in the short time remaining before the phone locks and data becomes encrypted.

In any event, as to remote wiping, law enforcement is not without specific means to address the threat. Remote wiping can be fully prevented by disconnecting a phone from the network. There are at least two simple ways to do this: First, law enforcement officers can turn the phone off or remove its battery. Second, if they are concerned about encryption or other potential problems, they can leave a phone powered on and place it in an enclosure that isolates the phone from radio waves. See Ayers 30–31. Such devices are commonly called "Faraday bags," after the English scientist Michael Faraday. They are essentially sandwich bags made of aluminum foil: cheap, lightweight, and easy to use. See Brief for Criminal Law Professors as *Amici Curiae* 9. They may not be a complete answer to the problem, see Ayers 32, but at least for now they provide a reasonable response. In fact, a number of law enforcement agencies around the country already encourage the use of Faraday bags. See, e.g., Dept. of Justice, National Institute of Justice, Electronic Crime Scene Investigation: A Guide for First Responders 14, 32 (2d ed. Apr. 2008); Brief for Criminal Law Professors as *Amici Curiae* 4–6.

To the extent that law enforcement still has specific concerns about the potential loss of evidence in a particular case, there remain more targeted ways to address those concerns. If "the police are truly confronted with a 'now or never' situation,"—for example, circumstances suggesting that a defendant's phone will be the target of an imminent remote-wipe attempt—they may be able to rely on exigent circumstances to search the phone immediately. *Missouri v. McNeely*, 569 U.S. ___, ___ (2013) (Slip op., at 10) (quoting

Roaden v. Kentucky, 413 U.S. 496, 505 (1973); some internal quotation marks omitted). Or, if officers happen to seize a phone in an unlocked state, they may be able to disable a phone's automatic-lock feature in order to prevent the phone from locking and encrypting data. See App. to Reply Brief in No. 13–132, p. 3a (diagramming the few necessary steps). Such a preventive measure could be analyzed under the principles set forth in our decision in *McArthur*, 531 U.S. 326, which approved officers' reasonable steps to secure a scene to preserve evidence while they awaited a warrant. See *id.*, at 331–333.

B

The search incident to arrest exception rests not only on the heightened government interests at stake in a volatile arrest situation, but also on an arrestee's reduced privacy interests upon being taken into police custody. *Robinson* focused primarily on the first of those rationales. But it also quoted with approval then-Judge Cardozo's account of the historical basis for the search incident to arrest exception: "Search of the person becomes lawful when grounds for arrest and accusation have been discovered, and the law is in the act of subjecting the body of the accused to its physical dominion." 414 U.S., at 232 (quoting *People v. Chiagles*, 237 N.Y. 193, 197, 142 N.E. 583, 584 (1923)); see also 414 U.S., at 237 (Powell, J., concurring) ("an individual lawfully subjected to a custodial arrest retains no significant Fourth Amendment interest in the privacy of his person"). Put simply, a patdown of Robinson's clothing and an inspection of the cigarette pack found in his pocket constituted only minor additional intrusions compared to the substantial government authority exercised in taking Robinson into custody. See *Chadwick*, 433 U.S., at 16, n. 10 (searches of a person are justified in part by "reduced expectations of privacy caused by the arrest").

The fact that an arrestee has diminished privacy interests does not mean that the Fourth Amendment falls out of the picture entirely. Not every search "is acceptable solely because a person is in custody." *Maryland v. King*, 569 U.S. ___, ___, (2013) (slip op., at 26). To the contrary, when "privacy-related concerns are weighty enough" a "search may require a warrant, notwithstanding the diminished expectations of privacy of the arrestee." Ibid. One such example, of course, is *Chimel*. *Chimel* refused to "characteriz[e] the invasion of privacy that results from a top-to-bottom search of a man's house as 'minor.'" 395 U.S., at 766–767, n. 12. Because a search of the arrestee's entire house was a substantial invasion beyond the arrest itself, the Court concluded that a warrant was required.

Robinson is the only decision from this Court applying *Chimel* to a search of the contents of an item found on an arrestee's person. In an earlier case, this Court had approved a search of a zipper bag carried by an arrestee, but the Court analyzed only the validity of the arrest itself. See *Draper v. United States*, 358 U.S. 307, 310–311 (1959). Lower courts applying *Robinson* and *Chimel*, however, have approved searches of a variety of personal items carried by an arrestee. See, e.g., *United States v. Carrion*, 809 F.2d 1120, 1123, 1128 (CA5 1987) (billfold and address book); *United States v. Watson*, 669 F.2d 1374, 1383–1384 (CA11 1982) (wallet); *United States v. Lee*, 501 F.2d 890, 892 (CADC1974) (purse).

The United States asserts that a search of all data stored on a cell phone is "materially indistinguishable" from searches of these sorts of physical items. Brief for United States in No. 13–212, p. 26. That is like saying a ride on horseback is materially indistinguishable from a flight to the moon. Both are ways of getting from point A to point B, but little else justifies lumping them together. Modern cell phones, as a category, implicate privacy concerns far beyond those implicated by the search of a cigarette pack, a wallet, or a purse. A conclusion that inspecting the contents of an arrestee's pockets works no substantial additional intrusion on privacy beyond the arrest itself may make sense as applied to physical items, but any extension of that reasoning to digital data has to rest on its own bottom.

1

Cell phones differ in both a quantitative and a qualitative sense from other objects that might be kept on an arrestee's person. The term "cell phone" is itself misleading shorthand; many of these devices are in fact minicomputers that also happen to have the capacity to be used as a telephone. They could just as easily be called cameras, video players, rolodexes, calendars, tape recorders, libraries, diaries, albums, televisions, maps, or newspapers.

One of the most notable distinguishing features of modern cell phones is their immense storage capacity. Before cell phones, a search of a person was limited by physical realities and tended as a general matter to constitute only a narrow intrusion on privacy. See Kerr, Foreword: Accounting for Technological Change, 36 Harv. J.L. & Pub. Pol'y 403, 404–405 (2013). Most people cannot lug around every piece of mail they have received for the past several months, every picture they have taken, or every book or article they have read—nor would they have any reason to attempt to do so. And if they did, they would have to drag behind them a trunk of the sort held to require a search warrant in *Chadwick, supra*, rather than a container the size of the cigarette package in *Robinson*.

But the possible intrusion on privacy is not physically limited in the same way when it comes to cell phones. The current top-selling smart phone has a standard capacity of 16 gigabytes (and is available with up to 64 gigabytes). Sixteen gigabytes translates to millions of pages of text, thousands of pictures, or hundreds of videos. See Kerr, *supra*, at 404; Brief for Center for Democracy & Technology et al. as *Amici Curiae* 7–8. Cell phones couple that capacity with the ability to store many different types of information: Even the most basic phones that sell for less than $20 might hold photographs, picture messages, text messages, Internet browsing history, a calendar, a thousand-entry phone book, and so on. See *id.*, at 30; *United States v. Flores–Lopez*, 670 F.3d 803, 806 (C.A.7 2012). We expect that the gulf between physical practicability and digital capacity will only continue to widen in the future.

The storage capacity of cell phones has several interrelated consequences for privacy. First, a cell phone collects in one place many distinct types of information—an address, a note, a prescription, a bank statement, a video—that reveal much more in combination than any isolated record. Second, a cell phone's capacity allows even just one type of information to convey far more than previously possible. The sum of an individual's private life can be reconstructed through a thousand photographs labeled with dates, locations, and descriptions; the same cannot be said of a photograph or two of loved ones tucked into a wallet. Third, the data on a phone can date back to the purchase of the phone, or even earlier. A person might carry in his pocket a slip of paper reminding him to call Mr. Jones; he would not carry a record of all his communications with Mr. Jones for the past several months, as would routinely be kept on a phone.

Finally, there is an element of pervasiveness that characterizes cell phones but not physical records. Prior to the digital age, people did not typically carry a cache of sensitive personal information with them as they went about their day. Now it is the person who is not carrying a cell phone, with all that it contains, who is the exception. According to one poll, nearly three-quarters of smart phone users report being within five feet of their phones most of the time, with 12% admitting that they even use their phones in the shower. See Harris Interactive, 2013 Mobile Consumer Habits Study (June 2013). A decade ago police officers searching an arrestee might have occasionally stumbled across a highly personal item such as a diary. See, e.g., *United States v. Frankenberry*, 387 F.2d 337 (CA2 1967) (*per curiam*). But those discoveries were likely to be few and far between. Today, by contrast, it is no exaggeration to say that many of the more than 90% of American adults who own a cell phone keep on their person a digital record of nearly every aspect of their lives—from the mundane to the intimate. See *Ontario v. Quon*, 560 U.S. 746, 760 (2010). Allowing the police to scrutinize such records on a routine basis is quite different from allowing them to search a personal item or two in the occasional case.

Although the data stored on a cell phone is distinguished from physical records by quantity alone, certain types of data are also qualitatively different. An Internet search and browsing history, for example, can be found on an Internet-enabled phone and could reveal an individual's private interests or concerns—perhaps a search for certain symptoms of disease, coupled with frequent visits to WebMD. Data on a cell phone can also reveal where a person has been. Historic location information is a standard feature on many smart phones and can reconstruct someone's specific movements down to the minute, not only around town but also within a particular building. See *United States v. Jones*, 565 U.S. ___, ___, (2012) (SOTOMAYOR, J., concurring)(slip op., at 3) ("GPS monitoring generates a precise, comprehensive record of a person's public movements that reflects a wealth of detail about her familial, political, professional, religious, and sexual associations.").

Mobile application software on a cell phone, or "apps," offer a range of tools for managing detailed information about all aspects of a person's life. There are apps for Democratic Party news and Republican Party news; apps for alcohol, drug, and gambling addictions; apps for sharing prayer requests; apps for tracking pregnancy symptoms; apps for planning your budget; apps for every conceivable hobby or pastime; apps for improving your romantic life. There are popular apps for buying or selling just about anything, and the records of such transactions may be accessible on the phone indefinitely. There are over a million apps available in each of the two major app stores; the phrase "there's an app for that" is now part of the popular lexicon. The average smart phone user has installed 33 apps, which together can form a revealing montage of the user's life. See Brief for Electronic Privacy Information Center as *Amicus Curiae* in No. 13–132, p. 9.

In 1926, Learned Hand observed (in an opinion later quoted in *Chimel*) that it is "a totally different thing to search a man's pockets and use against him what they contain, from ransacking his house for everything which may incriminate him." *United States v. Kirschenblatt*, 16 F.2d 202, 203 (CA2). If his pockets contain a cell phone, however, that is no longer true. Indeed, a cell phone search would typically expose to the government far more than the most exhaustive search of a house: A phone not only contains in digital form many sensitive records previously found in the home; it also contains a broad array of private information never found in a home in any form—unless the phone is.

2

To further complicate the scope of the privacy interests at stake, the data a user views on many modern cell phones may not in fact be stored on the device itself. Treating a cell phone as a container whose contents may be searched incident to an arrest is a bit strained as an initial matter. See *New York v. Belton*, 453 U.S. 454, 460, n. 4 (1981) (describing a "container" as "any object capable of holding another object"). But the analogy crumbles entirely when a cell phone is used to access data located elsewhere, at the tap of a screen. That is what cell phones, with increasing frequency, are designed to do by taking advantage of "cloud computing." Cloud computing is the capacity of Internet-connected devices to display data stored on remote servers rather than on the device itself. Cell phone users often may not know whether particular information is stored on the device or in the cloud, and it generally makes little difference. See Brief for Electronic Privacy Information Center in No. 13–132, at 12–14, 20. Moreover, the same type of data may be stored locally on the device for one user and in the cloud for another.

The United States concedes that the search incident to arrest exception may not be stretched to cover a search of files accessed remotely—that is, a search of files stored in the cloud. See Brief for United States in No. 13–212, at 43–44. Such a search would be like finding a key in a suspect's pocket and arguing that it allowed law enforcement to unlock and search a house. But officers searching a phone's data would not typically know whether the information they are viewing was stored locally at the time of the arrest or has been pulled from the cloud.

Although the Government recognizes the problem, its proposed solutions are unclear. It suggests that officers could disconnect a phone from the network before searching the device—the very solution whose feasibility it contested with respect to the threat of remote wiping. Compare Tr. of Oral Arg. in No. 13–132, at 50–51, with Tr. of Oral Arg. in No. 13–212, pp. 13–14. Alternatively, the Government proposes that law enforcement agencies "develop protocols to address" concerns raised by cloud computing. Reply Brief in No. 13–212, pp. 14–15. Probably a good idea, but the Founders did not fight a revolution to gain the right to government agency protocols. The possibility that a search might extend well beyond papers and effects in the physical proximity of an arrestee is yet another reason that the privacy interests here dwarf those in *Robinson*.

C

Apart from their arguments for a direct extension of *Robinson*, the United States and California offer various fallback options for permitting warrantless cell phone searches under certain circumstances. Each of the proposals is flawed and contravenes our general preference to provide clear guidance to law enforcement through categorical rules. "[I]f police are to have workable rules, the balancing of the competing interests . . . 'must in large part be done on a categorical basis—not in an ad hoc, case-by-case fashion by individual police officers.'" *Michigan v. Summers*, 452 U.S. 692, 705, n. 19 (1981) (quoting *Dunaway v. New York*, 442 U.S. 200, 219–220 (1979) (White, J., concurring)).

The United States first proposes that the *Gant* standard be imported from the vehicle context, allowing a warrantless search of an arrestee's cell phone whenever it is reasonable to believe that the phone contains evidence of the crime of arrest. But *Gant* relied on "circumstances unique to the vehicle context" to endorse a search solely for the purpose of gathering evidence. 556 U.S., at 343. Justice SCALIA's *Thornton* opinion, on which *Gant* was based, explained that those unique circumstances are "a reduced expectation of privacy" and "heightened law enforcement needs" when it comes to motor vehicles. 541 U.S., at 631; see also *Wyoming v. Houghton*, 526 U.S., at 303–304. For reasons that we have explained, cell phone searches bear neither of those characteristics.

At any rate, a *Gant* standard would prove no practical limit at all when it comes to cell phone searches. In the vehicle context, Gant generally protects against searches for evidence of past crimes. See 3 W. LaFave, Search and Seizure § 7.1(d), at 709, and n. 191. In the cell phone context, however, it is reasonable to expect that incriminating information will be found on a phone regardless of when the crime occurred. Similarly, in the vehicle context *Gant* restricts broad searches resulting from minor crimes such as traffic violations. See *id.*, § 7.1(d), at 713, and n. 204. That would not necessarily be true for cell phones. It would be a particularly inexperienced or unimaginative law enforcement officer who could not come up with several reasons to suppose evidence of just about any crime could be found on a cell phone. Even an individual pulled over for something as basic as speeding might well have locational data dispositive of guilt on his phone. An individual pulled over for reckless driving might have evidence on the phone that shows whether he was texting while driving. The sources of potential pertinent information are virtually unlimited, so applying the *Gant* standard to cell phones would in effect give "police officers unbridled discretion to rummage at will among a person's private effects." 556 U.S., at 345.

The United States also proposes a rule that would restrict the scope of a cell phone search to those areas of the phone where an officer reasonably believes that information relevant to the crime, the arrestee's identity, or officer safety will be discovered. See Brief for United States in No. 13–212, at 51–53. This approach would again impose few meaningful constraints on officers. The proposed categories would sweep in a great deal of information, and officers would not always be able to discern in advance what information would be found where.

We also reject the United States' final suggestion that officers should always be able to search a phone's call log, as they did in Wurie's case. The Government relies on *Smith v. Maryland*, 442 U.S. 735 (1979), which held that no warrant was required to use a pen register at telephone company premises to identify numbers dialed by a particular caller. The Court in that case, however, concluded that the use of a pen register was not a "search" at all under the Fourth Amendment. See *id.*, at 745–746. There is no dispute here that the officers engaged in a search of Wurie's cell phone. Moreover, call logs typically contain more than just phone numbers; they include any identifying information that an individual might add, such as the label "my house" in Wurie's case.

Finally, at oral argument California suggested a different limiting principle, under which officers could search cell phone data if they could have obtained the same information from a pre-digital counterpart. See Tr. of Oral Arg. in No. 13–132, at 38–43; see also *Flores–Lopez*, 670 F.3d, at 807 ("If police are entitled to open a pocket diary to copy the owner's address, they should be entitled to turn on a cell phone to learn its number."). But the fact that a search in the pre-digital era could have turned up a photograph or two in a wallet does not justify a search of thousands of photos in a digital gallery. The fact that someone could have tucked a paper bank statement in a pocket does not justify a search of every bank statement from the last five years. And to make matters worse, such an analogue test would allow law enforcement to search a range of items contained on a phone, even though people would be unlikely to carry such a variety of information in physical form. In Riley's case, for example, it is implausible that he would have strolled around with video tapes, photo albums, and an address book all crammed into his pockets. But because each of those items has a pre-digital analogue, police under California's proposal would be able to search a phone for all of those items—a significant diminution of privacy.

In addition, an analogue test would launch courts on a difficult line-drawing expedition to determine which digital files are comparable to physical records. Is an e-mail equivalent to a letter? Is a voicemail equivalent to a phone message slip? It is not clear how officers could make these kinds of decisions before conducting a search, or how courts would apply the proposed rule after the fact. An analogue test would "keep defendants and judges guessing for years to come." *Sykes v. United States*, 564 U.S. 1, ___, (2011)

(SCALIA, J., dissenting) (slip op., at 7) (discussing the Court's analogue test under the Armed Career Criminal Act).

IV

We cannot deny that our decision today will have an impact on the ability of law enforcement to combat crime. Cell phones have become important tools in facilitating coordination and communication among members of criminal enterprises, and can provide valuable incriminating information about dangerous criminals. Privacy comes at a cost.

Our holding, of course, is not that the information on a cell phone is immune from search; it is instead that a warrant is generally required before such a search, even when a cell phone is seized incident to arrest. Our cases have historically recognized that the warrant requirement is "an important working part of our machinery of government," not merely "an inconvenience to be somehow 'weighed' against the claims of police efficiency." *Coolidge v. New Hampshire*, 403 U.S. 443, 481 (1971). Recent technological advances similar to those discussed here have, in addition, made the process of obtaining a warrant itself more efficient. See *McNeely*, 569 U.S., at ___, (slip op., at 11-12); *id.*, at ___, (ROBERTS, C.J., concurring in part and dissenting in part) (slip op., at 8) (describing jurisdiction where "police officers can e-mail warrant requests to judges' iPads [and] judges have signed such warrants and e-mailed them back to officers in less than 15 minutes").

Moreover, even though the search incident to arrest exception does not apply to cell phones, other case-specific exceptions may still justify a warrantless search of a particular phone. "One well-recognized exception applies when "'the exigencies of the situation" make the needs of law enforcement so compelling that [a] warrantless search is objectively reasonable under the Fourth Amendment.'" *Kentucky v. King*, 563 U.S., at ___, (slip op., at 6) (quoting *Mincey v. Arizona*, 437 U.S. 385, 394 (1978)). Such exigencies could include the need to prevent the imminent destruction of evidence in individual cases, to pursue a fleeing suspect, and to assist persons who are seriously injured or are threatened with imminent injury. 563 U.S., at ___. In *Chadwick*, for example, the Court held that the exception for searches incident to arrest did not justify a search of the trunk at issue, but noted that "if officers have reason to believe that luggage contains some immediately dangerous instrumentality, such as explosives, it would be foolhardy to transport it to the station house without opening the luggage." 433 U.S., at 15, n. 9.

In light of the availability of the exigent circumstances exception, there is no reason to believe that law enforcement officers will not be able to address some of the more extreme hypotheticals that have been suggested: a suspect texting an accomplice who, it is feared, is preparing to detonate a bomb, or a child abductor who may have information about the child's location on his cell phone. The defendants here recognize—indeed, they stress—that such fact-specific threats may justify a warrantless search of cell phone data. See Reply Brief in No. 13–132, at 8–9; Brief for Respondent in No. 13–212, at 30, 41. The critical point is that, unlike the search incident to arrest exception, the exigent circumstances exception requires a court to examine whether an emergency justified a warrantless search in each particular case. See *McNeely*, supra, at ___, (slip op., at 6).

* * *

Our cases have recognized that the Fourth Amendment was the founding generation's response to the reviled "general warrants" and "writs of assistance" of the colonial era, which allowed British officers to rummage through homes in an unrestrained search for evidence of criminal activity. Opposition to such searches was in fact one of the driving forces behind the Revolution itself. In 1761, the patriot James Otis delivered a speech in Boston denouncing the use of writs of assistance. A young John Adams was there, and he would later write that "[e]very man of a crowded audience appeared to me to go away, as I did, ready to take arms against writs of assistance." 10 Works of John Adams 247–248 (C. Adams ed. 1856). According to Adams, Otis's speech was "the first scene of the first act of opposition to the arbitrary claims of Great Britain. Then and there the child Independence was born." *Id.*, at 248 (quoted in *Boyd v. United States*, 116 U.S. 616, 625 (1886)).

Modern cell phones are not just another technological convenience. With all they contain and all they may reveal, they hold for many Americans "the privacies of life," *Boyd, supra*, at 6304. The fact that technology now allows an individual to carry such information in his hand does not make the information any less worthy of the protection for which the Founders fought. Our answer to the question of what police must do before searching a cell phone seized incident to an arrest is accordingly simple—get a warrant.

We reverse the judgment of the California Court of Appeal in No. 13–132 and remand the case for further proceedings not inconsistent with this opinion. We affirm the judgment of the First Circuit in No. 13–212.

It is so ordered.

[Justice Alito's opinion, concurring in part and concurring in the judgment, has been omitted.]

Source: U.S. Supreme Court. *Riley v. California*. 573 U.S.__(2014). www.supremecourt.gov/opinions /13pdf/13-132_8l9c.pdf.

Other Historic Documents of Interest

From previous *Historic Documents*

- Supreme Court Rules on Privacy, *2012*, p. 43

Supreme Court Rules on Affordable Care Act Birth Control Mandate

JUNE 30, 2014

On June 30, 2014, the Supreme Court, on the last day before leaving for summer recess, ruled on its second major challenge to the Patient Protection and Affordable Care Act of 2010 (ACA), President Barack Obama's signature health care law. Almost exactly two years earlier, the Court had largely upheld the law against a challenge to the constitutionality of its so-called "individual mandate," the requirement that everyone purchase health insurance or pay a penalty. That case had shocked most court observers when Chief Justice John G. Roberts Jr. wrote the controlling opinion upholding the mandate, joining with the more liberal justices on the court in result if not in rationale. There was no such surprise in the outcome of *Burwell v. Hobby Lobby Stores, Inc. et al.*, which involved a challenge to the law's requirement that employers provide coverage for contraceptive services in their employee's health care plans. The challengers to this provision were closely held corporations whose owners objected to the requirement on religious grounds. In a 5–4 decision, Justice Samuel A. Alito Jr. writing for the majority, sided with the law's challengers. The federal government could not, he wrote, require family-owned corporations to provide health insurance coverage for methods of birth control that violate the sincerely held religious beliefs of the companies' owners. For such businesses, the Court concluded, the contraceptive mandate runs afoul of another federal statute, the Religious Freedom Restoration Act of 1993.

TWO FEDERAL STATUTES ON A COLLISION COURSE

Generally, the ACA requires employers of fifty or more full-time employees to offer health insurance that provides "minimum essential coverage." Employers who fail to provide the required coverage are subject to substantial financial penalties. Congress left it to Health and Human Services (HHS) to determine just what "minimum essential coverage" requires. In 2011, HHS promulgated regulations that required businesses to cover "all FDA approved contraceptive methods, sterilization procedures, and patient education and counseling." Churches were granted exemptions from this requirement as were certain religious nonprofit organizations. For these organizations, the law requires the insurance companies to provide the contraceptive services without any cost to the employee or the employer.

This contraceptive mandate was challenged by two corporations: Hobby Lobby, a nationwide chain of arts-and-crafts stores, and Conestoga Wood Specialties, a company that makes wood cabinets. As for-profit corporations, neither of these companies qualifies for the religious exemptions to this mandate, and yet the families who own each corporation say that they try to run their businesses in accordance with their deeply held religious beliefs. The two families believe that life begins at conception and, of the twenty methods of contraception required by the ACA, they object on the grounds that four of them, including "morning after" pills and IUDs, may have the effect of preventing an already fertilized egg from developing further by interfering with its attachment in the uterus. They considered these to be abortifacients and objected on religious principles to providing insurance that would cover the costs associated with these birth control methods to their employees. The Hahn family, devout members of the Mennonite Church, who own Conestoga, argued that "it is immoral and sinful for [them] to intentionally participate in, pay for, facilitate, or otherwise support these drugs." Both corporations sued in federal court, and differing appellate court results in their cases led the Supreme Court to agree to hear their two cases at the same time.

Hobby Lobby and Conestoga argued that forcing them to comply with the contraception mandate in violation of their sincere religious beliefs would violate the Religious Freedom Restoration Act of 1993 (RFRA). When it passed RFRA, Congress was reacting to a 1990 Supreme Court decision, *Employment Division v. Smith*, in which the Court dramatically narrowed the way it analyzed First Amendment free-exercise of religion claims. The *Smith* case involved two members of the Native American Church who were fired for ingesting peyote for sacramental purposes and were denied unemployment benefits on the grounds that consumption of peyote was a crime. In rejecting the Native Americans claims, the Court dispensed with the earlier test that had required the government to show a "compelling governmental interest" before burdening a religious practice. In its place, the Court advanced a significantly less rigorous analysis holding that any "neutral, generally applicable laws" that advance a "legitimate government interest" may satisfy the Constitution's requirements when applied to religious practices. In other words, a law that burdened someone's exercise of religion would not violate the Free Exercise Clause of the First Amendment as long as the law did not target religious groups for discrimination. This raised a significant outcry from religious groups, and Congress responded by passing RFRA with the explicit purpose to return to the earlier, pre-*Smith* standards and to provide broader protection for religious liberty. The law was based on the congressional finding that even though a law may be "neutral" toward religion, it still "may burden religious exercise as surely as laws intended to interfere with religious exercise."

BIRTH CONTROL MANDATE VIOLATES CORPORATE RELIGIOUS RIGHTS

In an opinion written by Justice Alito and joined by Chief Justice Roberts Jr. and Justices Antonin Scalia, Anthony M. Kennedy, and Clarence Thomas, the Court addressed whether it violates the RFRA to mandate that closely held corporations provide health insurance coverage for methods of contraception that violate the religious beliefs of their owners. But, before it could even reach this question, it first had to determine if the RFRA applies at all to for-profit corporations such as Hobby Lobby and Conestoga. There was a potential issue here because the birth control mandate, by its terms, applies only to companies and not to their owners as individuals. At the same time, the terms of RFRA prohibit the government from substantially burdening "a person's exercise of religion." RFRA had already been held to apply in the context of non-profit corporations but, as Justice Ruth Bader Ginsburg noted in her dissent, it had never been applied to "the commercial, profit-making world." The government had argued that corporations cannot be protected by RFRA because they cannot practice religion.

The Court majority, however, had no trouble dispensing with this initial issue and finding that RFRA applies to for-profit corporations. When can a corporation be treated like a person is the same question addressed in *Citizens United v. Federal Election Commission* (2010) where the Court ruled that corporations have free speech rights. Here, instead of free speech, the Court concluded that corporations, like people, have rights to religious liberty. "A corporation is simply a form of organization used by human beings to achieve desired ends," Justice Alito wrote. "When rights, whether constitutional or statutory, are extended to corporations, the purpose is to protect the rights of these people." To say that the owners of corporations forfeit their rights under RFRA when they decide to organize their businesses as corporations would force them to "either give up the right to seek judicial protection of their religious liberty or forgo the benefits, available to their competitors, of operating as corporations." The majority found no evidence that this is what Congress intended when it passed the very broad RFRA. "Congress," Justice Alito wrote, "did not discriminate in this way against men and women who wish to run their businesses as for-profit corporations in the manner required by their religious beliefs."

Once the Court determined that RFRA applies to corporations, it had to address whether the contraception mandate violated the terms of the federal law that prohibits the government from imposing a "substantial burden" on a person's exercise of religion, unless there is a "compelling governmental interest" and the measure is the "least restrictive means" of achieving that interest. The Court acknowledged that the companies' owners possess sincere religious beliefs that would be substantially burdened if they were to provide the coverage required by the birth control mandate. Failure to comply would lead to severe economic sanctions. The Court also assumed that the interest in guaranteeing cost-free access to birth control is a compelling governmental interest.

Where the Court had trouble was with the final prong of the test: whether the birth control mandate is the "least restrictive means" of satisfying the government's interest in guaranteeing free birth control. The opinion discussed a number of possible alternative solutions that would not burden the religious rights of corporations like Hobby Lobby. Justice Alito suggested that the most direct solution would be for the government to pay for the four contraceptives at issue. Alternatively, the government could extend to objecting for-profit corporations the same accommodations it already provides to religious organizations.

Because other avenues exist to fund employees' birth control access without burdening the employers' religious freedom, the Court held that the government could not enforce the birth control mandate against corporations with religious conflicts. It is important to note that the Court based this ruling on RFRA, a federal statute. It did not address any constitutional claims.

JUSTICES DISAGREE ABOUT SCOPE OF DECISION

There was intense disagreement among the justices regarding the scope of this decision and how expansively it will be applied to other challenges by businesses that claim that laws burden their religious beliefs. Justice Alito emphasized the narrowness and specificity of his opinion. "Our decision," he wrote, "should not be understood to hold that an insurance coverage mandate must necessarily fall if it conflicts with an employer's religious beliefs." He emphasized that the holding "is concerned solely with the contraceptive mandate" and was restricted to closely held corporations controlled by individuals with "sincerely held religious beliefs." He left open whether RFRA could apply to a publically traded corporation but he dismissed the issue, stating that "it seems unlikely" that such "corporate giants" would make a religious liberty claim. He also did not anticipate "a flood of religious objections regarding a wide variety of medical procedures and drugs."

By contrast, Justice Ginsburg, who wrote the principal dissent, described the case as a "decision of startling breadth." Her dissent was joined in its entirety by Justice Sonia Sotomayor and in part by Justices Stephen Breyer and Elena Kagan. "The Court's expansive notion of corporate personhood," according to Justice Ginsburg, "invites for-profit entities to seek religion-based exemptions from regulations they deem offensive to their faiths." She argued that the logic relied on by the Court would make it hard to limit the scope of the decision the way that Justice Alito outlined. The language used by the majority extends to "corporations of any size, public or private." She raised the specter of other law suits from corporations claiming to object on religious grounds to providing insurance coverage for all sorts of specific medical interventions, including blood transfusions (Jehovah's Witnesses), vaccinations (Christian Scientists, among others), or antidepressants (Scientologists), to name just a few. Corporations may also object on religious grounds to paying the minimum wage, or paying women and men equally for the same work. Some employers may argue that their religious beliefs must exempt them from all sorts of antidiscrimination laws. According to Justice Ginsburg, this decision means that claims like these may come before the courts putting them where they should not be: in the middle of evaluating the relative merits and sincerity of differing religious claims. "The Court, I fear, has ventured into a minefield."

Justice Kennedy joined with the majority on this case, but wrote a separate concurring opinion to support Justice Alito's contention that the holding in this case is a narrow one. In his view, the "Court's opinion does not have the breadth and sweep ascribed to it by the respectful and powerful dissent."

AFTERMATH OF THE DECISION

The owners of Hobby Lobby described themselves as "overjoyed" with the result and said that they would continue to provide sixteen of the twenty mandated contraceptives that they do not find objectionable. It is unclear how many companies will be affected by the specifics of this ruling. According to a Kaiser Family Fund poll, 85 percent of large companies were already offering birth control in their insurance coverage before they were required to do so by the ACA. To satisfy the requirements of the *Hobby Lobby* ruling, the Obama administration has published new proposed rules on extending an exemption to the mandate for certain closely held corporations and is seeking comment from the public.

Groups that have been watching to see how expansively the ruling will be interpreted by other federal courts have included those supporting equal rights for gays and lesbians who question how it would be applied if individuals claiming to have sincere religious objections to conducting business with gay people seek exemptions from various antidiscrimination laws.

—Melissa Feinberg

Following is the edited text of the Supreme Court decision in Burwell v. Hobby Lobby *in which the Court ruled 5–4 that the ACA's mandate to require family-owned companies to provide birth control and contraceptive coverage to all employees was an unconstitutional violation of religious beliefs.*

Burwell v. Hobby Lobby

June 30, 2014

Nos. 13-354 and 13-356

Sylvia Burwell, Secretary of Health
and Human Services, et al.,
petitioners

v.

Hobby Lobby Stores, Inc., et al.

Conestoga Wood Specialties
Corporation et al., petitioners

v.

Sylvia Burwell, Secretary of Health
and Human Services, et al.

On writ of certiorari
to the United States
Court of Appeals for
the Tenth Circuit

On writ of certiorari
to the United States
Court of Appeals for
the Third Circuit

[June 30, 2014]

JUSTICE ALITO delivered the opinion of the Court.

We must decide in these cases whether the Religious Freedom Restoration Act of 1993 (RFRA), 107 Stat. 1488,42 U. S. C. §2000bb *et seq.*, permits the United States Department of Health and Human Services (HHS) to demand that three closely held corporations provide health-insurance coverage for methods of contraception that violate the sincerely held religious beliefs of the companies' owners. We hold that the regulations that impose this obligation violate RFRA, which prohibits the Federal Government from taking any action that substantially burdens the exercise of religion unless that action constitutes the least restrictive means of serving a compelling government interest.

In holding that the HHS mandate is unlawful, we reject HHS's argument that the owners of the companies forfeited all RFRA protection when they decided to organize their businesses as corporations rather than sole proprietorships or general partnerships. The plain terms of RFRA make it perfectly clear that Congress did not discriminate in this way against men and women who wish to run their businesses as for-profit corporations in the manner required by their religious beliefs.

Since RFRA applies in these cases, we must decide whether the challenged HHS regulations substantially burden the exercise of religion, and we hold that they do. The owners of the businesses have religious objections to abortion, and according to their religious beliefs the four contraceptive methods at issue are abortifacients. If the owners comply with the HHS mandate, they believe they will be facilitating abortions, and if they do not comply, they will pay a very heavy price—as much as $1.3 million per day, or about $475 million per year, in the case of one of the companies. If these consequences do not amount to a substantial burden, it is hard to see what would.

Under RFRA, a Government action that imposes a substantial burden on religious exercise must serve a compelling government interest, and we assume that the HHS regulations satisfy this requirement. But in order for the HHS mandate to be sustained, it must also constitute the least restrictive means of serving that interest, and the mandate plainly fails that test. There are other ways in which Congress or HHS could equally ensure that every woman has cost-free access to the particular contraceptives at issue here and, indeed, to all FDA-approved contraceptives.

In fact, HHS has already devised and implemented a system that seeks to respect the religious liberty of religious nonprofit corporations while ensuring that the employees of these entities have precisely the same access to all FDA-approved contraceptives as employees of companies whose owners have no religious objections to providing such coverage. The employees of these religious nonprofit corporations still have access to insurance coverage without cost sharing for all FDA-approved contraceptives; and according to HHS, this system imposes no net economic burden on the insurance companies that are required to provide or secure the coverage.

Although HHS has made this system available to religious nonprofits that have religious objections to the contraceptive mandate, HHS has provided no reason why the same system cannot be made available when the owners of for-profit corporations have similar religious objections. We therefore conclude that this system constitutes an alternative that achieves all of the Government's aims while providing greater respect for religious liberty. And under RFRA, that conclusion means that enforcement of the HHS contraceptive mandate against the objecting parties in these cases is unlawful.

As this description of our reasoning shows, our holding is very specific. We do not hold, as the principal dissent alleges, that for-profit corporations and other commercial enterprises can "opt out of any law (saving only tax laws) they judge incompatible with their sincerely held religious beliefs." *Post,* at 1 (opinion of GINSBURG, J.). Nor do we hold, as the dissent implies, that such corporations have free rein to take steps that impose "disadvantages . . . on others" or that require "the general public [to] pick up the tab." And we certainly do not hold or suggest that "RFRA demands accommodation of a for-profit corporation's religious beliefs no matter the impact that accommodation may have on . . . thousands of women employed by Hobby Lobby." The effect of the HHS-created accommodation on the women employed by Hobby Lobby and the other companies involved in these cases would be precisely zero. Under that accommodation, these women would still be entitled to all FDA-approved contraceptives without cost sharing.

[Sections I and II, containing background on the case, have been omitted.]

III

A

RFRA prohibits the "Government [from] substantially burden[ing] *a person's* exercise of religion even if the burden results from a rule of general applicability" unless the Government "demonstrates that application of the burden to *the person*—(1) is in furtherance of a compelling governmental interest; and (2) is the least restrictive means of furthering that compelling governmental interest." 42 U. S. C. §§2000bb–1(a), (b) (emphasis added).The first question that we must address is whether this provision applies to regulations that govern the activities of for-profit corporations like Hobby Lobby, Conestoga, and Mardel.

HHS contends that neither these companies nor their owners can even be heard under RFRA. According to HHS, the companies cannot sue because they seek to make a profit for their owners, and the owners cannot be heard because the regulations, at least as a formal matter, apply only to the companies and not to the owners as individuals. HHS's argument would have dramatic consequences. . . .

As we have seen, RFRA was designed to provide very broad protection for religious liberty. By enacting RFRA, Congress went far beyond what this Court has held is constitutionally required. Is there any reason to think that the Congress that enacted such sweeping protection put small-business owners to the choice that HHS suggests? An examination of RFRA's text, to which we turn in the next part of this opinion, reveals that Congress did no such thing.

As we will show, Congress provided protection for people like the Hahns and Greens by employing a familiar legal fiction: It included corporations within RFRA's definition of "persons." But it is important to keep in mind that the purpose of this fiction is to provide protection for human beings. A corporation is simply a form of organization used by human beings to achieve desired ends. An established body of law specifies the rights and obligations of the *people* (including shareholders, officers, and employees) who are associated with a corporation in one way or another. When rights, whether constitutional or statutory, are extended to corporations, the purpose is to protect the rights of these people. For example, extending Fourth Amendment protection to corporations protects the privacy interests of employees and others associated with the company. Protecting corporations from government seizure of their property without just compensation protects all those who have a stake in the corporations' financial well-being. And protecting the free-exercise rights of corporations like Hobby Lobby, Conestoga, and Mardel protects the religious liberty of the humans who own and control those companies.

In holding that Conestoga, as a "secular, for-profit corporation," lacks RFRA protection, the Third Circuit wrote as follows:

> "General business corporations do not, *separate and apart from the actions or belief systems of their individual owners or employees,* exercise religion. They do not pray, worship, observe sacraments or take other religiously-motivated actions separate and apart from the intention and direction of their individual actors." 724 F. 3d, at 385 (emphasis added).

All of this is true—but quite beside the point. Corporations, "separate and apart from" the human beings who own, run, and are employed by them, cannot do anything at all. . . .

[Sections 1, 2, and 3, further describing previous cases and the RFRA, have been omitted.]

IV

Because RFRA applies in these cases, we must next ask whether the HHS contraceptive mandate "substantially burden[s]" the exercise of religion. 42 U. S. C. §2000bb– 1(a). We have little trouble concluding that it does.

A

As we have noted, the Hahns and Greens have a sincere religious belief that life begins at conception. They therefore object on religious grounds to providing health insurance that covers methods of birth control that, as HHS acknowledges, see Brief for HHS in No. 13–354, at 9, n. 4, may result in the destruction of an embryo. By requiring the Hahns and

Greens and their companies to arrange for such coverage, the HHS mandate demands that they engage in conduct that seriously violates their religious beliefs.

If the Hahns and Greens and their companies do not yield to this demand, the economic consequences will be severe. If the companies continue to offer group health plans that do not cover the contraceptives at issue, they will be taxed $100 per day for each affected individual. 26 U. S. C. §4980D. For Hobby Lobby, the bill could amount to $1.3 million per day or about $475 million per year; for Conestoga, the assessment could be $90,000 per day or $33 million per year; and for Mardel, it could be $40,000 per day or about $15 million per year. These sums are surely substantial. . . .

C

In taking the position that the HHS mandate does not impose a substantial burden on the exercise of religion, HHS's main argument (echoed by the principal dissent) is basically that the connection between what the objecting parties must do (provide health-insurance coverage for four methods of contraception that may operate after the fertilization of an egg) and the end that they find to be morally wrong (destruction of an embryo) is simply too attenuated. HHS and the dissent note that providing the coverage would not itself result in the destruction of an embryo; that would occur only if an employee chose to take advantage of the coverage and to use one of the four methods at issue. *Ibid.*

This argument dodges the question that RFRA presents (whether the HHS mandate imposes a substantial burden on the ability of the objecting parties to conduct business in accordance with *their religious beliefs*) and instead addresses a very different question that the federal courts have no business addressing (whether the religious belief asserted in a RFRA case is reasonable). The Hahns and Greens believe that providing the coverage demanded by the HHS regulations is connected to the destruction of an embryo in a way that is sufficient to make it immoral for them to provide the coverage. This belief implicates a difficult and important question of religion and moral philosophy, namely, the circumstances under which it is wrong for a person to perform an act that is innocent in itself but that has the effect of enabling or facilitating the commission of an immoral act by another. Arrogating the authority to provide a binding national answer to this religious and philosophical question, HHS and the principal dissent in effect tell the plaintiffs that their beliefs are flawed. For good reason, we have repeatedly refused to take such a step. . . .

V

Since the HHS contraceptive mandate imposes a substantial burden on the exercise of religion, we must move on and decide whether HHS has shown that the mandate both "(1) is in furtherance of a compelling governmental interest; and (2) is the least restrictive means of furthering that compelling governmental interest." §2000bb–1(b).

A

. . . We will assume that the interest in guaranteeing cost-free access to the four challenged contraceptive methods is compelling within the meaning of RFRA, and we will proceed to consider the final prong of the RFRA test, *i.e.*, whether HHS has shown that the contraceptive mandate is "the least restrictive means of furthering that compelling governmental interest." §2000bb–1(b)(2).

B

The least-restrictive-means standard is exceptionally demanding, see *City of Boerne*, 521 U. S., at 532, and it is not satisfied here. HHS has not shown that it lacks other means of achieving its desired goal without imposing a substantial burden on the exercise of religion by the objecting parties in these cases. . . .

The most straightforward way of doing this would be for the Government to assume the cost of providing the four contraceptives at issue to any women who are unable to obtain them under their health-insurance policies due to their employers' religious objections. This would certainly be less restrictive of the plaintiffs' religious liberty, and HHS has not shown, see §2000bb–1(b)(2), that this is not a viable alternative. . . .

In the end, however, we need not rely on the option of a new, government-funded program in order to conclude that the HHS regulations fail the least-restrictive-means test. HHS itself has demonstrated that it has at its disposal an approach that is less restrictive than requiring employers to fund contraceptive methods that violate their religious beliefs. As we explained above, HHS has already established an accommodation for nonprofit organizations with religious objections. Under that accommodation, the organization can self-certify that it opposes providing coverage for particular contraceptive services. If the organization makes such a certification, the organization's insurance issuer or third-party administrator must "[e]xpressly exclude contraceptive coverage from the group health insurance coverage provided in connection with the group health plan" and "[p]rovide separate payments for any contraceptive services required to be covered" without imposing "any cost-sharing requirements . . . on the eligible organization, the group health plan, or plan participants or beneficiaries." 45 CFR §147.131(c)(2); 26 CFR §54.9815–2713A(c)(2).

We do not decide today whether an approach of this type complies with RFRA for purposes of all religious claims. At a minimum, however, it does not impinge on the plaintiffs' religious belief that providing insurance coverage for the contraceptives at issue here violates their religion, and it serves HHS's stated interests equally well. . . .

C

HHS and the principal dissent argue that a ruling in favor of the objecting parties in these cases will lead to a flood of religious objections regarding a wide variety of medical procedures and drugs, such as vaccinations and blood transfusions, but HHS has made no effort to substantiate this prediction. HHS points to no evidence that insurance plans in existence prior to the enactment of ACA excluded coverage for such items. Nor has HHS provided evidence that any significant number of employers sought exemption, on religious grounds, from any of ACA's coverage requirements other than the contraceptive mandate. . . .

In any event, our decision in these cases is concerned solely with the contraceptive mandate. Our decision should not be understood to hold that an insurance coverage mandate must necessarily fall if it conflicts with an employer's religious beliefs. Other coverage requirements, such as immunizations, may be supported by different interests (for example, the need to combat the spread of infectious diseases) and may involve different arguments about the least restrictive means of providing them.

The principal dissent raises the possibility that discrimination in hiring, for example on the basis of race, might be cloaked as religious practice to escape legal sanction. Our decision today provides no such shield. The Government has a compelling interest in providing an equal opportunity to participate in the workforce without regard to race, and prohibitions on racial discrimination are precisely tailored to achieve that critical goal. . . .

* * *

The contraceptive mandate, as applied to closely held corporations, violates RFRA. Our decision on that statutory question makes it unnecessary to reach the First Amendment claim raised by Conestoga and the Hahns.

The judgment of the Tenth Circuit in No. 13–354 is affirmed; the judgment of the Third Circuit in No. 13–356 is reversed, and that case is remanded for further proceedings consistent with this opinion.

It is so ordered.

[Justice Kennedy's concurring opinion has been omitted.]

JUSTICE GINSBURG, with whom JUSTICE SOTOMAYOR joins, and with whom JUSTICE BREYER and JUSTICE KAGAN join as to all but Part III–C–1, dissenting.

In a decision of startling breadth, the Court holds that commercial enterprises, including corporations, along with partnerships and sole proprietorships, can opt out of any law (saving only tax laws) they judge incompatible with their sincerely held religious beliefs. Compelling governmental interests in uniform compliance with the law, and disadvantages that religion-based opt outs impose on others, hold no sway, the Court decides, at least when there is a "less restrictive alternative." And such an alternative, the Court suggests, there always will be whenever, in lieu of tolling an enterprise claiming a religion-based exemption, the government, *i.e.,* the general public, can pick up the tab.

The Court does not pretend that the First Amendment's Free Exercise Clause demands religion-based accommodations so extreme, for our decisions leave no doubt on that score. Instead, the Court holds that Congress, in the Religious Freedom Restoration Act of 1993 (RFRA), 42 U. S. C. §2000bb *et seq.*, dictated the extraordinary religion-based exemptions today's decision endorses. In the Court's view, RFRA demands accommodation of a for-profit corporation's religious beliefs no matter the impact that accommodation may have on third parties who do not share the corporation owners' religious faith—in these cases, thousands of women employed by Hobby Lobby and Conestoga or dependents of persons those corporations employ. Persuaded that Congress enacted RFRA to serve a far less radical purpose, and mindful of the havoc the Court's judgment can introduce, I dissent.

[The remainder of the dissent has been omitted.]

SOURCE: U.S. Supreme Court. *Burwell v. Hobby Lobby Stores, Inc.* 573 U.S.__(2014). www.supremecourt .gov/opinions/13pdf/13-354_olp1.pdf.

OTHER HISTORIC DOCUMENTS OF INTEREST

FROM PREVIOUS *HISTORIC DOCUMENTS*

Supreme Court Rules on Union Contributions by Public Employees

JUNE 30, 2014

Unions have come under attack in a variety of ways in recent years, mainly from governors who have sought to weaken their power at the bargaining table by passing right-to-work legislation. Such laws weaken a union's ability to force all public employees to pay union dues. On June 30, 2014, at the close of its term, the Supreme Court issued its ruling in the case of a specific subset of quasi-government employees—home care workers in Illinois—who were required to pay union dues even though they chose not to seek union membership. The Court ultimately ruled 5–4 that, in the case of these workers, they could not be forced to pay union dues because they are hired and fired by individual patients and are therefore not full-fledged state employees. The Court did not go so far in its ruling as to determine whether other groups of public employees could be forced to pay union dues; however, the narrow ruling did leave the door open for future cases of this nature.

Home Health Care Workers in Illinois

Union membership has declined steadily in the private sector since its heyday in the 1960s and 1970s. Today, only 7 percent of that portion of the American workforce is unionized. In the public sector, however, union membership remains strong, covering nearly a third of all government employees. In 2003 in Illinois, a state long known for its strong public unions, then Governor Rod Blagojevich decided that home care workers who aid disabled individuals would be classified as state employees. These employees were already paid by the state through Medicaid funds. The intent, in Illinois and in the approximately twenty other states that categorize employees in this manner, is to keep disabled individuals out of institutions to lower their cost of care. Often, those who provide the in-home care are relatives of the disabled individual.

Once these workers were considered state employees, they gained representation from the Service Employees International Union (SEIU) Healthcare Illinois-Indiana. The collective bargaining agreement between this union and the state of Illinois says that all state employees covered by the union will pay union dues, even those who do not wish to be members of the union—the union's argument being that even nonmembers benefit from gains made during collective bargaining. In 2010, the National Right to Work Legal Defense Foundation filed a claim against Illinois' Public Labor Relations Act on behalf of Pamela Harris, who provides care for her disabled adult son, and seven other home care workers, arguing that their First Amendment rights were violated when they were forced to pay union dues and that these workers had been improperly classified as state employees only for the benefit of union dues.

The district court that first heard the case ruled that Harris and her colleagues were appropriately classified as state employees, even though both the state and the individual are considered the employer. The court found that the long-held standard in such suits has been that employees can be required to pay dues for any nonpolitical activities. Harris appealed the case, but the Seventh Circuit Court of Appeals of Chicago affirmed the lower court's ruling. Harris asked the Supreme Court to weigh in. The Court, in turn, looked to the state of Illinois and the federal government to determine if it should hear the case.

The state waived its right to respond, and the federal government encouraged the Supreme Court not to take up the case, stating that the court of appeals was correct in its assumption that the home care workers were legally state employees and that prior Supreme Court cases should be upheld and applied to the Harris case. There was nothing in the case, the government said, that could necessitate a review of First Amendment rights as they apply to union dues. Ultimately, the Court decided to hear the case.

Court Rules for the Plaintiffs

Justice Samuel A. Alito Jr. wrote the majority opinion, released on June 30, 2014, and was joined by Chief Justice John G. Roberts Jr. and Justices Antonin Scalia, Anthony Kennedy, and Clarence Thomas. His opinion offered no apologies to public unions operating in Illinois and instead lashed out at the state's determination of who qualifies as a public employee as simply a nod to union control. "Illinois deems personal assistants to be state employees for one purpose only, collective bargaining," he wrote.

The majority decision rested heavily on the 1977 ruling in *Abood v. Detroit Board of Education*. In that case, the Court found that there must be standards in place that prevent nonunion members from taking advantage of their union dues-paying counterparts, because both groups benefit from work done at the collective bargaining table. Ultimately, in *Abood*, the Court determined that public sector workers in areas where union dues are compulsory could not refuse to pay dues for work done by the union that is nonpolitical in nature.

In the *Harris* ruling, the Court found that the justifications in *Abood* essentially ignored the difference between public- and private-sector workers and misconstrued earlier Court decisions regarding union dues and membership. In its *Harris* ruling, the Court found that the precedent set in *Abood* could not apply here because the home care workers are "partial public employees" and were only categorized as such to support union dues collection. Therefore, Harris and her home care colleagues could not be forced to pay dues for positions of the union with which they disagree, even if they ultimately benefit from the union's work. "If we accepted Illinois' argument, we would approve an unprecedented violation of the bedrock principle that, except perhaps in the rarest of circumstances, no person in this country may be compelled to subside speech by a third party that he or she does not wish to support," Alito wrote. "The First Amendment prohibits the collection of an agency fee from personal assistants in the Rehabilitation Program who do not want to join or support the union," he added. The Court added that the union had no compelling interest to force such a small group of partial employees to contribute.

The home care workers in the *Harris* case had hoped that the Court would overturn the *Abood* decision completely, but Alito rejected that idea, finding that the 1977 precedent did not fully apply in the *Harris* case because *Abood* only impacted "full-fledged state employees," not the home care workers in this case who did not enjoy some of the benefits of state employment, such as retirement plans.

A dissenting opinion was written by Justice Elena Kagan and joined by Justices Ruth Bader Ginsburg, Stephen G. Breyer, and Sonia Sotomayor. The dissent disagreed with the majority finding that *Abood* did not fully apply in this case because the home care workers were not full public employees. Kagan argued that because these workers were overseen and paid for by the state, there was nothing to distinguish the home care workers from any other state employee. "Today's opinion takes the tack of throwing everything against the wall in the hope that something might stick," she wrote.

Justice Kagan wrote that the majority ruling should have respected the decision in *Abood*. Alito noted that the Court neither affirmed nor overturned *Abood*, but instead refused to extend its protections to Illinois home-health workers. Kagan used most of the dissent to defend *Abood* and its principles, which help prevent government employees from taking advantage of their coworkers who are paying union dues. "Union supporters (no less than union detractors) have an economic incentive to free ride," Kagan wrote.

The ruling was celebrated by right-to-work organizations, including the National Right to Work Foundation that represented the plaintiffs in the case. The group's president, Mark Mix, applauded the "effort to convince the Supreme Court to strike down this constitutionally dubious scheme, thus freeing thousands of home care providers from unwanted union control." The SEIU and other public sector unions decried the ruling as yet another attempt at union busting and argued that with union representation, home care workers who often provide round-the-clock care have realized better working conditions and wages. "The extreme views of today's Supreme Court aimed at home care workers aren't just bad for unions—they're bad for all workers and the middle class," said AFL-CIO president Richard Trumka. Home care workers "do backbreaking, thankless work, often for low wages. By forming a union these workers are helping to combat income inequality and the rise of low wage jobs, ensuring that these are good jobs with good benefits," he added.

The ruling will likely have an impact on membership and dues collection in SEIU Healthcare Illinois-Indiana, which had 93,000 members at the time of the ruling, a quarter of whom were home care workers who pay a collective $3.6 million in dues each year.

POTENTIAL IMPACT ON CALIFORNIA CASE

The ruling in *Harris* makes it increasingly likely that the Supreme Court will hear a similar case out of California, *Friedrichs v. California Teachers Association*, in which public school teachers are suing the state over the requirement that they pay union dues even if they choose not to join the union. As noted in the *Harris* case, the justices found the ruling in *Abood* questionable (even though they ultimately decided not to overturn it) and might not believe that public employees can be compelled in this case to pay union dues. The unions disagree and believe that anyone who benefits from their efforts at the collective bargaining table should be subject to dues.

A ruling in favor of the teachers in California could deal a serious blow to the California Teachers Association, which in 2011 raised $178 million of its $191 million in revenue from dues, which can cost teachers as much as $1,000 per year. Evidence suggests that by removing the requirement to pay dues, union membership will decrease. In Wisconsin, where Republican governor Scott Walker signed a law in 2011 that limited collective bargaining and prohibited unions from collecting dues from nonmembers, the Wisconsin Education Council lost one-third of its members, while the American Federation of Teachers' Wisconsin affiliate lost 60 percent of its membership. At the end of 2014, the California case was still pending before the Ninth Circuit but will likely reach the Supreme Court sometime in its next term.

—Heather Kerrigan

Following are excerpts from the Supreme Court ruling in Harris v. Quinn *in which the Court ruled 5–4 on June 30, 2014, that Illinois home care workers cannot be forced to contribute dues to a union in which they do not desire to be members.*

| DOCUMENT | *Harris v. Quinn* |

June 30, 2014

[Footnotes have been omitted.]

No. 11-681

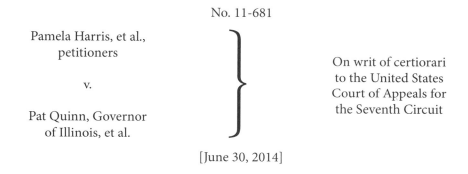

Pamela Harris, et al.,
petitioners

v.

Pat Quinn, Governor
of Illinois, et al.

On writ of certiorari
to the United States
Court of Appeals for
the Seventh Circuit

[June 30, 2014]

JUSTICE ALITO delivered the opinion of the Court.

This case presents the question whether the First Amendment permits a State to compel personal care providers to subsidize speech on matters of public concern by a union that they do not wish to join or support. We hold that it does not, and we therefore reverse the judgment of the Court of Appeals.

[Section I, which offers background on the case and home care workers in Illinois, has been omitted.]

II

In upholding the constitutionality of the Illinois law, the Seventh Circuit relied on this Court's decision in *Abood supra*, which held that state employees who choose not to join a public-sector union may nevertheless be compelled to pay an agency fee to support union work that is related to the collective-bargaining process. *Id.*, at 235–236. Two Terms ago, in *Knox v. Service Employees*, 567 U. S. ___ (2012), we pointed out that *Abood* is "something of an anomaly." *Id.*, at ___ (slip op., at 11). "'The primary purpose' of permitting unions to collect fees from nonmembers," we noted, "is 'to prevent non-members from free-riding on the union's efforts, sharing the employment benefits obtained by the union's collective bargaining without sharing the costs incurred.'" *Id.*, at ___ (slip op., at 10) (quoting *Davenport v. Washington Ed. Assn.*, 551 U. S. 177, 181 (2007)). But "[s]uch free-rider arguments . . . are generally insufficient to overcome First Amendment objections." 567 U. S., at ___ (slip op., at 10–11).

For this reason, *Abood* stands out, but the State of Illinois now asks us to sanction what amounts to a very significant expansion of *Abood*—so that it applies, not just to full-fledged public employees, but also to others who are deemed to be public employees solely for the purpose of unionization and the collection of an agency fee. Faced with this argument, we begin by examining the path that led to this Court's decision in *Abood*.

[Sections II A and B, detailing earlier Supreme Court cases, have been omitted.]

C

This brings us to *Abood*, which, unlike *Hanson* and *Street*, involved a public-sector collective-bargaining agreement. The Detroit Federation of Teachers served "as the exclusive representative of teachers employed by the Detroit Board of Education." 431 U. S., at 211–212. The collective-bargaining agreement between the union and the board contained an agency-shop clause requiring every teacher to "pay the Union a service charge equal to the regular dues required of Union members." *Id.*, at 212. A putative class of teachers sued to invalidate this clause. Asserting that "they opposed collective bargaining in the public sector," the plaintiffs argued that "'a substantial part'" of their dues would be used to fund union "'activities and programs which are economic, political, professional, scientific and religious in nature of which Plaintiffs do not approve, and in which they will have no voice.'" *Id.*, at 212-213.

This Court treated the First Amendment issue as largely settled by *Hanson* and *Street*. 431 U. S., at 217, 223. The Court acknowledged that *Street* was resolved as a matter of statutory construction without reaching any constitutional issues, 431 U. S., at 220, and the Court recognized that forced membership and forced contributions impinge on free speech and associational rights, *id.*, at 223. But the Court dismissed the objecting teachers' constitutional arguments with this observation: "[T]he judgment clearly made in *Hanson* and *Street* is that such interference as exists is constitutionally justified by the legislative assessment of the important contribution of the union shop to the system of labor relations established by Congress." *Id.*, at 222.

The *Abood* Court understood *Hanson* and *Street* to have upheld union-shop agreements in the private sector based on two primary considerations: the desirability of "labor peace" and the problem of "'free riders[hip].'" 431 U. S., at 220–222, 224.

The Court thought that agency-shop provisions promote labor peace because the Court saw a close link between such provisions and the "principle of exclusive union representation." *Id.*, at 220. This principle, the Court explained, "prevents inter-union rivalries from creating dissension within the work force and eliminating the advantages to the employee of collectivization." Id., at 220–221. In addition, the Court noted, the "designation of a single representative avoids the confusion that would result from attempting to enforce two or more agreements specifying different terms and conditions of employment." *Id.*, at 220. And the Court pointed out that exclusive representation "frees the employer from the possibility of facing conflicting demands from different unions, and permits the employer and a single union to reach agreements and settlements that are not subject to attack from rival labor organizations." *Id.*, at 221.

Turning to the problem of free ridership, *Abood* noted that a union must " 'fairly and equitably . . . represent all employees'" regardless of union membership, and the Court wrote as follows: The "union-shop arrangement has been thought to distribute fairly the cost of these activities among those who benefit, and it counteracts the incentive that employees might otherwise have to become 'free riders' to refuse to contribute to the union while obtaining benefits of union representation." *Id.*, at 221–222.

The plaintiffs in *Abood* argued that *Hanson* and *Street* should not be given much weight because they did not arise in the public sector, and the Court acknowledged that public-sector bargaining is different from private sector bargaining in some notable respects. 431 U. S., at 227–228. For example, although public and private employers both desire to keep costs down, the Court recognized that a public employer "lacks an important discipline against agreeing to increases in labor costs that in a market system would require price increases." *Id.*, at 228. The Court also noted that "decisionmaking by a public employer is above all a political process" undertaken by people "ultimately responsible to the electorate." *Ibid.* Thus, whether a public employer accedes to a union's demands, the Court wrote, "will depend upon a blend of political ingredients," thereby giving public employees "more influence in the decisionmaking process that is possessed by employees similarly organized in the private sector." *Ibid.* But despite these acknowledged differences between private- and public-sector bargaining, the Court treated *Hanson* and *Street* as essentially controlling.

Instead of drawing a line between the private and public sectors, the *Abood* Court drew a line between, on the one hand, a union's expenditures for "collective-bargaining, contract administration, and grievance-adjustment purposes," 431 U. S., at 232, and, on the other, expenditures for political or ideological purposes. *Id.*, at 236.

D

The *Abood* Court's analysis is questionable on several grounds. Some of these were noted or apparent at or before the time of the decision, but several have become more evident and troubling in the years since then.

The *Abood* Court seriously erred in treating *Hanson* and *Street* as having all but decided the constitutionality of compulsory payments to a public-sector union. As we have explained, Street was not a constitutional decision at all, and Hanson disposed of the critical question in a single, unsupported sentence that its author essentially abandoned a few years later. Surely a First Amendment issue of this importance deserved better treatment.

The *Abood* Court fundamentally misunderstood the holding in *Hanson*, which was really quite narrow. As the Court made clear in *Street*, "all that was held in *Hanson* was that [the RLA] was constitutional *in its bare authorization* of union-shop contracts requiring workers to give 'financial support' to unions legally authorized to act as their collective bargaining agents." 367 U. S., at 749 (emphasis added). In *Abood*, on the other hand, the State of Michigan did more than simply *authorize* the imposition of an agency fee. A state instrumentality, the Detroit Board of Education, actually *imposed* that fee. This presented a very different question.

Abood failed to appreciate the difference between the core union speech involuntarily subsidized by dissenting public-sector employees and the core union speech involuntarily funded by their counterparts in the private sector. In the public sector, core issues such as wages, pensions, and benefits are important political issues, but that is generally not so in the private sector. In the years since *Abood*, as state and local expenditures on employee wages and benefits have mushroomed, the importance of the difference between bargaining in the public and private sectors has been driven home.

Abood failed to appreciate the conceptual difficulty of distinguishing in public-sector cases between union expenditures that are made for collective-bargaining purposes and those that are made to achieve political ends. In the private sector, the line is easier to see. Collective bargaining concerns the union's dealings with the employer; political advocacy and lobbying are directed at the government. But in the public sector, both collective bargaining and political advocacy and lobbying are directed at the government.

Abood does not seem to have anticipated the magnitude of the practical administrative problems that would result in attempting to classify public-sector union expenditures as either "chargeable" (in *Abood's* terms, expenditures for "collective-bargaining, contract administration, and grievance-adjustment purposes," *id.*, at 232) or nonchargeable (i.e., expenditures for political or ideological purposes, *id.*, at 236). In the years since *Abood*, the Court has struggled repeatedly with this issue. . . .

Abood likewise did not foresee the practical problems that would face objecting nonmembers. Employees who suspect that a union has improperly put certain expenses in the "germane" category must bear a heavy burden if they wish to challenge the union's actions. . . .

[Section III, detailing the differences between partial state employees and full-fledged state employees, Section IV, discussing the constitutionality of union payments in this case, and Section V, reviewing other claims by the plaintiffs and defendant, have been omitted.]

***

For all these reasons, we refuse to extend *Abood* in the manner that Illinois seeks. If we accepted Illinois' argument, we would approve an unprecedented violation of the bedrock principle that, except perhaps in the rarest of circumstances, no person in this country may be compelled to subsidize speech by a third party that he or she does not wish to support. The First Amendment prohibits the collection of an agency fee from personal assistants in the Rehabilitation Program who do not want to join or support the union.

The judgment of the Court of Appeals is reversed in part and affirmed in part and the case is remanded for further proceedings consistent with this opinion.

It is so ordered.

JUSTICE KAGAN, with whom JUSTICE GINSBURG, JUSTICE BREYER, and JUSTICE SOTOMAYOR join, dissenting.

Abood v. Detroit Bd. of Ed., 431 U. S. 209 (1977), answers the question presented in this case. *Abood* held that a government entity may, consistently with the First Amendment, require public employees to pay a fair share of the cost that a union incurs negotiating on their behalf for better terms of employment. That is exactly what Illinois did in entering into collective bargaining agreements with the Service Employees International Union Healthcare (SEIU) which included fair-share provisions. Contrary to the Court's decision, those agreements fall squarely within *Abood's* holding. Here, Illinois employs, jointly with individuals suffering from disabilities, the in-home care providers whom the SEIU represents. Illinois establishes, following negotiations with the union, the most important terms of their employment, including wages, benefits, and basic qualifications. And Illinois's interests in imposing fair-share fees apply no less to those caregivers than to other state workers. The petitioners' challenge should therefore fail.

And that result would fully comport with our decisions applying the First Amendment to public employment. *Abood* is not, as the majority at one point describes it, "something of an anomaly," allowing uncommon interference with individuals' expressive activities. *Ante*, at 8. Rather, the lines it draws and the balance it strikes reflect the way courts generally evaluate claims that a condition of public employment violates the First Amendment. Our decisions have long afforded government entities broad latitude to manage their workforces, even when that affects speech they could not regulate in other contexts. *Abood* is of a piece with all those decisions: While protecting an employee's most significant expression, that decision also enables the government to advance its interests in operating effectively—by bargaining, if it so chooses, with a single employee representative and preventing free riding on that union's efforts.

For that reason, one aspect of today's opinion is cause for satisfaction, though hardly applause. As this case came to us, the principal question it presented was whether to over-rule *Abood*: The petitioners devoted the lion's share of their briefing and argument to urging us to over-turn that nearly 40-year-old precedent (and the respondents and amici countered in the same vein). Today's majority cannot resist taking potshots at Abood, see *ante*, at 17–20, but it ignores the petitioners' invitation to depart from principles of stare decisis. And the essential work in the majority's opinion comes from its extended (though mistaken) distinction of *Abood*, see *ante*, at 20–28, not from its gratuitous dicta critiquing *Abood*'s foundations. That is to the good—or at least better than it might be. The *Abood* rule is deeply entrenched, and is the foundation for not tens or hundreds, but thousands of contracts between unions and governments across the Nation. Our precedent about precedent, fairly understood and applied, makes it impossible for this Court to reverse that decision.

[The body of the opinion, detailing the background of the case and the majority's arguments, has been omitted.]

III

For many decades, Americans have debated the pros and cons of right-to-work laws and fair-share requirements. All across the country and continuing to the present day, citizens have engaged in passionate argument about the issue and have made disparate policy choices. The petitioners in this case asked this Court to end that discussion for the entire public sector, by overruling *Abood* and thus imposing a right-to-work regime for all government employees. The good news out of this case is clear: The majority declined that radical request. The Court did not, as the petitioners wanted, deprive every state and local government, in the management of their employees and programs, of the tool that many have thought necessary and appropriate to make collective bargaining work.

The bad news is just as simple: The majority robbed Illinois of that choice in administering its in-home care program. For some 40 years, *Abood* has struck a stable balance—consistent with this Court's general framework for assessing public employees' First Amendment claims—between those employees' rights and government entities' interests in managing their workforces. The majority today misapplies *Abood*, which properly should control this case. Nothing separates, for purposes of that decision, Illinois's personal assistants from any other public employees. The balance *Abood* struck thus should have defeated the petitioners' demand to invalidate Illinois's fair-share agreement. I respectfully dissent.

SOURCE: U.S. Supreme Court. *Harris v. Quinn*. 573 U.S.__ (2014). www.supremecourt.gov/opinions /13pdf/11-681_j426.pdf.

OTHER HISTORIC DOCUMENTS OF INTEREST

FROM PREVIOUS *HISTORIC DOCUMENTS*

- Chicago Teachers Union and Mayor Address Strike, *2012*, p. 393

July

United Nations High Commissioner for Refugees Details Growing Refugee Crisis in Iraq and Syria

JULY 3 AND 18, AND AUGUST 19 AND 29, 2014

As the Islamic State of Iraq and the Levant (ISIL) continued its campaign to capture cities across Syria and Iraq, tens of thousands of civilians fled their countries, many of whom entered Turkey and thus created an acute crisis as the government and international aid organizations attempted to provide for the influx. Valerie Amos, the United Nation's top relief official, urged the international community to continue providing "sustained funding and support" and also called on the Iraqi government to develop "a clear strategy" for slowing ISIL's rise.

Iraqi Refugees Flee ISIL

As ISIL moved across Iraq, it targeted women, children, and religious minorities. Women were kidnapped and sold into slavery, while young girls were reportedly raped by ISIL fighters or forced into marriage. Religious minorities had their belongings stolen, houses of worship razed, shrines desecrated, and they were systematically killed. Of the violence targeting Christians, Pope Francis said, "I learned with great concern the news that came from the Christian communities in Mosul and other parts of the Middle East, where they have lived since the birth of Christianity and where they have made significant contributions for the good of their societies." He added, "Today they are persecuted. . . . They've been driven away. They must leave their homes without being able to take anything with them." United Nations secretary-general Ban Ki-moon said that those carrying out such heinous acts against any minority must be brought to justice, adding that he condemned "in the strongest terms the systematic persecution of minority populations in Iraq by Islamic State (IS) and associated armed groups."

In September, the UN announced that an estimated 1.8 million Iraqis had been internally displaced since January 2014, and nearly half sought refuge in the Kurdistan region. That number grew in the final months of the year. In October, the United Nations said that an estimated 180,000 people fled from the Iraqi town of Hit over the course of a weekend when it was captured by ISIL. Those primarily Sunni refugees had originally sought refuge in Hit after fleeing earlier violence in Ramadi, Fallujah, and Anbar. "The exodus from Hit represents the fourth major wave of displacement in less than a year in Iraq, and for many of those caught up in it, it is the second, third or even fourth time that they have had to flee since January," said United Nations High Commissioner for Refugees (UNHCR) chief spokesperson Melissa Fleming. "Tens of thousands of desperate Iraqis are now caught in a rolling wave of multiple displacement amidst the conflict's shifting frontlines."

In response to the growing number of refugees, the Iraqi government said it would create a committee to support those who had been displaced by ISIL violence. The committee established a project called The Network Reaches You, which entered the most remote areas of Iraq to find refugee families and offer them social assistance and money for basic necessities.

According to Ammar Moneim, the media director for the Ministry of Labour and Social Affairs, the committee "is seeking, with all of its available resources, to meet the needs of displaced persons and to include those below the poverty [line] within the network of beneficiaries from salaries of social protection." Those who had been displaced would receive $128 per person or $345 for a family of four.

Syria's Refugees Escape Civil War and ISIL

Following the start of the Syrian civil war in 2011, hundreds of thousands of Syrians fled into neighboring countries, mainly Turkey, Lebanon, Jordan, Egypt, and Iraq. As ISIL militants continued their reign of terror, the number of Syrian refugees increased to 3.2 million, and the number of those internally displaced increased to six million by September 2014. "The levels of suffering are unimaginable," said António Guterres, head of UNHCR. "We need to be prepared for things to get worse before they get better."

In late September, ISIL entered Kurdish villages in northern Syria. Their campaign of destruction pushed tens of thousands into the outskirts of Syria and across the border into Turkey. Turkey had already handled a large influx of refugees since the start of the Syrian civil war in 2011, and the United Nations called the September outflow from Syria into Turkey the largest single instance of refugees leaving Syria. The United Nations estimated that more than 140,000 had crossed the border over the course of five days, which UNHCR Turkey representative Carol Batchelor said indicated "how this situation is unfolding and the very deep fear people have about the circumstances inside Syria and, for that matter, Iraq."

Between the Syrian civil war and ISIL's rise, the Turkish government spent more than $3.5 billion on relief efforts. The nation promised that it would continue to accept refugees from Syria, and prior to the September influx, it already had approximately 850,000 refugees registered. But the government expressed concern that such an open door policy could have dangerous implications if members of the Kurdistan Workers' Party (PKK), an armed guerrilla group that has long opposed Turkey's government, also cross the border. The PKK, which has frequently clashed with Turkish security forces, seeks to create an independent Kurdish state, something Turkey's government opposes.

In September, the United Nations announced new aid for the Turkish government in an effort to help it prepare for the likelihood that hundreds of thousands more refugees would enter the country. Guterres said that he commended "Turkey's welcoming response to offer refuge and aid to this population so suddenly and violently driven from their homes in fear for their lives." In its renewed response, the United Nations supported Turkey's efforts to build two new camps and provided mobile registration units, coordination centers, and vital supplies for the refugees such as blankets, mats, and plastic sheets.

In Lebanon, the 1.1 million registered refugees from Syria make up about a quarter of the nation's population, and an already thinly stretched social services network was becoming increasingly unstable. The situation was similar in Jordan and Egypt. All three nations have spent millions in additional funds on basic human needs like food, electricity, and water for refugees. Jordan, Egypt, and Lebanon's own citizens have also felt the impact. Jobs have become scarcer as refugees, who are often willing to work for lower wages, have taken many open positions. And as demand for goods and services has risen, so have prices.

International Response

Around the world, countries and aid agencies struggled with how to respond to the ongoing crisis. The United Nations said in September that it was reaching a point where it might no longer be able to respond to the needs of Syria's refugees and displaced people. The United Nations told the international community that an inability to end the civil war in Syria and stop ISIL's rise was not just a regional problem, but one that "has become the most serious threat to global peace and security," according to Guterres.

With dwindling resources, the United Nations issued a variety of calls for humanitarian assistance from nations outside the Middle East, saying that the generosity of countries accepting refugees "needs to be matched by much stronger international support, in a true spirit of effective burden sharing." On July 3, 2014, the UN said that there could be severe consequences if international agencies did not begin making vital investments in the Syrian refugee response. "Failing to provide enough humanitarian support for Syrian refugees by the end of 2014 could result in dramatic consequences for refugees and the stability of the entire region," said Guterres. At the time of his remarks, the agency had only collected $1.1 billion for Syria, which was only 30 percent of the estimated need. "The international community simply cannot afford to let this growing and increasingly protracted population of refugees fall through the cracks. Nor can we fail to support the countries who generously host them," Guterres said.

In December, the United Nations issued an urgent plea for $7 billion in new assistance for Syrian refugees and announced that it would undertake a new method to assist those nations that were bearing the brunt of refugee influx. "A traditional humanitarian response is no longer enough," said Gina Casar, the under secretary-general and associate administrator of the UN Development Programme. "The task ahead requires a comprehensive response to the crisis that builds the resilience of these communities and government institutions" of those nations supporting refugees. The two new programs announced by the United Nations in December included the Syria Humanitarian Response Plan and the Regional Refugee and Resilience Plan. The former would provide assistance for Syrians who have been displaced within their own country, while the latter would aid host nations.

News of the UN's new programs came on the heels of an announcement by the World Food Programme (WFP) that it was restarting its food plan for Syria, which costs $64 million per month. The agency temporarily ended the program, which was assisting nearly 1.7 million Syrian refugees, because it was unable to cover the cost. However, after launching the campaign #ADollarALifeline and soliciting large donations from the UN's international partners, the agency was able to raise more than $80 million to cover the cost of food vouchers for the month of December.

—Heather Kerrigan

The following are four press releases from the United Nations on the refugee crises in Syria and Iraq issued on July 3 and 18, and August 19 and 29, 2014.

UN Raises Concerns About Dwindling Resources for Syrian Refugees

July 3, 2014

Faced with continued violence in Syria and a growing refugee influx into the region, UNHCR and its partners are warning of dire consequences if funding gaps are not closed and mounting refugee needs are not met.

In a revised 2014 Syria Regional Response Plan (RRP6) to be formally presented in Geneva tomorrow, UNHCR and partners call on donors to fund a $3.74 billion programme across Lebanon, Jordan, Turkey, Iraq and Egypt to save lives, prevent harm, protect the vulnerable and strengthen the capacity and resilience of refugees and host communities as the crisis deepens into its fourth year.

"Failing to provide enough humanitarian support for Syrian refugees by the end of 2014 could result in dramatic consequences for refugees and the stability of the entire region, including a serious security threat to Lebanon," said UN High Commissioner for Refugees António Guterres.

"We have a situation of heightened volatility in the region, a spillover of the conflict into Iraq and continued outflows of refugees into neighbouring countries grappling with very complex security and humanitarian issues," he added.

So far in 2014, donors have contributed some US$1.1 billion to the Syria Regional Response Plan, allowing UNHCR and its partners to meet many of the food, health, education and protection needs of refugees. However, this amount represents only 30 per cent of the revised requirements against the new estimate of 3.6 million Syrian refugees in the region by the end of 2014.

Thanking donors for their generous contributions so far, Guterres warned of some of the hardships and risks facing refugees if the rate of funding does not increase quickly enough to meet mounting needs. These may include reduced food rations, limited health services and contagious disease.

In addition, more than 2.4 million people will need extra support to prepare for winter in the coming months, while an estimated 860,000 refugees currently living outside of camps in sub-standard shelter also need assistance. Already, government and communal services are under strain, threatening social cohesion and stability.

"The international community simply cannot afford to let this growing and increasingly protracted population of refugees fall through the cracks. Nor can we fail to support the countries who generously host them," Guterres said.

At present there are 2.9 million Syrian refugees registered in the region, with numbers growing at a rate of 100,000 people every month.

Source: United Nations High Commission for Refugees. "UNHCR warns of dramatic consequences if funding gaps for Syrian refugees continue." July 2, 2014. www.unhcr.org/53b518499.html.

DOCUMENT   *UN Calls for Political Solution in Iraq*

July 18, 2014

UN High Commissioner for Refugees António Guterres warned on Friday that Iraq risks "full-fledged sectarian war and complete fragmentation" as Iraqis continue to flee their homes and minority groups are targeted.

Iraqi politicians and the international community are "running out of time to act," he said.

In high-level talks in Baghdad on Wednesday, he urged leaders to move urgently to a political solution and to "seize this last chance to bring everyone together in a non-sectarian approach. Otherwise, we risk a true sectarian war."

The UNHCR head encouraged regional and global governments to provide support. "Countries with influence also need to constructively work towards a solution," he said. "This is a threat to everybody—nobody is safe."

Guterres witnessed the dire conditions facing some of the more than 650,000 Iraqis displaced by conflict since January. At the Khazair transit camp, midway between the Iraqi cities of Erbil and Mosul, he walked the dusty paths between some 500 tents provided by UNHCR where Iraqi Shiites, Sunnis and others are now living.

A father who fled fighting in Mosul a month ago told Guterres his son had returned to the city last week to check on their house and found it occupied and partly destroyed.

Guterres noted the dramatic impact on the economy and society from the influx of more than 225,000 Syrian refugees and over 300,000 newly displaced Iraqis. He appealed to the international community to "enhance support to the government & people in the Kurdistan region in this very difficult moment."

"The Middle East is in flames," he said. "Kurdistan represents one of the few stable areas where protection can be granted."

The High Commissioner said a forthcoming $500 million contribution by the Kingdom of Saudi Arabia will help the UN provide critical humanitarian aid to Iraqis. "Others need to come forward to help Kurdistan cope with this terrible challenge," he said.

On Friday, the High Commissioner travelled to the new Arbat refugee camp in the northern city of Sulaymaniyah, now home to more than 3,000 Syrians who fled the civil war. Of almost three million Syrian refugees, 225,000 are in Iraq. Noting the region's stability, Guterres said "without Kurdistan, many people fleeing would have no place to go."

Guterres visited Iraq to pay respect to the internally displaced, Syrian refugees and their host communities and show solidarity during the Muslim holy month of Ramadan. He spoke of his concerns for all Iraqis, especially minorities, who are at risk.

"Everybody needs to be protected," he said. "Everybody seeking access should be given refuge without discrimination. Everybody deserves to be safe."

He praised the commitment by the president and prime Minister of the Kurdistan Region of Iraq to "maintain a policy of open borders and doors to all people in need of help regardless of ethnicity or religion. This attitude of tolerance and openness has an important symbolic meaning at a time when we need to avoid at all cost a sectarian civil war in Iraq."

He was blunt in assessing what UNHCR and the broader humanitarian community can accomplish. "What we do is minimize suffering. There is no humanitarian solution for this tragic humanitarian crisis. There is no way humanitarians can clean up the mess made by politicians. What they really need is peace."

SOURCE: United Nations High Commissioner for Refugees. "UNHCR head calls for urgent political solution to Iraq's deepening crisis." July 18, 2014. www.unhcr.org/53c91bbb6.html.

DOCUMENT *UN on New Humanitarian Push in Iraq*

August 19, 2014

As it prepares to ramp up its response to the population displacement in northern Iraq, the UN refugee agency is working closely with the authorities in Iraq's Kurdistan region to meet the immense challenges of helping the tens of thousands who have sought shelter there.

Barring delays, the stepped up air, road and sea operation will start with a four-day airlift using Boeing 747s from Aqaba in Jordan to Erbil, followed by road convoys from Turkey and Jordan, and sea and land shipments from Dubai via Iran over the next 10 days. Included in the initial aid shipments are 3,300 tents, 20,000 plastic sheets, 18,500 kitchen sets, and 16,500 jerry cans.

Some 200,000 people have made their way to Iraqi Kurdistan since early August, when the city of Sinjar and neighbouring areas were seized by armed groups. "The number of displaced people flowing [from Syria] into Duhok [province] across the Peshkabour border has slowed in the past week from thousands per day to a few hundred," UNHCR spokesman Adrian Edwards said in Geneva. "All still require our support," he added.

Iraq's current humanitarian challenges are immense. While most of the displaced are still living rough in schools, mosques, churches, unfinished buildings and elsewhere, UNHCR has been pitching hundreds of family tents every day.

Currently, almost a dozen sites are open or about to open in Iraqi Kurdistan's Dohuk and Erbil provinces. These are likely to be boosted by additional camps being set up by the International Humanitarian Partnership—with contributions from Denmark, Estonia, Germany, Norway, Sweden and the United Kingdom.

"At this stage we envisage there being 12–14 sites in all with capacity for 140,000 people," said the UNHCR spokesman, adding that technical staff were currently assessing additional possible camp sites identified by the Kurdistan Regional Government to determine their suitability and to prioritize locations.

The needs are not confined to the Kurdistan region. There are other camps or sites in other provinces where displaced people have gathered, including in Sulaymaniyah, Diyala and Kirkuk. The Iraqi government has also set up three centres for the displaced in Baghdad.

Meanwhile, the stepped up UNHCR aid push due to start on Wednesday is aimed at helping close to 500,000 people who have been forced to flee their homes amid the deteriorating situation in the north.

The major focus is on improving living conditions for the displaced in the region, particularly people without shelter or housing. Conditions remain desperate for those without access to suitable shelter, people struggling to find food and water to feed their families, and those without access to primary medical care.

"Many are still coming to grips with the tragedy they've been through in recent weeks—fleeing homes with nothing, and many trying to cope with the loss of loved ones. Emergency support is an urgent need that we are trying to meet," UNHCR's Edwards said.

Inside Syria, UNHCR continues to help Yazidi people fleeing the Sinjar area across the border. As of Tuesday, there were an estimated 8,000 people at the Newroz camp, about 60 kilometres from the Iraqi border, plus an estimated 3,000 who have moved to Yazidi villages in and around the towns of Malkia, Qahtania, Amuda, Derbassia.

Others who were staying at the Newroz camp last week have returned to Iraq to reunite with their families. UNHCR is continuing to help with providing transport for the refugees to and from the camp and is flying in more aid from its warehouses in Damascus. The first of six flights arrived in Qamishli last night from Damascus, and the mattresses and electric fans are being delivered to the refugees today, to help improve conditions in the heat.

UNHCR has now provided shelter and relief items to more than 210,000 people. It has also provided over 80,000 displaced people with protection monitoring and needs assessments, and nearly 3,500 individuals have been approved for cash assistance, with some already receiving it. Legal assistance will be provided to vulnerable families to ensure they can access their rights as Iraqi citizens, with referrals being made for those with specific assistance needs. Many also fled without documents, and UNHCR is helping them obtain new ones.

An estimated 1.2 million Iraqis have been displaced so far in 2014, including some 600,000 people uprooted by the Anbar province crisis which began in January, and 600,000 displaced from conflicts in and around Mosul and more recently Sinjar, since August.

SOURCE: United Nations High Commissioner for Refugees. "UNHCR in major air, land and sea humanitarian push into northern Iraq." August 19, 2014. www.unhcr.org/53f33a049.html.

UN Says Three Million Syrians Have Fled Their Homes

August 29, 2014

Syria's intensifying refugee crisis will today surpass a record three million people, amid reports of increasingly horrifying conditions inside the country—cities where populations are surrounded, people are going hungry and civilians are being targeted or indiscriminately killed.

Almost half of all Syrians have now been forced to abandon their homes and flee for their lives. One in every eight Syrians has fled across the border, fully a million people more than a year ago. A further 6.5 million are displaced within Syria. Over half of those uprooted are children.

UNHCR and other aid agencies say increasing numbers of families are arriving in a shocking state, exhausted, scared and with their savings depleted. Most have been on the run for a year or more, fleeing from village to village before taking the final decision to leave.

There are worrying signs too that the journey out of Syria is becoming tougher, with many people forced to pay bribes at armed checkpoints proliferating along the borders. Refugees crossing the desert into eastern Jordan are being forced to pay smugglers hefty sums (ranging from $100 per person or more) to take them to safety.

The vast majority remain in countries neighboring Syria, with the highest concentrations in Lebanon (1.14 million), Jordan (608,000) and Turkey (815,000). In addition to the three million registered refugees, governments estimate hundreds of thousands more Syrians have sought sanctuary in their countries. This has led to an enormous strain on their economies, infrastructures and resources. More than four in five refugees are struggling to make a living in towns and cities outside of camps, with 38 per cent living in sub-standard shelter, according to a recent survey.

Syrians are now the world's largest refugee population under UNHCR care, second only in number to the decades-long Palestinian crisis. The Syria operation is now the largest in UNHCR's 64-year history.

"The Syrian crisis has become the biggest humanitarian emergency of our era, yet the world is failing to meet the needs of refugees and the countries hosting them," said António Guterres, the UN High Commissioner for Refugees.

"The response to the Syrian crisis has been generous, but the bitter truth is that it falls far short of what's needed," said Guterres.

A recent upsurge in fighting appears to be worsening an already desperate situation. As frontlines shift, new areas are emptying out. Recent arrivals to Jordan, for example, are running from attacks in the areas of Raqaa and Aleppo.

UNHCR is also deeply concerned for the wellbeing of several hundred Syrians trapped inside the Al Obaidy refugee camp in Al Qa'im, Iraq, after UN agencies and international NGOs were forced to abandon their offices and warehouses. UNHCR says national partners are continuing to provide supplies and maintenance, but the situation is volatile.

Many newly arriving refugees say they only left Syria as a last resort. A growing number, including more than half of those coming to Lebanon, have moved at least once before fleeing, and one in ten have moved more than three times. One woman told UNHCR she moved no fewer than 20 times before finally crossing into Lebanon.

In addition to worsening security, the latest refugees report increasing difficulty in finding work, skyrocketing food and commodity prices, and failing services. A packet of bread in one village near the city of Idlib costs ten times more this year than last, according to a new arrival in Jordan.

A growing share of recent arrivals—up to 15% in Jordan, for example—are suffering from long term medical conditions such as diabetes, heart disease and cancer, and left because they were no longer able to get adequate care at home.

UNHCR is working with 150 other agencies and groups, together with the governments of neighbouring countries, to help refugees pay the rent, and get food, education and medical care, as well as giving basic goods such as tents, mattresses and plastic sheeting.

In the past year alone, 1.7 million refugees received food aid, 350,000 children were enrolled in school, and shelter in camps was provided for more than 400,000 refugees. Since the beginning of the crisis in 2011, UNHCR has registered refugees faster than at any time in its history.

Donors have contributed more than USD 4.1 billion to successive regional response plans since 2012. However, more than 2 billion more is needed by the end of this year alone to meet the urgent needs of refugees. Most urgently, more than 2.4 million people are expected to need support in the coming weeks to prepare for next winter.

SOURCE: United Nations High Commissioner for Refugees. "Refugee total hits 3 million as Syrians flee growing insecurity and worsening conditions." August 29, 2014. www.unhcr.org/53ff78ac9.html.

OTHER HISTORIC DOCUMENTS OF INTEREST

FROM THIS VOLUME

- ISIL Captures Fallujah; U.S. Vows Support for Iraq, p. 21

FROM PREVIOUS HISTORIC DOCUMENTS

- Lebanese Prime Minister on Impact of Syrian Civil War, *2013*, p. 69
- United Nations Fails to Take Action in Syria, *2012*, p. 81

U.S. and Iraqi Officials
on New Iraqi Leadership

JULY 15 AND SEPTEMBER 24, 2014

On April 30, 2014, Iraqis went to the polls to choose new members of parliament in their third national election since the new democratic constitution was written in 2005. The elections were considered largely peaceful and successful, but following the vote, parliament struggled to choose a new president, prime minister, and speaker. As the various blocs jockeyed for position, pressure mounted for selection as the Islamic State of Iraq and the Levant (ISIL) increased in strength and moved into strategically situated locations approximately an hour outside of Baghdad. British educated political moderate Haider al-Abadi was ultimately chosen as the new prime minister, but he will face an uphill battle to stem ISIL's expansion and ensure security.

Successful Parliamentary Election

The April 30 election marked the first since U.S. troop withdrawal. In total, more than 9,000 candidates and 276 political entities appeared on the ballot. Of the twenty-two million eligible Iraqis, 62 percent cast a ballot. A reported six polling stations were attacked by suicide bombers in the run-up to the election on April 28 while security forces cast their ballots.

The election of Iraq's new parliament in April 2014 was highly successful and largely considered credible. There were some instances of irregularities, including a reported 300 polling stations that had their results annulled for violations, and 1,000 poll workers were dismissed for ballot rigging. Additionally, a large segment of Anbar province, where ISIL had taken control of many major cities, did not participate in the vote. Even so, United Nations Special Representative for Iraq Nickolay Mladenov praised Iraq for its handling of the election: "The security situation in Iraq is very difficult and inevitably this places a burden on the voting process and on the country at large. Therefore, the fact that 60 percent of people did come out to vote is even more remarkable." President Barack Obama expressed similar sentiments, adding, "There will be more difficult days ahead, but the United States will continue to stand with the Iraqi people as partners in their pursuit of a peaceful, unified and prosperous future."

The results of the election were published on May 26, 2014, but results were not officially certified until June 16 when the Iraqi Independent High Electoral Commission had reviewed all appeals and accusations filed. Current prime minister Nouri al-Maliki's State of Law coalition took the most seats—92 of 328. Together with its allied parties, State of Law would control enough seats to be given the first opportunity to choose a prime minister and form a government.

New Parliament Struggles to Seat Government

The Iraqi constitution dictates that once the elections have concluded and the new members of the Council of Representatives are chosen, during the new body's first session it must choose a speaker and first and second deputy by absolute majority. The body then chooses a president, who must be elected by two-thirds of its members. The largest bloc in the Council of Representatives chooses a leader to act as prime minister, and the new president then charges that designee to form the Council of Ministers. An informal agreement that has held since Iraq set up its first government after the 2003 U.S.-led invasion dictates that the president will be a Kurd, the prime minister a Shiite, and the speaker a Sunni.

When the election results were certified and the new members were installed, they held their first sitting on July 1, 2014. The session quickly came to an end when Kurdish and Sunni Arab members boycotted the session over conflicts with other lawmakers. Less than two weeks later, on July 13, the body met again to attempt to choose its leaders. However, the session was ended after only thirty minutes "due to the absence of any agreement on the names of the nominees for the three posts," according to acting speaker Mahdi al-Hafidh. The various factions within parliament were also at odds over whether the president, prime minister, and speaker should be chosen as a group or individually. The inability for parliament to quickly act to seat a government was not without precedent. Following the 2010 parliamentary elections, it took almost ten months to finally choose a government. However, there was more pressure to seat a government quickly this time because ISIL continued to gain power by toppling cities in northern Iraq, and the government needed to mount a strong response.

On July 15, 2014, parliament finally chose the new speaker and two deputy speakers. U.S. secretary of state John Kerry celebrated the seating of these leaders and urged the government "to follow this achievement with rapid formation of a new government pursuant to Iraq's constitutional timelines." He added, "This is a moment when the stakes for Iraq's future could not be clearer as much depends on the ability of Iraq's leaders to come together and take a united stand against ISIL."

New Prime Minister Chosen

Maliki's reelection as prime minister was in doubt before election day. He has become a highly polarizing figure among the various religious sects, including his own. Mohammed al-Hamdani, a senior leader in State of Law allied Sadrist party, said Maliki "did not serve the people and did not deliver on his promises to the other political blocs." Others opposing his rule pointed to his attempts at consolidating power since first taking office in 2006, and his ongoing failure to end sectarian violence. But Maliki said from the outset that he intended to seek a third term. On August 11, while the State of Law coalition debated whom to put forth for presidential approval as the new prime minister, Maliki announced that he would submit a case in the Iraqi courts against the president for violating the constitution, which indicates that a prime minister must be named within fifteen days of the president's election. Maliki, who at the time was leader of the coalition and could have been named prime minister at the coalition's failure to nominate another member, said that the president was committing a "coup against the constitution and the political process."

On September 8, 2014, the governing State of Law Coalition chose Haider Al-Abadi as the new prime minister of Iraq. Abadi's background is in economics and electric engineering, and he held various positions with high-tech companies in the United Kingdom until 2002. During his time in London, two of Abadi's brothers were killed by Saddam

Hussein's Baathist regime. When Hussein's government was overthrown in 2003, Abadi returned to his native Iraq with the intent of helping the nation form a new, more inclusive democratic government. In 2003, he was named minister of communications and was elected to parliament in 2005 where he served a term as deputy speaker in 2014. Abadi is known as a political moderate, and he is a strong advocate for reconciling the various religious sects in Iraq. "We have to be careful not to become involved in a sectarian war," Abadi said. "Shias are not against Sunnis and Sunnis are not against Shias."

COMBATTING ISIL

The most pressing challenge facing Abadi will be how to respond to the security situation created by ISIL. Sunni leaders have criticized Maliki for fueling ISIL's rise, arguing that those dissatisfied with the former prime minister's government took up arms with the group. Abadi, it seems, wants to reach consensus with Sunnis on how best to combat the extremist group.

Speaking after his election, Abadi promised to "back the military operations in all the areas of confrontation against the armed gangs and the forces of terrorism and ensuring their continuation till victory is achieved." Abadi has said that he will accept any foreign assistance to fight the terrorists, even from Iran. "If U.S. air strikes [happen], we don't need Iranian air strikes. If they don't, then we may need Iranian air strikes," he said in June.

The United States had been holding back on giving support to Iraq to fight ISIL until it formed a new government, and in September, President Obama authorized airstrikes against the militants. On September 24, President Obama met with Abadi and noted that the new prime minister "understands that in order for Iraq to succeed it's not just a matter of a military campaign," but that political outreach is also necessary. "I want to say directly to the prime minister that we fully support his political vision," Obama said. The United States recommitted itself to Iraq but was cautious of becoming overly involved, something Abadi said he appreciated as he sought to retain the nation's sovereignty. During their talks, Abadi said he "emphasized the importance of the respect of the sovereignty of Iraq and the territorial integrity of Iraq" and "reaffirmed the importance for all forces that want to help Iraq to respect the sovereignty of Iraq and its territorial integrity." Abadi further thanked the United States and its allies "for maintaining and respecting the territorial integrity of Iraq and its sovereignty."

Early in his term, Abadi tackled another hot button issue, that of oil revenues for the autonomous Kurdish region. During his time as leader, Maliki distanced his government from the Kurds, which ignited ethnic tensions. Reconciliation with the Kurdish region was necessary for Abadi if he was to effectively fight ISIL. Initially, when the Kurds took control of the Kirkuk oil fields in June in an attempt to protect them from ISIL, they exported the oil independently and refused to share the profits with Baghdad, arguing that the central government had not been providing much-needed payments to the Kurdish region to combat ISIL. In December, the prime minister managed to secure an agreement to share the nation's oil wealth and military resources. International analysts believe that this will likely stop, at least for some time, the Kurdish drive to become an independent state.

—Heather Kerrigan

Following is a statement by Secretary of State John Kerry on July 15, 2014, congratulating the people of Iraq on seating a new government; and the text of a press conference between President Barack Obama and new Iraqi prime minister Haider al-Abadi on September 24, 2014.

Secretary Kerry Congratulates New Parliamentary Leaders

July 15, 2014

We congratulate the Iraqi people on the election of a new parliamentary Speaker and two Deputy Speakers. The election of a Speaker is the first step in the critical process of forming a new government that can take into account the rights, aspirations, and legitimate concerns of all Iraq's communities.

We urge Iraq's leaders to follow this achievement with rapid formation of a new government pursuant to Iraq's constitutional timelines. We further urge the international community to support Iraq's democratic political process, which reflects the aspirations of the nearly 14 million Iraqis who voted for new representatives from all parts of the country. These representatives are now charged, through the Iraqi parliament, to form a new government with leaders who reflect a broad national consensus.

As I said in Baghdad, this is a moment when the stakes for Iraq's future could not be clearer as much depends on the ability of Iraq's leaders to come together and take a united stand against ISIL. Iraq faces an existential threat and Iraq's leaders need to confront that threat with the urgency that it demands. As they do, the United States will remain a steadfast partner in support of their fight for the democratic process and against ISIL.

SOURCE: U.S. Department of State. "U.S. Congratulates Iraqis on the Election of a Parliamentary Speaker." July 15, 2015. www.state.gov/secretary/remarks/2014/07/229288.htm.

President Obama Meets With New Prime Minister Abadi

September 24, 2014

President Obama. Well, I want to thank Prime Minister Abadi and his delegation for the opportunity to meet here this morning.

As I've said previously, the United States and Iraq have a strategic relationship that is important to both countries. We believe in a vision of an Iraq that is inclusive, in which Sunni, Shia, Kurd are all able to come together to peacefully iron out their differences and to achieve prosperity and peace for all the people of the country.

Obviously, Iraq is under enormous threat at the moment from the organization that calls itself ISIL. And as I've discussed today and for many weeks now, we consider ISIL to be a threat not only to Iraq, but to the region, to the world, and to the United States.

We are committed to working in support of Iraq regaining territory that ISIL has currently taken over, and making sure that an inclusive Iraqi government is able to control its territory and push ISIL back. In doing that, we are coordinating closely in our military campaign. And the airstrikes and air support that we're able to provide, as well as the training and assistance, I think will be critical in partnership with Iraqi forces on the ground.

One of the things I'm very impressed with, however, is the fact that Prime Minister Abadi understands that in order for Iraq to succeed it's not just a matter of a military campaign; it's also the need for political outreach to all factions within the country. And I've been very impressed with Prime Minister Abadi's vision.

Since he took over the prime-ministership, he has reached out systematically to all the peoples of Iraq. He has articulated a vision of reform and a commitment to moving forward with many of the laws that had previously stalled but offer the potential of unleashing energy and entrepreneurship inside of Iraq.

And so, in addition to the military campaign in which we're going to be coordinating, I want to say directly to the Prime Minister that we fully support his political vision, and we are also encouraged by his willingness to reach out and work with other countries in the region who are going to be very important in supporting our overall effort to defeat ISIL.

The last point I would make: I think that the Prime Minister recognizes this is not something that is going to be easy and it is not going to happen overnight. But after talking with the Prime Minister, I'm confident that he's the right person to help work with a broad-based coalition of like-minded Iraqis and that they will be successful.

And my main message to the Prime Minister is that although we cannot do this for you, we can be a strong partner, and we are fully committed to your success. We wish you Godspeed. And we are grateful for your willingness to take on this leadership mantle at such a critical time in your country's history.

Prime Minister Abadi. [as interpreted] In the name of God, Most Compassionate, Most Merciful, I would like to thank President Obama for allowing for this opportunity for Iraq to explain its points of view towards the confrontation that is happening in Iraq and in which Iraq is at the forefront of the confrontation against the forces of ISIL.

The Iraqi people have confronted this very brutal, ruthless attack on the Iraqi territory with bravery, and I am very proud to say that I am the commander of the Iraqi armed forces. Our armed forces have also offered a lot of sacrifices when they confronted the Daesh attack. And I can say today that in many of the areas we are now turning around the ground.

Today, I am also proud to say that our people are brave, and the popular effort on the ground has been of utmost importance. I am keen to protect our brave people on the ground, and I am proud of the sacrifices and protect them and protect all that they have been doing to protect their communities on the ground, their religious sites, and to stand a firm stance against the terrorist attacks that targeted the minorities, and targeted and killed children, men and women.

In my discussion with President Obama, I emphasized the importance of the respect of the sovereignty of Iraq and the territorial integrity of Iraq. And as a Prime Minister of Iraq, I reaffirmed the importance for all forces that want to help Iraq to respect the sovereignty of Iraq and its territorial integrity. I am very thankful for President Obama and all the allies, all who are helping, for maintaining and respecting the territorial integrity of Iraq and its sovereignty.

Finally, one of the requests that I have put forth for President Obama is the importance of equipping and arming the Iraqi army and to provide the Iraqi armed forces with weapons. As you know, our armed forces are in dire need for equipment and for weapons, mostly because we lost a lot of the equipment and the weapons in our confrontation and our fight against ISIL, and specifically when the ISIL groups came through the borders from Syria, many of the weapons were destroyed. Some of the weapons fell in the hand of ISIL. Therefore, I am very thankful for President Obama that he promised that weapons and supplies would be delivered to Iraq as soon as possible so Iraq can defeat ISIL and Iraq can overcome this crisis.

We are keen in Iraq to promote further the strategic relationship between our two countries, a strategic relationship that is based on mutual respect within the Strategic Framework Agreement that was signed between the two governments back in 2008. I am pleased to say that President Obama has promised to reinvigorate the Strategic Framework Agreement not only to put the focus on the military and security aspect of that agreement, but also on all other levels—scientific, educational, economic, cultural and academic, social and other aspects of our relationship.

Mr. President, I thank you for all your support and all the promises that you have given us. And I hope to see that these promises will be concretely fulfilled on the ground as soon as possible. Thank you.

Prime Minister Abadi.   Thank you Mr. President.

President Obama.   Appreciate it.

Prime Minister Abadi.   Thank you very much.

President Obama.   Thank you very much, everybody.

SOURCE: Executive Office of the President. "Remarks Following a Meeting With Prime Minister Haider al-Abadi of Iraq in New York City." September 24, 2014. *Compilation of Presidential Documents* 2014, no. 00700 (September 24, 2014). www.gpo.gov/fdsys/pkg/DCPD-201400700/pdf/DCPD-201400700.pdf.

OTHER HISTORIC DOCUMENTS OF INTEREST

FROM PREVIOUS *HISTORIC DOCUMENTS*

California Death Penalty Declared Unconstitutional

JULY 16, 2014

California, one of the thirty-two U.S. states with the death penalty in 2014, has the largest population of inmates awaiting execution of any state. Of the 748 people on California's death row, more than 40 percent have been there longer than nineteen years, many much longer. No executions have been carried out since 2006, when Judge Jeremy Fogel ordered a moratorium on use of the death penalty after finding that the state had illegally bypassed its own rules when passing an execution protocol. In fact, since the death penalty was adopted by voters in California, 900 people have been sentenced to death, but only thirteen have actually been executed; more inmates died of natural and other causes, and this will likely increase as the prison population ages. The majority of inmates on death row are still litigating their appeals, a process that can take twenty-five years and is growing longer every year. This was the situation that federal district court judge Cormac J. Carney found on July 16, 2014, to be "broken" and "completely dysfunctional." "For most," the judge wrote in a decision that could have broad implications, "systemic delay has made their execution so unlikely that the death sentence carefully and deliberately imposed by the jury has been quietly transformed into one no rational jury or legislature could ever impose: *life in prison with the remote possibility of death.*" Ruling on a petition by death row inmate Ernest Dewayne Jones, Judge Carney declared that the inordinate and unpredictable delays in California's death penalty system constitute unconstitutional cruel and unusual punishment. This decision, stunning for its breadth, declared California's whole death penalty administration to be unconstitutional.

CALIFORNIA'S DEATH PENALTY: DELAYS AND UNCERTAINTY

The U.S. Supreme Court has never held that capital punishment itself violates the Eighth Amendment's prohibition of "cruel and unusual punishment." The closest it came to doing so was in 1972 when its decision in *Furman v. Georgia* effectively placed a moratorium on the death penalty as practiced at the time. The Supreme Court struck down a system that gave states almost complete discretion as to which cases merited the ultimate penalty, resulting in arbitrary sentencing. The decision was 5–4, but there is no controlling decision because the five justices who agreed that this was unconstitutional could not agree on why. After *Furman*'s historic decision invalidating the death penalty as practiced across the country, many states rewrote their death penalty guidelines adding, for instance, lists of aggravating and mitigating factors to guide the discretion of the jury and separating the trial on the merits from the sentencing portion of the case. In 1978, California voters passed Proposition 7, reintroducing the death penalty to California. In 2012, a ballot proposition to replace the death penalty with life in prison without parole narrowly lost.

Since 1978, the state of California has sentenced more than 900 people to death. Of these people, only thirteen have actually been executed, 94 have died of other causes, and

39 have had their sentences reduced. Currently, 748 people are on death row, but only 17 of them have exhausted their appeals processes and are currently awaiting execution. It takes a prisoner more than twenty-five years to run through the complete process of court review in California, two times longer than the national average.

California's lengthy appeals process for death row inmates was a central issue in the ruling. Judge Carney described the process and the delay that comes with each stage in great detail. While on death row, prisoners spend much of that time on appeals after waiting for the state to appoint them an attorney. Under California law, everyone sentenced to death is entitled to an automatic direct appeal to the California Supreme Court of the issues that arose during their trial. They are also entitled to the assistance of a lawyer who is qualified by the state to accept death penalty appeals. Inmates generally wait three to five years on death row to have a qualified lawyer appointed to take their appeals. Once appointed, the lawyer must learn the trial record, which is generally tens of thousands of pages, and file a brief, to which the state will respond. This briefing process often takes an additional four years. Then the inmate must wait to be put on the court's calendar. The Supreme Court hears twenty to twenty-five death penalty appeals a year, so it takes the inmates another two to three years to have their argument scheduled and a decision rendered. Judge Carney wrote, "From the sentence of death to the California Supreme Court's disposition of the automatic appeal, between 11.7 and 13.7 years will have elapsed, with inmates spending much of that time waiting for counsel to be appointed and for oral argument to be scheduled."

The purpose of this Supreme Court disposition is to resolve issues raised at the trial and sentencing. If a prisoner has other issues, such as ineffective assistance of counsel, that prisoner must raise them through a different appeals process, namely, habeas corpus petitions. These petitions may raise state or federal issues, but the rule is that all state issues must be resolved before an inmate can file in federal court. Each of these stages adds additional years of delay. California law directs that a different lawyer be provided for each stage of the appeals. Habeas corpus counsel is generally comprised of private attorneys, but because these attorneys are paid substantially below the market rate with low caps on funds available for investigations and experts, it can be difficult to find lawyers willing to take the assignments, and the backlog continues to grow every year. By June 2014, 352 inmates were still waiting to be assigned lawyers for these appeals, and almost half of them had been waiting more than ten years.

By the time most inmates have had their direct appeal heard and all their state habeas corpus issues reviewed, typically seventeen years have passed on death row. Only then can the inmate seek relief in federal court, a process that takes from beginning to end an average of 10.4 years. Since the death penalty restarted in 1978, only eighty-one inmates have made it all the way through this process. More than half of those had their sentence reduced in some way, taking them off death row. Thirteen were executed, leaving only seventeen ready for execution, each of whom has been on death row more than twenty-five years.

In addition to the seemingly endless delay built in to California's death penalty appeals process, the population on death row continues to grow, adding further delays to the system. No executions have taken place since 2006 when Judge Fogel prevented the execution of an inmate on the grounds that, as administered, California's lethal injection protocol created "an undue and unnecessary risk that an inmate will suffer pain so extreme" as to rise to the level of constitutionally prohibited "cruel and unusual punishment." California rewrote its execution protocols but the state Supreme Court ruled that when it did so, it failed to comply with its own procedural law and enjoined all executions until the state properly adopted procedures. Currently, Governor Jerry Brown's administration is working toward adopting a single-drug method of execution, but, according to the *Los Angeles Times*, "drug suppliers have balked at having their products used in executions."

In 2008, the bipartisan California Commission on the Fair Administration of Justice made recommendations on reforming the death penalty system to eliminate unnecessary delays. Many of the proposed reforms included adequately funding the system. According to the Commission, if these reforms were enacted, the state could reduce the time between sentencing and execution to between eleven and fourteen years. The national average for the time it takes a death row prisoner to exhaust available appeals is approximately fifteen years.

DELAYS AND UNCERTAINTIES VIOLATE CONSTITUTION

On July 16, 2014, Santa Ana–based U.S. District Court judge Carney, an appointee of former president George W. Bush, issued an order vacating the death sentence of Ernest Dewayne Jones, who had been on death row since his 1995 conviction for the rape and murder of his girlfriend's mother. Carney, a judge with a reputation for independence and meting out tough sentences, did not rule that the death penalty was inherently unconstitutional; rather, he focused his opinion on the dysfunctional way California enforces the death penalty. He concluded that the decades-long delays and the uncertainty as to whether an inmate will ever be executed violate the Constitution's Eighth Amendment prohibition on cruel and unusual punishment.

The judge's conclusion stems from two separate but related arguments. His first argument is based on the fact that, despite large numbers of people sentenced to death, only "a trivial few" will ever be executed. How those few inmates are selected does not depend on "whether their crime was one of passion or of premeditation, [or] whether they killed one person or ten," or on neutral criteria such as the order in which they were convicted. Rather, who is executed on death row depends on a factor that is out of the inmate's control, that is, "how quickly the inmate proceeds through the State's dysfunctional post-conviction review process." Although there was no controlling opinion in *Furman v. Georgia* in 1972, Judge Carney quoted from subsequent Supreme Court cases that described *Furman* as asserting the fundamental principle that the death penalty "could not be imposed under sentencing procedures that created a substantial risk that it would be inflicted in an arbitrary and capricious manner." While the U.S. Supreme Court precedent only prohibits the states from randomly selecting which convicted prisoners to condemn to death, Judge Carney argues that the principle applies with equal force to prevent states from randomly selecting "which trivial few of those condemned it will actually execute." Due to the fact that the delays in the California system have resulted in a system that arbitrarily imposes the ultimate punishment of death, according to Judge Carney, the death penalty violates constitutional principles.

In addition to arguing that California's death penalty process is unconstitutionally arbitrary, Judge Carney argued that it is unconstitutionally excessive because it does not further society's goals for punishment: deterrence and retribution. The extraordinary delays alone would undermine any deterrent of the death penalty; but, in a system where only thirteen of the 900 individuals sentenced to death have been executed, a reasonable person thinking of committing a capital crime would assume he would realistically face life imprisonment even if sentenced to death. Here, Judge Carney concluded, "the death penalty is about as effective a deterrent to capital crime as the possibility of a lightning strike is to going outside in the rain." The systemic delays also undermine capital punishment's retributive roll of serving as "an expression of society's moral outrage at particularly offensive conduct." Judge Carney wrote, "As for the random few for whom execution does become a reality, they will have languished for so long on Death Row that their execution will serve no retributive or deterrent purpose and will be arbitrary."

Finally, the opinion addresses the fact that no other judge has held delays in death penalty cases to be cruel and unusual punishment. Generally the cases that have rejected this argument have done so for two reasons: that a lengthy appeal is necessary to protect the accuracy of the conviction and that the delay is caused by the petitioner himself. In this case, however, the judge writes that the state itself is to blame for allowing "such dysfunction to creep into its death penalty system."

AFTER THE RULING

In August, California state attorney general Kamala Harris announced that she would appeal Judge Carney's ruling to the Ninth Circuit Court of Appeals. In a statement, she said, "I am appealing the court's decision because it is not supported by the law, and it undermines important protections that our courts provide to defendants." No executions can proceed in California while this decision is in place. If the Ninth Circuit upholds the opinion, it is likely to be appealed to the U.S. Supreme Court.

Jones's lead attorney, Michael Laurence of the Habeas Corpus Resource Center, expressed gratitude for the decision in a statement, saying, "The execution of Mr. Jones, and others like him whose meritorious legal claims have gone unheard for decades, serves no valid state interest." Kent S. Scheidegger of the Criminal Justice Legal Foundation expressed his disagreement with the idea that lengthy delays undermine the retribution interest in the death penalty: "The defendant still deserves this punishment for the very worst murders, and society has a valid interest in carrying it out, no matter how long it takes."

Regardless of whether the decision makes it to the U.S. Supreme Court, it is likely to inspire similar arguments in death penalty appeals in other states that, like California, have large and growing populations on death row but few recent executions. It may also bring attention to the fact that although politicians generally express their support for the death penalty, they have not voted to adequately fund its administration.

—Melissa Feinberg

Following is the edited text of the ruling in Jones v. Chappell *in which the U.S. District Court for the Central District of California found California's death penalty to be unconstitutional.*

DOCUMENT ## Jones v. Chappell

July 16, 2014

[Footnotes have been omitted.]

United States District Court

Central District of California
Ernest Dewayne Jones,
Petitioner

vs.

Kevin Chappell, Warden of
California State Prison at San
Quentin, Respondent

Case No. CV
09-02158-CJC

Order declaring
California's death
penalty system
unconstitutional and
vacating petitioner's
death sentence

On April 7, 1995, Petitioner Ernest Dewayne Jones was condemned to death by the State of California. Nearly two decades later, Mr. Jones remains on California's Death Row, awaiting his execution, but with complete uncertainty as to when, or even whether, it will ever come. Mr. Jones is not alone. Since 1978, when the current death penalty system was adopted by California voters, over 900 people have been sentenced to death for their crimes. Of them, only 13 have been executed. For the rest, the dysfunctional administration of California's death penalty system has resulted, and will continue to result, in an inordinate and unpredictable period of delay preceding their actual execution. Indeed, for most, systemic delay has made their execution so unlikely that the death sentence carefully and deliberately imposed by the jury has been quietly transformed into one no rational jury or legislature could ever impose: *life in prison, with the remote possibility of death.* As for the random few for whom execution does become a reality, they will have languished for so long on Death Row that their execution will serve no retributive or deterrent purpose and will be arbitrary.

That is the reality of the death penalty in California today and the system that has been created to administer it to Mr. Jones and the hundreds of other individuals currently on Death Row. Allowing this system to continue to threaten Mr. Jones with the slight possibility of death, almost a generation after he was first sentenced, violates the Eighth Amendment's prohibition against cruel and unusual punishment.

[The background section has been omitted.]

Analysis

The Eighth Amendment prohibits the imposition of cruel and unusual punishment by the state. Although reasonable people may debate whether the death penalty offends that proscription, no rational person can question that the execution of an individual carries with it the solemn obligation of the government to ensure that the punishment is not arbitrarily imposed and that it furthers the interests of society. As the American tradition of law has long recognized, death is a punishment different in kind from any other. *See, e.g., Harmelin v. Michigan*, 501 U.S. 957, 995 (1991) (noting the "qualitative difference between death and all other penalties"); *Coleman v. McCormick*, 874 F.2d 1280, 1288 (9th Cir. 1989) ("The finality and severity of a death sentence makes it qualitatively different from all other forms of punishment."). Indeed, in its finality, the punishment of death "differs more from life imprisonment than a 100-year prison term differs from one of only a year or two. Because of that qualitative difference, there is a corresponding difference in the need for reliability in the determination that death is the appropriate punishment in a specific case." *Woodson v. North Carolina*, 428 U.S. 280, 305 (1976).

Recognizing that solemn obligation, in 1972 the United States Supreme Court invalidated the death sentences of the three petitioners appearing before it, and signaled that as it was then being imposed across much of the country, the death penalty violated the Eighth Amendment. *See Furman v. Georgia*, 408 U.S. 238 (1972) (per curiam). In *Furman*, the Court encountered state sentencing schemes by which judges and juries were afforded virtually untrammeled discretion to decide whether to impose the ultimate sanction. The result was that the death penalty was being imposed in an at best random manner against some individuals, with "no meaningful basis for distinguishing the few cases in which it [was] imposed from the many cases in which it [was] not." *See id.* at 313 (White, J., concurring). While no majority opinion controlled in *Furman*, the Supreme Court agreed that such an outcome was abhorrent to the Constitution, holding that the death penalty "could not be imposed under sentencing procedures that created a substantial risk that it would be inflicted in an arbitrary and capricious manner." *See Gregg v. Georgia*, 428 U.S. 153, 188 (1976) (plurality opinion) (describing *Furman*'s holding). Put another way, the Constitution quite simply "cannot tolerate the infliction of a sentence of death under legal systems that permit this unique penalty to be so wantonly and so freakishly imposed." *Furman*, 408 U.S. at 310 (Stewart, J., concurring). In the 40 years since *Furman*, the Supreme Court has never retreated from that fundamental principle . . . .

Arbitrariness in California's Death Penalty System

California's death penalty system is so plagued by inordinate and unpredictable delay that the death sentence is actually carried out against only a trivial few of those sentenced to death. Of the more than 900 individuals that have been sentenced to death since 1978, only 13 have been executed. For every one inmate executed by California, seven have died on Death Row, most from natural causes. The review process takes an average of 25 years, and the delay is only getting longer. Indeed, no inmate has been executed since 2006, and there is no evidence to suggest that executions will resume in the reasonably near future. Even when executions do resume, the current population of Death Row is so enormous that, realistically, California will still be unable to execute the substantial majority of Death Row inmates. In fact, just to carry out the sentences of the 748 inmates currently on Death Row, the State would have to conduct more than one execution a week for the next 14 years. Such an outcome is obviously impossible for many reasons, not the least of which is that as a result of extraordinary delay in California's system, only 17 inmates currently on Death Row have even completed the post-conviction review process and are awaiting their execution. For all practical purposes then, a sentence of death in California is a sentence of life imprisonment with the remote possibility of death—a sentence no rational legislature or jury could ever impose.

Of course, for an arbitrarily selected few of the 748 inmates currently on Death Row, that remote possibility may well be realized. Yet their selection for execution will not depend on whether their crime was one of passion or of premeditation, on whether they killed one person or ten, or on any other proxy for the relative penological value that will be achieved by executing that inmate over any other. Nor will it even depend on the perhaps neutral criterion of executing inmates in the order in which they arrived on Death Row. Rather, it will depend upon a factor largely outside an inmate's control, and wholly divorced from the penological purposes the State sought to achieve by sentencing him to death in the first instance: how quickly the inmate proceeds through the State's dysfunctional post-conviction review process.

Mr. Jones's case is illustrative. Mr. Jones is now in his fifth year of federal review, and given that the final briefing on the merits of his claims was completed in January, a decision from this Court could be rendered by the end of the year. On average, review at the Ninth Circuit will take another 2.2 years. *See* Commission Report at 123. Accounting then for the time spent seeking *en banc* review from the Circuit and certiorari from the United States Supreme Court, and assuming relief is denied at every level, the federal stay on Mr. Jones's execution could be lifted and he could be ready for execution within three or four years—about 23 years after he was first sentenced to death.

By comparison, of the 380 inmates who are currently on Death Row, 285 have been there longer than Mr. Jones. Over a third of them are engaged in state court proceedings. In all likelihood, given the delays in the post-conviction review process, most of them will never face execution as a realistic possibility, unlike Mr. Jones. Similarly, of the 38 Death Row inmates who like Mr. Jones were sentenced to death in 1995, only 7, including Mr. Jones, have completed the state habeas review process. Were his petition denied today, Mr. Jones would be one of three inmates sentenced in 1995 to have his federal habeas petition under review by the Ninth Circuit, effectively the last available stage before execution. Again, because of the inordinate delays inherent in California's system, many of the rest will never be executed. They will instead live out their lives on Death Row . . . .

For Mr. Jones to be executed in such a system, where so many are sentenced to death but only a random few are actually executed, would offend the most fundamental of constitutional protections—that the government shall not be permitted to arbitrarily inflict the ultimate punishment of death. *See Furman*, 408 U.S. at 293 (Brennan, J., concurring) ("When the punishment of death is inflicted in a trivial number of the cases in which it is legally available, the conclusion is virtually inescapable that it is being inflicted arbitrarily. Indeed, it smacks of little more than a lottery system.") To be sure, *Furman* specifically addressed arbitrariness in the selection of who gets sentenced to death. But the principles on which it relied apply here with equal force. The Eighth Amendment simply cannot be read to proscribe a state from randomly selecting which few members of its criminal population it will sentence to death, but to allow that same state to randomly select which trivial few of those condemned it will actually execute. Arbitrariness in execution is still arbitrary, regardless of when in the process the arbitrariness arises.

B. The Penological Purpose of California's Death Penalty System

The systemic delay and dysfunction that result in the arbitrary execution of California's Death Row inmates give rise to a further constitutional problem with the State's administration of its death penalty system. In California, the execution of a death sentence is so infrequent, and the delays preceding it so extraordinary, that the death penalty is deprived of any deterrent or retributive effect it might once have had. Such an outcome is antithetical to any civilized notion of just punishment.

1. Deterrence

Whether the death penalty has any deterrent effect when administered in a functional system is a widely contested issue upon which no clear empirical consensus has been reached. But even when administered in a functional system, few could dispute that long delays preceding execution frustrate whatever deterrent effect the death penalty may have. Indeed, the law, and common sense itself, have long recognized that the deterrent effect of *any* punishment is contingent upon the certainty and timeliness of its imposition. *See, e.g., Harmelin*, 501 U.S. at 989 ("[D]eterrent effect depends not only upon the amount of the penalty but upon its certainty . . . ."); *United States v. Panico*, 308 F.2d 125, 128 (2d Cir. 1962) ("There can be little doubt that the effectiveness of punishment as a deterrent is related not only to the quality of the possible punishment but to the certainty and promptness as well."), *vacated on other grounds*, 375 U.S. 29 (1963); *see also* Commission Report at 115 n.8 (agreeing that "[i]f there is a deterrent value [to the death penalty], . . . it is certainly dissipated by long intervals between judgment of death and its execution"). In the death penalty context, where finality of punishment is not achieved until the actual execution of the inmate, the case is no different.

In California, the system in which the death penalty is administered can only be described as completely dysfunctional. The delay inherent in California's system is so extraordinary that it alone seriously undermines the continued deterrent effect of the State's death penalty. But delay is not the only problem. Executions by the State are so few and far between that since 1978, of the 900 individuals sentenced to death in California, only 13 have been executed. The reasonable expectation of an individual contemplating a capital crime in California then is that if he is caught, it does not matter whether he is sentenced to death—he realistically faces only life imprisonment. Under such a system, the death penalty is about as effective a deterrent to capital crime as the possibility of a lightning strike is to going outside in the rain.

2. Retribution

Just as inordinate delay and unpredictability of executions eliminate any deterrent effect California's death penalty might have, so too do such delay and unpredictability defeat the death penalty's retributive objective. It is true that the Supreme Court has consistently affirmed the view that retribution, as "an expression of society's moral outrage at particularly offensive conduct," is a constitutionally permissible aim of capital sentencing schemes. *See Gregg*, 428 U.S. at 183. But no reasonable jurist could dispute that inordinate delay frustrates that aim. *See Coleman*, 451 U.S. at 960 (Rehnquist, J., dissenting from the denial of certiorari) ("There can be little doubt that delay in the enforcement of capital punishment frustrates the purpose of retribution."); *Ceja v. Stewart*, 134 F.3d 1368, 1374 (9th Cir. 1998) (Fletcher, J., dissenting) ("[T]he ability of an execution to provide moral and emotional closure to a shocked community diminishe[s] as the connection between crime and punishment [becomes] more attenuated and more arbitrary."); Lewis Powell, *Capital Punishment*, Commentary, 102 Harv. L. Rev. 1035, 1041 (1989) ("The retributive value of the death penalty is diminished as imposition of sentence becomes ever farther removed from the time of the offense.") . . . .

C. Petitioners' Fault in Creating Delay

. . . The Court pauses first to note the arguments that the State is not making in opposition to Mr. Jones's claim. The State is not arguing that the delay in Mr. Jones's execution is an isolated incident in a system that otherwise operates as expeditiously as possible to execute those sentenced to death. Nor does the State argue that it is rational or necessary for it to take more than two decades to provide Death Row inmates with the process required to ensure that their death sentence comports with constitutional requirements. Indeed, the State cannot reasonably make these arguments.

On the record before it, the Court finds that much of the delay in California's post-conviction review process is created by the State itself, not by inmates' own interminable efforts to delay . . . .

These delays—exceeding 25 years on average—are inherent to California's dysfunctional death penalty system, not the result of individual inmates' delay tactics, except perhaps in isolated cases . . . . That such delays are not reasonably necessary to the fair administration of justice is evident. In 2008, the Commission recommended a series of related reforms that, in its view, would help alleviate delay inherent in California's death penalty system . . . .

The Commission's proposal, and the experience of other states across the country—which, on average, take substantially less than 20 years, let alone 25 or 30 years, to adjudicate their post-conviction review process—demonstrate that the inordinate delay in California's death penalty system is not reasonably necessary to protect an inmate's rights. Moreover, there is no basis to conclude that inmates on California's Death Row are simply more dilatory, or have stronger incentives to needlessly delay the capital appeals process, than are those Death Row inmates in other states. Most of the delay in California's post-conviction process then is attributable to California's own system, not the inmates themselves.

Of course, the Court's conclusion should not be understood to suggest that the post-conviction review process should be curtailed in favor of speed over accuracy. Indeed, it bears noting that in more than half of all cases in which the federal courts have reviewed a California inmate's death sentence on habeas review, the inmate has been granted relief from the death sentence. The post-conviction review process is, therefore, vitally important. It serves both the inmate's interest in not being improperly executed, as well as the State's interest in ensuring that it does not improperly execute any individual. Nevertheless, the Court holds that where the State permits the post-conviction review process to become so inordinately and unnecessarily delayed that only an arbitrarily selected few of those sentenced to death are executed, the State's process violates the Eight Amendment. Fundamental principles of due process and just punishment demand that any punishment, let alone the ultimate one of execution, be timely and rationally carried out . . . .

* * *

When an individual is condemned to death in California, the sentence carries with it an implicit promise from the State that it will actually be carried out. That promise is made to the citizens of the State, who are investing significant resources in furtherance of a punishment that they believe is necessary to achieving justice. It is made to jurors who, in exercise of their civic responsibility, are asked to hear about and see evidence of undeniably horrific crimes, and then participate in the agonizing deliberations over whether the perpetrators of those horrific crimes should be put to death. It is made to victims and their loved ones, for whom just punishment might provide some semblance of moral and emotional closure from an otherwise unimaginable loss. And it is made to the hundreds of individuals on Death Row, as a statement their crimes are so heinous they have forfeited their right to life.

But for too long now, the promise has been an empty one. Inordinate and unpredictable delay has resulted in a death penalty system in which very few of the hundreds of individuals sentenced to death have been, or even will be, executed by the State. It has resulted in a system in which arbitrary factors, rather than legitimate ones like the nature of the crime or the date of the death sentence, determine whether an individual will actually be executed. And it has resulted in a system that serves no penological purpose. Such a system is unconstitutional. Accordingly, the Court hereby VACATES Mr. Jones's death sentence.

DATED: July 16, 2014
CORMAC J. CARNEY
UNITED STATES DISTRICT JUDGE

[Appendix A: Death Sentences in California, 1978–1997 has been omitted.]

SOURCE: U.S. District Court for the Central District of California. *Jones v. Chappell.* Case No. CV-09-02158-CJC. www.cacd.uscourts.gov/sites/default/files/documents/Jones%20v.%20Chappell.pdf.

OTHER HISTORIC DOCUMENTS OF INTEREST

FROM PREVIOUS *HISTORIC DOCUMENTS*

Preliminary Report on Downing of Malaysian Flight Released

JULY 17 AND 21, AND SEPTEMBER 9, 2014

On July 14, 2014, during a scheduled flight from Amsterdam, The Netherlands, to Kuala Lumpur, Malaysia, a passenger plane with 298 onboard crashed in eastern Ukraine. The initial investigation into the crash found that Malaysia Airlines Flight 17 (MH17) was likely shot down by a missile, and speculation was rampant that the weapon was supplied to pro-Russian separatists by the Russian government. This further ignited tensions in the region and ultimately led many Western nations to impose additional sanctions on Russia for their failure to draw down troops. This was the second Malaysia Airlines plane crisis that occurred in 2014, the first being MH370, which went missing in March and by the end of 2014 had not yet been found. The MH17 crash was the deadliest airline shoot down and the first downing of a passenger plane since Siberian Airlines Flight 1812 crashed into the Black Sea after being mistakenly shot down during a Ukrainian military training exercise in 2001.

MH17 Crashes in Eastern Ukraine

On July 17, MH17 left Amsterdam's Schiphol airport at 12:31 p.m. local time, en route to Kuala Lumpur, where it was due to arrive at 6:10 a.m. local time. At approximately 1:20 p.m. GMT, the plane lost contact with air traffic controllers thirty-one miles from the Russia-Ukraine border. The plane crashed near Hrabove, in eastern Ukraine near the Russian border. There were a total of 283 passengers and fifteen crew onboard, none of whom survived. A majority—193—were citizens of The Netherlands. Other nationalities represented on the plane included forty-three Malaysians, twenty-seven Australians, twelve Indonesians, ten Britons, four Belgians, four Germans, three Filipinos, one Canadian, and one New Zealander. Approximately eighty passengers were under age eighteen. A member of the Dutch Senate, Willem Witteveen, was onboard the flight, as was the former president of the International AIDS society who, with other delegates, was en route to the 20th International AIDS Conference.

The area of eastern Ukraine in which the plane went down has been controlled primarily by pro-Russian separatists following the March 2014 referendum during which the Crimean Peninsula of Ukraine voted to become part of Russia. In the months leading up to the attack, Ukrainian military planes were shot down in increasing numbers; this included the downing of a military transport plane which left forty-nine dead. Many of the flights were brought down by shoulder-carried missiles.

Because of the ongoing fighting prior to the crash, the International Civil Aviation Organisation issued a warning making the airspace on the eastern edge of Ukraine off limits up to 32,000 feet. MH17, however, was flying at 33,000 feet. A number of airlines had been using the airspace, and even at the time of the crash, there were multiple other flights in the area. Some airlines had issued flight restrictions for their own fleets, including

Korean Air, British Airways, and Asiana Airlines. The U.S. Federal Aviation Administration (FAA) issued some restrictions for other areas of Ukraine and urged all U.S.-flag airlines to "exercise extreme caution" in the region. Even so, given the altitude of the plane and light air traffic, the airspace was considered safe for travel by Malaysia Airlines.

INVESTIGATION INDICATES MISSILE ATTACK

The crash site was not immediately sealed off, and reports and photographs note that the separatists were the first to reach the area, with some indication that they looted the luggage and other items found on the victims. During the initial days after the crash, separatist rebels kept Ukrainian and Organization for Security and Co-operation in Europe (OSCE) investigators from reaching the site. Andrei Purgin, the leader of the Donetsk People's Republic, where the plane crashed, said, "We will guarantee the safety of international experts on the scene as soon as Kiev concludes a ceasefire agreement." These separatists recovered both the plane's black boxes but quickly handed them over to the Malaysian government. Malaysian officials reported that there was no evidence the data contained in the flight recorders had been tampered with.

On July 21, international investigators were allowed by local officials to begin viewing 272 of the bodies that had been recovered and were being stored on a refrigerated train; the bodies were later sent to The Netherlands for identification and forensics work but as of February 2015, three bodies are still unaccounted for. The full offsite investigation of the crash began on July 23. The investigation was led by the Dutch Safety Board and included assistance from the United States, Russia, United Kingdom, Ukraine, Germany, Malaysia, and Australia. The team of investigators was unable to access the crash site until early August because, according to a Ukrainian official, the separatists had placed mines around the site. By August 6, investigators left the site because of safety concerns. It was not until October 13 that the team was able to reenter the crash site to begin collecting evidence and the belongings of the victims. The plane was removed from the site in November and was taken to The Netherlands where it was reassembled.

Igor Girkin, leader of the separatists in Donbass, initially took credit for the downing of the plane on a social media account, but when he learned that it was a passenger plane, the message was removed and his group denied any involvement. The Ukrainian government immediately blamed Russia and the separatists for the crash, while the separatists blamed Ukraine. Russia disputed any allegation that it was involved and instead suggested that a Ukrainian fighter plane or missile system may have caused the crash. During a press conference on July 21, Russian air force chief Lt. Gen. Igor Makushev said that a second aircraft had been spotted on Russia's radar shortly before the crash near flight MH17. He said that the country's satellite data also indicated that the Ukrainian military had moved missile systems into the region, which were quickly moved back out on July 18. There was little evidence provided by the Russian defense ministry to back up such claims, and the United States called them "desperate" propaganda and added that Ukrainian fighter jets can't operate at 30,000 feet. White House press secretary Josh Earnest said that the ongoing investigation seemed to indicate that Russia had supplied the separatists with antiaircraft missiles. "Russian claims to the contrary are getting both more desperate and much harder to believe," Earnest said.

After reviewing some of the evidence from the crash, American and Ukrainian officials said that it is highly likely that the plane was shot down by a Buk missile system, primarily because of its ability to reach such a high altitude. Further, both nations believe that the weapon was supplied by Russia. "We have compelling evidence that this terrorist act was committed with the help of the Russian Federation. We know clearly that the crew of this system were Russian citizens," Vitaly Nayda, chief of Ukraine's Security Service Counter Intelligence Department, said on July 19. Nayda noted that Ukrainian officials had access to recorded conversations during which the separatists spoke with Russian leaders about the crash. Witnesses, including Associated Press journalists reporting from the separatist-controlled regions, reported seeing Buk missile launchers moved into the region the day before the crash.

In its preliminary report released on September 9, 2014, the Dutch Safety Board said the "damage observed on the forward fuselage and cockpit section of the aircraft appears to indicate that there were impacts from a large number of high-energy objects from outside the aircraft." This impact likely led the plane to breakup in mid-air. The preliminary report also found no indication of technical or operational errors. The Board made its initial assessment based on the location of puncture holes in the plane, the six-mile-by-three-mile-wide field of debris, and "non-airline metal" found in the bodies of some of the crash victims. The report did not specifically state that a missile had caused the crash; however, the use of the term "high-energy object" is consistent with that form of weapon. Although many experts believe that the plane likely disintegrated before the passengers knew what was happening, in October, Dutch foreign minister Frans Timmermans said that one of the bodies was found with an oxygen mask around its neck, indicating that at least some passengers were alive after the missile strike. The Dutch Safety Board is expected to release its final report in August 2015.

Ongoing Investigations and Response

Some of the families of the crash victims called on the United Nations to conduct its own investigation, claiming that the work of the Dutch Safety Board was flawed. The families demanded that the Dutch Safety Board hand over all its materials to a special envoy from the United Nations. The Netherlands has rejected the request. There is also an ongoing criminal investigation being conducted by the Dutch Ministry of Justice. The 200 investigators on the case noted that they are specifically looking at metal debris found on the bodies to determine whether it did in fact come from a surface-to-air missile.

Western leaders urged Russia to use the downing of MH17 as a reason to change course on the situation with Ukraine. President Barack Obama called on Russian leaders to "pivot away from the strategy they've been taking and get serious about trying to resolve hostilities within Ukraine." Unwilling to do so, the Russian government received a new round of sanctions from the United States and European Union, which included expanded travel bans and asset freezes; Russia called the sanctions "destructive and short-sighted." By the end of 2014, neither Russian President Vladimir Putin nor Ukrainian president Petro Poroshenko had reached a lasting ceasefire with each other or with the separatists.

—Alexis Atwater

Following are statements by the prime minister of The Netherlands and prime minister of Ukraine on July 17, 2014, and July 21, 2014, respectively, with regard to the crash of flight MH17; and the Summary of Findings from the Dutch Safety Board's initial report into the downing of Malaysian Airlines Flight 17, issued on September 9, 2014.

DOCUMENT *Prime Minister Rutte on MH17*

July 17, 2014

I am deeply shocked by the dramatic reports of the air disaster involving Malaysia Airlines flight MH17 from Amsterdam to Kuala Lumpur over Ukrainian territory. Much remains unclear as regards the cause and circumstances of the crash and those on board the aircraft. I have just spoken to the Ukrainian president.

I am now on my way back to the Netherlands to monitor and address the situation from The Hague.

Our thoughts are with those who were on board the aircraft and their family and friends.

SOURCE: Government of Netherlands. "Statement by Prime Minister Mark Rutte in response to the Ukraine air disaster." July 17, 2014. www.government.nl/issues/mh17-incident/news/2014/07/17/statement-by-prime-minister-mark-rutte-in-response-to-the-ukraine-air-disaster.html.

DOCUMENT *Ukrainian Prime Minister on Malaysia Airlines Crash*

July 21, 2014

First let me express once again my deepest condolences to the families who lost their beloved ones. We pray for everyone, we pray for these families, and the Ukrainian nation mourns.

Let me provide an update on the latest developments. The Ukrainian authorities discovered 272 bodies, 251 of which are already loaded into the refrigerator train. We sent two trains, with four cars each. They are right now located in Torez city.

These bloody guerrillas do not allow the train to leave the area. We expect that the train will leave the area as soon as possible.

The Ukrainian Government is ready to transfer an international investigation to our Dutch friends. The Dutch side could lead the process of investigation together with the entire international community and the Ukrainian authorities.

We are ready to transfer all bodies directly to Amsterdam as one of the best well equipped forensic laboratories is located in Amsterdam.

The Ukrainian Security Service has already started a comprehensive and thorough investigation of this deadly terrorist attack, of this crime against humanity under the existing bilateral agreement between Ukraine and Netherlands. We are ready in the full cooperation with the Dutch side and another international and foreign agencies to conduct this type of investigation.

Those who committed this international crime, those responsible will be held accountable, and together with the entire international community we will bring to justice everyone responsible, including the country which is behind the scenes, but which supplied a lethal weapon, provided financial support, trained these bastards, and supported and even orchestrated this kind of despicable crime.

The Ukrainian Government will do everything to investigate this crime, to transfer the bodies, to provide any support to all respective Governments, and to unfold the truth to the entire world.

Question:	Can I ask if the priority at the moment is the recovery of the bodies, removing those bodies from the crash site and moving them to Amsterdam—if so, does the train have to go through Donetsk? And if so—was it wise to begin military action in Donetsk this morning?
Prime Minister Arseniy Yatsenuyk:	The key priority for us is to recover the bodies, to collect all evidence of this crime. As I already said, we recovered 272 bodies, 251 of which are already loaded in the refrigerators. We facilitated a route how to deliver these bodies to any destination which is needed, including capital Kyiv or Amsterdam as I already said. In Amsterdam we can get a perfect forensic expertise as our Dutch partners can provide well-equipped facilities. There is no indication about any military activity or counter-terrorist operation in the area of the crash site. We do understand our responsibility, because the key priority is to collect all evidence and to have a thorough investigation.
Question:	How are the negotiations going on, how do they happen? Are you discussing with the terrorist bastards or whatever you call them about the train—you said "as soon as possible"—what's the timetable for it and how are you talking to them and who is talking to them?
PM:	The government has established a special commission in order to recover these bodies, in order to have this investigation. We have to talk to these bastards and we did it and due to this fact we recovered and collected the bodies and collected a number of evidences. This is an ongoing and never ending process, we are doing it 24/7 to make it as quick as possible.
Question:	You mentioned several times that you are willing to give the lead in the investigation to the Netherlands. Are you responding to demand from Russia or from the rebels that the investigation be taken out of the direct hands of the Ukrainian government? And is there a proposal from the other side that all of this be handled through Russia?
PM:	We are responding to the request of our Dutch partners. It was our Dutch friends who launched this request. And you know, that Dutch people suffered mostly. This is I would say even a humanitarian gesture. This is the right thing to do. And this will provide more independence to this investigation.
Question:	And do the rebels want to go through Russia?
PM:	I don't care about these not rebels, but Russian lead guerillas. They are not rebels.
Question:	Do you expect the Russian government to increase its co-operation in this case or—according to you information, to your feelings as

Prime minister—the situation is getting worse at the moment, in these hours? Thank you.

PM: I expect nothing from the Russian government. What they can do: they can supply weapons, they can send well-trained agents, they can support these guerillas, but they have to stop and President Putin is to realize that enough is enough. This is not the conflict just between Ukraine and Russia. After they shot down the MH-17, this is an international and global conflict. So, what we expect from Russia and Russian regime is to deescalate the situation, to withdraw their agents, to close the border, to stop to support these bastards and to stick to international law and to international obligations and to present an unfold every information and every single evidence they have to get the real picture of what happened and to investigate this drama sorrowfully and as quick as possible.

Question: I have a question about the experts who are sitting in Kyiv and cannot go to Donetsk and cannot investigate the scene where the aircraft came down. Can you say if they can go there in the next hours or days?

PM: I want to update you with the latest information. The presidential plane touched down few hours ago. And let me give you the correct numbers. At 10 in the morning there were 31 international experts landing in Kharkiv city. 23 are Dutch experts, 2 German, 2 from the U.S., one from the U.K., and 3 representatives of Australian embassy. So the plane touched down just few hours ago.

Question: Do you expect they will go there today or tomorrow?

PM: It depends on the security situation. We are doing everything, what is possible to provide the humanitarian corridor and to deliver them exactly to the crash site.

Question: Will Ukraine provide its missile inventory to the investigating agency as the Russians demand? And what's your response to Putin's statement that no one should use this crisis for cheap and selfish political achievement? Thank you.

PM: Ukrainian government and Ukrainian authorities, Department of Defense is ready to present an entire picture and comprehensive information in relation to all anti-aircraft missiles and surface-to-air missiles that are deployed on Ukrainian territory and used by Ukrainian military. Or—to be correct—that never have been used by Ukrainian military.

Question: Can you clarify what seems to be a somewhat complicated situation where you seem to be in control of emergency workers and volunteers at the site, but you said that rebels are blocking the train? How much control does the Ukrainian Government have there and what are they actually doing to stop that train? Could you also comment on the reports that the anti-terrorist operation is moving to the city of Donetsk? Thank you.

PM: We were allowed to get to the crash site and to recover the bodies only after we had very long talks with these Russian-led guerillas.

But they still control the area. And they still control the railway station in the city of Torez. How? With guns and grenade launchers—this is the way how they control the area. So if we get the deal and if they allow us to transfer these bodies to the area that will be determined by the international rescue team, we will do it as quick as possible. On any other military issues we expect that the Security service of Ukraine will give a press conference, I want them to disclose the relevant information from the relevant agencies . . . .

Question: The Western media says the Ukrainian government already defined this tragic crash that the flight was shut down with Buk by the rebels before the international investigation and how do you explain that? And another question—how would you ensure the international rescue team their safety?

PM: Thank you for the question. We are interested in having a comprehensive large-scale widespread and thorough international investigation. But let's speak about facts—what's on the ground, what's really on the table? The first one: Ukrainian military never used surface-to-air missiles. Second one: Ukrainian Department of Defense will unfold all relevant information about the locations of anti-aircraft missiles. The third one: we got the footage and pictures of Russian-made anti-aircraft vehicle moving in the area that is fully and entirely controlled by Russian-led guerillas. The fourth one: we have the pictures of the missile launch. The fifth one: we got an intercept of the telephone calls between Russian-led guerillas and Russian FSB agents. The sixth one: we got the preliminary evidence of the clear fact that MH17 was shot down by a surface-to-air missile. The seventh one: on the Internet, this bunch of idiots posted a chat saying that we downed Ukrainian military plane, then they deleted it in 30 seconds. In addition to this, we got a number of statements of intelligence agencies and respective governments clearly saying that they do share the opinion that MH17 was shot down by a missile. And it's crystal clear that some Russian drunken guerilla cannot manage this system. This is to be a well-trained agent and what the Department of Defense reported to me is that to acquire this target and to shoot down the plane they need to work in collaboration with other radar systems that we don't have on the Ukrainian territory. And we want an international investigation to get the real facts on who targeted MH17, who supported and provided the intelligence to those who committed this international crime. And I urge the Russian government to respond to all questions that have been raised.

Thank you.

SOURCE: Government of Ukraine. "Press-briefing of Prime Minister of Ukraine Arseniy Yatsenuyk on MH17 attack." July 21, 2014. www.kmu.gov.ua/control/en/publish/article?art_id=247471550&cat_id=244851734.

Preliminary Dutch Safety Board Report on MH17

September 9, 2014

[All other sections, containing photos and factual data about the flight, and footnotes have been omitted.]

3. SUMMARY OF FINDINGS

Crew

According to the information received from Malaysia Airlines the crew was properly licensed and had valid medical certificates to conduct the flight.

Aircraft

According to the documents, the aircraft was in an airworthy condition at departure from Amsterdam Airport Schiphol, there were no known technical malfunctions.

CVR/FDR

No evidence or indications of manipulation of the recorders were found.

No aural alerts or warnings of aircraft system malfunctions were heard on the Cockpit Voice Recorder. The communication between the flight crew members gave no indication of any malfunction or emergency prior to the occurrence.

The engine parameters were consistent with normal operation during the flight. No engine or aircraft system warnings or cautions were detected.

No technical malfunctions or warnings in relation to the event flight were found on Flight Data Recorder data.

Both recordings ended at 13.20:03.

ATC / Airspace

At the time of the occurrence, flight MH17 was flying at FL330 in unrestricted airspace of the Dnipropetrovs'k (UKDV) FIR in the eastern part of the Ukraine, the aircraft flew on a constant heading, speed and altitude when the Flight Data Recording ended. UkSATSE had issued NOTAMs that restricted access to the airspace below FL320.

The last radio transmission made by the crew began at 13.19:56 hrs and ended at 13.19:59 hrs.

The last radio transmissions made by Dnipropetrovs'k air traffic control centre to flight MH17 began at 13.20:00 hrs and ended at 13.22:02 hrs. The crew did not respond to these transmissions.

No distress messages were received by the ATC.

According to radar data three commercial aircraft were in the same Control Area as flight MH17 at the time of the occurrence. All were under control of Dnipro Radar. At 13.20 hrs the distance between the closest aircraft and MH17 was approximately 30 km.

Damage

Damage observed on the forward fuselage and cockpit section of the aircraft appears to indicate that there were impacts from a large number of high-energy objects from outside the aircraft.

The pattern of damage observed in the forward fuselage and cockpit section of the aircraft was not consistent with the damage that would be expected from any known failure mode of the aircraft, its engines or systems.

The fact that there were many pieces of aircraft structure distributed over a large area, indicated that the aircraft broke up in the air.

Based on the preliminary findings to date, no indications of any technical or operational issues were found with the aircraft or crew prior to the ending of the CVR and FDR recording at 13.20:03 hrs.

The damage observed in the forward section of the aircraft appears to indicate that the aircraft was penetrated by a large number of high-energy objects from outside the aircraft. It is likely that this damage resulted in a loss of structural integrity of the aircraft, leading to an in-flight break up.

5. FURTHER INVESTIGATIONS

This report is preliminary. The information must necessarily be regarded as tentative and subject to alteration or correction if additional evidence becomes available. Further work will at least include the following areas of interest to substantiate the factual information regarding:

- detailed analyses of data, including CVR, FDR and other sources, recorded onboard the aircraft;
- detailed analyses of recorded ATC surveillance data and radio communication;
- detailed analyses of the meteorological circumstances;
- forensic examination of wreckage if recovered and possible foreign objects, if found;
- results of the pathological investigation;
- analyses of the in-flight break up sequence;
- assessment of the operator's and State of Occurrence's management of flight safety over a region of conflict or high security risk;
- any other areas that are identified during the investigation.

SOURCE: Dutch Safety Board. "Preliminary report involving Malaysia Airlines Boeing 777-200 flight MH17." September 9, 2014. www.onderzoeksraad.nl/uploads/phase-docs/701/b3923acad0ceprem-rap port-mh-17-en-interactief.pdf.

OTHER HISTORIC DOCUMENTS OF INTEREST

FROM THIS VOLUME

Iranian, European Union, and U.S. Leaders Remark on Nuclear Talks

JULY 18 AND 19, 2014

During the first half of 2014, a group of countries known as the P5+1—comprised of China, France, Germany, Russia, the United Kingdom, and the United States—continued negotiations with Iran to identify solutions to the ongoing international dispute over that country's nuclear program. Western countries and the United Nations had for many years sought to limit Iran's nuclear activities, primarily through economic sanctions, amid suspicions that the country has been attempting to build nuclear weapons in violation of the Nuclear Non-Proliferation Treaty. Iran has long maintained that its nuclear program is intended to generate electricity for its citizens, but it has a history of attempting to conceal these activities and their possible military applications from the international community. In November 2013, amid a perceived warming of diplomatic relations between Iran and the West, negotiators reached a six-month agreement that required Iran to take several immediate steps to reduce its nuclear activities in return for some easing of sanctions, with the goal of providing additional time for the parties to reach a longer-term agreement. The plan set a deadline of July 20, 2014, for a final agreement to be reached, but while negotiators reportedly made progress in their deliberations, "significant gaps" between the two sides remained, prompting the group to extend the agreement deadline twice.

THE JOINT PLAN OF ACTION

International efforts to restrict Iran's nuclear program had been ongoing for roughly twenty years, but the June 2013 election of Hassan Rouhani as Iran's new president raised hopes of greater cooperation and an easing of tensions between Iran and the West. While Rouhani's predecessor, Mahmoud Ahmadinejad, was a hardline conservative who refused to make any concessions on Iran's nuclear program, Rouhani was a moderate reformer who called for more negotiations and "mutual confidence-building" around the nuclear issue. In September, two historic conversations between U.S. and Iranian officials took place, indicating first steps toward normalization of diplomatic relations. President Barack Obama and Rouhani spoke by phone, the first time leaders from the two countries directly communicated since the 1979 Iranian Revolution, and Secretary of State John Kerry met with Iranian foreign minister Javad Zarif, the first time in a generation that the two countries publicly met one-on-one. Also in September, Rouhani participated in the UN General Assembly meeting in New York, where he stated that Iran's goal "is resolving problems" and called for a nuclear deal with the international community in the next three to six months.

The P5+1 and Iranian negotiators began a new round of talks earlier in 2013, and U.S. officials held several separate secret talks with Iran through the year but had so far failed to reach an agreement. Their final meeting of the year began on November 20. Four days later, the parties announced that they had reached an interim agreement. Known as the

Joint Plan of Action, the agreement was meant to last for six months to provide negotiators additional time to work out a longer agreement to ensure Iran's nuclear program would remain peaceful.

Through the plan, Iran agreed to reduce some of its nuclear activities in return for approximately $7 billion worth of sanctions relief from the UN, United States, and EU. One of the plan's key elements was a requirement that Iran dilute its stockpile of uranium that had been enriched to 20 percent down to a maximum of 5 percent or convert that uranium into oxide so that it could not be used militarily. Uranium that has been enriched to 20 percent is considered medium-grade purity and can easily be further enriched to become weapons-grade material, while uranium enriched between 3.5 percent and 5 percent is sufficient to run nuclear power stations. Iran also promised that it would not enrich any additional uranium over the 5 percent level during the six-month agreement period; advance its work at its Natanz, Fordo, or Arak facilities; build any new uranium enrichment facilities; install new centrifuges at existing facilities; or begin using facilities that already existed but were not yet operational, among other measures. Iran also agreed to participate in enhanced monitoring of its nuclear activities, such as providing detailed information about operations at its nuclear facilities to the International Atomic Energy Association (IAEA) and greater access to those facilities to IAEA inspectors.

If Iran complied, the P5+1 would halt efforts to further reduce Iran's crude oil sales; allow Iran to repatriate approximately $4.2 billion of oil sales revenue that is currently held in foreign banks; suspend U.S. and EU sanctions on insurance and transportation services related to crude oil sales, petrochemical exports, and Iran's auto industry; not implement any new nuclear-related sanctions; and establish a financial channel to facilitate humanitarian trade for Iran's domestic needs. The deal did not allow for any additional Iranian oil to enter the market nor did it affect the Western embargo of Iranian oil or a ban preventing Iranians from using the international banking system.

A New Round of Negotiations Begins

The Joint Plan of Action went into effect on January 20, 2014, and set a deadline of July 20 for reaching a final agreement. Before a new round of talks began, the IAEA issued a report stating that Iran was complying with the terms of the plan, and the United States and EU released statements indicating that they had waived some sanctions, as called for by the plan, and had established a schedule of payments for Iran to receive the agreed upon interim funds. Once the agreement went into effect, the IAEA also began conducting more frequent and extensive inspections of Iran's nuclear facilities.

Negotiators first met in February in Vienna to discuss the details of a long-term plan. Both Zarif and Iranian deputy foreign minister Abbas Araghchi said the talks started well but shared some concerns. "To us, what has been announced as dismantling Iran's program and facilities is not on the agenda," said Araghchi. Zarif noted that calls for new sanctions from some in the U.S. Congress had created a "great deal of concern in Iran on whether the U.S. is serious about wanting to reach an agreement."

In May, several reports indicated that representatives involved in the negotiations found progress to be slow and that there were "significant gaps" between the two sides. The primary point of disagreement reportedly centered on the number and type of centrifuges—used to enrich uranium—that Iran would be permitted to have under a final plan. Iranian officials wanted to expand the number of modern centrifuges installed in the country to 50,000; at the time of negotiations, it had 19,000 centrifuges installed with

10,000 in operation. They also wanted to maintain the ability to continue enriching uranium for nuclear power purposes. Officials insisted both measures would be critical to ensuring the country could meet its power needs when its fuel-supplying agreement with Russia expired in 2021. By contrast, U.S. negotiators did not want Iran to have more than a few thousand centrifuges—and preferably outdated equipment. Their concern was that if Iran had more centrifuges, and if there were not sufficient restrictions on those centrifuges, they would be able to convert the machinery for weapons production and build a nuclear bomb much more quickly. Before the Joint Plan of Action was in place, Iran had enough equipment and low-level enriched uranium to be able to produce fuel for a nuclear weapon within one to two months, according to the Institute for Science and International Security. U.S. officials wanted to extend that timeframe to at least one year to allow sufficient time for the international community to intervene. The P5+1 also noted that Russia would be willing to extend the fuel supply deal beyond 2021, thus rendering additional fuel producing capabilities unnecessary.

The impasse reportedly continued through June. "We are still hitting a wall on one absolutely fundamental point, which is the number of centrifuges which allow enrichment," said French foreign minister Laurent Fabius. "We say that there can be a few hundred centrifuges, but the Iranians want thousands. We're not in the same framework." The final meeting before the July 20 deadline began on July 13. Despite several days of continued negotiations, the group was unable to reach an agreement. On July 19, High Representative of the Union for Foreign Affairs and Security Policy Catherine Ashton and Zarif issued a statement announcing an extension of the Joint Plan of Action until November 24, 2014. "While we have made tangible progress on some of the issues and have worked together on a text for a Joint Comprehensive Plan of Action, there are still significant gaps on some core issues which will require more time and effort," the statement read. "Iran and the E3/EU+3 reaffirm that they will continue to implement all their commitments described in the Joint Plan of Action in an efficient and timely manner." Kerry also issued a statement, emphasizing how far negotiators had progressed in a short period of time and calling the interim agreement "a clear success," pointing to Iran's reduction of its nuclear activities. "This effort remains as intense as it is important," Kerry said. "Diplomacy takes time, and persistence is needed to determine whether we can achieve our objectives peacefully. To turn our back prematurely on diplomatic efforts when significant progress has been made would deny ourselves the ability to achieve our objectives peacefully, and to maintain the international unity that we have built."

Under the extension, all parties would continue meeting the terms of the interim plan. Iran also committed to taking several additional steps, including converting enriched uranium that it had already diluted under the plan into fuel for the Tehran Research Reactor—a process that would make it very difficult to use the uranium for weapons material. The United States also agreed to allow Iran to access $2.8 billion of its $100 billion in restricted assets during the extension.

While parties to the negotiations insisted they would not have extended the deadline if they did not believe achieving a final agreement was possible, the decision stoked concerns among some in the U.S. Congress that any final deal would not go far enough. Some lawmakers called for new and tougher sanctions. Sens. John McCain, R-Ariz., Lindsey Graham, R-S.C., and Kelly Ayotte, R-N.H., issued a statement in the fall saying that a "bad deal" with Iran would ignite a nuclear arms race in the Middle East and that an extension of the interim agreement should involve increased sanctions. Obama administration officials continued to oppose new sanctions as long as the negotiations continued, stating that they would consider such measures if the talks collapsed. Israeli prime minister Benjamin Netanyahu also continued to insist that any final agreement must require Iran to stop all enrichment activity, having previously characterized the Joint Plan of Action as a "historic mistake."

Talks Continue

Talks resumed in September and continued with periodic meetings through November. On November 24, negotiators announced another, seven-month extension for the talks. "We remain convinced that, based on the progress made and on the new ideas which continue to be explored, there is a credible path through which a comprehensive solution can be reached," Zarif and Ashton said in a joint statement. "We intend to build on the current momentum in order to complete these negotiations within the shortest possible time." Negotiators are now working toward reaching a final agreement by June 30, 2015.

—Linda Fecteau Grimm

Following is the text of a statement by U.S. secretary of state John Kerry on July 18, 2014, on the delay of Iranian nuclear talks; and the text of a joint statement on July 19, 2014, from the European Union's high representative Catherine Ashton and Iranian foreign minister Mohammad Javad Zarif, regarding the extension of the nuclear agreement discussion.

DOCUMENT

Secretary Kerry on the Delay of Nuclear Talks With Iran

July 18, 2014

As President Obama and our entire administration has made clear, we are committed to testing whether we can address one of the world's most pressing priorities—ensuring that Iran does not obtain a nuclear weapon—through the diplomatic negotiations in which we and our international partners are currently engaged.

This effort remains as intense as it is important, and we have come a long way in a short period of time. Less than a year ago, President Obama and Iranian President Rouhani spoke for the first time to try to usher in a new diplomatic moment, and I held the first bilateral meeting between a Secretary of State and an Iranian Foreign Minister in more than three decades.

Since that time, we've been intensely engaged in a constant and comprehensive effort—the best chance we've ever had to resolve this issue peacefully. This effort has been made possible by the Joint Plan of Action, which stopped the progress of Iran's nuclear program—and rolled parts of it back—for the first time in a decade.

The JPOA was a six-month understanding that went into effect on January 20, and it has been a clear success. Since its implementation, Iran has complied with its obligations to neutralize its stockpile of 20 percent enriched uranium; cap its stockpile of 5 percent enriched uranium; not install advanced centrifuges; not install or test new components at its Arak reactor; and submit to far more frequent inspections of its facilities. The International Atomic Energy Agency has regularly verified that Iran has lived up to these commitments. Meanwhile, we and our P5+1 and EU partners have provided limited sanctions relief, as agreed to in the Joint Plan of Action, while vigorously enforcing the broader sanctions regime that remains in place.

As I said on Monday in Vienna, it is clear to me that we have made tangible progress in our comprehensive negotiations, but there are very real gaps in some areas. Today, we have a draft text that covers the main issues, but there are still a number of brackets and blank spaces in that text.

In terms of progress, we have been working together to find a long-term solution that would effectively close off the plutonium path to a bomb through the reactor at Arak. We have been working on a different purpose for Fordow that would ensure it cannot be used to build a nuclear weapon. We have been working to guarantee Iran's stockpile of low enriched uranium can't be turned into higher enriched uranium suitable for a bomb. And we have agreed that any long-term, comprehensive solution will involve enhanced monitoring and verification measures that go well beyond the status quo—measures that are absolutely critical in creating the confidence we need that Iran will not be able to build a weapon in secret. There are other areas where we've made progress; these are just some of the most important. Of course, on all these issues there is still work to do and differences to resolve, but we have made real progress.

Still, there are very real gaps on issues such as enrichment capacity at the Natanz enrichment facility. This issue is an absolutely critical component of any potential comprehensive agreement. We have much more work to do in this area, and in others as well.

Diplomacy takes time, and persistence is needed to determine whether we can achieve our objectives peacefully. To turn our back prematurely on diplomatic efforts when significant progress has been made would deny ourselves the ability to achieve our objectives peacefully, and to maintain the international unity that we have built. While we've made clear that no deal is better than a bad deal, the very real prospect of reaching a good agreement that achieves our objectives necessitates that we seek more time.

As a result, we have decided—along with the EU, our P5+1 partners, and Iran—to extend the Joint Plan of Action until November 24, exactly one year since we finalized the first step agreement in Geneva. This will give us a short amount of additional time to continue working to conclude a comprehensive agreement, which we believe is warranted by the progress we've made and the path forward we can envision.

Under this short extension, all parties have committed to upholding their obligations in the Joint Plan of Action. For the next four months, we will continue to halt the progress of Iran's nuclear program in key areas. In addition, Iran has committed to take further nuclear-related steps in the next four months that are consistent with the types of steps that they committed to in the JPOA. These include a continued cap on the amount of 5 percent enriched uranium hexafluoride and a commitment to convert any material over that amount into oxide.

In the JPOA, Iran diluted half of its 20 percent enriched uranium hexafluoride and converted the rest to oxide. In this extension, Iran has committed to go one step further and make all of this 20 percent into fuel for the Tehran Research Reactor. Twenty-five kilograms of this material will be converted into fuel by the end of the extension. Once the 20 percent material is in fuel form, it will be very difficult for Iran to use this material for a weapon in a breakout scenario. Attempting to do so would be readily detected by the IAEA and would be an unambiguous sign of an intent to produce a weapon.

In return, we will continue to suspend the sanctions we agreed to under the JPOA and will allow Iran access to $2.8 billion dollars of its restricted assets, the four-month pro-rated amount of the original JPOA commitment. Let me be clear: Iran will not get any more money during these four months than it did during the last six months, and the vast majority of its frozen oil revenues will remain inaccessible. And, just as we have over the last six months, we will continue to vigorously enforce the sanctions that remain in place.

Ultimately, our goal in pursuing this brief extension is to capitalize on the progress we've already made, while giving us the best chance of success at the end of this process. Critically, Iran's nuclear program will remain halted during the next four months. This is in our interest, and in the interest of our allies. And as we pursue this path, we will continue to consult with those allies and with the Congress about this critical issue.

We do so mindful not just of where we hope to arrive, but of how far we have come. One year ago, few would have predicted that Iran would have kept all its commitments under a first step nuclear agreement, and that we would be actively negotiating a long-term comprehensive agreement. Now we have four additional months to determine the next miles of this difficult diplomatic journey. Let's all commit to seize this moment, and to use the additional time to make the fundamental choices necessary to conclude a comprehensive agreement that makes the entire world a safer place.

SOURCE: U.S. Department of State. "Extension of Iran Nuclear Talks." July 18, 2014. www.state.gov/secretary/remarks/2014/07/229491.htm.

EU, Iranian Leaders on Nuclear Talks Extension

July 19, 2014

The High Representative of the European Union for Foreign Affairs and Security Policy, Catherine Ashton, and the Foreign Minister of the Islamic Republic of Iran, Mohammad Javad Zarif, made today the following statement:

"We, together with the Political Directors of the E3+3 (China, France, Germany, Russia, the United Kingdom and the United States), have worked intensively towards a Joint Comprehensive Plan of Action, building on the political momentum created by the adoption and smooth implementation by both sides of the Joint Plan of Action agreed on 24 November 2013. We are grateful to the Austrian government and the United Nations for their tremendous support in hosting these negotiations in Vienna.

We have held numerous meetings in different formats, and in a constructive atmosphere, to reach a mutually agreed long-term comprehensive solution that would ensure Iran's nuclear programme will be exclusively peaceful.

During the past few weeks, we have further intensified our efforts, including through the active involvement of E3+3 Foreign Ministers or their Vice Ministers, who came to Vienna on 13 July 2014 to take stock of progress in the talks. While we have made tangible progress on some of the issues and have worked together on a text for a Joint Comprehensive Plan of Action, there are still significant gaps on some core issues which will require more time and effort.

We, together with the Foreign Ministers of the E3+3, have therefore decided to extend the implementation of measures of the Joint Plan of Action until 24 November 2014, in line with the timeframe that we envisaged in the Joint Plan of Action. Iran and the E3/EU+3 reaffirm that they will continue to implement all their commitments described in the Joint Plan of Action in an efficient and timely manner.

We will reconvene in the coming weeks in different formats with the clear determination to reach agreement on a Joint Comprehensive Plan of Action at the earliest possible moment."

SOURCE: European Union. European External Action Service. "Joint Statement by EU High Representative Catherine Ashton and Iranian Foreign Minister Mohammad Javad Zarif." July 19, 2014. © European Union http://eeas.europa.eu/statements/docs/2014/140719_01_en.pdf.

OTHER HISTORIC DOCUMENTS OF INTEREST

FROM PREVIOUS *HISTORIC DOCUMENTS*

Local Officials Respond to Officer-Involved Shootings

JULY 18 AND AUGUST 19, 2014

In 2014, two shooting deaths by white police of unarmed black men gained national attention. In both instances, the grand juries decided not to indict the police officers involved in the shooting. The two cases sparked widespread protests and led public officials to launch reviews of police department policies and the president to call for a dialogue to improve the relationship between police and the African American community.

THE ERIC GARNER CASE

On July 17, 2014, Eric Garner was allegedly selling black market cigarettes in Staten Island, New York. He was approached by a plainclothes New York City police officer, Daniel Pantaleo. Garner told Pantaleo to "get away," adding "every time you see me, you want to mess with me. I'm tired of it. It stops today . . . . I'm minding my own business. Please just leave me alone." Pantaleo approached Garner and attempted to handcuff him for the alleged illegal sales. Garner tried to get away, at which point Pantaleo placed Garner in a chokehold and attempted to bring him to the ground. Pantaleo and Garner were surrounded by other NYPD officers, and once Garner was on the ground, Pantaleo released his chokehold. In the video taken by bystander Ramsey Orta, Garner could be heard saying "I can't breathe" multiple times. The officers did not appear to take any action until they noticed that Garner was unresponsive. An ambulance was called, but police made no attempt to resuscitate the man before paramedics arrived. When the ambulance arrived, there was no medical aid provided. On the way to the hospital, Garner suffered a heart attack and was pronounced dead an hour later.

In the police report following the incident, the supervising sergeant at the scene, an African American woman named Kizzy Adoni, said that the officer did not end the chokehold because "the perpetrator's condition did not seem serious and he did not appear to get worse." The other officers at the scene noted that they did not administer CPR because Garner was still breathing on his own. The medical examiner's investigation, which concluded on August 1, ruled the death a homicide and said that the chokehold directly contributed to Garner's death. It was further noted that Garner had a history of asthma, obesity, and high blood pressure that made the chokehold and subsequent pressure on his chest when he was forced to the ground contributing factors.

THE MICHAEL BROWN CASE

On August 9, 2014, police in the small St. Louis, Missouri, suburb of Ferguson were called to respond to a robbery at a convenience store. On the way to the store, the responding officer, Darren Wilson, found eighteen-year-old Michael Brown walking with a friend down the center of the street. Wilson asked the two men to move to the sidewalk and continued driving. After the pair refused, Wilson backed up and stopped nearby. From there, eyewitness accounts of what happened vary widely. A struggle apparently took place between Brown and Wilson through the window of his police vehicle. At one point during this confrontation, Wilson fired at least six shots and killed Brown, who was unarmed. The entire event, from when Wilson first spotted Brown until he was killed, lasted approximately ninety seconds. Brown's body lay in the street where he was killed for nearly four hours before being taken to the morgue.

One day later, the St. Louis Police Department announced that it would complete an investigation into the officer-involved shooting. A grand jury was convened and began meeting on August 20. Robert McCulloch was named the prosecuting attorney. His appointment was heavily criticized by those who believed he would be unable to remain impartial because his father, a former police officer, was killed by a black suspect. In an attempt to alleviate public concern, McCulloch said that all the proceedings of the grand jury would be transcribed, and if an indictment was not returned, all the materials would be made public.

Immediately following Brown's death, protesters took to the streets to demonstrate against police use of force. The protests turned violent with looting and attacks on local businesses. On August 14, President Barack Obama criticized the Ferguson police department for its excessive use of force against protesters and called on Attorney General Eric Holder to "do what is necessary to help determine exactly what happened and to see that justice is done." The Missouri National Guard was called into Ferguson on August 18 to calm the unrest and protect citizens. The police department initially refused to release the name of the officer involved in the shooting, in an attempt to protect him from the protesters, but as anger mounted over the nearly nonexistent release of information related to the shooting, on August 15 Wilson's name was released.

GRAND JURY RULES IN BROWN CASE

The Brown grand jury met for twenty-five days over the course of three months and heard from sixty separate witnesses, including Wilson. According to Wilson, Brown "started swinging and punching at me from outside the vehicle" and had his body positioned against the door so that Wilson could not exit. Wilson said that Brown hit him in the face and that he "felt like a five-year-old holding onto Hulk Hogan." Wilson testified that he was unable to reach his mace or baton, so he drew his weapon and told Brown to step back or he would shoot. Brown then grabbed the gun and turned it toward Wilson, who was able to regain control and made three attempts to fire at Wilson but the gun did not discharge. Brown ran from the car and Wilson followed on foot, telling Brown to stop and get on the ground. Brown then allegedly made a "grunting noise" and charged Wilson with his hand in his waistband. Wilson fired several shots, paused, and shot again. Brown was still coming at Wilson, so he shot again, this time hitting Brown in the head.

Eyewitnesses presented a slightly different picture of the events, saying that there was a confrontation at Wilson's vehicle, but that when Wilson asked Brown to put his hands up and stop running, Brown complied. There were also questions about whether Brown had attempted to gain control of Wilson's gun or whether he had indeed reached into his waistband, which made Wilson believe the suspect had a weapon. The medical examiner did not take any pictures at the scene but noted that Brown's left hand was under his body near the waistband. Audio of the confrontation and a video of the robbery that eventually led to the shooting were shown to the grand jury during their deliberations.

On the evening of November 24, McCulloch announced that the grand jury had reached the decision not to indict Wilson. In a twenty-minute press conference, McCulloch detailed the known facts in the case and the jury's verdict. Following the announcement, McCulloch released thousands of pages of grand jury documents, transcripts, statements, audio recordings, and videos. As the announcement was made on live television, some protesters in Ferguson could be seen running through the streets, looting stores, and setting fire to buildings and police cars.

GARNER CASE JURY DOES NOT INDICT

The Staten Island district attorney announced on August 19 that the Garner case would go before a grand jury, based on the findings of the medical examiner's office. The twenty-three member grand jury met for two months, at one point hearing two hours of testimony from Pantaleo and viewing the video of the confrontation and arrest taken by Orta. On December 3, just one week after the grand jury ruled in Ferguson, the Staten Island grand jury decided not to indict Pantaleo. Pantaleo issued a public apology following the decision, stating, "It was never my intention to harm anyone and I feel very bad about the death of Mr. Garner. My family and I include him and his family in our prayers and I hope that they will accept my personal condolences for their loss."

The Garner family expressed disappointment in the grand jury's decision. "He's still feeding his kids, when my husband is six feet under and I'm looking for a way to feed my kids now," said Garner's widow Esaw. "I am determined to get justice for my husband because he shouldn't have been killed in that way."

Demonstrations began immediately following the grand jury's decision in New York, with thousands gathering in Boston, Chicago, Baltimore, Atlanta, and Washington, DC. In New York City, tens of thousands of protesters marched through the streets. Hundreds were arrested in New York during the protests, mainly for refusing to comply with police orders to clear the streets. On December 20, in an apparent retaliation for the Garner ruling, Ismaaiyl Brinsley killed two NYPD officers after writing on his Instagram account, "I'm putting wings on pigs today."

PUBLIC REACTION; CALLS FOR GREATER COOPERATION

The deaths of Brown and Garner raised questions across the country about use of police force against suspected criminals, and especially against African Americans. President Obama steered clear of making the deaths an issue of race and instead said that the two situations spoke "to the larger issues" of trust between police and civilians. As such, the president created a task force to look into how to fix the relationship between police and minority communities and promised to take steps to improve police training.

In New York, Police Commissioner William Bratton called for a review of the police force's tactics, including use of force when detaining a suspect and training provided on how to handle such situations. The commissioner also said that he would continue to roll out the body camera pilot program, which he hoped would make officers more accountable for their actions and would provide evidence when police action is called into question.

Following the deaths of Brown and Garner, the #BlackLivesMatter movement, which was first created as a Twitter hashtag after the 2012 shooting of unarmed black teenager Trayvon Martin by community watch activist George Zimmerman, gained momentum. To date, there are approximately twenty-three chapters of the group around the world, mainly in the United States and Canada. According to the organization, it is "a unique contribution that goes beyond extrajudicial killings of Black people by police and vigilantes." The various chapters held protests around the country following the grand jury decisions, and these protest organizers have met with President Obama and other leaders to discuss methods for stopping police brutality against black individuals, high rates of incarceration, and building a greater community of trust between officials and the black community. In Ferguson, in response to the questions raised about whether Brown had his hands up, protesters rallied around the phrase "Hands Up, Don't Shoot." NFL players came onto the field the weekend after the grand jury decision with their hands up in a show of solidarity. Professional athletes also took up the Garner cause, wearing "I can't breathe" shirts during pregame warm-ups before NFL and NBA games.

Prominent black leaders, including Rev. Al Sharpton and Jesse Jackson, joined the protest movement but called for demonstrators to remain peaceful. "We have no choice, but to keep on fighting because it could be your child next," said Sharpton. "All of our protests, we will not have violence, or inflict pain on others. Eric Garner was not doing anything violent, Michael Brown did not do anything violent."

In December, the Department of Justice announced a federal civil rights investigation into the shooting death of Garner. A separate investigation led by the Federal Bureau of Investigation into Brown's death was launched in August. In March 2015, the Justice Department released the findings of its investigation and said that it did not have enough evidence to indicate that Brown's civil rights had been violated, and Wilson would therefore not be further charged.

—Heather Kerrigan

Following is the text of a press conference held on July 18, 2014, by New York City mayor Bill de Blasio and Police Commissioner William Bratton on the shooting of Eric Garner; and the text of a statement from Missouri governor Jay Nixon on August 19, 2014, in response to the situation in Ferguson, Missouri.

New York City Officials
Discuss Garner Shooting

DOCUMENT

July 18, 2014

| **Mayor Bill de Blasio:** | Joined by Commissioner Bratton, Deputy Commissioner Ben Tucker, Chief Robert Boyce, who is Acting Chief of Department, and Corporation Counsel Zach Carter. I join you today with a heavy heart. On behalf of all New Yorkers I want to offer my deepest condolences to the family and loved ones of Eric Garner. He was a loving husband and a caring father and grandfather. This is a terrible tragedy that occurred yesterday. A terrible tragedy that no family should have to experience. And our thoughts and prayers go out to Eric's family and his friends. |

Like so many New Yorkers I was very troubled by the video I reviewed earlier today. I have instructed Commissioner Bratton to ensure that there will be a full and thorough investigation of this incident. We at City Hall will be working closely with Commissioner Bratton, with Richmond

County DA Dan Donovan, with elected officials and community leaders —in fact we have been in constant conversation with elected officials, community leaders and clergy throughout the day. I want to note something that is true every day in New York City—the men and women of the NYPD are handed an enormous responsibility. The responsibility of keeping us safe, but also the responsibility of making very difficult, split-second decisions in trying circumstances. It is too early to jump to any conclusions about this case—we must wait for all the facts and details of the incident to emerge. But I assure all New Yorkers, there will be a full and thorough investigation. Commissioner Bratton and I are deeply committed to strengthening the relationship between community and police in New York City in all of our neighborhoods. As Commissioner Bratton has said repeatedly: our police must be compassionate, constitutional and respectful in all we do. The NYPD is the most effective police force in this nation and is at its best and at its most effective when it has the support and respect of those that it protects. That is what we are working for every day. In light of yesterday's events, now more than ever we must come together as New Yorkers. As we search for answers and come to terms with this tragedy, let us keep Eric Garner and his family in our hearts. With that, let me call upon Commissioner Bratton.

Commissioner Bill Bratton, NYPD:

Good afternoon. On Thursday July 17th, two New York City police officers assigned to the 120th precinct on Staten Island and assigned to the Plainclothes Anti-Crime Unit, were directed by a superior officer to address specific conditions in the vicinity of Tompkinsville Park near the intersection of Victory Boulevard and Bay Street in Staten Island. It's a little triangular park in a very small commercial area almost directly across from the Staten Island Ferry terminal. The immediate area had been the subject of numerous community complaints by local residents and merchants. Year to date at that location there have been 98 arrests for various offenses, 100 cease summonses issued mostly for quality of life offenses, as well as 646 nine-eleven calls for service within the immediate area of that very small park.

At approximately 3:30 pm the officers approached a 43 year old male, later identified as Eric Garner, of 50 Vaughn Street, Staten Island, concerning the sale of illegal cigarettes in front of 202 Bay Street, Staten Island, directly across from the park. In attempting to take Mr. Garner into custody, there was a physical struggle during which Mr. Garner repeatedly complained of difficulty breathing as the officers wrestled him to the ground. An ambulance was immediately called to the scene and Mr. Garner was transported by EMS to Richmond University Medical Center. He went into cardiac arrest, if I understand, while he was in the vehicle. He was pronounced dead approximately one hour later at the hospital.

The medical examiner will rule on the cause of death. The Richmond County District Attorney's office is leading the investigation—the criminal investigation—into this matter, assisted by the New York City Police Department's Internal Affairs Bureau. And this morning I had the opportunity to go to Staten Island, visited the location of the incident. Met at length with the District Attorney and his staff. I also met with the commanding officer of the Staten Island borough police division, Ed Delatorre. I met with the City Council member who represents that area, Debi Rose, as well as James Oddo, the borough president. I also had conversations with the inspector general—or the newly named inspector general—for the City of New York to brief him on the circumstances of the case. So those are in fact the circumstances as we now know them. As the mayor has indicated, he has directed that there be a full, thorough, transparent investigation and myself and the district attorney are in fact committed to doing just that.

Mayor:	Thank you. I'm going to take questions just on this topic.
Question:	Commissioner, has the dropped status of the officers involved been changed at all, modified, or suspended, and could you tell us about their work history?
Commissioner Bratton:	The two officers who were engaged in the arrest of the deceased, one is an 8-year veteran, the other is a 4-year veteran. Both officers have been assigned to desk duty pending the investigation going forward, and until its conclusion.
Question:	Commissioner, why do chokeholds remain a persistent problem 20 years after you [inaudible]?
Commissioner Bratton:	The issue of chokeholds has been one that the Department began to address back as early as the 1980s, and over years has refined its policies and procedures relative to it. As recently as last year, when another order was issued to the effect that chokeholds are in fact prohibited by the NYPD, as they are, in fact, by most police departments in the United States, because of the concerns of potential death arising from them. So I have instructed, and you see with us Deputy Commissioner of Training Ben Tucker, to review the video but also to review all of our policies and to move forward, if necessary, with a reminder, retraining if appropriate, but at the minimum a reminder of the department's policies as it relates to the use of a chokehold which is in fact prohibited by the department.
Question:	Do you view their usage as still a widespread problem?
Commissioner Bratton:	We do not. No. This is my first exposure to it in the six months I've been Police Commissioner and my seven years at the Los Angeles Police Department, which was a frequent user of that policy prior to 2002, that it was a relatively infrequent occurrence.
Question:	Was this a chokehold, Commissioner Bratton? You've seen the video, I assume.
Commissioner Bratton:	Yes, as defined in the department's patrol guide, this would appear to have been a chokehold. But the investigation, both by the District Attorney's office as well as by our Internal Affairs, will seek to make that final determination as part of our investigation. For purposes of the department, it would be an issue of if it's a violation of our policies and procedures. As to whether in any way shape or form a violation of law, that would be a determination of the District Attorney's criminal investigation.

Question: Selling cigarettes is not a violent crime or anything, yet pretty strong reaction from the officers, the back and forth according to the video, I wanted to get your thoughts on that aspect. And to the Mayor, a lot of people were looking to you to reform the NYPD, to change things, and what would you say to them today?

Commissioner Bratton: The issue of the sale of individual cigarettes, "loosies" as they're called, which is apparently the action that the officers were asked to address at this location, while seemingly a small, maybe innocuous matter to most people, that quite obviously to the shop owners in that area who lost sales of cigarettes that in fact has tax stamps to this illegal type of activity, it was a concern to them, because they repeatedly called to ask the police to do something about this violation of the law. And it was for that reason that the officers were in fact directed to that location. So again, a seemingly minor quality of life offense, if you will, but it's one that the New York City Police Department is asked to address every day, because in fact it is complained about, it is the subject of 911 calls, and it is of concern to the quality of life as well as the business vitality in some of these neighborhoods.

Mayor: To the other part of your question, Commissioner Bratton and I are moving very consistently and energetically to create a series of reforms. And I think we can say, having spoken to community leaders all over the city, that the effect of those reforms is being felt on the ground. This incident was a tragedy. There will be a very thorough investigation. But if you look at what's happening all over the city, I think we can safely say that real progress is being made, that the relationship between police and community is starting to heal and improve. And it's something we are committed to for the long haul. Marcia?

Question: Mayor, [inaudible] you could tell me what your thoughts were after you saw the video? And Commissioner, if you could also tell me what your thoughts were [inaudible]?

Mayor: It was very troubling. I watched it the same way a family member would watch it, and it was very sad to watch. But that being said, we can't pass ultimate judgment based on one video. We need the facts of a full and detailed investigation.

Commissioner Bratton: I think we all, all of us, unequivocally understand that this was a tragedy. The loss of a life is always a tragedy—a tragedy for all involved. Certainly, Mr. Garner, his family, community, for the members of the New York City Police Department. Nobody began the day with the expectation it would end as it did. And so it is a tragedy that needs to be addressed, it needs to be thoroughly investigated, reviewed, and questions answered, and that is what we're committed to doing.

Question: [inaudible] still looking at the video, it's still under investigation. But circling back to what this initial call was about—the sale of illegal cigarettes. Would such a crime—alleged crime—warrant such an aggressive physical response?

Mayor: I'll start and pass it to the Commissioner. Look, if police officers are asked to enforce the law because there's a community concern, we require that—we expect that of them. We wouldn't want a situation where community members call with a concern and the police did not respond. The question of how you respond is a different matter. And I have real confidence that there's going to be, again, a very full and thorough investigation. I also have confidence—and I think the way the Commissioner framed it is exactly right—that if we have to go back and retrain people in what's appropriate, we're ready to do that, to make sure that members of the police force of course do enforce the law regularly and consistently, but do it in the right way.

Commissioner Bratton: Part of our investigation will be—despite the video that appears to show all that occurred—to understand all the circumstances surrounding it. The video made it quite apparent that the officers made it known to the deceased that they were intending to arrest him. He made it quite known to them that he was not going to allow that arrest to occur. I do not expect my officers to walk away from that type of situation. So in terms of our investigation going forward, it will be, as the mayor indicated, to determine were all the actions appropriate that led to this unfortunate circumstance and tragedy. But let's be quite clear that one of the things the video appears to show is that the officers were in fact in the performance of their lawful duties. They were there for that purpose, and in the course of that event, that they met resistance. Now the investigation will determine—was the actions that they took appropriate to the resistance that they were experiencing. Thank you.

Mayor: Thank you everyone.

SOURCE: City of New York. "Transcript: Mayor de Blasio Holds Media Availability With Police Commissioner Bratton on the Death of Eric Garner." July 18, 2014. www1.nyc.gov/office-of-the-mayor/news/360-14/transcript-mayor-de-blasio-holds-media-availability-police-commissioner-bratton-the-death.

Missouri Governor Remarks on Situation in Ferguson

August 19, 2014

Ten days ago, a police officer shot and killed Michael Brown, in broad daylight. Since then, the world has watched a community become engulfed in grief, anger, fear and at times violence.

For a family mourning the loss of a son, it has been a profound personal tragedy. For Ferguson and our entire nation, it has ripped open old wounds that have festered for generations, and exposed difficult issues that communities across our country must still resolve.

But amid all the pain and distrust and anger, we've also seen tremendous acts of grace, courage, and kindness as the people of Ferguson try to maintain peace, while they call for justice for the family of Michael Brown. In Ferguson, people of all races and creeds are joining hands to pray for justice. Teenagers cooking meals for law enforcement officers. Community leaders demonstrating courage and heroism throughout the night in standing against armed and violent instigators. Volunteers coming out to pick up littered neighborhoods.

They are the faces of Ferguson. They are the faces of this region. They are the faces and soul of Missouri.

For them, for the family of Michael Brown, for all the parents who have had their sons taken from them much too soon, and for all the children dreaming of a brighter and better future, we now have a responsibility to come together and do everything we can to achieve justice for this family, peace for this community, and have the courage to address the problems that have divided us for too long. Real problems of poverty, education inequality, and race.

So how do we do that?

First, we must protect the people of Ferguson.

The officers of the Missouri Highway Patrol, St. Louis County, St. Louis City, and other jurisdictions are united in working valiantly to protect the public, while at the same time preserving citizens' rights to express their anger peacefully.

As we've seen over the past week, it is not an easy balance to strike. And it becomes much more difficult in the dark of night, when organized and increasingly violent instigators take to the streets intent on creating chaos and lawlessness.

But we will not be defeated by bricks and guns and Molotov cocktails. With the help of peaceful demonstrators, pastors and community leaders, Captain Johnson and law enforcement will not give up trying to ensure that those with peace in their hearts are not drowned out by those with senseless violence in their hands.

Second, a vigorous prosecution must now be pursued.

The democratically elected St. Louis County prosecutor and the Attorney General of the United States, each have a job to do. Their obligation to achieve justice in the shooting death of Michael Brown must be carried out thoroughly, promptly, and correctly; and I call upon them to meet those expectations.

Finally, once we have achieved peace in Ferguson and justice for the family of Michael Brown, we must remain committed to rebuilding the trust that has been lost, mending what has been broken, and healing the wounds we have endured.

This is hard. Nothing about this is simple. We won't always get it right, but we're going to keep trying. Because Ferguson is a test, a test not just for the people of this community, but for all Americans. And it is a test we must not fail.

Last week I met with and prayed with the mother of Michael Brown. She has lost a son who she can never bring back. But what we can do is work together to ensure that Michael Brown's death is not remembered as the tragedy that sparked a cycle of violence and distrust, but rather marks the beginning of a process of healing and reconciliation.

So I ask that we continue to stand together as we work to achieve justice for Michael Brown, restore hope and peace to the streets of Ferguson, and march together toward a future of greater opportunity and understanding for all of us."

SOURCE: Office of the Governor of Missouri. "A message from Gov. Jay Nixon about the situation in Ferguson." August 19, 2014. https://governor.mo.gov/news/archive/message-gov-jay-nixon-about-situation-ferguson.

OTHER HISTORIC DOCUMENTS OF INTEREST

FROM PREVIOUS *HISTORIC DOCUMENTS*

President Obama Signs
LGBT Employment Protection
Executive Order

JULY 21, 2014

Making good on a promise from his 2008 campaign, on July 21, 2014, President Barack Obama signed an executive order extending workplace and hiring protections based on sexual orientation and gender identity. The president had been pushed by the lesbian, gay, bisexual, and transgender (LGBT) community for years to create a protected class for these individuals, arguing that they face hiring discrimination akin to that experienced by other minority groups. Congressional inaction on the issue forced the president to use his executive authority to enact such protections. The executive order was not as far-reaching as some had hoped because it only extends to employees of federal contractors and federal employees. Still, the presidential order provides new protections to approximately 28 million working Americans.

LGBT DISCRIMINATION

According to the Williams Institute, an LGBT think tank, there are an estimated seven million LGBT employees working in the private sector and approximately 1.2 million working in the public sector. A majority of those who work for state and local government are located in California and New York. Although anecdotal evidence abounds, research organizations have found it difficult to develop statistics to measure the level of discrimination LGBT individuals face during the hiring process and in the workplace.

A study conducted in 2011, the largest of its kind to look at discrimination against gay men, attempted to tackle this problem. The lead researcher, András Tilcsik of Harvard University, sent two fake résumés to 1,700 entry-level jobs in a variety of industries. Both résumés had similar qualifications; the only distinction between the two was that one indicated that the individual had participated in a gay organization while in college. This individual was called for an interview in 7.2 percent of the jobs, while the second résumé without the gay affiliation received a callback for 11.5 percent of open positions. The largest variance in callback rates were in Florida, Ohio, and Texas, which have been traditionally more conservative in their policies on same-sex issues.

Organizations that support LGBT rights have conducted studies of their communities to gain a baseline understanding of discrimination. For example, the National Center for Transgender Equality reports that 90 percent of respondents to a 2011 survey said that they had been harassed or mistreated on the job, or had to hide their transgender identity to avoid such treatment. In 2007, a similar survey conducted by the Williams Institute found discrimination rates among respondents anywhere between 15 percent and 57 percent.

LGBT Protections

In 2014, twenty-nine states did not have workplace protections based on sexual orientation and thirty-two did not have written protection based on gender identity. Private sector corporations have been most active in implementing their own workplace gender identity and sexual orientation protections. According to Human Rights Campaign (HRC) statistics cited by the president during his signing ceremony, more than 90 percent of Fortune 500 companies have a workplace policy that includes sexual orientation, while 61 percent include gender identity.

According to the HRC, the largest LGBT civil rights organization, public sentiment has been shifting toward support for laws that protect individuals from discrimination based on gender identity or sexual orientation. In June 2014, just one month before President Obama's executive order, a public opinion poll conducted by the HRC found that 63 percent of those surveyed supported the idea of federal legislation protecting LGBT workers from employment and workplace discrimination. Only 25 percent of those surveyed opposed such a law. Surprisingly, the HRC poll found higher than anticipated support from those groups that have traditionally been less likely to support LGBT rights. The poll found 58 percent support among regular church-goers, 55 percent support among Southerners, 52 percent support among men over age forty, and a 43 percent rate of support among Republicans.

Congressional Action

The first iteration of a workplace protection bill for LGBT individuals was introduced on May 14, 1974. The Equality Act was intended to change the Civil Rights Act of 1964 by adding "sexual orientation" as a protected class, thus prohibiting discrimination in hiring, employment, and access to public facilities. The sponsors failed to garner enough support to implement the modification.

Since 1994, every Congress except the 109th has introduced the Employment Non-Discrimination Act (ENDA). The legislation would prohibit any company with fifteen or more employees from discriminating in hiring and employment based on sexual orientation. The bill had its best chance at passing when Democrats controlled both houses of Congress from 2007 to 2010. On April 24, 2007, openly gay Rep. Barney Frank, D-Mass., introduced a version of ENDA that included protections for gender identity, but it failed to gain enough support during the committee process to pass to the full House. Facing strong criticism from LGBT activists, five months later Rep. Frank introduced a new version of ENDA that stripped out the protection for gender identity; he subsequently submitted a separate bill seeking such protection. Frank's ENDA passed the House on November 7, 2007, with a vote of 235–184. The Senate did not consider the legislation.

Frank introduced another version of ENDA, this time including both sexual orientation and gender identity protections, in June 2009; two months later, similar legislation was introduced in the Senate. Neither bill garnered enough support to pass before the end of the 111th Congress. The 112th Congress also failed to consider such legislation. A reintroduction of the bill in 2013 gained enough support to pass in the Senate, but the bill was not considered in the Republican-controlled House.

Executive Order 13672

On July 21, 2014, President Obama signed Executive Order 13672, which banned workplace discrimination against LGBT individuals employed by the federal government or federal contractors. "America's federal contracts should not subsidize discrimination against the American people," the president said during the signing ceremony. "It doesn't make much sense, but today in America millions of our fellow citizens wake up and go to work with the awareness that they could lose their job, not because of anything they do or fail to do but because of who they are—lesbian, gay, bisexual, transgender—and that's wrong. We're here to do what we can to make it right."

The executive order was divided into two parts. The first, which went into effect on April 8, 2015, targets federal contractors by making it illegal for them to harass or fire someone based on gender identity or sexual orientation. The second part of the law prohibits discrimination against transgender federal employees and was effective immediately. While some hoped to see greater protections for all employers, the order does cover a wide swath of the American workforce—approximately 28 million workers. HRC believes that fourteen million LGBT Americans will be protected under the new order. The five largest federal contractors already had similar protections in place internally.

The signing of the order was the culmination of a campaign promise made by the president in 2008, for which he has faced criticism for not acting sooner. Obama's executive order amended Executive Order 11246, first signed by President Lyndon Johnson in 1965, which protected those employed by federal contractors from bias because of race, color, religion, sex, or national origin. That original order was amended in 2002 by President George W. Bush to allow federal contractors with a religious affiliation to give priority hiring status to individuals of that religion. Obama also amended Executive Order 11478, which prohibits discrimination against federal civilian employees. Obama did not, as some had feared, insert an exemption into the order for religiously affiliated federal contractors.

The signing was celebrated across the LGBT community. "With this action, President Obama has cemented his legacy as a transformative leader," said HRC president Chad Griffin. He went on to call on the House of Representatives to pass ENDA: "A bipartisan coalition of Americans is standing behind LGBT equality. A bipartisan coalition of our elected leaders should be doing the same."

Ongoing Debate

On September 17, 2014, in an attempt to force a vote in the House on ENDA, openly gay Rep. Jared Polis, D-Colo., filed a discharge petition. On December 3, a majority of the Republican cosponsors of the bill asked Speaker of the House John Boehner, R-Ohio, to allow the legislation to be voted on as a piece of a separate, unrelated bill before the end of the 113th Congress; the House Rules Committee voted against allowing such a provision for ENDA within the defense authorization bill.

In February 2015, Kansas Republican governor Sam Brownback sparked controversy when he issued an executive order ending the prohibition on hiring and workplace discrimination against LGBT state employees. The protections were initially established by executive order by his Democratic predecessor, Kathleen Sebelius, in 2007. In repealing the prohibition, Brownback said his decision "ensures that state employees enjoy the same civil rights as all Kansans without creating additional 'protected classes' as the previous order did" and added that "the order also reaffirms our commitment to hiring, mentoring and recognizing veterans and individuals with disabilities." Brownback further stated his belief that adding protected classes was the job of the state legislature, not the executive. LGBT groups immediately expressed their disapproval. Thomas Witt, the executive director of Equality Kansas, called the legislation a declaration of "open season" on workplace harassment. He said, "If you work for the state and have felt comfortable being 'out' at work knowing you had protection from bigotry, that protection is gone."

—Heather Kerrigan

Following is the text of the executive order signed by President Barack Obama on July 21, 2014, and his remarks at the signing ceremony.

DOCUMENT *Executive Order 13672*

July 21, 2014

By the authority vested in me as President by the Constitution and the laws of the United States of America, including 40 U.S.C. 121, and in order to provide for a uniform policy for the Federal Government to prohibit discrimination and take further steps to promote economy and efficiency in Federal Government procurement by prohibiting discrimination based on sexual orientation and gender identity, it is hereby ordered as follows:

Section 1.   *Amending Executive Order 11478.* The first sentence of section 1 of Executive Order 11478 of August 8, 1969, as amended, is revised by substituting "sexual orientation, gender identity" for "sexual orientation".

Sec. 2.   *Amending Executive Order 11246.* Executive Order 11246 of September 24, 1965, as amended, is hereby further amended as follows:

    (a) The first sentence of numbered paragraph (1) of section 202 is revised by substituting "sex, sexual orientation, gender identity, or national origin" for "sex, or national origin".

    (b) The second sentence of numbered paragraph (1) of section 202 is revised by substituting "sex, sexual orientation, gender identity, or national origin" for "sex or national origin".

    (c) Numbered paragraph (2) of section 202 is revised by substituting "sex, sexual orientation, gender identity, or national origin" for "sex or national origin".

    (d) Paragraph (d) of section 203 is revised by substituting "sex, sexual orientation, gender identity, or national origin" for "sex or national origin".

Sec. 3.   *Regulations.* Within 90 days of the date of this order, the Secretary of Labor shall prepare regulations to implement the requirements of section 2 of this order.

Sec. 4.   *General Provisions.* (a) Nothing in this order shall be construed to impair or otherwise affect:

    (i) the authority granted by law to an agency or the head thereof; or

    (ii) the functions of the Director of the Office of Management and Budget relating to budgetary, administrative, or legislative proposals.

(b) This order is not intended to, and does not, create any right or benefit, substantive or procedural, enforceable at law or in equity by any party against the United States, its departments, agencies, or entities, its officers, employees, or agents, or any other person.

Sec. 5.   *Effective Date*. This order shall become effective immediately, and section 2 of this order shall apply to contracts entered into on or after the effective date of the rules promulgated by the Department of Labor under section 3 of this order.

BARACK OBAMA
The White House,
July 21, 2014.

SOURCE: Executive Office of the President. "Executive Order 13672—Further Amendments to Executive Order 11478, Equal Employment Opportunity in the Federal Government, and Executive Order 11246, Equal Employment Opportunity." July 21, 2014. *Compilation of Presidential Documents* 2014, no. 00553 (July 21, 2014). www.gpo.gov/fdsys/pkg/DCPD-201400553/pdf/DCPD-201400553.pdf.

Obama Remarks on Signing LGBT Protections

July 21, 2014

The President. Thank you. All right, everybody, have a seat, have a seat. Well welcome to the White House, everybody. I know I'm a little late. [Laughter] But that's okay because we've got some big business to do here.

Many of you have worked for a long time to see this day coming. You organized, you spoke up, you signed petitions, you sent letters. I know because I got a lot of them. *[Laughter]* And now, thanks to your passionate advocacy and the irrefutable rightness of your cause, our Government—Government of the people, by the people, and for the people—will become just a little bit fairer.

Audience member. Amen.

The President. It is—*[applause]*—doesn't make much sense, but today in America, millions of our fellow citizens wake up and go to work with the awareness that they could lose their job, not because of anything they do or fail to do, but because of who they are: lesbian, gay, bisexual, transgender. And that's wrong. We're here to do what we can to make it right, to bend that arc of justice just a little bit in a better direction.

In a few moments, I will sign an Executive order that does two things. First, the Federal Government already prohibits employment discrimination on the basis of sexual orientation. Once I sign this order, the same will be explicitly true for gender identity.

And second, we're going to prohibit all companies that receive a contract from the Federal Government from discriminating against their LGBT employees. America's Federal contracts should not subsidize discrimination against the American people.

Now, this Executive order is part of a long, bipartisan tradition. President Roosevelt signed an order prohibiting racial discrimination in the national defense industry.

President Eisenhower strengthened it. President Johnson expanded it. Today I'm going to expand it again.

Currently, 18 States have already banned workplace discrimination based on sexual orientation and gender identity. And over 200 cities and localities have done the same. Governor Terry McAuliffe is here; his first act as Governor was to prohibit discrimination against LGBT employees of the Commonwealth of Virginia. Where did Terry go? Right back here.

I've appointed a record number of lesbian, gay, bisexual, and transgender public servants to positions across my administration. They are Ambassadors and Federal judges, special assistants, senior advisers from the Pentagon to the Labor Department. Every day, their talent is put to work on behalf of the American people.

Equality in the workplace is not only the right thing to do, it turns out to be good business. That's why a majority of Fortune 500 companies already have nondiscrimination policies in place. It is not just about doing the right thing, it's also about attracting and retrain—retaining the best talent. And there are several business leaders who are here today who will attest to that.

And yet, despite all that, in too many States and in too many workplaces, simply being gay, lesbian, bisexual, or transgender can still be a fireable offense. There are people here today who've lost their jobs for that reason. This is not speculative, this is not a matter of political correctness; people lose their jobs as a consequence of this. Their livelihoods are threatened; their families are threatened. In fact, more States now allow same-sex marriage than prohibit discrimination against LGBT workers. So I firmly believe that it's time to address this injustice for every American.

Now, Congress has spent 40 years—four decades—considering legislation that would help solve the problem. That's a long time. [Laughter] And yet they still haven't gotten it done. Senators Terry [Tammy]* Baldwin and Jeff Merkley are here. They have been champions of this issue for a long, long time. We are very proud of them. I know they will not stop fighting until fair treatment for all workers is the Federal law of the land. And we want to thank them for that. *[Applause]*

But I'm going to do what I can, with the authority I have, to act. The rest of you, of course, need to keep putting pressure on Congress to pass Federal legislation that resolves this problem once and for all.

Audience member. Amen!

The President. Amen. Amen! Got the "amen" corner here. [Laughter]

[At this point, the President sang.]

The President. "Well"—*[laughter]*. You don't want to get me preaching, now. *[Laughter]*

For more than two centuries, we have strived, often at great cost, to form a more perfect Union,—to make sure that we the people applies to all the people. Many of us are only here because others fought to secure rights and opportunities for us. And we've got a responsibility to do the same for future generations. We've got an obligation to make sure that the country we love remains a place where no matter who you are or what you look like or where you come from or how you started out or what your last name is or who you love—no matter what, you can make it in this country.

That's the story of America. That's the story of this movement. I want to thank all of you for doing your part. We've got a long way to go, but I hope as everybody looks around this room you are reminded of the extraordinary progress that we have made not just in our lifetimes, but in the last 5 years. In the last 2 years. In the last 1 year. We're on the right side of history.

I'm going to sign this Executive order. Thank you, everybody.

[The President signed the Executive order.]

The President. We made it. Thank you.

* White House correction.

SOURCE: Executive Office of the President. "Remarks on Signing an Executive Order on Lesbian, Gay, Bisexual, and Transgender Employment Discrimination." July 21, 2014. *Compilation of Presidential Documents* 2014, no. 00552 (July 21, 2014). www.gpo.gov/fdsys/pkg/DCPD-201400552/pdf/DCPD-201400552.pdf.

OTHER HISTORIC DOCUMENTS OF INTEREST

FROM PREVIOUS *HISTORIC DOCUMENTS*

European Court of Human Rights Rules on Poland's Involvement With CIA Secret Prisons

JULY 24, 2014

The Strasbourg-based European Court of Human Rights on July 27, 2014, delivered a rebuke both to the Polish government and the Central Intelligence Agency (CIA) for their roles in a counter-terrorism program hatched in response to the September 11, 2001, attacks on the United States. The court found that Poland had violated the 1950 European Convention on Human Rights by allowing the CIA to operate a secret prison in northeastern Poland from 2002 to 2003 where the CIA detained and interrogated men it suspected of being al Qaeda operatives plotting terrorist attacks against the United States. The court ordered the Polish government to pay compensation to the two plaintiffs for having facilitated the CIA's activities. It could not pronounce a verdict against the CIA because the agency fell outside its purview; the United States is not a party to the convention. The CIA program, which its critics say made torture an instrument of the U.S. government, had received the green light from President George W. Bush in 2001. It was abolished by his successor, Barack Obama, as soon as he took office in January 2009.

Spotlight on CIA Torture Allegations

The European Court of Human Rights, established in 1959, is the judicial arm of the Council of Europe, an international organization founded in 1949 to promote human rights and democracy that currently has forty-seven member states. The Council membership is notably broader than the twenty-eight-country European Union, stretching across the Eurasian continent, from Portugal to Russia, from Iceland to Turkey. The Council's fundamental legal text is the European Convention on Human Rights, which enumerates the human rights and fundamental freedoms the member countries are obliged to uphold. If an individual believes that a member country has breached its obligations under the convention, he or she can petition the court directly to obtain a remedy and may receive financial compensation if the court finds in his or her favor.

The judgment grouped together cases filed by two former residents of Saudi Arabia: Abd Al Rahim Hussayn Muhammad Al Nashiri, of Yemeni origin, and Zayn Al-Abidin Muhammad Husayn, of Palestinian background. Both plaintiffs are currently detained by the United States at its custom-built terrorist suspect prison at the U.S. naval station at Guantánamo Bay in Cuba. In the immediate aftermath of the 9/11 attacks perpetrated by the Islamist militant group al Qaeda, which killed nearly three thousand people in the United States, President Bush faced enormous pressure to capture those responsible. He agreed to empower the CIA to detain and interrogate terrorist suspects, although the precise details of what he agreed to continue to be a subject of debate. With its enhanced powers, the CIA devised a new program that involved capturing terrorist suspects overseas and moving them between countries to be detained and interrogated at secret sites. The sites were deliberately located outside the United States to deprive the detainees of basic legal protections that the U.S. constitution would have afforded them, such as the right to challenge their detention before a court of law. The CIA developed rigorous methods of questioning, which it called "enhanced interrogation techniques," that included mock executions, sleep deprivation, and waterboarding—a procedure involving water being continuously poured over a detainee's face to simulate a sensation of drowning.

The CIA negotiated agreements with several foreign governments that allowed the CIA to hold and interrogate detainees at undisclosed locations. Poland was one of those countries. When the Cold War ended in 1989, Poland had chosen to distance itself from Russia and become an ally of the United States. At the time the CIA program was being set up, the Polish government was on the verge of attaining a major foreign policy goal—membership in the North Atlantic Treaty Organization (NATO)—and was consequently anxious to keep on good terms with the United States. It thus agreed to help the CIA in implementing the new program by providing a host venue: a remote villa in a military zone in Stare Kiejkuty, a village situated in the lake district of northeastern Poland. The United States paid the Polish government millions of dollars for use of the site and equipped it with security cameras. The CIA meanwhile made similar arrangements with other foreign governments, including Lithuania, Morocco, Romania, Thailand, and Uzbekistan, to transfer, host, or interrogate detainees. The process by which the detainees were moved between countries was known as "extraordinary rendition" to differentiate it from a more established process called "rendition" by which individuals are transferred via a judicial process such as an extradition. With the CIA program, the courts were bypassed.

Husayn was the first of the two men to be apprehended, seized in Pakistan in March 2002 and sent to a CIA secret prison in Thailand before being transferred to the Polish site on December 5, 2002, and kept there until September 22, 2003, when he was moved to Guantánamo Bay. Al Nashiri was taken into U.S. custody in October 2002 in Dubai in the United Arab Emirates. He was then moved to a secret CIA facility in Afghanistan before being sent to the Polish site on December 5, 2002, and kept there until June 6, 2003. The United States suspected Al Nashiri of involvement in the October 2000 bombing of the USS *Cole* warship in the harbor of Aden in Yemen and of helping plan the 9/11 attacks. Both men were labeled "high value detainees," a term coined by the Bush administration to describe individuals whom they believed were prominent members of al Qaeda.

The seven judges assigned to the case were from Albania, Bulgaria, Cyprus, Finland, Latvia, Malta, and Poland. Determining precisely what treatment the men were subjected to while in Poland was difficult because the plaintiffs were imprisoned in Guantánamo and the judges therefore had limited contact with them, and neither the Polish nor the U.S. governments provided much, if any, cooperation. By this time, the CIA program had been discontinued and had become a major embarrassment for all governments associated with it. The program had come to the wider public's attention in late 2005 as a result of an investigative report published by *The Washington Post* newspaper. Initially, the Polish government denied it had hosted a secret prison but as the evidence against it mounted, the authorities switched their strategy from outright denial to evasiveness. Parliamentary inquiries from two pan-European legislatures, the European Parliament (an arm of the EU) and the Council of Europe's Parliamentary Assembly, shed further light on the collaboration between governments in the CIA program. However, these parliamentary investigators often struggled to substantiate specifics in the face of the persistent stonewalling of their inquiries by national governments.

Confronted with a similarly uncooperative attitude from the Polish government, the court had to rely to a large extent on publicly available sources. The judges ultimately came to the conclusion that the allegations made by the two plaintiffs were "sufficiently convincing" to warrant a judgment against Poland. In particular, the court said that Poland had breached Article 38 of the convention by refusing to supply evidence that the court had requested. In addition, the Polish government facilitated the program by allowing the CIA to use Polish airspace and airports to move detainees and assisting the CIA in transporting detainees over land. The court outlined the various articles of the convention that it considered were violated. They included the ban on torture, the right of freedom and security, respect for family and private life, the right to an effective redress, and the right of due process. The court ruled that the Polish authorities should have known that giving the CIA permission to detain and interrogate the plaintiffs would have put them at serious risk of being subject to treatments that violated their rights under the convention. The Polish government was ordered to pay $114,000 to each of the plaintiffs in compensation for the violations and $34,000 to cover the legal expenses of Husayn. Nashiri's legal team did not request such expenses.

Controversial Program Casts Long Shadow

In October 2014, the Polish government announced that it was appealing the ruling. While the current Polish administration seems intent on continuing to fight, the former president of Poland who was head of state at the time that the secret prison was in use has since publicly acknowledged his role in assisting the CIA with it. At a press conference on December 10, 2014, Aleksander Kwasniewski, president from 1995 to 2005, said, "The US asked the Polish side to find a quiet place where it could carry out activities to gain information from people who had declared themselves willing to cooperate." He insisted, however, that there was "no agreement on torture." He added that "the Americans conducted their activities in such secrecy, that it raised our concerns. The Polish authorities acted to end these activities and they were stopped under pressure from Poland." He claimed that the United States had drafted a memorandum in which it pledged to treat the detainees as prisoners of war but had not signed the memo due to lack of time. And Kwansniewski said that he had mentioned the secret prison during a 2003 meeting with President Bush. In fact, responding to growing criticism the Bush administration in September 2006 decided to put the whole program on ice, transferring the fourteen detainees still held by the CIA into military custody by emptying the CIA facilities and moving them to Guantánamo.

The former Polish president's revelations came as the U.S. Senate published the results of a five-year investigation into the CIA program. That 528-page report, which had been spearheaded by Sen. Dianne Feinstein, D-Calif., concluded that the CIA had held 119 prisoners for the duration of the program, including at least twenty-six cases of mistaken identities due to bad intelligence. Enhanced interrogation techniques used by the CIA included waterboarding and "rectal feeding," where detainees had pureed foods injected to their rectum involuntarily. The report did not take a position regarding whether or not these practices constituted torture. However, it did conclude that the techniques had not produced valuable intelligence as former senior officials in the Bush administration, including the current CIA director, John Brennan, claimed.

The court ruling is far from being the final say on the matter. In the short-term, the Polish government's appeal against the judgment will proceed. More broadly, parliaments, courts, the media, and historians will continue to try to learn more about the program, not only the Polish chapter but also the wider story in which numerous African, Asian, and European governments are alleged to have been involved in various ways. The future of the plaintiffs themselves remains in suspense. Despite having been detained at Guantánamo for more than a decade, neither has been convicted either by a military or civilian court yet of a specific crime. There is similar uncertainty about the future of the CIA officials involved. President Obama has abolished the program, strongly condemned it, and said he personally considered interrogation techniques like waterboarding to be torture. However, the U.S. Department of Justice in 2012 ruled out the possibility of pursuing criminal charges against the CIA employees in question.

—Brian Beary

Following are excerpts from the European Court of Human Rights ruling issued on July 24, 2014, regarding Poland's hosting of secret CIA torture facilities.

EU Court Rules on Polish Involvement in CIA Torture

DOCUMENT

July 24, 2014

[The table of contents, summary of the proceedings, evidence before the court, and background on the case and those involved, have been omitted.]

In the case of Al Nashiri v. Poland,

The European Court of Human Rights (Fourth Section), sitting as a Chamber composed of:

Ineta Ziemele, *President,*

Päivi Hirvelä,

George Nicolaou,

Ledi Bianku,

Zdravka Kalaydjieva,

Vincent A. De Gaetano,

Krzysztof Wojtyczek, *judges,*

and Françoise Elens-Passos, *Section Registrar,*

Having deliberated in private on 2 and 3 December 2013 and 1, 2 and 8 July 2014, Delivers the following judgment, which was adopted on the last of these dates . . . .

B. The so-called "High-Value Detainees Programme"

47. After 11 September 2001 the US Government began operating a special interrogation and detention programme designed for suspected terrorists. On 17 September 2001 President Bush signed a classified Presidential Finding granting the Central Intelligence Agency ("the CIA") extended competences relating to its covert actions, in particular

authority to detain terrorist suspects and to set up secret detention facilities outside the United States, in cooperation with the governments of the countries concerned.

48. On an unspecified later date the CIA established a programme in the Counterterrorist Center to detain and interrogate terrorists at sites abroad. In further documents the American authorities referred to it as "the CTC program" (see also paragraph 51 below) but, subsequently, it was also called "the High-Value Detainees Program" ("the HVD Programme") or the Rendition Detention Interrogation Program ("the RDI Programme"). In the Council of Europe's documents it is also described as "the CIA secret detention programme" or "the extraordinary rendition programme" (see also paragraphs 244-261 below). For the purposes of the present case, it is referred to as "the HVD Programme".

1. The establishment of the HVD Programme

49. On 24 August 2009 the American authorities released a report prepared by John Helgerson, the CIA Inspector General, in 2004 ("the 2004 CIA Report"). The document, dated 7 May 2004 and entitled "Special Review Counterterrorism Detention and Interrogation Activities September 2001-October 2003", with appendices A-F, had previously been classified as "top secret". It was considerably redacted; overall, more than one-third of the 109-page document was blackened out.

50. The report, which covers the period from September 2001 to mid-October 2003, begins with a statement that in November 2002 the CIA Deputy Director for Operations ("the DDO") informed the Office of Inspector General ("OIG") that the Agency had established a programme in the Counterterrorist Centre ("CTC") to detain and interrogate terrorists at sites abroad . . . .

52. As further explained in the 2004 CIA Report, "terrorist targets" and detainees referred to therein were generally categorised as "high value" or "medium value". This distinction was based on the quality of intelligence that they were believed likely to be able to provide about current terrorist threats against the United States. "Medium-Value Detainees" were individuals believed to have lesser direct knowledge of terrorist threats but to have information of intelligence value. "High-Value Detainees" (also called "HVD") were given the highest priority for capture, detention and interrogation. In some CIA documents they are also referred to as "High-Value Targets" ("HVT").

The applicant fell into this category.

2. Enhanced Interrogation Techniques

53. According to the 2004 CIA Report, in August 2002 the US Department of Justice had provided the CIA with a legal opinion determining that 10 specific "Enhanced Interrogation Techniques" ("EITs"), as applied to suspected terrorists, would not violate the prohibition of torture. This document provided "the foundation for the policy and administrative decisions that guided the CTC Program".

54. The EITs are described in paragraph 36 of the 2004 CIA Report as follows:

"[1.]   The attention grasp consists of grasping the detainee with both hands, with one hand on each side of the collar opening, in a controlled and quick motion. In the same motion as the grasp, the detainee is drawn toward the interrogator.

 [2.]   During the walling technique, the detainee is pulled forward and then quickly and firmly pushed into a flexible false wall so that his shoulder blades hit the wall. His head and neck are supported with a rolled towel to prevent whiplash.

[3.] The facial hold is used to hold the detainee's head immobile. The interrogator places an open palm on either side of the detainee's face and the interrogator's fingertips are kept well away from the detainee's eyes.

[4.] With the facial or insult slap, the fingers are slightly spread apart. The interrogator's hand makes contact with the area between the tip of the detainee's chin and the bottom of the corresponding earlobe.

[5.] In cramped confinement, the detainee is placed in a confined space, typically a small or large box, which is usually dark. Confinement in the smaller space lasts no more than two hours and in the larger space it can last up to 18 hours.

[6.] Insects placed in a confinement box involve placing a harmless insect in the box with the detainee.

[7.] During wall standing, the detainee may stand about 4 to 5 feet from a wall with his feet spread approximately to his shoulder width. His arms are stretched out in front of him and his fingers rest on the wall to support all of his body weight. The detainee is not allowed to reposition his hands or feet.

[8.] The application of stress positions may include having the detainee sit on file floor with his legs extended straight out in front of him with his anus raised above his head or kneeling on the floor while leaning back at a 45 degree angle.

[9.] Sleep deprivation will not exceed 11 days at a time.

[10.] The application of the waterboard technique involves binding the detainee to a bench with his feet elevated above his head. The detainee's head is immobilized and an interrogator places a cloth over the detainee's mouth and nose while pouring water onto the cloth in a controlled manner. Airflow is restricted for 20 to 40 seconds and the technique produces the sensation of drowning and suffocation."

[Additional information on CIA detention procedures, reviews of the CIA program by U.S. authorities, information on the defendant, background on Polish criminal code, international laws on torture, media coverage, the court's assessment of the case, and international inquiries on the secret CIA sites have been omitted.]

4. Assessment of the facts and evidence relevant for Poland's alleged knowledge of and complicity in the CIA HVD Programme. . . .

(c) The alleged existence of a "special" bilateral agreement with the CIA and authorisation of Poland's role in the CIA operations by Polish officials

423. Several sources of evidence before the Court have suggested the existence of a special bilateral agreement between Poland and the USA on the setting up and running of a secret prison in Poland.

424. The 2007 Marty Report, based on evidence from confidential sources, states that the CIA brokered an "operating agreement" with Poland to hold its High-Value Detainees in a secret detention facility and that Poland agreed to "provide the premises in which [that facility was] established, the highest degrees of physical security and secrecy, and steadfast guarantees of non-interference" (see paragraphs 254-255 above).

In the context of the authorisation of Poland's role in the CIA rendition operations, the 2007 Report mentioned a number of names of the Polish high-ranking officials, stating that they had known and authorised the country's role "in the CIA operation of secret detention facilities for High-Value Detainees on Polish territory" and that they "could therefore be held accountable for these activities" (see paragraph 257, see also paragraph 240 above).

Senator Marty confirmed those statements before the Court and added that the operation had been organised within the framework of NATO. It had been decided that the CIA would be in sole charge of the operation and, if requested, the member countries would provide cooperation. As regards the specific names of Polish officials that had been given in the 2007 Marty Report, he explained that they had been indicated "because the sources that [had] provided us with these names [had been] of such value, they [had been] so authoritative and there [had been] so much concurring evidence of the involvement of those persons" (see paragraph 321 above).

425. Mr J.G.S., when heard by the Court, said that whilst in the course of the Marty Inquiry they had not seen the classified documents in question, they had been made aware of the existence of authorising agreements, which granted extraordinary protections and permissions to the CIA in its execution of the rendition operations (see paragraph 329 above).

426. Senator Pinior, both in his affidavit and oral testimony before the Court, stated that he had been informed by an authoritative confidential source of a document—a draft prepared by the Polish intelligence—drawn up under the auspices of Mr Miller's Government for the purpose of regulating the operation of the CIA prison in Poland. According to him, that document, which was currently in the Polish prosecution authority's possession, contained precise regulations concerning the functioning of the prison and, among other things, a proposed protocol for action in the event of a prisoner's death. The word "detainees" was used in the text. The draft had not been signed on behalf of the US (see paragraphs 303 and 334 above).

427. The 2007 EP Resolution "note[d] with concern" that the Polish authorities' official reply of 10 March 2006 to the Secretary General of the Council of Europe, "indicate[d] the existence of secret cooperation agreements initialled by the two countries' secret services themselves, which exclude[d] the activities of foreign secret services from the jurisdiction of the Polish judicial bodies" (see paragraph 275 above).

428. The Court does not find it necessary for its examination of the present case to establish whether such agreement or agreements existed and if so, in what format and what was specifically provided therein.

It considers that it is inconceivable that the rendition aircraft crossed Polish airspace, landed in and departed from a Polish airport and that the CIA occupied the premises in Stare Kiejkuty without some kind of pre-existing arrangement enabling the CIA operation in Poland to be first prepared and then executed.

(d) Poland's lack of cooperation with the international inquiry bodies

429. The Court considers that the respondent State's lack of cooperation in the course of the international inquiries into the CIA rendition operations in Europe undertaken in 2005-2007 is an element that is relevant for its assessment of Poland's alleged knowledge of, and complicity in, the CIA rendition operations.

430. To begin with, in their response dated 10 March 2006 to the Secretary General of the Council of Europe's questions in the procedure launched under Article 52 of the Convention, the authorities "fully denied" the allegations of "the alleged existence in Poland of secret detention centres and related over-flights (see paragraph 242 above; the relevant letter is also mentioned above in paragraph 427 above). In that regard, they relied

on the findings of "the Polish Government's internal inquiry". It is not clear what kind of "internal inquiry" was carried out and whether the authorities in fact meant the Parliamentary inquiry conducted in November-December 2005 (see paragraph 128 above) but, be that as it may, they could not have been unaware of the CIA operations in the country in 2002-2003 (see paragraphs 423-428 above).

431. A similar obstructive attitude was displayed during the Marty Inquiry. In the 2006 Marty Report it was noted that "the Polish authorities ha[d] been unable, despite repeated requests, to provide [the rapporteur] with information from their own national aviation records to confirm any CIA-connected flights into Poland" (see paragraph 248 above). The 2007 Marty Report noted that "in over eighteen months of correspondence, Poland ha[d] failed to furnish [the] inquiry with any data from its own records confirming CIA-connected flights into its airspace or airports" (see paragraph 259 above).

Senator Marty, at the fact-finding hearing, added that "Poland [had been] no exception" and that practically all governments that [had] had links with the secret detention centres or with 'extraordinary rendition' not only [had] not cooperate[d] but [had done] everything that they could in order to stifle the truth, to create obstacles in the search for the truth" (see paragraph 320 above).

432. The conduct adopted by the authorities in respect to the Fava Inquiry was no different. The Fava Report explicitly stated that the Polish authorities cooperation with the TDIP delegation had been "regrettably poor", that the delegation had not been able to meet any representatives of Parliament and that the Government had been "reluctant to offer full cooperation . . . and receive [the] delegation at an appropriate political level". It was also noted that there had been confusion about flight registers of CIA planes transiting through Poland and contradictory statements about the existence of flight logs (see paragraph 270 above). The same observations were made in the 2007 EP Resolution (see paragraph 275 above).

In his testimony before the Court, Mr Fava stated that the Polish Government had "cooperated very little" with the TDIP and that almost all representatives of the Government whom they had asked for a meeting had declined the TDIP's request. He also confirmed that during his visit to Poland with the TDIP delegation he had "definitely" had the impression that there had been attempts on the authorities' part to conceal information (see paragraph 308 above).

433. Having regard to the above facts, the Court finds that in the course of the relevant international inquiries the Polish authorities displayed conduct that can be characterised as denial, lack of cooperation with the inquiry bodies and marked reluctance to disclose information of the CIA rendition activities in Poland.

(e) Informal transatlantic meeting

434. Mr Fava, in his oral testimony described in detail a document—the records or "the debriefing" of the informal transatlantic meeting of the European Union and North Atlantic Treaty Organisation foreign ministers with the US Secretary of State Condoleezza Rice, which had taken place on 7 December 2005. The meeting was convened in connection with recent international media reports concerning the CIA secret detentions and rendition, naming European countries that had allegedly had CIA black sites on their territory. The debriefing, obtained by the TDIP from a credible confidential source in the offices of the European Union, confirmed that the member States had had knowledge of the CIA rendition programme and there had been an "animated discussion" on the practices applied by the CIA. While Mr Fava could not recall whether there had been any

intervention by the Polish Government at that meeting, he said that it had appeared from Ms Rice's statement "we all know about these techniques" that there had been an attempt on the USA's part to share "the weight of accusations" (see paragraph 306 above).

(f) Relations of cooperation between the Polish intelligence and the CIA

435. The Court further notes that Mr Fava also referred to the meeting held in the context of the Fava Inquiry with the former Polish head of the security service who, "although . . . with great diplomacy", had confirmed that the CIA officials often landed in Szymany and that the Polish intelligence and the CIA had had "frequent relations of cooperation . . . consisting in sharing certain practices and objectives" (see paragraphs 269 and 310 above).

436. Former President of Poland, Mr Kwaśniewski, in his press interview given on 30 April 2012, also referred to the "intelligence cooperation" with the CIA and stated that "the decision to cooperate with the CIA carried the risk that the Americans would use inadmissible methods" (see paragraph 240 above).

(g) Circumstances surrounding detainees transfer and reception at the black site

437. Having regard to the procedure for High-Value Detainees' transfers under which, as established above, a detainee such as the applicant was blindfolded, wore black goggles and was shackled by his hands and feet for the duration of his transfer (see paragraphs 64, 282 and 409 above), the Court considers that those of the Polish authorities who received the CIA personnel on the Szymany airport runway, put them on the vans and drove them to the black site could not be unaware that the persons brought there with them were the CIA prisoners.

In particular, the Court finds it inconceivable they would not have seen or, as described by Mr J.G.S., "witnessed . . . the unloading of bound and shackled detainees from aircraft" (see paragraph 330 above).

(h) Other elements

438. There are also other elements that the Court considers relevant for its assessment of Poland's knowledge of the nature and purposes of the CIA activities on its territory at the material time.

As recounted by Senator Pinior in his affidavit and subsequently confirmed in his oral testimony given to the Court, "in the period when the CIA prisoners were detained in Stare Kiejkuty" the authorities of the military base ordered from a Polish company a metal cage of the size fitting a grown man with the option of adding a portable chemical toilet (see paragraphs 303 and 335 above). No explanations have been offered by the respondent Government as to what kind of purposes that cage was to serve.

Furthermore, there were, as pointed out by one of the experts (see paragraph 330 above), other aspects of the CIA activity in Poland that were extraordinary from the perspective of the normal operation of an airport like Szymany.

For instance, the landing of the Boeing 737 (N313P on which Mr Abu Zubaydah was transferred from Poland; see *Husayn (Abu Zubaydah)*, cited above, §§ 408, 419 and 440) on 22 September 2003 at Szymany took place despite the fact that the airport did not have the necessary technical conditions for receiving such a large aircraft, in particular the facilities to refuel it, and the fact that the airport fire brigade was not adequately equipped for that purpose (see paragraphs 295 and 318 above). In the view of Ms M.P., the airport manager at the relevant time, "there must have been some very pressing reasons" for allowing that landing (see paragraph 296 above).

On another occasion in the winter, notwithstanding the severe weather conditions and the fact that snow had not been cleared at the airport for six weeks, the airport management were not in a position to refuse the CIA aircraft's landing and had to clear the runway because "if the aircraft concerned did not land, 'heads w[ould] roll'" (see paragraph 300 above).

For the airport civilian staff, the landing of the CIA aircraft was a "major event". Despite the fact that they were excluded from the handling of the aircraft and were taken to the airport terminal building during the CIA landings and departures (see paragraph 418 above), they perceived those events as "spies" coming or a "changeover of intelligence staff" (see paragraph 297 above).

(i) **Public knowledge of treatment to which captured terrorist-suspects were subjected in US custody**

439. Lastly, the Court attaches importance to the fact that already between January 2002 and August 2003 ill-treatment and abuse to which captured terrorist suspects were subjected in US custody at different places, including Guantánamo Bay or Bagram base in Afghanistan was largely in the public domain through numerous statements or reports of international organisations (see paragraphs 214-228 and 389–390 above).

At the material time that topic was also present in the international and Polish media, which paid considerable attention to the situation of Al'Qaeda prisoners in US custody (see paragraphs 230–239 above).

5. Court's conclusions as to Poland's alleged knowledge of and complicity in the CIA HVD Programme

440. The Court has taken due note of the fact that knowledge of the CIA rendition and secret detention operations and the scale of abuse to which High-Value Detainees were subjected in CIA custody evolved over time (see paragraphs 47-71, 78-81, 214-239, 241-261, 266-275 and 281-286 above). In particular, the CIA's various secret or top secret documents, including the 2004 CIA Report, the CIA Background Paper and the 2009 DOJ Report—which, in the present case and in *Husayn (Abu Zubaydah)*, are among important items of documentary evidence relevant for the establishment of the facts relating to both applicants' rendition, secret detention and treatment by the US authorities—were disclosed to the public, in a heavily redacted form, as late as 2009-2010 (see paragraphs 49-50, 57 and 62 above). The 2007 ICRC Report, including the applicant's account of the treatment and material conditions of detention to which he was subjected under the HVD Programme, was leaked into the public domain in 2009 (see paragraph 277 above). The reports following the Marty Inquiry and the Fava Inquiry emerged earlier, in 2006-2007 (see paragraphs 246-261 and 266-272), but this was between three and a half and five years after the events complained of. As stated by Senator Marty, even "the picture provided by the 2007 [Marty] Report is still very much a partial one", having regard to the subsequent developments, such as the publication of the CIA materials and the availability of statements from detainees (see paragraph 323 above).

As already stated above (see paragraphs 42 and 397-400 above), the Court has relied extensively on those sources of evidence in its retrospective reconstruction and establishment of the facts concerning the applicant's transfers to and from Poland and his secret detention and ill-treatment by the CIA in Poland. However, the Polish State's knowledge of and complicity in the HVD Programme must be established with reference to the elements that it knew or ought to have known at or closely around the relevant time, that is, between December 2002 and June 2003 in respect of the applicant and between December 2002 and September 2003 in respect of Mr Abu Zubaydah.

441. In that regard, the Court has taken into account the various attendant circumstances referred to above (see paragraphs 418-439 above). In the Court's view, those elements taken as a whole demonstrate that at that time the Polish authorities knew that the CIA used its airport in Szymany and the Stare Kiejkuty military base for the purposes of detaining secretly terrorist suspects captured within the "war on terror" operation by the US authorities. It is inconceivable that the rendition aircraft could have crossed Polish airspace, landed in and departed from a Polish airport, or that the CIA occupied the premises in Stare Kiejkuty and transported detainees there, without the Polish State being informed of and involved in the preparation and execution of the HVD Programme on its territory. It is also inconceivable that activities of that character and scale, possibly vital for the country's military and political interests, could have been undertaken on Polish territory without Poland's knowledge and without the necessary authorisation being given at the appropriate level of the State authorities.

The Court would again refer to the testimony given by the experts who, in the course of their inquiries, had the benefit of contact with various, including confidential, sources. They all stated, in unambiguous terms, that at the relevant time Poland had had, or should have had, knowledge of the CIA rendition operations. Poland had ensured the security of the area and had collaborated in concealing the rendition flights. The Polish officials' liaison units must have been aware of the preparation or execution of particular operations and their timing. They had known that the CIA interrogations had contributed intelligence to the United States' war on terror (see paragraphs 307, 321-323, 326 and 330-331 above).

This did not mean, in the experts' view, that the Polish authorities had known the details of what went on inside the black site, since the interrogations had been the exclusive responsibility of the CIA, or that they had witnessed treatment to which High-Value Detainees had been subjected in Poland (see paragraphs 322-323 and 330-331 above). The Court, being confronted with no evidence to the contrary, accepts the experts' above-mentioned assessment.

Notwithstanding the foregoing proviso as to the lack of direct knowledge of the treatment to which the applicant was subjected in Poland, as noted above, already between January 2002 and August 2003 numerous public sources were consistently reporting ill-treatment and abuse to which captured terrorist suspects were subjected in US custody in different places. Moreover, in the 2003 PACE Resolution adopted in June 2003—of which Poland, as any other Contracting State was aware—the Parliamentary Assembly of the Council of Europe was "deeply concerned at the conditions of detention" of captured "unlawful combatants" held in the custody of the US authorities. All these sources reported practices resorted to or tolerated by the US authorities that were manifestly contrary to the principles of the Convention (see paragraphs 214-224, 229-239 and 389-390 above). Consequently, there were good reasons to believe that a person in US custody under the HVD Programme could be exposed to a serious risk of treatment contrary to those principles (see also *El-Masri*, cited above, § 218).

442. Taking into consideration all the material in its possession (see paragraphs 418-439 above), the Court finds that there is abundant and coherent circumstantial evidence, which leads inevitably to the following conclusions:

(a) that Poland knew of the nature and purposes of the CIA's activities on its territory at the material time and that, by enabling the CIA to use its airspace and the airport, by its complicity in disguising the movements of rendition aircraft and by its provision of logistics and services, including the special security arrangements, the special procedure for landings, the transportation of the CIA teams with detainees on land, and the securing of the Stare Kiejkuty base for the CIA's secret detention, Poland cooperated in the preparation and execution of the CIA rendition, secret detention and interrogation operations on its territory;

(b) that, given that knowledge and the emerging widespread public information about ill-treatment and abuse of detained terrorist suspects in the custody of the US authorities, Poland ought to have known that, by enabling the CIA to detain such persons on its territory, it was exposing them to a serious risk of treatment contrary to the Convention (see also *El-Masri,* cited above, §§ 217-221).

443. Consequently, Poland was in a position where its responsibility for securing "to everyone within [its] jurisdiction the rights and freedoms defined . . . in [the] Convention" set forth in Article 1 was engaged in respect of the applicant at the material time.

[Further discussion of the court's findings has been omitted.]

XI. OTHER ALLEGED VIOLATIONS OF THE CONVENTION

580. Lastly, the applicant complained under Article 10 of the Convention that Poland, by its refusal to acknowledge, disclose and promptly and effectively investigate details of his secret detention, ill-treatment and rendition, had violated his and the public's right to the truth under Articles 2, 3, 5 and 10 of the Convention . . . .

581. The Court notes that a similar complaint was raised in *El-Masri* and declared inadmissible as being manifestly ill-founded (see *El-Masri,* cited above, § 264-265).

582. It finds no reason to hold otherwise and concludes that this complaint must be rejected in accordance with Article 35 §§ 3 (a) and 4 of the Convention . . . .

FOR THESE REASONS, THE COURT, UNANIMOUSLY,

1. *Decides* to join to the merits the Government's preliminary objection of non-exhaustion of domestic remedies and dismisses it;

2. *Holds* that the respondent State failed to comply with its obligations under Article 38 of the Convention;

3. *Declares* the complaints under Articles 2, 3, 5, 6 § 1, 8 and 13 of the Convention and Article 1 of Protocol No. 6 to the Convention admissible and the remainder of the application inadmissible;

4. *Holds* that there has been a violation of Article 3 of the Convention in its procedural aspect on account of the respondent State's failure to carry out an effective investigation into the applicant's allegations of serious violations of the Convention, including torture, ill-treatment and undisclosed detention;

5. *Holds* that there has been a violation of Article 3 of the Convention in its substantive aspect, on account of the respondent State's complicity in the CIA High-Value Detainees Programme in that it enabled the US authorities to subject the applicant to torture and ill-treatment on its territory and to transfer the applicant from its territory despite the existence of a real risk that he would be subjected to treatment contrary to Article 3;

6. *Holds* that there has been a violation of Article 5 of the Convention on account of the applicant's undisclosed detention on the respondent State's territory and the fact that the respondent State enabled the US authorities to transfer the applicant from its territory, despite the existence of a real risk that he would be subjected to further undisclosed detention;

7. *Holds* that there has been a violation of Article 8 of the Convention;

8. *Holds* that there has been a violation of Article 13 of the Convention on account of the lack of effective remedies in respect of the applicant's grievances under Article 3 of the Convention;

9. *Holds* that there has been a violation of Article 6 § 1 of the Convention on account of the transfer of the applicant from the respondent State's territory despite the existence of a real risk that he could face a flagrant denial of justice;

10. *Holds* that there has been a violation of Articles 2 and 3 of the Convention taken together with Article 1 of Protocol No. 6 to the Convention on account of the transfer of the applicant from the respondent State's territory despite the existence of a real risk that he could be subjected to the death penalty;

11. *Holds*

(a) that the respondent State is to pay the applicant, within three months from the date on which the judgment becomes final in accordance with Article 44 § 2 of the Convention, EUR 100,000 (one hundred thousand euros), plus any tax that may be chargeable in respect of non-pecuniary damage;

(b) that from the expiry of the above-mentioned three months until settlement simple interest shall be payable on the above amount at a rate equal to the marginal lending rate of the European Central Bank during the default period plus three percentage points;

12. *Dismisses* the remainder of the applicant's claim for just satisfaction.

Done in English, and notified in writing on 24 July 2014, pursuant to Rule 77 §§ 2 and 3 of the Rules of Court.

Françoise Elens-Passos   Ineta Ziemele

Registrar   President

Source: European Union Court of Human Rights. "Case of *Al Nashiri v. Poland.*" July 24, 2014. http:// hudoc.echr.coe.int/sites/eng/pages/search.aspx?i=001-146044.

OTHER HISTORIC DOCUMENTS OF INTEREST

FROM THIS VOLUME

- Senate Committee Releases Report on CIA Detention and Interrogation Program, p. 596

International Leaders Announce Sanctions against Russia

JULY 30 AND SEPTEMBER 11, 2014

Following President Vladimir Putin's decision to annex Ukraine's Crimea Peninsula in February 2014, Western leaders issued sanctions against the Russian government over what they considered continuing encroachment in Ukraine. Despite a series of ceasefire agreements between Russia and Ukraine, by the end of the year, Russian troops were again seen stationing themselves along the border and flowing into Ukrainian territory.

Tensions Escalate; New President of Ukraine Elected

Following the February 2014 unseating of Ukrainian president Viktor Yanukovych's government and subsequent March referendum by Crimea to become part of the Russian Federation, tensions between Russia and Ukraine, a former Soviet-bloc nation, intensified. Pro-Russian troops had already been moving into Crimea and eastern Ukraine Yanukovych's government collapsed, and the buildup intensified after the referendum. Russia fiercely denied accusations that its own government troops were part of the militias; however, photographic evidence from Western nations showed official Russian military vehicles in Ukraine and those involved in the fighting wearing Russian uniforms.

On April 17, Russia and Ukraine agreed to a ceasefire, but by April 22, Ukraine announced a resumption of military operations against Russian forces in eastern Ukraine, believing that Russia had continued to station its troops inside Ukraine in direct violation of the ceasefire. On May 11, separatists in the areas of Donetsk and Luhansk declared their own independence. The declaration went unrecognized by any nation.

On May 24, Ukrainians went to the polls to choose a new president. Although many areas in eastern Ukraine did not participate in the election, it was still hailed a success by the international community, especially considering that it was held under unusual circumstances. Petro Poroshenko, the pro-Western former minister of foreign affairs and economic development, was declared president on May 25.

G7 Convenes in Brussels

The Group of 8 (G8), made up of the world's largest industrialized democracies—Canada, France, Germany, Italy, Japan, Russia, the United Kingdom, and the United States—meets each year at an annual summit to discuss issues of global significance. Following Russia's incursion in Ukraine, in June 2014 the body became the G7 when it banned Russia from attending its meeting for the first time since the nation joined in 1997. Russia was supposed to have hosted the 2014 summit in Sochi, the Black Sea resort town that held the 2014 Olympic Winter Games, but the other seven nations announced in a joint statement that they would instead meet in Brussels. The group said it was "united in condemning the Russian Federation's continuing violation of the sovereignty and territorial integrity of Ukraine," adding that "Russia's illegal annexation of Crimea, and actions to de-stabilise eastern Ukraine, are unacceptable and must stop." Putin was asked for a reaction at an event in St. Petersburg and replied only, "I would like to wish them bon appetit."

In statements following the summit, the group worked to present a united front in their disapproval of Russia's actions, but there were some clear indications that there was tension among the seven nations. The United States, which began imposing sanctions on Russia in March, stood ready to further isolate the country. "If Russia's provocations continue, it's clear from our discussions here that the G7 nations are ready to impose additional costs on Russia," said President Barack Obama. Obama had been working behind the scenes with the German government to encourage France to cancel the sale of two warships to Putin's government, but he admitted that the deal would likely go ahead (by the end of the year, France had not yet transferred the ships to Russia). Japan appeared to favor diplomacy over sanctions. "I want Russia to be involved in various issues concerning the international community in a constructive manner," Prime Minister Shinzo Abe said. "To this end I'm hoping to continue dialogue with President Putin."

At the conclusion of the summit on June 4, the group released a communiqué outlining its foreign policy stance. On Ukraine, the group said it would "stand by the Ukrainian government and people." The group further confirmed "the decision by G7 countries to impose sanctions on individuals and entities who have actively supported or implemented the violation of Ukraine's sovereignty and territorial integrity and who are threatening the peace, security, and stability of Ukraine," adding that it stood "ready to intensify targeted sanctions and to implement significant additional restrictive measures to impose further costs on Russia should events so require."

MOUNTING SANCTIONS

The United States and European Union issued their first sets of sanctions against Russia on March 17, one day after the Crimean referendum. These sanctions banned specific Russian leaders from traveling into the United States or European Union and also froze assets held by these same individuals. For the sanctions to be lifted, President Obama said Russia would have to "move back its troops" and deescalate tensions. Russia responded by issuing its own sanctions against U.S. leaders, including Speaker of the House John Boehner, R-Ohio, two presidential advisers, and Sen. John McCain, R-Ariz., stating, "Treating our country in such a way . . . is inappropriate and unproductive." The United States extended its sanctions on April 28, stopping business transactions within its territory for specific Russian officials and companies. The same day, the EU expanded its travel ban against Russians.

Following the downing of Malaysia Airlines Flight 17 on July 17 over Ukraine, which resulted in the deaths of all 298 onboard, the G7 released a joint statement expressing "grave concern about Russia's continued actions to undermine Ukraine's sovereignty, territorial integrity, and independence." The G7 stated its opinion that the crash should have marked a course change for Russia that would cause it to cease supporting illegal armed groups in Ukraine. The group said that it remained committed to finding a political solution to the ongoing crisis, and one that Russia would participate in. However, given that the country failed to change direction following the crash, all seven member nations enacted additional sanctions against Russia. Non-G7 nations followed suit throughout the summer.

In response to the new rounds of sanctions, Putin signed a decree that called for a one-year embargo on imports of most agricultural products from those countries that had "adopted the decision on introduction of economic sanctions in respect of Russian legal and (or) physical entities." The measure had the greatest impact on the European Union, whose exports to Russia of fruits, vegetables, meat, fish, and dairy products made up 10 percent of its total exports.

On September 11, President Obama announced that the United States, in partnership with the European Union, would impose another round of sanctions on Russia. "Together with G-7 and European partners and our other Allies, we have made clear that we are prepared to impose mounting costs on Russia," the president said. "We are implementing these new measures in light of Russia's actions to further destabilize Ukraine over the last month, including through the presence of heavily armed Russian forces in eastern Ukraine." The new measures, which were outlined on September 12, broadened sanctions in the financial, energy, and defense sectors, including sanctions against Russia's largest bank, biggest oil companies, and a major arms maker. The president called on Russia "to work with Ukraine and other international partners, within the context of the Minsk agreement and without setting unreasonable conditions, to reach a lasting resolution to the conflict." If such a political agreement were reached, the president said, the sanctions would be rolled back. Following rounds of failed legislation, in mid-December, the U.S. House and Senate passed bills to add another round of sanctions, while authorizing the sale of arms, services, and training to Ukraine.

Although sanctions never targeted the Russian president himself, as international leaders wanted to meet him face-to-face for negotiations, Putin attacked the ongoing sanctions that further isolate his government, saying that such attempts to "blackmail" Russia would not produce the desired results. "Our partners should be well aware that attempts to put pressure on Russia with unilateral and illegitimate restrictive measures will not bring about a settlement, but rather impede the dialogue," Putin said. The Russian economy, which was already struggling prior to the Ukraine conflict, began to teeter on the brink of recession. Weak investment and capital flight reaching $75 billion by September deepened concerns that the nation would fall into economic collapse as more sanctions were piled on.

TENSIONS REIGNITE FOLLOWING A TRUCE

Despite a June decision by Putin to call on parliament to revoke the authorization for military intervention in Ukraine, the fighting between Ukrainians and pro-Russian separatists continued to rage into the fall and winter of 2014. International leaders called on Putin to cease the movement of weapons into Eastern Ukraine, but Putin has consistently denied any involvement with the separatists. In August, the leader of the separatist movement in Ukraine, Alexander Zakharchenko, said that as many as 4,000 Russian civilians had joined their ranks.

On September 5, Ukraine agreed to a truce, known as the Minsk Protocol, with pro-Russian rebels, and less than three weeks later, the North Atlantic Treaty Organization (NATO) announced that there had been a notable decrease in the number of Russian troops stationed in eastern Ukraine. This was followed by Putin's order on October 12 for troops stationed near the border to withdraw from their posts. By the end of October, the European Union brokered an agreement between Russia and Ukraine for the former to resume sending gas supplies to the latter.

However, in November, tensions ignited again when Russia supported elections held by separatists in eastern Ukraine to elect their own leaders. Poroshenko said the vote could derail "the entire peace process." NATO reported a subsequent rise in the number of military troops and vehicles seen entering Ukraine; the Pentagon indicated that 8,000 Russian troops were re-positioned on Ukraine's border. According to NATO commander general Philip Breedlove, "The cease-fire is in name only at this point. The violence increases day by day." Russia continued to publicly deny involvement. "Russian soldiers are not taking part in military activities in the east of Ukraine," said Deputy Defense Minister Nikolay Pankov.

—Heather Kerrigan

Following is a statement by the leaders of the Group of 7 on July 30, 2014, regarding the conflict between Russia and Ukraine; and a September 11, 2014, statement by President Barack Obama announcing new sanctions against Russia.

DOCUMENT

G7 Leaders on Continuing Conflict in Ukraine

July 30, 2014

We, the leaders of Canada, France, Germany, Italy, Japan, the United Kingdom, the United States, the President of the European Council, and the President of the European Commission, join in expressing our grave concern about Russia's continued actions to undermine Ukraine's sovereignty, territorial integrity, and independence. We once again condemn Russia's illegal annexation of Crimea, and actions to de-stabilize eastern Ukraine. Those actions are unacceptable and violate international law.

We condemn the tragic downing of Malaysia Airlines Flight 17 and the deaths of 298 innocent civilians. We demand a prompt, full, unimpeded, and transparent international investigation. We call upon all sides to establish, maintain, and fully respect a cease-fire at and around the crash site, as demanded by UN Security Council resolution 2166, so that the investigators can take up their work and to recover the remains of all victims and their personal possessions.

This terrible event should have marked a watershed in this conflict, causing Russia to suspend its support for illegal armed groups in Ukraine, secure its border with Ukraine, and stop the increasing flow of weapons, equipment, and militants across the border in order to achieve rapid and tangible results in de-escalation.

Regrettably, however, Russia has not changed course. This week, we have all announced additional coordinated sanctions on Russia, including sanctions on specific companies operating in key sectors of the Russian economy. We believe it is essential to demonstrate to the Russian leadership that it must stop its support for the separatists in eastern Ukraine and tangibly participate in creating the necessary conditions for the political process.

We remain convinced that there must be a political solution to the current conflict, which is causing rising numbers of civilian casualties. We call for a peaceful settlement of the crisis in Ukraine and underline the need to implement President Poroshenko's peace plan without any further delay. To this end, we urge all parties to establish a swift, genuine, and sustainable general cease-fire on the basis of the Berlin Declaration of 2 July with the aim of maintaining Ukraine's territorial integrity. We call upon Russia to use its influence with the separatist groups and ensure effective border control, including through OSCE observers. We support the OSCE and the Trilateral Contact Group as central players in creating the conditions for a ceasefire.

Russia still has the opportunity to choose the path of de-escalation, which would lead to the removal of these sanctions. If it does not do so, however, we remain ready to further intensify the costs of its adverse actions.

SOURCE: The White House. Office of the Press Secretary. "G-7 Leaders Statement on Ukraine." July 31, 2014. www.whitehouse.gov/the-press-office/2014/07/30/g-7-leaders-statement-ukraine.

President Obama Announces New Sanctions

September 11, 2014

Today, we join the European Union in announcing that we will intensify our coordinated sanctions on Russia in response to its illegal actions in Ukraine. I have said from the very beginning of this crisis that we want to see a negotiated political solution that respects Ukraine's sovereignty and territorial integrity. Together with G-7 and European partners and our other allies, we have made clear that we are prepared to impose mounting costs on Russia. We are implementing these new measures in light of Russia's actions to further destabilize Ukraine over the last month, including through the presence of heavily armed Russian forces in eastern Ukraine. We are watching closely developments since the announcement of the ceasefire and agreement in Minsk, but we have yet to see conclusive evidence that Russia has ceased its efforts to destabilize Ukraine.

We will deepen and broaden sanctions in Russia's financial, energy, and defense sectors. These measures will increase Russia's political isolation as well as the economic costs to Russia, especially in areas of importance to President Putin and those close to him. My administration will outline the specifics of these new sanctions tomorrow.

The international community continues to seek a genuine negotiated solution to the crisis in Ukraine. I encourage President Putin to work with Ukraine and other international partners, within the context of the Minsk agreement and without setting unreasonable conditions, to reach a lasting resolution to the conflict. As I said last week, if Russia fully implements its commitments, these sanctions can be rolled back. If, instead, Russia continues its aggressive actions and violations of international law, the costs will continue to rise.

SOURCE: Executive Office of the President. "Statement on International Sanctions Against Russia." September 11, 2014. *Compilation of Presidential Documents* 2014, no. 00656 (September 11, 2014). www.gpo.gov/fdsys/pkg/DCPD-201400656/pdf/DCPD-201400656.pdf.

OTHER HISTORIC DOCUMENTS OF INTEREST

FROM THIS VOLUME

International Leaders on
Ebola Outbreak in West Africa

JULY 31, SEPTEMBER 18, AND OCTOBER 28, 2014

In 2014, amid the largest outbreak of the Ebola virus disease, the global community struggled to respond as numbers of those infected continue to rise. The United Nations adopted a resolution to address the disease, formerly known as hemorrhagic fever, as it spread almost unchecked across borders due to weak health care infrastructure in West Africa following a period of political instability. The virus eventually made its way to the United States, where a man who traveled from West Africa died from the disease and a number of nurses and doctors were infected.

History of Ebola and Outbreaks

According to the Centers for Disease Control and Prevention (CDC), the virus was discovered in 1976 near the Ebola River. Though the virus is named for the Ebola River in what is now the Democratic Republic of the Congo, Ebola is not a water-borne illness. The five species of Ebola virus disease (EVD) are believed to be transmitted by animals, with bats being the most likely carrier of the disease, but very little is known definitively about the cause of this virus. There is no Food and Drug Administration (FDA)-approved vaccine or antiviral available. Currently, there are multiple experimental, preventative drugs in development. During the 2014 outbreak, these drugs were used to treat patients diagnosed with EVD, but without any clinical trials of the drugs, their effectiveness cannot be assessed beyond anecdotal evidence. Providing intravenous fluids, balancing electrolytes, maintaining blood pressure, and the saturation of oxygen in the blood in the early stages of the disease have been shown to increase the chance of survival. Though it is not known if survivors of EVD are immune for life, studies show that the antibodies developed during the course of the illness last in excess of ten years.

Persons with Ebola exhibit many flu-like symptoms including: prolonged fever, headaches, muscle pain or weakness, general fatigue, diarrhea, and vomiting. It is nearly impossible in the early stages to distinguish Ebola from other infectious diseases without confirmation from laboratory testing. Later stages of infection can include abdominal pain, unexplained bruising, or bleeding from the eyes, ears, nose, mouth, and rectum. Death results from prolonged dehydration, sepsis, and loss of organ function. Transmission of the virus occurs through direct contact with blood or body fluids of an infected person. Symptoms of infection typically appear within ten days of exposure. Those most at risk for infection are health care providers caring for Ebola patients and those patients' primary household or family caregivers. The virus can survive on dried surfaces for only hours, but it can survive several days in bodily fluids outside the body at room temperature. For this reason, those in close contact with sick persons are at extremely high risk of becoming ill if the proper precautions are not observed, including when preparing the body of a person known to have died from EVD for burial. Taking these precautions into consideration, it is recommended that bodies of Ebola victims be cremated.

It is generally thought that the risk of transmission is low after having recovered from Ebola, though traces of the virus may still exist in the blood or bodily fluids of the infected individual. Some evidence supports the idea that the disease may be transmitted as long as bodily fluids contain the virus. According to the World Health Organization (WHO), it may be possible for men to transmit the virus through their semen even up to seven weeks after recovery. Many medical professionals recommend abstaining from sex for three months or using condoms when abstinence is not possible. The virus can be killed with household bleach, and all medical instruments must be either disposed of and contained or sterilized between uses to prevent accidental transmission.

2014 Outbreak

The current outbreak in West Africa, with the first death traced to December of 2013, is considered to be the deadliest Ebola outbreak since the initial discovery of the virus. The mortality rate in West Africa from EVD during this outbreak was estimated to be 70 percent, according to Dr. Daniel Bausch, a leading expert in tropical medicine and infectious disease. In an interview with BBC News, Dr. David Mabey, a professor of communicable diseases at the London School of Hygiene and Tropical Medicine, stated, "Very few other viruses approach that [mortality rate]." He added, "The really terrifying thing about Ebola [is] you can be a perfectly fit 20 year-old and be dead within 10 days." This is in stark comparison to contagious viruses like influenza where deaths occur mostly in older populations with additional comorbidities.

In March 2014, a disease believed to be the Ebola virus was reported by hospital staff to Guinea's Ministry of Health. This information was also reported to Doctors Without Borders, and the WHO, which confirmed the disease as EVD. The outbreak remained centralized in Guinea, Sierra Leone, and Liberia. These countries are known to have deficits in infrastructure to counter such an outbreak, as the region has historically been plagued by long periods of instability. On August 8, 2014, on the heels of the 2014 U.S.-Africa Leaders Summit held in Washington, DC, the outbreak was declared by WHO to be a "Public Health Emergency of International Concern," as deaths and cases continued to rise. Prior to the summit, concerns regarding the spread of EVD to the United States threatened to sway public opinion against President Barack Obama for hosting the summit with leaders from across Africa. The summit focused on regional security and economic investment in Africa. Sessions also highlighted food security issues in Africa. This particular issue, also mentioned in UN Security Council Resolution 2177, influenced the international community to put pressure on the three most effected states to lift quarantines to ensure that those who remained free of Ebola or who are recovering from the disease, especially in remote areas, continued to have access to food and aid.

Initially the governments of the affected states, in particular Liberia, made attempts to quarantine entire areas. The hope was that restricting movement would slow the spread of the disease. Fearing that prolonged quarantines would irrevocably disturb the economics and tenuous political stability in the area, the international community encouraged a lift of quarantines and the placement of a travel advisory restricting "nonessential travel." As noted by Dr. Thomas Frieden, head of the CDC, during a briefing on July 31, 2014, risking nonessential travel could result in hospitalizations for reasons unrelated to Ebola such as car accidents. These hospitalizations would expose the public unnecessarily to the virus.

When lifting the quarantine, public buildings and even retailers employed a simple yet effective method for sterilization. Numerous reports describe buckets of bleach diluted with water placed at the entrances of buildings, with visitors required to submerge their hands in the water prior to entering. Though the strict quarantines were lifted, schools remained closed, threatening to reverse decades of literacy work in the region with many doubting that students would return if the schools remained closed for an extended period of time.

As of March 2015, the death toll was estimated to have surpassed 10,000 between Guinea, Liberia, Mali, Nigeria, Sierra Leone, Spain, and the United States. Due to difficulties collecting data in more rural areas, it is believed that the true death toll may be much higher. In February, WHO officials discovered a mass grave of bodies that had not previously been reported, supporting the idea that the true size of this outbreak may yet be unknown.

Ebola Travels Outside of West Africa

In all but three cases of EVD treated outside of West Africa, the patient was infected while in West Africa. In these three cases, a health care worker was infected as a result of treating a previously infected patient. The first case of Ebola virus infection outside the primarily affected region was reported in Madrid, Spain. The nurse in this case did not recover. Following the case in Madrid, two health care professionals in Dallas, Texas, tested positive for Ebola and have since recovered. In Dallas, the medical personnel contracted the disease from Thomas Duncan who died while receiving care after having traveled to the United States from Liberia prior to becoming symptomatic.

In his statement to the press on October 28, 2014, President Barack Obama referred to both Nina Pham, a nurse working at Texas Health Presbyterian Hospital and the first to contract the virus in the United States, and to Amber Vinson, the second health care worker diagnosed with the virus after treating Duncan. The president urged restraint regarding health care workers in the fight against Ebola. The statement came after public ridicule of Vinson's decision to travel to Cleveland, Ohio, to shop for bridesmaid dresses and plan her wedding following caring for the Ebola patient who died just two days earlier. She maintains that she was not symptomatic prior to or even immediately upon return from her trip to Cleveland. The CDC completed a mandatory monitoring period and cleared all persons with whom she interacted during her stay in Cleveland and those on her flight.

President Obama attempted to diminish both the public backlash against the nurses and the public hysteria about the potential spread of Ebola within the United States, saying, "It's also important for the American people to remind themselves that only two people so far have contracted Ebola on American soil . . . . Today, both of them are disease-free." In a highly publicized photo, the president was shown giving Pham a hug during a visit to the White House. Pham continued to make headlines into 2015 after she filed a lawsuit seeking damages from the parent company of the hospital where she worked, siting invasions of her privacy and lack of adequate training for treating Ebola patients.

Resistance and Challenge

Cultural resistance to outside intervention continues to be a challenge to health care professionals working to end the outbreak of Ebola in West Africa. There are reports of aid workers having been attacked and forced from villages. This aversion to outside assistance has enabled new cases to crop up, with the total number of new diagnoses rising in February 2015 following a downturn in new transmissions in January 2015. Aid workers are struggling to stop the spread before the rainy season begins, because many areas could be cut off from assistance during that period.

—Sarah Gall

Following is a news release from the World Health Organization on July 31, 2014, regarding the response to the Ebola outbreak; excerpts from a July 31, 2014, briefing by the Centers for Disease Control and Prevention; excerpts from the UN Security Council resolution on Ebola, released on September 18, 2014; and an October 28, 2014, statement by President Barack Obama on the ongoing response to Ebola.

WHO Details Response to Ebola in West Africa

July 31, 2014

The Director-General of WHO and presidents of west African nations impacted by the Ebola virus disease outbreak will meet Friday in Guinea to launch a new joint US$ 100 million response plan as part of an intensified international, regional and national campaign to bring the outbreak under control.

"The scale of the Ebola outbreak, and the persistent threat it poses, requires WHO and Guinea, Liberia and Sierra Leone to take the response to a new level, and this will require increased resources, in-country medical expertise, regional preparedness and coordination," says Dr Chan. "The countries have identified what they need, and WHO is reaching out to the international community to drive the response plan forward."

The Ebola Virus Disease Outbreak Response Plan in West Africa identifies the need for several hundred more personnel to be deployed in affected countries to supplement overstretched treatment facilities. Hundreds of international aid workers, as well as 120-plus WHO staff, are already supporting national and regional response efforts. But more are urgently required. Of greatest need are clinical doctors and nurses, epidemiologists, social mobilization experts, logisticians and data managers. The plan also outlines the need to increase preparedness systems in neighbouring nations and strengthen global capacities.

Key elements of the new plan, which draws on lessons learnt from other outbreaks, include strategies to:

- stop transmission of Ebola virus disease in the affected countries through scaling up effective, evidence-based outbreak control measures; and
- prevent the spread of Ebola virus disease to the neighbouring at-risk countries through strengthening epidemic preparedness and response measures.

WHO and affected and neighbouring countries will renew efforts to mobilize communities and strengthen communication so that people know how to avoid infection and what to do if they fear they may have come into contact with the virus.

Improving prevention, detecting and reporting suspected cases, referring people infected with the disease for medical care, as well as psychosocial support, are key. The plan also emphasizes the importance of surveillance, particularly in border areas, of risk assessments and of laboratory-based diagnostic testing of suspected cases. Also highlighted is the need to improve ways to protect health workers, a scarce resource in all three countries, from infection.

Finally, reinforcing coordination of the overall health response is critical. In particular, this includes strengthening capacities of the WHO-run Sub-regional Outbreak Coordination Centre, which was opened this month in Conakry, Guinea, to consolidate and streamline support to West African countries by all major partners and assist in resource mobilization.

The scale of the ongoing outbreak is unprecedented, with approximately 1323 confirmed and suspected cases reported, and 729 deaths in Guinea, Liberia and Sierra Leone since March 2014.

SOURCE: World Health Organization. "WHO Director-General, west African presidents to launch intensified Ebola outbreak response plan." July 31, 2014. www.who.int/mediacentre/news/releases/2014/ebola-outbreak-response-plan/en/.

DOCUMENT   *CDC Briefing on Ebola Outbreak*

July 31, 2014

[Introductory remarks by the CDC director of public affairs and Dr. Tom Frieden, CDC director, have been omitted.]

Dr. Tom Frieden: ". . . . Let me start with the big picture. Then I will go through considerable detail about what's happening with the Ebola outbreak in West Africa. It is complex. I would be happy to take your questions and with some final remarks. The bottom line is that Ebola is worsening in West Africa. CDC along with others are surging to begin to turn the tide. It's not going to be quick. It's not going to be easy.

". . . The current outbreak is bad. It's the biggest, most complex and the first time it's been present in this region of the world which means that response systems and community understanding of the disease is not what it is elsewhere . . . .

"There are two major challenges which the countries are facing in control of Ebola. The first is that many of the health systems in these countries are not highly functional. They may not reach into rural areas. Health care workers may not reliably be present at facilities and health care facilities may have limited capacities. Second, in some areas, as has been well covered by the media, there has been lack of understanding and hostility or violence against some of the groups that are trying to respond to the outbreaks.

"The key priority and the key means of stopping Ebola fundamentally is by doing three things. First, finding patients. So that we rapidly identify patients, get them isolated, find out who their contacts are, keep them from spreading it to others, get them diagnosed accurately and promptly. Second, responding to cases, providing supportive care and treatment centers and preventing spread and protecting health care workers. Finding every single contact of each Ebola patient and following each of the contacts for 21 days . . . . Third, after finding and responding, preventing future cases and that's through messages to the community and health centers, avoiding close contact with sick people or bodies, reporting suspected cases, isolating cases in treatment centers to prevent spread and for the prevention of initial spread from animals to humans, avoiding consumption of bush meat and contact with bats.

"CDC is surging our response with the current challenges that we are facing. Over the next 30 days, we plan to send an additional 50 CDC disease control specialists into the three countries. These individuals will help countries establish emergency operations centers that can develop a structured and effective way of addressing the outbreak. This is being done in close collaboration with the World Health Organization. They will also help strengthen laboratory networks so testing for the disease can be done rapidly and patients determined whether or not they have Ebola. If they do, that whole chain of contact investigation continuing. And, third, building the capacity of individuals from within the area to do these functions for this outbreak and future threats as well . . . .

"We also are today issuing a travel advisory recommending against nonessential travel to the West African nations of Guinea, Liberia and Sierra Leone because the ongoing Ebola outbreak in these countries poses a potential risk to travelers particularly if you are traveling and happen to fall ill or be injured in a car crash and needed to go to a medical facility which might have recognized or unrecognized spread of Ebola. It also supports these three countries in their abilities to preserve and improve their response to the outbreaks. It allows them to focus on control to protect the travelers who do go because we are continuing, as we are at CDC, to surge our response and send additional disease control experts to the region and humanitarian assistance continues to go in. We have had conversations with the air carriers and we understand they will continue to fly which is very important to continue to support the response and maintain essential functions in the country. The objectives of our surge are really to improve the ability of the countries to manage the current outbreaks. And over the next 30 days we'll be deploying 50 epidemic intelligence service officers, other epidemiologists, health communication experts to the affected area.

"In addition, we recognize that there will be concerns in the U.S. Ebola poses little risk to the U.S. general population. It's important to understand how it spreads . . . . First, it doesn't spread from people who aren't sick with it. If someone has been exposed but they are not sick and someone else has contact with that individual, they are not at risk of getting Ebola. Ebola is spread as people get sicker and sicker, they have fever and they may develop severe symptoms. Those symptoms and the body fluids that may be shed during that time, those are the infectious risk entities. In Africa, burial rites where people who have very large quantities of virus and have died from Ebola can be a major way of spread of a disease. But in this country, we are confident that we will not have significant spread of Ebola, even if we were to have a patient with Ebola here. We work actively to educate American health care workers on how to isolate patients and how to protect themselves against infection. In fact, any advanced hospital in the U.S., any hospital with an intensive care unit has the capacity to isolate patients . . . .

"On Monday of this week we sent out a health alert notice to remind U.S. health care workers of the importance of taking steps to prevent spread of the virus . . . . I'm confident that as we make progress over the coming weeks and months, we will not only begin to tamp down these outbreaks, but leave behind stronger systems that will be able to find, stop before they spread and prevent more effectively Ebola and other health threats . . . . We are working in this surge both to begin to get better control in these three countries and to strengthen the capacity of these countries to improve their ability to find, stop and prevent future outbreaks.

"So bottom line, Ebola has been worsening in West Africa. CDC and others are surging our response to begin to turn the tide. It's not going to be quick or easy. Even in a best case scenario, it could take three to six months or more. Given the weak health care systems and the violence that some areas have seen, we are not in the best of circumstances. And we have strong measures in place to protect Americans if there is the possibility of somebody coming in with Ebola. So I will stop here. We'll turn it over for questions."

[Questions regarding items answered in the opening statement have been omitted.]

Question: "... I think there are a lot of Americans who have this idea that there are teams of CDC experts at all the airports with their, you know, biocontrol suits to rush out to the airplane and grab anybody coming off with a fever from West Africa. Can you paint a better picture of what it's like ...?"

Dr. Frieden: "... We have at CDC quarantine stations in all of the major ports of entry. If a patient is ill on a plane, we are called to assess and if appropriate, we would undertake tracking or tracing of the people around that individual on the plane. In fact, for the individual who traveled to Nigeria, our staff is assisting authorities in several countries, tracing patients—passengers who shared a flight with that individual. But, remember, Ebola to spread generally requires close contact ... to people with whom they have very close contact with body fluids ..."

Question: "... You just said the transmission of Ebola is through close contact. But it seems it's going beyond that ... people are scared at the rate at which it is being transmitted and moving very fast. I would like to know how Ebola is contracted."

Dr. Frieden: "... [Ebola] seems mysterious to people when it's spreading. It is very clear that it is not a food-borne illness. It is not a water-borne illness .... The overwhelming risk, the overwhelming way it spreads is by close contact with infected and very sick people. So if we look at the cases that are occurring in the three countries, a large portion of them are in people who are exposed in health care facilities. So that includes health care workers who account for a substantial proportion of the cases and, sadly, a substantial proportion of the deaths as well. That includes burial traditions where there may be handling of the remains of someone who died from Ebola .... So the communication is so important to get out into the communities that burial needs to be done in a way that is safe so that other people don't become ill and die from Ebola. For every facility caring for people in that area there needs to be meticulous infection control to protect not just the health care workers but also patient's families, other patients. Hospitals become amplification points if there isn't meticulous infection control. We know how Ebola spreads. We know how to stop the spread of Ebola. But we need to make progress informing communities and implementing good control measures.

"I will give you a positive example. In Uganda where we worked for many years with the government, Ebola is more familiar. We have worked with traditional healers so they will recognize a potential Ebola patient and refer them to a diagnostic and treatment center. We have worked with the hospitals to isolate patients. We have ensured where there are Ebola or possible cases the burial practices are safe. As a result, where there used to be large outbreaks, now there have been sometimes just single cases where the spread stops or much smaller outbreaks. We know that not only is it possible biologically to control Ebola with our current tools, but it's also possible in Africa working with community strengths and community leaders to do that as well. . . ."

Question:	". . . Starting this weekend and into the early part of next week, something like 50 airplanes from Africa, including some of these countries will be landing in Washington for this summit. I'm wondering whether the CDC is taking special precautions to protect the president and the president's team and everybody else here in Washington given the fact that some of the planes might be coming outside of the normal, you know, travel network and travel procedures that commercial flights might come on."
Dr. Frieden:	"We are certainly looking at all options for ensuring that travelers from this region in particular are accorded all possible health care if they become sick and don't expose others to illness if they do become sick. Remember, this is limited to three countries. The key is to identify people as soon as they develop fever, if they have contact with Ebola cases. We have also strongly encouraged anyone who's had contact not to travel. . . ."
Question:	"Are you guys recommending to any of the three countries that they not attend the summit?"
Dr. Frieden:	"No. But we do understand that some of the heads of state are so focused on controlling these outbreaks that they may or may not come."

[Duplicate questions and answers about travel advisories and WHO budget questions have been omitted.]

Question:	". . . I wonder if you could tell us what you know about the two Samaritans First volunteers coming back to the U.S., if that's going to happen. And also the experimental serum one of them has received."
Dr. Frieden:	". . . it's really up to the organization what they do. There are a lot of complexities and we stand willing to help them in their decision and to support them in that. In terms of experimental treatment, I don't know any details of what may have been given. I will say that we have reviewed the evidence of the treatments out there and don't find any treatment that's had proven effectiveness against Ebola disease."

[Duplicate exchanges regarding experimental drug treatment and travel advisories, and closing statements, have been omitted.]

Source: Centers for Disease Control and Prevention. "CDC Telebriefing on the Update on Ebola outbreak in West Africa." July 31, 2014. www.cdc.gov/media/releases/2014/t0731-ebola.html.

UN Security Council
Adopts Resolution on Ebola

DOCUMENT

September 18, 2014

[References to a previous resolution and general opening statements have been omitted.]

"*Recognizing* that the peacebuilding and development gains of the most affected countries concerned could be reversed in light of the Ebola outbreak and *underlining* that the outbreak is undermining the stability of the most affected countries concerned and, unless contained, may lead to further instances of civil unrest, social tensions and a deterioration of the political and security climate,

"*Determining* that the unprecedented extent of the Ebola outbreak in Africa constitutes a threat to international peace and security,

"*Expressing* concern about the particular impact of the Ebola outbreak on women,

[Portions of the resolution commending member states for their assistance in fighting Ebola and urging increased assistance have been omitted.]

"*Expressing* concern about the impact, including on food security, of general travel and trade restrictions in the region and taking note of the AU call on its Member States to lift travel restrictions to enable the free movement of people and trade to the affected countries,

"*Emphasizing* the role of all relevant United Nations System . . . in supporting the national, regional and international efforts to respond to the Ebola outbreak and *recognizing*, in this regard, the central role of the World Health Organization (WHO), which designated the Ebola outbreak a public health emergency of international concern. . . .

"*Taking* note of the WHO Ebola Response Roadmap of 28 August 2014 that aims to stop transmission of the Ebola virus disease worldwide, while managing the consequences of any further international spread and *also taking note* of the 12 Mission Critical Actions, including infection control, community mobilization and recovery, to resolve the Ebola outbreak,

"*Taking* note of the WHO protocols to prevent the transmission of the Ebola virus disease between individuals, organizations and populations, *underlining* that the Ebola outbreak can be contained, including through the implementation of established safety and health protocols . . .,

". . . to consolidate the operational work of the United Nations System, Member States, non-governmental organizations and other partners focused on providing assistance to the affected countries in response to the Ebola outbreak, as well as to ensure . . . an effective response to the broader dimensions of the outbreak that include food security and access to basic health services,

"*Welcoming* the intention of the Secretary-General to convene a high-level meeting on the margins of the sixty-ninth United Nations General Assembly to urge an exceptional and vigorous response to the Ebola outbreak,

"1. *Encourages* the governments of Liberia, Sierra Leone and Guinea to accelerate the establishment of national mechanisms to provide for the rapid diagnosis and isolation of suspected cases of infection, treatment measures, effective medical services for responders, credible and transparent public education campaigns, and strengthened preventive and preparedness measures to detect, mitigate and respond to Ebola exposure . . . ;

"2. *Encourages* the governments of Liberia, Sierra Leone and Guinea to continue efforts to resolve and mitigate the wider political, security, socio-economic and humanitarian dimensions of the Ebola outbreak, as well as to provide sustainable, well-functioning and responsive public health mechanisms, *emphasizes* that responses to the Ebola outbreak should address the specific needs of women and stresses the importance of their full and effective engagement in the development of such responses;

"3. *Expresses concern* about the detrimental effect of the isolation of the affected countries as a result of trade and travel restrictions imposed on and to the affected countries;

"4. *Calls on* Member States, including of the region, to lift general travel and border restrictions, imposed as a result of the Ebola outbreak, and that contribute to the further isolation of the affected countries and undermine their efforts to respond to the Ebola . . . ;

"5. *Calls on* Member States, especially of the region, to facilitate the delivery of assistance . . . ;

"6. *Calls on* Member States, especially of the region, and all relevant actors providing assistance in response to the Ebola outbreak, to enhance efforts to communicate to the public, as well as to implement, the established safety and health protocols and preventive measures to mitigate against misinformation and undue alarm about the transmission and extent of the outbreak . . . ;

"7. *Calls on* Member States to provide urgent resources and assistance, including deployable medical capabilities such as field hospitals with qualified and sufficient expertise, staff and supplies, laboratory services, logistical, transport and construction support capabilities, airlift and other aviation support and aeromedical services and dedicated clinical services in Ebola Treatment Units and isolation units, to support the affected countries in intensifying preventive and response activities and strengthening national capacities in response to the Ebola outbreak and to allot adequate capacity to prevent future outbreaks;

"8. *Urges* Member States, as well as bilateral partners and multilateral organizations . . . to mobilize and provide immediately technical expertise . . . and to continue to exchange expertise, lessons learned and best practices . . . to respond effectively and immediately to the Ebola outbreak . . . ;

"9. *Urges* Member States to . . . lead the organization, coordination and implementation of national preparedness and response activities, including, where and when relevant, in collaboration with international development and humanitarian partners;

"10. *Commends* the continued contribution and commitment of international health and humanitarian relief workers to respond urgently to the Ebola outbreak and calls on all relevant actors to put in place the necessary repatriation and financial arrangements, including medical evacuation capacities and treatment and transport provisions, to facilitate their immediate and unhindered deployment to the affected countries;

"11. *Requests* the Secretary-General to help to ensure that all relevant United Nations System entities . . . accelerate their response to the Ebola outbreak, including by supporting the development and implementation of preparedness and operational plans and liaison and collaboration with governments of the region and those providing assistance;

"12. *Encourages* the WHO to continue to strengthen its technical leadership and operational support to governments and partners, monitor Ebola transmission, assist in identifying existing response needs and partners to meet those needs to facilitate the availability of essential data and hasten the development and implementation of therapies and vaccines according to best clinical and ethical practices and also encourages Member States to provide all necessary support in this regard, including the sharing of data in accordance with applicable law."

[The closing has been omitted.]

SOURCE: United Nations. "With Spread of Ebola Outpacing Response, Security Council Adopts Resolution 2177 (2014) Urging Immediate Action, End to Isolation of Affected States." September 18, 2014. www.un.org/press/en/2014/sc11566.doc.htm.

DOCUMENT *President Obama on Ebola Response*

October 28, 2014

[Introductory remarks have been omitted.]

We know that the best way to protect Americans ultimately is going to stop this outbreak at the source. And I just had the privilege of speaking with some of the men and women who are working to do just that: our Disaster Assistance Response Team on the ground in West Africa . . . .

We deployed this DART team to West Africa back in early August . . . . They've increased the number of Ebola treatment units and burial teams. They've expanded the pipeline of medical personnel and equipment and supplies. They've launched an aggressive education campaign in country. The bottom line is . . . folks from the United States who are leading the way in helping Liberia, Guinea, and Sierra Leone . . . .

The truth is that we're going to have to stay vigilant here at home until we stop the epidemic at its source. And for that, we're going to need to make sure that our doctors and our health care professionals here in the United States are properly trained and informed and that they are coordinated if and when an Ebola case crops up here in the United States . . . .

And that's why yesterday the CDC announced that we're going to have new monitoring and movement guidance that is sensible, based in science, and tailored to the unique circumstances of each health worker that may be returning from one of these countries after they have provided the kind of help that they need . . . .

It's also important for the American people to remind themselves that only two people so far have contracted Ebola on American soil. . . . Today, both of them are disease-free. I met with one of them, Nina Pham, last week, and she is doing wonderfully. And I just had a chance to get off the phone with Amber Vinson, who is on her way back home and . . . doing well also . . . .

Meanwhile, the West African nations of Senegal and Nigeria have now been declared Ebola-free . . . .

. . . this disease can be contained . . . . We have to keep leading the global response. America cannot look like it is shying away, because other people are watching what we do, and if we don't have a robust international response in West Africa, then we are actually endangering ourselves here back home.

[Repetitive statements regarding containment of Ebola and support of health care workers and closing remarks have been omitted.]

SOURCE: Executive Office of the President. "Remarks on the United States Response to the Ebola Epidemic in West Africa and an Exchange With Reporters." October 28, 2014. *Compilation of Presidential Documents* 2014, no. 00798 (October 28, 2014). www.gpo.gov/fdsys/pkg/DCPD-201400798/pdf/DCPD-201400798.pdf.

Senator Feinstein and the White House Remark on CIA Hacking

JULY 31, 2014

The U.S. Senate Select Committee on Intelligence's investigation into the Central Intelligence Agency's (CIA) detention and interrogation of suspected terrorists—and its subsequent critical report—fueled tensions between the two organizations that culminated in 2014, when the leadership of each organization accused the other's staff of inappropriate activities. Committee chairman Dianne Feinstein, D-Calif., claimed the CIA had hacked into committee staff computers, possibly violating the Constitution in the process. Meanwhile, CIA officials alleged that committee staffers had accessed internal agency documents that they were not authorized to review. The controversy prompted an internal review by the CIA's inspector general, who later concluded that CIA staff had improperly accessed a computer network committee staff was using to conduct their research.

STUDYING CIA DETENTION AND INTERROGATION PROGRAMS

Congress established House and Senate intelligence committees in the 1970s to "provide vigilant legislative oversight" of the CIA, National Security Administration, and other intelligence agencies. These responsibilities include conducting routine and periodic investigations into intelligence programs and events to help ensure that they conform to U.S. law.

The Senate Select Committee on Intelligence took up one such investigation in May 2009, launching a review of the CIA's detention and interrogation of suspected terrorists during President George W. Bush's administration. For purposes of the investigation, the CIA established a secure offsite location in northern Virginia and a "stand-alone computer system" and network that was "segregated from CIA networks" for committee staff to use to access the documents they needed. The CIA also provided more than six million pages of records for the staff to review. A third-party contractor was required to review the materials before committee staff could.

The investigation was initially meant to take one year to complete, but the volume of material led to significant delays. The review also faced a number of challenges, including Republican committee members' withdrawal from the investigation after Attorney General Eric Holder announced the Justice Department was considering prosecutions against CIA employees who had been involved in "enhanced interrogation" programs. In addition, more than 800 documents reportedly disappeared from the computers committee staff was using—an incident for which the CIA later apologized.

Four years and $40 million later, the committee released its final report in December 2013. The 6,400-page classified report was highly critical of the CIA's detention and interrogation programs. It described in detail a number of controversial interrogation techniques—including sleep deprivation, death threats, "rectal feeding" or "rectal hydration," and waterboarding—that the agency had employed, and found that such techniques had been used more harshly and more frequently than previously believed. It concluded that these techniques had produced little valuable intelligence, citing at least 20 instances in which a detainee who had been subjected to such practices had not provided information that played a role in apprehending terrorists, foiling planned attacks or finding al Qaeda leader Osama bin Laden. The report's findings also included that CIA officials had consistently misled the White House and Congress about the efficacy of their interrogation techniques, and that the agency did not provide sufficient oversight of the secret prisons it had established around the world. Upon the report's release, Feinstein called the interrogation program "a stain on our values and our history."

Prior to releasing the report, the committee had submitted its findings to the CIA for comment. The agency responded in June 2013 with a report of its own that challenged some of the facts and conclusions included in the committee report. CIA director John Brennan acknowledged that the CIA had made mistakes, but also called the committee's report an "incomplete and selective picture of what occurred." The agency's response also said that for the committee's conclusions to be accurate, "there would have had to have been a years long conspiracy among C.I.A. leaders at all levels, supported by a large number of analysts and other line officers."

The CIA's pushback came as a surprise to committee staff, as their findings were similar to those of an internal CIA investigation that had examined the same programs and found evidence of significant wrongdoing. Portions of the investigation, which became known as the Panetta Review, were included among the materials the CIA provided to committee staff for their report. Yet the CIA's response to the committee report appeared to conflict with the Panetta Review.

CIA, Committee Trade Accusations

The Panetta Review soon became the focus of the dispute between the CIA and the Senate committee. Both Feinstein and then-committee member Sen. Mark Udall, D-Colo., called for the CIA to provide the intelligence committee with the complete internal report, but the agency refused, saying the documents were privileged.

Then on January 15, 2014, Brennan called an emergency meeting with Feinstein and Sen. Saxby Chambliss, R-Ga., the committee's vice chairman, to tell them the CIA had conducted a search of the documents and the computer network used by committee staff at the offsite facility. Brennan told the senators that the search had been conducted because they suspected the staffers had gained unauthorized access to the Panetta Review and had made copies of it.

Shortly after this meeting took place, CIA inspector general David Buckley learned about the incident and began conducting an investigation to determine whether the CIA had acted improperly by searching staff computers. In March, Buckley referred the matter to the Justice Department to help determine whether CIA staff committed any criminal acts; around the same time, CIA counsel also filed allegations surrounding committee staff actions with the Justice Department. The department would later determine that it did not have sufficient evidence to launch a criminal probe into either set of allegations.

On March 11, what had been a relatively discreet dispute was thrust into the public eye when Feinstein delivered a forty-minute speech on the Senate floor, rebuking the CIA. Feinstein accused the CIA of hacking into the committee's computers, removing key documents, and attempting to impede the committee's investigation. She also accused the agency of trying to intimidate her staff, citing the appearance of anonymous reports in the press that the matter had been referred to the Department of Justice for a criminal investigation.

"I have grave concerns that the CIA search may well have violated the separation-of-powers principles embodied in the United States Constitution, including the speech and debate clause," she said. "It may have undermined the constitutional framework essential to effective congressional oversight of intelligence activities or any other government function." Feinstein also demanded the CIA apologize, adding, "How Congress responds and how this is resolved will show whether the Intelligence Committee can be effective in monitoring and investigating our nation's intelligence activities, or whether our work can be thwarted by those we oversee." The speech's tone was particularly notable because Feinstein had staunchly defended the intelligence community throughout the previous year, despite the controversy surrounding the NSA's surveillance program.

Brennan denied her allegations. "As far as the allegations of the CIA hacking into Senate computers, nothing could be further from the truth," he said. "That's beyond the scope of reason."

THE INSPECTOR GENERAL'S REPORT

On July 31, Buckley released a summary of his findings, concluding that three of the CIA's IT staff and two of its lawyers "improperly accessed or caused access" to the computer network designated for the committee staff's use. Buckley also found that CIA employees had read the e-mail of Senate investigators and created a false online identity to gain access to the staff's computers. In addition, he concluded the CIA staff had sent a criminal referral to the Department of Justice that was based on false information. The IT staff, he said, had given inaccurate information to the CIA's lawyers.

The same day, CIA spokesperson Dean Boyd told the press that Brennan had informed Feinstein and Chambliss of the report's findings and "apologized to them for such actions by CIA officers as described in the OIG report." Boyd also said that Brennan planned to establish an internal accountability board to review the issue. The board, to be led by former Indiana Sen. Evan Bayh, could recommend "potential disciplinary measures" and "steps to address systemic issues" if needed.

In a statement, Feinstein said, "The investigation confirmed what I said on the Senate floor in March—CIA personnel inappropriately searched Senate Intelligence Committee computers in violation of an agreement we had reached, and I believe in violation of the constitutional separation of powers." Chambliss also responded to the findings, describing them as "serious violations" and calling for CIA employees to be "dealt with very harshly." Udall took a step further, calling for Brennan's resignation. "These offenses, along with other errors in judgment by some at the CIA, demonstrate a tremendous failure of leadership, and there must be consequences," he said. "From the unprecedented hacking of congressional staff computers and continued leaks undermining the Senate Intelligence Committee's investigation of the CIA's detention and interrogation program to his abject failure to acknowledge any wrongdoing by the agency, I have lost confidence in John Brennan." Yet the White House defended Brennan. "He has been candid about the inconsistencies the IG found," said White House press secretary Josh Earnest. He added that Brennan had "taken all the responsible steps to address this situation. That's the kind of proactive leadership the president would expect." Brennan was not asked to resign.

The accountability board led by former senator Bayh is expected to release its findings in 2015.

—Linda Fecteau Grimm

Following is a statement from Sen. Dianne Feinstein, D-Calif., on July 31, 2014, on the hacking of Senate Select Intelligence Committee computers; and the text of a press conference with White House press secretary Josh Earnest on July 31, 2014, with regard to the hacking scandal.

Sen. Feinstein Reacts to CIA Report on Hacking

July 31, 2014

"I was briefed Tuesday by CIA Inspector General David Buckley on the results of an IG investigation. The investigation confirmed what I said on the Senate floor in March—CIA personnel inappropriately searched Senate Intelligence Committee computers in violation of an agreement we had reached, and I believe in violation of the constitutional separation of powers.

"Director Brennan apologized for these actions and submitted the IG report to an accountability board. These are positive first steps. This IG report corrects the record and it is my understanding that a declassified report will be made available to the public shortly."

Source: Sen. Dianne Feinstein. "Feinstein Statement on CIA IG Report." July 31, 2014. http:// www.feinstein.senate.gov/public/index.cfm/press-releases?ID=e1cf9543-5d61-4674-8c47-a824856f20c3.

White House Press Conference on Hacking Scandal

July 31, 2014

[Questions and answers unrelated to the CIA case have been omitted.]

Q: Can I ask you about the internal CIA report that suggests that indeed the CIA was spying on the Senate Intelligence Committee, and the conversations on the Hill that John Brennan had with Dianne Feinstein and Saxby Chambliss? Back in March, he said that when the facts come out a lot of people who are claiming there has been all this spying and monitoring and hacking will be proved wrong. Given what this report says, and the fact that he went to the Hill and has apologized, does the President believe that there is a credibility issue for John Brennan there?

MR. EARNEST: Not at all. The fact of the matter is, Director Brennan is the one who suggested that the inspector general investigate this situation in the first place.

In response to that report, the CIA Public Affairs Office put out a statement in which they said that Director Brennan was briefed on the IG's findings, and noted that that finding included, "a judgment that some CIA employees acted in a manner inconsistent with the common understanding reached between the Senate Intelligence Committee and the CIA."

So Director Brennan is the one who suggested that this situation be investigated. He supported the IG launching that investigation. He now has been briefed on those results, has affirmed the conclusion that the employees acted in a manner inconsistent with the common understanding reached between the CIA and the committee. Director Brennan has taken the further step of appointing an accountability board to review this situation, review the conduct of these individuals who are involved, and if necessary ensure that they are properly held accountable for that conduct. He has appointed somebody who doesn't work at the CIA, former Senator Evan Bayh, a member of the Senate Intel Committee, to lead that accountability board and to offer him some recommendations about steps that can be taken to ensure that these kind of misunderstandings don't happen again.

So Director Brennan has taken all of the kinds of responsible steps to address this situation. The fact of the matter is Director Brennan is somebody who over the course of the last five and a half years has played an instrumental role in helping the President make the kinds of decisions that I mentioned to Jon earlier that have decimated the leadership of core al Qaeda in Afghanistan and Pakistan. And he currently is operating in a very difficult environment to ensure the safety of the American public. He is somebody who had a very difficult job who does that job extraordinarily well.

Q: So no concern about the fact that he stated so certainly in March that this hadn't happened? Or any perception problems that may arise over the fact that obviously the President has a close relationship with him, that he was formerly, obviously, as you know, the NSC Deputy Director for Terrorism—no action anticipated as a result of this disconnect?

MR. EARNEST: Absolutely not. As I mentioned, Director Brennan has done what is necessary to get to the bottom of what exactly happened. He has been candid about the inconsistencies that the IG found, and he has taken the additional step of appointing somebody who does not work at the CIA to conduct a review, an accountability review of what exactly happened and to determine what's necessary to hold those individuals accountable.

That's the kind of proactive leadership that the President would expect from somebody who has an important job like running the CIA. And it in no way impacts any judgment on John Brennan's strong record of making the kinds of difficult decisions that are necessary to keep the American public safe.

Q: Josh, and is it accurate that it's an apology he's making today to the leaders of the Intelligence Committee?

MR. EARNEST: In terms of communication between the Director of the Central Intelligence Agency and the Senate Select Committee on Intelligence, I'd refer you to the CIA.

Q: And do you know if it's right that Senator Feinstein is here today to have a conversation with the President about this?

MR. EARNEST: I believe—we'll have to check—that she is among those who is participating in the discussion that the President has convened with Democrats and Republicans on Capitol Hill about a range of foreign policy matters in the Cabinet Room. I know that some of you were actually in that room taking photographs of that meeting. I was not actually in that room.

So I believe Senator Feinstein was there.

Q: (Inaudible.)

MR. EARNEST: Okay. Your colleague confirms that Senator Feinstein was in the room for that meeting. And so that was the reason that she's at the White House today. I do not know whether or not she and the President will have the opportunity to discuss this specific issue.

SOURCE: The White House. Office of the Press Secretary. "Press Briefing by Press Secretary Josh Earnest, 7/31/2014." July 31, 2014. www.whitehouse.gov/the-press-office/2014/07/31/press-briefing-press-secretary-josh-earnest-7312014.

OTHER HISTORIC DOCUMENTS OF INTEREST

FROM THIS VOLUME

■ Senate Committee Releases Report on CIA Detention and Interrogation Program, p. 596

United Nations Accuses
Hamas of War Crimes

JULY 31, 2014

After another failed peace attempt between Israel and Palestine in 2014, the two sides continued attacks on each other. Following the June kidnapping and murder of three Israeli teenagers by Hamas militants, Israel launched an attack against Hamas that resulted in the deaths of more than 2,000 individuals over a seven-week period. The attacks ended with an Egyptian-brokered ceasefire in late August. The United Nations High Commissioner on Human Rights categorized the attacks by Hamas as war crimes and called on the two sides to come back to the negotiating table to reach a lasting peace agreement.

Ongoing Israeli-Palestinian Conflict

The Israeli-Palestinian relationship has been marked by conflict since the establishment of the State of Israel in 1948. Palestinian resentment regarding Jewish settlements in ancestral Palestinian lands, Israeli military deployments, and disputed custody of shared holy sites found expression in a series of intifadas, or uprisings, which began in 1987. The term "intifada" comes from the Arabic phrase "to shake off" and was first applied when a spontaneous public rebellion erupted in response to an apparent truck accident that killed four Palestinians in December 1987. Grievances expanded to include calls for the removal of all Israeli military personnel and settlers and recognition of Palestinian territory. Significantly, the internal nature of conflict also precluded participation by the Palestinian diaspora, limiting territorial claims to residents within the West Bank, the Gaza strip on Israel's eastern coast, and parts of East Jerusalem, the location of many sacred Abrahamic sites. The Israeli government had not anticipated the scope of the protests, which included strikes and boycotts and were led by the Palestinian Liberation Organization (PLO).

The first intifada was resolved through the mutual acknowledgement of the need for a two-state solution to the conflict, enshrined in the 1993 Oslo Accords, which were brokered with U.S. and Norwegian mediation. The agreement was opposed by Hamas, the militant Islamist faction of the Palestinian leadership. Hamas continued to call for the elimination of the State of Israel.

A second intifada occurred in 2000 following a visit by then Israeli prime minister Ariel Sharon, to the Al Aqsa mosque, a holy Islamic site built on the Temple Mount, which is sacred to Israel. Sharon's tour of the contested area prompted violent riots and Palestinian clashes with Israeli police in the Old City of East Jerusalem, precipitating wider demonstrations that continued sporadically throughout the decade. Israel responded by building a series of defenses, including a security wall around Palestinian territory in 2002. The wall was declared illegal by the International Criminal Court (ICC) in 2004. Israel, which does not recognize the court, responded that the wall was necessary to protect its citizens. In an additional bid to bolster security, Israel withdrew troops and Jewish settlers from the Gaza Strip in 2005 amid protests by right-leaning groups.

Following the Israeli withdrawal from Gaza, internal Palestinian tensions were inflamed by Hamas's victory in legislative elections in January 2006. Fatah, the erstwhile dominant moderate block, attempted to undermine the Hamas mandate by increasing the powers of the presidency, which it still controlled through Fatah's leader, Mahmood Abbas. The two factions' inability to form a unity government acceptable to Israel and external parties resulted in a brief war for the eastern Gaza Strip in July 2007. Hamas won the conflict and established control in the area, countered by a rival Fatah government in the West Bank. Fatah and Hamas remained estranged until the announcement of a unity government in April 2014, cutting short the latest round of peace negotiations between Fatah and Israel, which had begun under the auspices of the United States in July 2013.

While in control of the Gaza Strip, Hamas established a network of tunnels to circumvent the Israeli blockade of the area. Israel, in cooperation with Egypt, had sealed the area's borders within the state and with Egypt's Sinai Peninsula to prevent Hamas from receiving new arms shipments. The ban also resulted in regular shortages of staples for the local population. Observers posited that a secondary Israeli motive for the blockade was to lessen support for the Hamas-led government by increasing general economic hardship in the area, where unemployment averages over 40 percent. Nevertheless, the cyclical nature of militant attacks on Israeli targets, followed by reprisals in the densely populated Gaza Strip, stiffened Palestinian animosity toward Israel and benefited Hamas.

In addition to supplying arms and commodities, Hamas used its tunnel network to stage cross-border attacks on Israeli territory. On December 27, 2008, Israel responded to recent rocket launches by Hamas with Operation Cast Lead, a twenty-two-day air and ground offensive marked by approximately 1,400 deaths before a unilateral Israeli ceasefire on January 18, 2009. This initiative was followed in 2012 by another combined campaign, Pillar of Defense, from November 14 to November 21, causing upwards of 2,000 casualties. Both operations also resulted in significant civilian injuries and destruction of property.

In response to accusations of war crimes, Israel maintained that the attacks were necessary responses to successive assaults on its own civilians. The country has rejected the jurisdiction of institutions such as the ICC. It also declined to cooperate with various external investigative reports, such as the Goldstone Report commissioned by the United Nations Human Rights Council in December 2009, dismissing them as biased. Hamas, meanwhile, faced criticism that it had knowingly endangered people living under its government by launching its attacks from within highly populated areas, guaranteeing significant civilian casualties and attendant Palestinian outrage toward the Israeli government. Palestinian interest groups have continued to lobby for increased scrutiny of Israeli actions at the international level.

New Outbreak of War

The most recent outbreak of war began in July 2014, after the kidnapping and murder of three Israeli teenagers by Hamas militants in June. Following a series of rocket attacks by Hamas, Israel launched Operation Protective Edge on July 8, resulting in more than 2,000 casualties over seven weeks of conflict that ended with an Egyptian-brokered ceasefire on August 26. An earlier draft under Egyptian mediation was derailed by Hamas's insistence that the Rafah checkpoint, the only international border crossing into the Gaza Strip, be opened to commerce.

Israel's stated purpose for Operation Protective Edge was the comprehensive elimination of Hamas's tunnel network. Although the Israeli military stated that it had bombed thirty-two tunnels, observers cautioned that additional routes could remain undetected, providing a base for future asymmetrical attacks. Israel also aimed to destroy Hamas's arms supply, disposing of some 3,000 rockets, while estimating that Hamas retained an additional 3,000 in reserve. International observers were concerned to note that a UN school being used as a civilian shelter was bombed, as was a hospital and other civilian facilities. On July 31, 2014, Navi Pillay, the UN High Commissioner for Human Rights, noted civilians had been killed during an apparent ceasefire for the Muslim Eid holiday, including children. Separate reports indicated that some 18,000 homes had been destroyed, displacing an esti-mated 250,000 people. Pillay also faulted Hamas for launching attacks from within crowded areas close to critical infrastructure, including the area's only electricity plant, which was demolished. Hamas launched more than 3,500 rockets and 800 mortars from its bases in Gaza during the recent conflict.

Commissioner Pillay cautioned that both parties had a responsibility to limit harm to civilians, regardless of whether alarms were issued prior to specific attacks. She concluded with a call for redoubled international efforts to enforce accountability for both parties with more robust investigations, lamenting that the recommendations highlighted in the 2009 Goldstone Report had not been implemented. These recommendations included support for thorough internal investigations by both Israeli and Palestinian authorities. Israel initiated investigation of forty-four cases within a month of the August 2014 ceasefire, but indicated that it would not cooperate with an external investigation by the United Nations due to presumed bias.

Human Rights Watch, an international lobby group, accused Israel of deliberately tar-geting civilian structures, while criticizing Hamas's attacks on populated Israeli areas. Amnesty International, which published the first comprehensive report on the conflict, faulted both sides but was criticized by Israel for insufficiently acknowledging the militant nature of Hamas, which is considered a terrorist group by the U.S. and UK governments. Hamas was removed from the EU terror blacklist in December 2014.

Meanwhile, external observers argue that the end of the blockade is a prerequisite for lasting peace. This is unlikely to transpire so long as Israel views rocket launches by Hamas as a threat to its civilian population, which suffered sixty-seven deaths in the last bout of violence. Israel also views Hamas as a proxy group of the Iranian government, which the government considers an existential threat. Eviatar Manor, Israel's ambassador to the UN Human Rights Commission, rejected the commission's perceived implication of "moral symmetry between a terrorist aggressor and a democracy defending itself." The United States adheres to this view and allocated an additional $47 million to alleviate blockade-induced shortages before the August ceasefire to quell calls to lift the ban.

OUTLOOK ON PEACE

Given successive outbreaks of internal violence and failed bids for a peace settlement, Palestinians have increasingly resorted to "internationalizing" the conflict through appli-cations to various external authorities. Palestinians have engaged in "lawfare" to invoke international norms to gain leverage over Israeli authorities. This approach was most clearly typified by Palestine's decision to join the ICC in April 2015. Palestine plans to spearhead investigations of alleged Israeli war crimes through the body, but this tactic entails risk for it as well, since the ICC would hypothetically have jurisdiction to prosecute all crimes committed in Palestinian territory, including attacks by Hamas on civilians.

Israel does not recognize the ICC and argues that Palestine lacks the sovereignty required to unilaterally join external organizations. It responded to Palestine's ICC bid by freezing its monthly transfer of $127 million in taxes levied on behalf of the Palestinian Authority (PA), potentially complicating PA efforts to pay public sector salaries. Israel has also accused the PA of paying pensions to families of suicide bombers and Islamists held in Israeli prisons. The United States, for its part, promised to suspend $400 million in annual aid to the PA if Palestine led claims against Israel at the ICC. The United States is the PA's largest donor after the European Union.

Notwithstanding U.S. and Israeli efforts, the Palestinian approach of internationalization appears more successful than previous attempts to leverage its influence. As of November 2014, 135 countries had recognized Palestine as a state, and the European Union voted in favor of Palestinian statehood in December that year. Given this momentum, Palestinian attempts to prosecute alleged Israeli war crimes through external bodies is likely to yield some symbolic victories. Israel, however, will not acknowledge any investigative finding that discounts the security threat presented by Hamas and other militant groups. It will continue to maintain its right to protect its citizens and assign blame for both Israeli and Palestinian civilian deaths to jihadists.

—Anastazia Clouting

Following is the text of a press release issued on July 31, 2014, by the United Nations Office of the High Commissioner for Human Rights regarding ongoing civilian attacks in Gaza that indicate war crimes.

UN Human Rights Commissioner on Attacks in Gaza

July 31, 2014

UN High Commissioner for Human Rights Navi Pillay on Thursday strongly condemned the 30 July shelling by Israeli military forces of a UN school in Gaza sheltering people fleeing the violence, as well as other attacks on schools, hospitals, places of worship and vital infrastructure such as Gaza's only electric power plant.

She underlined the need for "real accountability considering the increasing evidence of war crimes and an ever-growing number of civilian casualties, including some 250 children."

"Six UN schools have now been hit, including another deadly strike on 24 July that also killed civilians," Pillay said. "The shelling and bombing of UN schools which have resulted in the killing and maiming of frightened women and children and civilian men, including UN staff, seeking shelter from the conflict are horrific acts and may possibly amount to war crimes," Pillay said. "If civilians cannot take refuge in UN schools, where can they be safe? They leave their homes to seek safety—and are then subjected to attack in the places they flee to. This is a grotesque situation."

"Under international law, humanitarian relief personnel and objects used for relief operations—this would include UNRWA schools in Gaza being used as shelters—must be respected and protected," Pillay said. "An attack against humanitarian relief personnel and objects used exclusively for relief operations, is a violation of international humanitarian law and may amount to a war crime."

The situation in the Gaza strip has markedly deteriorated in recent days, as Israeli military forces expanded their bombardment and military ground operations. Since the Israeli military operation began on the night of 7 July, more than 2,700 air raids, firing more than 4,000 missiles, have been conducted in addition to artillery and naval bombardment.

As of 4:00 p.m. on Wednesday, more than 1,200 Palestinians had been killed, including at least 850 civilians. More than 250,000 have been displaced, many on multiple occasions, with the shelters overflowing and unable to accommodate terrified new arrivals.

"The numbers don't begin to adequately tell the tale of the ongoing human tragedy in Gaza," said Pillay. "What we are witnessing is the killing of entire families, and of children in the street either playing or trying to find safety. Waves and waves of ordinary people continue to flee their homes as the already weak infrastructure in Gaza caves in under the relentless bombardment."

Pillay expressed alarm at how this crisis has gravely affected civilians in Gaza, including an attack on Beach camp on 28 July, in which 12 children and an elderly man were killed while playing, walking or buying supplies in shops. There were reports of a similar attack in the Shi'jaiya neighbourhood of Gaza yesterday, an area already subjected to intense bombardment, when a marketplace was bombed during a supposed humanitarian ceasefire, with many civilians killed.

"The killing of civilians, including children, as they played or shopped in Beach Camp in Gaza during the end-of-Ramadan *Eid*, traditionally a time of celebration and happiness, is profoundly disturbing," the High Commissioner said. "According to initial reports there were no military activities in the area, which begs the question—what possible justification could there be for such an attack?"

Pillay reiterated her condemnation of the indiscriminate firing of rockets into Israel by armed groups in Gaza and emphasized that military assets should not be located in densely populated areas nor should attacks be launched from such areas. More than 3,500 rockets and 800 mortars have been fired by armed groups in Gaza since the beginning of the crisis. Reportedly, three civilians in Israel have been killed so far. "The launching of indiscriminate attacks is a war crime," Pillay said. In addition, 57 Israeli soldiers have been killed in the course of the hostilities.

She emphasized that issuing warnings to civilians, or any alleged violation of the laws of war by one party, does not excuse either party from their continuing obligations to protect civilians and respect the core principles of distinction, proportionality and precautions in attack.

Pillay cited what a Palestinian child had said to one of her staff in Gaza: "This little 7 year-old boy talked of his dream—and his dream is to have a Palestinian 'Iron Dome' protecting him and his family from Israeli attacks, just as the Israelis have their 'Iron Dome' system protecting them against rockets attacks from Gaza.

She also condemned the repeated attacks on Gaza's overburdened hospitals which are packed with people injured and dying as a result of airstrikes and shelling.

"Like any other civilian object, hospitals are prima facie protected from attack," she said. "However, because of their vital importance, international humanitarian law specifically provides for their protection. Under the Fourth Geneva Convention, 'civilian hospitals . . . may in no circumstances be the object of attack, but shall at all times be respected and protected by the Parties to the conflict.' Intentional attacks on hospitals being exclusively used as hospitals amounts to a war crime."

Accountability for any violations of international law is essential to end the recurrent cycle of violence. The Commission of Inquiry established by the Human Rights Council at its Special Session on 23 July 2014 will play a key role in addressing accountability issues related to the current hostilities in Gaza. "However, true justice will only be achieved by bringing cases in front of a fair and competent court," Pillay said. "The international community has a collective responsibility to end this climate of impunity."

The High Commissioner noted that the 2009 report of the Gaza Fact-Finding Mission set up by the Human Rights Council provided a contextual, factual and legal analysis, as well as a set of recommendations for follow up, that "remain compellingly relevant in light of what is happening today."

The report's recommendations, including regarding referral of the situation to the International Criminal Court, remain relevant in view of the lack of progress in ensuring effective accountability through investigations at the domestic level.

"That accountability and justice is unlikely to be achieved through domestic proceedings is evident in the lack of adequate investigations, to this day, into even the most serious reports of violations contained in the Fact-Finding Mission's report," she added. "Instead, a huge orchestrated effort was made to denigrate the report and its authors to the point where its findings are being shamefully ignored."

"It's unforgivable that the international community could not find the political resolve to take the practical steps that the report said were essential," she said. "These were designed to deter future violations, by ending the longstanding impunity that has been such a feature of this situation."

SOURCE: United Nations. Office of the High Commissioner for Human Rights. "Pillay condemns continuing attacks on civilians in Gaza." July 31, 2014. www.ohchr.org/EN/NewsEvents/Pages/DisplayNews .aspx?NewsID=14916&LangID=E

OTHER HISTORIC DOCUMENTS OF INTEREST

FROM THIS VOLUME

- U.S., Palestinian, and Israeli Leaders Remark on Peace Process, p. 118
- U.S., United Nations, and Swedish Leaders on Installation of Palestinian Unity Government, p. 231

FROM PREVIOUS *HISTORIC DOCUMENTS*

- Israel and Palestine Remark on Prisoner Swap, *2011*, p. 549
- Israel Raids Gaza Flotilla, *2010*, p. 282

August

Massachusetts Passes
Nation's Toughest Gun Law

AUGUST 1 AND 13, 2014

Following inaction at the federal level to increase gun control regulations, the Massachusetts state legislature took up consideration of a bill that would tighten gun control in the state through many provisions, including giving police chiefs the ability to petition the issuance of a firearms identification (FID) that is required for gun purchase. The legislation, which is not supported by gun rights organizations like the National Rifle Association (NRA), is one of the strictest in the nation.

LEGISLATORS WORK TO DRAFT LEGISLATION

In December 2012, Adam Lanza walked into Sandy Hook Elementary in Newtown, Connecticut, and systematically gunned down six teachers and twenty students. The tragedy instantly brought national attention to gun laws in the United States and raised questions about whether President Barack Obama or Congress would take action to impose tighter regulations. Because Lanza was carrying a semiautomatic weapon in addition to two handguns, one of the major questions was whether the president would attempt to reinstate the assault weapons ban that had expired in 2004 and thus far had not been renewed by Congress. Early in his first term, the president had loosened some gun restrictions, including allowing concealed carry in national parks and on Amtrak trains. During his 2012 campaign, the president reiterated that he did not have any intention to "take guns away" from licensed holders.

In response to the events in Newtown, the president created a task force that would make recommendations by January 2013 on all possible solutions to curb gun violence, including how to set provisions for those with mental health problems. The recommendations developed by the task force and released by President Obama on January 16, 2013, were folded into executive actions and legislative proposals. They included adding new incentives to push states to share information with the national background check system, and closing a loophole in the background check system for people associated with trusts or corporations (which had allowed some felons to obtain access to firearms). "Even as Congress fails to act on common-sense proposals, like expanding criminal background checks and making gun trafficking a federal crime, the president and vice president remain committed to using all the tools in their power to make progress toward reducing gun violence," the White House said in a 2013 statement.

The NRA immediately came out in defense of gun ownership, with Executive Vice President Wayne LaPierre arguing that "the only thing that stops a bad guy with a gun is a good guy with a gun." The NRA proposed placing armed police officers in every school to stop another shooting like in Newtown, but offered no support for further gun control legislation. Teachers groups came out against such a proposal, stating that it would create greater risk for students and staff.

In Congress, Republicans shied away from gun control legislation, with Sen. Lindsey Graham, R-S.C., saying, "Every bad event in the world can't be fixed by government action." Democrats, however, submitted a variety of bills in the House and Senate aimed at greater gun restrictions, including the Safe Communities, Safe Schools Act of 2013, which combined many of the already submitted bills into one piece of legislation. Notably absent from this piece of legislation was a reinstatement of the assault weapons ban. As debate continued on the bill, Sens. Pat Toomey, R-Pa., and Joe Manchin, D-W.V., submitted an amendment that would extend background checks to gun show and Internet purchases. The amendment failed, and the ultimate inability of Congress to pass the bill was seen by many as an indication that Congress would not be able to approve any kind of meaningful gun control legislation.

MASSACHUSETTS TAKES ACTION

Without Congressional action on the issue, some states decided to implement their own gun control legislation. Arkansas, Kansas, and Texas relaxed gun control regulations in 2013, while Colorado, Connecticut, Delaware, Maryland, and New York passed tighter gun control laws.

Massachusetts, a state that already had some of the nation's toughest gun control laws, worked throughout 2013 and 2014 to craft its own legislation. In an effort to develop a widely accepted bill, during the drafting process legislators invited gun control supporters and opponents, including the Gun Owners' Action League of Massachusetts (GOAL), to submit input. GOAL opposed initial measures considered for the bill but worked with legislators to create something palatable for their membership. Early in 2014, state Sen. Robert DeLeo, who was driving the legislation, appointed a task force to review a set of forty-four recommendations submitted by supporters and opponents of the bill. Some of the recommendations included maintaining restrictions on large-magazine capacity sales, creating a single-licensing standard, and requiring gun sales to be processed only through licensed gun dealers.

During debate, the state House placed into the legislation a provision that would allow police chiefs to reject issuing a firearms identification card. This provision is similar to one already in place that allows police chiefs to use their discretion when issuing concealed carry permits. The Senate rejected such a provision, saying that it gave too much subjective power to police chiefs. The two chambers developed a compromise that would instead give police chiefs ninety days after receiving a request for an FID to file a court petition to deny such an FID if the chief feels that the person requesting the FID is not suitable for gun ownership. If a chief chooses to deny an application for gun ownership, written justification based on public safety would have to be submitted with the rejection. Most other states do not allow for such authority, and instead issue FIDs to anyone who properly completes the applications. Of the compromise, John Rosenthal, founder of Stop Handgun Violence, expressed disappointment, calling it "a burden on chiefs who are simply trying to save lives," but he said the compromise "is far better than nothing."

Other provisions in the draft legislation included creating a website that would allow for real-time background checks for private sellers, the creation of a firearms trafficking unit, harsher penalties for gun crimes, two-way communication devices between schools and police/fire departments, and mandated suicide awareness prevention and training for school staff. The background check provision is intended to close the gun show sale loophole, which allows any individual with an FID to purchase a firearm without a background check.

The legislation drafted by lawmakers in July 2014 not only placed focus on gun ownership restrictions, but also called for greater support of mental health issues, including mandating that schools develop plans to address any mental health needs of their students. It also required the state to join the National Instant Criminal Background Check System (NICS), which collects information about substance abuse and mental health issues and is used by police when determining whether to approve a firearms application.

The NRA initially came out in support of the Senate version of Massachusetts's gun bill, which did not include the ability to deny FIDs, feeling that the House version gave too much authority to local police chiefs. In contrast, police chiefs and gun safety organizations fought the Senate version. Ed Davis, a former Boston police commissioner, spoke at a rally in support of the House bill, noting that he had once issued an ID despite his own suspicions, and that an eighty-year-old man later went on to hold police hostage with the gun he obtained with his FID.

Once the House and Senate reconciled the ID provision, the NRA said it could no longer give support to the bill because "it isn't difficult to imagine" ways government officials might abuse such power. GOAL's executive director Jim Wallace said he was happy with the efforts made to soften the original language of the House bill, but added, "I don't think it should be a model for the rest of the country because Massachusetts' gun laws are still very convoluted."

On July 9, the House passed the reconciled bill 112–28. The state Senate passed an altered version of the bill 28–10 on July 17. The changes made by the Senate sent the bill back to the House. Ultimately, both chambers agreed to final passage on August 1.

Gov. Patrick Signs Gun Legislation

On August 13, Governor Deval Patrick signed the gun control legislation into law, making Massachusetts the first in the nation to increase record keeping aimed at reducing gun trafficking and investing in police chiefs a significant amount of control over who would be issued an FID. The final bill included provisions to allow individuals committed for mental health problems to petition the court five years after date of commitment to request an ability to possess a firearm; required all licensed gun dealers to run criminal background checks on their employees; required personal sales and transfers of firearms to be completed through a web portal that will ensure the transaction complies with state law; created new criminal offenses involving the use of firearms including assault with battery with a firearm and disarming a police officer; imposed new requirements on tracking firearms involved in crimes; and required additional reporting to the NICS on substance abuse, mental illness commitments, and domestic violence convictions.

The bill was celebrated by gun control activists around the state. Molly Malloy, director of the Massachusetts chapter of Moms Demand Action, said, "The single most effective thing we can do to keep guns out of dangerous hands and reduce the number of Americans killed with guns every day is require criminal background checks on all sales to close the loophole that allows felons, domestic abusers and the dangerously mentally ill to buy guns. Real leadership is what will keep guns out of the hands of dangerous people, and we are grateful to have leaders on this issue taking action to protect our families in the commonwealth."

Massachusetts's tightening of its gun laws was in stark contrast to regulations in other states that have loosened gun ownership and concealed carry provisions. In nearby New Jersey, Governor Chris Christie vetoed a bill to ban high-capacity magazines with more than ten rounds of ammunition. And in Georgia, Governor Nathan Deal signed a law that took effect on July 1 that gave residents the right to carry guns into a variety of buildings that lack security personnel, including nightclubs, bars, some government buildings, and classrooms.

—Heather Kerrigan

Following is a statement by Boston mayor Martin J. Walsh on the passage of gun control legislation on August 1, 2014; and an August 13, 2014, summary of the new gun legislation provided by the Massachusetts Department of Criminal Justice Information Services.

Mayor Walsh on Gun Control Legislation

August 1, 2014

Today, the House of Representatives and the Senate made history with the passage of comprehensive gun safety legislation that will make our neighborhoods, streets and homes safer places to live. In particular, I would like to thank Speaker DeLeo and Senate President Murray for their leadership throughout the entire process. With this legislation, the Commonwealth will once again be a national model for not only the contents of this bill, but also the process by which we arrived at this point. The bipartisan efforts exhibited by members of the Massachusetts Legislature are truly commendable. Our legislators put aside their differences and, by working together, created a bill that will have a tremendous impact on our efforts to reduce gun violence in the Commonwealth. I look forward to Governor Patrick signing this bill into law so that we can begin to utilize the tools provided by this legislation.

Source: City of Boston. "Statement of Mayor Martin J. Walsh on Gun Safety Legislation." August 1, 2014. www.cityofboston.gov/news/Default.aspx?id=14742.

Massachusetts Department of Justice Information Services Releases Bill Summary

August 13, 2014

On August 13, 2014, the Governor signed House Bill 4376, "An Act Relative to the Reduction of Gun Violence." The full text of H4376 is available at: https://malegislature.gov/Laws/SessionLaws/Acts/2014/Chapter284.

The bill:

- Requires Massachusetts to submit more data to the federal National Instant Check System (NICS), including state commitments for alcohol and/or substance abuse, commitments for mental illness or as dangerous persons, and convictions for domestic violence cases;
- Allows an individual who has been committed for certain mental health reasons, for an alcohol use disorder, substance use disorder, or guardianship appointment to petition the court 5 years from the date of commitment requesting that his/her ability to possess a firearms, rifle, or shotgun be restored;

- Requires all Massachusetts licensed gun dealers to run criminal offender record information (CORI) checks on current and new employees;
- Requires all Massachusetts licensed gun dealers to post information about suicide awareness and prevention;
- Eliminates the requirement to obtain a firearms identification card or license to carry to purchase or possess self-defense spray, unless under the age of 18 or otherwise disqualified by law;
- Requires personal sales/transfers of all firearms, rifles, and shotguns to be completed through a web portal to be developed by the Department of Criminal Justice Information Services; the portal will, among other things, verify the identity of both buyer and seller, and ensure the sale/transfer complies with the law;
- Expands the eligibility disqualifications for firearms identification cards and licenses to carry;
- Allows licensing authorities to petition the district court to deny, suspend, or revoke firearms identification cards on the grounds of unsuitability;
- Requires that a licensing authority provide each applicant with a receipt indicating that either a new or renewal firearms license application has been received;
- Provides an indefinite grace period if an applicant submits a renewal application prior to the expiration of his/her current license;
- Eliminates the Class B license to carry firearms, though current Class B licenses to carry will remain valid until the said expiration of the license;
- Exempts active duty military personnel from the requirement to take a Basic Firearms Safety Course before obtaining an FID or LTC;
- Reduces the firearms application fee to $25 for retired law enforcement officers;
- Exempts law enforcement officers from the assault weapon and large capacity feeding device ban;
- Changes the definition and some punishments relative to firearms trafficking crimes;
- Creates several new crimes involving the use of firearms, including assault and battery with a firearm and disarming a law enforcement officer;
- Requires all licensing authorities to trace and collect specific data on any firearm used in a crime within its jurisdiction.

Some changes to the statute go into effect immediately, while others will go into effect in accordance with the schedule indicated in H4376. Please call your local licensing authority or the Firearms Records Bureau (617.660.4782) should you have any questions.

SOURCE: Massachusetts Department of Criminal Justice Information Services. "Changes to the Laws Concerning Firearms Licensing and Gun Sales in Massachusetts." August 13, 2014. www.mass.gov/eopss/agencies/dcjis/key-changes-to-the-massachusetts-gun-laws-august-2014.pdf.

OTHER HISTORIC DOCUMENTS OF INTEREST

FROM PREVIOUS *HISTORIC DOCUMENTS*

President Obama Authorizes Airstrikes Against ISIL Targets

AUGUST 7, 2014

Responding to the growing threat posed by the Islamic State in Iraq and the Levant (ISIL), in August 2014, President Barack Obama authorized the use of targeted airstrikes to protect U.S. interests in Iraq. The president also pledged further humanitarian aid and distanced himself from any suggestion that he might want to send ground troops into the country. Although the Pentagon reported that ISIL's movements had been somewhat hampered by the airstrikes, officials stated that a longer-term, nonmilitary policy was needed to help ensure the group could be weakened.

AIRSTRIKES AUTHORIZED

In a nationally televised address on August 7, the president told Americans that he had authorized targeted airstrikes against ISIL in an attempt to protect U.S. interests in Iraq and protect troops who were helping deliver humanitarian assistance to Iraqi refugees stranded on Mount Sinjar. "Earlier this week, one Iraqi in the area cried to the world, 'There is no one coming to help.' Well, today, America is coming to help," the president said. Obama said that some of the strikes would be focused on helping evacuate Iraqis from Mount Sinjar who became stranded there after attempting to flee ISIL. "These innocent families are faced with a horrible choice—descend the mountain and be slaughtered or stay and slowly die of thirst and hunger . . . . We can act responsibly to prevent an act of genocide."

On August 8, targeted airstrikes led by Air Force and Navy fighters, began near Erbil, Iraq. Unmanned drones were also used to protect citizens and forces near Erbil and help troops free citizens trapped on Mount Sinjar. On August 21, Defense Secretary Chuck Hagel said that the airstrikes were working as intended: "Overall, these operations have stalled ISIL's momentum and enabled Iraqi and Kurdish forces to regain their footing and take the initiative. As Iraqi and Kurdish forces continue to take the initiative, the United States will continue to support them." Hagel added that moving forward the United States would continue to work with the newly seated government of Iraq to push for political reform and a comprehensive strategy on targeting ISIL. "The president, the chairman and I are all very clear eyed about the challenges ahead. We are pursuing a long-term strategy against ISIL because ISIL clearly poses a long-term threat," Hagel said. The Pentagon echoed Hagel's remarks but added in its own statement that they were "unlikely to affect ISIL's overall capabilities or its operations in other areas of Iraq and Syria." Within one month of their authorization, a reported 133 airstrikes had been conducted across Iraq.

INTERNATIONAL RESPONSE TO GROWING ISIL THREAT

In addition to announcing airstrikes against ISIL in September, President Obama discussed other nonmilitary responses to the terrorist group that the nation would undertake with its international partners. This included sending 475 troops to Iraq for a support mission that would include training and intelligence but would not include any direct combat duties. The president also promised that the United States would work to improve intelligence about foreign fighters in the Middle East in an effort to find ways to cut funding to various terrorist organizations and stem their movement.

Obama increased the level of humanitarian assistance for those affected by ISIL. New airdrops of water, medical supplies, and food began on August 7 and targeted those stranded on Mount Sinjar. The United States also deployed the U.S. Agency for International Development Disaster Assistance response team and sent military advisers to assess the humanitarian crisis in northern Iraq. The findings were better than many had expected: there were not as many stranded on Mount Sinjar as originally expected, and their situation was not as dire as first thought. The United States said it intended to continue its humanitarian mission on an as-needed basis.

In his statement about America's ISIL response, the president was careful to ensure that the nation understood he had no intention of involving ground forces in the region. "American combat troops will not be returning to fight in Iraq, because there is no American military solution to the larger crisis in Iraq," Obama said. "This effort will be a steady and relentless approach to take out terrorists who threaten us, while supporting our partners on the front lines." Obama did not give the airstrike mission a target end date, but senior officials said the mission would not be sustained.

Close allies of the United States were slower to determine whether to become involved in the fighting. On September 5, the United Kingdom's foreign secretary, William Hague, stated, "We in Britain have made no commitment to take part in any air strikes as yet," but "we'll certainly consider that possibility if we think that it is the best and most effective way to support a credible and inclusive Iraqi government." The United Kingdom did partner with the United States on humanitarian assistance, conducting its own airdrops on Mount Sinjar.

Other nations, including Canada, Denmark, France, Germany, and Italy, worked with the United States to equip and train Kurdish fighters to help them respond to the ISIL threat in the Kurdistan region of Iraq. The United Kingdom in late August agreed to "supply non-lethal equipment to Kurdish forces . . . including night vision equipment and body armour."

Ongoing Support

In late September during an interview with *60 Minutes*, Obama admitted that the United States had initially underestimated ISIL's threat, while subsequently overestimating the abilities of the Iraqi army to combat the group's rise. He said the militant group was able to gain power because of the ongoing unrest in the region. "During the chaos of the Syrian civil war, where essentially you have huge swaths of the country that are completely ungoverned, they were able to reconstitute themselves and take advantage of that chaos," the president said.

Speaker of the House John Boehner, R-Ohio, was critical of the president's airstrike approach and said he did not believe it would succeed. He added on ABC's *This Week* that the president was wrong to state that he would not send in ground troops because "we have no choice. If we don't destroy them first, we're gonna pay the price." Obama responded, "Rather than play whack-a-mole and send U.S. troops wherever this occurs, we have to build strong partnerships." The president added, "We have to get the international community to recognize this is a problem. We've got to get Arab and Muslim leaders to say very clearly, 'These folks do not represent us. They do not represent Islam.'"

In December, Congress provided new funds within its 2015 defense authorization to help combat ISIL. On February 11, 2015, President Obama somewhat changed course and asked

Congress to authorize the use of military force against ISIL. "Make no mistake, this is a difficult mission and it will remain difficult for some time," the president said at a press conference the same day. But, he added, "ISIL is on the defensive and ISIL is going to lose." The proposal submitted by the president did not call for immediately sending troops to the region, but it left open the possibility of a combat mission. "I am convinced that the U.S. should not get back into another ground war in the Middle East," the president said. On the one hand, Republicans in the House supported an authorization but said that the president should not have such limited options. "Any authorization for the use of military force must give our military commanders the flexibility and authorities they need to succeed and protect our people. . . . I have concerns that the president's request does not meet this standard," Speaker Boehner said. Democrats, on the other hand, hoped to win bipartisan support for the president's proposal as is.

ISIL Releases Videos Showing Beheadings of Americans

As the United States carried out airstrikes, ISIL was finding new ways to target those opposed to its existence. This included a growing number of beheadings, many of which were carried out by a man who became known as "Jihadi John," who covered himself in head-to-toe black with only a small space for his eyes peeking out of a mask. On August 19, a video surfaced of James Foley, a freelance journalist who was abducted in Syria in November 2012. In the video, Foley read a prepared statement that was critical of the United States and its airstrikes against ISIL. Before beheading the journalist, Jihadi John called on the United States to stop its invasion. Jihadi John stated in the Foley video that he would next kill *Time* journalist Steven Sotloff if the United States did not meet his demands. Sotloff was killed on September 2, followed by the beheading of Peter Kassig, a humanitarian aid worker, on November 16. Countless Syrian soldiers and international aid workers were also beheaded by Jihadi John and his associates throughout the fall and winter of 2014.

The FBI and British intelligence organizations MI5 and Scotland Yard called for the capture of Jihadi John and worked together to determine his identity and whereabouts. Initial reports indicated that he was likely British, because he spoke with a "multicultural London English" accent. In September, British prime minister David Cameron announced that the terrorist's identity had been determined, but no further information was released. It was not until late February 2015 that *The Washington Post* identified Jihadi John as Mohammed Emwazi, a British citizen with Iraqi parents. British intelligence agencies would not confirm the report. The United States has announced a $10 million bounty for anyone with information leading to his capture.

—Heather Kerrigan

Following is the text of a statement by President Barack Obama on August 7, 2014, authorizing airstrikes against ISIL targets.

DOCUMENT *President Obama Authorizes Airstrikes*

August 7, 2014

Good evening. Today I authorized two operations in Iraq: targeted airstrikes to protect our American personnel and a humanitarian effort to help save thousands of Iraqi civilians who are trapped on a mountain without food and water and facing almost certain death. Let me explain the actions we're taking and why.

First, I said in June, as the terrorist group ISIL began an advance across Iraq, that the United States would be prepared to take targeted military action in Iraq if and when we determined that the situation required it. In recent days, these terrorists have continued to move across Iraq and have neared the city of Erbil, where American diplomats and civilians serve at our consulate and American military personnel advise Iraqi forces.

To stop the advance on Erbil, I've directed our military to take targeted strikes against ISIL terrorist convoys should they move toward the city. We intend to stay vigilant and take action if these terrorist forces threaten our personnel or facilities anywhere in Iraq, including our consulate in Erbil and our Embassy in Baghdad. We're also providing urgent assistance to Iraqi Government and Kurdish forces so they can more effectively wage the fight against ISIL.

Second, at the request of the Iraqi Government, we've begun operations to help save Iraqi civilians stranded on the mountain. As ISIL has marched across Iraq, it has waged a ruthless campaign against innocent Iraqis. And these terrorists have been especially barbaric towards religious minorities, including Christian and Yazidis, a small and ancient religious sect. Countless Iraqis have been displaced, and chilling reports describe ISIL militants rounding up families, conducting mass executions, and enslaving Yazidi women.

In recent days, Yazidi women, men, and children from the area of Sinjar have fled for their lives. And thousands—perhaps tens of thousands—are now hiding high up on the mountain, with little but the clothes on their backs. They're without food; they're without water. People are starving, and children are dying of thirst. Meanwhile, ISIL forces below have called for the systematic destruction of the entire Yazidi people, which would constitute genocide. So these innocent families are faced with a horrible choice: descend the mountain and be slaughtered or stay and slowly die of thirst and hunger.

Now, I've said before, the United States cannot and should not intervene every time there's a crisis in the world. So let me be clear about why we must act and act now. When we face a situation like we do on that mountain, with innocent people facing the prospect of violence on a horrific scale; when we have a mandate to help, in this case, a request from the Iraqi Government; and when we have the unique capabilities to help avert a massacre, then I believe the United States of America cannot turn a blind eye. We can act carefully and responsibly to prevent a potential act of genocide. That's what we're doing on that mountain.

I've therefore authorized targeted airstrikes, if necessary, to help forces in Iraq as they fight to break the siege of Mount Sinjar and protect the civilians trapped there. Already, American aircraft have begun conducting humanitarian airdrops of food and water to help these desperate men, women, and children survive. Earlier this week, one Iraqi in the area cried to the world, "There is no one coming to help." Well, today America is coming to help. We're also consulting with other countries—and the United Nations—who have called for action to address this humanitarian crisis.

I know that many of you are rightly concerned about any American military action in Iraq, even limited strikes like these. I understand that. I ran for this office in part to end our war in Iraq and welcome our troops home, and that's what we've done. As Commander in Chief, I will not allow the United States to be dragged into fighting another war in Iraq. And so even as we support Iraqis as they take the fight to these terrorists, American combat troops will not be returning to fight in Iraq, because there is no American military solution to the larger crisis in Iraq. The only lasting solution is reconciliation among Iraqi communities and stronger Iraqi security forces.

However, we can and should support moderate forces who can bring stability to Iraq. So even as we carry out these two missions, we will continue to pursue a broader strategy that empowers Iraqis to confront this crisis. Iraqi leaders need to come together and forge a new Government that represents the legitimate interests of all Iraqis and that can fight back against the threats like ISIL. Iraqis have named a new President, a new Speaker of Parliament, and are seeking consensus on a new Prime Minister. This is the progress that needs to continue in order to reverse the momentum of the terrorists who prey on Iraq's divisions.

Once Iraq has a new Government, the United States will work with it and other countries in the region to provide increased support to deal with this humanitarian crisis and counterterrorism challenge. None of Iraq's neighbors have an interest in this terrible suffering or instability.

And so we'll continue to work with our friends and allies to help refugees get the shelter and food and water they so desperately need and to help Iraqis push back against ISIL. The several hundred American advisers that I ordered to Iraq will continue to assess what more we can do to help train, advise, and support Iraqi forces going forward. And just as I consulted Congress on the decisions I made today, we will continue to do so going forward.

My fellow Americans, the world is confronted by many challenges. And while America has never been able to right every wrong, America has made the world a more secure and prosperous place. And our leadership is necessary to underwrite the global security and prosperity that our children and our grandchildren will depend upon. We do so by adhering to a set of core principles: We do whatever is necessary to protect our people, we support our allies when they're in danger, we lead coalitions of countries to uphold international norms, and we strive to stay true to the fundamental values—the desire to live with basic freedom and dignity—that is common to human beings wherever they are. That's why people all over the world look to the United States of America to lead. And that's why we do.

So let me close by assuring you that there is no decision that I take more seriously than the use of military force. Over the last several years, we have brought the vast majority of our troops home from Iraq and Afghanistan. And I've been careful to resist calls to turn, time and again, to our military, because America has other tools in our arsenal than our military. We can also lead with the power of our diplomacy, our economy, and our ideals.

But when the lives of American citizens are at risk, we will take action. That's my responsibility as Commander in Chief. And when many thousands of innocent civilians are faced with the danger of being wiped out, and we have the capacity to do something about it, we will take action. That is our responsibility as Americans. That's a hallmark of American leadership. That's who we are.

So tonight we give thanks to our men and women in uniform, especially our brave pilots and crews over Iraq who are protecting our fellow Americans and saving the lives of so many men, women, and children that they will never meet. They represent American leadership at its best. As a nation, we should be proud of them and of our country's enduring commitment to uphold our own security and the dignity of our fellow human beings.

God bless our Armed Forces, and God bless the United States of America.

SOURCE: Executive Office of the President. "Remarks on the Situation in Iraq." August 7, 2014. *Compilation of Presidential Documents* 2014, no. 00602 (August 7, 2014). www.gpo.gov/fdsys/pkg/DCPD-201400602/pdf/DCPD-201400602.pdf.

OTHER HISTORIC DOCUMENTS OF INTEREST

FROM THIS VOLUME

European Commission on Slow Growth and New Investment Plans

AUGUST 28 AND NOVEMBER 26, 2014

Economic figures released in late August showed a slower than anticipated recovery rate in the second quarter of 2014 for the eighteen countries that form part of the European Union's single currency area known as the eurozone. In addition, there was a dip in the economic sentiment indicator, which measures how confident consumers and businesses feel about the future prospects for their economy. One of the causes for this negative trend was the crisis in Ukraine that developed in spring 2014 when Russia annexed the Black Sea peninsula of Crimea from Ukraine, and two pro-Russian regions in eastern Ukraine seceded, triggering separatist conflicts on the Russian-Ukrainian border. With the eurozone still struggling to emerge from its sovereign debt crisis of 2010–2012, this was a setback for its recovery efforts. Some economists warned that the European Union was in danger of suffering its third recession since the 2008 financial crisis, although these fears had subsided somewhat by the end of the year.

SUMMER OF DISCONTENT

When the European Commission, the EU's executive arm, published its monthly Economic Sentiment Indicator on August 28, it raised alarm bells because it showed a decrease back to December 2013 levels. Among the eighteen eurozone members, the weighted average indicator was 100.6 points, down 1.2 points compared with the previous month, while for the twenty-eight-member European Union the indicator was 104.6 points, a decrease of 1.5 points. The indicator showed particular weaknesses in the construction, industry, and retail sectors, with the services sectors showing a slight uptick.

Meanwhile, the German Bundesbank's monthly report for August painted a picture of an economy hanging in the balance. Germany, widely seen as the economic motor of Europe, had a bumpy start in the first quarter of 2014, with growth picking up in the second quarter. However, its annual economic growth rate still hovered around a disappointing 1 percent, just as the United States was seeing its growth rate increase to 3 percent a year. The eurozone was not the only region in the doldrums: Brazil and Japan also experienced low growth. In neighboring Russia, the situation was even worse. The Russian economy took a nosedive throughout the year with two key factors at play: a fall in the prices of crude oil from $115 to $60 a barrel in the second half of 2014—Russia relies heavily on its oil exports—and the escalating conflict in Ukraine.

Meanwhile, the Frankfurt-based European Central Bank continued its efforts to stimulate the eurozone's economy using the powerful tools at its disposal. On June 5, it further reduced already-low interest rates, bringing them down by 0.1 percent to 0.15 percent for deposits and by 0.35 percent to 0.40 percent for lending. It also injected money directly into the markets by buying up sovereign bonds, with one such spree in early January 2015 worth

€600 billion ($674 billion). On the currency markets, the euro began to lose value against the dollar, falling by 2.5 percent between March and August; a trend that continued through the end of year, with the dollar gaining in strength against most other currencies. Meanwhile, the Russian ruble tumbled to half of its value, further adding to its economic and fiscal woes.

ANTIAUSTERITY SENTIMENT GROWS

Many international economists—including officials at the International Monetary Fund (IMF)—urged the eurozone's leaders, especially Germany, the architect and strongest advocate of so-called austerity policies, to ease off debt-reduction efforts and focus more on growth-promoting investments. But the message seemed to fall on deaf ears in Berlin where staying on the austerity course remained the dominant mantra. The Bundesbank's August report lauded the fact that Germany's public finances were in "comparatively good shape," with small surpluses registered in 2012 and 2013 and balanced budgets forecast for 2014 and 2015. But rather than concluding that the time was ripe to end austerity, it said that "given the extremely favourable conditions for public finances and the ongoing budgetary risks, it would, in fact, be advisable to pursue a more ambitious budgetary policy rather than loosening fiscal policy." It urged the German government to continue to push the country's debt-to-GDP ratio below 60 percent, the threshold below which all eurozone countries are required to keep their debt levels under its membership rules. Hitting this target would "lessen the impact in particular, of the demographic challenges that lie ahead," it said. "Experience shows the importance of prudent budgetary policy in good times. . . . This is equally true of Germany as the euro area's stability anchor," it concluded.

When the financial crisis and Great Recession first hit Europe in the fall of 2008, Germany's relative robustness—after a severe contraction in 2009, it quickly bounced back to positive growth—was seen as the eurozone's saving grace. It was the countries on the periphery, notably Greece, Ireland, Portugal, and Spain, who before the recession had been growing rapidly, were suddenly plunged into sovereign debt crises. This triggered the creation of a bailout fund, the European Stability Mechanism, aimed at preventing them from defaulting on their debts or having to exit the eurozone. As the single largest contributor to this fund, Germany was in a position where it could demand that bailout recipients drastically reduce public spending and push through radical, painful structural reforms to make their economies more competitive.

Several years into this process, by mid-2014 a shift in the economic situation of the eurozone members was perceptible. Ireland emerged from the crisis and was the fastest-growing economy in the European Union, while Portugal and Spain both enjoyed growth again, although Spain was saddled with a disturbingly high unemployment rate of 25 percent. Even Greece, viewed by many as the economic basket-case of Europe, turned a corner, ending five successive years of economic contraction, although it still had a huge mountain of sovereign debt: 170 percent of its GDP. By contrast, the "sick men" of Europe were two large countries at the core of the eurozone: France and Italy. They both had socialist governments that wanted to end austerity but they faced pressure by Germany to maintain efforts to improve their public finances.

According to Kit Juckes, currency strategist at Société Générale, the eurozone's problem was "too little growth to stop the debt snowball, a vicious cycle of fiscal austerity and lack of aggregate demand staying in place and dooming Europe to Japanification." The term "Japanification" referred to relative economic stagnation that Japan has experienced since the late 1990s. Germany's economics minister, Sigmar Gabriel, said, "The German economy is steering through rough foreign waters. Geopolitical crises have also increased uncertainty in Germany and moderate growth is weighing on the German economy." Germany's finance minister, Wolfgang Schäuble, was more upbeat, saying that the weakness was only temporary and not indicative of a new impending crisis. Schäuble was adamant that this was no time to ease up on debt-reduction efforts.

As the year progressed, Schäuble's prediction seemed to be borne out because the economic data for the third quarter showed higher levels of growth than had been expected. It looked as though those who had predicted a "triple-dip-recession" had been overly pessimistic because the eurozone's sluggish but steady recovery resumed. The International Monetary Fund's (IMF) World Economic Outlook, released in October, said the eurozone's "fundamentals are slowly improving." Ireland, Poland, and the United Kingdom (the latter two countries are not in the eurozone but are EU members) were the fastest-growing EU economies, while three EU members—Croatia, Cyprus, and Finland—saw their economies contract in 2014. The countries with the lowest unemployment rates were Austria, Germany, and Malta, and those with the highest rates were Greece and Spain. The IMF's economic prescription for the eurozone was to invest more in infrastructure to spur demand in the short term and supply in the medium term. The IMF said that Germany could afford to use public money for this purpose and still be in compliance with the eurozone's rules on deficit and debt levels. Another priority, the Fund said, was to go beyond speaking the mantra of structural reform and identify specific actions to be taken. The IMF urged the eurozone governments to avoid "self-defeating" additional fiscal consolidation efforts.

€315 Billion Investment Fund

Meanwhile, the EU institutions experienced a changing of the guard with the election of a new European Commission and Parliament. The new commission president, Jean-Claude Juncker, had a strong economic background, having for many years chaired the Eurogroup—the regular meetings of eurozone finance ministers. One of Juncker's flagship projects was a new infrastructure investment fund worth €315 billion aimed at reviving the EU's economy. In the final weeks of 2014, he and his new team of twenty-eight commissioners set about identifying projects and sectors where these funds could be channeled, as well as the source of these funds. By early 2015, progress had been made in developing the fund as a wave of antiausterity sentiment swept through Europe. It was generally agreed by the leaders that most of the capital for the fund would have to come from the private sector but that initial spending needed to be injected from public sources to leverage private sector money.

Despite supporting the new investment fund, Germany still kept up the pressure on eurozone members to improve their public finances. The focus of its energies fell on Greece, which remained in deep debt despite having recently returned to economic growth. Tensions increased following the Greek elections of January 25, 2015, in which the left-wing Syriza party, which had campaigned on a platform of antiausterity, emerged as the winning party and quickly formed a new government. Germany and its pro-austerity allies in the eurozone, which include Finland and the Netherlands, doubled down on demands that Greece continue its debt repayments plan enshrined in EU and IMF bailout packages. The Greek government, led by Prime Minister Alexis Tsipras, pushed for debt relief. But its eurozone partners held firm, making Athens stick to past commitments of reducing public spending levels, making the government function more efficiently—notably by clamping down on tax evasion—and making the economy more competitive and diverse. The German-Greek standoff was in many ways a microcosm of wider tensions that persist between eurozone nations and stem from deep-rooted cultural differences over how to manage debt, while at the same time stimulate the economy.

—Brian Beary

Following is a press release from the European Commission on August 28, 2014, on the economic situation in the eurozone; and the text of a statement delivered on November 26, 2014, by European Commission president Jean-Claude Juncker on a new European Union investment plan.

European Commission on Economic Sentiment

August 28, 2014

[All graphs, charts, and footnotes have been omitted.]

In August the *Economic Sentiment Indicator* (ESI) fell in the euro area (by 1.5 points to 100.6) and the EU (by 1.2 points at 104.6).

Euro area developments

After a broadly flat development over the last five months, August's decrease shifted the euro area headline indicator back to its December 2013 level. Worsened sentiment resulted from deterioration in retail trade, consumer, industry, and, to a lesser extent, services confidence. Construction confidence remained broadly unchanged. Amongst the largest euro area economies, sentiment dropped significantly in Italy (−4.1), sending the ESI below its long-term average of 100, and in Germany (−1.9). Milder contractions were booked also in France (−0.6) and the Netherlands (−0.8), while sentiment remained flat in Spain.

Weakened ***industry confidence*** (−1.5) was caused by managers' more careful views on *expected production*, while assessments of the *current level of overall order books* and the *stocks of finished products* stayed broadly unchanged. By contrast, managers' assessments of the level of *past production* and, to a lesser extent, *export order books*, which do not enter the calculation of the confidence indicator, improved. ***Services confidence*** slid somewhat (−0.5) owing to downward revisions of managers' assessments of the *past business situation* and *past demand*, while their *demand expectations* remained virtually unchanged. The deterioration in ***consumer confidence*** (−1.6) was driven by more negative assessments of *future unemployment* and the *future general economic situation*, and, to a lesser extent, *future savings* and *households' future financial situation*. Falling ***retail trade confidence*** (−2.3) was the result of managers' more pessimistic views on both the *present and expected business situation* together with a worsened assessment of the adequacy of the *volume of stocks*. The broadly flat development of ***construction confidence*** (−0.2) reflected downward revisions of the level of *order books* partially offset by a small improvement in *employment expectations*. The slight increase (+0.4) in ***financial services confidence*** (not included in the ESI) was backed by more positive appraisals of the *past business situation* and *past demand*, while *demand expectations* were revised downward.

Employment plans saw an upward revision in services, while they remained broadly unchanged in industry and construction and deteriorated in the retail trade sector. *Selling price expectations* increased in services and construction, but declined in the other two surveyed business sectors (industry and retail trade). Consumers' price expectations were revised downward.

EU DEVELOPMENTS

The relatively more moderate decrease of the headline indicator in the two largest non-euro area EU economies, the UK (−1.1) and Poland (−1.0), resulted in a less severe contraction for the EU ESI (−1.2) compared to the euro area. EU construction confidence improved, while, as in the euro area, industry, retail trade, services and consumer confidence slipped. Financial services confidence booked a more robust improvement (+1.9).

Contrary to the euro area, EU-wide employment plans were revised downwards in industry but increased slightly in construction and remained flat in retail trade. EU price expectations were in line with those for the euro area apart from a broadly flat development in services.

SOURCE: European Commission. "August 2014: Economic Sentiment falls in the euro area and the EU." August 28, 2014. © European Union. http://europa.eu/rapid/press-release_IP-14-952_en.htm.

President of European Commission Lays Out New Investment Plan

November 26, 2014

1. INTRODUCTION—TURNING A PAGE

Dear President, dear honourable Members of Parliament, Ladies and Gentlemen,

I addressed this house just over a month ago and I promised to present an ambitious Investment Plan before Christmas. One month later and Christmas has come early—I am here to deliver on my promise.

And I am presenting it in the Parliament, because that is where important things should happen.

Today Europe is turning a page. After years of fighting to restore our fiscal credibility and to promote reform, today we are adding the third point of a virtuous triangle: An ambitious, yet realistic 'Investment Plan for Europe'. Europe needs a kick-start and today the Commission is supplying the jump cables.

Investing in Europe: It means much more than figures and projects, money and rules. We need to send a message to the people of Europe and to the rest of the world: Europe is back in business. This is not the moment to look back. Investment is about the future.

Of course, we should never neglect the sacrifices that many in Europe made over the past 6 years to overcome the crisis. Nor should we stop the push to bring down barriers, open up markets and reform what doesn't work in our economies. These are necessary, but not sufficient conditions for growth.

We need structural reforms to modernise and preserve our social market economy. We need fiscal responsibility to restore confidence and the sustainability of our public finances. And to complete this virtuous *omne trium perfectum* (rule of three) we now need to boost investment. No tree can grow on soil and air alone, the Investment Plan we are presenting today is the watering can.

For the first time, the European Commission is presenting all three components of Europe's future economic success together. Not pitched one against the other, but grouped in one single, simple message: Namely, that Europe can offer hope both to its future generations and to the rest of the world, as a promising, attractive hub for jobs, growth and investment.

2. WHY ARE WE DOING THIS?

First, because not only are we faced with a serious investment gap; we are caught in an investment trap. When I talk to investors, they all agree that Europe is an attractive place to invest in. But then I look at the figures, they tell a different story: investment levels in the EU are down to €370 billion below the historical pre-crisis norms. While investment is taking off in the U.S., Europe is lagging behind. Why? Because investors lack confidence, credibility and trust.

Secondly, because we are confronted with a major paradox: despite the huge liquidity in the world's money markets and corporate bank accounts, investment in Europe is not rebounding.

Thirdly, because our public resources are stretched: our debt levels have increased from 60% of our GDP to 90% in the space of just a few years. Public expenditure already represents close to 50% of EU GDP. What we need is a smart use of public money, geared to unlocking investment. Public expenditure should be used for what it is best at doing: funding our schools and welfare systems, not servicing our debt.

Today we are responding to these European pathologies and keeping our eye on the one ball that matters: the real economy. This is not the time for national, political or ideological fights. It is time for a major political and social consensus, a grand bargain to put Europe back to work.

I often hear that we need 'fresh' money. What I believe we really need is a fresh start and fresh investment. Others say we need more debt. We do not. National budgets are already stretched. The EU operates on balanced budgets and the abundant liquidity can allow Europe to grow without creating new debt. We will not betray our children and grandchildren and write more checks that they will ultimately have to pay off. We will not betray the rules of the Stability and Growth Pact that we have agreed jointly—this is a matter of credibility. However, if Member States chip in capital to the Fund, we will not take these contributions into account in our assessments under the Pact.

What we are going to do is to set up the right system that will use available public money to leverage additional capital that would have never otherwise been mobilised. Every public euro mobilised can generate additional investment that would not have happened otherwise. And it can create jobs.

We will need to look carefully at projects. Destinations for the fresh investment drive should be attractive, free of regulatory burdens and linked to economic reality, not political expedience.

Let me [be] clear about one thing—the money we are putting forward today comes on top of what already exists. It comes on top of the €630 billion that is about to be unlocked from the structural and investment funds at national and regional level[s]. It comes on top of what the European Investment Bank has already been able to do so far. After the capital increase of €10 billion, the EIB shipped €180 billion to the real economy. It comes on top of EU programmes such as the Connecting Europe Facility, Horizon 2020 and 'COSME' which are already investing in infrastructure, innovation and Europe's SMEs.

Perhaps most importantly, it comes on top of what Member States can do to help themselves. For Member States must also support the investment environment through a better use of public money and a greater commitment to structural reforms.

Let me explain what my vision is for where this money should go:

- I have a vision of school children in Thessaloniki walking into a brand new class-room, decked out with computers.
- I have a vision of a hospital in Florence saving lives with state-of-the-art medical equipment.
- I have a vision of a French commuter being able to charge his electric car along the motorway in the same way we fill up on petrol today.
- Households and companies want to benefit from technological progress and are crying out for action to become more energy-efficient.
- Our energy sector needs to interconnect networks and markets, integrate renewable sources of energy and diversify our sources of supply.
- Our transport sector has to modernise its infrastructure, reduce congestion and improve trade connections. Our environment needs better waste, recycling and water treatment facilities.
- We need far-reaching and faster broadband and smarter data centres across Europe.
- And we need to invest in our education and innovation systems that are often underfunded and less equipped than those of our key competitors. Investing in people—this is what the social market economy is about. In Europe; we spell 'social' with a capital 'S'.]

The needs are vast. This is the challenge of a generation. Europe will have to face it head on.

3. HOW IS IT GOING TO WORK?

Money will not fall from the sky. We do not have a money printing machine. We will have to attract money and make it work for us. Today we are setting up a new architecture that will make this possible. The key is to provide a risk-bearing capacity that can unlock additional investment.

Our Plan is built on three main pillars ("filières"):

1. We are creating a new European Fund for Strategic Investments, guaranteed with public money from the EU budget and the European Investment Bank (EIB). The Fund will be able to mobilise €315 billion over the next three years.

The Commission has put up €8 billion from the EU budget. This backs up a €16 billion guarantee given to the Fund. Topped up by another €5 billion from the EIB. That makes €21 billion. With a €21 billion reserve, the EIB can give out loans of €63 billion. That's €63 billion of fresh financing we've just injected into the economy. But the EIB will not be acting alone. The EIB will be financing the riskier parts of projects worth 315 billion, meaning private investors will be pitching in the remaining €252 billion.

And yet some say this is not enough. This is the greatest effort in European history to mobilise the EU's budget to trigger additional investment—and without changing the rules. We have managed to pull an unprecedented €8 billion out of the EU budget! Just ask your national governments how difficult it is to make those kinds of savings.

I know some of you are worried about the impact on the research and infrastructure allocations. You fear that redirecting money from the Horizon 2020 and Connecting Europe budget lines will mean that money is lost. But this is not the case. Every euro from these programmes paid into the Fund creates €15 euros for those very same research and infrastructure projects. We are not just moving money around, we are maximising its input.

If Member States step up to the plate and contribute to the Fund, then the knock-on effect of this significant amount will be even bigger.

2. We are setting up a credible project pipeline backed by a technical assistance programme to link investments to mature, growth-generating projects of European significance. It is not the job of politicians to choose projects. It will be done by the technicians who have the experience and know-how to do so. The Fund will have a dedicated Investment Committee made up of experts that will have to validate every project from a commercial and societal perspective and based on what value-added they can have to the EU as a whole.

3. We are proposing an ambitious roadmap to make Europe more attractive and remove red-tape and regulatory bottlenecks. The answer is not just financial. It is also regulatory. A single EU Regulation can replace 28 sets of laws. This is the best simplification machine.

The EIB has done a great job in recent years, and I am delighted that they will remain a central player and partner in Europe's new Investment Plan. Werner, the triple-A of your institution is a European treasure that we will now put to even better use for Europe. We couldn't have done this without you. I wish to pay tribute to you, Werner, and your team for everything you have done so far and thank you for what you will still have to do over the next three years. Indeed, Werner and I had a comprehensive exchange of views on this already in July.

There are still important steps that we need to take as of tomorrow. This is only the beginning.

That is why today I want to call on all those who say they to want to put Europe back on the path of strong growth:

1. Member States should join in and multiply the impact of the Fund even further. Every public Euro mobilised in the Fund can generate about €15 of investment. My pledge to you in turn, as I already mentioned, is that in the assessment of public finances under the Stability and Growth Pact, the Commission will not count such capital contributions to the Fund. That's European solidarity. That's what working together for the greater good looks like.

Some of you will ask me—what's in it for me? Why would Member States contribute to the fund when there is no guarantee how much they will get back? Because geographical silos will not serve anyone. France growing is good for Italy. Southern Europe growing is good for Germany. We are all in this together. Our fates are linked. We should stand shoulder to shoulder.

2. The €315 billion of total expected investment is not a ceiling. If we are successful, as I believe we will be, we can even go beyond this.

3. We need a broad political consensus in the European Parliament and the European Council that will endorse the Investment Plan and validate its content, structure and objectives. We need a Coalition of the 'willing to invest'.

Honourable members, I will notably count on the commitment of this House to fast-track the legislation necessary to set up the Fund. I will ask colleagues at the European Council for the same commitment. We have to get the Fund up and running by June next year so that it can start delivering.

The European Parliament is a key partner in bringing Europe back to growth. We will be accountable to you. High-level representatives of the new Fund should regularly report to you on the activities of the Fund. I will also guarantee [sic] that the relevant Vice-Presidents and European Commissioners responsible for the different areas of activities of the Fund, as well as EIB representatives will regularly report to you and your relevant Committees.

Let me, however, be very clear: we need political endorsement and backing, but not *politicisation* of the Plan. No political fiddling with projects, no national wish-lists. This is a major credibility test that has to be convincing to private investors and the world financial markets. Here too, I count on the EIB's professionalism, experience and expertise.

The Plan is not an ATM and the Fund will not be a bank. We need something agile. Something which is simple for investors and public authorities to use. Something that can evolve and develop over time. Not constrained by the "silo" logic of thematic, sectoral or geographic pre-allocations. Something credible that builds on established structures and guarantees accountability.

What we propose here can be done at EU level alone. Less than a month into the mandate of my Commission, we are taking responsibility and we are delivering. I now invite others to follow suit and show they too are ready to play ball.

And this does not have to be one-off. Today's Plan is a first test case. If it works, who is to say it could not become a permanent feature?

4. No way back

This is an investment offensive that optimises our economic policy. We are focusing on long-term, large-scale European investment to create jobs. We are also targeting SMEs—Europe's job creators—to give a boost to the real economy.

We are turning a corner, completing fiscal responsibility and structural reform with innovative investment plans and instruments. This ground-breaking investment plan, mobilising all levels of government, is the missing part of the puzzle, the third point in the virtuous triangle. The *omne trium perfectum* made whole.

We will stand tall on three pillars: the money, the projects and the rules to create the right business environment.

We are offering hope to millions of Europeans disillusioned after years of stagnation. Yes, Europe can still become the epicentre of a major investment drive. Yes, Europe can grow again. Yes, the European social model will persevere.

Now that we are going in the right direction, there will be no turning back.

SOURCE: European Commission. "Investing in Europe: speech by President Juncker in the European Parliament plenary session on the €315 billion Investment Plan." November 26, 2014. © European Union. http://europa.eu/rapid/press-release_SPEECH-14-2160_en.htm.

OTHER HISTORIC DOCUMENTS OF INTEREST

FROM PREVIOUS *HISTORIC DOCUMENTS*

Chinese Standing Committee Reviews Universal Suffrage in Hong Kong

---

AUGUST 31, 2014

Hong Kong, a semiautonomous region of China, has been somewhat more democratic than its parent nation since coming under China's rule in 1997. One of the freedoms sought by many in Hong Kong is universal suffrage, which China agreed to grant to allow Hong Kong to select a new chief executive in 2017. However, in August 2014, the powerful Chinese Standing Committee decided that, while all citizens would be allowed to vote, the candidates would have to win approval of a separate committee, one that many in Hong Kong considered pro-Beijing, to appear on the ballot. This decision provoked tens of thousands of Hong Kongers to take to the streets.

Tense Relationship Continues

For decades, Hong Kong was a colony of the British Empire. But, under an agreement signed by China and Great Britain in 1984, authority over the East Asian nation was given back to China in 1997. At the time of the agreement, Chinese leader Deng Xiaoping established a governance structure for Hong Kong known as "One Country, Two Systems." As stated in 1997, this policy would be kept in place for fifty years and would give Hong Kong a high degree of day-to-day authority—including many rights that are restricted in China, such as the freedom of assembly and freedom of speech. The nation would not, however, have any control over foreign and military policy. The country has its own court system and own governing document, known as the Basic Law, but Hong Kong's leader, known as the chief executive, is chosen by an election committee comprised mainly of pro-Beijing representatives.

Hong Kong's long-standing intent has been to elect its leader by popular vote, something the Chinese government supported and said it would implement beginning in 2017. However, when new leadership came into power in China in 2012, the premier stated that while an election would be held to choose Hong Kong's new leader in 2017, an election committee would choose those who could run for the office. This was largely seen as an attempt to subvert Hong Kong's goal of democratic governance by placing those loyal to Beijing in charge. The premier said that he would put this issue before the National People's Congress Standing Committee in August 2014 for a final decision on how the 2017 election would be handled.

Hong Kong Protests

With the announcement that Hong Kong's 2017 election would not be truly democratic in nature, two pro-democracy protest groups emerged: Occupy Central and an unnamed coalition of student groups. The student groups held a variety of protests, sit-ins, and boycotts, including street occupations that at their height numbered a reported 100,000 participants. Occupy Central held an unofficial referendum in June 2014 on universal suffrage. Approximately 20 percent of eligible voters cast a ballot, and 42 percent of those backed the proposal that the public, political parties, or a nominating committee should be able to select those candidates who are eligible to run for chief executive, not the pro-Beijing election committee. The vote was opposed by Beijing and those in Hong Kong who support the central government; over the course of ten days of balloting, some pro-Beijing protesters sought signatures for a petition to encourage Hong Kongers not to participate in the unsanctioned election.

For its part, the Chinese government has lashed out at the pro-democracy movement, calling their protests and occupations illegal. The central government has also argued that the new system proposed for the 2017 election improves upon the current structure of Hong Kong's governance system. China's deputy secretary general for the National People's Congress Standing Committee said that allowing any candidate to seek a leadership position in Hong Kong would create chaos. In June, the Chinese government released a report on the impact of One Country, Two Systems in Hong Kong. The paper indicated that many in the country have a "confused or lopsided" understanding of the policy and that such misunderstanding has the potential to impact its "economy, society and development of its political structure." An article released by the state-run news agency Xinhua following the release of the report claimed that "the policy enjoys growing popularity in Hong Kong, winning the wholehearted support from Hong Kong compatriots as well as people in all other parts of China." Noting the advances that have been made in Hong Kong under this practice, the article concluded that "Firmly advancing the cause of 'one country, two systems' is the common wish of all the Chinese people, Hong Kong compatriots included, and is in the fundamental interests of the country and people, the general and long-term interests of Hong Kong and the interests of foreign investors."

The current chief executive in Hong Kong, CY Leung, generally agrees with Beijing's stance on selecting specific candidates to seek the leadership position, calling it a "major step forward in the development of Hong Kong's society." He added that the current policy of One Nation, Two Systems has widely benefitted Hong Kong's residents, most of whom support Beijing's decision.

On July 1, in response to the release of the One Country, Two Systems report, Hong Kong saw its largest ever pro-democracy rally. The date marks the anniversary of the reinstatement of Chinese rule over Hong Kong in 1997, and there is at least a small rally held opposing Chinese rule every year. Estimates of the number of participants varied from 92,000 to one million. As they marched through the central part of the city, demonstrators chanted "Our own government, our own choice" and carried signs with phrases like "Say no to Communist China." Mainland China's media did not cover the event, at which more than 500 demonstrators were arrested for illegal assembly.

There is also a strong pro-China contingency in Hong Kong. These groups include Silent Majority for Hong Kong and Caring Hong Kong Power. Collectively, the groups claim that the protests being held by the pro-democracy movement only serve to further damage the relationship between Beijing and Hong Kong, which could have a detrimental effect on Hong Kong's economy. Pro-Beijing groups organized their own protests, holding their largest on August 17, when thousands came out to support China's central government in what was called a "march for peace."

CHINESE LEGISLATURE LIMITS VOTING REFORMS

On August 31, the Standing Committee of the National People's Congress met and called for strict restrictions on the 2017 democratic vote in Hong Kong. Regulations would include a requirement that any candidate chosen to run for chief executive "love the country, and love Hong Kong" and would "protect the broad stability of Hong Kong now and in the future," according to Li Fei, the deputy secretary general of the committee. The limits would require candidates who want to run in 2017 to first win an endorsement from at least half the members of a nominating committee. This nominating committee would be created based on the current composition of Hong Kong's Election Committee, which is generally pro-Beijing. According to Li, this committee is "broadly representative" of all Hong Kong's citizens, a statement rejected by the pro-democracy movement. According to Michael Davis, a professor at the University of Hong Kong, the new restrictions raise the bar on qualifying to run for a leadership position in Hong Kong, because only the support of one-eighth of the Election Committee members was required in prior elections. "Democrats have no chance of getting nominated," under the new system, Davis said.

Pro-democracy leaders called the limits a mockery of the promises that had been made to Hong Kong since 1997. "After having lied to Hong Kong people for so many years, it finally revealed itself today," Alan Leong, a pro-democracy legislator, said of the Chinese Standing Committee. "Hong Kong people are right to feel betrayed. It's certain now that the central government will be effectively appointing Hong Kong's chief executive." In response to the Standing Committee's decision, Occupy Central called for another round of protests, and several thousand people turned out. One of the group's cofounders, Benny Tai, said the hope for the protests was to begin "an era of civil disobedience, an era of resistance."

According to Leung, Hong Kong's government would use the Standing Committee framework to draft electoral reform legislation that would permit universal suffrage ahead of the 2017 election. The Democratic Party promised to veto any electoral reform bill put forward, believing that it would largely be written by those favorable toward the Chinese central government. But Leung said not passing electoral reform would be a setback for all Hong Kong citizens: "Five million Hong Kong people would be deprived of the voting right that they would be otherwise entitled to." Leung added, "We cannot afford a standstill in our constitutional development or else the prosperity or stability of Hong Kong will be at stake."

The decision of the Standing Committee is considered important for all of China, including the other semiautonomous regions of Macau and Taiwan. Among mainland China and its territories, Hong Kong enjoys the greatest democratic freedom. By limiting these in Hong Kong, China's central government has sent a strong message across its population that greater freedoms will not soon be realized.

ONGOING ACTION AGAINST PRO-DEMOCRACY MOVEMENT

Following its August decision, the Chinese government undertook a campaign to crackdown on pro-democracy protesters. In November, a group of Hong Kong's student leaders were restricted from traveling to mainland China to push for free elections after their return-home cards (akin to a visa) were revoked by Chinese officials. Carrie Lam, a top civil servant in Hong Kong, told the students that "not all of Hong Kong's problems can be solved by the Hong Kong government" and that there was "no need" for them to travel to mainland China. This did not deter the student activists. "The movement in Hong Kong will be ongoing," said Alex Chow, one of the students denied entry. "Hong Kong people have been pursuing democracy and democratic reform for more than three decades and we are still on our way to restructure the concept of democracy."

On December 9, Hong Kong's high court ruled that three portions of the protest camp that had clogged major arteries throughout Hong Kong since summer could be cleared. The number of those in the camps had been falling steadily since November because transportation firms obtained court-ordered injunctions to remove protesters from major streets. Protesters were encouraged to leave the area by 9:00 a.m.; however, the demonstrators, many of whom were students, refused. Because the order requested "the assistance of the police where necessary," the protesters were eventually forcibly removed. The earlier injunctions were met with violent resistance, but the clearing of the camps on December 9, 10, and 11 took place largely peacefully, with dozens of arrests but no violence. Chow said that leaving the camp peacefully "delivers the political message that while we will resist to the last moment, we respect the rule of law and we are not barbarians."

—Heather Kerrigan

Following is the text of the August 31, 2014, National People's Congress decision on the election of Hong Kong's chief executive; the text of a transcript from remarks delivered by Hong Kong's Chief Executive CY Leung on August 31, 2014, following the Standing Committee's decision on the 2017 election; and a press release from the National People's Congress on August 31, 2014, regarding its universal suffrage deliberations.

National People's Congress on Election of Hong Kong's Chief Executive

August 31, 2014

The Standing Committee of the Twelfth National People's Congress considered at its Tenth Session the Report on whether there is a need to amend the methods for selecting the Chief Executive of the Hong Kong Special Administrative Region in 2017 and for forming the Legislative Council of the Hong Kong Special Administrative Region in 2016 submitted by Leung Chun-ying, the Chief Executive of the Hong Kong Special Administrative Region, on 15 July 2014. In the course of deliberation, the relevant views and suggestions of the Hong Kong community were given full consideration.

The Session points out that according to the Decision of the Standing Committee of the National People's Congress on Issues Relating to the Methods for Selecting the Chief Executive of the Hong Kong Special Administrative Region and for Forming the Legislative Council of the Hong Kong Special Administrative Region in the Year 2012 and on Issues Relating to Universal Suffrage adopted by the Standing Committee of the Tenth National People's Congress at its Thirty-first Session on 29 December 2007, the election of the fifth Chief Executive of the Hong Kong Special Administrative Region in the year 2017 may be implemented by the method of universal suffrage; at an appropriate time prior to the selection of the Chief Executive of the Hong Kong Special Administrative Region by universal suffrage, the Chief Executive shall make a report to the Standing Committee of the National People's Congress as regards the issue of amending the method for selecting the Chief Executive in accordance with the relevant provisions of the Hong Kong Basic Law and the Interpretation by the Standing Committee of the National People's Congress of Article 7 of Annex I and Article III of Annex II to the Basic Law of the Hong Kong Special Administrative Region of the People's Republic of China, and a determination thereon shall be made by the Standing Committee of the National People's Congress. From 4 December 2013 to 3 May 2014, the Government of the Hong Kong Special Administrative Region conducted an extensive and in-depth public consultation on the methods for selecting the Chief Executive in 2017 and for forming the Legislative Council in 2016. In the course of consultation, the Hong Kong community generally expressed the hope to see the selection of the Chief Executive by universal suffrage in 2017, and broad consensus was reached on important principles such as: the method for selecting the Chief Executive by universal suffrage shall comply with the Hong Kong Basic Law and the relevant Decisions of the Standing Committee of the National People's Congress and the Chief Executive shall be a person who loves the country and loves Hong Kong. With respect to the methods for selecting the Chief Executive by universal suffrage in 2017 and for forming the Legislative Council in 2016, the Hong Kong community put forward various views and suggestions. It was on this basis that the Chief Executive of the Hong Kong Special Administrative Region made a report to the Standing Committee of the National People's Congress on issues relating to amending the methods for selecting the Chief Executive in 2017 and for forming the Legislative Council in 2016. The Session is of the view that the report complies with the requirements of the Hong Kong Basic Law, the Interpretation by the Standing Committee of the National People's Congress of Article 7 of Annex I and Article III of Annex II to the Hong Kong Basic Law and the relevant Decisions of the Standing Committee of the National People's Congress, and reflects comprehensively and objectively the views collected during the public consultation; and is thus a positive, responsible and pragmatic report.

The Session is of the view that implementing universal suffrage for the selection of the Chief Executive represents a historic progress in Hong Kong's democratic development and a significant change in the political structure of the Hong Kong Special Administrative Region. Since the long-term prosperity and stability of Hong Kong and the sovereignty, security and development interests of the country are at stake, there is a need to proceed in a prudent and steady manner. The selection of the Chief Executive of the Hong Kong Special Administrative Region by universal suffrage has its origin in Paragraph 2 of Article 45 of the Hong Kong Basic Law: "The method for selecting the Chief Executive shall be specified in the light of the actual situation in the Hong Kong Special Administrative Region and in accordance with the principle of gradual and orderly progress. The ultimate aim is the selection of the Chief Executive by universal suffrage upon nomination by a broadly representative nominating committee in accordance with democratic procedures." The formulation of the method for selecting the Chief Executive by universal suffrage must strictly comply with the relevant provisions of the Hong Kong Basic Law, accord with the principle of "one country, two systems", and befit the legal status of the Hong Kong Special Administrative Region. It must meet the interests of different sectors of the society, achieve balanced participation, be conducive to the development of the capitalist economy, and make gradual and orderly progress in developing a democratic system that suits the actual situation in Hong Kong. Given the divergent views within the Hong Kong community on how to implement the

Hong Kong Basic Law provisions on universal suffrage for selecting the Chief Executive, and in light of the constitutional responsibility of the Standing Committee of the National People's Congress for the proper implementation of the Hong Kong Basic Law and for deciding on the method for the selection of the Chief Executive, the Standing Committee of the National People's Congress finds it necessary to make provisions on certain core issues concerning the method for selecting the Chief Executive by universal suffrage, so as to facilitate the building of consensus within the Hong Kong community and the attainment of universal suffrage for the selection of the Chief Executive smoothly and in accordance with law.

The Session is of the view that since the Chief Executive of the Hong Kong Special Administrative Region shall be accountable to both the Hong Kong Special Administrative Region and the Central People's Government in accordance with the provisions of the Hong Kong Basic Law, the principle that the Chief Executive has to be a person who loves the country and loves Hong Kong must be upheld. This is a basic requirement of the policy of "one country, two systems". It is determined by the legal status as well as important functions and duties of the Chief Executive, and is called for by the actual need to maintain long-term prosperity and stability of Hong Kong and uphold the sovereignty, security and development interests of the country. The method for selecting the Chief Executive by universal suffrage must provide corresponding institutional safeguards for this purpose.

The Session is of the view that the amendments made to the method for forming the fifth term Legislative Council in 2012 represented major strides towards the direction of enhancing democracy. The existing formation method and voting procedures for the Legislative Council as prescribed in Annex II to the Hong Kong Basic Law will not be amended, and will continue to apply in respect of the sixth term Legislative Council in 2016. This is consistent with the principle of gradual and orderly progress in developing a democratic system that suits Hong Kong's actual situation and conforms to the majority view in the Hong Kong community. It also helps the various sectors of the Hong Kong community to focus their efforts on addressing the issues concerning universal suffrage for selecting the Chief Executive first, thus creating the conditions for attaining the aim of electing all the members of the Legislative Council by universal suffrage after the implementation of universal suffrage for the selection of the Chief Executive.

Accordingly, pursuant to the relevant provisions of the Basic Law of the Hong Kong Special Administrative Region of the People's Republic of China, the Interpretation by the Standing Committee of the National People's Congress of Article 7 of Annex I and Article III of Annex II to the Basic Law of the Hong Kong Special Administrative Region of the People's Republic of China and the Decision of the Standing Committee of the National People's Congress on Issues Relating to the Methods for Selecting the Chief Executive of the Hong Kong Special Administrative Region and for Forming the Legislative Council of the Hong Kong Special Administrative Region in the Year 2012 and on Issues Relating to Universal Suffrage, the Standing Committee of the National People's Congress makes the following decision:

I.   Starting from 2017, the selection of the Chief Executive of the Hong Kong Special Administrative Region may be implemented by the method of universal suffrage.

II. When the selection of the Chief Executive of the Hong Kong Special Administrative Region is implemented by the method of universal suffrage:

(1) A broadly representative nominating committee shall be formed. The provisions for the number of members, composition and formation method of the nominating committee shall be made in accordance with the number

of members, composition and formation method of the Election Committee for the Fourth Chief Executive.

(2) The nominating committee shall nominate two to three candidates for the office of Chief Executive in accordance with democratic procedures. Each candidate must have the endorsement of more than half of all the members of the nominating committee.

(3) All eligible electors of the Hong Kong Special Administrative Region have the right to vote in the election of the Chief Executive and elect one of the candidates for the office of Chief Executive in accordance with law.

(4) The Chief Executive-elect, after being selected through universal suffrage, will have to be appointed by the Central People's Government.

III. The specific method of universal suffrage for selecting the Chief Executive shall be prescribed in accordance with legal procedures through amending Annex I to the Basic Law of the Hong Kong Special Administrative Region of the People's Republic of China: The Method for the Selection of the Chief Executive of the Hong Kong Special Administrative Region. The bill on the amendments and the proposed amendments to such bill shall be introduced by the Hong Kong Special Administrative Region Government to the Legislative Council of the Hong Kong Special Administrative Region in accordance with the Hong Kong Basic Law and the provisions of this Decision. Such amendments shall obtain the endorsement of a two-thirds majority of all the members of the Legislative Council and the consent of the Chief Executive before being submitted to the Standing Committee of the National People's Congress for approval.

IV. If the specific method of universal suffrage for selecting the Chief Executive is not adopted in accordance with legal procedures, the method used for selecting the Chief Executive for the preceding term shall continue to apply.

V. The existing formation method and voting procedures for the Legislative Council as prescribed in Annex II to the Hong Kong Basic Law will not be amended. The formation method and procedures for voting on bills and motions of the fifth term Legislative Council will continue to apply to the sixth term Legislative Council of the Hong Kong Special Administrative Region in 2016. After the election of the Chief Executive by universal suffrage, the election of all the members of the Legislative Council of the Hong Kong Special Administrative Region may be implemented by the method of universal suffrage. At an appropriate time prior to the election of the Legislative Council by universal suffrage, the Chief Executive elected by universal suffrage shall submit a report to the Standing Committee of the National People's Congress in accordance with the relevant provisions of the Hong Kong Basic Law and the Interpretation by the Standing Committee of the National People's Congress of Article 7 of Annex I and Article III of Annex II to the Basic Law of the Hong Kong Special Administrative Region of the People's Republic of China as regards the issue of amending the method for forming the Legislative Council. A determination thereon shall be made by the Standing Committee of the National People's Congress.

The Session stresses that it is the consistent position of the central authorities to implement resolutely and firmly the principles of "one country, two systems", "Hong Kong people administering Hong Kong" and a high degree of autonomy, strictly adhere to the Hong Kong Basic Law and steadily take forward the selection of the Chief Executive by universal suffrage in 2017. It is hoped that the Hong Kong Special Administrative Region Government and all sectors of the Hong Kong community will act in accordance with the provisions of the Hong Kong Basic Law and this Decision and jointly work towards the attainment of the aim of selecting the Chief Executive by universal suffrage.

SOURCE: Xinhua News Agency. "Full text of NPC decision on universal suffrage for HK Chief Executive selection." August 31, 2014. http://news.xinhuanet.com/english/china/2014-08/31/c_133609238.htm.

Hong Kong's Chief Executive Responds to Universal Suffrage Decision

August 31, 2014

Following is the transcript of remarks by the Chief Executive, Mr. C Y Leung, at a media session at the ground floor lobby of the Office of the Chief Executive at Tamar today (August 31) on the Decision of the Standing Committee of the National People's Congress on Issues Relating to the Selection of the Chief Executive of the Hong Kong Special Administrative Region by Universal Suffrage and on the Method for Forming the Legislative Council of the Hong Kong Special Administrative Region in the Year 2016:

Reporter: Mr. Leung, do you find the proposal acceptable to the people of Hong Kong and how confident are you that you will secure, the Government will secure a two-thirds majority in LegCo?

Chief Executive: We have work to do, we have a lot of work to do and we will ask the people of Hong Kong to understand that this is the first time, the first time ever, in the history of Hong Kong that eligible voters will be given, and each and every one of them, will be given the right to vote in the universal suffrage to elect the leader of this government, and the leader of this city. It is a precious offer from the National People's Congress Standing Committee. Obviously we have work to do, I think it is an important and historical moment for Hong Kong.

SOURCE: Government of Hong Kong. "Transcripts of remarks by CE at media session." August 31, 2014. www.info.gov.hk/gia/general/201408/31/P201408310944.htm.

Standing Committee Votes on Universal Suffrage in Hong Kong

August 31, 2014

Top Chinese legislator Zhang Dejiang has hailed a newly adopted decision on how the leader of Hong Kong will be elected by universal suffrage in 2017 as "another important decision" for the region's constitutional development.

Zhang, chairman of the National People's Congress (NPC) Standing Committee, the country's top legislature, made the remarks at the closing meeting of the 10th session of the 12th NPC Standing Committee on Sunday.

It unanimously adopted a decision that candidates for elections to choose the Chief Executive of the Hong Kong Special Administrative Region (HKSAR) will have to be nominated by a "broadly representative" committee.

Deliberating on and adopting the "Decision of the Standing Committee of the National People's Congress on Issues Relating to the Selection of the Chief Executive of the Hong Kong Special Administrative Region by Universal Suffrage and on the Method for Forming the Legislative Council of the Hong Kong Special Administrative Region in the Year 2016" was a key task for the session, he said.

The decision is of great significance to implementing the principles of "one country, two systems," "Hong Kong people administering Hong Kong," and ensuring the region maintains a high degree of autonomy while following the Hong Kong Basic Law, according to Zhang.

"The decision is vital for steadily developing democracy in Hong Kong and implementing the selection of the HKSAR Chief Executive by universal suffrage according to law," he said.

Zhang told the meeting, "It is the central government's consistent and clear stance to support the HKSAR in developing a democratic system in line with the actual conditions of Hong Kong based on the regulations of the Hong Kong Basic Law."

The decision accords with the fundamental interests of Hong Kong compatriots, gives clear stipulations on many key factors in the universal suffrage system for the HKSAR Chief Executive, and charts the direction for the HKSAR to decide in detail how universal suffrage will be applied in the election, the top legislator said.

Zhang expressed hope that Hong Kong society can continue a rational and practical discussion on this matter and reach consensus within the framework of the Hong Kong Basic Law and the decision made by the NPC Standing Committee.

He said he hoped that with the joint efforts of the HKSAR government and Hong Kongers, Hong Kong could properly handle its constitutional development issues according to law and smoothly realize the goal of selecting a Chief Executive by universal suffrage in 2017.

SOURCE: The National People's Congress of the People's Republic of China. "Top legislator hails HK election method decision." August 31, 2014.

OTHER HISTORIC DOCUMENTS OF INTEREST

FROM PREVIOUS HISTORIC DOCUMENTS

September

Census Bureau Reports on Poverty in the United States

SEPTEMBER 16 AND OCTOBER 16, 2014

The U.S. poverty rate decreased from 2012 to 2013, according to a U.S. Census Bureau report released on September 16, 2014, marking the first year-over-year decrease since 2006. According to the report, in 2013, the poverty rate was 14.5 percent, or 45.3 million Americans living in poverty, down from 15 percent and 46.5 million individuals in 2012. Although the rate declined, the number of those living in poverty did not record a statistically significant drop. Median household income was $51,939 in 2013, which again was not a statistically significant difference from 2012. Income inequality, although still high according to the Gini index, was largely unchanged from 2012 to 2013.

POVERTY RATE DECREASES; NUMBER OF AMERICANS IN POVERTY REMAINS UNCHANGED

Overall, the United States has seen gradual economic improvement since the official end of the recession in 2009. Unemployment fell from a peak of 10 percent in October 2009 to 5.6 percent by December 2014 as both public and private sector employers added jobs. The annual *Income, Poverty, and Health Insurance Coverage in the United States* report echoed the improvement, as a statistically significant year-over-year decrease in the poverty rate was recorded. The 2013 percentage of those in poverty, set at an income level below $23,624 for a family of four, was 14.5 percent.

Overall, the number and type of families in poverty did not show a significant change from 2013. By age group, those under eighteen had a 19.9 percent poverty rate, the eighteen to sixty-four group was 13.6 percent, and those sixty-five and older were 9.5 percent. None of the four Census regions showed a statistically significant difference from 2012. In the South, which continued to have the highest poverty rate of the four regions, 16.1 percent, or 18.9 million people, were in poverty. In the Midwest, these numbers were 12.9 percent and 8.6 percent. The Northeast had a 12.7 percent poverty rate, or 7 million individuals, and the West had a 14.7 percent poverty rate, or 10.8 million individuals.

The poverty rate was varied between racial groups: non-Hispanic whites had a poverty rate of 9.6 percent, while blacks had a rate of 27.2 percent, Hispanics of 23.5 percent, and Asians of 10.5 percent. Hispanics were the only racial group to experience a statistically significant decline in poverty, down from 25.6 percent in 2012. The poverty rate for black and Hispanic individuals remains twice as high as that of non-Hispanic whites and Asians. According to the New York City Coalition Against Hunger, the United States has the highest level of racial income inequality among any Western industrialized nation.

Shared households increased slightly in 2013, from 19 percent of all households in 2012 to 19.1 percent in Spring 2014; this number was still markedly higher than 2007's pre-recession 17 percent. The Census Bureau indicated in its report that it is difficult to determine what impact shared households have on poverty rates because those aged twenty-five to thirty-four who live with their parents had an official poverty rate of 9.3 percent, but if only their own finances are taken into account, these young people had a poverty rate of 43.7 percent. Additionally, 9 percent of the families in poverty have an adult child aged twenty-five to thirty-four in the household; this number would grow to 14 percent if the adult child was not living in the household.

Although the poverty rate did not increase, federal officials said the statistics issued by the Census Bureau indicated that there is still more that can be done. "The typical family has still not seen its income recover from the deep recession, which came on top of a decade in which incomes stagnated for the middle class, itself part of a longer-term trend of increasing income inequality," said Jason Furman, the chair of the White House Council of Economic Advisers. Rep. Paul Ryan, R-Wis., chair of the powerful House Budget Committee, said, "We can do better," adding "the status quo simply isn't good enough."

Number of Children in Poverty Falls

Even though the number of people in poverty remained largely unchanged from 2012 to 2013, the number of children under age eighteen in poverty did fall for the first time since 2000, by 1.4 million. This decline was coupled with a rise in median income for families with children. This left the number of children in poverty at 14.7 million, or 19.9 percent. The lowest ever recorded rate of childhood poverty was in 1969 when the number was 13.8 percent. The 2013 decrease was significant because children have often had a higher poverty rate than adults, at approximately one in five. Much like the decline in the overall population, falling childhood poverty was linked to an improving job market and growing labor force—from 2012 to 2013, the number of full-time year-round working adults increased by approximately 960,000. Child poverty fell among all ethnic groups except for black children. White non-Hispanic children made up approximately 50 percent of the reduction in childhood poverty. Geographically, child poverty rates did not record a statistically significant change.

While the gains are positive, it still means that of the 45 million Americans living in poverty, one third are children. According to the United Nations' Children's Fund, the United States ranks 34th out of 35 developed countries for childhood poverty. Hannah Matthews, who heads CLASP, a nonprofit group seeking to improve the conditions of low-income individuals, said there is still work to be done. "Top among the policies that will help working parents is making child care more affordable," she said. "Congress is expected to pass legislation very soon to improve child care quality and make receipt of child care assistance a smoother process for parents. . . . We also need additional resources to expand access to child care assistance," Matthews continued. With this in mind, one of President Barack Obama's talking points during his 2015 State of the Union Address was helping middle-class and low-income families afford quality childcare: "In today's economy, when having both parents in the workforce is an economic necessity for many families, we need affordable, high-quality childcare more than ever. It's not a nice-to-have—it's a must have."

Supplemental Poverty Measure Also Remains Unchanged

The official Census estimate of poverty does not account for food stamps, cash assistance, tax credits, and a variety of other government support systems, all of which can have a significant impact on the number of Americans considered impoverished. And it is these official Census figures that are used to determine government aid funding allocation. In

2010, the Census released its first supplemental poverty report, which was hailed as a more accurate method for determining the number of Americans living in poverty by taking into account both government assistance programs and expenses like health insurance, child care, housing, and job expenses such as transportation.

On October 16, the Census released its fourth annual supplemental poverty estimate, which found that the nation's poverty rate fell from 16 percent in 2012 to 15.5 percent in 2013. This rate is still higher than the official poverty measure at 14.5 percent. According to the supplemental report, 48.7 million Americans fell below the poverty line in 2013, which was not a statistically significant change from 2012. In thirteen states, including Alaska, California, Connecticut, Florida, Hawaii, Illinois, Maryland, Massachusetts, Nevada, New Hampshire, New Jersey, New York, and Virginia, and the District of Columbia, the supplemental poverty rate was higher than official statewide poverty rates.

AMERICANS STILL BELIEVE RECESSION ONGOING

After the Census Bureau release in September, many economists noted that the small decline in the poverty rate is simply a regular part of the ebb and flow of a postrecession economy. "If you look at the last 40 years, this (poverty) line wiggles up and down 3 or 4 percentage points, and that's all it ever does," said Robert Rector, a research fellow at the conservative Heritage Foundation think tank. "It really hasn't changed much. The poverty rate today is essentially the same as it was in 1966, two years after Lyndon Johnson launched the War on Poverty."

According to Justin Wolfers, an economist at the University of Michigan, the ongoing struggle of those in poverty to make significant income gains is a major factor regarding why half of Americans believe the United States is still in recession, even though it was officially declared over in 2009. In recent recessions, after significant job and income loss, those in poverty have not been able to recover as quickly as they had during earlier economic downturns. Some economists believe this has to do with Congressional action on cutting welfare spending for Americans in the lowest income brackets. Extended unemployment benefits were ended in 2014, and billions have been pulled from the Supplemental Nutrition Assistance Program (SNAP), or food stamps.

Added to this is the challenge that wages are not keeping pace with inflation. Although there are more people working full time, median household income is still sitting just around $52,000, 11 percent below what it was in 2000 and 8 percent lower than in 2007. According to Sheldon Danziger, president of the Russell Sage Foundation, a social research group, the growth that has occurred has mainly been for the highest income earners. "Through the Bush years and now the Obama years, through periods of economic growth and severe recession, the bottom half has continued to have difficulty moving forward," he said. "It's great that more people are working full-time. But if we really want to do something about poverty, inequality and the struggles of the middle class, economic growth on its own is not sufficient."

—Heather Kerrigan

Following are excerpts from the U.S. Census Bureau report on the poverty level in the United States, released on September 16, 2014; and a press release detailing the findings of a supplemental poverty report released by the U.S. Census Bureau on October 16, 2014.

Census Bureau Report on Poverty in the United States

September 16, 2014

[All portions of the report not corresponding to poverty have been omitted.]

[Tables, graphs, and footnotes, and references to them, have been omitted.]

POVERTY IN THE UNITED STATES

Highlights

- In 2013, the official poverty rate was 14.5 percent, down from 15.0 percent in 2012. This was the first decrease in the poverty rate since 2006.
- In 2013, there were 45.3 million people in poverty. For the third consecutive year, the number of people in poverty at the national level was not statistically different from the previous year's estimate.
- The 2013 poverty rate was 2.0 percentage points higher than in 2007, the year before the most recent recession.
- The poverty rate for children under 18 fell from 21.8 percent in 2012 to 19.9 percent in 2013.
- The poverty rate for people aged 18 to 64 was 13.6 percent, while the rate for people aged 65 and older was 9.5 percent. Neither of these poverty rates was statistically different from its 2012 estimates.
- Both the poverty rate and the number in poverty decreased for Hispanics in 2013.
- Despite the decline in the national poverty rate, the 2013 regional poverty rates were not statistically different from the 2012 rates.

RACE AND HISPANIC ORIGIN

Hispanics were the only group among the major race and ethnic groups to experience a statistically significant change in their poverty rate and the number of people in poverty. For Hispanics, the poverty rate fell from 25.6 percent in 2012 to 23.5 percent in 2013, while the number of Hispanics in poverty fell from 13.6 million to 12.7 million.

The poverty rate for non-Hispanic Whites was 9.6 percent in 2013. Non-Hispanic Whites accounted for 62.4 percent of the total population and 41.5 percent of people in poverty. For Blacks, the 2013 poverty rate was 27.2 percent, and there were 11.0 million people in poverty. For Asians, the 2013 poverty rate was 10.5 percent, which represented 1.8 million people in poverty.

AGE

In 2013, both the poverty rate and the number in poverty decreased for children, defined as those under age 18. The poverty rate fell from 21.8 percent to 19.9 percent. The number of children in poverty fell from 16.1 million to 14.7 million. Children represented 23.5 percent of the total population and 32.3 percent of people in poverty.

The poverty rate for children was higher than the rates for people aged 18 to 64 and those aged 65 and older. Neither the poverty rate nor the number of people in poverty aged 18 to 64 were statistically different in 2013 than 2012, at 13.6 percent and 26.4 million in 2013. The number of people aged 65 and older in poverty increased from 3.9 million in 2012 to 4.2 million in 2013. The 2013 poverty rate for this group was 9.5 percent, which was not statistically different from the 2012 poverty rate.

Related children are people under age 18 related to the householder by birth, marriage, or adoption who are not themselves householders or spouses of householders. The poverty rate and the number in poverty for related children under age 18 were 19.5 percent and 14.1 million in 2013, down from 21.3 percent and 15.4 million in 2012. For related children in families with a female householder, 45.8 percent were in poverty in 2013, not statistically different from 2012. The poverty rate for related children in married-couple families decreased from 11.1 percent in 2012 to 9.5 percent in 2013.

About 1 in 5 related children under age 6 were in poverty in 2013. The poverty rate and the number in poverty for these children were 22.2 percent and 5.2 million in 2013, down from 24.4 percent and 5.8 million in 2012. Among related children under age 6 in families with a female householder, more than half (55.0 percent) were in poverty. This was more than five times the rate for related children in married-couple families (10.2 percent).

Sex

Between 2012 and 2013, poverty rates fell for both males and females. In 2013, 13.1 percent of males and 15.8 percent of females were in poverty, down from 13.6 percent and 16.3 in 2012.

Gender differences in poverty rates were more pronounced for those aged 65 and older. The poverty rate for women aged 65 and older was 11.6 percent, while the poverty rate for men aged 65 and older was 6.8 percent. The poverty rate for women aged 18 to 64 was 15.3 percent, while the poverty rate for men aged 18 to 64 was 11.8 percent. On the other hand, for children under age 18, the poverty rate for girls (20.0 percent) was not statistically different from the poverty rate for boys (19.8 percent).

Nativity

The foreign-born population was estimated to be 13.1 percent of the total population. In 2013, the poverty rate for the foreign born decreased from 19.2 percent in 2012 to 18.0 percent in 2013, while the number in poverty was not statistically different from 2012 at 7.4 million. In contrast, the 2013 poverty rate and the number in poverty for the native born were not statistically different from the previous year at 13.9 percent and 37.9 million.

Within the foreign-born population, 46.7 percent were naturalized citizens. The poverty rate and the number in poverty in 2013 were 12.7 percent and 2.4 million for foreign-born naturalized citizens, neither statistically different from 2012. On the other hand, both the poverty rate and the number in poverty fell for foreign-born noncitizens. The rate fell from 24.9 percent in 2012 to 22.8 percent in 2013, while the number fell from 5.4 million to 5.0 million.

Region

None of the four regions experienced a significant change in the poverty rate or the number in poverty between 2012 and 2013. In 2013, the poverty rate and the number in poverty were 12.7 percent and 7.0 million for the Northeast, 12.9 percent and 8.6 million for the Midwest, 16.1 percent and 18.9 million for the South, and 14.7 percent and 10.8 million for the West. The South continued to have a higher poverty rate than the other three regions.

RESIDENCE

Inside metropolitan statistical areas, the poverty rate and the number of people in poverty were 14.2 percent and 37.7 million in 2013, which were not statistically different from 2012. Among those living outside metropolitan statistical areas, the poverty rate and the number in poverty decreased from 17.7 percent and 8.5 million in 2012 to 16.1 percent and 7.6 million in 2013.

The 2013 poverty rate and the number of people in poverty for those living inside metropolitan areas but not in principal cities were 11.1 percent and 18.2 million. Among those who lived in principal cities, the 2013 poverty rate and the number in poverty were 19.1 percent and 19.5 million. Neither estimate was statistically different from 2012.

Within metropolitan areas, people in poverty were more likely to live in principal cities in 2013. While 38.4 percent of all people living in metropolitan areas lived in principal cities, 51.7 percent of poor people in metropolitan areas lived in principal cities.

WORK EXPERIENCE

In 2013, the percentage of workers aged 18 to 64 in poverty was 7.3 percent, not statistically different from 2012. For those who worked full time, year round, the poverty rate was 2.7 percent in 2013, which was not statistically different from 2012. One of the only major groups to experience higher poverty in 2013 than in 2012 was the group working less than full time, year round. The poverty rate for this group increased from 16.6 percent in 2012 to 17.5 percent in 2013. However, the number of workers who worked less than full time, year round fell from 47.1 million in 2012 to 45.4 million in 2013.

Among those who did not work at least 1 week in 2013, the poverty rate and the number in poverty were 32.3 percent and 15.7 million in 2013, not statistically different from the 2012 estimates. Those who did not work at least 1 week in 2013 represented 24.9 percent of all people aged 18 to 64, compared with 59.4 percent of people aged 18 to 64 in poverty.

FAMILIES

The poverty rate for families fell from 11.8 percent in 2012 to 11.2 percent in 2013. The number of families in poverty fell from 9.5 million to 9.1 million over the same period.

For married-couple families, both the poverty rate and the number in poverty decreased to 5.8 percent and 3.5 million in 2013, down from 6.3 percent and 3.7 million in 2012. The poverty rate and the number in poverty showed no statistical change in 2013 for other families. The poverty rate for families with a female householder was 30.6 percent, while the poverty rate for families with a male householder was 15.9 percent. There were 4.6 million female-householder families in poverty and 1.0 million male-householder families in poverty in 2013.

Depth of Poverty

Categorizing a person as "in poverty" or "not in poverty" is one way to describe his or her economic situation. The income-to-poverty ratio and the income deficit or surplus describe additional aspects of economic well-being. While the poverty rate shows the proportion of people with income below the relevant poverty threshold, the income-to-poverty ratio gauges the depth of poverty and shows how close a family's income is to its poverty threshold. The income-to-poverty ratio is reported as a percentage that compares a family's or an unrelated person's income with the applicable poverty threshold. For example, a family with an income-to-poverty ratio of 125 percent has income that is 25 percent above its poverty threshold.

The income deficit or surplus shows how many dollars a family's or an individual's income is below (or above) their poverty threshold. For those with an income deficit, the measure is an estimate of the dollar amount necessary to raise a family's or a person's income to their poverty threshold.

Ratio of Income to Poverty

Table 5 *[omitted]* presents the number and the percentage of people with specific income-to-poverty ratios—those below 50 percent of poverty ("Under 0.50"), those below 125 percent of poverty ("Under 1.25"), those below 150 percent of poverty ("Under 1.50"), and those below 200 percent of poverty ("Under 2.00").

In 2013, 19.9 million people lived in families with an income below one-half of their poverty threshold. They represented 6.3 percent of all people and 43.8 percent of those in poverty. One in 5 people (19.2 percent) had a family income below 125 percent of their threshold, 1 in 4 people (24.3 percent) had a family income below 150 percent of their poverty threshold, while approximately 1 in 3 (33.9 percent) had a family income below 200 percent of their threshold.

Of the 19.9 million people with a family income below one-half of their poverty threshold, 6.5 million were children under age 18, 12.2 million were aged 18 to 64, and 1.2 million were aged 65 years and older. The percentage of people aged 65 and older with an income below 50 percent of their poverty threshold was 2.7 percent, less than one-half the percentage of the total population at this poverty level (6.3 percent).

The demographic makeup of the population differs at varying degrees of poverty. In 2013, children represented:

- 23.5 percent of the overall population.
- 32.6 percent of the population below 50 percent of their poverty threshold.
- 27.5 percent of people with an income between 100 percent and 200 percent of their poverty threshold.
- 20.4 percent of the people with an income above 200 percent of their poverty threshold.

By comparison, people aged 65 and older represented:

- 14.2 percent of the overall population.
- 6.1 percent of people below 50 percent of their poverty threshold.
- 17.3 percent of people between 100 percent and 200 percent of their poverty threshold.
- 14.4 percent of people with an income above 200 percent of their poverty threshold.

Income Deficit

The income deficit for families in poverty (the difference in dollars between a family's income and its poverty threshold) averaged $9,834 in 2013, which was not statistically different from the inflation-adjusted 2012 estimate. The average income deficit was larger for families with a female householder ($10,691) than for married-couple families ($9,013) and families with a male householder ($8,717).

For families in poverty, the average income deficit per capita for families with a female householder ($3,183) was higher than for married-couple families ($2,442) and families with a male householder ($2,841). For unrelated individuals, the average income deficit for those in poverty was $6,422 in 2013. The $6,041 deficit for women was lower than the $6,905 deficit for men.

Shared Households

Shared households are defined as households that include at least one "additional" adult, a person aged 18 years or older who is not the householder, spouse, or cohabiting partner of the householder. Adults aged 18 to 24 years who are enrolled in school are not counted as additional adults.

In 2014, the number and percentage of shared households was higher than in 2007, prior to the recession. In 2007, there were 19.7 million shared households, representing 17.0 percent of all households; by 2014, there were 23.5 million shared households representing 19.1 percent of all households. The number of adults in shared households grew from 61.7 million (27.7 percent) in 2007 to 73.9 million (30.9 percent) in 2014.

Between 2013 and 2014, the change in the number and percentage of shared households was not statistically significant. However, the number of additional adults residing in shared households increased by 1.8 million (0.6 percentage points) between 2013 and 2014.

In 2014, an estimated 10.7 million adults aged 25 to 34 (25.2 percent) were additional adults in someone else's household. Of these young adults, 6.1 million (14.4 percent) lived with their parents. The change between 2013 and 2014 in the number and percentage of additional adults in this age group living in their parents' household was not statistically significant. Further, there has been no significant annual change since 2011 in the number or percent of adults aged 25 to 34 living with their parents.

It is difficult to assess the precise impact of household sharing on overall poverty rates. In 2014, adults aged 25 to 34 living with their parents had an official poverty rate of 9.3 percent (when the entire family's income is compared with the threshold that includes the young adult as a member of the family). However, if poverty status were determined using only the additional adult's own income, 43.7 percent of those aged 25 to 34 would have been below the poverty threshold for a single person under age 65. Moreover, although 9.0 percent of families including an adult child of the householder aged 25 to 34 years of age were poor, 14.0 percent of these families would be poor if the young adult was not living in the household.

Source: U.S. Census Bureau. "Income, Poverty, and Health Insurance Coverage in the United States: 2013." September 16, 2014. www.census.gov/content/dam/Census/library/publications/2014/demo/p60-249.pdf.

Census Bureau Releases
Supplemental Poverty Measures

October 16, 2014

The nation's poverty rate was 15.5 percent in 2013, down from 16.0 percent in 2012, according to the supplemental poverty measure released today by the U.S. Census Bureau. The 2013 rate was higher than the official measure of 14.5 percent, but similarly declined from the corresponding rate in 2012.

Meanwhile, 48.7 million were below the poverty line in 2013 according to the supplemental poverty measure, not statistically different from the number in 2012. In 2013, 45.3 million were poor using the official definition released last month in Income and Poverty in the United States: 2013.

These findings are contained in the Census Bureau report The Supplemental Poverty Measure: 2013, released with support from the Bureau of Labor Statistics and describing research showing different ways of measuring poverty in the United States.

The supplemental poverty measure serves as an additional indicator of economic well-being and provides a deeper understanding of economic conditions and policy effects.

Unlike the official poverty rate, the supplemental poverty measure takes into account the impact of different benefits and necessary expenses on the resources available to families, as well as geographic differences in housing costs. For example, the measure adds refundable tax credits to cash income, which reduces the supplemental poverty rate for all people by nearly three percentage points (18.4 percent to 15.5 percent). For children, the supplemental poverty rate of 16.4 percent would rise to 22.8 percent if refundable tax credits were excluded.

"The supplemental poverty measure is an important tool that helps policymakers and the public judge the effectiveness of social safety-net programs in a way that the official poverty measure cannot," said Kathleen Short, a Census Bureau economist and the report's author. "It also helps us track how necessary expenses, such as paying taxes or work-related and medical-out-of-pocket expenses, affect the economic well-being of all families."

The supplemental poverty measure deducts various necessary expenses from income; these include medical out-of-pocket expenses, income and payroll taxes, child care expenses and work-related expenses. These expenses reduce income available for purchasing essential basic goods, including food, clothing, shelter and utilities and a small additional amount to allow for other needs. Deducting medical out-of-pocket expenses increases the supplemental poverty rate by 3.6 percentage points. Without accounting for medical out-of-pocket expenses, the number of people living below the poverty line would have been 37.5 million rather than the 48.7 million people classified as poor with the supplemental poverty measure.

Without adding Social Security benefits to income, the supplemental poverty rate overall would have been 8.6 percentage points higher (or 24.1 percent rather than 15.5 percent). People 65 and older had a supplemental poverty rate of 14.6 percent, equating to 6.5 million. Excluding Social Security would leave the majority of this population (52.6 percent or 23.4 million) in poverty.

The supplemental poverty measure's poverty thresholds vary by geography, family size, and if a family pays a mortgage, rents or owns their home free and clear. For example, among the lowest thresholds for families with two adults and two children, about $18,000, were those for homeowners without a mortgage living outside metropolitan areas in Alabama, Arkansas, Georgia, Iowa, Kentucky, Louisiana, Missouri, Mississippi, North Dakota, Oklahoma, South Dakota, Tennessee and West Virginia. Among the highest for this family type were those for homeowners with a mortgage in the San Jose-Sunnyvale-Santa Clara, Calif.; San Francisco-Oakland-Fremont, Calif.; Santa Cruz-Watsonville, Calif.; and Honolulu, Hawaii, metropolitan statistical areas, around $35,000. The $23,624 official poverty threshold for a family of four was the same no matter where a family lives.

ESTIMATES FOR STATES

The differences between the official and supplemental poverty measures varied considerably by state. The supplemental rates were higher than the official statewide poverty rates in the District of Columbia and 13 states: Alaska, California, Connecticut, Florida, Hawaii, Illinois, Maryland, Massachusetts, Nevada, New Hampshire, New Jersey, New York and Virginia.

For another 26 states, supplemental rates were lower than the official statewide poverty rates. The states were Alabama, Arkansas, Idaho, Indiana, Iowa, Kansas, Kentucky, Louisiana, Maine, Michigan, Mississippi, Missouri, Montana, Nebraska, New Mexico, North Carolina, North Dakota, Ohio, Oklahoma, South Carolina, South Dakota, Tennessee, Texas, West Virginia, Wisconsin and Wyoming. Rates in the remaining 11 states were not statistically different using the two measures.

COMPARING POVERTY RATES FOR DIFFERENT DEMOGRAPHIC GROUPS

The supplemental poverty measure can show the effects of tax and transfer policies on various subgroups, unlike the current official poverty measure. According to the report:

- Including tax credits and noncash benefits results in lower poverty rates for some groups. For instance, the supplemental poverty rate was lower for children than the official rate: 16.4 percent compared with 20.4 percent.
- Subtracting necessary expenses from income results in higher poverty rates for other groups. The supplemental poverty rate for those 65 and older was 14.6 percent compared with only 9.5 percent using the official measure. Medical out-of-pocket expenses were a significant element for this group.
- Even though supplemental poverty rates were lower than the official rates for children and higher for those 65 and older, the rates for children were still higher than the rates for both 18- to 64-year-olds and people 65 and older.
- Supplemental poverty rates were higher than the official measure for all race groups and for Hispanics, with one exception: blacks, whose 24.7 percent supplemental poverty rate was lower than the official rate of 27.3 percent.
- Supplemental poverty rates differed by region primarily because the supplemental poverty measure has thresholds that vary geographically. The rates were higher than official rates for the Northeast and West, and not statistically different from the official measure in the South and Midwest. These results reflect differences in housing costs, which are not captured by the official poverty measure.

BACKGROUND

The supplemental poverty measure is an effort to take into account many of the government programs designed to assist low-income families and individuals that were not included in the current official poverty measure, released Sept. 16.

While the official poverty measure includes only pretax money income, the supplemental measure adds the value of in-kind benefits, such as the Supplemental Nutrition Assistance Program, school lunches, housing assistance and refundable tax credits. Additionally, the supplemental poverty measure deducts necessary expenses for critical goods and services from income. Expenses that are deducted include taxes, child care and commuting expenses, out-of-pocket medical expenses and child support paid to another household.

Today's report compares 2013 supplemental poverty estimates to 2013 official poverty estimates for numerous demographic groups at the national level. In addition, the report presents supplemental poverty estimates for states using three-year averages. At the national level, the report also compares 2012 supplemental poverty estimates with 2013 estimates.

There has been a continuing debate about the best approach to measure income and poverty in the United States since the publication of the first official U.S. poverty estimates in 1964. In 2009, an interagency group asked the Census Bureau, in cooperation with the Bureau of Labor Statistics, to develop a new, supplemental measure to allow for an improved understanding of the economic well-being of American families and the way that federal policies affect those living in poverty.

The measures presented in this report used the 2014 Current Population Survey Annual Social and Economic Supplement with income information that referred to calendar year 2013 to estimate supplemental poverty measure resources, including the value of various in-kind benefits beyond cash income. (The official poverty measure is based solely on cash income.)

SOURCE: U.S. Census Bureau. "Poverty Rate Declines, Number of Poor Unchanged, Based on Supplemental Measure of Poverty." October 16, 2014. www.census.gov/newsroom/press-releases/2014/cb14-188.html.

OTHER HISTORIC DOCUMENTS OF INTEREST

FROM THIS VOLUME

- State of the Union Address and Republican Response, p. 3

FROM PREVIOUS *HISTORIC DOCUMENTS*

- White House Report Details Benefits of Unemployment Insurance, *2013*, p. 609
- Census Bureau Reports on Poverty in the United States, *2013*, p. 437
- President Obama Issues Sequestration Order, *2013*, p. 79

President Obama Launches Campaign to Curb Campus Sexual Assault

SEPTEMBER 19, 2014

In 2014, President Barack Obama took a number of steps to encourage colleges and universities to work to curb sexual assault against women on their campuses, including establishing a task force to make recommendations on the issue. His work culminated in the "It's On Us" campaign, unveiled on September 19, 2014, which encourages both men and women to become involved in preventing sexual assault.

SEXUAL ASSAULT ON CAMPUS

Under the Jeanne Clery Disclosure of Campus Security Policy and Campus Crime Statistics Act of 1990, schools are required to report data on sexual assault to the Department of Education and notify students about such crime on campus. Reporting was strengthened in 2013 under the Violence Against Women Reauthorization Act, and schools are now required to report instances of sexual assault as well as domestic violence, dating violence, and stalking incidents. According to the Department of Justice, 20 percent of women are targets of attempted or completed sexual assault as a college student, while that number is one in sixteen for men. Such statistics are heavily debated, but researchers agree that somewhere between one in four and one in five women will experience sexual assault during their college careers.

There are a litany of annual reports on the statistics of sexual violence against women on college campuses, including the National Intimate Partner and Sexual Violence Survey (published by the Centers for Disease Control and Prevention), the Campus Sexual Assault study (funded by the Department of Justice), and the National Crime Victimization Survey. Each survey differs in how it collects its data, which has led many to criticize how reliable some of the information is. For example, in December 2014, when the National Crime Victimization survey released its newest report, it found that women aged eighteen to twenty-four who are not college students are more likely to be victims of sexual violence. But at the same time, 80 percent of college students said they did not report a sexual assault, while this number was only 67 percent for nonstudents. Some took this data to mean that the information about sexual assault on college campuses has been overblown. John Foubert, a sexual violence researcher at Oklahoma State University, finds the study somewhat questionable because it did not go through the peer review process and does not work with the data to remove false positives. Still, he adds, "even if there are more women outside than inside college who experience rape, so what? There is still a lot of rape out there."

ANALYSIS OF CAMPUS ASSAULT DATA

In May, the Department of Education released a report that listed fifty-five colleges that have open sexual violence investigations. These ongoing investigations are part of regular examinations by the Office for Civil Rights into whether schools are complying with Title IX, which prohibits gender-based discrimination. Some of these schools were potentially violating the law's requirements regarding how to handle sexual violence cases. Prominent Ivy League schools that appeared on the list include Harvard University, Princeton University, and Dartmouth College. Others included many large state universities like The Ohio State University, the University of Michigan, Pennsylvania State University, and Florida State University.

In July, Sen. Claire McCaskill, D-Mo., released the findings of a study she commissioned that reviewed how 440 four-year colleges and universities report, investigate, and adjudicate cases of sexual assault. The report found a variety of failings across most schools participating in the report, including a failure to encourage students to report sexual violence, a lack of assault training for staff, failure to investigate sexual assault cases, lack of services for survivors, failed adjudication systems, no training on sexual assault response for law enforcement, and lack of oversight. McCaskill called "most alarming" the finding that schools reported a higher number of sexual assault incidents than had been investigated. "That means that they are reporting some incidents that they clearly have not even bothered to investigate," she said. McCaskill submitted a bill on February 3, 2015, to address many of these failings.

The Washington Post conducted its own analysis of 2012 data on college and university sexual assault reports, finding that there were more than 3,900 reports of alleged forcible sex offenses. The reports included acts such as forcible rape, forcible sodomy, forcible fondling, and sexual assault with an object. A large number of these cases, according to the *Post*, do not result in prosecution. According to the *Post* report, Penn State University had the highest number of reported forcible sex offenses in 2012 at fifty-six. University officials said this tally is likely related to the reports made in relation to the case against former assistant football coach Jerry Sandusky. The second highest number was at the University of Michigan's main campus in Ann Arbor, where thirty-four assaults were reported, followed by Harvard University at thirty-one. Larger universities tend to have a higher number of reported cases, but these same institutions often struggle to compile and report complete data because they have large populations of graduate students living off campus. The University of North Carolina at Greensboro, for example, had no reported instances of sexual assault in 2012, but admitted that "it is improbable that there would be no actual incidents."

White House Encourages Action

The Obama administration has aggressively searched for ways to fight sexual assault on college campuses. In January, the White House created the Task Force to Protect Students from Sexual Assault to promote the president's efforts at curbing campus sexual assault. In April, the group released its first report, "Not Alone," which included a list of recommended actions and guidelines for schools to protect victims, while still encouraging them to report assault. "One in five women is sexually assaulted in college. Most often, it's by someone she knows—and also most often, she does not report what happened. . . . We are here to tell sexual assault survivors that they are not alone. And we're also here to help schools live up to their obligation to protect students from sexual violence," the report states in its opening.

The recommendations in the report include providing training to school officials on trauma, improving discipline systems, and increasing transparency. The most prominent of the recommendations was to promote bystander intervention to motivate witnesses to report sexual assault. "When men think their peers don't object to abusive behavior, they are much less likely to step in and help," the report states. The task force report also encouraged schools to be more diligent about reporting and documenting the extent of sexual assault on college campuses. McCaskill, a strong proponent of the work being done by the White House, said that it is important to help schools understand that they will not be targeted for revealing a fuller picture of the sexual assault rate on their campuses.

On September 19, President Obama launched the "It's On Us" campaign, aimed at encouraging everyone to become involved in combatting sexual violence against women on college campuses. "From sports leagues to pop culture to politics, our society does not sufficiently value women," Obama said, urging a shift in the way women are treated. "We still don't condemn sexual assault as loudly as we should." To kick-off the program, the White House unveiled a thirty-second video featuring well-known actors, musicians, and athletes, including Jon Hamm, Questlove, and Kevin Love. In announcing the campaign, the president noted that only 12 percent of sexual assaults on campuses are reported, and of those, few offenders face punishment:

> *For anybody whose once-normal, everyday life was suddenly shattered by an act of sexual violence, the trauma, the terror can shadow you long after one horrible attack. It lingers when you don't know where to go or who to turn to. It's there when you're forced to sit in the same class or stay in the same dorm with the person who raped you; when people are more suspicious of what you were wearing or what you were drinking, as if it's your fault, not the fault of the person who assaulted you. It's a haunting presence when the very people entrusted with your welfare fail to protect you.*

Obama stressed the importance of engaging men of all ages in the conversation. "It is not just on parents of young women to caution them, it is on the parents of young men to teach them respect for women," he said. "It is on grown men to set an example and be clear about what it means to be a man." A variety of companies have partnered with the White House to promote the campaign, including MTV, VH1, the NCAA, and video game maker Electronic Arts, which will be placing the "It's On Us" logo on many of its games.

FRATERNITIES PARTNER TO RAISE AWARENESS

On September 23, 2014, Lambda Chi Alpha, Phi Delta Theta, Pi Kappa Alpha, Sigma Alpha Epsilon, Sigma Alpha Mu, Sigma Chi, Tau Kappa Epsilon, and Triangle announced that, in the spirit of the president's campaign, they would work together to educate their members on sexual misconduct. The Fraternal Health and Safety Initiative was organized by fraternity insurance company James R. Favor & Company and will provide training to fraternity members in retreat-like settings. "If you think of the power of having all of these fraternities on a particular campus going through similar programming and similar messaging, it could definitely impact the culture on that campus fairly quickly," said Marc Mores, executive vice president of the company.

In November, the University of Virginia suspended all fraternities on campus following the publication of the article "A Rape on Campus" in *Rolling Stone* written by Sabrina Erdely. According to the article, in 2012, a female student, referred to as "Jackie," was gang raped by seven members of the Phi Kappa Psi fraternity. The article was reportedly based on interviews with the alleged victim, but Erdely did not interview any of those whom Jackie accused of rape. After publication, journalists across the country began questioning the accuracy of the article and the university said that it had noted a number of discrepancies in the story.

Rolling Stone issued an apology on December 5, but Erdely continued to stand by her story, saying she could not have done it "any better." Even though the article was largely discredited, it had a serious emotional impact on those accused who were targeted by the campus student body. There has been some speculation about whether fraternity members will consider civil charges against *Rolling Stone*.

—Heather Kerrigan

Following is the text of the speech delivered by President Barack Obama on September 19, 2014, unveiling the "It's On Us" campaign.

President Obama Unveils White House Campaign Against Sexual Assault

September 19, 2014

Thank you so much, everybody. Please have a seat. Well, welcome to the White House, everybody. And thank you to Joe Biden not just for the introduction, not just for being a great Vice President, but for decades, since long before he was in his current office, Joe has brought unmatched passion to this cause. And—*[applause]*. He has.

And at a time when domestic violence was all too often seen as a private matter, Joe was out there saying that this was unacceptable. Thanks to him and so many others, last week, we were able to commemorate the 20th anniversary of the law Joe wrote, a law that transformed the way we handle domestic abuse in this country: the Violence Against Women Act.

And we're here to talk today about an issue that is a priority for me, and that's ending campus sexual assault. I want to thank all of you who are participating. I particularly want to thank Lilly for her wonderful presentation and grace. I want to thank her parents for being here. As a father of two daughters, I on the one hand am enraged about what has happened; on the other hand, am empowered to see such an incredible young woman be so strong and do so well. And we're going to be thrilled watching all of the great things she is going to be doing in her life. So the—we're really proud of her.

I want to thank the White House Council on Women and Girls. Good Job. Valerie, thank you. I want to thank our White House Adviser on Violence Against Women, the work that you do every day partnering with others to prevent the outrage, the crime of sexual violence.

We've got some outstanding lawmakers with us. Senator Claire McCaskill is right here from the great State of Missouri, who I love. And we've got Dick Blumenthal from the great State of Connecticut, as well as Congresswoman Susan Davis. So thank you so much, I'm thrilled to have you guys here.

I also want to thank other Members of Congress who are here and have worked on this issue so hard for so long. A lot of the people in this room have been on the front lines in fighting sexual assault for a long time. And along with Lilly, I want to thank all the survivors who are here today and so many others around the country. Lilly, I'm sure, took strength from a community of people—some who came before, some who were peers—who were able to summon the courage to speak out about the darkest moment of their lives. They endure pain and the fear that too often isolates victims of sexual assault. So when they give voice to their own experiences, they're giving voice to countless others—women and men, girls and boys—who still suffer in silence.

So to the survivors who are leading the fight against sexual assault on campuses, your efforts have helped to start a movement. I know that, as Lilly described, there are times where the fight feels lonely, and it feels as if you're dredging up stuff that you'd rather put behind you. But we're here to say today, it's not on you. This is not your fight alone. This is on all of us, every one of us, to fight campus sexual assault. You are not alone, and we have your back, and we are going to organize campus by campus, city by city, State by State. This entire country is going to make sure that we understand what this is about and that we're going to put a stop to it.

And this is a new school year. We've been working on campus sexual assault for several years, but the issue of violence against women is now in the news every day. We've started to, I think, get a better picture about what domestic violence is all about. People are talking about it. Victims are realizing they're not alone. Brave people have come forward; they're opening up about their own experiences.

And so we think today's event is all that more relevant, all that more important for us to say that campus sexual assault is no longer something we as a nation can turn away from and say that's not our problem. This is a problem that matters to all of us.

An estimated one in five women has been sexually assaulted during her college years—one in five. Of those assaults, only 12 percent are reported, and of those reported assaults, only a fraction of the offenders are punished. And while these assaults overwhelmingly happen to women, we know that men are assaulted too. Men get raped. They're even less likely to talk about it. We know that sexual assault can happen to anyone, no matter their race, their economic status, sexual orientation, gender identity. And LGBT victims can feel even more isolated, feel even more alone.

For anybody whose once normal, everyday life was suddenly shattered by an act of sexual violence, the trauma, the terror can shadow you long after one horrible attack. It lingers when you don't know where to go or who to turn to. It's there when you're forced to sit in the same class or stay in the same dorm with the person who raped you; when people are more suspicious of what you were wearing or what you were drinking, as if it's your fault, not the fault of the person who assaulted you. It's a haunting presence when the very people entrusted with your welfare fail to protect you.

Now, students work hard to get into college. I know. I'm watching Malia right now. She's a junior. [Laughter] She's got a lot of homework. [Laughter] And parents can do everything they can to support their kids' dreams of getting a good education. When they finally make it onto campus, only to be assaulted, that's not just a nightmare for them and their families; it's not just an affront to everything they've worked so hard to achieve. It is an affront to our basic humanity. It insults our most basic values as individuals and families and as a nation. We are a nation that values liberty and equality and justice. And we're a people who believe every child deserves an education that allows them to fulfill their God-given potential, free from fear of intimidation or violence. And we owe it to our children to live up to those values. So my administration is trying to do our part.

First of all, 3 years ago, we sent guidance to every school district, every college, every university that receives Federal funding, and we clarified their legal obligations to prevent and respond to sexual assault. And we reminded them that sexual violence isn't just a crime, it is a civil rights violation. And I want to acknowledge Secretary of Education Arne Duncan for his department's work in holding schools accountable and making sure that they stand up for students.

Number two, in January, I created a White House task force to prevent—a Task Force To Protect Students From Sexual Assault. Their job is to work with colleges and universities on better ways to prevent and respond to assaults, to lift up best practices. And we held conversations with thousands of people: survivors, parents, student groups, faculty, law enforcement, advocates, academics. In April, the Task Force released the first report, recommending a number of best practices for colleges and universities to keep our kids safe. And these are tested, and they are commonsense measures, like campus surveys to figure out the scope of the problem, giving survivors a safe place to go and a trusted person to talk to, training school officials in how to handle trauma. Because when you read some of the accounts, you think, what were they thinking? I mean, you just get a sense of too many people in charge dropping the ball, fumbling something that should be taken with the most—the utmost seriousness and the utmost care.

Number three, we're stepping up enforcement efforts and increasing the transparency of our efforts. So we're reviewing existing laws to make sure they're adequate. And we're going to keep on working with educational institutions across the country to help them appropriately respond to these crimes.

So that's what we have been doing, but there's always more that we can do. And today we're taking a step and joining with people across the country to change our culture and help prevent sexual assault from happening. Because that's where prevention—that's what prevention is going to require. We've got to have a fundamental shift in our culture.

As far as we've come, the fact is that from sports leagues to pop culture to politics, our society still does not sufficiently value women. We still don't condemn sexual assault as loudly as we should. We make excuses. We look the other way. The message that sends can have a chilling effect on our young women.

And I've said before, when women succeed, America succeeds. Let me be clear, that's not just true in America. If you look internationally, countries that oppress their women are countries that do badly. Countries that empower their women are countries that thrive.

And so this is something that requires us to shift how we think about these issues. One letter from a young woman really brought this point home. Katherine Morrison, a young student from Youngstown, Ohio, she wrote: "How are we supposed to succeed when so many of our voices are being stifled? How can we succeed when our society says that as a woman, it's your fault if you are at a party or walked home alone. How can we succeed when people look at women and say, 'You should have known better,' or, 'Boys will be boys'?"

And Katherine is absolutely right. Women make up half this country, half its workforce, more than half of our college students. They are not going to succeed the way they should unless they are treated as true equals and are supported and respected. And unless women are allowed to fulfill their full potential, America will not reach its full potential. So we've got to change.

And this is not just the work of survivors, it's not just the work of activists. It's not just the work of college administrators. It's a responsibility of the soccer coach and the captain of the basketball team and the football players. And it's on fraternities and sororities, and it's on the editor of the school paper and the drum major in the band. And it's on the English department and the engineering department, and it's on the high schools and the elementary schools, and it's on teachers, and it's on counselors, and it's on mentors, and it's on ministers.

It's on celebrities and sports leagues and the media to set a better example. And it's on parents and grandparents and older brothers and sisters to sit down young people and talk about this issue.

SEPTEMBER

And it's not just on the parents of young women to caution them. It is on the parents of young men to teach them respect for women. And it's on grown men to set an example and be clear about what it means to be a man.

It is on all of us to reject the quiet tolerance of sexual assault and to refuse to accept what's unacceptable. And we especially need our young men to show women the respect they deserve and to recognize sexual assault and to do their part to stop it. Because most young men on college campuses are not perpetrators. But the rest—we can't generalize across the board. But the rest of us can help stop those who think in these terms and shut stuff down. And that's not always easy to do with all the social pressures to stay quiet or go along; you don't want to be the guy who's stopping another friend from taking a woman home even if it looks like she doesn't or can't consent. Maybe you hear something in the locker room that makes you feel uncomfortable or see something at a party that you know isn't right, but you're not sure whether you should stand up, not sure it's okay to intervene.

Here—and I think Joe said it well. The truth is, it's not just okay to intervene, it is your responsibility. It is your responsibility to speak your mind. It is your responsibility to tell your buddy when he's messing up. It is your responsibility to set the right tone when you're talking about women, even when women aren't around, maybe especially when they're not around. *[Laughter]*

And it's not just men who should intervene, women should also speak up when something doesn't look right, even if the men don't like it. It's all of us taking responsibility. Everybody has a role to play.

And in fact, we're here with Generation Progress to launch, appropriately enough, a campaign called "It's On Us." I mean, the idea is to fundamentally shift the way we think about sexual assault. So we're inviting colleges and universities to join us in saying, we are not tolerating this anymore: not on our campuses, not in our community, not in this country. And the campaign is building on the momentum that's already being generated by college campuses by the incredible young people around the country who have stepped up and are leading the way. I couldn't be prouder of them.

And we're also joined by some great partners in this effort, including the Office of Women's Health, the college sports community, media platforms. We've got universities who have signed up, including, by the way, our military academies, who are represented here today. So the goal is to hold ourselves and each other accountable and to look out for those who don't consent and can't consent. And anybody can be a part of this campaign.

So the first step on this is to go to ItsOnUs.org—that's ItsOnUs.org. Take a pledge to help keep women and men safe from sexual assault. It's a promise not to be a bystander to the problem, but to be part of the solution. I took the pledge. Joe took the pledge. You can take the pledge. You can share it on social media; you can encourage others to join us.

And this campaign is just part of a broader effort, but it's a critical part, because even as we continue to enforce our laws and work with colleges to improve their responses and to make sure that survivors are taken care of, it won't be enough unless we change the culture that allows assault to happen in the first place.

And I'm confident we can. I'm confident because of incredible young people like Lilly who speak out for change and empower other survivors. They inspire me to keep fighting. I'm assuming they inspire you as well. And this is a personal priority not just as a President, obviously, not just as a husband and a father of two extraordinary girls, but as an American who believes that our Nation's success depends on how we value and defend the rights of women and girls.

So I'm asking all of you, join us in this campaign. Commit to being part of the solution. Help make sure our schools are safe havens where everybody, men and women, can pursue their dreams and fulfill their potential. Thank you so much for all the great work.

SOURCE: Executive Office of the President. "Remarks Announcing the 'It's On Us' Campaign to Prevent Sexual Assault on College Campuses." September 19, 2014. *Compilation of Presidential Documents* 2014, no. 00680 (September 19, 2014). www.gpo.gov/fdsys/pkg/DCPD-201400680/pdf/DCPD-201400680.pdf.

OTHER HISTORIC DOCUMENTS OF INTEREST

FROM PREVIOUS *HISTORIC DOCUMENTS*

Scotland Votes Against Independence

SEPTEMBER 19 AND NOVEMBER 27, 2014

In 2014, Scotland put a referendum before voters to determine whether the country should become a nation independent of the United Kingdom. Advocates for such a decision argued that the country would see impressive gains in its economy because of oil reserve revenues it is currently required to share with its parent nation. Opponents said that Scotland would struggle alone, not only because of declining oil revenues but also because it would have to seek entry into international organizations such as the European Union. Ultimately, voters decided to remain a part of the United Kingdom, but the country did gain additional powers for itself through the referendum process.

DEVOLUTION ATTEMPTS

In 1707, Scotland and England united to form the Kingdom of Great Britain. There are a variety of arguments regarding why the two nations chose to merge, including bribes and failed economies. Since that time, a number of parties have attempted to rise to power in Scotland with the aim of seeking independence. The Labour Party made the first legitimate attempt in the 1920s, but seeking home rule, or Scottish devolution, fell lower on its agenda as the years went on, until the party became against such a proposition. In 1979, the Labour government held power and the Scottish National Party (SNP), which was initially formed in the 1930s on an independence platform, pressured the government to put a referendum on the ballot to create a devolved Scottish parliament. The measure succeeded but did not meet the 40 percent threshold that it needed to go into effect. The devolution issue did not come up again until 1997 when the Labour Party came back into power. At that time, it managed to pass the devolution referendum, and in 1998, the Scotland Act created a new parliament for Scotland.

In 2011, the SNP placed a devolution referendum before the Scottish parliament to do one of the following: seek full independence; seek full devolution to be able to oversee "all laws, taxes and duties in Scotland" with the exception of financial regulation, monetary policy, and defense; or seek full devolution with the power to tax. The SNP failed to secure opposition support, and eventually withdrew the referendum from consideration.

In January 2012, with knowledge that the SNP intended to again attempt to pass a devolution referendum, the United Kingdom's central government said it would assist in the vote and would allow Scotland to abide by the decision of the resolution, so long as the country adhered to certain guidelines, including bringing no harm to the United Kingdom. This compromise, known as the Edinburgh Agreement, would also give additional powers to Scotland if the referendum ultimately failed to win voter support. The Scottish Independence Referendum Act 2013 passed parliament on June 27, 2013, allowing the question of full independence to be put before the voters. In November, Scotland's government published a white paper for public viewing that outlined how Scotland could seek to become an independent nation and what such a vote might mean for citizens.

Scotland Campaigns for Independence

In late March 2014, the election date for the independence referendum was set for September 18, 2014. In the lead-up to the election, there was debate across the United Kingdom regarding whether such a referendum was legal and whether all UK citizens should be allowed to vote, because independence of one nation would impact everyone. Regarding the former, because Scotland and the United Kingdom's government agreed to the Edinburgh Agreement, which temporarily granted the Scottish parliament the right to hold such an election before December 31, 2014, Scotland was well within its legal right. The latter issue was rejected by Britain's leaders. Lord Wallace, the advocate general for Scotland, called the decision to seek independence "a matter for Scotland."

The campaign was organized to allow one organization each to represent those in support of and opposed to the referendum. Each side was allowed to spend up to £1.5 million ($2.3 million), and each major party was given a separate spending cap. Neither organization was permitted to run television or radio ads; instead, they had to rely on approved political party broadcasts.

Yes Scotland, the campaign supporting independence, launched its operations on May 25, 2012, with support from the SNP, the Scottish Socialist Party, and the Scottish Green Party. The aim of the group at the outset was to get one million signatures in support of the referendum, a goal that it reached in August 2014.

The anti-independence campaign, Better Together, opened its operations one month after Yes Scotland with support from the Conservative Party, Labour Party, and Liberal Democrats. In August 2014, the group announced that it had raised enough to cover its spending limit and could no longer accept donations; most of the money raised came from large sum donations from prominent figures including author J. K. Rowling, who donated £1 million.

The issue that dominated the referendum vote was the economy. Scotland has profitable North Sea oil and gas reserves off its coast. The Scottish government has argued that the nation stands to gain great economic benefit if it fully controlled those revenues instead of sharing them with the United Kingdom. That belief has been debated, however. The Institute for Fiscal Studies, an economic and social research organization, released a report in March 2014 indicating that oil revenues were falling and the Scottish economy had weakened relative to that of the United Kingdom.

Voters Reject Independence

The referendum was held on September 18, 2014. At the polls, voters were asked the question "Should Scotland be an independent country?" a change from the initially desired wording of "Do you agree that Scotland should be an independent country?" which some deemed too leading. According to the UK government, as long as the referendum received a simple majority, the nation would be granted independence "after a process of negotiations." If the referendum lost and Scotland remained part of the United Kingdom, the nation's parliament would receive additional authority as stated under the Edinburgh Agreement.

Ultimately, on September 19, it was announced that the referendum had lost, by a vote of 55.3 percent against and 44.7 percent in favor. Turnout was nearly 85 percent of eligible voters. Prime Minister David Cameron said that "it would have broken my heart to see our United Kingdom come to an end and I know that this sentiment was shared not just by people across our country but also around the world." He added, "We now have a chance—a great opportunity—to change the way the British people are governed, and change it for the better."

Scottish first minister Alex Salmond called on everyone to respect the outcome of the vote but said he would step down as leader of the SNP. "For me as leader my time is nearly over but for Scotland the campaign continues and the dream shall never die," he said. "Today of all days as we bring Scotland together let us not dwell on the distance we have fallen short. Let us dwell on the distance we have travelled and have confidence that the movement is so broad in Scotland that it will take this nation forward and we shall go forward as one nation."

MOVING FORWARD

The Scottish referendum on independence sparked many hurt feelings across the United Kingdom, with one British member of parliament even calling on Scotland to explain why 45 percent of their population wanted to leave the United Kingdom. Cameron's government, however, was dedicated to moving forward. The UK's three leading parties, the Conservatives, Labour Party, and Liberal Democrats, all agreed that Scotland should be given further devolution of powers on tax, spending, and welfare. These new powers would include levying of new taxes, expanded borrowing powers, and a new rate of income tax.

Following the vote, the three parties, led by Cameron, set a timeline for such new powers, on which work would begin immediately. In October 2014, proposals of legislation granting further devolution would be published, and in January 2015, there would be a draft Scotland Bill published. That bill would be included in the Queen's annual speech before parliament in May 2015. Any legislation related to devolution would not be voted on until after May 2015 when the UK parliament was set to hold elections.

There are a number of areas of disagreement that will need to be addressed before the final proposal is drafted. These include how far reaching the taxation powers will be and whether there will be changes for Scottish members of parliament in voting on England-only issues in the UK's parliament. On the latter, many have argued that there is an unfair balance of power that shifts to Scotland if they are the only ones allowed to vote on devolved issues, while the Scots can vote on issues that impact only England. It is also likely that the United Kingdom's other two countries, Wales and Northern Ireland, might begin asking for expanded powers of their own. A major issue for members of parliament from Wales regards whether the Barnett funding formula, which sets public spending in Northern Ireland, Scotland, and Wales, will be continued. Under the formula, Scotland receives more funding per head than the UK average, which leaves Wales with £300 million less per year, despite having a significantly poorer population.

Lord Smith, who was tasked with leading the commission that would develop the new proposals on devolution, called for "courage" and "compromise" as talks began. "Time is tight but this is not an exercise in thinking about what we could do; that has been done. It is about agreeing on what we will do," he said. The first task of the Smith Commission was to bring together the five major political parties in Scotland to agree on how to move forward by the end of November.

On November 27, 2014, the Smith Commission released recommendations, which would guide the creation of draft legislation. The recommendations took into account 18,400 e-mail and other submissions from organizations and individuals across the United

Kingdom. The recommendations included giving the Scottish parliament complete power to set income tax rates and bands, increased borrowing powers, control over various social benefits, onshore oil and gas extraction licensing powers, and a portion of the value-added tax raised in Scotland would go back to the nation's government.

In the opening of the report, Smith wrote, "This agreement is, in itself, an unprecedented achievement. It demanded compromise from all of the parties. In some cases that meant moving to devolve greater powers than they had previously committed to, while for other parties it meant accepting the outcome would fall short of their ultimate ambitions. It shows that, however difficult, our political leaders can come together, work together, and reach agreement with one another."

—Heather Kerrigan

Following is the text of two statements, one by Prime Minister David Cameron and one by Scottish first minister Alex Salmond, both on September 19, 2014, following the failure of the Scottish independence referendum; and a statement by Alistair Carmichael before the House of Commons on November 27, 2014, regarding the decision of the Smith Commission on Scottish devolution.

Prime Minister Cameron Remarks on Failure of Scottish Independence Referendum

September 19, 2014

The people of Scotland have spoken. It is a clear result. They have kept our country of 4 nations together. Like millions of other people, I am delighted. As I said during the campaign, it would have broken my heart to see our United Kingdom come to an end.

And I know that sentiment was shared by people, not just across our country, but also around the world because of what we've achieved together in the past and what we can do together in the future.

So now it is time for our United Kingdom to come together, and to move forward. A vital part of that will be a balanced settlement—fair to people in Scotland and importantly to everyone in England, Wales and Northern Ireland as well.

Let us first remember why we had this debate—and why it was right to do so.

The Scottish National Party (SNP) was elected in Scotland in 2011 and promised a referendum on independence. We could have blocked that; we could have put it off, but just as with other big issues, it was right to take—not duck—the big decision.

I am a passionate believer in our United Kingdom—I wanted more than anything for our United Kingdom to stay together.

But I am also a democrat. And it was right that we respected the SNP's majority in Holyrood and gave the Scottish people their right to have their say.

Let us also remember why it was right to ask the definitive question, Yes or No. Because now the debate has been settled for a generation or as Alex Salmond has said, perhaps for a lifetime.

So there can be no disputes, no re-runs—we have heard the settled will of the Scottish people.

Scotland voted for a stronger Scottish Parliament backed by the strength and security of the United Kingdom and I want to congratulate the No campaign for that—for showing people that our nations really are better together.

I also want to pay tribute to Yes Scotland for a well-fought campaign and to say to all those who did vote for independence: "we hear you".

We now have a chance—a great opportunity—to change the way the British people are governed, and change it for the better.

Political leaders on all sides of the debate now bear a heavy responsibility to come together and work constructively to advance the interests of people in Scotland, as well as those in England, Wales and Northern Ireland, for each and every citizen of our United Kingdom.

To those in Scotland sceptical of the constitutional promises made, let me say this we have delivered on devolution under this government, and we will do so again in the next Parliament.

The 3 pro-union parties have made commitments, clear commitments, on further powers for the Scottish Parliament. We will ensure that they are honoured in full.

And I can announce today that Lord Smith of Kelvin—who so successfully led Glasgow's Commonwealth Games—has agreed to oversee the process to take forward the devolution commitments, with powers over tax, spending and welfare all agreed by November and draft legislation published by January.

Just as the people of Scotland will have more power over their affairs, so it follows that the people of England, Wales and Northern Ireland must have a bigger say over theirs. The rights of these voters need to be respected, preserved and enhanced as well.

It is absolutely right that a new and fair settlement for Scotland should be accompanied by a new and fair settlement that applies to all parts of our United Kingdom. In Wales, there are proposals to give the Welsh government and Assembly more powers. And I want Wales to be at the heart of the debate on how to make our United Kingdom work for all our nations. In Northern Ireland, we must work to ensure that the devolved institutions function effectively.

I have long believed that a crucial part missing from this national discussion is England. We have heard the voice of Scotland—and now the millions of voices of England must also be heard. The question of English votes for English laws—the so-called West Lothian question—requires a decisive answer.

So, just as Scotland will vote separately in the Scottish Parliament on their issues of tax, spending and welfare, so too England, as well as Wales and Northern Ireland, should be able to vote on these issues and all this must take place in tandem with, and at the same pace as, the settlement for Scotland.

I hope that is going to take place on a cross-party basis. I have asked William Hague to draw up these plans. We will set up a Cabinet Committee right away and proposals will also be ready to the same timetable. I hope the Labour Party and other parties will contribute.

It is also important we have wider civic engagement about to improve governance in our United Kingdom, including how to empower our great cities. And we will say more about this in the coming days.

This referendum has been hard fought. It has stirred strong passions. It has electrified politics in Scotland, and caught the imagination of people across the whole of our United Kingdom.

It will be remembered as a powerful demonstration of the strength and vitality of our ancient democracy. Record numbers registered to vote and record numbers cast their vote. We can all be proud of that. It has reminded us how fortunate we are that we are able to settle these vital issues at the ballot box, peacefully and calmly.

"Now we must look forward, and turn this into the moment when everyone—whichever way they voted—comes together to build that better, brighter future for our entire United Kingdom."

Source: Prime Minister's Office. Scotland Office. "Scottish Independence Referendum: statement by the Prime Minister." September 19, 2014. www.gov.uk/government/news/scottish-independence-referendum-statement-by-the-prime-minister. License: www.nationalarchives.gov.uk/doc/open-government-licence/version/3/.

DOCUMENT

Scotland First Minister on Failure of Referendum

September 19, 2014

Thank you Scotland for 1.6 million votes for Scottish independence. Our friends in the Highlands of Scotland are still to speak, so the final results aren't in but we know that there is going to be a majority for the No campaign.

It's important to say that our referendum was an agreed and consented process and Scotland has by majority decided not at this stage to become an independent country. I accept that verdict of the people and I call on all of Scotland to follow suit in accepting the democratic verdict of the people of Scotland.

But I think all of us in this campaign say that that 45 per cent, that 1.6 million votes, is a substantial vote for Scottish independence and the future of this country. Let us say something which I hope that unites all campaigns and all Scots. I think the process by which we have made our decision as a nation reflects enormous credit upon Scotland. A turnout of 86 per cent is one of the highest in the democratic world for any election or any referendum in history. This has been a triumph for the democratic process and for participation in politics.

For example, the initiative by which 16 and 17 year olds were able to vote has proved to be a resounding success. I suspect that no one will ever again dispute their right and ability to participate fully and responsibly in democratic elections.

So we now face the consequences of Scotland's democratic decision. Firstly, Clause 30 of the Edinburgh Agreement is now in operation. On behalf of the Scottish Government I accept the results and I pledge to work constructively in the interest of Scotland and the rest of the United Kingdom.

Secondly, the unionist parties made vows late in the campaign to devolve more powers to Scotland. Scotland will expect these to be honoured in rapid course. Just as a reminder, we have been promised a second reading of a Scotland Bill by the 27th of March next year and not just the 1.6 million Scots who voted for independence will demand that that timetable is followed but all Scots who participated in this referendum will demand that that timetable is followed.

I'll be speaking to the Prime Minister shortly after this statement but can I return thirdly to the empowerment of so many Scots entering the political process for the very first time. It is something that is so valuable it has to be cherished, preserved and built upon.

I've said before many times in this campaign that the most moving things I saw was the queue of people in Dundee two or three weeks ago patiently waiting to register to vote. Most of them for the first time ever deciding to participate in the democratic process. Today in Inverurie I met a 61 year old lady just coming out of the polling station who had never voted before in her life. I met a soldier, a former soldier, who hadn't voted since he left the army some 24 years ago. And these people were inspired to enter democratic politics by the thought that they could make a difference in building something better for the country.

These are people who all of us as we campaigned have met and been inspired by. And all of us are a part of all of that experience that we have encountered. Whatever else we can say about this referendum campaign, we have touched sections of the community who've never before been touched by politics. These sections of the community have touched us and touched the political process. I don't think that will ever be allowed to go back to business as usual in politics again.

So friends, sometimes it's best to reflect where we are on a journey. 45 per cent, 1.6 million of our fellow citizens voting for independence, I don't think that any of us whenever we entered politics would have thought such a thing to be either credible or possible.

Today of all days as we bring Scotland together let us not dwell on the distance we have fallen short. Let us dwell on the distance we have travelled and have confidence that the movement is so broad in Scotland that it will take this nation forward and we shall go forward as one nation. Thank you very much.

Source: The Scottish Government. "First Minister on Referendum Outcome." September 19, 2014. www.scotreferendum.com/2014/09/first-minister-on-referendum-outcome/. License: www.nationalar chives.gov.uk/doc/open-government-licence/version/3/.

Secretary of State for Scotland on Smith Commission Recommendations

November 27, 2014

[All commentary given before the House of Commons, aside from Alistair Carmichael's remarks on the Smith Commission, has been omitted.]

SMITH COMMISSION

11.2 am

The Secretary of State for Scotland (Mr Alistair Carmichael): With permission, Mr Speaker, I shall make a statement to the House about the further devolution process in Scotland and the publication of the heads of agreement resulting from Lord Smith's five-party talks. As the Prime Minister has already said this morning, we back the agreement and its recommendations, and will produce draft legislation in January.

The referendum on independence that was held on 18 September 2014 saw Scotland vote decisively to remain within our UK family of nations of England, Wales, Scotland and Northern Ireland, backed by the strength, security and stability of the United Kingdom. The turnout across Scotland was nearly 85%, and more than 2 million people made a positive choice for Scotland to remain part of the UK.

During the referendum campaign, the Prime Minister, the Deputy Prime Minister and the Leader of the Opposition made a joint commitment to deliver more powers to the Scottish Parliament. The Smith commission, chaired by Lord Smith of Kelvin, was up and running on 19 September, and Lord Smith convened cross-party talks to reach agreement on the proposals for further devolution to Scotland. The process has been thorough and extensive. The party representatives were drawn from the five main political parties in Scotland; this was the first time ever that all five had participated in a devolution process.

I would echo the comments of Lord Smith in the foreword to his report:

"This agreement is, in itself, an unprecedented achievement. It demanded compromise from all of the parties. In some cases that meant moving to devolve greater powers than they had previously committed to, while for other parties it meant accepting the outcome would fall short of their ultimate ambitions. It shows that, however difficult, our political leaders can come together, work together, and reach agreement with one another."

In preparing the report, Lord Smith heard from a wide range of Scottish civic institutions and members of the public. Over 400 submissions were received from organisations and groups, and over 18,000 submissions, including e-mails, letters and signatures to petitions, from people across Scotland.

The Smith commission has today produced comprehensive heads of agreement ahead of the St Andrew's day deadline contained in the timetable. This is a significant achievement and historic moment for Scotland. I thank Lord Smith and the party representatives for their work. They have worked hard against a challenging timetable, covering an enormous area of ground. This work will deliver a substantial package of new powers to the Scottish Parliament.

The heads of agreement provide for a durable but responsive constitutional settlement for Scotland within the United Kingdom. They give greater financial responsibility to the Scottish Parliament, with an updated fiscal framework for Scotland, consistent with the UK fiscal framework. For the first time, over 50% of the money spent by the Scottish Government will be raised by the Scottish Government. That is an important step which builds on the measures brought forward by this Government in the Scotland Act 2012, and further increases the financial accountability of the Scottish Parliament to the Scottish people.

The recommendations provide for key welfare measures to be designed by and delivered in Scotland. That will give the Scottish Parliament the tools—and the responsibility— to tackle a range of issues with specific consideration of local circumstances, including those related to social care, long-term unemployment and housing, while continuing to benefit from the strength and stability of the UK-wide system.

The recommendations build on the already significant powers of the Scottish Parliament in social justice and a range of other policy areas. Together, those recommendations give greater responsibility for more decisions affecting Scotland to be made in the Scottish Parliament and paid for by revenue raised by the Scottish Parliament. However, further devolution is just one part of this story. People in Scotland were unequivocally clear on 18 September that Scotland should retain the security of being part of our United Kingdom. The Smith commission's remit was clear—to set out proposals for further devolution within the United Kingdom—and that remit was signed up to by all parties participating in the process, including the Scottish Government. The conclusions reached by the parties ensure a set of proposals that do not cause detriment to the UK as a whole or any of its constituent parts. The Government are committed to ensuring that Scotland and the whole of the United Kingdom continue to prosper from our single domestic market, our social union and the strength that comes from the pooling and sharing of risks.

People in Scotland voted on 18 September for the jobs and opportunities that are created by being part of a larger United Kingdom with one currency, no borders and more money to spend on public services. People in Scotland want to keep the advantages of the UK pound, UK pensions, UK armed forces and a strong UK voice in the world. The package that has been announced today allows that to happen.

As the Prime Minister has already made clear, the Government back the heads of agreement and their recommendations and we shall get on with producing draft legislation. The draft clauses will be produced by Burns night, 25 January, meeting the next phase in our commitment to the people in Scotland. That work begins today. A team has been brought together with leading officials in the Scotland Office, HM Treasury, the Department for Work and Pensions and the Cabinet Office. That team will work closely with all lead policy Departments within the UK Government. The team will remain in place to deliver a Bill in the UK Parliament following the next general election.

To support the preparation of the draft legislation, I have invited key Scottish stakeholders representing a wide range of sectors to form a stakeholder group. I shall provide further details of the membership and terms of reference of the group in due course, but it is my intention that it will support the Government's work translating the heads of agreement into the draft legislation that we shall publish by 25 January. As Lord Smith said in his foreword:

"Through this process I have worked closely with people who can argue passionately with one another while sharing an equal concern and love for their country. I would like to thank them all for their input, challenge and support. I hope that, in the end, they can work together, maintain their energy and use it to create a Scotland which is even stronger and even better."

Having a more powerful Scottish Parliament inside a strong United Kingdom is the best outcome for the people of Scotland and the people of the United Kingdom. This is what we voted for on 18 September. Today's report is an affirmation of the vow that was made in September. It is a historic moment for Scotland.

The cause of home rule has been at the heart of Scottish politics since the days of Gladstone. This agreement provides a modern blueprint: Scottish home rule within our strong United Kingdom—home rule for Scotland that can open the door to constitutional reform for the rest of the United Kingdom. We can achieve home rule all round.

Source: House of Commons. "Oral Answers to Questions." November 27, 2014. www.publications .parliament.uk/pa/cm201415/cmhansrd/cm141127/debtext/141127-0001.htm#14112763000001. License: www.nationalarchives.gov.uk/doc/open-government-licence/version/3/.

Secret Service Remarks on White House Security Breaches

SEPTEMBER 20 AND 30, 2014

On September 19, 2014, Omar J. Gonzalez, a forty-two-year old ex-Marine from Texas, scaled the northern fence of the White House, which runs along the iconic Pennsylvania Avenue, dashed toward the mansion, and entered through the North Portico door. Inside the White House, Gonzalez, who carried a small knife, made his way to the East Room, which lay just one flight of stairs away from President Barack Obama's living quarters, before he was finally subdued. Although President Obama had just departed, the event marked one of the most serious breaches in Secret Service history; for the first time since the agency's founding in 1865, an intruder was able to enter the White House. The event also punctuated the Secret Service's spotty history under President Obama. Several embarrassing, high-profile incidents—including an event in the spring of 2012 in which dozens of agents on a presidential trip to Cartagena, Colombia, were ordered to return home after they allegedly hired prostitutes—hinted at deep institutional flaws and monumental gaps in leadership. In the months following the September incident, an internal Secret Service review found "performance, organizational and technical failings" at the agency. Numerous Congressional hearings described systemic problems, including a striking lack of candor about recent security breaches, and members of Congress from both sides of the aisle publicly signaled their lost confidence in the service. Finally, amid continued Congressional, media, and public scrutiny, Julia Pierson, the first woman to head the agency, resigned as Secret Service director, just a year and a half after her appointment.

FENCE JUMPER EVADES SECRET SERVICE, ENTERS WHITE HOUSE

On the afternoon of September 19, 2014, Gonzalez approached the White House northern fence, which runs along Pennsylvania Avenue, and without prompting, climbed over. After landing on the northern lawn, Gonzalez sprinted across the grounds, weaving between the circular fountain and a security guard booth before reaching the Northern Portico doors. He then entered through an unlocked and unattended door and maneuvered to the East Room. There, mere feet away from the Obamas' personal residence, he was finally subdued and arrested by a plainclothes officer.

While Gonzalez did not express any intent to harm the president, the arresting officers found a folding-knife with a two-and-a-half-inch serrated blade on his person. A subsequent search of his car revealed additional weapons, including a hatchet and nearly 800 rounds of ammunition. Gonzalez, a decorated former Marine who served three tours in Iraq, also suffered from a series of mental health issues, including obsessive-compulsive disorder, schizophrenia, and post-traumatic distress disorder (PTSD). After his arrest, Gonzalez recounted how "the atmosphere was collapsing" and that he "needed to get the information to the president of the United States so that he could get the word out to the people."

The incident was particularly concerning because not only did Gonzalez breach the security perimeter, but he also entered the building in a largely unsophisticated manner—jumping the fence and running for the door. Officers openly worried that Gonzalez's success may serve as an example for or embolden more serious threats, such as suicide bombers or terrorists. Most important, it potentially undermined what Secret Service training manuals describe as "one of the best tools for deterring future attempts"—the White House's aura of invulnerability.

Gonzalez had already come to the attention of the Secret Service twice that year. In the summer, he was interviewed by the agency after raising alarms during a routine traffic stop in rural Virginia. Over the course of the stop, the police allegedly found eleven weapons, including a sawed-off shotgun, two sniper rifles, an assault rifle, a bolt-action rifle, a shotgun, and five handguns. Among the weapons lay a map of Washington with a line pointed toward the White House. Later that summer, he was stopped while walking along the south fence of the White House with a hatchet in his waistband but was not arrested.

SERIES OF SECURITY BREACHES SIGNAL SYSTEMIC ISSUES

The September incident was the latest in a series of high-profile security lapses and public embarrassments for the Secret Service during the Obama administration. While the agency's failings culminated in Secret Service director Pierson's resignation, the issues began under her predecessor.

In November 2009, Tareq and Michaele Salahi crashed Obama's first state dinner after the Secret Service failed to check whether they were on the guest list. Two years later, the Secret Service ordered officers to stand down after mistaking four semiautomatic rifle gunshots fired at the White House for car backfire. It took the service four days to realize that the shots struck the front facade, and only then because a cleaning crew noticed broken glass. At the time, President Obama and the First Lady were not home, but their daughters, Sasha and Malia, were inside and on her way home, respectively.

In perhaps the most widely reported blunder, a dozen Secret Service agents, including two supervisors, preparing for a presidential trip to the sixth Summit of the Americas in Cartagena, Colombia, were fired in April 2012 after reports that several of them hired prostitutes. Following the incident, then-director Mark Sullivan resigned. President Obama appointed Sullivan's chief-of-staff, Pierson, as head of the Secret Service and charged her with cleaning up the agency's image.

The problems continued. A year after Director Pierson's appointment, an investigation into an incident in which a Secret Service supervisor left a bullet in a room in the Hay-Adams hotel overlooking the White House uncovered that the officer and a colleague sent sexually suggestive e-mails to a female subordinate officer. The supervisor was later fired, and the colleague reassigned.

In March 2014, three Secret Service agents, part of the counter assault team, the President's last line of defense, were placed on leave after violating Secret Service regulations following a night of drinking in Amsterdam. Finally, just three days before Gonzalez jumped the White House fence, the Secret Service failed to properly screen an armed security contractor who shared an elevator with President Obama in Atlanta. The man had a gun on him at the time and an assault record, neither of which the Secret Service knew until the man was fired later that day. The service did not disclose the security breach to President Obama.

Following the Atlanta and the fence-jumping incidents, Congressional leaders from both sides of the aisle called Pierson in to testify about the breach and answer for the troubling lapses in security.

CONGRESSIONAL HEARINGS PROBE HOW SIX RINGS OF SECURITY FAILED

On September 30, 2014, Director Pierson testified before the House Committee on Oversight and Government Reform. In her statement to the committee, the director took full responsibility for the fence-jumping incident, describing it as "unacceptable," and outlined how the security plan "was not executed properly." Pierson touched on the agency's many security lapses under President Obama but described how she would "redouble" her efforts "to bring the Secret Service to a level of performance that lives up to the vital mission we perform, the important individuals we protect, and the American people we serve."

Despite Pierson's pledge to address the internal issues and to issue a comprehensive internal review of the incidents, it appeared to little satisfy committee members. Rep. Darrell Issa, R-Calif., the ranking member of the committee, in particular rebuked Pierson's efforts, scoffing at seemingly simple security measures that were mishandled. "Why was there no guard stationed at the front door of the White House," Chair Issa asked, adding, "and yes, how much would it cost to lock the front door of the White House?"

In particular, the committee questioned how Gonzalez was able to breach what Pierson called the "six rings of security." First, a team of plainclothes Secret Service agents in crowds on the public sidewalk did not spot Gonzalez as he climbed over. Next, agents failed to hit the alarm found in several of the "crash boxes" on the White House grounds, which automatically locks the door to the residence. In the third tier, an agent stationed in a guard booth near the fountain should stop the intruder and raise an alarm. That alarm, a review later discovered, had been muted at the White House staff's request. If that officer is unable to catch him, the officer should release an attack dog, a Belgian Malinois trained to tackle an intruder. However, as Pierson noted, the officer may not have released the dog because there were other Secret Service officers pursuing Gonzalez by foot; the officer may have worried that the dog would attack the trailing agents rather than the intruder. Nonetheless, if the officer does not pursue the intruder or release the attack dog, the guard should send a heavily armed SWAT team to the front door. That measure was created in the 1990s specifically to address jumpers after a study by the Army's Delta Force warned that the White House was vulnerable to fence jumpers. However, neither of those measures was tripped. Finally, in the sixth ring of security, a guard at the front desk should have apprehended the intruder.

Several other committee members declared that they had lost confidence in the Secret Service's ability to protect the first family and questioned whether Pierson was fit to confront the systemic issues and "striking lack of candor" about the recent security breaches. The lawmakers were ultimately proven correct. One week after testifying before Congress, Pierson resigned after just a year and a half in the position.

INTERNAL REVIEW FINDS "PERFORMANCE, ORGANIZATIONAL, AND TECHNICAL FAILINGS"

Two months after the initial event, the Secret Service released its internal report. The report offered not only an overview of the facts surrounding the incident, but also outlined the "performance, organizational, and technical failings" at the heart of the organization.

In all, nearly a dozen failures allowed Gonzalez to get inside the White House. The portion of the fence Gonzalez scaled was missing an ornate yet practical spike, which would have impeded his progress. Some of the alarms were muted, and many responding officers were delayed because of poor lines of sight with the front fence because of construction on the northern grounds. Other officers stood down because they thought the door was locked or that the shrubbery was impassable, assumptions that proved false.

In particular, poor communication plagued the agency. Many radios were muted or failed to function properly, including one of a crisis command center officer. Another officer did not realize that there was a fence jumper because of "unintelligible traffic over the radio." In another example, an attack dog handler was not at his post, instead talking on his personal cellphone in a nearby van that lacked monitors or speakers.

The report also found a number of inconsistencies with how the event was originally described to the media. For example, officials had previously said that Gonzalez only made it just inside the North Portico doors before he was tackled when in fact he was arrested in the East Room, much deeper into the residence than originally reported.

Finally, many agents feared that the breach was directly related to a severe staffing shortage. In particular, the agency struggled to staff the Uniform Division, which has primary responsibility for securing the White House grounds, and reportedly flew in agents from field offices around the country for temporary assignments.

—Robert Howard

Following is the text of a press release issued on September 20, 2014, by the U.S. Secret Service regarding the White House fence-jumping incident; and the text of a statement delivered on September 30, 2014, by Julia Pierson, director of the U.S. Secret Service, before the United States House of Representatives Committee on Oversight and Government Reform.

DOCUMENT

Secret Service Remarks on Fence Jumper

September 20, 2014

Yesterday at approximately 7:20PM, Omar J. Gonzalez, W/M/42, of Copperas Cove, TX, climbed over the fence on the north side of the White House complex and ran toward the front of the mansion. Gonzalez failed to comply with responding Secret Service Uniformed Division Officers' verbal commands, and was physically apprehended after entering the White House North Portico doors. The first family was not in the residence at the time of the incident and was en route to Camp David, MD.

Every day the Secret Service is challenged to ensure security at the White House complex while still allowing public accessibility to a national historical site. The challenge of securing the White House complex from security threats is ever present. Although last night the officers showed tremendous restraint and discipline in dealing with this subject, the location of Gonzalez's arrest is not acceptable.

In addition to the criminal investigation of Gonzalez by the Secret Service's Washington Field Office, Director Julia Pierson immediately ordered the Secret Service's Office of Professional

Responsibility to conduct a comprehensive after action review of the incident. The review findings will be submitted to Department of Homeland Secretary, Jeh Johnson. This review began last night with a physical assessment of the site and personnel interviews. In addition, the Secret Service will review all operational policies and security procedures during this process.

In the interim, Director Pierson has ordered the immediate enhancement of officer patrols and surveillance capabilities along the Pennsylvania Avenue fence line around the White House complex. These measures went into effect last night.

The men and women of the Secret Service are committed to providing the highest level of security for those we are charged to protect, and will do whatever is necessary to successfully accomplish our mission.

SOURCE: U.S. Secret Service. "U.S. Secret Service Statement Regarding Fence Jumper." September 20, 2014. www.secretservice.gov/press/Secret-Service-Statement-Regarding-Fence%20Jumpe.pdf.

Secret Service Director on Security Breach

September 30, 2014

INTRODUCTION

Good morning, Chairman Issa, Ranking Member Cummings and distinguished members of the Committee. I am here today to address the concern that we all share, following the incident on September 19th at the White House. It is clear that our security plan was not executed properly.

I take full responsibility; what happened is unacceptable and it will never happen again. As Director, my primary concern is the operational readiness of my workforce and, over the past 18 months, I have worked hard to proactively address all aspects of Presidential protection and the security of the White House Complex. I have also been aggressive in addressing human capital challenges, professionalism, and leadership development with the goal of ensuring operational readiness.

As I have informed you and your staff, given that much of what we do to protect the President and the White House involves information that is highly sensitive or classified, I will be limited in what I can say in a public hearing. However, I will share as much information as I responsibly can during the open portion of today's hearing. I am willing to give more complete responses in a closed session after this session is complete.

SEPTEMBER 19TH INCIDENT

On September 19th, a man scaled the north fence of the White House, crossed the lawn while ignoring verbal commands from armed Uniformed Division officers, entered through the front door, and was arrested on the state floor. Immediately that night, I ordered security enhancements around the Complex. Additionally, Secretary of Homeland Security Jeh Johnson has directed, in clear and very strong terms, that he receive a thorough, beginning-to-end accounting of what transpired on Friday, September 19th. Specifically, he has directed that a full investigation be conducted of the event and that he receive a report of investigation. As a result, I initiated a comprehensive review of the incident and protective measures to ensure this will not happen again.

The review began with a physical assessment of the site and personnel interviews. All decisions made that evening are being evaluated, including decisions on tactics and use of force, in light of the totality of the circumstances confronting those officers.

I am committed to the following:

1. A complete and thorough investigation of the facts of this incident, to include necessary personnel actions;

2. A complete and thorough review of all policies, procedures and protocols in place that govern the security of the White House Complex and our response to this incident; and

3. A coordinated, informed effort to make any and all adjustments necessary to properly ensure the safety and security of the President and First Family and those who work and visit the White House.

White House emergency action plans are multi-faceted and tailored to each threat. The Secret Service has apprehended 16 individuals who have jumped the fence over the last five years, including six this year alone. In fact, on September 11, 2014, a week prior to the events that are the subject of today's hearing, officers apprehended an individual seconds after he scaled the fence and ran onto the grounds.

In addition to fence-jumpers, over the last five years, hundreds of individuals have approached the White House fence verbalizing threats toward our protectees, or acting in a suspicious manner. Our officers and agents routinely leverage their training and experience to make decisions to arrest or transfer these individuals to appropriate facilities for mental health evaluations.

PROTECTING THE PEOPLE'S HOUSE

Protecting the White House Complex is a challenge in any threat environment. In addition to being a national icon, the complex consists of public spaces, executive offices where our nation's highest leaders congregate, and the private residence of the President and First Family. Ensuring the safety and well-being of all who work and live at the White House, while preserving accessibility to millions of visitors per year, requires a unique balance.

Since becoming Director, and in the years before that, the security of the President and White House has been my top priority. With the help of Congress, the Secret Service has been undertaking significant enhancements of protective countermeasures and security features at the White House. We are constantly adjusting the security measures for the President and First Family and the White House. There is no such thing as "business as usual" in our line of work; we have to be successful 100 percent of the time, and we are constantly making changes and doing everything possible to ensure that we are.

In the past five years, the Secret Service has upgraded perimeter cameras, officer booths, vehicle access gates, and command and control systems, along with enhancements to highly classified programs that have made the President and Complex more secure. We thank Congress for their support in a time of constrained resources. We have generated many of these enhancements in direct response to intelligence information on known and emerging terrorist tactics.

Beyond technology, approximately 75% of our annual budget is dedicated to payroll costs, which supports our most valuable asset—our people. The agency relies heavily on the training, experience, and judgment of our men and women to make critical, split-second decisions.

CONCLUSION

With respect to the many questions that have been raised and opinions proffered in the wake of the September 19th incident, I do not want to get ahead of the investigation that is underway.

Let me also say that I recognize that these events did not occur in a vacuum. The Secret Service has had its share of challenges in recent years—some during my tenure and some before—of which this is the most recent. I intend over the coming months to redouble my efforts, not only in response to this incident, but in general to bring the Secret Service to a level of performance that lives up to the vital mission we perform, the important individuals we protect, and the American people we serve.

As Director, I am proud of all Secret Service employees who serve each day with honor and distinction, and put their lives on the line throughout the world. It is my responsibility to ensure that these men and women have the resources and training they need for mission success. From my first days as Director, I have worked with DHS Headquarters and Secretary Johnson, the Administration, and Congress, including members of this Committee, to develop a comprehensive, forward leaning strategy to further enhance the Secret Service's capabilities. We remain dedicated and committed to protecting the President and First Family and the sanctity of the White House Complex within the bounds of the Constitution and laws of the United States.

I'd like to thank the Committee for the opportunity to appear before you today. I look forward to your questions.

SOURCE: House Committee on Oversight and Government Reform. "Statement of Julia A. Pierson, Director, United States Secret Service, Department of Homeland Security." September 30, 2014. http://oversight.house.gov/wp-content/uploads/2014/09/Pierson-Statement-USSS-9-30.pdf.

OTHER HISTORIC DOCUMENTS OF INTEREST

FROM PREVIOUS *HISTORIC DOCUMENTS*

Yemen's President and Rebel Groups Sign Peace Agreement

SEPTEMBER 21, 2014

Following the slashing of fuel subsidies by Yemen's central government in August 2014, the Houthis, a rebel movement that operates mainly in the northern part of the country, called for protests against the government. These eventually devolved into the Houthis taking control of the central city of Sana'a, which forced the hand of the central government into signing a peace agreement. Such an agreement did not last, and the central government resigned en masse in January 2015. Calming instability in Yemen is a key priority for Middle Eastern and Western diplomats because the nation is home to one of the most notorious al Qaeda offshoots, al Qaeda in the Arabian Peninsula.

Energy Subsidies

In January 2011, Yemen became swept up in the Arab Spring movement when opponents of then President Ali Abdullah Saleh took to the streets to protest the president's power grab. As the protests raged on, Saleh wavered between promising to accept international power transfer deals and using force to dispel the protesters. It was not until February 25, 2012, that Saleh formally ceded power to his vice president, Abdu Rabbu Mansour Hadi, following a presidential election in which Hadi was the sole candidate and received 65 percent of the vote. Even with Saleh out of power, political battles raged across the country, driven by falling oil revenues that account for a majority of the nation's economy.

Declining oil revenues placed the government in a difficult position, because it was no longer able to keep up with desperately needed energy subsidies for its population, half of whom live on less than $2 per day. Yemen has some of the highest energy subsidies in the Middle East, which is one of the few reliable social benefits offered by the government. These subsidies have allowed the nation's highest income earners to purchase oil at low prices and then smuggle the oil into neighboring countries to make large profits.

Instead of reducing the subsidy when its economy first began to falter, Yemen's government instead reached out to the International Monetary Fund (IMF) for a loan. To qualify for financial assistance, the IMF required that the government not only eliminate fuel subsidies, but also subsequently gradually adjust the price of fuel. To further reduce the impact on citizens, the IMF suggested that the government bolster its safety net programs to support those who would be most affected. Under pressure, on July 30, 2014, the government announced that it would reform fuel subsidies and increase prices. In reaction, the Houthis, a rebel group that follows Shia Zaidi Islam, called for protests against the central government's decision. Hadi agreed to make slight concessions, but those were rejected by the Houthis as not going far enough.

The Houthis have been in a constant state of conflict with Yemen's central government for decades. They want more control over the territory in the northern part of Yemen in which most of their supporters live, and some have claimed that the Houthis will continue to challenge the government until they are given a semi-independent state. Houthi leadership has denied such claims. In 2011, the Houthis protested Saleh's government and expanded their own control in the northern part of the country. They agreed to participate in a national dialogue with Yemeni leaders, but when President Hadi announced in February 2014 that the nation would become a federation of six regions, one of which was not Houthi-dominated, the group took up arms.

The growing instability in the country, which has been largely linked to unequal access to resources and high unemployment, resulted in many uprisings against the government, led by both the Houthis and pro-democracy activists.

SEPTEMBER 21ST CAPTURE AND PEACE DEAL

The intent of the Houthi rebels was to oust the central government, and they intended to take advantage of public discontent over the end of fuel subsidies to do so. On September 18, the group moved into the capital city of Sana'a. They evacuated armed forces headquarters and took control of the state-run television offices. By September 21, the Houthis had taken control of most of the central city of Sana'a. The armed forces put up little resistance, reportedly because they had been directed by the central government to offer "support for the people's revolution" in an attempt to get the Houthis to sign a UN-brokered peace agreement.

The prime minister, Mohammed Basindawa, resigned in response to the Houthi invasion and condemned Hadi, who he believed supported the rebels along with the military. "I do not want to be an obstacle in front of any ceasefire deal that takes place between President Abdurabu Hadi and Ansarullah," he said in a resignation letter.

The same day it took control of Sana'a, the Houthis, Yemen's president, and representatives from Yemen's major political parties signed the UN-brokered peace agreement, the Peace and National Partnership Agreement, which called for an immediate ceasefire. The agreement also dictated "the formation of a technocratic national government, which will work to enhance government transparency, implement economic reforms, in addition to continuing military and security reforms," according to a statement released by the signatories. The Houthis promised to respect Hadi's position as president under the agreement and work with him to form a new government. It would be Hadi's responsibility to appoint a prime minister within three days and then form his caretaker government within a month after the signing of the agreement. An agenda would be set within thirty days of the signing, and it would include a decrease of gas and diesel prices. Once seated, the new government would have one week to establish a committee to begin studying the economic situation in Yemen, including whether fuel subsidies would be reinstated.

In forming his government, Hadi first chose his chief of staff, Ahmed Awad Bin Mubarak, to take over as prime minister, but Mubarak was pressured by the Houthis to reject the seat. On October 13, Khaled Bahah took the prime minister's post. The new government officially took over on November 9, but the Houthis and General People's Congress did not participate, arguing that they had not been consulted on the makeup of the cabinet. The Houthis also refused to sign the annex of the peace agreement, which stipulated that conflicts should be resolved through dialogue and that all hostility in the capital of Sana'a would end immediately to allow the government to continue the work outlined in the agreement. Some viewed this refusal as an indication that the Houthis would not soon leave Sana'a and accept the terms of the agreement. Publicly, the Houthis argued that they chose not to sign the annex because it was not included in the original agreement prior to the signing. "President Hadi did not insist on signing the annex, therefore we did not, but the agreement was a success whether the annex was signed or not," said Ali Al-Imad, a member of the Houthi political office.

Questions were raised by the Houthis regarding the United States' role in the ongoing instability and peace agreement. When Saleh left power under the peace agreement in 2012, he was replaced by Hadi, an ally of the United States. Because the rebel uprising in Yemen threatened the Hadi government, the United States faced accusations that it was meddling in Yemen's affairs, something the Obama administration vehemently denied. According to Prime Minister Saleh's supporters, Gerald Michael Feierstein, the U.S. ambassador to Yemen, tried to force Saleh to leave the country. The State Department called such accusations "completely false."

The United States did, however, call on the United Nations Security Council to impose sanctions on Saleh and two senior leaders in the Houthi group for obstructing the political process during the recent uprisings. According to a UN diplomat, there was "broad support" for such action. Saleh said he would not accept any sanctions, nor did he have any intention of stepping down and leaving the country. Instead, his party rallied around him and called for demonstrations against the United States. The UN sanctions passed on November 7 and included travel and asset bans. In response, Saleh's General People's Congress accused Hadi of working behind the scenes to win approval for such sanctions; Hadi was subsequently stripped of his party leadership role.

RENEWED FIGHTING

Despite the peace agreement, the Houthis continued their attempt to subvert the power of the government. This included blocking top officials, including the army chief, state oil company officials, and the port director from entering their offices. Salah told the Houthis that if the attempts to overthrow his government continued, he would resign.

On January 20, 2015, Houthi fighters raided and took control of the presidential palace and placed Hadi under house arrest. Two days later, on January 22, President Hadi and his cabinet resigned, and less than a month later, the Houthis dissolved parliament and set up a Revolutionary Committee to act as the interim government. According to Houthi leaders, this government would rule for up to two years. Such a move threatens to further destabilize Yemen, because Sunni leaders in the southern part of the country refuse to recognize the Houthi Shia leadership.

On February 11, 2015, in response to the ongoing instability, the United States temporarily closed its embassy in Yemen and evacuated staff. "The United States remains firmly committed to supporting all Yemenis who continue to work toward a peaceful, prosperous and unified Yemen," said State Department spokesperson Jen Psaki. "We will explore options for a return to Sana'a when the situation on the ground improves." The embassy was reopened for routine consular services in June.

—Heather Kerrigan

Following is the text of the peace agreement signed by the Yemeni government and Houthi rebel group on September 21, 2014.

Yemen's Government Signs
Peace Agreement With Rebels

September 21, 2014

Preamble: Pursuant to the outcomes of the Comprehensive National Dialogue Conference, which have been agreed upon by all Yemeni constituencies and which laid the foundations for building a new, federal democratic Yemeni state based on the rule of law, equal citizenship, human rights and good governance; resolved to the unity, sovereignty, independence and territorial integrity of Yemen; committed to responding to the peoples' demand for peaceful change, economic, financial and administrative reforms, and to achieving economic welfare; dedicated to furthering the higher national interest through a spirit of partnership and consensus in diagnosis, solutions, and implementation; and committed to stabilizing the country and realizing a bright promising democratic future, the Parties, in the interest of national unity and building and promoting peace, commit to the following:

Article 1: The President of the Republic shall engage in inclusive and transparent consultations with all of the constituencies represented in the National Dialogue Conference, immediately following the signing of this Agreement. The purpose of these consultations shall be to establish a competency-based government in a period not to exceed one (1) month. The current government shall remain responsible for the normal affairs until the formation of the new government. In establishing the new government, the principles of competence, integrity and national partnership shall be upheld, and broad participation of political constituencies shall be ensured.

Through this consultation process, constituencies shall be meaningfully engaged, and they shall be represented in the executive bodies at the central and governorate levels to ensure efficiency and national partnership.

Article 2: Within three (3) days following the entry into force of this Agreement, the President of the Republic shall appoint political advisers from Ansarallah and the Southern Peaceful Movement. The President of the Republic shall define the authorities and functions of his political advisers.

A new Prime Minister, who shall be a neutral and impartial national figure of competence and high integrity and who shall enjoy broad political support, shall be appointed. The President of the Republic shall issue a presidential decree charging the new Prime Minister to form a new government.

The political advisers to the President of the Republic shall develop criteria for candidates for posts in the new government. These criteria shall include: integrity, competency, requisite expertise in a field relevant to the ministerial portfolio, commitment to the protection of human rights and the rule of law, and impartiality in the conduct of state affairs.

The political advisers to the President of the Republic shall make recommendations to the President of the Republic and Prime Minister regarding the allocation of Cabinet seats to the political constituencies, ensuring representation of women and youth.

Within three (3) days following the announcement of the new Prime Minister, all constituencies shall nominate their candidates for the Cabinet to the President of the Republic and the Prime Minister. If any constituency fails to submit their nominees within an additional three (3) days after the initial three-day period, the President of the Republic and the new Prime Minister shall have the right to name candidates, as they see appropriate for the portfolios, provided that they meet the criteria listed above and that they reinforce the principle of national partnership.

The President of the Republic and the Prime Minister shall consult with a representative of each constituency of his political advisers in order to decide on any objections raised by the constituencies regarding whether candidates of other constituencies meet the criteria listed above within a period not to exceed three (3) days.

The President of the Republic shall, after consultations, select the Ministers of Defence, Finance, Foreign Affairs and Interior, provided that they meet the criteria listed above, and does not belong or is not loyal to any political party.

The Prime Minister shall, in consultation with the President of the Republic, select the Ministers for the remaining portfolios, provided they meet the criteria listed above.

The government shall, within thirty (30) days following the appointment of the Cabinet, develop a programme that is consensual and based primarily on implementation of the Outcomes of the National Dialogue Conference. The programme shall be submitted to the Parliament for a vote of confidence.

Within fifteen (15) days following the signing of this Agreement, the President shall issue a decree expanding the Shura Council according to the recommendations of the National Dialogue Conference, and in a manner that ensures national partnership.

Article 3: Alleviating the burden of the people is a mutual responsibility and requires the collaborative efforts of all constituencies. To this end, the new government shall establish an economic committee of qualified experts and economists drawn from various political constituencies and relevant government ministries with expertise in the field of financial and economic regulation and management. The recommendations of the committee shall be binding on the government. The committee shall be formed within one (1) week after the formation of the government. The committee shall study the economic and fiscal situation in Yemen by reviewing the state budget and spending, and shall make recommendations on how the savings will be used to benefit people living in poverty and previously marginalised areas.

The committee shall prepare an overall economic reform programme that is timebound, specific and clear, and that is primarily aimed at eradicating corruption in all sectors, addressing the imbalance in the public budget and rationalising expenditures. The committee shall identify and report on the deficiencies caused by pervasive corruption and lack of adequate oversight, and shall propose solutions regarding the required comprehensive reforms for the oil and electricity sectors, together with the new government, in a manner that will achieve the demands and aspirations of the people.

A new decision shall be issued immediately providing for a new price of 20 liters of petrol and diesel at 3000 YR. The abovementioned economic committee shall reconsider this within three (3) months, based on the liberalization of the import and distribution of oil and the reform of the electricity sector, which will lead to real price reform based on a scientific and economic assessment, and meet the aspirations of the people.

The committee shall develop a detailed and comprehensive plan, which will include a package of measures to address the financial and economic crisis now facing Yemen in a way that protects and promotes the rights and livelihoods of all Yemenis, particularly the vulnerable and those living in poverty. The plan shall aim to create an enabling environment whereby all Yemenis are able to maximize their full economic potential and provide a decent standard of living for their families.

In developing this plan, the committee shall examine all economic and financial issues, to primarily include the following issues:

(a) opening up competition and export/import for the private sector;

(b) the price of basic commodities;

(c) ensuring tax and customs revenue collection, and tax and customs reform;

(d) collecting revenue owed to all statement institutions, including for taxes, customs or utilities, amongst others, from everyone, focusing on the key land holders;

(e) eliminating ghost workers and double dippers in all state civil, military and security institutions, and any new recruitments in state civil institutions shall be done through the Ministry of Civil Service without prejudice to exceptional remedies agreed to in the National Dialogue Conference outcomes;

(f) applying the biometric (fingerprint) system in all state, civil, military and security institutions;

(g) alleviating the burden on the citizens from fuel subsidy reform;

(h) infrastructure investment;

(i) financial and administrative corruption; and

(j) social protection programmes.

The committee shall also make recommendations to the Ministry of Civil Service on reform of salary scales with a view to alleviating the burden on low-income Yemenis.

The committee shall include in its plan a proposal to activate the monitoring and audit bodies, notably the Central Organization of Control and Audit and the Anti-Corruption Authority, and to make their annual reports accessible to the public.

The committee shall present its binding plan and implementation matrix to the new government within three (3) months. The President and the new government shall work closely with all constituencies to implement the recommendations of the committee.

Article 4: The new government shall undertake the following:

(a) increase the Social Welfare Fund payments by 50 per cent and deliver the payments to the beneficiaries immediately, while reviewing beneficiary eligibility criteria to ensure that those who are ineligible are eliminated and those who are eligible are enrolled;

(b) increase civil service, military and security sector salaries, and expedite the process for eliminating ghost workers and double dippers by making all payments through bank or post office transfers; and

(c) increase the budget for the next fiscal year for education and health, which shall be targeted toward people living in poverty and in marginalised areas.

Article 5: The new government shall commit to the full implementation of the outcomes of the National Dialogue Conference relevant to countering corruption and shall provide the necessary resources in this regard.

Article 6: The President of the Republic shall exercise his constitutional authorities to ensure fair representation of all constituencies in executive bodies at the central and governorate levels, as well as in oversight bodies, to ensure national partnership, competence, integrity and efficiency. Fair participation in judicial bodies shall be ensured according to the outcomes of the National Dialogue Conference.

A government operating under the principle of national partnership shall respect the high interests of Yemen in both domestic and foreign policies, and reflect the will of all of the people.

Article 7: All constituencies shall participate in the preparations for the new biometric voter registry and the referendum on the constitution based on the new voter registry, and shall participate in the preparations and monitoring of elections according to the outcomes of the National Dialogue Conference.

Article 8: The President of the Republic shall work closely with all constituencies in order to develop a consensus on a new constitution, through the mechanisms of the Constitution Drafting Commission and the National Body.

Article 9: The membership of the National Body shall be revisited, within a period not to exceed fifteen (15) days to ensure fair representation of constituencies. The National Body shall prepare its rules of procedure through the committee established to undertake this task in accordance with the outcomes of the National Dialogue Conference.

Article 10: The National Body, through its oversight of the Constitution Drafting Commission, shall, among other things, address the structure of the state in a manner that adheres to the outcomes of the National Dialogue Conference.

Article 11: The government shall designate a committee with Ansarallah to develop an expedited implementation matrix to execute the outcomes of the Sa'ada Working Group of the National Dialogue Conference. The Government shall designate a similar committee, in agreement with all constituencies, including the Peaceful Southern Movement, to develop an expedited implementation matrix to execute the outcomes of the Southern Issues Working Group of the National Dialogue Conference.

Article 12: The outcomes of the Working Group on Building the Foundations for the Security and Military Institutions of the National Dialogue Conference shall be strictly implemented according to an agreed-upon timeline, with monitoring and follow-up by the National Body.

Article 13: The military and security situation in and the issues related to Amran, Al Jawf, Mareb, Sana'a and any other governorate shall be dealt with in the Annex.

Article 14: The political, public and media escalation shall end, and manifestations of the threat or use of force shall cease. This includes obliging State media and urging the private and partisan media to stop their inflammatory campaigns of a sectarian and regional nature.

Article 15: Following the signing of this Agreement, the announcement of the new fuel price and the announcement of the new Prime Minister, the camps in the vicinity of high security facilities, including Hezyaz, Al Sabaha and the airport, shall be dismantled and removed.

With the start of the formation of the new government, the camps established around the capital, Sana'a, as well as camps within the city limits, shall be dismantled and removed. Unofficial checkpoints in and around Sana'a shall also be dismantled.

Article 16: The Parties commit to resolve any disputes regarding this Agreement through direct dialogue, within the framework of the outcomes of the Comprehensive National Dialogue Conference, and to continue negotiations through a joint committee established with the support of the United Nations. This joint committee shall be the appropriate forum to raise any concerns related to the interpretation and implementation of this Agreement.

Article 17: The Parties request the Special Adviser to the Secretary-General on Yemen to continue United Nations support for the implementation of the measures agreed upon in this Agreement. In this regard, the Parties request the Special Adviser to continue to monitor any violations.

SIGNATURES

ANNEX

The Military and Security Situation in and the issues related to Amran, Al Jawf, Mareb, Sana'a and any other governorate.

Article 1: The Parties pledge to defuse all elements of political and security tensions, to resolve any conflict through dialogue, as well as to enable the State to fulfil its functions. All hostilities being conducted by all sides inside the capital, Sana'a, and its surroundings shall cease.

Article 2: The Parties reaffirm the need for the re-establishment of state authority and the restoration of control over all the territory in line with the outcomes of the National Dialogue Conference.

Article 3: With the technical support of the United Nations, an agreement shall be reached on a mechanism for the implementation of the recommendations of the National Dialogue Conference relating to the "disarmament and recovery of State-owned heavy and medium weapons from all parties, groups and individuals that were plundered or seized nationwide, within a specific time frame and simultaneously." The mechanism shall provide for the representation of all constituencies. No parties, groups or individuals shall be exempted from the work of the mechanism. The mechanism shall include a detailed plan and timeline for implementation, and in line with the outcomes of the National Dialogue Conference.

Article 4: Regarding Amran, the new Prime Minister shall establish a joint committee, within five (5) days, mandated to normalise the situation, and to complete the organisation of the administrative, security and military authorities in a manner that achieves the establishment of state authority and that achieves security, stability and sustainable development.

The local officials in Amran shall fully carry out their responsibilities. The state military and security forces shall carry out their functions in ensuring security and stability in the governorate.

The joint committee shall be primarily responsible for the supervision and the implementation of this Agreement, including the withdrawal of all armed groups coming from outside Amran.

The Parties undertake to provide the joint committee, immediately on request, with all relevant information necessary for carrying out its duties.

The joint committee shall provide all necessary support and assistance to the local officials so that they may fully carry out their responsibilities, and shall ensure the principle of national partnership. The joint committee shall serve as a venue to discuss and resolve any barriers to the carrying out of those responsibilities.

Article 5: There shall be an immediate cessation of hostilities and a ceasefire in Al Jawf and Mareb. All armed groups coming from outside Al Jawf and Mareb shall withdraw, while simultaneously the administrative, security and military authorities are restructured.

A robust implementation and joint monitoring and verification committee shall be established by the Parties, with impartial participation. The details of the ceasefire and the joint mechanism, with a strict timeline, shall be established in a supplemental document. The new government shall be responsible for the organisation of the administrative, security and military authorities in Al Jawf and Mareb, in a manner that achieves the security, stability and national partnership. The state military and security forces shall carry out their functions in ensuring security and stability in the two governorates.

Article 6: The supplemental document shall include the following issues:

- Principles governing the ceasefire;
- Set of definitions in order to avoid confusion during the implementation of the ceasefire;
- Identification of phases of implementation;
- Creation of a joint monitoring and verification committee, joint monitoring and verification field teams, and joint technical monitoring and review teams;
- Clear listing of acts that constitute ceasefire violations;
- Clear timeline for implementation.

Article 7: The Parties commit to facilitate safe and unhindered access for humanitarian actors to reach people in need of humanitarian assistance. The Parties also commit to ensure the safety of civilians, including those receiving assistance, as well as the need to ensure the security of humanitarian personnel and United Nations and its associated personnel.

Article 8: The State shall undertake to protect the citizens in Al Beidha from Al Qaeda in the Arabian Peninsula (AQAP), and shall stand by them in facing the dangers posed by AQAP and terrorism.

Article 9: Normalisation in areas where camps were established after their removal. The establishment of military positions shall be prevented on the land vacated by the camps.

Article 10: The State shall commit to abolish any punitive administrative, financial or other measures on military personnel and civilians in the context of their participation in peaceful demonstrations, and their support, by peaceful means, of legitimate, popular demands.

SOURCE: European Union. European Parliament. "The Peace and National Partnership Agreement." September 21, 2014. © European Union, 2014. www.europarl.europa.eu/meetdocs/2014_2019/docu ments/darp/dv/darp20141204_05_/darp20141204_05_en.pdf.

OTHER HISTORIC DOCUMENTS OF INTEREST

FROM PREVIOUS *HISTORIC DOCUMENTS*

October

Unemployment Rate Falls; Federal Reserve Ends Controversial Bond Buying Program

OCTOBER 3 AND 29, 2014

In October 2014, the U.S. Bureau of Economic Analysis (BEA) released its September unemployment report and found that the United States had reached its lowest unemployment rate in six years, at 5.9 percent. That number would fall even further, to 5.6 percent, by the year's end. Despite halted growth around the world, the U.S. economy continued to expand, reaching an annualized growth rate of 2.4 percent. The economic expansion led the Federal Reserve to end its controversial bond buying program that had helped keep long-term interest rates low. Despite all the positive gains, wages barely rose, which unequally impacted the various economic classes.

September BEA Report Release

On October 3, the BEA reported that the U.S. economy added 248,000 jobs in September, bringing the unemployment rate to 5.9 percent and far surpassing analysts' expectations of 215,000 added jobs (the BEA later revised this number upwards in December 2014 to 271,000). The last time the unemployment rate was below 5.9 percent was in July 2008, prior to the recession. Job gains were seen in factories, which added 4,000 jobs; the retail sector, which added 35,000 jobs; and construction and healthcare, which added 16,000 and 23,000 jobs, respectively. The largest growth was seen in the professional and business services sector, which added 81,000 jobs in September.

Other factors in the report were mixed. Workforce participation declined from 62.8 percent to 62.7 percent from August to September, the lowest percentage since 1978. This factor was driven by a greater number of retiring workers, as well as individuals frustrated by the job market who gave up the search for a job. The number of those unemployed for longer than twenty-seven weeks had barely changed, and the number of part-time workers who desire, but cannot find, full-time employment dropped to 7.1 percent. When taken together, the underemployment rate fell from 12 percent in August to 11.8 percent in September. However, said Janet Yellen, chair of the Federal Reserve, "There are still too many people who want jobs but cannot find them, too many who are working part-time but would prefer full-time work." According to Yellen, this directly impacts slow wage growth.

Middle Class Squeeze

With only one month before the midterm elections, the report became a key talking point for Democrats and Republicans alike, who attempted to appeal specifically to the middle class. "The data underscore that six years after the Great Recession—thanks to the hard work of the American people and in part to the policies the President has pursued—our economy has bounced back more strongly than most others around the world," said Jason Furman, the chair of the White House Council of Economic Advisers. President Barack Obama echoed those remarks: "The United States has put more people back to work than Europe, Japan and every other advanced economy combined." The president said that such growth is indicative of the fact that the economy has become stronger since he took office, thanks in part to his policies.

One point in the report—stagnant average wages that were $24.53 per hour in September—was used by Republicans as an attack on Democratic strategies and by the president to call on Congress to pass a minimum wage increase. "Every day I hear from people in my district who say no matter how hard they work, they still struggle to make ends meet," House Speaker John Boehner, R-Ohio, said of the residents in his district. "Instead of trying to convince Americans that things are great, Washington Democrats ought to show they're serious about helping middle-class families get ahead, not just get by." In December, President Obama, when calling on Congress to help raise the minimum wage, countered, "Even though corporate profits and the stock market have hit all-time highs, the typical family isn't bringing home more than they did 15 years ago." He added, "A vibrant jobs market gives us the opportunity to keep up this progress, and begin to undo that decades-long middle-class squeeze."

Research groups painted a fuller picture than that offered by politicians and the BEA of the true disparity between the nation's various economic classes. In mid-December, the Pew Research Center reported that the income gap between the middle-class (46 percent of the country) and high-income earners (21 percent of the country) had grown to a record high. According to the report, in 2013, the median wealth of middle-income families was $96,500, while the nation's high-income families made seven times that amount at $639,400. These high-income families also had a net worth seventy times that of low-income families.

FEDERAL RESERVE ENDS BOND BUYING PROGRAM

The September jobs report release came just ahead of a meeting of the Federal Reserve Board of Governors during which it ended the quantitative easing program, which was first adopted in 2008 to encourage borrowing and spending by buying bonds and driving long-term rates lower. According to Allan Meltzer, a Federal Reserve scholar and professor at Carnegie Mellon University, the program "prevented a failure of a financial system, a run on banks, collapse of the payment system." The program was controversial throughout its run and added $3.5 trillion to the Federal Reserve balance sheet. Although the program was kept open ended, and the Federal Reserve said it would not stop the program until the economy had "improved substantially," in December 2013, the Federal Reserve announced that it would begin tapering off the program, which heightened anxiety over how global markets might respond and how high U.S. interest rates would increase as a result. To the latter, Federal Reserve chair Yellen said that interest rates would remain near zero for a "considerable time."

In its official release on the matter, the Federal Reserve stated "that there has been a substantial improvement in the outlook for the labor market since the inception of its current asset purchase program" and that it "continues to see sufficient underlying strength in the broader economy to support ongoing progress toward maximum employment in a context of price stability. Accordingly, the Committee decided to conclude its asset purchase program this month." Although economists had anticipated the end of the program, the markets reacted to the news more strongly than expected.

CONTINUING ECONOMIC GROWTH

In October, the U.S. economy added 214,000 jobs (later revised upwards to 261,000 in January 2015), pushing the unemployment rate even lower to 5.8 percent. Wage growth continued to be a persistent problem, as a majority of the jobs added were for low-wage, low-skill positions. "Although the headline number is decent, the details behind the curtain will be particularly concerning to investors and Main Street," said Todd Schoenberger, a managing partner at hedge-fund firm LandColt Capital. He added, "Wage growth is embarrassingly low, especially considering where we are in terms of the so-called economic recovery." In November, the unemployment rate held steady, but 321,000 jobs were added (this number was later revised upwards in February 2015 to 423,000 jobs). Average hourly earnings in November grew by nine cents, the largest increase since June 2013. By December, the unemployment rate dropped again to 5.6 percent when 252,000 jobs were added (later revised in February 2015 to 329,000 jobs). "American businesses are on a hiring binge," Sal Guatieri, a senior economist at BMO Capital Markets said at the time. "It clearly suggests the economy is on a much stronger growth track than the first four years of the recovery."

In 2014, the economy added approximately 2.95 million jobs, the strongest year for job creation since 1999, and the unemployment rate fell more than one point since December 2013 when it was 6.7 percent. The Federal Reserve predicted in December 2013 that the unemployment rate would likely be between 6.8 percent and 7.3 percent by the close of 2014. Still, wages failed to keep pace with inflation and only grew 1.7 percent from December 2013 to December 2014. Economists generally agree that wages will increase in 2015. "If you don't see wages picking up over the coming year, it means there's something fundamentally wrong with the recovery," said Gennadiy Goldberg, a U.S. strategist at TD Securities. An estimated three million workers were already expected to see their wages rise in January 2015, because twenty states and Washington, D.C., were set to raise their in-state minimum wages.

The sustained strong growth appeared to be building confidence for employers and the American public. The consumer sentiment index released in December 2014 by Thomson Reuters and the University of Michigan found that Americans feel more confident about the economy than they have over the past seven years. That confidence has driven spending, which helped the economy grow at an annualized rate of 2.4 percent. "That is the kind of speed that we really need to see to get more people back to work, to get inflation rising a bit more and for the Federal Reserve to finally conclude that their work is essentially done," said Bernard Baumohl, chief global economist at The Economic Outlook Group.

The still-struggling global economy and falling oil prices seen late in the year will continue to be a concern for investors, individuals, and the U.S. government. Secretary of Labor Thomas Perez said he will be "carefully monitoring the unemployment effects in the energy sector." There is concern that falling oil prices will cause a large number of job losses; however, there is also the potential for the counter effect if falling oil prices help boost consumer spending, and thus the economy as a whole.

—Heather Kerrigan

Following is the Bureau of Labor Statistics commissioner's statement on October 3, 2014, announcing September job growth; and a press release from the Federal Reserve on October 29, 2014, announcing the end of its quantitative easing program.

Bureau of Labor Statistics
Commissioner on Job Growth

DOCUMENT

October 3, 2014

Nonfarm payroll employment rose by 248,000 in September, and the unemployment rate declined to 5.9 percent. Employment increased in professional and business services, retail trade, and health care.

Incorporating the revisions for July and August, which increased total nonfarm payroll employment by 69,000 on net, monthly job increases have averaged 224,000 over the past 3 months. In the 12 months prior to September, employment growth averaged 213,000 per month.

Professional and business services added 81,000 jobs in September, compared with an average monthly gain of 56,000 over the prior 12 months. In September, job gains occurred in employment services (+34,000), management and technical consulting services (+12,000), and architectural and engineering services (+6,000).

Retail trade employment rose by 35,000 in September. Most of the increase occurred in food and beverage stores (+20,000), largely reflecting the return of workers who had been off payrolls in August due to employment disruptions at a grocery store chain in New England. Over the year, retail trade employment has increased by 264,000.

Employment in health care increased by 23,000 in September. Over the month, job gains occurred in home health care services (+7,000) and in hospitals (+6,000). Over the year, health care has added 256,000 jobs.

In September, the information industry added 12,000 jobs, with a gain of 5,000 in telecommunications. Over the year, employment in information has shown little net change.

Among other service-providing industries, employment in food services and drinking places and in financial activities continued to trend up in September (+20,000 and +12,000, respectively).

In the goods-producing sector, mining employment rose by 9,000 in September and is up by 50,000 over the year. Construction employment continued on an upward trend in September (+16,000). Within the industry, residential building gained 6,000 jobs. Over the year, construction employment has grown by 230,000. Employment in manufacturing showed little change over the month.

Average hourly earnings of all employees on private nonfarm payrolls were little changed at $24.53 in September (-1 cent), following an increase of 8 cents in August. Over the 12 months ending in September, average hourly earnings grew by 2.0 percent. From August 2013 to August 2014, the Consumer Price Index for All Urban Consumers (CPI-U) increased by 1.7 percent.

Turning to measures from the survey of households, the unemployment rate declined in September by 0.2 percentage point to 5.9 percent. Over the year, the jobless rate is down by 1.3 percentage points.

In September, there were 9.3 million unemployed persons, a decrease of 329,000 from August. The number of long-term unemployed (those unemployed 27 weeks or more) was essentially unchanged over the month, at 3.0 million.

The labor force participation rate, at 62.7 percent, changed little in September. The employment-population ratio remained at 59.0 percent; it has been at this level for 4 consecutive months.

Among the employed, the number of people working part time for economic reasons was little changed at 7.1 million in September. (These individuals, also referred to as involuntary part-time workers, would have preferred full-time employment, but had their hours cut or were unable to find full-time work.)

Among people who were neither working nor looking for work in September, 2.2 million were classified as marginally attached to the labor force, about unchanged over the year. (These individuals had not looked for work in the 4 weeks prior to the survey but wanted a job, were available for work, and had looked for a job within the last 12 months.) The number of discouraged workers, a subset of the marginally attached who believed that no jobs were available for them, was 698,000 in September, a decline of 154,000 over the year.

In summary, nonfarm payroll employment increased by 248,000 in September, and the unemployment rate declined to 5.9 percent.

SOURCE: Bureau of Labor Statistics. "Commissioner's Statement on the Employment Situation News Release." October 3, 2014. www.bls.gov/news.release/archives/jec_10032014.pdf.

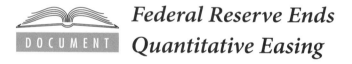

Federal Reserve Ends Quantitative Easing

October 29, 2014

Information received since the Federal Open Market Committee met in September suggests that economic activity is expanding at a moderate pace. Labor market conditions improved somewhat further, with solid job gains and a lower unemployment rate. On balance, a range of labor market indicators suggests that underutilization of labor resources is gradually diminishing. Household spending is rising moderately and business fixed investment is advancing, while the recovery in the housing sector remains slow. Inflation has continued to run below the Committee's longer-run objective. Market-based measures of inflation compensation have declined somewhat; survey-based measures of longer-term inflation expectations have remained stable.

Consistent with its statutory mandate, the Committee seeks to foster maximum employment and price stability. The Committee expects that, with appropriate policy accommodation, economic activity will expand at a moderate pace, with labor market indicators and inflation moving toward levels the Committee judges consistent with its dual mandate. The Committee sees the risks to the outlook for economic activity and the labor market as nearly balanced. Although inflation in the near term will likely be held down by lower energy prices and other factors, the Committee judges that the likelihood of inflation running persistently below 2 percent has diminished somewhat since early this year.

The Committee judges that there has been a substantial improvement in the outlook for the labor market since the inception of its current asset purchase program. Moreover, the Committee continues to see sufficient underlying strength in the broader economy to support ongoing progress toward maximum employment in a context of price stability. Accordingly, the Committee decided to conclude its asset purchase program this month. The Committee is maintaining its existing policy of reinvesting principal payments from its holdings of agency debt and agency mortgage-backed securities in agency mortgage-backed securities and of rolling over maturing Treasury securities at auction. This policy, by keeping the Committee's holdings of longer-term securities at sizable levels, should help maintain accommodative financial conditions.

To support continued progress toward maximum employment and price stability, the Committee today reaffirmed its view that the current 0 to 1/4 percent target range for the federal funds rate remains appropriate. In determining how long to maintain this target range, the Committee will assess progress—both realized and expected—toward its objectives of maximum employment and 2 percent inflation. This assessment will take into account a wide range of information, including measures of labor market conditions, indicators of inflation pressures and inflation expectations, and readings on financial developments. The Committee anticipates, based on its current assessment, that it likely will be appropriate to maintain the 0 to 1/4 percent target range for the federal funds rate for a considerable time following the end of its asset purchase program this month, especially if projected inflation continues to run below the Committee's 2 percent longer-run goal, and provided that longer-term inflation expectations remain well anchored. However, if incoming information indicates faster progress toward the Committee's employment and inflation objectives than the Committee now expects, then increases in the target range for the federal funds rate are likely to occur sooner than currently anticipated. Conversely, if progress proves slower than expected, then increases in the target range are likely to occur later than currently anticipated.

When the Committee decides to begin to remove policy accommodation, it will take a balanced approach consistent with its longer-run goals of maximum employment and inflation of 2 percent. The Committee currently anticipates that, even after employment and inflation are near mandate-consistent levels, economic conditions may, for some time, warrant keeping the target federal funds rate below levels the Committee views as normal in the longer run.

Voting for the FOMC monetary policy action were: Janet L. Yellen, Chair; William C. Dudley, Vice Chairman; Lael Brainard; Stanley Fischer; Richard W. Fisher; Loretta J. Mester; Charles I. Plosser; Jerome H. Powell; and Daniel K. Tarullo. Voting against the action was Narayana Kocherlakota, who believed that, in light of continued sluggishness in the inflation outlook and the recent slide in market-based measures of longer-term inflation expectations, the Committee should commit to keeping the current target range for the federal funds rate at least until the one-to-two-year ahead inflation outlook has returned to 2 percent and should continue the asset purchase program at its current level.

Source: Board of Governors of the Federal Reserve System. "Press Release." October 29, 2014. www.federalreserve.gov/newsevents/press/monetary/20141029a.htm.

Other Historic Documents of Interest

From this volume

- State of the Union Address and Republican Response, p. 3
- Census Bureau Reports on Poverty in the United States, p. 439
- President Obama and Speaker Boehner Respond to 2014 Midterm Elections, p. 501

From previous *Historic Documents*

- White House Details Benefits of Unemployment Insurance, *2013*, p. 609
- Federal Reserve Board Chair Announces End of Recession, *2009*, p. 430
- Federal Reserve Board on the State of the U.S. Economy, *2007*, p. 449

Supreme Court Rejects
Same-Sex Marriage Appeals

OCTOBER 6 AND 7, 2014

The year's most impactful legal case concerning same-sex marriage came on October 6, 2014, when the Supreme Court decided *not* to take up the issue. Without explanation, the Court declined to hear appeals from decisions by three federal appeals courts that had overturned same-sex marriage bans in five states—Indiana, Oklahoma, Utah, Virginia, and Wisconsin. The lower court rulings had been put on hold, pending review by the Supreme Court, but, by denying review, the Supreme Court let the lower rulings stand, effectively legalizing same-sex marriage in those five states. The Court's inaction immediately brought the total number of states allowing same-sex marriage from nineteen to twenty-four, and shortly after included another six states whose laws are controlled by those three federal circuits. In this way, the Supreme Court's nonaction led to a historic watershed moment for this issue because, for the first time, same-sex couples could marry in a majority of states.

The Impact of the Supreme Court's Earlier Decisions on Same-Sex Marriage

The Supreme Court has only ever addressed issues involving same-sex marriage in two decisions, both released on the final day of the Court's 2012–2013 term. Both decisions ducked the key issue of whether the Constitution requires recognition of these marriages. Of the two decisions, the most far reaching was *United States v. Windsor*, where the Court, in a 5–4 decision, struck down portions of the federal Defense of Marriage Act (DOMA). The 1996 DOMA, passed by Congress before any states had legalized single-sex marriage, defined the word "marriage" for purposes of all federal law or regulation to mean "only a legal union between one man and one woman as husband and wife." In *Windsor*, the Supreme Court ruled, in an opinion by Justice Anthony M. Kennedy, that DOMA unconstitutionally violates the rights of equal liberty protected by the Fifth Amendment by "creating two contradictory marriage regimes within the same state." According to Justice Kennedy, "DOMA's principal effect" was "to identify a subset of state-sanctioned marriages and make them unequal."

When the *Windsor* opinion was handed down, only twelve states and the District of Columbia had legalized same-sex marriage and the Court opinion explicitly did not resolve whether recognition of such marriages is constitutionally required. Justice Kennedy wrote: "The court does not have before it, and the logic of its opinion does not decide, the distinct question whether the states, in the exercise of their 'historic and essential authority to define the marital relation,' may continue to utilize the traditional definition of marriage." In his scathing dissent, Justice Antonin Scalia countered that this sentiment was disingenuous as the majority opinion and in his view "arms well every challenger to a state law restricting marriage to its traditional definition."

The impact of the *Windsor* decision bore out Justice Scalia's prediction. Immediately following the ruling, federal courts across the country exploded with constitutional challenges to same-sex marriage bans. As of this writing, these bans are currently facing active court challenges in every single state that has them. Of the federal and state courts that have ruled on the issue, forty have found them to violate constitutional guarantees of due process and equal protection. Only two lower courts have ruled opposingly.

The three appeals court rulings that the Supreme Court let stand came out of the Fourth, Seventh, and Tenth federal circuits. All of those decisions overturned state bans on same-sex marriages.

IMMEDIATE IMPACT OF THE COURT'S REFUSAL TO DECIDE

When the Supreme Court decided not to hear the appeals in these cases, the stays on the lower appeals court rulings were lifted and they could go into effect almost immediately. In fact, on October 7, Virginia governor Terry McAuliffe released an executive order stating, "Same-sex marriage is now legal in Virginia." Within hours, the first same-sex couples were married in Fairfax County, Virginia. The same day, the Court of Appeals for the Tenth Circuit issued an order lifting the stay in the Utah and Oklahoma proceedings. In Indiana, where the state had unsuccessfully supported its same-sex marriage ban in court, Governor Mike Pence released a statement recognizing the impact of the Supreme Court's decision: "While it is disappointing to many that the Supreme Court has chosen not to hear arguments on this important issue, under our system of government, people are free to disagree with court decisions but we are not free to disobey them." By declining to review the court of appeals decisions that had overturned same-sex marriage bans, the Supreme Court effectively granted marriage rights to same-sex couples in all the states that comprise these circuits: the states at issue in the case—Indiana, Oklahoma, Utah, Virginia, and Wisconsin—as well as the other states in the circuits—Colorado, Kansas, North Carolina, South Carolina, West Virginia, and Wyoming. The Supreme Court's denial of review, however, had no binding impact on federal courts in other circuits, all of which had cases working their way through the courts.

The day after the Supreme Court denied review of three federal appellate court rulings in favor of same-sex marriage rights, the Ninth Circuit Court of Appeals struck down same-sex marriage bans in Idaho and Nevada, holding that the constitutional guarantee of equal protection required that same-sex and opposite-sex couples be treated equally under the law. Same-sex marriage bans in Alaska, Arizona, and Montana, also in the Ninth Circuit, fell the next month. This decision brought the number of states recognizing legal same-sex marriage to thirty-five, and the District of Columbia. Of these states, twenty-five legalized the marriages through court action, eight by the actions of state legislatures and three by popular vote. By the end of 2014, only thirteen states still had intact state constitutional amendments limiting marriage to one man and one woman.

REACTION TO THE DENIAL OF REVIEW

The strongest and most universal reaction to the Court's inaction on same-sex marriage was one of surprise. More than thirty states had petitioned the Court to take the appeal and decide the constitutional issues definitively, as had advocacy groups on both sides of the issue. Ed Whelan, the president of the Ethics and Public Policy Center, wrote in the *National Review* that "the court's denial of review in all the pending cases strikes me as grossly irresponsible." Many who oppose same-sex marriage had seen hopeful signs that the Supreme Court would act in their favor after the justices had stepped in to put a hold on decisions allowing same-sex marriage in Virginia and Utah. Proponents of same-sex marriage were also impatient for the Court to address the issue. Evan Wolfson, the founder and president of Freedom to Marry, was quoted in *The New York Times* urging the justices to step in. He said, "The court's delay in affirming the freedom to marry nation-wide prolongs the patchwork of state-to-state discrimination and the harms and indignity that the denial of marriage still inflicts on too many couples in too many places."

Those who were not surprised by the Court's failure to act decisively on the constitutional issues point to recent public comments by the liberal stalwart on the Court, Justice Ruth Bader Ginsburg. She has often spoken of the need to move slowly on contentious and polarizing cultural issues in order not to get ahead of popular opinion. This was a lesson she said she had learned from the backlash following the 1973 decision in *Roe v. Wade*, which declared a constitutional right to an abortion. Although she is pro-choice, she has said that this decision "moved too far, too fast" and that it "stopped the momentum that was on the side of change." Many see her view as having clear implications for the timing of a sweeping ruling on same-sex marriage.

Most commentators attempted to read into what the refusal to review might mean for the future of same-sex marriage given that the Supreme Court did not have the four willing justices necessary to grant review. Many opine that the longer the Supreme Court waits to resolve the issue, the more states will have laws recognizing same-sex marriage, the more people will marry, and the harder it will be to overturn, particularly after letting stand so many court decisions striking down same-sex marriage bans. Walter E. Dellinger III, acting U.S. solicitor general in the Clinton administration, predicted, "Once a substantial part of the country has experienced gay marriage, then the court will be more willing to finish the job."

Debate Continues in Court

In November 2014, the Sixth Circuit broke the streak of victories for same-sex marriage supporters by bucking the legalization trend and becoming the first of the federal courts of appeals to uphold same-sex marriage bans in cases that came out of Kentucky, Michigan, Ohio, and Tennessee. This ruling created a conflict in the circuits that will need to be resolved.

On January 16, 2015, the Supreme Court agreed to take on the legally and culturally important same-sex marriage issue, potentially resolving it once and for all. The Court made clear its intention to face the constitutional issues involved head on. When it accepted the Sixth Circuit case for appeal, the Court ordered the parties to address two questions in their legal briefs: whether the Constitution requires states to issue marriage licenses to same-sex couples, and whether states must recognize same-sex marriages performed in other states where they are legal. Oral arguments were heard in April, and a final ruling is expected in late June.

—Melissa Feinberg

Following is the text of a statement by Indiana governor Mike Pence on October 6, 2014, in favor of traditional marriage; a press release issued by the office of Utah governor Gary Herbert on October 6, 2014, responding to the Supreme Court's decision not to review same-sex marriage; and an October 7, 2014, press release from the office of Virginia governor Terry McAuliffe directing state agencies to comply with the same-sex marriage ruling.

Indiana Governor Responds to Same-Sex Marriage Decision

October 6, 2014

"I will always believe in the importance of traditional marriage and I will always abide by the rule of law.

"While it is disappointing to many that the Supreme Court has chosen not to hear arguments on this important issue, under our system of government, people are free to disagree with court decisions but we are not free to disobey them.

"Hoosiers may be assured that I and my administration will uphold the rulings of our federal courts concerning marriage in the policies and practices of our state.

"As Governor of all the people of Indiana I am confident that Hoosiers will continue to demonstrate the civility for which we are known and respect the beliefs of all people in our state."

SOURCE: State of Indiana. Office of Governor Mike Pence. "Governor Pence Issues Statement Regarding U.S. Supreme Court's Decision Regarding Same-sex Marriage in Indiana." October 6, 2014. www.in.gov/activecalendar/EventList.aspx?fromdate=10/1/2014&todate=10/31/2014&display=Month&type=public&eventidn=187506&view=EventDetails&information_id=206779.

Utah Governor on Supreme Court Decision

October 6, 2014

In response to the Supreme Court's decision not to hear *Kitchen v. Herbert* or other same-sex marriage cases, Utah Governor Gary R. Herbert issued the following statement:

"As I have said all along, the people of Utah and people across the country deserve clarity with respect to the law. It is best if that clarity comes from the nation's highest court. I am surprised—as are many on both sides of the issue—that the Supreme Court has made the decision not to consider Utah's case, or any similar case from another state.

"I believe states should have the right to determine their own laws regarding marriage. That said, we are a society of laws and we will uphold the law. I have instructed state agencies to implement necessary changes in light of today's news.

"Once again, I encourage all Utahns—regardless of their personal beliefs on this issue—to treat each other with respect."

The Governor's Office also issued a memo to all state agencies:

Dear Cabinet members,

As you are all aware, the United States Supreme Court announced this morning it will not grant certiorari in the *Kitchen v. Herbert* case, or any other case related to same-sex marriage. The effect of this decision is that the stay that has been in place in Utah's case has been lifted and Utah's laws regarding same-sex marriage have been ruled to be unconstitutional.

We have also just received the mandate from the 10th Circuit Court finalizing its order and lifting its own stay. Accordingly, each agency should conduct business today and going forward, recognizing all legally performed same-sex marriages. Please make adjustments to any forms or other processes, as appropriate.

If there are any specific questions that arise, please consult with the Governor's Office so we can work with the Attorney General to resolve those questions.

Thank you all for you dedicated service to the citizens of the State of Utah. We trust that you and your employees will make sure this transition in the application of our laws occurs as smoothly and professionally as possible.

Sincerely,

Justin Harding
Chief of Staff

Jacey Skinner
General Counsel

Source: Office of Utah Governor Gary Herbert. "Gov. Herbert Statement on Supreme Court Decision Regarding Same-sex Marriage." October 6, 2014. www.utah.gov/governor/news_media/article.html?article=10431.

Virginia Governor Signs Executive Order on Same-Sex Marriage

October 7, 2014

Today Governor Terry McAuliffe signed Executive Order #30, directing all Virginia state agencies, authorities, commissions and other entities to make the necessary policy changes to comply with yesterday's U.S. Supreme Court decision not to review the Fourth Circuit Court of Appeals' decision legalizing gay marriage in Virginia. The text of the Executive Order is as follows:

NUMBER THIRTY (2014)

Marriage Equality in the Commonwealth of Virginia

Importance of the Issue

The highest priority of state government should be to guarantee every person's right to live, learn, work, and do business, regardless of their race, gender, creed or sexual orientation. This principle guided my first act as Governor when I signed Executive Order #1 banning discrimination in the state workplace based on sexual orientation or gender identity. This principle also guided the Virginia leaders, advocates and allies who fought for marriage equality and won when the Supreme Court declined to review the Fourth Circuit Court of Appeals' ruling in *Bostic v. Schaefer*. Same-sex marriage is now legal in Virginia. This is a historic and long overdue moment for our Commonwealth and our country.

The decision has opened new doors to my administration's guiding principle of equality. An open and welcoming environment is imperative to grow as a Commonwealth, and to build a new Virginia economy that will attract vital businesses, innovative entrepreneurs, and thriving families.

On issues ranging from recognizing same-sex marriages to extending health care benefits to same-sex spouses of state employees, state government is already well-prepared to implement this landmark decision. My administration will act quickly to continue to bring all of our policies and practices into compliance so that we can give married same-sex couples the full array of benefits they deserve.

Pursuant to the authority vested in me as the Chief Executive Officer of the Commonwealth, and pursuant to Article V of the Constitution and the laws of Virginia, I hereby order, effective immediately, that all entities in the executive branch, including agencies, authorities, commissions, departments, and all institutions of higher education further evaluate all policies and take all necessary and appropriate legal measures to comply with this decision.

In addition, the Director of the Department of Human Resource Management shall notify all state agencies that employees whose same-sex marriage is recognized as legal in the Commonwealth, and who are eligible, may enroll their spouse and eligible dependents in the health benefits program for state employees within sixty (60) days of marriage.

A full and complete report of all appropriate measures will be reviewed by the Counselor to the Governor and presented to the Governor on or before November 15, 2014.

Effective Date of the Executive Order

This Executive Order shall become effective upon its signing, and shall remain in full force and effect unless amended or rescinded by further executive order.

Given under my hand and under the Seal of the Commonwealth of Virginia this 7th day of October, 2014.

Terence R. McAuliffe, Governor

SOURCE: Office of Virginia Governor Terry McAuliffe. "Governor McAuliffe Signs Executive Order Directing State Agencies to Comply with Same-Sex Marriage Ruling." October 7, 2014. https://governor .virginia.gov/newsroom/newsarticle?articleId=6780.

OTHER HISTORIC DOCUMENTS OF INTEREST

FROM PREVIOUS *HISTORIC DOCUMENTS*

November

President Obama and Speaker Boehner Respond to 2014 Midterm Elections

NOVEMBER 4 AND 5, 2014

On November 4, 2014, voters across the country went to the polls for the midterm election. In addition to nearly 150 ballot measures, voters also chose all 435 seats in the House of Representatives, thirty-six Senate seats, thirty-six governors, and forty-six state legislatures, in addition to a multitude of local races. The elections marked a major victory for the Republican Party, which took control of the Senate and would hold both houses of Congress during the 2015–2016 legislative session. The party also won a majority of the governorships and state legislative races. Campaign spending reached an all-time high at nearly $4 billion, which some called a direct reflection of the Supreme Court's 2010 *Citizens United* ruling that gave corporations and labor unions the ability to spend unlimited sums of money on ads and other political methods to call for the support of or opposition to specific candidates. Turnout was at its lowest level for a midterm election since 1942, with less than 37 percent of eligible Americans casting a vote.

PRIMARY UPSETS

On May 27, 2014, Rep. Ralph Hall, R-Texas, who represented the state's 4th Congressional District, became the first House incumbent to lose a primary that year. Hall, who was first elected to Congress in 1980 as a Democrat and was the oldest sitting member in the House, was defeated by John Ratcliffe, a former mayor and U.S. attorney, by approximately 4 percent of the vote. "I entered this race because I want a better path for America than the one we're on right now," Ratcliffe said of his primary victory. "Tonight, the voters of this district confirmed what I've been hearing on the campaign trail for the last six months." Ratcliffe went on to run unopposed in the November general election.

The biggest upset of the primary season came on June 10, when Rep. Eric Cantor, R-Va., the current House majority leader, lost his primary bid to David Brat, a professor at Randolph-Macon College. Brat won 55.5 percent of the primary vote to Cantor's 44.5 percent, even though he spent only $200,000 to Cantor's more than $2 million. The loss was the first ever suffered by a sitting House majority leader. "This is the political version of the San Francisco earthquake. It came out of nowhere," said Stuart Rothenberg, publisher of *The Rothenberg & Gonzales Political Report*. Cantor, who had held his seat since 2000, subsequently resigned from his leadership position on July 31 and was replaced by Rep. Kevin McCarthy of California. Cantor resigned his House seat soon after on August 18. "I want to make sure that the constituents in the 7th District will have a voice in what will be a very consequential lame-duck session," Cantor said upon resigning. He asked Virginia governor Terry McAuliffe to call a special election to allow a candidate to be seated immediately rather than leaving the seat open until January 2015. Political analyst Larry Sabato said Cantor's resignation may have been somewhat self-serving. "It's highly probable that he has a very lucrative deal in the works for his post-Congress life, and he's eager to get started," Sabato said. Brat won both the special election and the general election.

HOUSE AND SENATE VICTORIES

Going into the general election, political analysts said that turnout would be low, as it has been in midterm elections dating back to the 1840s. The composition of the electorate also tends to be slightly different during midterms, with higher percentages of white and older Americans coming out to vote, both factors that benefit Republicans. Historically, Democrats were set up to lose. Since the Great Depression, midterm elections held during the sixth year of a president's two terms often see the incumbent's party lose seats. Both parties, however, faced a voting public with strong anti-incumbent sentiment. According to a Pew Research Center poll conducted in July, only 48 percent of all registered voters surveyed said they wanted their representative to be reelected, while 24 percent said they wanted most members of Congress to be reelected.

The most closely watched races were in the Senate, where Republicans needed a net gain of six seats to take majority control from the Democrats. On election night, it was clear that Republicans would gain at least a slight majority in the Senate and would hold control of the House. The remaining question was how big the ultimate majority would be in the Senate after multiple races faced delayed results and recounts. A runoff in Louisiana between incumbent Democrat Sen. Mary Landrieu and her opponent Bill Cassidy was held on December 6 and was the last race to be decided. Landrieu's loss left the Republicans with 54 seats in the Senate. The party had held all its seats and won nine new seats, which included the unseating of incumbent Democrats in Alaska, Arkansas, Colorado, Louisiana, and North Carolina. The last House seat, in Arizona's 2nd Congressional District, went to Republican Martha McSally, giving her party 247 seats to the Democrats' 188, the largest Republican total since 1928. McSally's seat was formerly held by Rep. Gabrielle Giffords, who was shot and critically injured in 2011 while meeting with constituents in Tucson.

Democrats took the loss in stride. "I do not believe what happened the other night is a wave," said House minority leader Nancy Pelosi, D-Calif. "There was no wave of approval for the Republicans. I wish them congratulations, they won the election, but there was no wave of approval for anybody. There was an ebbing . . . for us." As Pelosi would go on to explain, the problem for Democrats was not their message or the president's low approval rating, but rather the party's failure to engage voters. "Two-thirds of the electorate did not vote in this election," Pelosi said. "That's shameful."

Democrats suffered big losses at the state level as well. In the traditionally Democratic states of Illinois, Massachusetts, and Maryland, Republicans won the gubernatorial races; in the case of Illinois, a Democratic incumbent was unseated. This means that in 2015 Republicans will hold thirty-one of the nation's governorships. The party would also be in control of sixty-eight of the country's ninety-eight partisan legislative chambers. Twenty-one states would be wholly Republican controlled, with Republicans leading both the executive and the legislature. Matt Walter, president of the Republican State Leadership Committee, said that the key to the overwhelming victories "was recruiting diverse candidates and women candidates who made the critical difference."

Obama Remarks on Democratic Defeat

Shortly after their election night victories, Congressional Republicans began outlining some of their key strategies heading into the new Congress in January 2015. One of the major initiatives House Speaker John Boehner, R-Ohio, and soon-to-be Majority Leader Mitch McConnell, R-Ky., pledged was a vote to repeal the Affordable Care Act, often referred to as ObamaCare. In a *Wall Street Journal* op-ed, the pair said that supporting the middle class through job creation "means renewing our commitment to repeal ObamaCare, which is hurting the job market along with Americans' health care." But the leaders indicated, both behind closed doors and publicly, that they wanted to avoid the brinksmanship that had eroded public confidence in Congress. "There will be no government shutdown, and there will be no national default," McConnell said. Of the newly elected Republicans, McConnell said, "The vast majority of them don't feel they were sent to Washington to fight all the time." As opposed to the 2012 election, many Republican victories came through the backing of establishment candidates and even some of the more moderate Republicans, rather than Tea Party candidates, which could mean greater unity for the party, and thus a greater ability to pass bills. "We're not veering hard right," Rep. Steve Stivers, R-Ohio, said of the new Congress. "We're playing it straight down the fairway." Republican leaders in both houses seemed to be wary of the slim majority in the Senate. Sen. John Thune, R-S.D., the third most powerful member in the Senate, said that while there would be more potential for the House and Senate to work together with Republicans in control, he thinks Republicans "will have to keep expectations realistic of what we can accomplish."

During a November 5 press conference, Obama addressed the outcome of the midterm elections and spoke about how he planned to partner with House and Senate leadership, at one point remarking, "I would enjoy having some Kentucky bourbon with Mitch McConnell." Obama admitted that "Republicans had a good night" but that the major takeaway from the election should be that Americans "expect the people they elect to work as hard as they do. They expect us to focus on their ambitions and not ours. They want us to get the job done."

The president said there were a number of areas on which both parties could agree—creating jobs, growing exports, and expanding trade. "The key is to make sure that those ideas that I have overlap somewhere with some of the ideas that Republicans have," Obama said. Noting that there would be clear areas of disagreement, Obama said, "There are going to be some ideas that I've got that, I think the evidence backs up, would be good for the economy, and Republicans disagree. . . . I'm going to keep on arguing for them because I think they're the right thing for the country to do. There are going to be some ideas that they've got that they believe will improve the economy or create jobs that, from my perspective, isn't going to help middle class families improve their economic situation."

Despite the rhetoric, there were few areas heading into 2015 on which the two parties agreed. And Republicans were already promising to use the appropriations process to attempt to stall or turn back some of the president's policies, including weakening the Dodd-Frank consumer protection bill and pushing through stalled legislation including the Keystone XL pipeline. "It's reasonable to assume that we will use the power of the purse to try to push back against this overactive bureaucracy," McConnell said.

Attention Turns to 2016

Even before Election Day 2014, political commentators were already discussing what effect the midterm election might have on the 2016 presidential race, and, particularly, which speculative candidates might rise to the top. Brendan Nyhan, an assistant professor of government at Dartmouth College, noted that history indicates that midterm elections have little bearing on the outcome of subsequent presidential elections. In an article for *The New York Times*, Nyhan wrote, "Midterm results, which are typically unfavorable to the president's party, tell us relatively little about the coming presidential election." But, he added, "[t]he record shows that the president's party can rebound from major losses to win at the polls in two years." Political analyst Charlie Cook said the election "was not a representative cross-section of the country" and warned against "extrapolating too much" from the outcome. GOP consultant Ford O'Connell put it bluntly: "Whatever happens in 2014 stays in 2014."

—Heather Kerrigan

Following is a statement by Speaker of the House John Boehner, R-Ohio, on November 4, 2014, on Republican election victories; and the text of a press conference with President Barack Obama on November 5, 2014, following the midterm elections.

Speaker Boehner on Midterm Elections

November 4, 2015

We are humbled by the responsibility the American people have placed with us, but this is not a time for celebration. It's time for government to start getting results and implementing solutions to the challenges facing our country, starting with our still-struggling economy.

Americans can expect the new Congress to debate and vote soon on the many common-sense jobs and energy bills that passed the Republican-led House in recent years with bipartisan support but were never even brought to a vote by the outgoing Senate majority, as well as solutions offered by Senate Republicans that were denied consideration. I've also put forth a five-point roadmap for harnessing the emerging energy boom in America, resetting our economy and restoring the American Dream for our children and grandchildren. It calls for fixing our tax code, solving our spending problem, reforming our legal system, reforming our regulatory system, and improving our education system.

Republicans have made these our priorities by listening to the people we take an oath to serve. Our proposals provide an opportunity for President Obama to begin the last two years of his presidency by taking some bipartisan steps toward a stronger economy. We hope he'll work with us to enact them into law, and that he'll disavow reports that he plans to react to the loss of the Senate with a "counterattack" on the new majority. This is a time for solutions to get our economy moving again, and we're eager to get to work.

SOURCE: Office of the Speaker of the House John Boehner. "Statement by Speaker Boehner on Outlook for the 114th Congress." November 4, 2014. www.speaker.gov/press-release/statement-speaker-boehner-outlook-114th-congress.

President Obama Responds to Midterm Elections

November 5, 2014

The President. Good afternoon, everybody. Have a seat.

Today I had a chance to speak with John Boehner and congratulated Mitch McConnell on becoming the next Senate Majority Leader. And I told them both that I look forward to finishing up this Congress's business and then working together for the next 2 years to advance America's business. And I very much appreciated Leader McConnell's words last night about the prospect of working together to deliver for the American people. On Friday, I look forward to hosting the entire Republican and Democratic leadership at the White House to chart a new course forward.

Obviously, Republicans had a good night, and they deserve credit for running good campaigns. Beyond that, I'll leave it to all of you and the professional pundits to pick through yesterday's results. What stands out to me, though, is that the American people sent a message, one that they've sent for several elections now. They expect the people they elect to work as hard as they do. They expect us to focus on their ambitions and not ours. They want us to get the job done.

All of us, in both parties, have a responsibility to address that sentiment. Still, as President, I have a unique responsibility to try and make this town work. So, to everyone who voted, I want you to know that I hear you. To the two-thirds of voters who chose not to participate in the process yesterday, I hear you too. All of us have to give more Americans a reason to feel like the ground is stable beneath their feet, that the future is secure, that there's a path for young people to succeed, and that folks here in Washington are concerned about them. So I plan on spending every moment of the next 2-plus years doing my job the best I can to keep this country safe and to make sure that more Americans share in its prosperity.

Now, this country has made real progress since the crisis 6 years ago. The fact is, more Americans are working; unemployment has come down. More Americans have health insurance. Manufacturing has grown. Our deficits have shrunk. Our dependence on foreign oil is down, as are gas prices. Our graduation rates are up. Our businesses aren't just creating jobs at the fastest pace since the 1990s, our economy is outpacing most of the world. But we've just got to keep at it until every American feels the gains of a growing economy where it matters most, and that's in their own lives.

Obviously, much of that will take action from Congress. And I'm eager to work with the new Congress to make the next 2 years as productive as possible. I am committed to making sure that I measure ideas not by whether they are from Democrats or Republicans, but whether they work for the American people. And that's not to say that we won't disagree over some issues that we're passionate about. We will. Congress will pass some bills I cannot sign. I'm pretty sure I'll take some actions that some in Congress will not like. That's natural. That's how our democracy works. But we can surely find ways to work together on issues where there's broad agreement among the American people.

So I look forward to Republicans putting forward their governing agenda. I will offer my ideas on areas where I think we can move together to respond to people's economic needs.

So just take one example: We all agree on the need to create more jobs that pay well. Traditionally, both parties have been for creating jobs rebuilding our infrastructure: our roads, bridges, ports, waterways. I think we can hone in on a way to pay for it through tax reform that closes loopholes and makes it more attractive for companies to create jobs here in the United States.

We could also work together to grow our exports and open new markets for our manufacturers to sell more American-made goods to the rest of the world. And that's something I'll be focused on when I travel to Asia next week.

We all share the same aspirations for our young people. And I was encouraged that this year, Republicans agreed to investments that expanded early childhood education. I think we've got a chance to do more on that front. We've got some common ideas to help more young people afford college and graduate without crippling debt so that they have the freedom to fill the good jobs of tomorrow and buy their first homes and start a family.

And in the five States where a minimum wage increase was on the ballot last night, voters went five for five to increase it. And that will give about 325,000 Americans a raise in States where Republican candidates prevailed. So that should give us new reason to get it done for everybody, with a national increase in the minimum wage.

So those are some areas where I think we've got some real opportunities to cooperate. And I am very eager to hear Republican ideas for what they think we can do together over the next couple of years. Of course, there's still business on the docket that needs attention this year. And here are three places where I think we can work together over the next several weeks, before this Congress wraps up for the holidays.

First, I'm submitting a request to Congress for funding to ensure that our doctors, scientists, and troops have the resources that they need to combat the spread of Ebola in Africa and to increase our preparedness for any future cases here at home.

Second, I'm going to begin engaging Congress over a new Authorization to Use Military Force against ISIL. The world needs to know we are united behind this effort, and the men and women of our military deserve our clear and unified support.

Third, back in September, Congress passed short-term legislation to keep the Government open and operating into December. That gives Congress 5 weeks to pass a budget for the rest of the fiscal year. And I hope that they'll do it in the same bipartisan, drama-free way that they did earlier this year. When our companies are steadily creating jobs, which they are, we don't want to inject any new uncertainty into the world economy and to the American economy.

The point is, it's time for us to take care of business. There are things this country has to do that can't wait another 2 years or another 4 years. There are plans this country has to put in place for our future.

And the truth is, I'm optimistic about our future. I have good reason to be. I meet Americans all across the country who are determined and big-hearted and ask that—what they can do and never give up and overcome obstacles. And they inspire me every single day. So the fact is, I still believe in what I said when I was first elected 6 years ago last night. For all the maps plastered across our TV screens today, and for all the cynics who say otherwise, I continue to believe we are simply more than just a collection of red and blue States. We are the United States.

 And whether it's immigration or climate change or making sure our kids are going to the best possible schools, to making sure that our communities are creating jobs; whether it's stopping the spread of terror and disease, to opening up doors of opportunity to everybody who's willing to work hard and take responsibility, the United States has big things to do. We can and we will make progress if we do it together. And I look forward to the work ahead.

So with that, let me take some questions. I think that our team has got my list. And we're going to start with Julie Pace at Associated Press.

Midterm Elections/Bipartisanship/Minimum Wage/National Economy

Q. You said during this election that while your name wasn't on the ballot, your policies were. And despite the optimism that you're expressing here, last night was a devastating night for your party. Given that, do you feel any responsibility to recalibrate your agenda for the next 2 years? And what changes do you need to make in your White House and in your dealings with Republicans in order to address the concerns that voters expressed with your administration?

The President. Well, as I said in my opening remarks, the American people overwhelmingly believe that this town doesn't work well and that it is not attentive to their needs. And as President, they rightly hold me accountable to do more to make it work properly. I'm the guy who's elected by everybody, not just from a particular State or a particular district. And they want me to push hard to close some of these divisions, break through some of the gridlock, and get stuff done. So the most important thing I can do is just get stuff done and help Congress get some things done.

In terms of agenda items, though, Julie, if you look, as I just mentioned, to a minimum wage increase, for example, that's something I talked about a lot during the campaign. Where voters had a chance to vote directly on that agenda item, they voted for it. And so I think it would be hard to suggest that people aren't supportive of it. We know that the surveys consistently say they want to see that happen.

The key is to find areas where the agenda that I've put forward, one that I believe will help strengthen the middle class and create more ladders of opportunity into the middle class and improve our schools and make college more affordable to more young people and make sure that we're growing faster as an economy and we stay competitive—the key is to make sure that those ideas that I have overlap somewhere with some of the ideas that Republicans have.

There's not going to be perfect overlap. I mean, there are going to be some ideas that I've got that, I think the evidence backs up, would be good for the economy, and Republicans disagree. They're not going to support those ideas. But I'm going to keep on arguing for them because I think they're the right thing for the country to do. There are going to be some ideas that they've got that they believe will improve the economy or create jobs that, from my perspective, isn't going to help middle class families improve their economic situation, so I probably won't support theirs.

But I do think there are going to be areas where we do agree: on infrastructure, on making sure that we're boosting American exports. And part of my task, then, is to reach out to Republicans, make sure that I'm listening to them. I'm looking forward to them putting forward a very specific agenda in terms of what they would like to accomplish. Let's compare notes in terms of what I'm looking at and what they're looking at, and let's get started on those things where we agree. Even if we don't agree 100 percent, let's get started on those things where we agree 70, 80, 90 percent. And if we can do that and build up some trust and improve how processes work in Washington, then I think that's going to give the American people a little bit more confidence that, in fact, their Government is looking after them.

Q. But is there anything specific that you feel like you and your administration need to change given this disastrous election for your party and the message that voters sent?

The President. Julie, I think every single day I'm looking for, how can we do what we need to do better. Whether that is delivering basic services the Government provides to the American people, whether that is our capacity to work with Congress so that they're passing legislation, whether it's how we communicate with the American people about what our priorities and vision is, we are constantly asking ourselves questions about how do we make sure that we're doing a better job. And that's not going to stop. I think that every election is a moment for reflection, and I think that everybody in this White House is going to look and say, all right, what do we need to do differently?

But the principles that we're fighting for, the things that motivate me every single day and motivate my staff every day, those things aren't going to change. There's going to be a consistent focus on how do we deliver more opportunity to more people in this country, how do we grow the economy faster, how do we put more people back to work.

And I maybe have a naive confidence that if we continue to focus on the American people and not on our own ambitions or image or various concerns like that, that at the end of the day, when I look back, I'm going to be able to say the American people are better off than they were before I was President. And that's my most important goal.

So—but the other thing I just want to emphasize is I'm—I've said this before, I want to reiterate it: If there are ideas that the Republicans have that I have confidence will make things better for ordinary Americans, the fact that the Republicans suggesting it as opposed to a Democrat, that will be irrelevant to me. I want to just see what works.

And there are some things like rebuilding our infrastructure or early childhood education that we know works. And I'm hoping that the kind of attitude and approach that Mitch McConnell and John Boehner have already expressed, their desire to get things done, allows us to find some common ground.

Jeff Mason [Reuters].

Midterm Elections/Bipartisanship/Immigration Reform

Q. Thank you, Mr. President. In 2010, you called the result of the midterm election "a shellacking." What do you call this? And can you give us an update on your feelings about the immigration Executive order in the result—in the aftermath of this election? Does the election affect your plans to release it? Will it still—is it likely to come out before the lame duck session is over? And have you reduced its scope to just a couple million people?

The President. Well, as I said in my opening statement, there's no doubt that Republicans had a good night. And what we're going to make sure that we do is to reach out to Mitch McConnell and John Boehner, who are now running both Chambers in Congress, and find out what their agenda is. And my hope is, is that they've got some specific things they want to do that correspond with some things that we want to get done. What's most important to the American people right now, the resounding message not just of this election, but basically, the last several is: Get stuff done. Don't worry about the next election. Don't worry about party affiliation. Do worry about our concerns. Worry about the fact that I'm a single mom and, at the end of the month, it's really hard for me to pay the bills, in part because I've got these huge childcare costs. Do worry about the fact that I'm a young person who's qualified to go to college, but I'm really worried about taking $50,000 a year out in debt, and I don't know how I'd pay that back. Do worry about the fact that I'm a construction worker who has been working all my life, and I know that there's construction work that should be done, but right now, for some reason, projects are stalled. If we're thinking about those folks, I think we're, hopefully, going to be able to get some stuff done.

In terms of immigration, I have consistently said that it is my profound preference and interest to see Congress act on a comprehensive immigration reform bill that would strengthen our borders; would streamline our legal immigration system so that it works better and we're attracting the best and the brightest from around the world; and that we give an opportunity for folks who've lived here, in many cases, for a very long time, may have kids who are U.S. citizens, but aren't properly documented—give them a chance to pay their back taxes, get in the back of the line, but get through a process that allows them to get legal.

The Senate, on a bipartisan basis, passed a good bill. It wasn't perfect, it wasn't exactly what I wanted, but it was a sound, smart piece of legislation that really would greatly improve not just our immigration system, but our economy, and would improve business conditions here in the United States and make sure that American-born workers aren't undercut by workers who are undocumented and aren't always paid a fair wage, and as a consequence, employers who are breaking the rules are able to undercut folks who are doing the right thing.

So we got a bipartisan bill out of the Senate. I asked John Boehner at that point, can we pass this through the House? There's a majority of votes in the House to get this passed. And Speaker Boehner, I think, was sincere about wanting to pass it, but had difficulty over the last year trying to get it done.

So when he finally told me he wasn't going to call it up this year, what I indicated to him is, I feel obliged to do everything I can lawfully with my executive authority to make sure that we don't keep on making the system worse, but that whatever executive actions that I take will be replaced and supplanted by action by Congress. You send me a bill that I can sign, and those executive actions go away.

That's a commitment I made not just to the American people and to businesses and the evangelical community and law enforcement folks and everybody who's looked at this issue and thinks that we need immigration reform; that's a commitment that I also made to John Boehner, that I would act in the absence of action by Congress.

So before the end of the year, we're going to take whatever lawful actions that I can take that I believe will improve the functioning of our immigration system that will allow us to surge additional resources to the border, where I think the vast majority of Americans have the deepest concern. And at the same time, I'll be reaching out to both Mitch McConnell, John Boehner, and other Republican as well as Democratic leaders to find out how it is that they want to proceed. And if they want to get a bill done, whether it's during the lame duck or next year, I'm eager to see what they have to offer.

But what I'm not going to do is just wait. I think it's fair to say that I've shown a lot of patience and have tried to work on a bipartisan basis as much as possible, and I'm going to keep on doing so. But in the meantime, let's figure out what we can do lawfully through executive actions to improve the functioning of the existing system.

Q. How will you make sure that that executive action has teeth if Republicans try to block it by blocking funding? And can you give us a sense of whether or not you're thinking about 2 million or more million now?

The President. Jeff, I think if you want to get into the details of it, I suspect that when I announce that executive action, it will be rife with detail. [*Laughter*] And I'm sure there will be a lot of follow-up questions. [*Laughter*]

Chris Jansing [NBC News].

Midterm Elections/National Economy/Immigration Reform

Q. Thank you, Mr. President. I want to follow up on a couple of things and start with immigration. And are you concerned that if you sign an Executive order on immigration before the end of the year it will scuttle whatever chances there may be for there to be some sort of compromise on the issues that you talked about? And I wonder that, given this unhappy electorate, clearly, and they seem to be disappointed with both sides pretty much, why they punished the Democrats more than the Republicans by far.

The President. Well, as I said, when it comes to the political analysis, that's your job. But what is also true is I am the President of the United States, and I think, understandably, people are going to ask for greater accountability and more responsibility from me than from anybody else in this town, appropriately so, and I welcome that. And the commitment that I will make to the American people and the way I've tried to conduct myself throughout this Presidency is that I'm going to wake up every single day doing my absolute best to deliver for them.

And there are areas where we've made real progress. I think, economically, I can look back and there is no doubt that almost—on almost every measure, we are better off economically than we were when I took office. But what is also true is, there are still a lot of folks out there who are anxious and are hurting and are having trouble making ends meet or are worried about their children's future. And it's my job to give them some confidence that this town can work to respond to some of those worries that folks have.

And we haven't done a good enough job convincing them of that. And I understand that. If they've been watching Washington over the last 2, 4 years, what they've seen is a lot of arguing and a lot of gridlock, but not a lot of concrete actions, at least legislatively, that have made a difference in their lives. And so we've got to make sure that we do a better job, and I'm committed to doing that.

On immigration, I know that concerns have been expressed that, well, if you do something through executive actions, even if it's within your own authorities, that that will make it harder to pass immigration reform. I just have to remind everybody, I've heard that argument now for a couple of years. This is an issue I actually wanted to get done in my first term, and we didn't see legislative action. And in my second term, I made it my top legislative priority; we got really good work done by a bipartisan group of Senators, but it froze up in the House.

And I think that the best way, if folks are serious about getting immigration reform done, is going ahead and passing a bill and getting it to my desk. And then the executive actions that I take go away. They're superseded by the law that has passed. And I will engage any Member of Congress who's interested in this in how we can shape legislation that will be a significant improvement over the existing system. But what we can't do is just keep on waiting. There is a cost to waiting. There's a cost to our economy. It means that resources are misallocated.

When the issue of unaccompanied children cropped up during this summer, there was a lot of folks who perceived this as a major crisis in our immigration system. Now, the fact is, is that those numbers have now come down, and they're approximately where they were a year ago or 2 years ago or a year before that. But it did identify a real problem in a certain portion of the border where we've got to get more resources.

But those resources may be misallocated, separating families right now that most of us, most Americans would say, probably, we'd rather have them just pay their back taxes, pay a fine, learn English, get to the back of the line, but we'll give you a pathway where you can be legal in this country.

So where I've got executive authorities to do that, we should get started on that. But I want to emphasize once again, if in fact Republican leadership wants to see an immigration bill passed, they now have the capacity to pass it. And hopefully, engaging with me and Democrats in both the House and the Senate, it's a bill that I can sign because it addresses the real concerns that are out there. And the sooner they do it, from my perspective, the better.

Jonathan Karl [ABC News].

President's Relations With Congress/Bipartisanship/
Senate Minority Leader A. Mitchell McConnell

Q. Thank you, Mr. President. Mitch McConnell has been the Republican Leader for 6 years, as long as you've been President. But his office tells me that he has only met with you one-on-one once or twice during that entire 6-year period. So I'm wondering, as somebody who came to Washington promising to end the hyperpartisanship that was here long before you became President, but it's gotten worse since you got here, was it a mistake for you to do so little to develop relationships with Republicans in Congress?

The President. I think that every day, I'm asking myself, are there some things I can do better. And I'm going to keep on asking that every single day. The fact is that most of my interactions with Members of Congress have been cordial and they've been constructive. Oftentimes, though, we just haven't been able to actually get what's discussed in a leadership meeting through caucuses in the House and the Senate to deliver a bill.

The good news is that now Mitch McConnell and John Boehner are from the same party; I think they can come together and decide what their agenda is. They've got sufficient majorities to make real progress on some of these issues. And I'm certainly going to be spending a lot more time with them now because that's the only way that we're going to be able to get some stuff done.

And I take them at their word that they want to produce. They're in the majority; they need to present their agenda. I need to put forward my best ideas. I think the American people are going to be able to watch us, and they're paying attention to see whether or not we're serious about actually compromising and being constructive. And my commitment to them—and I've said this when I spoke to them—is, is that anywhere where we can find common ground, I'm eager to pursue it.

Q. Are you going to have that drink with Mitch McConnell now that you joked about at the White House Correspondents Dinner?

The President. You know, actually, I would enjoy having some Kentucky bourbon with Mitch McConnell. [Laughter] I don't know what his preferred drink is, but—my interactions with Mitch McConnell, he has always been very straightforward with me. To his credit, he has never made a promise that he couldn't deliver. And he knows the legislative process well. He obviously knows his caucus well. He has always given me, I think, realistic assessments of what he can get through his caucus and what he can't. And so I think we can have a productive relationship.

Phil Mattingly [Bloomberg Television].

Congressional Authorization for Use of Military Force/Islamic State of Iraq and the
Levant (ISIL) Terrorist Organization/Iran

Q. Thank you, Mr. President. Another deadline coming up is on—your negotiators by November 24 have to figure out if they're going to reach a deal with Iran on a nuclear area—a nuclear agreement. I'm interested what your current perspective is on how those negotiations are going. Also, if it is your feeling that you have the power to implement any type of agreement that's reached without any action from Congress? And then, also, I just wanted to quickly touch on the AUMF that you mentioned earlier. Is that going to be more of a codification of the limits that you've put in place for the mission up to this point? Or what should we be looking for on that when you send it to the Hill? Thank you.

The President. On the AUMF, the leaders are going to be coming here on Friday. It will be an expanded group, not just the four leaders, but a larger group who all have an interest in the issues we're discussing today. And I'm actually going to invite Lloyd Austin, the CENTCOM commander, to make a presentation about how our fight against ISIL is proceeding and, I think, to answer questions and assure that Congress is fully briefed on what we're doing there.

With respect to the AUMF, we've already had conversations with members of both parties in Congress, and the idea is to right-size and update whatever authorization Congress provides to suit the current fight, rather than previous fights.

In 2001, after the heartbreaking tragedy of 9/11, we had a very specific set of missions that we had to conduct, and the AUMF was designed to pursue those missions. With respect to Iraq, there was a very specific AUMF.

We now have a different type of enemy. The strategy is different. How we partner with Iraq and other Gulf countries and the international coalition, that has to be structured differently. So it makes sense for us to make sure that the authorization from Congress reflects what we perceive to be not just our strategy over the next 2 or 3 months, but our strategy going forward.

And it will be a process of listening to Members of Congress, as well as us presenting what we think needs to be the set of authorities that we have. And I'm confident we're going to be able to get that done. And that may just be a process of us getting it started now. It may carry over into the next Congress.

On Iran, because of the unprecedented sanctions that we put in place that really did have a crippling effect on Iran's economy, they've come to the table, and they've negotiated seriously around providing assurances that they're not developing a nuclear weapon for the first time. And they have abided by the interim rules. We have been able to freeze their program, in some cases, reduce the stockpile of nuclear material that they already had in hand. And the discussions, the negotiations have been constructive.

The international community has been unified and cohesive. There haven't been a lot of cracks in our alliance. Even countries where we have some differences, like Russia, have agreed with us and have worked with us cooperatively in trying to find ways to make sure that we can verify and have confidence going forward that Iran doesn't have the capacity to develop a nuclear weapon that could not only threaten friends of ours like Israel, trigger a nuclear arms race in the region, but could over the long term, potentially threaten us.

Whether we can actually get a deal done, we're going to have to find out over the next 3 to 4 weeks. We have presented to them a framework that would allow them to meet their peaceful energy needs. And if in fact what their leadership says, that they don't want to develop a nuclear weapon, if that is in fact true, then they've got an avenue here to provide that assurance to the world community and in a progressive, step-by-step, verifiable way, allow them to get out from under sanctions so that they can reenter as full-fledged members of the international community.

But they have their own politics, and there is a long tradition of mistrust between the two countries. And there's a sizeable portion of the political elite that cut its teeth on anti-Americanism and still finds it convenient to blame America for every ill that there is. And whether they can manage to say yes to what clearly would be better for Iran, better for the region, and better for the world, is an open question. We'll find out over the next several weeks. All right?

Q. Sir, if the—on whether or not you have the power unilaterally to relax sanctions to implement an agreement?

The President. Yes. There are a series of different sanctions. There are multilateral sanctions; there are U.N. sanctions; there are sanctions that have been imposed by us, this administration, unilaterally. And I think it's different for each of those areas.

But it—I don't want to put the cart before the horse. What I want to do is see if we in fact have a deal. If we do have a deal that I have confidence will prevent Iran from getting a nuclear weapon and that we can convince the world and the public will prevent Iran from getting a nuclear weapon, then it will be time to engage in Congress. And I think that we'll be able to make a strong argument to Congress that this is the best way for us to avoid a nuclear Iran, that it will be more effective than any other alternatives we might take, including military action.

But that requires it being a good deal. And I've said consistently that I'd rather have no deal than a bad deal, because what we don't want to do is lift sanctions and provide Iran legitimacy, but not have the verifiable mechanisms to make sure that they don't break out and produce a nuclear weapon. Okay?

Ed Henry [FOX News]. I missed you guys. I haven't done this in a while. [*Laughter*]

U.S. Strategy To Combat the Islamic State of Iraq and the Levant (ISIL) Terrorist Organization/Syria/Midterm Elections/Bipartisanship

Q. I know. I've missed you. [*Laughter*] Thank you, Mr. President. I haven't heard you say a specific thing during this news conference that you would do differently. You've been asked it a few different ways. I understand you're going to reach out, but you've talked about doing that before. It's almost like you're doubling down on the same policies and approach you've had for 6 years. And so my question is, why not pull a page from the Clinton playbook and admit you have to make a much more dramatic shift in course for these last 2 years?

And on ISIS, there was pretty dramatic setback in the last few days, with it appearing that the Syrian rebels have been routed. There are some Gitmo detainees who have rejoined the battlefield, helping ISIS and other terror groups, is what the reports are suggesting. So my question is, are we winning?

The President. Yes, I—well, I think it's too early to say whether we are winning, because as I said at the outset of the ISIL campaign, this is going to be a long-term plan to solidify the Iraqi Government, to solidify their security forces, to make sure that in addition to our air cover, that they have the capacity to run a ground game that pushes ISIL back from some of the territories that they had taken, that we have a strong international coalition that we've now built, but that they are on the ground providing the training, providing the equipment, providing the supplies that are necessary for Iraqis to fight on behalf of their territory.

And what I also said was that in Syria, that's been complicated, and that's not going to be solved any time soon. Our focus in Syria is not to solve the entire Syria situation, but rather to isolate the areas in which ISIL can operate. And there is no doubt that because of the extraordinary bravery of our men and women in uniform and the precision of our pilots and the strikes that have taken place, that ISIL is in a more vulnerable position and it is more difficult for them to maneuver than it was previously.

Now, there's a specific issue about trying to get a moderate opposition in Syria that can serve as a partner with us on the ground. That's always been the hardest piece of business to get done. There are a lot of opposition groups in Syria along a spectrum from radical jihadists who are our enemies to folks who believe in inclusive democracy and everything in between. They fight among each other. They are fighting the regime.

And what we're trying to do is to find a core group that we can work with that we have confidence in, that we've vetted, that can help in regaining territory from ISIL, and then ultimately serve as a responsible party to sit at the table in eventual political negotiations that are probably some ways off in the future.

That's always been difficult. As you know, one of the debates has consistently been, should the Obama administration provide more support to the opposition? Could that have averted some of the problems that are taking place in Syria? And as I've said before, part of the challenge is, it's a messy situation. This is not a situation where we have one single unified, broad-based, effective, reliable——

Q.——the idea that maybe we have to have leadership——

The President. [*Laughter*] Let me answer the question, Ed. And so what we are going to continue to test is, can we get a more stable, effective, cohesive, moderate opposition?

But that's not the sole measure of whether we are "winning" or not. Remember, our first focus, Ed, here is to drive ISIL out of Iraq. And what we're doing in Syria is, first and foremost, in service of reducing ISIL's capacity to resupply and send troops and then run back in over the Syrian border; to eventually reestablish a border between Iraq and Syria so that slowly, Iraq regains control of its security and its territory. That is our number-one mission. That is our number-one focus.

There are aspects of what's going on in Syria that we've got to deal with in order to reduce the scope of ISIL's operations. So, for example, our support for Kurds in Kobani, where they've been able to hold off ISIL and where we've been able to effectively strike ISIL positions consistently, that's not just because we're trying to solve a Syria problem. That's also because it gives us an opportunity to further weaken ISIL so that we can meet our number-one mission, which is Iraq.

In terms of things to do differently, I guess, Ed, your—the question you're asking is one actually I think I have answered. If you're asking about personnel or if you're asking about position on issues or what have you, then it's probably premature because I want to hear what——

Q. Your leadership, your leadership. Is there something about your leadership—[*inaudible*]—is my question.

The President. Ed, what I'd like to do is to hear from the Republicans to find out what it is that they would like to see happen. And what I'm committing to is making sure that I am open to working with them on the issues that—where they think that there's going to be cooperation.

Now, that isn't a change, because I've suggested to them before that where they think there's areas of cooperation, I'd like to see us get some things done. But the fact that they now control both Chambers of Congress, I think, means that perhaps they have more confidence that they can pass their agenda and get a bill on my desk. It means that negotiations end up perhaps being a little more real because they have larger majorities, for example, in the House, and they may be able to get some things through their caucuses that they couldn't before.

But the bottom line that the American people want to know and that I'm going to repeat here today is that my number-one goal—because I'm not running again, I'm not on the ballot, I don't have any further political aspirations—my number-one goal is just to deliver as much as I can for the American people in these last 2 years. And wherever I see an opportunity, no matter how large or how small, to make it a little bit easier for a kid to go to college, make it a little more likely that somebody is finding a good-paying job, make it a little more likely that somebody has high-quality health care, even if I'm not getting a whole loaf, I'm interested in getting whatever legislation we can get passed that adds up to improved prospects and an improved future for the American people.

Sam Stein [Huffington Post].

Selection Process to Replace Attorney General Eric H. Holder, Jr./Patient Protection and Affordable Care Act

Q. Thank you, Mr. President. Following the elections, congressional Republicans are pushing once again for major reforms to your health care act.

The President. Yes.

Q. In the past, you've said you're open to good ideas, but you don't want to undermine the bill. Can you tell us what specific ideas you're ruling out? Have the election results changed your calculus on reforming the law? And how confident are you heading into the second enrollment period? And on a totally unrelated matter—[*laughter*]—have you settled on a nominee to replace Attorney General Eric Holder, and if so, who is it? [*Laughter*]

The President. You guys want to spread out your news a little bit, don't you? You don't want it all in just one big bang. The—[*laughter*].

On the Attorney General, we have a number of outstanding candidates who we're taking a look at now, and in due course I will have an announcement. And you'll be there, Sam, when that's announced. [*Laughter*] But I'm confident that we'll find somebody who is well qualified, will elicit the confidence of the American people, will uphold their constitutional obligations and rule of law, and will get confirmed by the Senate.

On health care, there are certainly some lines I'm going to draw. Repeal of the law I won't sign. Efforts that would take away health care from the 10 million people who now have it and the millions more who are eligible to get it we're not going to support. In some cases, there may be recommendations that Republicans have for changes that would undermine the structure of the law, and I'll be very honest with them about that and say, look, the law doesn't work if you pull out that piece or that piece.

On the other hand, what I have said is there's no law that's ever been passed that is perfect. And given the contentious nature in which it was passed in the first place, there are places where, if I were just drafting a bill on our own, we would have made those changes back then, and certainly, as we've been implementing, there are some other areas where we think we can do even better.

So if in fact one of the items on Mitch McConnell's agenda and John Boehner's agenda is to make responsible changes to the Affordable Care Act to make it work better, I'm going to be very open and receptive to hearing those ideas. But what I will remind them is that despite all the contention, we now know that the law works. You've got millions of people who have health insurance who didn't have it before. You've got States that have expanded Medicaid to folks who did not have it before, including Republican Governors who've concluded, this is a good deal for their State.

And despite some of the previous predictions, even as we've enrolled more people into the Affordable Care Act and given more people the security of health insurance, health care inflation has gone done every single year since the law passed, so that we now have the lowest increase in health care costs in 50 years, which is saving us about $180 billion in reduced overall costs to the Federal Government in its—in the Medicare program.

So we are I think really proud of the work that's been done. But there's no doubt that there are areas where we can improve it. So I'll look forward to seeing what list they've got of improvements.

Q. Is the individual mandate one of those lines you can't cross?

The President. Yes, the individual mandate is a line I can't cross because the concept, borrowed from Massachusetts, from a law instituted by a former opponent of mine, Mitt Romney, understood that if you're providing health insurance to people through the private marketplace, then you've got to make sure that people can't game the system and just wait until they get sick before they go try to buy health insurance. You can't ensure that people with preexisting conditions can get health insurance unless you also say, while you're healthy, before you need it, you've got to get health insurance.

And obviously, there are hardship exemptions. We understand that there are some folks who, even with the generous subsidies that have been provided, still can't afford it. But that's a central component of the law.

In terms of enrollment, we'll do some additional announcements about that in the days to come. Starting in the middle of this month, people can sign up again. I think there are a number of people who the first time around sat on the sidelines in part because of our screw-ups on healthcare.gov. That's one area, Ed, by the way, that's very particular. We're really making sure the website works super well before the next open enrollment period. [*Laughter*] We're double- and triple-checking it. And so I think a lot of people who maybe initially thought, we're not sure how this works, let's wait and see— they're going to have an opportunity now to sign up. And what's been terrific is to see how more private insurers have come into the marketplace so that there's greater competition in more markets all around the country. The premiums that have come in that are available to people and the choices that are available are better than a lot of people, I think, had predicted.

So the law is working. That doesn't mean it can't be improved.

Major Garrett. [CBS News]
Immigration Reform/Keystone XL Pipeline Project/
Domestic Energy Production/Tax Reform/Infrastructure

Q. Thank you, Mr. President. And if you do miss us, allow me to humbly suggest we do this every week. [*Laughter*]

The President. We might. Who knows? [*Laughter*] I'm having a great time.

Q. All right. Let me go back to immigration. Moments before you walked out here, sir, Mitch McConnell said, and I quote, that if you in fact use your executive authority to legalize a certain number of millions of undocumented workers, it would "poison the well"— direct quote—and it would be "like waving a red flag in front of a bull." Do you not believe that is the considered opinion of the new Republican majority in the House and Senate? And do you also not believe what they have said in the aftermath of last night's results, that the verdict rendered by voters should stop you or should prevent you from taking this action because it was a subtext in many of the campaigns?

The President. Yes.

Q. Let me ask you a couple of specifics. Republicans haven't made a mystery about some of the things they intend to say——

The President. Hold—do I have to write all of these down? [*Laughter*]

Q. You're very well familiar with these. These will not be mysteries to you.

The President. No, but I——

Q. Keystone XL pipeline.

The President. All right.

Q. They will send you legislation on that. They will ask you to repeal the medical device tax as a part of a funding mechanism of the Affordable Care Act. And they have said they would like to repatriate some maybe $2 trillion of offshore revenue at the corporate level by reforming the corporate Tax Code without touching the individual Tax Code. To use your words, Mr. President, are any of those three lines you cannot cross? And also deal with what you perceive to be Republican attitudes about immigration.

The President. All right. I think, Major, that I answered the question on immigration. I have no doubt that there will be some Republicans who are angered or frustrated by any executive action that I may take. Those are folks, I just have to say, who are also deeply opposed to immigration reform in any form and blocked the House from being able to pass a bipartisan bill.

I have said before that I actually believe that John Boehner is sincere about wanting to get immigration reform passed, which is why for a year, I held off taking any action beyond what we had already done for the so-called DREAM kids and did everything I could to give him space and room to get something done. And what I also said at the time was, if in fact Congress—if this Congress—could not get something done, then I would take further executive actions in order to make the system work better, understanding that any bill that they pass will supplant the executive actions that I take.

So I just want to reemphasize this, Major: If in fact there is a great eagerness on the part of Republicans to tackle a broken immigration system, then they have every opportunity to do it. My executive actions not only do not prevent them from passing a law that supersedes those actions, but should be a spur for them to actually try to get something done. And I am prepared to engage them every step of the way with their ideas.

I think we should have further broad-based debate among the American people. As I've said before, I do think that the episode with the unaccompanied children changed a lot of attitudes. I think what may also change a lot of attitudes is when the public now realizes that that was a very temporary and isolated event and that in fact we have fewer illegal immigrants coming in today than we did 5 years ago, 10 years ago, or 20 years go, but that what we also have is a system that is not serving our economy well. So——

Q. Do you agree with Republicans who say the election was a referendum, at least in part, on your intentions to use executive authority for immigration?

The President. As I said before, I don't want to try to read the tea leaves on election results. What I am going to try to do as President is to make sure that I'm advancing what I think is best for the country. And here's an opportunity where I can use my administrative authorities, executive authorities, and lawfully try to make improvements on the existing system, understanding that that's not going to fix the entire problem and we're much better off if we go ahead and pass a comprehensive bill. And I hope that the Republicans really want to get it passed. If they do, they're going to have a lot of cooperation from me.

So let me just tick off: On Keystone, there's an independent process. It's moving forward. And the—I'm going to let that process play out. I've given some parameters in terms of how I think about it: Ultimately, is this going to be good for the American people? Is it going to be good for their pocketbook? Is it going to actually create jobs? Is it actually going to reduce gas prices that have been coming down? And is it going to be, on net, something that doesn't increase climate change that we're going to have to grapple with?

There's a pending case before a Nebraska judge about some of the siting. The process is moving forward, and I'm just going to gather up the facts.

I will note, while this debate about Canadian oil has been raging—keep in mind this is Canadian oil, this isn't U.S. oil—while that debate has been raging, we've seen the— some of the biggest increases in American oil production and American natural gas production in our history. We are closer to energy independence than we've ever been before or at least as we've been in decades. We are importing less foreign oil than we produce for the first time in a very long time. We've got a hundred-year supply of natural gas that, if we responsibly tap, puts us in the strongest position when it comes to energy of any industrialized country around the world. If you—when I travel to Asia or I travel to Europe, their biggest envy is the incredible homegrown U.S. energy production that is producing jobs and attracting manufacturing, because locating here means you've got lower energy costs.

So our energy sector is booming. And I'm happy to engage Republicans with additional ideas for how we can enhance that. I should note that our clean energy production is booming as well. And so Keystone I just consider as one small aspect of a broader trend that's really positive for the American people.

And let's see—see, the—Okay, medical device tax. I've already answered the question. We are going to take a look at whatever ideas—let me take a look comprehensively at the ideas that they present. Let's give them time to tell me. I'd rather hear it from them than from you.

Q. For example——

The President. Major——

Q. I'm just telling you what they said.

The President. Conceivably, I could just cancel my meeting on Friday because I've heard everything from you. [*Laughter*] I think I'd rather let Mitch McConnell——

Q. I just asked if it was a line you couldn't cross. That's all.

The President. I'd rather hear from Mitch McConnell and John Boehner what ideas they'd like to pursue, and we'll have a conversation with them on that.

On repatriation, I said in my opening remarks that there is an opportunity for us to do a tax reform package that is good for business, good for jobs, and can potentially finance infrastructure development here in the United States.

Now, the devil is in the details. So I think, conceptually, it's something where we may have some overlap, and I'm very interested in pursuing ideas that can put folks to work right now on roads and bridges and waterways and ports and a better air traffic control system. If we had one, by the way, we would reduce delays by about 30 percent. We could reduce fuel costs for airlines by about 30 percent. And hopefully, that would translate into cheaper airline tickets, which I know everybody would be interested in.

So there's all kind of work we can do on our infrastructure. This may be one mechanism that Republicans are comfortable in financing those kinds of efforts. So that will be part of the discussion that I think we're prepared for on Friday and then in the weeks to come leading into the new Congress.

Whew! Major works me, man. [*Laughter*]

Jim Acosta [CNN].

Midterm Elections/President's Agenda During
Final Years in Office/President's Role in 2014 Electoral Campaign

Q. Thank you, Mr. President. I know you don't want to read the tea leaves, but it is a fact that your party rejected you in these midterms.

The President. [*Laughter*] Yes.

Q. By and large, they did not want you out on the campaign trail in these key battleground States. How do you account for that? And your aides have said that this is the fourth quarter of your administration, but I don't know if you saw the morning talk shows, but there were several potential candidates for 2016 who are out there already. Is the clock ticking? Are you running out of time? How much time do you have left? And what do you make of the notion that you're now a lame duck?

The President. Well, traditionally, after the last midterm of a two-term Presidency, since I can't run again, that's the label that you guys apply. [*Laughter*]

Here's what I tell my team. I told them this last week, and I told them this this morning: We had this incredible privilege of being in charge of the most important organization on Earth, the U.S. Government and our military and everything that we do for good around the world.

And there's a lot of work to be done to make Government work better, to make Americans safer, to make opportunity available to more people, for us to be able to have a positive influence in every corner of the globe, the way we're doing right now in West Africa. And I'm going to squeeze every last little bit of opportunity to help make this world a better place over these last 2 years.

And some of that is going to be what we can do administratively and simple things like how do we make customer service better in every agency. Are there things that we can do to streamline how our veterans access care? Are there better ways that we can make businesses understand the programs that are available to them to promote their business or exports?

So there's a whole bunch of stuff to do on that front. And as I said before, there's going to be opportunities to work with Democrats and Republicans on Capitol Hill to get laws done. And if you look at the history of almost every President, those last 2 years, all kinds of stuff happens, in some cases, stuff that we couldn't predict.

So the one thing I'm pretty confident about, Jim, is I'm going to be busy for the next 2 years. And the one thing that I want the American people to be confident about is that every day I'm going to be filling up my time trying to figure out how I can make their lives better. And if I'm doing that, at the end of my Presidency, I'll say, we played that fourth quarter well, and we played the game well.

And the only difference between, I guess, basketball and politics is that the only score that matters is how did somebody else do, not how you did. And that's the score I'm keeping. Am I going to be able to look back and say, are more people working? Are their bank accounts better? Are more kids going to college? Is housing improved? Is the financial system more stable? Are younger kids getting a better education? Do we have greater energy independence? Is the environment cleaner? Have we done something about climate change? Have we dealt with an ongoing terrorist threat and helped to bring about stability around the world? And those things—every single day, I've got an opportunity to make a difference on those fronts, which is——

Q. And you're not satisfied with where you are now?

The President. Absolutely not. I wouldn't be satisfied as long as I'm meeting somebody who has a—doesn't have a job and wants one. I'm not going to be satisfied as long as there's a kid who writes me a letter and says, "I've got $60,000 worth of debt, and I don't know how to pay it back." And the American people aren't satisfied. So I want to do everything I can to deliver for them.

Q. And how about Democrats, the fact that they kept you out of these battleground States? Does that, kind of, bug you a little bit?

The President. Listen, I—as I think some of you saw when I was out on the campaign trail, I love campaigning. I love talking to ordinary people. I love listening to their stories. I love shaking hands and getting hugs and just seeing the process of democracy and citizenship manifest itself during an election.

But I'm also a practical guy. And ultimately, every candidate out there had to make their own decisions about what they thought would be most helpful for them. And I wanted to make sure that I'm respectful of their particular region, their particular State or congressional district, and if it was more helpful for them for me to be behind the scenes, I'm happy to do it.

Q. You don't think it was a mistake?

The President. I'll let other people analyze that. But what I will emphasize is that one of the nice things about being in the sixth year of your Presidency is, you've seen a lot of ups and downs and you've gotten more than your fair share of attention. And I've had the limelight, and I've—there have been times where the request for my appearances were endless. There have been times where, politically, we were down. And it all kind of evens out, which is why what's most important, I think, is keeping your eye on the ball, and that is, are you actually getting some good done?

Scott Horsley [National Public Radio], last question.
President's Communication With the Electorate/
Voter Participation in Political Process

Q. Thank you, Mr. President. You mentioned that where your policies actually were on the ballot, they often did better than members of your party.

The President. Yes.

Q. Does that signal some shortcoming on your part or on the party's part in framing this election and communicating to the American people what it is that Democrats stand for?

The President. I do think that one area where I know we're constantly experimenting and trying to do better is just making sure that people know exactly what it is that we're trying to accomplish and what we have accomplished in clear ways that people can—that understand how it affects them. And I think the minimum wage I talked about a lot on the campaign trail, but I'm not sure it penetrated well enough to make a difference.

Part of what I also think we've got to look at is that two-thirds of people who were eligible to vote and just didn't vote. One of the things that I'm very proud of in 2008 and 2012 when I ran for office was, we got people involved who hadn't been involved before. We got folks to vote who hadn't voted before, particularly young people.

And that was part of the promise, and the excitement was, if you get involved, if you participate, if you embrace that sense of citizenship, then things change—and not just in abstract ways, they change in concrete ways. Somebody gets a job who didn't have it before. Somebody gets health care who didn't have it before. Or a student is able to go to college who couldn't afford it before. And sustaining that, especially in midterm's elections, has proven difficult; sustaining that sense of, if you get involved, then—and if you vote, then there is going to be big change out there. And partly, I think, when they look at Washington, they say, "Nothing is working, and it's not making a difference," and there's just a constant slew of bad news coming over the TV screen, then you can understand how folks would get discouraged.

But it's my job to figure this out as best I can. And if the way we are talking about issues isn't working, then I'm going to try some different things. If the ways that we're approaching the Republicans in Congress isn't working, I'm going to try different things—whether it's having a drink with Mitch McConnell or letting John Boehner beat me again at golf or what . . . .

But I'll close with what I said in my opening statement. I am really optimistic about America. I know that runs counter to the current mood, but when you look at the facts, our economy is stronger than just about anybody's. Our energy production is better than just about anybody's. We've slashed our deficit by more than half. More people have health insurance. Our businesses have the strongest balance sheets that they've had in decades. Our young people are just incredibly talented and gifted, and more of them are graduating from high school, and more of them are going on to college, and more women are getting degrees and entering into the workforce.

And what—part of the reason I love campaigning is, you travel around the country, folks are just good. They're smart, and they're hard working. And they're not always paying a lot of attention to Washington, and in some cases, they've given up on Washington. But their impulses are not sharply partisan, and their impulses are not ideological. They're really practical, good, generous people.

So—and we continue to be a magnet for the best and brightest from all around the world. We have all the best cards relative to every other country on Earth. Our Armed Forces, you talk to them—I had a chance this morning to just call some of the—our health service that is operating in Liberia, and the amount of hope and professionalism that they've brought has galvanized the entire country, and has built—they've built a platform effectively for other countries suddenly to start coming in. And we're seeing real progress in fighting the disease in a country that just a month or a month and a half ago was desperate and had no hope.

So all that makes me optimistic. And my job over the next couple of years is to do some practical, concrete things—as much as possible with Congress; where it's not possible with Congress, on my own—to show people why we should be confident and to give people a sense of progress and a sense of hope.

That doesn't mean there aren't going to be ongoing nagging problems that are stubborn and can't be solved overnight. And probably the biggest one is the fact that despite economic growth, wages and income have still not gone up. And that's a long-term trend that we've seen for 10, 20, 30 years. And it makes people worried about not just their own situation, but whether their kids are going to be doing better than they did, which is the essence of the American Dream. I think there are some concrete things we can do to make sure that wages and incomes do go up. Minimum wage in those five States was a good start.

But I think more than anything what I want to communicate over these next 2 years is the promise and possibility of America. This is just an extraordinary country. And our democracy is messy. And we're diverse, and we're big. And there are times where you're a politician and you're disappointed with election results. But maybe I'm just getting older, I don't know. It doesn't make me mopey. It energizes me because it means that this democracy is working. And people in America were restless and impatient, and we want to get things done. And even when things are going good, we want them to do better. And that's why this is the greatest country on Earth. That's why I'm so privileged to have a chance to be President for the next couple years.

All right? Thank you, everybody.

SOURCE: Executive Office of the President. "The President's News Conference." November 5, 2014. *Compilation of Presidential Documents* 2014, no. 00820 (November 5, 2014). www.gpo.gov/fdsys/pkg/DCPD-201400820/pdf/DCPD-201400820.pdf.

OTHER HISTORIC DOCUMENTS OF INTEREST

FROM THIS VOLUME

Response to 2014 Ballot Initiatives

NOVEMBER 5 AND 8, 2014

While Democrats lost control of both houses of Congress during the 2014 midterm elections, voters were decidedly more liberal-leaning in their opinions on ballot measures. The number of initiatives dropped from a peak of 188 in 2012 to 147 in 2014, reflecting both an effort by state legislators to keep issues from moving to the voters, and a desire by some to hold measures until the 2016 presidential election, when turnout will be higher. State ballot measures in 2014 covered varied subjects, including recreational marijuana, gun control, prohibition, and abortion rights. Combined, proponents and opponents of the ballot measures that were voted on in November 2014 spent upwards of $1 billion, with much of that going toward keeping referenda from being added to the ballot.

Overall, voters approved more liberal ballot measures, even while voting against the Democrats who backed their passage. For example, in an analysis of 2014 ballot measures by *The Washington Post*, the paper found that while the initiative to legalize recreational marijuana in Alaska won by 4.6 percent, the Republican candidate for governor, Dan Sullivan, won his race against incumbent Mark Begich by 3.2 percent. Therefore, voters were 7.8 percentage points more liberal on the issue of marijuana legalization. Political analysts had initially thought that the combination of marijuana and minimum wage referenda would help give Begich the win.

LEGALIZATION OF MARIJUANA USE

Alaska, Oregon, and Washington, D.C., all had recreational marijuana use on their ballots, with voters being asked whether the state or D.C. should allow adults to possess a small amount for personal use. Notably, the D.C. measure would not legalize the sale of marijuana. In Florida, voters were asked to decide whether to legalize marijuana for medical purposes only. Political analysts closely watched the Florida race because marijuana initiatives bring out a greater number of liberal-leaning voters. With former Democratic governor Charlie Crist on the ballot running as an independent, some thought increased turnout for the marijuana referendum might also increase Crist's share of the vote.

Ultimately, the three recreational ballot measures passed. Alaska and Oregon, which will join Colorado and Washington as the only states with legalized recreational marijuana, will now be free to modify state law for use of recreational marijuana and set up a system for the sale and taxing of the drug. Washington, D.C., can also move forward; however, Congress still has the opportunity to reject the vote and continue the ban on recreational marijuana use in the nation's capital. Florida's medical marijuana measure received only 57 percent of the vote, shy of the 60 percent required to pass. Kevin Sabet, president of Project SAM (Smart Approaches to Marijuana), said it is likely voters were rejecting "the big loopholes" in the amendment rather than medical marijuana itself.

Victory in Alaska, Oregon, and Washington, D.C., is expected to have an impact on the forthcoming California recreational marijuana legalization referendum that will appear on the 2016 ballot. "The pace of reform is accelerating, other states are sure to follow," said Ethan Nadelmann, executive director of the Drug Policy Alliance, adding that the victories were "a validation of what Colorado and Washington did two years ago, and it means that the wind's at our back as we move forward nationally in California and a range of other states in 2016."

RAISING THE MINIMUM WAGE

President Barack Obama made raising the federal minimum wage, currently at $7.25 per hour, a key provision of his 2013 and 2014 State of the Union addresses. Democrats in both the House and Senate have floated proposals to raise the minimum wage to $10.10 per hour, citing strikes by fast-food workers and other low-wage employees. Although he was unable to encourage Republicans in Congress to agree to any nationwide minimum wage increase, the president did use his executive authority in February to raise the minimum wage for employees of federal contractors to $10.10 per hour. The president also encouraged governors to take action on the issue within their borders. "A majority of Americans—not just Democrats, not just independents, but Republicans too—support raising the minimum wage," Obama said.

Traditionally, voters support minimum wage increases, and all ten ballot measures on the issue since 2002 have passed. In November 2014, five states—four red and one blue—had minimum wage hikes on their ballots: Alaska, Arkansas, Illinois, Nebraska, and South Dakota. The Illinois measure would represent the highest minimum wage among the five states at $10 per hour, Arkansas and South Dakota wanted to increase theirs to $8.50 per hour, and Alaska's proposal was to increase its minimum wage from $8.75 to $9.75 per hour.

The four Republican-leaning states—Alaska, Arkansas, Nebraska, and South Dakota—approved their minimum wage referendums. Voters in Nebraska approved the increase by a vote of 59.2 percent to 40.8 percent, as did voters in South Dakota by 55.1 percent to 44.9 percent. In Arkansas, the vote was 65.9 percent in favor and 34.1 percent opposed; there the measure will increase the minimum wage incrementally until 2017 when it reaches $8.50 per hour. Alaska voted 68.9 percent to 31.1 percent to raise the minimum wage to $9.75 by 2016. After that time, minimum wage will be tied to inflation. Illinois voters also approved their minimum wage issue, which would go into effect on January 1, 2015, with 66.7 percent of the vote. AFL-CIO president Richard Trumka said that with the victories, "It's clear that American workers and their families are way ahead of the political elite when it comes to envisioning the next American chapter . . . . Their desire for bold, comprehensive and lasting economic change is the most real thing I've ever heard."

GUN CONTROL

Voters in Alabama and Washington considered gun control measures in November. In Alabama, voters were asked whether a law should be created to make it more difficult to restrict gun ownership. Washington's dueling measures were more closely watched. Two competing issues, one asking voters whether the state should require background checks at gun shows or during private gun purchases, and the other asking voters whether the state should prevent extensive background checks, appeared on the ballot. Lawmakers admitted that it was the first time in history that two similar initiatives had appeared on one ballot, and they were unsure what would happen if both passed.

In Washington, voters approved the measure that expanded background checks and rejected the more prohibitive amendment. The measure to ban background checks was defeated by nearly 55 percent to 44 percent, while the referenda calling for such checks won more than 59 percent of the vote. In response, Governor Jay Inslee said, "Voters in Washington state approved a common sense gun safety law that takes a step toward protecting our families." Brady Campaign to End Gun Violence president Dan Gross said, "The bottom line is this law will save lives. Washingtonians should sleep better tonight knowing that their state will be a safer place thanks to expanded Brady background checks." Alabama voters approved their "right to bear arms" amendment with 72.4 percent of the vote. The measure, which was heavily backed by the National Rifle Association (NRA), made changes to the state's constitution to note, "Every citizen has a fundamental right to bear arms in defense of himself or herself and the state. Any restriction on this right shall be subject to strict scrutiny."

Abortion Rights

Abortion initiatives appeared on the ballot in three states—Colorado, North Dakota, and Tennessee. Tennessee's Amendment 1 would add language to the state constitution to allow the legislature to make determinations to change, repeal, or enact state laws on abortion, including instances when a mother's life is in jeopardy or in the case of rape or incest. Voters approved the measure 52.6 percent to 47.4 percent. Opposition groups felt that the amendment would ultimately allow lawmakers to ban all abortions in the state. "This constitutional amendment kicks open the door for Tennessee politicians to do what far too many of their neighboring colleagues have done over the last several years and run roughshod over women's rights and health," said Nancy Northup, the president and CEO of the Center for Reproductive Rights. Yes on 1 backers slammed pro-choice groups for their attempts to seek a recount. "Rather than accept defeat . . . the nation's pro-abortion movement are willing to disenfranchise Tennessee voters in order to ensure that Tennessee remains an abortion destination with uninspected, unlicensed abortion facilities," said Brian Harris, president of Tennessee Right to Life and the coordinator of the Yes on 1 campaign.

In Colorado, the ballot issue asked voters whether the state should include fetuses under the definition of "person" in the state's criminal code. Voters rejected the proposal 64.8 percent to 35.2 percent. North Dakota's "life begins at conception" amendment was somewhat similar and asked voters to determine whether the state constitution should be amended to provide an "inalienable right to life" from the moment of conception. If passed, North Dakota would have become the first state to define life as beginning at conception. Voters ultimately rejected the proposal 64.1 percent to 35.9 percent.

Additional Ballot Measures

A variety of other measures appeared on ballots around the country, including California's consideration of a softening of penalties for nonviolent offenders in an effort to reduce costs and alleviate prison overcrowding. Voters approved the measure 59 percent to 41 percent.

Alabama, Maine, and Mississippi all had hunting on their ballots. Alabama and Mississippi voters passed measures that would allow the state constitution to be amended to declare hunting a right; in both states, the vote was overwhelming, with 88 percent of Mississippi voters and nearly 80 percent of Alabama voters in favor. These amendments also make hunting the preferred method of animal population control. In Maine, a contentious issue on outlawing dogs and bait in bear hunting faced significant opposition from the National Rifle Association, which said it was overly restrictive. Voters rejected the referendum 53.4 percent to 46.6 percent.

In Arkansas, which has one of the largest numbers of dry counties, voters easily defeated a measure that would legalize alcohol sales across the state, 56.9 percent to 43.1 percent. And in Missouri, voters defeated a measure that would have linked teacher salaries directly to student performance. In Colorado and Oregon, voters rejected requirements for the addition of labels to foods that have been genetically modified. A similar measure appeared on Washington's ballot in 2012, and it was handily defeated, thanks in part by $22 million in spending by major food companies Coca Cola, Pepsi, and Monsanto.

Unsurprisingly, after a series of high-profile voter ID cases in states such as North Carolina and Texas, voting rights issues also appeared on November ballots. Voters in Connecticut and Missouri took up the issue of how early voters should be allowed to cast a ballot. In Connecticut, voters rejected a proposal to expand early voting and access to absentee ballots by approximately 52 percent to 47 percent. In Missouri, voters rejected a six-day window for early voting, with more than 70 percent voting against the measure. In Montana, a ballot measure asked whether the state should end same-day voter registration, and instead require voters to register by the Friday before an election. Voters rejected the change 56.9 percent to 43.1 percent.

—Heather Kerrigan

Following are press releases from advocacy groups responding to state ballot measures including remarks from the Brady Campaign and the National Rifle Association on gun restrictions, both on November 5, 2014; a statement from the Drug Policy Alliance on November 5, 2014, in support of ballot initiatives on marijuana use; a November 5, 2014, press release from the AFL-CIO in support of the minimum wage increases that appeared before voters; and press releases from the Center for Reproductive Rights and Tennessee Yes on 1 advocacy group in response to abortion rights initiatives, on November 5, 2014, and November 8, 2014, respectively.

Brady Campaign on Washington State Gun Sales Referendum

November 5, 2014

In the only place where guns were directly on the ballot this election day, Washington state voters overwhelmingly passed Initiative 594 to expand background checks to all gun sales, including online and at gun shows. A competing initiative (Initiative 591) designed to block the implementation of background checks and sponsored by the gun lobby is trailing significantly. Washington now becomes the seventh state to require background checks on all gun sales, the fifth state since the shootings at Sandy Hook Elementary School in December 2012 (Washington, Colorado, Connecticut, Delaware, and New York).

"The bottom line is this law will save lives. Washingtonians should sleep better tonight knowing that their state will be a safer place thanks to expanded Brady background checks," said Brady Campaign President Dan Gross.

The organization issued a report, Washington State Officers Attacked, Ambushed & Killed by Armed Criminals, which showed that there are 39 percent fewer law enforcement officers killed by firearms in states with expanded background checks. In addition, states that have expanded background checks show 38 percent fewer women killed by intimate partners. Washington was the only state in the country where background checks were voted on directly by citizens this election day. The last time voters cast ballots directly on background checks was in 2000, when Colorado and Oregon citizens voted to overwhelmingly pass laws that extended background checks. Colorado's initiative passed 70 percent to 30 percent, and Oregon's passed 62 percent to 38 percent.

Brady [Campaign] President Dan Gross went on to say, "Today's great success in Washington confirms what we already knew, that the American public, in every state of this nation, overwhelmingly supports expanding background checks to keep guns out of the hands of criminals and other dangerous people. Now we plan to keep building on this exciting momentum, taking this issue directly to voters in more states and showing the gun lobby 'lap dogs' in statehouses and Congress exactly where the American people stand." Initiative 594 was the top electoral priority for the Brady Campaign and its Washington Chapters. The Brady Campaign was pleased to partner with the Washington Alliance for Gun Responsibility, by placing thousands of calls to turn out voters and placing organizers on the ground to help achieve this monumental victory.

"Make no mistake, this is a huge victory for the gun violence prevention movement and for every American who wants to live in a safer nation. It is the first direct vote in years to show exactly where the American people really stand on the gun violence issue. Most importantly, it is an inspiring indication of things to come, as we work to 'finish the job' and expand lifesaving Brady background checks to all gun sales nationwide," said Gross.

SOURCE: Brady Campaign to Prevent Gun Violence. "Washington State Voters Overwhelmingly Approve Citizens' Initiatives to Expand Background Checks to All Gun Sales." November 5, 2014. www.bradycampaign.org/press-room/washington-state-voters-overwhelmingly-approve-citizens'-initiative-to-expand-background.

NRA on Second Amendment Ballot Measures

November 5, 2014

On Tuesday, voters in Alabama, Mississippi and Maine came out in full support of protecting America's hunting heritage and Second Amendment rights. The National Rifle Association Political Victory Fund (NRA-PVF) led the way to enshrine the Right to Hunt, Fish and Harvest Wildlife in the state constitutions of Alabama and Mississippi and worked with a coalition of sportsmen's groups to protect hunters in Maine from extreme anti-hunting groups who aimed to ban traditional bear hunting methods in the state.

"Sportsmen and hunters are the true conservationists in the United States and the NRA will continue to lead efforts on the state and federal level to defend their rights," said Chris W. Cox, chairman of the NRA-PVF. "Hunting laws should be set by wildlife biologists and experts in the field who rely on sound science for wildlife management plans. On behalf of the NRA's 5 million members, we want to thank the voters of Alabama,

Mississippi, and Maine for supporting America's hunting heritage and protecting our Second Amendment freedoms."

In Alabama, NRA-backed Amendment 5 passed with an overwhelming 80 percent of the vote. The Right to Hunt and Fish amendment provides permanent protection for current and future generations of sportsmen in Alabama and ensures wildlife conservation and management decisions will be based on sound science and not the misguided emotions of anti-hunting extremists.

Also in Alabama, voters approved NRA-backed Amendment 3 to strengthen the state's existing Right to Keep and Bear Arms amendment. The words "fundamental" and "strict scrutiny" will now be added to that amendment in Alabama's state constitution. "Strict scrutiny" is a standard of judicial review that provides the highest level of protection for constitutional rights.

In Mississippi, 88 percent of voters overwhelmingly approved NRA-backed Amendment 1, the Right to Hunt, Fish and Harvest Wildlife, creating permanent protections for current and future generations of sportsmen in Mississippi. Amendment 1 ensures wildlife conservation and management decisions will be based on sound science and prevents extreme anti-hunting organizations from diminishing the state's strong hunting heritage.

Voters in Maine, for the second time in a decade, defeated efforts to ban traditional hunting methods critical to the state's wildlife management and economy. The NRA strongly opposed the Maine Bear Hunting Initiative (MBHI). The restriction would have undermined the ability to control Maine's bear population. Bear hunting is a longstanding tradition that is deeply engrained both in Maine's heritage and economy. Bear hunting contributes an estimated $60 million to the economy and sustains 900 hunting and outfitting jobs annually.

SOURCE: National Rifle Association. Institute for Legislative Action. "Stinging Defeats for Radical Anti-Hunting and Gun Control Groups." November 5, 2014. www.nraila.org/articles/20141107/voters-come-out-in-strong-support-of-americas-hunting-heritage-and-second-amendment-right.

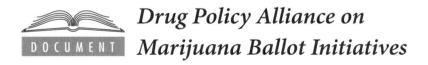

Drug Policy Alliance on Marijuana Ballot Initiatives

November 5, 2015

Voters across the country have accelerated the unprecedented momentum to legalize marijuana and end the wider drug war, with marijuana legalization measures passing in Oregon, Alaska and Washington, D.C., while groundbreaking criminal justice reforms passed in California and New Jersey.

"This Election Day was an extraordinary one for the marijuana and criminal justice reform movements," said Ethan Nadelmann, executive director of the Drug Policy Alliance. "Alaska and Oregon proved that Colorado and Washington were no flukes. Washington, D.C. voters sent a powerful message to Congress that federal marijuana prohibition has no place in the nation's capital. Voters in Florida and Guam demonstrated that medical marijuana could win big even in fairly conservative jurisdictions. And California and New Jersey revealed an electorate eager to reduce prison populations and the power of the prison industrial complex."

"These victories are even more notable for having happened in a year when Democrats were trounced at the polls," added Nadelmann. "Reform of marijuana and criminal justice policies is no longer just a liberal cause but a conservative and bipartisan one as well. On these issues at least, the nation is at last coming to its senses."

This November's successes will boost efforts already underway in states such as California, Massachusetts, Maine, Nevada and Arizona to end marijuana prohibition in 2016.

There [was] a wider spectrum of drug policy reforms on the ballot this November than ever before in American history, on everything from sentencing and bail reform to marijuana legalization, far-reaching decriminalization and medical marijuana. Among the highlights:

- Oregon voters overwhelmingly elected to make their state the third in the nation to legally regulate the production, distribution and sale of marijuana. Passage of Measure 91 accelerates the nationwide momentum in favor of legalizing marijuana and ending the wider drug war. Like the historic laws adopted in Colorado and neighboring Washington two short years ago, this new law will legalize possession of small amounts of marijuana for adults 21 and older and create a statewide system to regulate production and sales. DPA's lobbying arm, Drug Policy Action, was the single largest donor to the Oregon campaign and was deeply involved in the measure's drafting and on-the-ground campaign.
- Voters in the District of Columbia have approved Initiative 71, a ballot initiative that legalizes possession of up to two ounces of marijuana for adults over the age of 21 and allows individuals to grow up to six marijuana plants in their home. D.C. laws prevented the ballot initiative from addressing the taxation and sale of marijuana, but the D.C. Council is currently considering a bill that would tax, regulate and strictly control the sale of marijuana to adults. Drug Policy Alliance and its sister organization, Drug Policy Action, provided significant financial assistance and played a leadership role in the Initiative 71 campaign—coordinating efforts around coalition building, voter outreach, and advising on the drafting of the law. DPA's Dr. Malik Burnett also co-chaired the initiative's campaign. It's worth noting that this was the first legalization campaign in which the racial disproportionality of marijuana enforcement played a major role. (And it won with a whopping 69% of the vote—only 30 percent of voters cast ballots against the measure, and in only one of the city's 143 precincts were there more votes against it than for it!)
- Alaska became the first "red" state and the 4th nationally to approve the legal regulation of marijuana. With 36% of precincts reporting, it's leading with 53% support. DPA's lobbying arm, Drug Policy Action, supported this initiative with assistance on the drafting, as well as financial and other support for the campaign.
- Today, California voters took a significant step toward ending mass incarceration and the war on drugs by approving Proposition 47. On the heels of reforming the state's "three strikes" law in the 2012 election, Californians overwhelmingly voted to change six low-level, nonviolent offenses—including simple drug possession—from felonies to misdemeanors. DPA's lobbying arm, Drug Policy Action, supported this initiative with assistance on its drafting, as well as financial support for the campaign.

- New Jersey voters have approved Public Question No. 1 to reform New Jersey's bail system. This will reduce the number of people behind bars for low-level drug law violations and ushers in broader bail reform because it is linked to comprehensive legislation, already signed by the governor, that overhauls the state's broken bail system. DPA's New Jersey office played a pivotal role in this campaign.
- Fifty-seven percent of voters in Florida approved Amendment 2, a ballot initiative that makes Florida, with its huge population and bellwether status in American politics, the very first state in the South to see a majority vote in favor of a medical marijuana law. Nonetheless it won't be enacted into law because Florida is the only state that requires 60% to pass a ballot initiative. Even though it won't become law in Florida, it sends a powerful message throughout the South—and to Capitol Hill.
- Meanwhile, Guam's medical marijuana initiative won by 56%, making it the first U.S. territory to approve such a law. Guam is quite conservative politically, and home to a significant U.S. military presence, so this resounding victory is another confirmation of medical marijuana's broad support across the political spectrum. DPA's lobbying arm, Drug Policy Action, supported this initiative with assistance on its drafting.
- In New Mexico, voters in Santa Fe County and Bernalillo County voiced overwhelming support for marijuana decriminalization. Both the Santa Fe and Bernalillo County ballots asked voters whether they supported decriminalization of 1 ounce or less of marijuana at a city, county and state level. The passage of the advisory questions proves that voters in both counties want to decriminalize small amounts of marijuana. While this does not yet change the current law, it is a vital step in ensuring elected officials know where New Mexicans stand on this issue. Bernalillo and Santa Fe counties represent a third of the state's population. DPA's New Mexico office played a pivotal role in these campaigns.

SOURCE: Drug Policy Alliance. "Voters Across Country Accelerate Unprecedented Momentum to Legalize Marijuana, End Drug War." November 5, 2014. www.drugpolicy.org/news/2014/11/voters-across-country-accelerate-unprecedented-momentum-legalize-marijuana-end-drug-war.

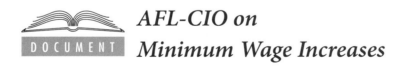 *AFL-CIO on*
Minimum Wage Increases

November 5, 2014

Despite some disappointing political results for millions of union members and all working families, the vast majority of Americans made clear that they want an economy that works for everyone. Months of unprecedented spending by corporate billionaires on television ads failed to turn voters against the idea of an economy that is built on a foundation of raising wages. This fact transcended simple Democratic and Republican political labels.

"The defining narrative of this election was confirmation, beyond a shadow of a doubt, that Americans are desperate for a new economic life," said AFL-CIO President Richard Trumka. "But the fact of the matter is that people are disillusioned by endless political bickering and eyed these elections with great dispirit. In way too many elections, they got a false choice. In these very difficult times, they did not a get a genuine economic alternative to their unhappiness and very real fear of the future. But when voters did have a chance to choose their future directly—through ballot measures—their decisions are unmistakable."

An election-night survey conducted by Peter D. Hart Research Associates found that while Republicans won many races on political grounds, voters heavily support working family issues. Voters favor increasing Social Security benefits by 61%-30%; raising the federal minimum wage by 62%-34%; taxing American corporations on profits they make overseas by 73%-21%; and increasing funding for public schools by 75%-21%. Additionally, voters opposed many traditional Republican issues such as raising the Social Security retirement age (27%-66%) and raising the Medicare eligibility age (18%-76%).

Voters sounded the loudest economic message in Alaska, Arkansas, Illinois, Nebraska and South Dakota, where minimum wage increases were overwhelmingly approved. San Francisco and Oakland also will likely raise minimum wage, and all four ballot initiatives supporting paid sick days passed. Successes such as these pave the way forward for a host of new ideas, ranging from how worker schedules are formulated to living wage legislation, paid sick leave and equal pay.

Trumka said, "It's clear that American workers and their families are way ahead of the political elite when it comes to envisioning the next American chapter. I was out there all fall. I was in almost every contested state. I spoke to hundreds and hundreds of workers. Their desire for bold, comprehensive and lasting economic change is the most real thing I've ever heard."

Where it counted, workers and their unions led intense, grassroots organizing on the ground. These efforts resulted in union members supporting working family governor candidates by 64%-32% and U.S. Senate candidates by 61%-35%.

Since its last convention, the AFL-CIO has been working to build a long-term, year-round mobilization structure that won't stop with elections. Already the AFL-CIO and allies are gearing up to press the interests of working people in the coming lame duck session of Congress, from immigration reform to trade deals that work for working families, while leading a national conversation on raising wages.

SOURCE: AFL-CIO. "Working-Class Voters Put the Economy First." November 5, 2014. www.aflcio.org/Press-Room/Press-Releases/Working-Class-Voters-Put-the-Economy-First.

Center for Reproductive Rights on Abortion Ballot Initiatives

November 5, 2014

The Center for Reproductive Rights issued the following statements on the defeat of anti-choice ballot measures in Colorado and North Dakota and passage of an anti-choice constitutional amendment in Tennessee.

Colorado

Colorado Voters Overwhelmingly Reject Measure Intended to Ban Abortion in the State

Colorado voters have resoundingly rejected a proposed constitutional amendment intended to ban abortion in Colorado. Amendment 67—which would have amended the Colorado constitution to define a "person" to include "unborn human beings"—would have also threatened to ban some forms of contraception and fertility treatments, as well as potentially criminalize both women in crisis pregnancy situations and reproductive health care providers.

Amendment 67—known as the "Brady Amendment" after a tragic case of a woman losing her pregnancy after being in a car crash with a drunk driver—was strongly supported by Personhood USA, the same extreme group that has advocated for the failed, so-called "personhood" measures on the Colorado ballot in 2008 and 2010.

Said Nancy Northup, president and CEO of the Center for Reproductive Rights:

"Voters in Colorado have, *for the third time*, seen through an attempt to advance an extreme measure that wouldn't just ban abortion, but potentially throw women and their doctors behind bars for obtaining or providing many basic reproductive health care services including contraception and fertility treatments.

"Pregnant women have a right to and deserve safe, healthy pregnancies, yet the politicians and anti-choice groups responsible for this measure have been cynically using a tragedy to strip women of their constitutional rights."

North Dakota

North Dakota Voters Reject Dangerous and Extreme Measure Designed to Cut off Access to Reproductive Health Care

The Center for Reproductive Rights applauds voters in North Dakota for rejecting Measure 1—a vaguely worded, permanent change to the State Constitution that would have severely threatened a range of essential reproductive health care services in the state, including abortion and some forms of contraception and fertility treatments.

Said Nancy Northup, president and CEO of the Center for Reproductive Rights:

"Today's victory at the North Dakota ballot box is yet another in a long history of voters from different political backgrounds and personal philosophies rejecting these extreme and unconstitutional ballot measures.

"North Dakota women are already subject to some of the most extreme abortion restrictions in the country, promoted by politicians hell-bent on choking off reproductive health care options until women have nowhere left to turn.

"North Dakotans have rejected this dangerous amendment that could have banned essential reproductive health care services like contraception, safe abortion and fertility treatments. The voters have sent a loud and clear message: women know what's best for their lives, their health, and their futures. It's time for North Dakota politicians to remember that message when they return to the capital for a new session in January."

The North Dakota legislature has already passed some of the most extreme abortion restrictions in the country, many of which are currently being challenged by the Center for Reproductive Rights on behalf of Red River Women's Clinic—the sole abortion provider in the state. The state's six week ban on abortion was permanently blocked in April 2014 by a federal district court judge and a medically unnecessary requirement that abortion providers obtain admitting privileges at a hospital within 30 miles was settled earlier this year. Just last week, the North Dakota Supreme Court upheld the state's law severely restricting access to medication abortion, effectively denying women access to an alternative to surgical abortion widely recognized as safe and effective by medical experts and organizations worldwide.

###

Tennessee

Tennessee Voters Approve Radical Constitutional Amendment Designed to Strip Women of Abortion Rights

Tennessee voters have approved a proposed constitutional amendment that strips the state constitution of its current protections for a woman's right to safe and legal abortion, becoming only the second state in the U.S. to include such extreme anti-choice language in its state constitution.

Said Nancy Northup, president and CEO of the Center for Reproductive Rights:

"In a region already devastated by underhanded abortion restrictions, Tennessee has stood up for women by providing strong constitutional protections for their reproductive rights.

"This constitutional amendment kicks open the door for Tennessee politicians to do what far too many of their neighboring colleagues have done over the last several years and run roughshod over women's rights and health.

"We call on the Governor and state legislature to consider the devastating impact restrictions on safe, legal abortion care have had on countless women in states like Mississippi and Texas before imposing similarly underhanded and harmful restrictions in Tennessee."

SOURCE: Center for Reproductive Rights. "Center for Reproductive Rights Statements on 2014 Anti-Choice Ballot Initiative Results." November 5, 2014. www.reproductiverights.org/press-room/center-for-reproductive-rights-statements-on-2014-anti-choice-ballot-initiative-results.

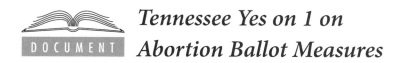

Tennessee Yes on 1 on Abortion Ballot Measures

November 8, 2014

Claiming that voter rights were violated and that ballots were not accurately counted in Tuesday's election, pro-abortion opponents of Amendment 1 have filed suit in federal court asking for the results to be nullified.

Yes on 1 responded and called the lawsuit one more example of pro-abortion activists refusing to trust the "common sense and compassion" of Tennesseans who voted to approve Amendment 1 on November 4.

"Amendment 1 was passed with a decisive majority of Tennesseans casting a vote to approve the language," said Brian Harris, president of Tennessee Right to Life and a coordinator for Yes on 1. "Even if you wrongly discount those who may have voted for Amendment 1 but not in the Governor's race, there is still a margin of almost 20,000 votes in favor of the amendment."

"Rather than accept defeat, Planned Parenthood and the nation's pro-abortion movement are willing to disenfranchise Tennessee voters in order to ensure that Tennessee remains an abortion destination with uninspected, unlicensed abortion facilities," said Harris. "That was unacceptable on election day and it remains so days after the passage of Amendment 1."

Yes on 1 remains confident that the pro-abortion lawsuit is a waste of resources and that courts will recognize the clear majority of voters who supported passage of Amendment 1.

"We are moving forward to prepare legislation that will restore common sense protections in our state and which reflect the will of the voters as clearly demonstrated in Tuesday's election," said Harris. "To do otherwise would be an abdication of the trust placed in us by Tennessee's electorate."

Review of Vote Counts:

1,353,728 combined votes were cast for all candidates running in Governor's race.

1,386,355 combined votes were cast for and against Amendment 1.

32,627 more votes were cast for Amendment 1 than the number cast in the Governor's race.

Amendment 1 required 676,865 YES votes to pass.

Amendment 1 received 729,163 YES votes or 52.6%.

Amendment 1 received 52,298 Yes votes in excess of those needed for passage.

Even if you disqualify the number of Amendment 1 votes not voting in the Governor's race but who cast a vote for or against the amendment, YES on 1 still enjoyed a margin of 19,671 votes above the number needed for approval.

SOURCE: Yes on 1. "Radical Pro-Abortion Lobby Continues Effort to Silence TN Voters." November 8, 2014. www.yeson1tn.org/pro-abortion_lawsuit.

OTHER HISTORIC DOCUMENTS OF INTEREST

FROM THIS VOLUME

FROM PREVIOUS *HISTORIC DOCUMENTS*

African Leaders Address Unrest in Burkina Faso

NOVEMBER 6 AND 17, 2014

In October 2014, riots broke out in the West African nation of Burkina Faso, sparked by an attempt by the president to extend his twenty-seven-year hold on power. The riots quickly spread across the country, and by October 30, President Blaise Compaoré dissolved the nation's government and fled the country. The military subsequently intervened and took control of the central government, a move the African Union (AU) declared illegal. The military worked with neighboring countries to complete a peaceful handover of power to an interim government.

COMPAORÉ'S TWENTY-SEVEN-YEAR RULE

Known by many as the Che Guevara of Africa, Compaoré headed a coup in 1983 to depose the government of Major Jean-Baptiste Ouedraogo. His supporter at the time, Captain Thomas Sankara, took over the presidency. But four years later, Compaoré organized another coup, this time grabbing power for himself; Sankara was killed during the coup, and the circumstances of his death have never been investigated, though many suspect Compaoré's involvement. Compaoré initially ruled Burkina Faso as one part of a three-member executive body. However, in 1989, he had his corulers arrested and executed and became the nation's sole leader, undoing a majority of the programs and policies put in place by Sankara. Compaoré easily won his election in 1991 after the major parties boycotted, and he was reelected in 1998, 2005, and 2010. The first major challenge to Compaoré's rule sprung up in 2011 when military bodyguards organized a revolt over alleged unpaid allowances. Compaoré fled the capital, but ultimately was able to hold power.

Internationally, Compaoré was one of few stable, strong allies for the West in West Africa. The United States has an air detachment stationed in the capital city of Ouagadougou, from which it conducts surveillance operations against al Qaeda-affiliated terrorist groups. Western nations have also relied heavily on Compaoré to help mediate regional tensions, specifically those in Ivory Coast.

Compaoré was closely allied with many African leaders, including former Libyan dictator Muammar Gaddafi, who was killed in 2011 during the Arab Spring uprisings, and Liberian warlord Charles Taylor. According to the International Crisis Group, Compaoré leveraged his ability to make deals with anyone, including securing hostage releases from al Qaeda in the Islamic Maghreb, to bring in an estimated $400 million in foreign aid every year, which accounted for 80 percent of Burkina Faso's expenditures. As the International Crisis Group (ICG) put it, Compaoré "developed a kind of 'mediation industry,' which has brought it political and economic dividends."

Compaoré was also known as a womanizer, and female members of the international press corps were often called to his presidential palace for late-night meetings. In a diplomatic cable posted to the WikiLeaks site, a French diplomat noted that Compaoré had a "reputation as a sexual 'gourmand' whose appetite was so strong that he had previously had 'Rasputin-like' escapades with the wife of at least one of his cabinet ministers."

OCTOBER UPRISING FORCES COLLAPSE OF GOVERNMENT

The Burkina Faso constitution, drafted in 2000, allows the president to remain in power for up to two five-year terms. Compaoré, who won his second term under the system in 2010, would be term limited in 2015, so in January 2014, his Congress for Democracy and Progress (CDP) party recommended he seek the approval of parliament to put a referendum before voters to amend the constitution and allow him another term in office. In response, some of the president's close allies and cabinet members stepped down to form an opposition party. The CDP did not back down. "The (Congress for Democracy and Progress) calls upon President Blaise Compaoré to organise the referendum to settle this and invites the political class to respect the verdict of the ballot box," CDP party official Paramanga Ernest Yonli said in June 2014 during a public rally. Assimi Kouanda, head of the party, added, "The Burkinabe people want peace and wish President Blaise Compaoré to continue his programme."

Compaoré never spoke publicly in favor of or against such a referendum. Instead, the CDP pushed for the nation's parliament to approve bringing a referendum before the voters. Opposition leaders criticized any such measure. "Today we have the proof that those in power want to fiddle with our constitution," said Bénéwendé Stanislas Sankara, the leader of the opposition Unity for the Renaissance/Sankarist Movement (UNIR/MS). "Those who try to torpedo the constitution will find themselves up against our supporters and the Burkinabe people." Sankara added, noting, "We have already said that we will call for civil disobedience."

The referendum was scheduled for debate on October 30, 2014. That morning, approximately 1,500 protesters stormed the parliament building, setting fire to cars and buildings. At least three protesters were killed in the incident, with dozens more wounded. In response, Compaoré pulled the referendum from consideration, dissolved parliament, and instituted a brief state of emergency. The protesters soon after began calling for Compaoré to resign.

Compaoré appeared on state-run television on October 30 in a brief recorded statement indicating that he would not resign, but would instead lead a transitional government with the intent of holding elections within one year to seat a new parliament. "I am available to open discussions with all parties," the president said. Western governments, including the United States, welcomed Compaoré's attempt to seat a democratically elected government and step aside at the end of his term.

MILITARY TAKEOVER AND PEACE AGREEMENT

On October 31, unable to find any consensus for his plan, Compaoré resigned his position, noting that he did so to preserve peace in the country. On his Twitter account, the former president called for "free elections to be held in Burkina Faso within 90 days at the most." Compaoré fled Burkina Faso for Ivory Coast with the assistance of France; French president François Hollande noted that the country merely ensured that Compaoré could leave "without drama" and did not actively participate in the escape.

In his absence, Gen. Honoré Nabéré Traoré, leader of the nation's military, took over as interim president to, as he put it, "save the life of the nation." Traoré vowed to hand over his position after new elections, although he did not immediately present a timeline for the establishment of a new government. Lieutenant Colonel Yacouba Isaac Zida, who had initially declared himself president, was given the position of interim prime minister.

The AU and opposition parties rejected the military takeover. "The victory of the popular uprising—and consequently the management of the transition—belongs to the people and should not in any way be confiscated by the army," the opposition coalition said in a statement. Zida responded saying, "This is not a coup d'état but a popular uprising." He added, "I salute the memory of the martyrs of this uprising and bow to the sacrifices made by our people." Still, the AU called for the immediate handover of power to a civilian body. "The Chairperson . . . stresses the duty and obligation of the defense and security forces to place themselves at the disposal of the civilian authorities who should lead the transition."

On November 5, the presidents of Ghana, Nigeria, and Senegal, acting on behalf of the Economic Community of West African States (ECOWAS), met with Zida to discuss a peaceful transition of power. In a November 6 communiqué from the group, ECOWAS expressed "deep appreciation to Lieutenant Colonel Yacouba Zida and the entire Armed Forces of Burkina Faso for demonstrating professionalism in maintaining security, law and order, as well as for their positive role in the establishment of a civilian led transitional arrangement." The AU and ECOWAS mediated talks between the military and opposition leaders and set a two-week deadline to hand over power to civilians, threatening that sanctions would be imposed if the timeline was not met.

The parties struggled to choose a new civilian leader, and Zida's inflammatory rhetoric over the threat of sanctions made reaching an agreement more difficult. Erastus Mwencha, AU deputy chairperson, accused the military of trying to take advantage of indecision to hold power for itself and said that the parties should "try to reach consensus for the sake of the country."

In mid-November, the parties developed a framework agreement that would return the nation to civilian rule, create a transitional government, and allow elections to be held in November 2015. A president was not named in the framework agreement, but it was noted that a group of religious, civil, and military leaders would choose the leader. Ultimately, former foreign minister and United Nations representative Michel Kafando was named president of the transitional government; Zida retained the position of prime minister. The AU said it "welcomes the significant progress made in Burkina Faso towards the establishment of a civilian-led transition, in conformity with the aspirations of the people of Burkina Faso for change and the consolidation of democracy." The AU added that it would "continue to support the efforts of the Burkinabe stakeholders for the completion of the Transition within the agreed timeframe" and urged other nations "to support these efforts and to mobilize the necessary support in favor of Burkina Faso."

On November 23, the interim government was announced, with six of twenty-six cabinet posts being held by military leaders, and the others held by members of political parties and civil groups. The body would be charged with ensuring adherence to the nation's timeline to hold presidential and parliamentary elections by November 2015.

—Heather Kerrigan

Following is a communiqué from the Economic Community of West African States (ECOWAS) on November 6, 2014, calling for the establishment of a transitional government in Burkina Faso; and a release from the African Union on November 17, 2014, welcoming the establishment of a transitional government in Burkina Faso.

Economic Community of West African States Summit on Burkina Faso

DOCUMENT

November 6, 2014

COMMUNIQUE BURKINA FASO CRISIS: EXTRAORDINARY SUMMIT OF THE ECOWAS AUTHORITY:

1. An Extraordinary Session of the Authority of Heads of State and Government of the Economic Community of West African States (ECOWAS) was convened in Accra, Republic of Ghana, on 6 November 2014 under the chairmanship of His Excellency John Dramani Mahama, President of the Republic of Ghana and Chairman of the Authority.

2. The Summit was convened to consider the political and security situation in Burkina Faso since the eruption of the crisis in the country on 30 October 2014, over the planed [*sic*] amendment to the Constitution.

3. The Heads of State and Government take note of the Memorandum of the President of the ECOWAS Commission on the situation in Burkina Faso.

4. Summit also welcome the outcome of the visit of H.E John Dramani Mahama of Ghana, H.E Goodluck Ebele Jonathan of Nigeria and H.E Macky Sall of Senegal which took place on 5 November in Ouagadougou, in order to help facilitate political dialogue after the recent events, namely the resignation of President Blaise Compaore [*sic*] and the dissolution of his Government.

5. The Heads of State and Government restate their commitment to the preservation of the democratic institutions, and to the Constitutional Convergence and Democratic Election Principles enshrined in the ECOWAS Supplementary Protocol on Democracy and Good Governance (2001).

6. In this regard, the Heads of State and Government endorse the Agreement reached by national stakeholders, particularly, with regard to the need to:

   i. Initiate an all-inclusive consultation among political party leaders, representatives of Civil Society Organizations, religious and traditional leaders as well as the military, to work out the composition of the transitional government.

   ii. Urgently designate a suitable eminent civilian person to lead the transition.

   iii. Immediately lift the suspension of the Constitution to enable the Constitutional Council to declare power vacancy and facilitate the establishment of a transitional government.

   iv. Secure all Burkinabe, including political party leaders, members of the Government and National Assembly, and protect human rights and property.

7. Authority decides to establish a Contact Group chaired by H.E. Macky Sall President of the Republic of Senegal and supported by the Chairman of the ECOWAS Authority, H.E John Dramani Mahama to facilitate the transition process. It further instructs the President of the Commission to appoint a Special Envoy to facilitate the process of dialogue between the stakeholders.

8. Authority expresses its heartfelt condolence to the families of those who lost their lives and its sympathy to those who have been victimized during the 30 October 2014 insurrection.

9. Summit expresses deep appreciation to Lieutenant Colonel Yacouba Zida and the entire Armed Forces of Burkina Faso for demonstrating professionalism in maintaining security, law and order, as well as for their positive role in the establishment of a civilian led transitional arrangement.

10. Summit welcomes the positive initiative of the Chairman of the Authority, H.E John Dramani Mahama, H.E Goodluck Ebele Jonathan and H.E Macky Sall, to undertake a visit to Ouagadougou and expresses its gratitude to them for their leadership in contributing to finding peaceful solution to the situation in Burkina Faso.

11. Summit commends the excellent work done by the joint UN-AU-ECOWAS Assessment Mission from 31 October to 05 November 2014 in Ouagadougou. It encourages the three organizations to continue to pursue their coordination towards ensuring the success of the transition.

12. In this regard, Summit appeals to the International Community and partners not to impose sanctions on Burkina Faso in the light of the on-going regional efforts and to continue supporting the country at these delicate times.

13. Authority remains seized with the situation in Burkina Faso and will issue further directives as it deem fit.

14. In the light of the up-coming elections in 2015, Authority reiterates its call on Member States to ensure that the processes preceding, and the actual conduct of these elections are peaceful, free, fair and credible.

15. Authority expresses profound gratitude to H.E John Dramani Mahama, President of the Republic of Ghana and the Chairman of the Authority for his personal commitment in the deepening of regional integration process and for the excellent facilities provided for the success of the Session.

DONE AT ACCRA, THIS 6TH DAY OF NOVEMBER 2014
THE AUTHORITY

SOURCE: Economic Community of West African States. "Communique Burkina Faso Crisis: Extraordinary Summit of the ECOWAS Authority." November 5, 2015. http://news.ecowas.int/presse show.php?nb=205&lang=en&annee=2014.

African Union Welcomes Agreement in Burkina Faso

DOCUMENT

November 17, 2014

The Chairperson of the Commission of the African Union (AU), Dr. Nkosazana Dlamini-Zuma, welcomes the significant progress made in Burkina Faso towards the establishment of a civilian-led transition, in conformity with the aspirations of the people of Burkina Faso for change and the consolidation of democracy.

In this regard, the Chairperson of the Commission welcomes the restoration of the Constitution and the signing, yesterday, 16 November 2014 in Ouagadougou, by all Burkinabe stakeholders, of the Transitional Constitutional Charter, in the presence of the AU Special Envoy for Burkina Faso, Mr. Edem Kodjo. She also notes with satisfaction the appointment of a civilian, Michel Kafando, as President of the Transition. She notes that these measures are in line with the communiqué of the 465th meeting of the Peace and Security Council (PSC), held on 3 November 2014. The Chairperson of the Commission expresses her deep appreciation to all the stakeholders and the Burkinabe people for their political maturity and sense of responsibility, which made it possible to take these crucial steps. She encourages them to persevere in their efforts to ensure a civilian-led transition, in accordance with the aspirations of the people of Burkina Faso and the PSC communiqué.

The Chairperson of the Commission also expresses her appreciation to the AU current Chairman, President Mohamed Ould Abel Aziz of Mauritania, as well as to Presidents Macky Sall of Senegal, Chair of the Contact Group on Burkina Faso of the Economic Community of West African States (ECOWAS), John Dramani Mahama of Ghana, current Chairman of ECOWAS, Goodluck Jonathan of Nigeria, and Faure Gnassingbe of Togo, for their important role in supporting the Burkinabe people and stakeholders. She also welcomes the contribution of the joint AU/ECOWAS/United Nations (UN) missions, comprising the AU Special Envoy, the President of the ECOWAS Commission, Kadre Desire Ouedraogo, and the UN Special Representative for West Africa, Mohamed Ibn Chambas.

The Chairperson of the Commission reiterates the AU's commitment, in close cooperation with ECOWAS and the UN, to continue to support the efforts of the Burkinabe stakeholders for the completion of the Transition within the agreed timeframe. She calls on the larger international community to support these efforts and to mobilize the necessary support in favor of Burkina Faso.

Source: African Union. "The African Union welcomes the steps taken towards a civilian-led transition in Burkina Faso." November 17, 2014. http://cpauc.au.int/en/content/african-union-welcomes-steps-taken-towards-civilian-led-transition-burkina-faso.

European Space Agency Successfully Lands Spacecraft on Comet

NOVEMBER 12, 2014

In November 2014, the European Space Agency (ESA) celebrated the culmination of a historic ten-year-long mission, the first to soft-land a spacecraft on a comet. Designed to study the comet's composition and travel through the solar system, the Rosetta mission was heralded as a tremendous scientific achievement, despite several challenges, and gathered new data that scientists believe will help them better understand our universe's origins.

The Rosetta Mission

The Rosetta mission was approved by ESA's Science Programme Committee in November 1993 as part of the agency's Horizons 2000 Science Programme. The $1.75 billion mission was designed to help scientists learn more about comets, which, as the oldest known and most primitive bodies in the solar system, could provide the earliest record of the materials from which the sun and planets formed. Scientists believe that comets crashing into the ancient Earth's surface spewed organic molecules, giving rise to life forms on the planet, and that they could also have helped fill Earth's oceans with water as they melted.

Rosetta would build on previous missions aimed at the study of comets, including ESA's Giotto mission, which flew past Halley's Comet in 1986, and NASA's Stardust mission, which collected surface samples from another comet in 2006. The Rosetta mission was to include a number of firsts: it would be the first mission to orbit and soft-land on a comet, the first spacecraft to travel alongside a comet as it enters the inner solar system, the first to provide images from a comet's surface and a subsurface analysis of the comet's composition, and the first to investigate a comet's nucleus and environment over an extended period of time.

The spacecraft designed for the mission included an orbiter known as Rosetta and a lander called Philae. The craft were named for the Rosetta Stone and an obelisk located on Philae Island in the Nile River, respectively. These ancient objects were key to understanding Egyptian hieroglyphics, and scientists hoped the mission would prove equally key to understanding the origins of the solar system and life on Earth.

The Philae probe weighed 220 pounds and was about the size of a standard washing machine. It featured ten instruments, including a drill for taking subsurface material samples, and was built by a consortium led by the German Aerospace Research Institute. During the primary phase of the mission, which was expected to last about two and a half days depending on the probe's battery life, Philae would complete several tasks and experiments. These would include taking a full panoramic view of the landing site, with some portions in 3D; capturing high resolution images of the surface immediately beneath the lander; conducting a spot analysis of the composition of the comet's surface material and collecting and analyzing subsurface materials; measuring the density, thermal properties and other characteristics of the comet's surface; and transmitting low-frequency radio signals back to the

Rosetta orbiter through the comet's nucleus to help gather data about its internal structure. ESA was hopeful that Philae's mission could be extended and it could continue collecting data for several months, but this would be dependent on the probe's solar panels and their ability to recharge its secondary battery.

At the same time, Rosetta would make remote observations of the comet and would continue to follow the object as it entered the inner solar system. Rosetta was principally an aluminum box with two solar panels that extended from its sides, spanning approximately 105 feet. Weighing in at 6,600 pounds, the orbiter was the first spacecraft to rely solely on solar cells to generate power. Its payload included eleven instruments designed to gather information about how a comet develops its coma (the field of gas and dust that surrounds it) and its tail; how its chemicals react with one another and with the solar wind; changes to the comet associated with changes in the seasons; and comet activity during perihelion, when it is in its closest position to the sun. While en route to the comet, Rosetta would also make observations of the Deep Impact Mission, Mars, and the asteroids Steins and Lutetia. Matt Taylor, ESA Rosetta project scientist, said, "Rosetta is trying to answer the very big questions about the history of our Solar System. What were the conditions like at its infancy and how did it evolve? What role did comets play in this evolution? How do comets work?"

Planning the mission and building the spacecraft was a collaborative effort spearheaded by ESA and involving scientists and engineers from across Europe and the United States. Approximately fifty contractors from fourteen European countries and the United States were also involved, with a total of 2,000 people contributing to the project. NASA, for example, contributed three of Rosetta's instruments and some of the electronics required for a spectrometer. It was also involved in conducting a number of experiments during the mission and contributed several scientists to help with other non-U.S. instruments.

The mission was originally scheduled to launch in January 2003 and land on a comet known as Wirtanen but was delayed after a failed test launch of the rocket that would carry Rosetta into space. The delay caused ESA to miss the window in which the mission could have reached Wirtanen, leading scientists to select Comet 67P/Churyumov-Gerasimenko as the mission's new target. First discovered by Ukrainian astronomers in 1969, Comet 67P is part of the "Jupiter Family" of comets, or those comets with orbits controlled by Jupiter's gravity. It is thought to have come from the Kuiper Belt, a region of space beyond Neptune's orbit that is filled with icy bodies. The comet orbits the sun every six and a half years, passing through the inner solar system between Earth and Jupiter.

"Ultimately, comets only have a limited amount of fuel and a limited lifetime," said Taylor. "We hope and expect that the comet will live up to the end of next year, hopefully, but it may not, it may break up. We don't know. That's part of the mission itself, is to try and understand how a comet works."

Those involved with the mission acknowledged the difficulty of attempting a soft-landing on a comet. "It is incredibly difficult with the low gravity, the unknown surface, the motion of the comet and spacecraft, and the lack of an active control system to land (having that would have made the lander much heavier and more complex)," Joel Parker, a planetary scientist at the Southwest Research Institute and deputy principal investigator for an ultraviolet spectrograph instrument on the Rosetta spacecraft, told *The New York Times*. "Simply put: If it was easy, it would have been done already."

The Landing

Rosetta launched on March 2, 2004, from ESA's launch station in Kourou, French Guiana. It took roughly ten years for the spacecraft to reach Comet 67P, in part because it had to complete several "flybys" of Earth and Mars to leverage their gravity to make it into the outer solar system. After traveling nearly four billion miles, Rosetta arrived at the comet on August 6, 2014.

The first images of the comet relayed to mission control in Darmstadt, Germany, showed it to have boulders, high cliffs, tall precipices and deep pits, with gas and dust spewing from the surface. Researchers had expected the comet to be semiround and regularly shaped, but it was in fact irregularly shaped with what were described as a "head," "neck," and "body." Six weeks after Rosetta arrived at the comet, ESA selected a landing site based on these initial images. Named Agilkia, the site was located on the "head" of the comet.

On November 12, the Rosetta mission successfully landed its Philae probe, with a signal confirming touchdown reaching Earth shortly after 11:00 a.m. EST. It took the lander about seven hours to reach the comet surface after beginning its descent at 3:35 a.m. At the time of the landing, the comet was approximately 310 million miles from Earth and was traveling through the solar system at about 40,000 miles an hour. Philae's descent was made without propulsion or guidance.

"Our ambitious Rosetta mission has secured a place in the history books: not only is it the first to rendezvous with and orbit a comet, but it is now also the first to deliver a lander to a comet's surface," said ESA director general Jean-Jacques Dordain. "With Rosetta we are opening a door to the origin of planet Earth and fostering a better understanding of our future. ESA and its Rosetta mission partners have achieved something extraordinary today."

Philae's descent was not without its challenges. The probe's three-legged landing gear was designed to absorb impact and prevent it from rebounding when it reached the comet surface, and ice screws—also called harpoons—in each foot were meant to drill into the comet's surface to provide stability. A small thruster on top of the lander was meant to push Philae down onto the surface while the screws drilled in. However, mission scientists discovered a problem with the thruster during descent, and it was unclear after landing whether it had performed as planned. The screw system also failed to engage, causing the probe to bounce twice as it landed. "Maybe we didn't just land once, we landed twice," quipped Dr. Stephan Ulamec, Philae lander manager.

Philae ultimately landed in a shadowy space near a cliff, leading ESA scientists to doubt whether it would be able to collect enough solar power to operate beyond its primary mission. The lander's instruments successfully relayed data to the Philae Science, Operations, and Navigation Centre at France's CNES space agency until November 14, when its batteries failed and the probe went silent.

Ongoing Research

While Philae may no longer be transmitting data, Rosetta is meant to continue traveling with the comet through December 2015, and collecting data and other observations from afar. ESA and its mission partners have also created the Rosetta Worldwide Ground-based Observing Program, through which amateur and professional astronomers are invited to help the mission team make additional observations of the comet as it approaches the sun and then begins its journey back to the outer part of the solar system. The program will collect observations between April and December 2015.

—Linda Fecteau Grimm

Following is a press release from the European Space Agency on November 12, 2014, announcing the touchdown of the Philae probe on a comet.

European Space Agency Announces Touchdown on Comet

November 12, 2014

ESA's Rosetta mission has soft-landed its Philae probe on a comet, the first time in history that such an extraordinary feat has been achieved.

After a tense wait during the seven-hour descent to the surface of Comet 67P/Churyumov–Gerasimenko, the signal confirming the successful touchdown arrived on Earth at 16:03 GMT (17:03 CET).

The confirmation was relayed via the Rosetta orbiter to Earth and picked up simultaneously by ESA's ground station in Malargüe, Argentina and NASA's station in Madrid, Spain. The signal was immediately confirmed at ESA's Space Operations Centre, ESOC, in Darmstadt, and DLR's Lander Control Centre in Cologne, both in Germany.

The first data from the lander's instruments were transmitted to the Philae Science, Operations and Navigation Centre at France's CNES space agency in Toulouse.

"Our ambitious Rosetta mission has secured a place in the history books: not only is it the first to rendezvous with and orbit a comet, but it is now also the first to deliver a lander to a comet's surface," noted Jean-Jacques Dordain, ESA's Director General.

"With Rosetta we are opening a door to the origin of planet Earth and fostering a better understanding of our future. ESA and its Rosetta mission partners have achieved something extraordinary today."

"After more than 10 years travelling through space, we're now making the best ever scientific analysis of one of the oldest remnants of our Solar System," said Alvaro Giménez, ESA's Director of Science and Robotic Exploration.

"Decades of preparation have paved the way for today's success, ensuring that Rosetta continues to be a game-changer in cometary science and space exploration."

"We are extremely relieved to be safely on the surface of the comet, especially given the extra challenges that we faced with the health of the lander," said Stephan Ulamec, Philae Lander Manager at the DLR German Aerospace Center.

"In the next hours we'll learn exactly where and how we've landed, and we'll start getting as much science as we can from the surface of this fascinating world."

Rosetta was launched on 2 March 2004 and travelled 6.4 billion kilometres through the Solar System before arriving at the comet on 6 August 2014.

"Rosetta's journey has been a continuous operational challenge, requiring an innovative approach, precision and long experience," said Thomas Reiter, ESA Director of Human Spaceflight and Operations.

"This success is testimony to the outstanding teamwork and the unique knowhow in operating spacecraft acquired at the European Space Agency over the decades."

The landing site, named Agilkia and located on the head of the bizarre double-lobed object, was chosen just six weeks after arrival based on images and data collected at distances of 30–100 km from the comet. Those first images soon revealed the comet as a world littered with boulders, towering cliffs and daunting precipices and pits, with jets of gas and dust streaming from the surface.

Following a period spent at 10 km to allow further close-up study of the chosen landing site, Rosetta moved onto a more distant trajectory to prepare for Philae's deployment.

Five critical go/no-go decisions were made last night and early this morning, confirming different stages of readiness ahead of separation, along with a final preseparation manoeuvre by the orbiter.

Deployment was confirmed at 09:03 GMT (10:03 CET) at a distance of 22.5km from the centre of the comet. During the seven-hour descent, which was made without propulsion or guidance, Philae took images and recorded information about the comet's environment.

"One of the greatest uncertainties associated with the delivery of the lander was the position of Rosetta at the time of deployment, which was influenced by the activity of the comet at that specific moment, and which in turn could also have affected the lander's descent trajectory," said Sylvain Lodiot, ESA Rosetta Spacecraft Operations Manager.

"Furthermore, we're performing these operations in an environment that we've only just started learning about, 510 million kilometres from Earth."

Touchdown was planned to take place at a speed of around 1 m/s, with the three-legged landing gear absorbing the impact to prevent rebound, and an ice screw in each foot driving into the surface.

But during the final health checks of the lander before separation, a problem was detected with the small thruster on top that was designed to counteract the recoil of the harpoons to push the lander down onto the surface. The conditions of landing—including whether or not the thruster performed—along with the exact location of Philae on the comet are being analysed.

The first images from the surface are being downlinked to Earth and should be available within a few hours of touchdown.

Over the next 2.5 days, the lander will conduct its primary science mission, assuming that its main battery remains in good health. An extended science phase using the rechargeable secondary battery may be possible, assuming Sun illumination conditions allow and dust settling on the solar panels does not prevent it. This extended phase could last until March 2015, after which conditions inside the lander are expected to be too hot for it to continue operating.

Science highlights from the primary phase will include a full panoramic view of the landing site, including a section in 3D, high-resolution images of the surface immediately underneath the lander, on-the-spot analysis of the composition of the comet's surface materials, and a drill that will take samples from a depth of 23 cm and feed them to an onboard laboratory for analysis.

The lander will also measure the electrical and mechanical characteristics of the surface. In addition, low-frequency radio signals will be beamed between Philae and the orbiter through the nucleus to probe the internal structure.

The detailed surface measurements that Philae makes at its landing site will complement and calibrate the extensive remote observations made by the orbiter covering the whole comet.

"Rosetta is trying to answer the very big questions about the history of our Solar System. What were the conditions like at its infancy and how did it evolve? What role did comets play in this evolution? How do comets work?" said Matt Taylor, ESA Rosetta project scientist.

"Today's successful landing is undoubtedly the cherry on the icing of a 4 km-wide cake, but we're also looking further ahead and onto the next stage of this ground-breaking mission, as we continue to follow the comet around the Sun for 13 months, watching as its activity changes and its surface evolves."

While Philae begins its close-up study of the comet, Rosetta must manoeuvre from its post-separation path back into an orbit around the comet, eventually returning to a 20 km orbit on 6 December.

Next year, as the comet grows more active, Rosetta will need to step further back and fly unbound 'orbits', but dipping in briefly with daring flybys, some of which will bring it within just 8 km of the comet centre.

The comet will reach its closest distance to the Sun on 13 August 2015 at about 185 million km, roughly between the orbits of Earth and Mars. Rosetta will follow it throughout the remainder of 2015, as they head away from the Sun and activity begins to subside.

"It's been an extremely long and hard journey to reach today's once-in-a-lifetime event, but it was absolutely worthwhile. We look forward to the continued success of the great scientific endeavour that is the Rosetta mission as it promises to revolutionise our understanding of comets," said Fred Jansen, ESA Rosetta mission manager.

SOURCE: European Space Agency. "Touchdown! Rosetta's Philae Probe Lands on Comet." November 12, 2014. www.esa.int/Our_Activities/Space_Science/Rosetta/Touchdown!_Rosetta_s_Philae_probe_lands_on_comet.

OTHER HISTORIC DOCUMENTS OF INTEREST

FROM PREVIOUS *HISTORIC DOCUMENTS*

United States and China Agree to Historic Climate Change Pact

NOVEMBER 12, 2014

The United States and China are the world's largest emitters of greenhouse gases, emitting 14 percent and 28 percent of the global total, respectively. Although China is party to the Kyoto Protocol, the preeminent international framework aimed at curbing climate change, the United States signed but never ratified the agreement. U.S. opponents of cutting greenhouse gas emissions have long argued that any reduction on the part of the United States would be outweighed by growing emissions in China. Accordingly, the announcement in November 2014 that the two countries had signed an agreement outlining steps they would each take to reduce emissions was met with excitement among climate and environmental advocates. Because the agreement is nonbinding, it remains to be seen whether China and the United States will follow through on their commitments. However, many hope that simply the intent might spur other nations to implement their own greenhouse gas reduction policies.

"Historic Agreement"

On November 12, 2014, President Barack Obama and Chinese president Xi Jinping met in Beijing, China, to announce their joint effort to limit greenhouse gas emissions in an effort to curb climate change. "As the world's two largest economies, energy consumers and emitters of greenhouse gases, we have a special responsibility to lead the global effort against climate change," Obama said during a press conference. "I commend President Xi, his team, and the Chinese Government for the commitment they are making to slow, peak, and then reverse the course of China's carbon emissions." President Xi said he stood ready to "work with the United States to make efforts in a number of priority areas," and "agreed to deepen practical cooperation on clean energy, environment protection, and other areas." The pair also said that they would work to ensure that the 2015 Paris conference on international climate change would reach an agreement to replace the Kyoto Protocol.

For its part of the agreement, which took nine months to negotiate, the United States said it would reduce net greenhouse gas emissions by 26 percent to 28 percent below 2005 levels by 2025. President Obama said such reduction is an "ambitious" but "achievable goal" that is "necessary to prevent the most catastrophic effects of climate change." The president added that the work toward such a reduction would help grow the clean energy sector, thus creating jobs. Already, the United States had agreed to reduce greenhouse gas emission levels by 17 percent below 2005 levels by 2020. At the time of the agreement with China, the nation had seen a reduction of approximately 10 percent below 2005 levels, which has mainly been caused by a weak economy, more fuel-efficient vehicles, and the greater use of natural gas and alternative energies over coal for electricity.

China's changes will come later. It is expected that carbon dioxide emissions will peak in China around 2030, at which point it will cap its pollution levels. The Chinese president expressed a desire to do so more quickly, an idea that was shared at the United Nations in September when Vice Premier Zhang Gaoli said the country would work "to peak total CO_2 pollution as soon as possible." The agreement marks the first time China has agreed to cap its carbon dioxide emissions. In addition to peaking its carbon emissions in 2030, China also agreed to get 20 percent of its energy from zero-carbon emission sources by 2030. China has already begun building nuclear, wind, and solar energy plants, and in 2014 its use of coal slowed by 1 percent for the first time this century.

Nonbinding Pact

The agreement between the two nations is not binding and has no enforcement authority, so it will be up to the two respective countries to hold up their end of the pact. Some have argued that this specifically benefits China. Senate minority leader Mitch McConnell, R-Ky., said the deal would be "creating havoc in my state and other states across the country" while "the Chinese . . . do nothing at all for 16 years." Such a statement has been refuted by climate change experts, who say it is impossible for China to flip a switch on December 31, 2029, and instantly begin capping emissions. "You can't stop your emissions immediately," said Ann Carlson, an environmental law professor at UCLA. "Imagine if China said they would stop emissions today. That would require massive changes to implement—no increases in driving unless cars were cleaner, no new economic growth without cutting emissions elsewhere, and so on. For China to achieve a cap in emissions by 2030, they will have to begin to find clean energy replacements very soon or seriously limit economic growth."

A majority of China's greenhouse gas emissions come from coal, which provides more than 70 percent of the nation's energy. In fact, ahead of the U.S.-China summit, the Chinese government ordered coal-burning factories in Beijing to stop production and gave time off to employees to reduce auto emissions and help clear the air in the heavily polluted city. In light of the thick, unbreathable smog in some regions, Chinese cities have begun attempting to implement their own cap-and-trade policies similar to those used in the United States and other Western nations. Depending on the success of these pilot programs, the Chinese government has said it might adopt a nationwide carbon program, which would be the largest in the world.

Reaction to the Pact

Climate change experts and environmental advocates celebrated the move. "For too long it's been too easy for both the United States and China to hide behind one another," said Bob Perciasepe, president of The Center for Climate and Energy Solutions. "People on both sides pointed to weak action abroad to delay action at home. This announcement hopefully puts those excuses behind us." However, many noted how ambitious the U.S. goals actually are. To achieve its target range of 26 percent to 28 percent reduction by 2030, the United States will have to double the pace of its current emissions cuts, set to 1.2 percent per year through 2020. Obama intends to meet this goal by encouraging new standards for and greater adoption of fuel-efficient vehicles, further reduction of emissions from power plants, and the continued development of technology to capture and store carbon. Following the summit with China, the White House noted that the president's ultimate goal is to reduce greenhouse gas emissions by 80 percent by 2050.

This ambitious effort will likely face resistance among some in the Republican Party, who the White House has deemed "leading climate deniers." The president's plan is to win support among lawmakers by making clear the energy savings that would come with reducing carbon emissions. "Consumers and businesses will save literally billions of dollars," an unnamed senior White House official told CNN. And with more energy coming from solar and wind power, job creation will increase in these sectors. McConnell argued that the opposite would be true. "Our economy can't take the President's ideological war on coal that will increase the squeeze on middle-class families and struggling miners," McConnell said. "This unrealistic plan, that the President would dump on his successor, would ensure higher utility rates and far fewer jobs." Obama will have some ability to use his executive authority to enact climate change policies, as he did in 2013 when he signed an executive order to cut power plant emissions. However, with Republicans winning control of both houses of Congress during the November 2014 midterm elections, steps toward meeting the goals outlined in the agreement will likely be limited.

The signing of the agreement raised hope among climate change experts that more countries will begin to follow suit. Robert Stavins, leader of the Project on Climate Agreements at Harvard University, called the agreement "potentially one of the most important developments in international climate negotiations in more than a decade." David Holmes, a researcher at Monash University in Australia said, "The announcement may mean climate will have to be higher on the G20 agenda despite host nation Australia trying to keep it off altogether," adding that the world's largest economies cannot ignore the impact of new climate policies on financial markets.

The U.S.-China agreement will also likely have an impact on the upcoming 20th annual UN Framework Convention on Climate Change, set to be held in December 2015 in Paris, during which delegates will complete new language to replace the Kyoto Protocol. Kyoto has faced international criticism since its inception in 1997 because of the imbalance in regulations for industrialized and developing nations. For example, those nations considered developing at the time of the agreement, including China and India, are now some of the leading contributors of greenhouse gases. Kyoto was set to expire at the close of 2012, and during the 18th annual United Nations climate change summit in Doha, Qatar, in December of that year, the agreement was extended to 2020. By that time, climate change delegates would be expected to draft and approve new climate change language to replace Kyoto. Nations who are party to the UN Framework Convention on Climate Change were expected to submit their greenhouse gas reduction pledges by March 2015. The timing of the U.S.-China agreement could encourage other countries to develop similarly ambitious plans. "[This] sends a powerful signal to those who have been sitting on the sidelines, like Australia and Canada and some developing nations," said Jake Schmidt, director of the International Program at the Natural Resources Defense Council.

—Heather Kerrigan

Following is the text of the climate change agreement between the United States and China, reached on November 12, 2014; and the edited text of a press conference between U.S. president Barack Obama and Chinese president Xi Jinping on bilateral relations between the two countries.

U.S.-China Climate Change Pact

November 12, 2014

Beijing, China, 12 November 2014

1. The United States of America and the People's Republic of China have a critical role to play in combating global climate change, one of the greatest threats facing humanity. The seriousness of the challenge calls upon the two sides to work constructively together for the common good.

2. To this end, President Barack Obama and President Xi Jinping reaffirmed the importance of strengthening bilateral cooperation on climate change and will work together, and with other countries, to adopt a protocol, another legal instrument or an agreed outcome with legal force under the Convention applicable to all Parties at the United Nations Climate Conference in Paris in 2015. They are committed to reaching an ambitious 2015 agreement that reflects the principle of common but differentiated responsibilities and respective capabilities, in light of different national circumstances.

3. Today, the Presidents of the United States and China announced their respective post-2020 actions on climate change, recognizing that these actions are part of the longer range effort to transition to low-carbon economies, mindful of the global temperature goal of 2°C. The United States intends to achieve an economy-wide target of reducing its emissions by 26%-28% below its 2005 level in 2025 and to make best efforts to reduce its emissions by 28%. China intends to achieve the peaking of CO_2 emissions around 2030 and to make best efforts to peak early and intends to increase the share of non-fossil fuels in primary energy consumption to around 20% by 2030. Both sides intend to continue to work to increase ambition over time.

4. The United States and China hope that by announcing these targets now, they can inject momentum into the global climate negotiations and inspire other countries to join in coming forward with ambitious actions as soon as possible, preferably by the first quarter of 2015. The two Presidents resolved to work closely together over the next year to address major impediments to reaching a successful global climate agreement in Paris.

5. The global scientific community has made clear that human activity is already changing the world's climate system. Accelerating climate change has caused serious impacts. Higher temperatures and extreme weather events are damaging food production, rising sea levels and more damaging storms are putting our coastal cities increasingly at risk and the impacts of climate change are already harming economies around the world, including those of the United States and China. These developments urgently require enhanced actions to tackle the challenge.

6. At the same time, economic evidence makes increasingly clear that smart action on climate change now can drive innovation, strengthen economic growth and

bring broad benefits—from sustainable development to increased energy security, improved public health and a better quality of life. Tackling climate change will also strengthen national and international security.

7. Technological innovation is essential for reducing the cost of current mitigation technologies, leading to the invention and dissemination of new zero and low-carbon technologies and enhancing the capacity of countries to reduce their emissions. The United States and China are two of the world's largest investors in clean energy and already have a robust program of energy technology cooperation. The two sides have, among other things:

- established the U.S.-China Climate Change Working Group (CCWG), under which they have launched action initiatives on vehicles, smart grids, carbon capture, utilization and storage, energy efficiency, greenhouse gas data management, forests and industrial boilers;
- agreed to work together towards the global phase down of hydrofluorocarbons (HFCs), very potent greenhouse gases;
- created the U.S.-China Clean Energy Research Center, which facilitates collaborative work in carbon capture and storage technologies, energy efficiency in buildings, and clean vehicles; and
- agreed on a joint peer review of inefficient fossil fuel subsidies under the G-20.

8. The two sides intend to continue strengthening their policy dialogue and practical cooperation, including cooperation on advanced coal technologies, nuclear energy, shale gas and renewable energy, which will help optimize the energy mix and reduce emissions, including from coal, in both countries. To further support achieving their ambitious climate goals, today the two sides announced additional measures to strengthen and expand their cooperation, using the existing vehicles, in particular the U.S.-China Climate Change Working Group, the U.S.-China Clean Energy Research Center and the U.S.-China Strategic and Economic Dialogue. These include:

- **Expanding Joint Clean Energy Research and Development:** A renewed commitment to the U.S.-China Clean Energy Research Center, including continued funding for three existing tracks on building efficiency, clean vehicles and advanced coal technology and launching a new track on the energy-water nexus;
- **Advancing Major Carbon Capture, Utilization and Storage Demonstrations:** Establishment of a major new carbon storage project based in China through an international public-private consortium led by the United States and China to intensively study and monitor carbon storage using industrial CO_2 and also work together on a new Enhanced Water Recovery (EWR) pilot project to produce fresh water from CO_2 injection into deep saline aquifers;
- **Enhancing Cooperation on HFCs:** Building on the historic Sunnylands agreement between President Obama and President Xi regarding HFCs, highly potent greenhouse gases, the two sides will enhance bilateral cooperation to begin phasing-down the use of high global warming potential HFCs

and work together in a multilateral context as agreed by the two Presidents at their meeting in St. Petersburg on 6 September 2013;

- **Launching a Climate-Smart/Low-Carbon Cities Initiative:** In response to growing urbanization and increasingly significant greenhouse gas emissions from cities and recognizing the potential for local leaders to undertake significant climate action, the United States and China will establish a new initiative on Climate-Smart/Low-Carbon Cities under the CCWG. As a first step, the United States and China will convene a Climate-Smart/Low-Carbon Cities Summit where leading cities from both countries will share best practices, set new goals and celebrate city-level leadership in reducing carbon emissions and building resilience;
- **Promoting Trade in Green Goods:** Encouraging bilateral trade in sustainable environmental goods and clean energy technologies, including through a U.S. trade mission led by Secretaries Moniz and Pritzker in April 2015 that will focus on smart low-carbon cities and smart low-carbon growth technologies; and
- **Demonstrating Clean Energy on the Ground:** Additional pilot programs, feasibility studies and other collaborative projects in the areas of building efficiency, boiler efficiency, solar energy and smart grids.

SOURCE: The White House. "U.S.-China Joint Announcement on Climate Change." November 9, 2014. www.whitehouse.gov/the-press-office/2014/11/11/us-china-joint-announcement-climate-change.

U.S. and Chinese Presidents Discuss Bilateral Agreements

November 12, 2014

President Xi. Honorable President Obama, distinguished guests, dear friends from the press, good morning. First of all, I wish to once again warmly welcome President Obama to China for this state visit.

Over the past 2 days, I had a constructive and productive discussion with President Obama. We had sincere and in-depth exchange of views and reached broad agreement on China-U.S. relations, major international and regional issues of shared interest, as well as on global issues.

We reaffirmed the agreement that we reached at the Annenberg Estate on developing the bilateral relations. We agreed to continue to advance the development of a new model of major-country relations between China and United States. We had in-depth discussions on the priority areas for advancing such relationship. We agreed to accelerate the negotiations of the BIT, and we'll make efforts to reach agreement on the core issues and the major articles of the treaty text and to initiate the negative list of negotiations in 2015.

We have reached agreement on the ITA expansion negotiations, and we are ready to work together for the early conclusion of relevant plural-lateral talks. We fully recognize the document signed between the two departments of defense on building two major confidence-building measures and agreed to continue to deepen military exchanges, mutual trust, and cooperation on that basis and develop a new type of military-to-military relations between the two countries.

We issued a joint statement on climate change and jointly announced our respective post-2020 targets. We agreed to make sure that international climate change negotiations will reach an agreement as scheduled at the Paris conference in 2015, and we agreed to deepen practical cooperation on clean energy, environment protection, and other areas.

We reaffirmed our firm opposition to terrorism of all forms and agreed to strengthen counterterrorism cooperation on intelligence sharing, terrorist financing, and cyber terrorism. And we will work together to remove the threats of various terrorists and extremist forces.

We agreed to make use of such channels as a meeting between the Chinese Ministry of Public Security and the U.S. Department of Homeland Security to have further discussions on law enforcement cooperation, which includes cracking down on transnational crimes, fugitives hunting, and recovery of criminal proceeds.

We have reached reciprocal arrangements on the visa for business travelers, tourists, and students. We have agreed to issue 10-year, multiple-entry visas for respective business travelers and tourists and 5-year, multiple-entry visas for each other's students. This will greatly promote people-to-people exchanges between our two countries and will help to promote our exchange and the cooperation in the various fields and promote the long-term development of bilateral relations. We agreed to follow such principles as mutual respect, seeking common ground while sharing differences, exchanges, and mutual learning, and manage our differences on sensitive issues in a constructive way so as to ensure the healthy and steady growth of the bilateral ties.

I told President Obama that China has proposed the Asian security concept at the CICA summit in May in order to encourage Asian countries to build common security in an inclusive and cooperative spirit. At the same time, I also said that the Pacific Ocean is broad enough to accommodate the development of both China and the United States, and our two countries should work together to contribute to security in Asia.

These are mutually complementary efforts instead of mutually exclusive ones. China and the U.S. should continue to enhance dialogue and the coordination on Asia-Pacific affairs and respect and accommodate each other's interests and concerns in this region and develop inclusive coordination.

I also introduced to President Obama China's initiatives of establishing the Asian Infrastructure Investment Bank and the Silk Road Fund. Underdeveloped infrastructure is the main bottleneck of obstructing the economic development in Asia. China has initiated the AIIB in order to offer support and facility to regional infrastructure development. These proposals and initiatives are open and inclusive in Asia; they are not exclusive. We welcome the active participation of the United States and other relevant countries so that together we can promote and share prosperity and peace in Asia-Pacific.

We recognize the positive actions both have taken in helping African countries affected by the Ebola virus to fight against the disease. We indicated that, based on the actual needs of African countries, we will leverage our respective strength and work with the rest of the international community to help affected countries to strengthen capacity-building on health and epidemic prevention so as to place the epidemic under control as soon as possible.

I thank President Obama and the U.S. team for their support to China's hosting of the APEC Economic Leaders' Meeting. Both are willing to strengthen coordination and cooperation on multilateral forums, including APEC and G–20, and to play a positive role in promoting global economic recovery and development.

China and the United States have worked closely on the negotiations of the Iranian nuclear issue, and we hope that relevant parties would persist in consensus, address differences, and make political decisions so as to promote the early conclusion of a win-win and a comprehensive agreement. China is firmly committed to achieving the denuclearization of the Korean Peninsula and to peace and the stability on the Korean Peninsula. We intend that we should address the Korean Peninsula issue through dialogue and negotiations. Relevant parties should have active contacts and dialogue so as to create conditions for the early launch—for the relaunch of the six-party talks. And the two sides also agreed to continue their exchange and the cooperation on the Afghan issue.

Ladies and gentlemen, friends, China is ready to work with the United States to make efforts in a number of priority areas and put into effect such principles as nonconfrontation, nonconflict, mutual respect, and win-win cooperation. And with unwavering spirit and unremitting efforts, we will promote new progress in building a new type—model of major-country relations between the two countries so as to bring greater benefits to our two peoples and two countries.

Thank you.

Moderator. Thank you, President Xi. I now give the floor to President Obama.

President Obama. Well, thank you, President Xi, for welcoming me and my delegation to Beijing and for the extraordinary hospitality that you and the Chinese people have shown to me on this state visit. I also want to take this opportunity to thank the people of China for the warmth and kindness they showed my wife Michelle and our daughters, as well as my mother-in-law, when they came to visit China earlier this year, another sign of the enduring friendship between our peoples.

This year marks the 35th anniversary of diplomatic relations between our two nations. I'm told that Deng Xiaoping said that we must "seek truth from facts." On this anniversary, it is a fact that the past three-and-a-half decades have seen an extraordinary growth in the ties between our two countries: more trade, more collaborations between our businesses and scientists and researchers, more connections between the Chinese and the American people, from tourists to our students. And it is a fact that when we work together, it's good for the United States, it's good for China, and it is good for the world.

As I've said many times, the United States welcomes the continuing rise of a China that is peaceful, prosperous, and stable and that plays a responsible role in the world. And we don't just welcome it, we support it. For decades, America's engagement in the Asia-Pacific, including our alliances and our stabilizing presence, have been a foundation for the region's progress, including contributing to China's remarkable economic growth. The United States has worked to expand trade and investment with China and to help integrate China into the global economy. And we want that progress to continue because, as I said before, it benefits all of us.

I believe that President Xi and I have a common understanding about how the relationship between our nations can move forward. We agree that we can expand our cooperation where our interests overlap or align. When we have disagreements, we will be candid and clear about our intentions, and we will work to narrow those differences where possible. Even as we compete and disagree in some areas, I believe we can continue to advance the security and prosperity of our people and people around the world. That's my vision for how we can develop the relationship between our countries. That's the vision that we've advanced during this visit, which has taken our bilateral, regional, and global cooperation to a new level. And I want to thank President Xi for his leadership in fostering that kind of atmosphere of cooperation.

First, President Xi and I agreed on the importance of continuing to exercise—to increase the trade that helps grow our economies and creates jobs. More U.S. exports to a growing China means more opportunities for American businesses, workers, and farmers. We agreed to work actively on a comprehensive bilateral investment treaty with high standards. And that provides the opportunity for Chinese businesses to invest in the United States, as well as opening up the opportunity for more U.S. businesses to invest here in China, creating jobs for both our countries.

We reached an understanding that will allow us to work with other nations to conclude the Information Technology Agreement, which will help us boost trade in the computer and IT products that power the 21st-century economy. We agreed to work together to promote innovation in agricultural and food security to help feed a growing planet. And our agreement to extend visas for business people, tourists, and students will help fuel growth and create jobs for Americans and Chinese.

I told President Xi that we welcome reforms being discussed here that would give the market a defining role in the Chinese economy. At the same time, I did emphasize the need for a level playing field so foreign companies can compete fairly, including against Chinese state-owned enterprises. I stressed the importance of protecting intellectual property as well as trade secrets, especially against cyber threats. And we welcomed continued progress towards a market-driven exchange rate.

Second, as the world's two largest economies, energy consumers, and emitters of greenhouse gases, we have a special responsibility to lead the global effort against climate change. That's why today I am proud that we can announce a historic agreement. I commend President Xi, his team, and the Chinese Government for the commitment they are making to slow, peak, and then reverse the course of China's carbon emissions.

Today I can also announce that the United States has set a new goal of reducing our net greenhouse gas emissions by 26 to 28 percent below 2005 levels by the year 2025. This is an ambitious goal, but it is an achievable goal. It will double the pace at which we're reducing carbon pollution in the United States. It puts us on a path to achieving the deep emissions reductions by advanced economies that the scientific community says is necessary to prevent the most catastrophic effects of climate change. It will help improve public health. It will grow our economy. It will create jobs. It will strengthen our energy security, and it will put both of our nations on the path to a low-carbon economy.

This is a major milestone in the U.S.-China relationship, and it shows what's possible when we work together on an urgent global challenge. In addition, by making this announcement today, together, we hope to encourage all major economies to be ambitious—all countries, developing and developed—to work across some of the old divides so we can conclude a strong global climate agreement next year.

Third, with respect to regional security, we agreed to a number of new measures to improve communications between our militaries in order to reduce the risk of accidents or miscalculations on the seas and in the air. President Xi and I reaffirmed our commitment to the complete denuclearization of the Korean Peninsula, and we agree that North Korea will not succeed in pursuing nuclear weapons and economic development, that it can't have both.

While the United States does not take a position on competing claims in the East and South China Seas, I made it clear that we do have a fundamental interest in freedom of navigation and that territorial disputes in the region should be resolved peacefully, in accordance with international law. And I congratulated President Xi on the initial contacts with Prime Minister Abe of Japan to help lower tensions with respect to that issue.

I reaffirmed my strong commitment to our "one China" policy based on the three joint communiqués and the Taiwan Relations Act. And we encourage further progress by both sides of the Taiwan Strait towards building ties, reducing tensions, and promoting stability on the basis of dignity and respect, which is in the interest of both sides as well as the region and the United States.

Fourth, I welcomed China's contributions to international security. This includes our mutual support for a stable, unified Afghanistan; our mutual interest in seeing the terrorist group ISIL is destroyed; the potential work we can do together in other counterterrorism activities, including those that were raised by President Xi; our mutual efforts as part of the P–5-plus-1 to reach a comprehensive solution that ensures Iran's nuclear program is exclusively peaceful. We agree that Iran should seize this historic opportunity by making the tough choices that are necessary to achieve a lasting diplomatic solution. And in addition, the United States is very appreciative of China's important contributions in West Africa in the fight against Ebola. We agreed to expand our cooperation against infectious diseases more broadly and to promote access to electricity across Africa, more examples of the difference we can make when we work together.

And finally, I reiterated to President Xi, as I have before, that America's unwavering support for fundamental human rights of all people will continue to be an important element of our relationship with China, just as it is with all the countries that we interact with around the world. And we had a very healthy exchange around these issues. President Xi gave me his sense of how China is moving forward. I described to him why it is so important for us to speak out for the freedoms that we believe are universal, rights that we believe are the birthright of all men and women, wherever they live, whether it is in New York or Paris or Hong Kong.

We think history shows that nations that uphold these rights—including for ethnic and religious minorities—are ultimately more prosperous, more successful, and more able to achieve the dreams of their people. In that context, I did note that we recognize Tibet as part of the People's Republic of China. We are not in favor of independence. But we did encourage Chinese authorities to take steps to preserve the unique cultural, religious, and linguistic identity of the Tibetan people.

In closing, I want to say that I am pleased that we continue to expand the ties between our peoples. The new visa extension that begins today will bring more Chinese tourists to the United States and more American tourists to see the magnificent sights of China. That will encourage more exchanges among our students. We welcome more Chinese students to the United States than from any other country. And I'm proud that this summer, my "100,000 Strong" program reached our goal of more than 100,000 Americans studying in China in recent years. With these visa extensions, we'll give more students this opportunity, both Chinese and American.

So every day, our people are coming to know each other better. Every day, our young people are forging friendships that will serve our countries for many decades to come. Every day, some of the barriers of mistrust are broken down, mutual understanding is promoted. And that lays the seeds for cooperation, not just today, but for future generations.

So, President Xi, thank you again for your hospitality, for the candid and very productive conversations, for your hosting of an excellent APEC summit, and for our work together.

As Deng Xiaoping said, we must seek facts from—"seek truth from facts." The truth is that we have made important progress today for the benefit of both of our nations and for the benefit of the world. The truth is that even more progress is possible as we continue to develop this important relationship. I am confident that we will be able to do so. So thank you. *Xie xie.*

[The question and answer segment with reporters has been omitted.]

SOURCE: Executive Office of the President. "The President's News Conference With President Xi Jinping of China in Beijing, China." November 12, 2014. *Compilation of Presidential Documents* 2014, no. 00848 (November 12, 2014). www.gpo.gov/fdsys/pkg/DCPD-201400848/pdf/DCPD-201400848.pdf.

OTHER HISTORIC DOCUMENTS OF INTEREST

FROM PREVIOUS *HISTORIC DOCUMENTS*

President Obama Announces Executive Action on Immigration

NOVEMBER 20 AND 21, 2014

Following another failed congressional effort at passing comprehensive immigration reform legislation, and amid growing pressure from immigration advocates and fellow Democrats, President Barack Obama announced several executive actions in the fall of 2014 that sought to address, in part, the presence of roughly eleven million illegal immigrants in the United States. In addition to improving border security and enforcement programs, the actions established a program of deferred deportations for a select population of undocumented immigrants who had been in the country for at least five years and expanded a similar, existing program for those who had been brought to the United States illegally as children. The new actions caused uproar among Republicans, who claimed Obama did not have the constitutional authority to issue such orders and raised several measures they could take to prevent their implementation.

BUILDING PRESSURE, CONGRESSIONAL INACTION

Beginning early in 2014, Obama and the House of Representatives' Republican leadership once again engaged in conversations about the need to pass immigration reform legislation. For more than ten years, Congress had debated immigration reform yet failed to approve any significant legislation. Most recently, the Senate passed a bipartisan bill in June 2013 that would increase the number of border patrol agents while establishing a pathway to citizenship for undocumented immigrants. Obama urged the House to pass a similar bill, but House Speaker John Boehner, R-Ohio, declared that the House would not vote on the Senate bill and would instead come up with its own legislation that adopted a piecemeal approach to immigration issues.

The first half of the year passed without the House taking up any of the several immigration measures that had been approved by the Judiciary Committee the previous summer. Meanwhile, a variety of Democratic lawmakers and interest groups continued pressuring Obama to take unilateral action. "We're begging the president. Go big. These [illegal immigrants] are a plus to our nation. Mr. President, please. You said you were going to do something. Do it. Act now," said Rep. Juan Vargas, D-Calif. Former House majority leader Steny Hoyer, D-Md., said Obama needed to "give immediate relief to families who are being wrenched apart and living in fear." Organizations including the AFL-CIO and the National Council of La Raza criticized Obama for deporting more than 1.4 million illegal immigrants since taking office—the most by any president since the 1950s. In the spring, the Congressional Hispanic Caucus reportedly considered a resolution condemning these deportations.

Then in June, House majority leader Eric Cantor, R-Va., lost the Republican primary to Tea Party candidate David Brat in a major upset. Political observers attributed this loss in part to criticisms that Cantor was too soft on immigration issues and speculated the development would make immigration reform much more difficult to pass in the House. Around the same time, Department of Homeland Security officials testified before Congress that border officials had apprehended more than 52,000 unaccompanied children at the Mexico border since the beginning of the year—more than double the 24,000 children apprehended in fiscal year 2014—prompting intensified calls for the administration to take action. Obama announced that he would "fix as much of our immigration system as I can on my own, without Congress" and that he would take action by the end of the summer. This timeline was delayed after Democrats urged the president to wait until after the 2014 midterm elections, for fear it would hurt their chances to win their respective races.

NEW EXECUTIVE ACTIONS

On November 20, Obama announced during a televised speech from the White House that he would take several new executive actions around immigration issues. Obama spoke in broad terms, saying the executive actions would provide additional resources for law enforcement personnel at the border, make it easier for high-skilled immigrants to remain in the United States, and "take steps to deal responsibly with the millions of undocumented immigrants who already live in our country" through a program of deferred deportation. He also issued a preemptive warning that Congress should not try to use the budget and appropriations process to prevent implementation of his actions—such as by threatening a government shutdown—adding, "[T]o those members of Congress who question my authority to make our immigration system work better, or question the wisdom of me acting where Congress has failed, I have one answer: Pass a bill."

Notably, Obama did not issue any executive orders related to these actions. With the exception of two presidential memos issued to the heads of federal departments and agencies, all other actions were revealed through intra-agency memos or fact sheets made available after Obama's speech. The president's plan would allow approximately four million undocumented immigrants who were parents of U.S. citizens or legal permanent residents to remain in the United States temporarily, without threat of deportation, as long as they registered with the government and agreed to a background check. Only those who had already been in the United States for at least five years would be eligible. By registering, they would also be allowed to apply for a three-year work permit, although they would not be eligible to vote or to receive health insurance subsidies through ObamaCare.

The actions also expanded the Deferred Action for Childhood Arrivals program, which Obama established in 2012 by executive order. Under this program, the Department of Homeland Security would defer any enforcement actions against an individual for a period of two years if an individual met the following criteria: was brought by his or her parents to the United States before the age of sixteen and was currently younger than thirty-one; had continuously lived in the United States for at least five years; was in school, had graduated high school or obtained a GED, or was an honorably discharged U.S. veteran; and had no criminal record and was not perceived as a threat to national security. The 2014 actions lifted the age cap and changed the cutoff date for eligibility from pre-June 2007 arrivals to pre-January 2010 arrivals. These changes extended eligibility to approximately 330,000 additional immigrants, according to Pew Research Center estimates. The 2014 actions also lengthened the work permits and timeframe for deferred deportations under the program from two years to three.

Other actions included "implement[ing] a Southern Border and Approaches Campaign Strategy to fundamentally alter the way in which we marshal resources to the border." Under this program, the Department of Homeland Security would commission three task forces to focus on enhancing security of the southern maritime border, the southern land border and West Coast, and investigations to support the other two task forces. They also increased the number of visas available for skilled workers and spouses of green card holders; granted deferred deportations to some immediate relatives of U.S. citizens and legal permanent residents who "seek to enlist in the Armed Forces"; provided a discount to the first 10,000 immigrant applicants to the new deferred deportation program to help increase participation; and shifted deportation priorities to focus on those who have been convicted of felonies or "significant" misdemeanors.

In addition to these actions, Obama issued two memos to heads of executive departments and agencies on November 21. The first one called for government officials to work with private and nonfederal public actors to develop recommendations for streamlining and improving the legal immigration system, including modernizing the IT systems used in visa processing, and to establish metrics to measure progress in implementing said recommendations. The second established an interagency White House Task Force on New Americans charged with identifying and supporting successful state and local efforts to integrate immigrants and to determine how those efforts could be expanded and replicated. The task force was given 120 days to develop and submit a plan to the president for advancing the integration of "new Americans." Within a year, the task force was expected to provide a status report on the memo's implementation.

CRITICISMS AND LEGAL QUESTIONS

Republicans immediately pounced on the announcement, claiming that Obama did not have the constitutional authority to issue such orders and criticizing him for acting unilaterally. "The American people want both parties to focus on solving problems together; they don't support unilateral action from a president who is more interested in partisan politics than working with the people's elected representatives. That is not how American democracy works," said Boehner. "By ignoring the will of the American people, President Obama has cemented his legacy of lawlessness and squandered what little credibility he had left." Interestingly, just a few days before, a poll conducted by NBC and *The Wall Street Journal* found that while 57 percent supported creating a pathway for illegal immigrants to eventually become U.S. citizens, only 38 percent supported Obama taking executive action on immigration without Congress's approval.

Some Republicans raised the possibility of suing the president for overstepping his authority, while others called for his impeachment. House minority leader Nancy Pelosi, D-Calif., defended the president, saying his actions "fall well within the clear constitutional and legal authority of his office, and the well-established precedent set by every president since Eisenhower." Angela Maria Kelley, vice president for immigration policy at the Center for American Progress, noted that executive action was a "tried and true component of immigration policy used by 11 presidents, 39 times in the last 60 years." *The New York Times* reported that Secretary of Homeland Security Jeh Johnson and a group of advisors had spent time in the months preceding Obama's announcement exploring the legal limits of presidential powers to determine whether such action would be allowed and concluded that the president did have the authority to issue these particular orders.

Obama and administration spokespeople sought to assuage concerns about the executive actions by stating that any congressional action would supersede his orders. Prior to the president's announcement, White House press secretary Josh Earnest said that if the House passed the immigration bill that had already been approved by the Senate, Obama would "retract" his executive actions.

NEXT STEPS

U.S. Citizenship and Immigration Services, part of the Department of Homeland Security, is expected to begin accepting applications for the expanded childhood immigrants program in February 2015 and for the new deferred deportation program in May 2015. As of publishing, Congress had not passed immigration reform legislation.

—Linda Fecteau Grimm

Following is the text of an address to the nation by President Barack Obama on November 20, 2014, on the issue of immigration reform; and two presidential memorandums issued on November 21, 2014, regarding integrating immigrants into American society and making changes to the visa system.

President Obama Addresses the Nation on Immigration Reform

November 20, 2014

My fellow Americans, tonight I'd like to talk with you about immigration.

For more than 200 years, our tradition of welcoming immigrants from around the world has given us a tremendous advantage over other nations. It's kept us youthful, dynamic, and entrepreneurial. It has shaped our character as a people with limitless possibilities, people not trapped by our past, but able to remake ourselves as we choose. But today, our immigration system is broken, and everybody knows it.

Families who enter our country the right way and play by the rules watch others flout the rules. Business owners who offer their workers good wages and benefits see the competition exploit undocumented immigrants by paying them far less. All of us take offense to anyone who reaps the rewards of living in America without taking on the responsibilities of living in America. And undocumented immigrants who desperately want to embrace those responsibilities see little option but to remain in the shadows or risk their families being torn apart. It's been this way for decades. And for decades, we haven't done much about it.

When I took office, I committed to fixing this broken immigration system. And I began by doing what I could to secure our borders. Today, we have more agents and technology deployed to secure our southern border than at any time in our history. And over the past 6 years, illegal border crossings have been cut by more than half. Although this summer there was a brief spike in unaccompanied children being apprehended at our border, the number of such children is now actually lower than it's been in nearly 2 years. Overall, the number of people trying to cross our border illegally is at its lowest level since the 1970s. Those are the facts.

Meanwhile, I worked with Congress on a comprehensive fix, and last year, 68 Democrats, Republicans, and Independents came together to pass a bipartisan bill in the Senate. It wasn't perfect. It was a compromise. But it reflected common sense. It would have doubled the number of border patrol agents while giving undocumented immigrants a pathway to citizenship if they paid a fine, started paying their taxes, and went to the back of the line. And independent experts said that it would help grow our economy and shrink our deficits.

Had the House of Representatives allowed that kind of bill a simple yes-or-no vote it would have passed with support from both parties, and today, it would be the law. But for a year and a half now, Republican leaders in the House have refused to allow that simple vote.

Now, I continue to believe that the best way to solve this problem is by working together to pass that kind of commonsense law. But until that happens, there are actions I have the legal authority to take as President—the same kinds of actions taken by Democratic and Republican Presidents before me—that will help make our immigration system more fair and more just.

Tonight I am announcing those actions. First, we'll build on our progress at the border with additional resources for our law enforcement personnel so that they can stem the flow of illegal crossings and speed the return of those who do cross over. Second, I'll make it easier and faster for high-skilled immigrants, graduates, and entrepreneurs to stay and contribute to our economy, as so many business leaders have proposed. Third, we'll take steps to deal responsibly with the millions of undocumented immigrants who already live in our country. I want to say more about this third issue, because it generates the most passion and controversy. Even as we are a nation of immigrants, we're also a nation of laws. Undocumented workers broke our immigration laws, and I believe that they must be held accountable, especially those who may be dangerous. That's why, over the past 6 years, deportations of criminals are up 80 percent. And that's why we're going to keep focusing enforcement resources on actual threats to our security: felons, not families; criminals, not children; gang members, not a mom who's working hard to provide for her kids. We'll prioritize, just like law enforcement does every day.

But even as we focus on deporting criminals, the fact is, millions of immigrants in every State, of every race and nationality, still live here illegally. And let's be honest: Tracking down, rounding up, and deporting millions of people isn't realistic. Anyone who suggests otherwise isn't being straight with you. It's also not who we are as Americans. After all, most of these immigrants have been here a long time. They work hard, often in tough, low-paying jobs. They support their families. They worship at our churches. Many of their kids are American-born or spent most of their lives here, and their hopes, dreams, and patriotism are just like ours. As my predecessor President Bush once put it, "They are a part of American life."

Now, here's the thing: We expect people who live in this country to play by the rules. We expect that those who cut the line will not be unfairly rewarded. So we're going to offer the following deal: If you've been in America for more than 5 years; if you have children who are American citizens or legal residents; if you register, pass a criminal background check, and you're willing to pay your fair share of taxes, you'll be able to apply to stay in this country temporarily without fear of deportation. You can come out of the shadows and get right with the law. That's what this deal is.

Now, let's be clear about what it isn't. This deal does not apply to anyone who has come to this country recently. It does not apply to anyone who might come to America illegally in the future. It does not grant citizenship or the right to stay here permanently or offer the same benefits that citizens receive. Only Congress can do that. All we're saying is, we're not going to deport you.

I know some of the critics of this action call it amnesty. Well, it's not. Amnesty is the immigration system we have today: millions of people who live here without paying their taxes or playing by the rules, while politicians use the issue to scare people and whip up votes at election time.

That's the real amnesty: leaving this broken system the way it is. Mass amnesty would be unfair. Mass deportation would be both impossible and contrary to our character. What I'm describing is accountability, a commonsense, middle-ground approach: If you meet the criteria, you can come out of the shadows and get right with the law. If you're a criminal, you'll be deported. If you plan to enter the U.S. illegally, your chances of getting caught and sent back just went up.

The actions I'm taking are not only lawful, they're the kinds of actions taken by every single Republican President and every single Democratic President for the past half century. And to those Members of Congress who question my authority to make our immigration system work better or question the wisdom of me acting where Congress has failed, I have one answer: Pass a bill.

I want to work with both parties to pass a more permanent legislative solution. And the day I sign that bill into law, the actions I take will no longer be necessary. Meanwhile, don't let a disagreement over a single issue be a deal breaker on every issue. That's not how our democracy works, and Congress certainly shouldn't shut down our Government again just because we disagree on this. Americans are tired of gridlock. What our country needs from us right now is a common purpose, a higher purpose.

Most Americans support the types of reforms I've talked about tonight. But I understand the disagreements held by many of you at home. Millions of us, myself included, go back generations in this country, with ancestors who put in the painstaking work to become citizens. So we don't like the notion that anyone might get a free pass to American citizenship.

I know some worry, immigration will change the very fabric of who we are or take our jobs or stick it to middle class families at a time when they already feel like they've gotten the raw deal for over a decade. I hear those concerns. But that's not what these steps would do. Our history and the facts show that immigrants are a net plus for our economy and our society. And I believe it's important that all of us have this debate without impugning each other's character.

Because for all the back and forth of Washington, we have to remember that this debate is about something bigger. It's about who we are as a country and who we want to be for future generations.

Are we a nation that tolerates the hypocrisy of a system where workers who pick our fruit and make our beds never have a chance to get right with the law? Or are we a nation that gives them a chance to make amends, take responsibility, and give their kids a better future?

Are we a nation that accepts the cruelty of ripping children from their parents' arms? Or are we a nation that values families and works together to keep them together?

Are we a nation that educates the world's best and brightest in our universities, only to send them home to create businesses in countries that compete against us? Or are we a nation that encourages them to stay and create jobs here, create businesses here, create industries right here in America?

That's what this debate is all about. We need more than politics as usual when it comes to immigration. We need reasoned, thoughtful, compassionate debate that focuses on our hopes, not our fears. I know the politics of this issue are tough. But let me tell you why I have come to feel so strongly about it.

Over the past years, I have seen the determination of immigrant fathers who worked two or three jobs without taking a dime from the government and at risk any moment of losing it all, just to build a better life for their kids. I've seen the heartbreak and anxiety of children whose mothers might be taken away from them just because they didn't have the right papers. I've seen the courage of students who, except for the circumstances of their birth, are as American as Malia or Sasha, students who bravely come out as undocumented in hopes they could make a difference in the country they love.

These people—our neighbors, our classmates, our friends—they did not come here in search of a free ride or an easy life. They came to work and study and serve in our military and, above all, contribute to America's success.

Tomorrow I'll travel to Las Vegas and meet with some of these students, including a young woman named Astrid Silva. Astrid was brought to America when she was 4 years old. Her only possessions were a cross, her doll, and the frilly dress she had on. When she started school, she didn't speak any English. She caught up to other kids by reading newspapers and watching PBS, and she became a good student. Her father worked in landscaping. Her mom cleaned other people's homes. They wouldn't let Astrid apply to a technology magnet school, not because they didn't love her, but because they were afraid the paperwork would out her as an undocumented immigrant. So she applied behind their back and got in. Still, she mostly lived in the shadows, until her grandmother, who visited every year from Mexico, passed away, and she couldn't travel to the funeral without risk of being found out and deported. It was around that time she decided to begin advocating for herself and others like her, and today, Astrid Silva is a college student working on her third degree.

Are we a nation that kicks out a striving, hopeful immigrant like Astrid, or are we a nation that finds a way to welcome her in? Scripture tells us that we shall not oppress a stranger, for we know the heart of a stranger; we were strangers once too.

My fellow Americans, we are and always will be a nation of immigrants. We were strangers once too. And whether our forebears were strangers who crossed the Atlantic or the Pacific or the Rio Grande, we are here only because this country welcomed them in and taught them that to be an American is about something more than what we look like or what our last names are or how we worship. What makes us Americans is our shared commitment to an ideal: that all of us are created equal and all of us have the chance to make of our lives what we will.

That's the country our parents and grandparents and generations before them built for us. That's the tradition we must uphold. That's the legacy we must leave for those who are yet to come.

Thank you. God bless you, and God bless this country we love.

Source: Executive Office of the President. "Address to the Nation on Immigration Reform." November 20, 2014. *Compilation of Presidential Documents* 2014, no. 00877 (November 20, 2014). www.gpo.gov/fdsys/pkg/DCPD-201400877/pdf/DCPD-201400877.pdf.

President Obama Issues Memorandum on Streamlining the Visa System

November 21, 2014

Memorandum for the Heads of Executive Departments and Agencies
Subject: Modernizing and Streamlining the U.S. Immigrant Visa System for the 21st Century

Throughout our Nation's history, immigrants have helped the United States build the world's strongest economy. Immigrants represent the majority of our PhDs in math, computer science, and engineering, and over one quarter of all U.S.-based Nobel laureates over the past 50 years were foreign-born. Immigrants are also more than twice as likely as native-born Americans to start a business in the United States. They have started one of every four American small businesses and high-tech startups, and more than 40 percent of Fortune 500 companies were founded by immigrants or their children.

But despite the overwhelming contributions of immigrants to our Nation's prosperity, our immigration system is broken and has not kept pace with changing times. To address this issue, my Administration has made commonsense immigration reform a priority, and has consistently urged the Congress to act to fix the broken system. Such action would not only continue our proud tradition of welcoming immigrants to this country, but also reduce Federal deficits, increase productivity, and raise wages for all Americans. Immigration reform is an economic, national security, and moral imperative.

Even as we continue to seek meaningful legislative reforms, my Administration has pursued administrative reforms to streamline and modernize the legal immigration system. We have worked to simplify an overly complex visa system, one that is confusing to travelers and immigrants, burdensome to businesses, and results in long wait times that negatively impact millions of families and workers. But we can and must do more to improve this system. Executive departments and agencies must continue to focus on streamlining and reforming the legal immigration system, while safeguarding the interest of American workers.

Therefore, by the authority vested in me as President by the Constitution and the laws of the United States of America, and in order to modernize and streamline the U.S. immigration system, I hereby direct as follows:

Section 1. Recommendations to Improve the Immigration System.

(a) Within 120 days of the date of this memorandum, the Secretaries of State and Homeland Security (Secretaries), in consultation with the Director of the Office of Management and Budget, the Director of the National Economic Council, the Assistant to the President for Homeland Security and Counterterrorism, the Director of the Domestic Policy Council, the Director of the Office of Science and Technology Policy, the Attorney General, and the Secretaries of Agriculture, Commerce, Labor, and Education, shall develop:

(i) in consultation with private and nonfederal public actors, including business people, labor leaders, universities, and other stakeholders, recommendations to streamline and improve the legal immigration system—including immigrant and non-immigrant visa processing—with a focus on reforms that reduce Government costs, improve services for applicants, reduce burdens on employers, and combat waste, fraud, and abuse in the system;

(ii) in consultation with stakeholders with relevant expertise in immigration law, recommendations to ensure that administrative policies, practices, and systems use all of the immigrant visa numbers that the Congress provides for and intends to be issued, consistent with demand; and

(iii) in consultation with technology experts inside and outside the Government, recommendations for modernizing the information technology infrastructure underlying the visa processing system, with a goal of reducing redundant systems, improving the experience of applicants, and enabling better public and congressional oversight of the system.

(b) In developing the recommendations as set forth in subsection (a) of this section, the Secretaries shall establish metrics for measuring progress in implementing the recommendations and in achieving service-level improvements, taking into account the Federal Government's responsibility to protect the integrity of U.S. borders and promote economic opportunity for all workers.

Sec. 2. General Provisions.

(a) Nothing in this memorandum shall be construed to impair or otherwise affect:

(i) the authority granted by law to an executive department, agency, or the head thereof; or

(ii) the functions of the Director of the Office of Management and Budget relating to budgetary, administrative, or legislative proposals.

(b) This memorandum shall be implemented consistent with applicable law and subject to the availability of appropriations.

(c) This memorandum is not intended to, and does not, create any right or benefit, substantive or procedural, enforceable at law or in equity by any party against the United States, its departments, agencies, or entities, its officers, employees, or agents, or any other person.

(d) The Secretary of State is hereby authorized and directed to publish this memorandum in the *Federal Register*.

BARACK OBAMA

SOURCE: Executive Office of the President. "Memorandum on Modernizing and Streamlining the United States Immigrant Visa System for the 21st Century." November 21, 2014. *Compilation of Presidential Documents* 2014, no. 00881 (November 21, 2014). www.gpo.gov/fdsys/pkg/DCPD-201400881/pdf/DCPD-201400881.pdf.

President Obama Issues Memorandum on Immigrants and Refugees

DOCUMENT

November 21, 2014

Memorandum for the Heads of Executive Departments and Agencies
Subject: Creating Welcoming Communities and Fully Integrating Immigrants and Refugees

Our country has long been a beacon of hope and opportunity for people from around the world. Nearly 40 million foreign-born residents nationwide contribute to their communities every day, including 3 million refugees who have resettled here since 1975. These new Americans significantly improve our economy. They make up 13 percent of the population, but are over 16 percent of the labor force and start 28 percent of all new businesses. Moreover, immigrants or their children have founded more than 40 percent of Fortune 500 companies, which collectively employ over 10 million people worldwide and generate annual revenues of $4.2 trillion.

By focusing on the civic, economic, and linguistic integration of new Americans, we can help immigrants and refugees in the United States contribute fully to our economy and their communities. Civic integration provides new Americans with security in their rights and liberties. Economic integration empowers immigrants to be self-sufficient and allows them to give back to their communities and contribute to economic growth. English language acquisition allows new Americans to attain employment or career advancement and be more active civic participants.

Our success as a Nation of immigrants is rooted in our ongoing commitment to welcoming and integrating newcomers into the fabric of our country. It is important that we develop a Federal immigrant integration strategy that is innovative and competitive with those of other industrialized nations and supports mechanisms to ensure that our Nation's diverse people are contributing to society to their fullest potential.

Therefore, I am establishing a White House Task Force on New Americans, an interagency effort to identify and support State and local efforts at integration that are working and to consider how to expand and replicate successful models. The Task Force, which will engage with community, business, and faith leaders, as well as State and local elected officials, will help determine additional steps the Federal Government can take to ensure its programs and policies are serving diverse communities that include new Americans.

By the authority vested in me as President by the Constitution and the laws of the United States of America, I hereby order as follows:

Section 1. White House Task Force on New Americans.

(a) There is established a White House Task Force on New Americans (Task Force) to develop a coordinated Federal strategy to better integrate new Americans into communities and support State and local efforts to do the same. It shall be co-chaired by the Director of the Domestic Policy Council and Secretary of Homeland Security, or their designees. In addition to the Co-Chairs, the Task Force shall consist of the following members:

  (i) the Secretary of State;

  (ii) the Attorney General;

  (iii) the Secretary of Agriculture;

   (iv) the Secretary of Commerce;

   (v) the Secretary of Labor;

   (vi) the Secretary of Health and Human Services;

   (vii) the Secretary of Housing and Urban Development;

   (viii) the Secretary of Transportation;

   (ix) the Secretary of Education;

   (x) the Chief Executive Officer of the Corporation for National and Community Service;

   (xi) the Director of the Office of Management and Budget;

   (xii) the Administrator of the Small Business Administration;

   (xiii) the Senior Advisor and Assistant to the President for Intergovernmental Affairs and Public Engagement;

   (xiv) the Director of the National Economic Council;

   (xv) the Assistant to the President for Homeland Security and Counterterrorism; and

   (xvi) the Director of the Office of Science and Technology Policy.

(b) A member of the Task Force may designate a senior-level official who is from the member's department, agency, or office, and is a full-time officer or employee of the Federal Government, to perform day-to-day Task Force functions of the member. At the direction of the Co-Chairs, the Task Force may establish sub-groups consisting exclusively of Task Force members or their designees under this subsection, as appropriate.

(c) The Secretary of Homeland Security shall appoint an Executive Director who will determine the Task Force's agenda, convene regular meetings of the Task Force, and supervise work under the direction of the Co-Chairs. The Department of Homeland Security shall provide funding and administrative support for the Task Force to the extent permitted by law and subject to the availability of appropriations. Each executive department or agency shall bear its own expenses for participating in the Task Force.

Sec. 2. Mission and Function of the Task Force.

(a) The Task Force shall, consistent with applicable law, work across executive departments and agencies to:

   (i) review the policies and programs of all relevant executive departments and agencies to ensure they are responsive to the needs of new Americans and the receiving communities in which they reside, and identify ways in which such programs can be used to increase meaningful engagement between new Americans and the receiving community;

   (ii) identify and disseminate best practices at the State and local level;

   (iii) provide technical assistance, training, or other support to existing Federal grantees to increase their coordination and capacity to improve long-term integration and foster welcoming community climates;

(iv) collect and disseminate immigrant integration data, policies, and programs that affect numerous executive departments and agencies, as well as State and local governments and nongovernmental actors;

(v) conduct outreach to representatives of nonprofit organizations, State and local government agencies, elected officials, and other interested persons that can assist with the Task Force's development of recommendations;

(vi) work with Federal, State, and local entities to measure and strengthen equitable access to services and programs for new Americans, consistent with applicable law; and

(vii) share information with and communicate to the American public regarding the benefits that result from integrating new Americans into communities.

(b) Within 120 days of the date of this memorandum, the Task Force shall develop and submit to the President an Integration Plan with recommendations for agency actions to further the integration of new Americans. The Integration Plan shall include:

(i) an assessment by each Task Force member of the status and scope of the efforts by the member's department, agency, or office to further the civic, economic, and linguistic integration of new Americans, including a report on the status of any offices or programs that have been created to develop, implement, or monitor targeted initiatives concerning immigrant integration; and

(ii) recommendations for issues, programs, or initiatives that should be further evaluated, studied, and implemented, as appropriate.

(c) The Task Force shall provide, within 1 year of the date of this memorandum, a status report to the President regarding the implementation of this memorandum. The Task Force shall review and update the Integration Plan periodically, as appropriate, and shall present to the President any updated recommendations or findings.

Sec. 3. General Provisions.

(a) Nothing in this memorandum shall be construed to impair or otherwise affect:

(i) the authority granted by law to an executive department, agency, or the head thereof; or

(ii) the functions of the Director of the Office of Management and Budget relating to budgetary, administrative, or legislative proposals.

(b) This memorandum shall be implemented consistent with applicable law and subject to the availability of appropriations.

(c) This memorandum is not intended to, and does not, create any right or benefit, substantive or procedural, enforceable at law or in equity by any party against the United States, its departments, agencies, or entities, its officers, employees, or agents, or any other person.

(d) The Secretary of Homeland Security is hereby authorized and directed to publish this memorandum in the *Federal Register*.

BARACK OBAMA

SOURCE: Executive Office of the President. "Memorandum on Creating Welcoming Communities and Fully Integrating Immigrants and Refugees." November 21, 2014. *Compilation of Presidential Documents 2014*, no. 00882 (November 21, 2014). www.gpo.gov/fdsys/pkg/DCPD-201400882/pdf/DCPD-201400 882.pdf.

OTHER HISTORIC DOCUMENTS OF INTEREST

FROM PREVIOUS *HISTORIC DOCUMENTS*

OPEC Fails to Respond
to Falling Oil Prices

NOVEMBER 27, 2014

After years of steadily high prices, from mid- to late 2014, the per-barrel price of oil fell by 40 percent. This negatively impacted countries that rely on oil exports to keep their economies afloat but marked a positive change for consumers who were paying lower prices at the pump. The Organization of the Petroleum the Exporting Countries (OPEC), whose members account for 40 percent of global oil production, failed to work with its members to convince them to reduce production, which left oil prices in free fall through the end of the year.

STEEP DECLINE IN OIL PRICES

Oil prices have remained at approximately $100 per barrel since 2010 because suppliers have been unable to meet demand from rapidly growing nations such as China, even given a global daily output of 75 million barrels. The situation became even more difficult as conflict spread in key oil-producing nations in the Middle East, including Iraq, Syria, and Libya, and control of oil fields fell into the hands of militant factions. It is estimated that the Islamic State of Iraq and the Levant (ISIL) is selling oil, procured through hostile take-over of oil fields, on the black market at as low as $30 per barrel. These ongoing conflicts, in addition to sanctions on Iranian oil imports into European Union nations, reduced supply by 3 million barrels per day.

However, as global economic powerhouses, such as those in Asia, Europe, and the United States felt the effects of the economic downturn, demand for oil began to rapidly decrease. At the same time, many western nations explored new energy efficiency measures to reduce dependence on foreign oil and lower greenhouse gas emissions. According to the International Energy Agency (IEA), the falling demand coupled with ramped-up production around the world meant that supply would outpace demand by late 2014, quickly driving prices to historic lows. According to the IEA, demand for crude oil in 2014 was estimated at 200,000 barrels per day, the lowest since 2009.

As prices began to fall in 2014 from their peak of $115 per barrel in June, analysts looked to OPEC to see whether it would work with its members to slow production. Many OPEC members rely on oil revenues to keep their economies afloat, and falling prices were having a growing impact. At OPEC's annual meeting on November 27, 2014, Saudi Arabia, the world's second-largest oil producer, positioned itself against smaller nations such as Iran and Venezuela. The latter two countries wanted OPEC to cut production, but Saudi Arabia refused to agree to any plan that would force it to reduce output because it feared losing its market share, especially in North America. Saudi Arabia argued that when oil prices fell in the 1980s, the country cut back production and lost market share, which it has struggled to gain back. "It is not in the interest of OPEC producers to cut their production, whatever the price is," said Ali al-Naimi, Saudi Arabia's oil minister.

Without the support of one of its biggest members, OPEC failed to take action. In a press release issued at the conclusion of the conference, the body agreed "in the interest of restoring market equilibrium, the Conference decided to maintain the production level of 30.0 mb/d [million barrels per day]," adding, "Member Countries confirmed their readiness to respond to developments which could have an adverse impact on the maintenance of an orderly and balanced oil market." At the conclusion of the summit, OPEC secretary-general Abdalla Salem El-Badri said, "We will produce 30 million barrels a day for the next six months, and we will watch to see how the market behaves." Inaction caused world oil prices to tumble to $80 per barrel following the meeting, and down again to $60 per barrel within a month.

NORTH AMERICAN OIL DRILLING

As oil prices rose in the early part of the decade and suppliers struggled to keep up, drilling companies in Canada and the United States took advantage and began further exploration into hard-to-extract areas including Canada's Alberta oil sands and shale formations across the United States.

In the United States, the new drilling method to extract shale from deep below the earth, known as hydraulic fracturing, or fracking for short, helped add four million additional barrels of oil each day to the global supply. In 2008, oil produced from American shale made up 0.5 percent of the global oil supply. By the end of 2014, that number rose to 3.7 percent. Fracking is a controversial issue because of its potential environmental impact. States including Arkansas, New York, North Dakota, Ohio, Oklahoma, Pennsylvania, Texas, and West Virginia, where there are large shale deposits, have debated the safety of the practice and have been faced with lawsuits from citizens who say their groundwater has been irreparably damaged by the practice. Additionally, fracking is expensive and new wells need to constantly be drilled. After its first year in production, a shale well's output will drop approximately 65 percent.

By late 2014, as oil prices fell, shale drillers were at risk of being driven out of business because the high cost of drilling was beginning to outweigh the profits. A survey by *The Economist* found that in 2013, of eight large independent oil firms, average operating costs ranged from $10 to $20 per barrel of oil, which means that even at $60 per barrel, the companies still stand to make a profit. However, once the newer wells hit their second and third years of production, this money will dry up and investment for new wells is required. Some drilling companies had already been operating at a loss, making up their difference in revenue and expenditures by issuing bonds, so any new investment required might not be feasible in light of falling profits. Falling oil prices will impact the various American oil companies differently—some are drilling in areas like Texas where it is cheap and easy to transport crude to market, but in North Dakota transportation can be far more costly. Shale drilling did decline somewhat by the start of 2015, but the U.S. Energy Information Administration (EIA) believes that in 2015, the United States will contribute an additional 700,000 barrels per day to the global market.

VARIED IMPACT

On December 2, International Monetary Fund (IMF) managing director Christine Lagarde said that falling oil prices would have a positive impact on the global economy: "if we have a 30 percent decline, [growth is] likely to be an additional 0.8 percent for most advanced economies, because all of them are importers of oil." However, she cautioned that net exporters of oil will likely feel the opposite effect. Mentioning nations like Iran, Russia, and Venezuela, Lagarde said they are "all countries that will be affected significantly by the decline in the oil price," adding, "Venezuela is clearly one . . . where it could be difficult."

For individuals, falling global oil prices meant lower prices on gasoline. In the United States, the EIA estimates that if prices remain low throughout 2015, drivers will spend an average of $550 less on gasoline than in 2014. And that is beneficial to the economy, because it means consumers will be spending that money elsewhere. Goldman Sachs economists estimated that if oil prices stayed low, it would equate to a tax break of $100 billion to $125 billion. But budgets in shale states are likely to see decreased revenues from production if oil companies in those states discontinue drilling due to its high cost.

Western Europe and the largest Asian nations including China, India, and Japan see falling prices as a boon to their own economies. Because these nations are largely oil importers—India, for example, imports 75 percent of its oil—lower prices put more money back in government coffers, a welcome relief after years of global recession. In Japan, the nation has suffered a severe trade deficit for the past few years, largely because of an increasing need to import energy resources following the 2011 Fukushima nuclear meltdown, so the decline could equate to billions of dollars in reduced spending.

However, for oil exporting nations the impact was far less positive. In Russia, one of the world's largest oil producers, oil revenues make up 45 percent of the nation's budget and 70 percent of its export income, so any fluctuation in price has a significant impact. For every dollar decrease in the price of a barrel of oil, Russia loses an estimated $2 billion in annual revenue. The steep decline at the end of 2014, coupled with ongoing tension in the region, put the nation's currency, the ruble, into free fall. In response, the country's central bank hiked interest rates to stop Russians from selling their money and halt the run on consumer goods like cars, electronics, and appliances. If oil prices remain low, global economists predict that the nation's economy will contract between 0.7 percent and 4.5 percent in 2015. Despite this, Russia views the situation similarly to Saudi Arabia—if it cuts production now, it risks losing market share when prices rise. "If we cut, the importer countries will increase their production and this will mean a loss of our niche market," said Russia's energy minister, Alexander Novak.

In Saudi Arabia, the government is relying on an estimated $750 billion fund set aside to cover its deficits from lost oil revenue, which are estimated at 14 percent of GDP in 2015, if oil prices remain low. Experts predict that, although the country could reverse the falling prices by cutting its own production, it has refused to do so because it fears the growth of the U.S. oil market. "In terms of production and pricing of oil by Middle East producers, they are beginning to recognize the challenge of U.S. production," said Robin Mills, the head of consulting at Manaar Energy.

In Venezuela, where oil exports account for 96 percent of the nation's total export market, the economy was already struggling before the oil crisis, and there is now concern that continuing downward pressure on oil prices could force the South American nation into default. The government faces difficult decisions to keep its economy out of recession and reduce inflation, which was above 60 percent in late 2014. One of the biggest potential revenue generators for the government of Nicolas Maduro would be to end, or at least drastically reduce, fuel subsidies, which cost an estimated $12.5 billion per year. But Maduro has stood by the subsidy, saying, "There's no rush, we're not going to throw more gasoline on the fire that already exists with speculation and induced inflation." Venezuela has repeatedly called on OPEC to aid in the crisis, even indicating that price manipulation might be the true cause of declining prices. "We are convinced that [the decline] does not result from fundamental market conditions but that there is price manipulation to create economic problems for the large oil-producing countries," said Venezuela's foreign minister, Rafael Ramírez.

Iran was already in a difficult position before oil prices began falling. The nation is heavily dependent on oil exports to keep its economy afloat, and sanctions from the European Union and United States on oil imports over Iran's failure to reach an agreement on its nuclear program hampered sales to the West. The IMF estimates that to balance its budget through oil exports, Iran needs the price of oil to rise to $131 per barrel. To alleviate some pressure, the Iranian government began cutting fuel subsidies for citizens, an unpopular move, and one that added to the weakening demand for oil worldwide.

—Heather Kerrigan

Following is a November 27, 2014, press release from the Organization of the Petroleum Exporting Countries (OPEC) at the conclusion of its annual conference.

OPEC Fails to Take Action Amid Falling Oil Prices

November 27, 2014

The 166th Meeting of the Conference of the Organization of the Petroleum Exporting Countries (OPEC) was held in Vienna, Austria, on Thursday, 27th November 2014 under the Chairmanship of its President, HE Abdourhman Ataher Al-Ahirish, Libyan Vice Prime Minister for Corporations and Head of its Delegation.

The Conference congratulated HE Adil Abd Al Mahdi on his appointment as Minister of Oil of Iraq, and thanked his predecessor in office, HE Abdul-Kareem Luaibi Bahedh, for his contribution to the work of the Organization.

The Conference elected HE Mrs. Diezani Alison-Madueke CON, Minister of Petroleum Resources of Nigeria and Head of its Delegation, as President of the Conference for one year, with effect from 1st January 2015, and HE Dr. Mohammed Bin Saleh Al Sada, Minister of Energy and Industry of Qatar and Head of its Delegation, as Alternate President, for the same period.

The Conference reviewed the Secretary General's report, the report of the Economic Commission Board (ECB) and a number of administrative matters. The Conference also exchanged views on developments in multilateral environment negotiations, including preparations for COP20/CMP10 which will be held shortly in Lima, Peru; the status of the Organization's on-going energy dialogue with the European Union (EU); its continued cooperative work with various other international organizations for the G-20; as well as its energy dialogue with the Russian Federation and others.

The Conference reviewed the oil market outlook, as presented by the Secretary General, in particular supply/demand projections for the first, second, third and fourth quarters of 2015, with emphasis on the first half of the year. The Conference also considered forecasts for the world economic outlook and noted that the global economic recovery was continuing, albeit very slowly and unevenly spread, with growth forecast at 3.2% for 2014 and 3.6% for 2015.

The Conference also noted, importantly, that, although world oil demand is forecast to increase during the year 2015, this will, yet again, be offset by the projected increase of 1.36 mb/d in non-OPEC supply. The increase in oil and product stock levels in OECD countries, where days of forward cover are comfortably above the five-year average, coupled with the on-going rise in non-OECD inventories, are indications of an extremely well-supplied market.

Recording its concern over the rapid decline in oil prices in recent months, the Conference concurred that stable oil prices—at a level which did not affect global economic growth but which, at the same time, allowed producers to receive a decent income and to invest to meet future demand—were vital for world economic wellbeing. Accordingly, in the interest of restoring market equilibrium, the Conference decided to maintain the production level of 30.0 mb/d, as was agreed in December 2011. As always, in taking this decision, Member Countries confirmed their readiness to respond to developments which could have an adverse impact on the maintenance of an orderly and balanced oil market.

Agreeing on the need to be vigilant given the uncertainties and risks associated with future developments in the world economy, the Conference directed the Secretariat to continue its close monitoring of developments in supply and demand, as well as non-fundamental factors such as speculative activity, keeping Member Countries fully briefed on developments.

The Conference appointed Dr. Bernard Mommer, Venezuelan Governor for OPEC, as Chairman of the Board of Governors for the year 2015, and Mr. Ahmed Messili, Algerian Governor for OPEC, as Alternate Chairman for the same period, with effect from 1st January 2015.

The Conference decided to extend the tenure of HE Abdalla S. El-Badri as Secretary General for a further period of six months, until 31st December 2015.

The Conference approved the Budget of the Organization for the year 2015.

The Conference resolved that its next Ordinary Meeting will convene in Vienna, Austria, on Friday, 5th June 2015, immediately after the OPEC International Seminar on "Petroleum: An Engine for Development" which will take place at the Vienna Hofburg Palace on 3rd and 4th June 2015.

Finally, the Conference again expressed its appreciation to the Government and the people of the Republic of Austria, as well as the authorities of the City of Vienna, for their warm hospitality and the excellent arrangements made for the Meeting.

SOURCE: Organization of the Petroleum Exporting Countries. "OPEC 166th meeting concludes." November 27, 2014. www.opec.org/opec_web/en/press_room/2938.htm.

OTHER HISTORIC DOCUMENTS OF INTEREST

FROM THIS VOLUME

- Russian President on the State of Russia's Economy, p. 627

FROM PREVIOUS *HISTORIC DOCUMENTS*

- House and EPA Release Reports on Natural Gas Drilling, *2011*, p. 210

December

Federal Response to Racial Profiling

DECEMBER 1, 8, AND 18, 2014

After five years of review and in the wake of two high-profile shootings of unarmed black men by white police officers, the Department of Justice released a series of rules for federal law enforcement agencies to ensure racial profiling and bias are not used during national security, intelligence, and law enforcement activities. The guidelines will also apply to state and local law enforcement officials who aid in federal activities; however, profiling will still be permitted in some federal policing. Attorney General Eric Holder called the revised regulations "a major and important step forward to ensure effective policing by federal law enforcement officials and state and local law enforcement participating in federal task forces throughout the nation."

RESPONSE TO SHOOTINGS

On July 17, 2014, Eric Garner, an unarmed black man, was approached by Staten Island, New York, police for allegedly selling black market cigarettes. When Garner refused to comply with the officer's instructions, he was placed in a chokehold. In a video of the incident taken by a bystander, Garner can be heard repeatedly saying "I can't breathe." The officer did not release the chokehold until Garner was secured in handcuffs on the ground. Garner subsequently became unresponsive and on the way to the hospital suffered a heart attack and died. The medical examiner reported that the chokehold, among other existing health conditions, contributed to Garner's death.

Less than one month later, in Ferguson, Missouri, eighteen-year-old African American Michael Brown was approached by a white police officer after refusing to comply with his instructions to move from the middle of the road to the sidewalk. Reports vary widely over what happened following the initial interaction. After an altercation between the officer and Brown at the officer's car, Brown ran away from the scene. He then turned and ran back toward the officer, at which point Brown was shot dead.

Both shootings sparked massive protests across the country and calls from the African American community to place greater regulations on law enforcement agencies to ensure that racial profiling is not a part of policing. In both the Brown and Garner cases, grand juries were convened, and they each declined to indict the officers involved in the incidents.

Following the outcry from the shootings, President Barack Obama called on Attorney General Holder to begin holding meetings with communities across the country to work toward building trust between minority groups and the police. The first meeting was held on December 1 in Atlanta, Georgia, at a church where Martin Luther King Jr. was once a pastor. Holder was repeatedly interrupted during his speech by protesters chanting "No justice, no peace." Holder allowed the protesters go on before they were escorted out. "There will be a tendency on the part of some to condemn what we just saw, but we should not," the attorney general said. "What we saw there was a genuine expression of concern and involvement. And it is through that level of involvement, that level of concern and I hope a level of perseverance and commitment, that change ultimately will come."

During his speech, Holder announced that he would issue revised federal racial profiling guidelines that would "institute rigorous new standards and robust safeguards to help end racial profiling once and for all." He also spoke about the ongoing civil rights investigations into the Missouri and New York shootings. He said the investigations "have been rigorous" and "independent from the beginning." Holder admitted that the bar is high in federal civil rights cases, but that his department "will see these investigations through to their appropriate conclusions, so that we can continue to work with the community to restore trust, to rebuild understanding, and to foster renewed cooperation between law enforcement and community members."

Holder held additional meetings in December and into 2015 in cities including Chicago, Illinois; Cleveland, Ohio; Memphis, Tennessee; Oakland, California; and Philadelphia, Pennsylvania. The meetings culminated in March 2015 in the selection of six cities to act as pilot sites for a new Department of Justice initiative that will work toward racial reconciliation between police departments and communities.

New Federal Regulations

The Justice Department's first federal profiling guidelines were released in 2003, pertained only to intelligence and law enforcement activities, and only spoke to profiling by race and ethnicity. The revised guidelines, issued after five years of review on December 8, 2014, added national security to those activities covered under the regulations and also expanded profiling to include gender, national origin, religion, sexual orientation, and gender identity. According to the Department of Justice, the new guidance "reaffirms the Federal government's deep commitment to ensuring that its law enforcement agencies conduct their activities in an unbiased manner. Biased practices, as the Federal government has long recognized, are unfair, promote mistrust of law enforcement, and perpetuate negative and harmful stereotypes." Additionally, the regulations state "biased practices are ineffective."

Two overarching provisions were presented in the new regulations. The first said that when federal law enforcement officers are carrying out routine activities, they cannot base those activities on race, gender, ethnicity, national origin, gender identity, sexual orientation, or religion, the exception being that officers may use such information as it is given in a suspect's description. The second provision said that federal officers may consider these characteristics "only to the extent that there is trustworthy information . . . that links persons possessing a particular listed characteristic to an identified criminal incident, scheme, or organization, a threat to national or homeland security, a violation of Federal immigration law, or an unauthorized intelligence activity."

One notably absent activity in the new regulations pertains to Department of Homeland Security (DHS) functions. During airline passenger screening, border inspections, and activities initiated by the Secret Service, law enforcement will be permitted to continue using profiling tactics. According to a DHS statement, "This does not mean that officers and agents are free to profile. To the contrary, DHS' existing policies make it categorically clear that profiling is prohibited, while articulating limited circumstances where it is permissible to rely in part on these characteristics, because of the unique nature of border and transportation security as compared to traditional law enforcement." Minority groups, specifically those who have faced the effects of racial profiling from DHS, took issue with the absence of regulations and called for better protection. According to Rajdeep Singh, senior director of law and policy at the Sikh Coalition, the new federal regulations are "flawed and misleading" and resemble "a used car with new paint." He continued, "The car looks better, but once you look underneath the hood, you realize it's unsafe to drive."

Civil rights groups, while happy with movement on the federal level, continued to call for similar regulations at the state and local level that deal specifically with nonfederal policing activities. Such regulations, many hoped, would help prevent future incidents similar to the Brown and Garner cases. Speaking about the new federal regulations, Laura Murphy, the American Civil Liberties Union (ACLU) Washington Legislative Office director, said that "several components . . . do little to nothing to protect some minority populations that have to endure unfair targeting by law enforcement every day." She added that the federal guidance "is not an adequate response to the crisis of racial profiling in America."

The Congressional Black Caucus has also taken up the issue. "The fact that our country—the greatest country in the world—remains mired in race relations issues in the year 2014 is an embarrassment," said Rep. Marcia Fudge, D-Ohio, the chair of the caucus. "If we are to learn anything from the tragic death of Michael Brown, we must first acknowledge that we have a race issue that we are not addressing." The caucus had already introduced a number of racial profiling bills in the years prior to the Garner and Brown shootings, and Rep. Sheila Jackson Lee, D-Texas, said she hoped Congress "would look to legislative fixes with our colleagues to make America better." Rep. Elijah Cummings, D-Md., sent a letter to the president calling on him to work with the Justice Department to develop training for law enforcement officers that combats racial bias.

EXECUTIVE ACTION

President Obama used his executive power to further the work done by the attorney general and Justice Department. The president called for $263 million in new funding for police training and body cameras. The plan would require Congressional approval and would help pay for 50,000 body cameras, matching state funding of the devices at 50 percent. The president's announcement was one in a series of moves intended to help calm the "simmering distrust" particularly between minority communities and police. "This is not a problem just of Ferguson, Missouri," the president said. "This is a national problem." The president added that his administration would focus on better oversight and training of the federal program that transfers military equipment to state and local law enforcement agencies in an effort to prevent a "militarized culture" in local police departments.

The president also announced that he would establish the Task Force on 21st Century Policing, to be led by Laurie Robinson, former Office of Justice Programs assistant attorney general, and Philadelphia police commissioner Charles Ramsey. The task force would "identify the best means to provide an effective partnership between law enforcement and local communities that reduces crime and increases trust," according to the executive order. Obama said he was aware of the failings of similar efforts, but that "this time will be different because the president of the United States is deeply vested in making it different."

The task force would be made up of representatives from law enforcement, community leaders, youth leaders, and academics. According to the White House, the task force will be charged with reviewing "how to strengthen public trust and foster strong relationships between local law enforcement and the communities that they protect, while also promoting effective crime reduction." Throughout the course of its work, the task force would hold listening sessions, hear testimony from invited witnesses, and also take recommendations and comments from the public.

The first listening session was scheduled for mid-January in Washington, D.C., and the task force's initial report was set to be delivered to the president on March 2, 2015.

—Heather Kerrigan

Following is the text of a speech delivered by Attorney General Eric Holder on December 1, 2014, on the work of the federal government to build trust between police and communities of color; an executive summary of the Department of Justice's revised guidelines on use of racial profiling, released on December 8, 2014; and the text of an executive order issued by President Barack Obama on December 18, 2014, establishing the Task Force on 21st Century Policing.

Attorney General
Holder on Race Relations

December 1, 2014

Thank you all for being here. It is my honor to bring warm greetings from President Obama, who asked that I share his best wishes with you this evening.

I'd like to thank Reverend [Raphael] Warnock, and his colleagues and counterparts throughout Atlanta's thriving community of faith, for inviting me to join you tonight. I also want to thank Mayor [Kasim] Reed and Police Chief [George] Turner for welcoming me to this beautiful city. Earlier today, I had the opportunity to meet with the two of them—along with a number of law enforcement, faith, civil rights, and community leaders from here in Atlanta—for the first in what will be a series of meetings with law enforcement, civic, and community leaders around the country in the coming weeks. I heard about the great work they are doing to foster strong and mutually-respectful relationships throughout this region. And I was particularly encouraged to learn about robust engagement strategies like the one that's in place in this area—thanks to the leadership of DeKalb County Director of Public Safety Cedric Alexander and his colleagues—as people have reacted to events in Ferguson.

I want to take a moment to recognize the Justice Department leaders who took part in this meeting, and who are here with us tonight—including Karol Mason, the Assistant Attorney General for the Office of Justice Programs; senior leaders from the Office of Community Oriented Policing Services; Vanita Gupta, the Assistant Attorney General for the Civil Rights Division; and Atlanta's very own Sally Yates, our outstanding U.S. Attorney for the Northern District of Georgia.

Most importantly, I want to thank each of the passionate citizens—and especially the young people—who have taken the time to reflect, to pray, and to engage with us this evening. It is a privilege to stand with this community as you convene a forum to help build cooperation, to foster inclusion, and to make your voices heard. And it is a particular honor to do so in the shadow of the historic sanctuary where a young man of faith named

Dr. Martin Luther King Jr. first found the voice that would stir millions to action; where he first articulated the vision that pushes us forward even today; and where he first bound himself to the enduring struggle for equal justice—a cause that he would pioneer, for which he would lay down his life, and in which every successive generation must be both trained and invested.

It was here at Ebenezer Baptist, well over half a century ago, that our nation's greatest advocate for justice, for peace, and for righteousness began the work that would help to transform the nation—and usher in decades of extraordinary, once-unimaginable progress. It was here that Dr. King set out not merely to change our laws, but to change the world—and to pull the country he loved ever closer to its founding principles. And it was here, too, that he issued a prophetic warning that, although brighter days undoubtedly lay ahead, progress would not come without considerable hardship, struggle, setback—and profound sacrifice.

"The winds," he told us, "are going to blow. The storms of disappointment are coming. The agonies and the anguishes of life are coming."

Dr. King knew then—as we know, today—that with the strength conferred by abiding faith, together, we can "stand up amid the storms." By placing our trust in the Divine, and in one another, we can "walk with [our] feet solid to the ground and [our] head[s] to the air." He assured us that, come what may, we need not feel discouraged or afraid; in fact, we need not fear any challenge that comes before us. But the struggles will continue. The storms will come. And the road ahead will be anything but smooth or straight.

As we look down this road tonight, it's clear that our nation continues to face persistent challenges—along with the countless opportunities that Dr. King helped make possible, but that he himself did not live to see. As we recommit ourselves to the cause with which he entrusted us, it's apparent that our nation's journey is not yet over. And so we return once more to this hallowed place to seek shelter from a terrible storm—a storm that I'm certain we will weather, so long as we continue to stand united—and unafraid to address realities too long ignored.

Like millions of Americans, I know many of you have spent the past few days with family members, friends, and loved ones, giving thanks for the blessings of the past year—but also mindful of recent news, the anguished emotions, and the images of destruction that have once again focused this country's attention on Ferguson, Missouri.

While the grand jury proceeding in St. Louis County has concluded, I can report this evening that the Justice Department's investigation into the shooting death of Michael Brown, as well as our investigation into allegations of unconstitutional policing patterns or practices by the Ferguson Police Department, remain ongoing and active. They have been rigorous and independent from the very beginning. While federal civil rights law imposes an extremely high legal bar in these types of cases, we have resisted prejudging the evidence or forming premature conclusions. And as these investigations proceed, I want to assure the American people that they will continue to be conducted both thoroughly and in a timely manner—following the facts and the law wherever they may lead. We will see these investigations through to their appropriate conclusions, so that we can continue to work with the community to restore trust, to rebuild understanding, and to foster renewed cooperation between law enforcement and community members.

Like you, I understand that the need for this trust was made clear in the wake of the intense public reaction to last week's grand jury announcement. But the problems we must confront are not only found in Ferguson. The issues raised in Missouri are not unique to that state or that small city. We are dealing with concerns that are truly national in scope and that threaten the entire nation. Broadly speaking, without mutual understanding between citizens—whose rights must be respected—and law enforcement officers—who make tremendous and often-unheralded personal sacrifices every day to preserve public safety—there can be no meaningful progress. Our police officers cannot be seen as an occupying force disconnected from the communities they serve. Bonds that have been broken must be restored. Bonds that never existed must now be created.

But the issue is larger than just the police and the community. Our overall system of justice must be strengthened and made more fair. In this way, we can ensure faith in the justice system. Without that deserved faith, without that reasoned belief, there can be no justice. This is not an unreasonable desire—it is a fundamental American right enshrined in our founding documents.

There can be no question that Michael Brown's death was a tragedy. Any loss of life—and particularly the loss of someone so young—is heart-rending, regardless of the circumstances. But in the months since this incident occurred, it has sparked a significant national conversation about the need to ensure confidence in the law enforcement and criminal justice processes. The rifts that this tragedy exposed, in Ferguson and elsewhere, must be addressed—by all Americans—in a constructive manner. And it is deeply unfortunate that this vital conversation was interrupted, and this young man's memory dishonored, by destruction and looting on the part of a relatively small criminal element.

Dr. King would be the first to remind us that acts of mindless destruction are not only contrary to the rule of law and the aims of public safety; they threaten to stifle important debate, "adding deeper darkness to a night already devoid of stars." They actively impede social progress by drowning out the legitimate voices of those attempting to make themselves heard. And they are not consistent with the wishes of Michael Brown's father, who asked that his son be remembered peacefully.

Time and again, America's proud history has shown that the most successful and enduring movements for change are those that adhere to principles of non-aggression and nonviolence. As this congregation knows better than most, peaceful protest has long been a hallmark, and a legacy, of past struggles for progress. This is what Dr. King taught us, half a century ago, in his eloquent words from the Ebenezer pulpit and in the vision he shared from the steps of the Lincoln Memorial.

So this evening, I renew his call for all those who seek to lend their voices to important causes and discussions, and who seek to elevate these vital conversations, to do so in ways that respect the gravity of their subject matter. I urge all Americans to stand in solidarity with those brave citizens, in Ferguson, who stopped looters from destroying even more local businesses, who isolated people responsible for acts of violence, and who rejected lawless and destructive tactics—just as I have urged them to stand with law enforcement personnel to ensure the rights of protesters and defuse tense situations whenever and wherever possible.

I also want to reaffirm my own steadfast dedication, and the commitment of my colleagues at every level of the U.S. Department of Justice, to keep working with citizens and law enforcement leaders alike in building this inclusive, national dialogue—so we can close these gaps, improve police and community relations, and open a new era of collaboration in pursuit of public safety, especially among the vulnerable and underserved populations that need our assistance the most.

This has been a top priority for my colleagues and me over the past six years. In fact, in just the last few months, under the leadership of Assistant Attorney General Mason and

COPS Director Ron Davis, our Office of Justice Programs and COPS Office have worked to develop and disseminate guidance to law enforcement officers about how to maintain order during peaceful protests and other First Amendment-protected events—while safeguarding the rights of demonstrators. As we speak, the COPS Office and Community Relations Service are doing great work on the ground in Ferguson—conducting an after-action review, recommending constructive steps we can take to resolve persistent tensions, and identifying areas where law enforcement priorities and community concerns must fall into alignment.

As this critical effort unfolds, we will remain firmly resolved to stand shoulder-to-shoulder with you in driving this work into the future. And this commitment will also fuel our broader efforts to bring change—and meaningful reform—to urgent challenges far beyond the realm of community policing.

Through the Smart on Crime initiative I launched last year, we are already strengthening the federal criminal justice system, moving away from outdated sentencing regimes, and embracing a holistic approach to law enforcement, incarceration, rehabilitation, and reentry. Through important, bipartisan legislation like the Smarter Sentencing Act—and in cooperation with Congressional leaders from both parties—we're striving to give judges more discretion in determining sentences for people convicted of certain federal drug crimes. And we're marshaling a broad coalition of bipartisan leaders to urge state lawmakers to repeal and rethink misguided and unjust policies like felon disenfranchisement, so voting rights can be restored to those individuals who have served their time, paid their fines, and completed their probation or parole.

Through the groundbreaking My Brother's Keeper initiative that President Obama announced in February, we are also working tirelessly to address persistent opportunity gaps faced by boys and young men of color—and to ensure that all young people can reach their full potential. Under the leadership of Vanita Gupta, the Department's Civil Rights Division is deeply engaged in reinvigorated police reform work. Over the last five fiscal years, they've opened more than 20 investigations into police departments across the country—and entered into 15 consent decrees or memoranda of understanding—to correct unconstitutional policing practices. And through the new National Initiative for Building Community Trust and Justice, which I launched in September, we are forging robust relationships between police officers and their communities—so we can bridge long-simmering divides from coast to coast; so we can provide innovative training on bias reduction and procedural fairness, to ensure that everyone is treated equitably; and so we can minimize needless confrontation, preserve peace, and maintain the public trust at all times—particularly in moments of heightened community tension.

Earlier today, I was proud to join President Obama at the White House to discuss this ongoing work. And I am pleased to note this evening that the President has announced a series of steps to take these efforts to a new level—to strengthen promising practices by local police while bolstering law enforcement and community relations.

First: based on an exhaustive, Administration-wide review of the distribution of military hardware to state and local police—which the President ordered in August, and which uncovered a lack of consistency in the way this equipment is distributed—the White House has released a detailed report outlining next steps for ensuring appropriate use of federal programs. And the President has instructed his staff to draft an Executive Order directing relevant agencies to work with law enforcement and civil rights organizations to find ways to improve the effectiveness, integrity, accountability, and transparency of these initiatives.

Second: the President made clear that this Administration will continue to strongly support the use of body cameras by local police. And he announced a commitment of more than $200 million to support a three-year initiative that will invest in body-worn cameras, expand training for law enforcement agencies, add more resources for police department reform, and multiply the number of cities where Justice Department leaders facilitate greater engagement between residents and local authorities.

Third: in the coming days, I will announce updated Justice Department guidance regarding profiling by federal law enforcement, which will institute rigorous new standards—and robust safeguards—to help end racial profiling, once and for all. This new guidance will codify our commitment to the very highest standards of fair and effective policing.

Finally: the President took the historic step of creating a new Task Force on 21st Century Policing—a body composed of law enforcement executives and community leaders from around the country, led by Philadelphia Police Commissioner Charles Ramsey, former Assistant Attorney General Laurie Robinson, and COPS Director Ron Davis, who will convene in the coming weeks to examine the present state of policing, to identify best practices, and to make recommendations for the future. This important Task Force will ask tough questions, examine thorny challenges, and consider the state of the law enforcement profession in a broad and inclusive way. It will offer suggestions for new ways to advance community policing throughout the country. And it will help to provide strong, national direction on a scale not seen since President Lyndon Johnson's Commission on Law Enforcement nearly 50 years ago.

I want to be very clear that, although frank dialogue is a necessary first step and sign of commitment, these efforts aren't just about talking—and they're certainly not about imposing solutions from Washington. They're about bringing leaders together—from every perspective—to confront specific challenges, to spur renewed engagement, and to translate healthy dialogue into concrete, coordinated action and results.

Because police officers have an indispensable role to play in securing our neighborhoods and building a brighter future. Because these public servants shoulder enormous burdens, and incur significant personal risks, to fulfill their critical responsibilities. Because all lives matter and all lives must be valued. And because all Americans deserve fair and equal treatment in the eyes of the law.

After all, at a fundamental level, this is about much more than effective policy. It's about the progress that can only spring from thoughtful, peaceful gatherings like this one. It's about leaders like all of you—the men and women in this crowd tonight. And it's about the power that passionate, engaged citizens can and must exercise in shaping our nation's future: so we can reclaim the promise, and the singular opportunity born of tragedy, that brings us together—here and now. So we can keep our steadfast commitment to prevent future tragedies and promote mutual understanding. And so we can fulfill the sacred responsibility that all Americans share—a responsibility to Dr. King, and untold millions of others, who sacrificed everything they had to bring our nation to this point; a responsibility to our fellow citizens, as well as the law enforcement officers who keep us safe; and—most of all—a responsibility to our children, black and white, from all backgrounds, races, and walks of life, in cities and towns across this country—as to generations yet to come.

It was Dr. King who reminded us—in his very last speech, on the night before his life was taken—that it's only when it is dark enough that the stars can be seen.

Tonight, once again, it is dark enough. Yet even in recent weeks, there have arisen great sparks of humanity, and hope, that illuminate the way forward.

Out of this darkness shine the actions of those who reject destruction in favor of peaceful protest; the bravery of others who faced down mobs; the valor of law enforcement officers who risked their lives to restore public safety to their communities; and the humble words of a father who lost a son, but raised his voice in pursuit of peace.

These are the moments that remind us of the values that bind us together as a nation. These are the times—of great challenge and great consequence—that point the way forward in our ongoing pursuit of a more perfect Union. And these are the lights that will help us beat back the encroaching darkness—and the stars that will guide us, together, out of this storm.

May God grant us safe passage. May He continue to watch over our journey. And may He always bless the United States of America.

SOURCE: U.S. Department of Justice. "Attorney General Eric Holder Delivers Remarks During the Interfaith Service and Community Forum at Ebenezer Baptist Church." December 1, 2014. www.justice.gov/opa/speech/attorney-general-eric-holder-delivers-remarks-during-interfaith-service-and-community.

Justice Department Releases
Revised Racial Profiling Guidelines

December 8, 2014

INTRODUCTION AND EXECUTIVE SUMMARY

This Guidance supersedes the Department of Justice's 2003 Guidance Regarding the Use of Race by Federal Law Enforcement Agencies. It builds upon and expands the framework of the 2003 Guidance, and it reaffirms the Federal government's deep commitment to ensuring that its law enforcement agencies conduct their activities in an unbiased manner. Biased practices, as the Federal government has long recognized, are unfair, promote mistrust of law enforcement, and perpetuate negative and harmful stereotypes. Moreover—and vitally important—biased practices are ineffective. As Attorney General Eric Holder has stated, such practices are "simply not good law enforcement."

Law enforcement practices free from inappropriate considerations, by contrast, strengthen trust in law enforcement agencies and foster collaborative efforts between law enforcement and communities to fight crime and keep the Nation safe. In other words, fair law enforcement practices are smart and effective law enforcement practices.

Even-handed law enforcement is therefore central to the integrity, legitimacy, and efficacy of all Federal law enforcement activities. The highest standards can—and should—be met across all such activities. Doing so will not hinder—and, indeed, will bolster—the performance of Federal law enforcement agencies' core responsibilities.

This new Guidance applies to Federal law enforcement officers performing Federal law enforcement activities, including those related to national security and intelligence, and defines not only the circumstances in which Federal law enforcement officers may take into account a person's race and ethnicity—as the 2003 Guidance did—but also when gender, national origin, religion, sexual orientation, or gender identity may be taken into account. This new Guidance also applies to state and local law enforcement officers while participating in Federal law enforcement task forces. Finally, this Guidance promotes training and accountability, to ensure that its contents are understood and implemented appropriately.

Biased law enforcement practices, as the 2003 Guidance recognized with regard to racial profiling, have a terrible cost, not only for individuals but also for the Nation as a whole. This new Guidance reflects the Federal government's ongoing commitment to keeping the Nation safe while upholding our dedication to the ideal of equal justice under the law.

Two standards in combination should guide use by Federal law enforcement officers of race, ethnicity, gender, national origin, religion, sexual orientation, or gender identity in law enforcement or intelligence activities:

- In making routine or spontaneous law enforcement decisions, such as ordinary traffic stops, Federal law enforcement officers may not use race, ethnicity, gender, national origin, religion, sexual orientation, or gender identity to any degree, except that officers may rely on the listed characteristics in a specific suspect description. This prohibition applies even where the use of a listed characteristic might otherwise be lawful.
- In conducting all activities other than routine or spontaneous law enforcement activities, Federal law enforcement officers may consider race, ethnicity, gender, national origin, religion, sexual orientation, or gender identity only to the extent that there is trustworthy information, relevant to the locality or time frame, that links persons possessing a particular listed characteristic to an identified criminal incident, scheme, or organization, a threat to national or homeland security, a violation of Federal immigration law, or an authorized intelligence activity. In order to rely on a listed characteristic, law enforcement officers must also reasonably believe that the law enforcement, security, or intelligence activity to be undertaken is merited under the totality of the circumstances, such as any temporal exigency and the nature of any potential harm to be averted. This standard applies even where the use of a listed characteristic might otherwise be lawful.

[A more in-depth discussion of the guidance has been omitted.]

SOURCE: U.S. Department of Justice. "Guidance for Federal Law Enforcement Agencies Regarding the Use of Race, Ethnicity, Gender, National Origin, Religion, Sexual Orientation, or Gender Identity." December 8, 2014. www.justice.gov/sites/default/files/ag/pages/attachments/2014/12/08/use-of-race-policy.pdf.

President Obama Establishes Task Force on 21st Century Policing

December 18, 2014

By the authority vested in me as President by the Constitution and the laws of the United States of America, and in order to identify the best means to provide an effective partnership between law enforcement and local communities that reduces crime and increases trust, it is hereby ordered as follows:

Section 1. Establishment. There is established a President's Task Force on 21st Century Policing (Task Force).

Sec. 2. Membership.

(a) The Task Force shall be composed of not more than eleven members appointed by the President. The members shall include distinguished individuals with relevant experience or subject-matter expertise in law enforcement, civil rights, and civil liberties.

(b) The President shall designate two members of the Task Force to serve as Co-Chairs.

Sec. 3. Mission.

(a) The Task Force shall, consistent with applicable law, identify best practices and otherwise make recommendations to the President on how policing practices can promote effective crime reduction while building public trust.

(b) The Task Force shall be solely advisory and shall submit a report to the President by March 2, 2015.

Sec. 4. Administration.

(a) The Task Force shall hold public meetings and engage with Federal, State, tribal, and local officials, technical advisors, and nongovernmental organizations, among others, as necessary to carry out its mission.

(b) The Director of the Office of Community Oriented Policing Services shall serve as Executive Director of the Task Force and shall, as directed by the Co-Chairs, convene regular meetings of the Task Force and supervise its work.

(c) In carrying out its mission, the Task Force shall be informed by, and shall strive to avoid duplicating, the efforts of other governmental entities.

(d) The Department of Justice shall provide administrative services, funds, facilities, staff, equipment, and other support services as may be necessary for the Task Force to carry out its mission to the extent permitted by law and subject to the availability of appropriations.

(e) Members of the Task Force shall serve without any additional compensation for their work on the Task Force, but shall be allowed travel expenses, including per diem, to the extent permitted by law for persons serving intermittently in the Government service (5 U.S.C. 5701–5707).

Sec. 5. Termination. The Task Force shall terminate 30 days after the President requests a final report from the Task Force.

Sec. 6. General Provisions.

(a) Nothing in this order shall be construed to impair or otherwise affect:

   (i) the authority granted by law to a department, agency, or the head thereof; or

   (ii) the functions of the Director of the Office of Management and Budget relating to budgetary, administrative, or legislative proposals.

(b) This order is not intended to, and does not, create any right or benefit, substantive or procedural, enforceable at law or in equity by any party against the United States, its departments, agencies, or entities, its officers, employees, or agents, or any other person.

(c) Insofar as the Federal Advisory Committee Act, as amended (5 U.S.C. App.) (the "Act") may apply to the Task Force, any functions of the President under the Act, except for those in section 6 of the Act, shall be performed by the Attorney General.

BARACK OBAMA

The White House,
December 18, 2014

Source: Executive Office of the President. "Executive Order 13684—Establishment of the President's Task Force on 21st Century Policing." December 18, 2014. *Compilation of Presidential Documents* 2014, no. 00943 (December 18, 2014). www.gpo.gov/fdsys/pkg/DCPD-201400943/pdf/DCPD-201400943.pdf.

OTHER HISTORIC DOCUMENTS OF INTEREST

FROM THIS VOLUME

FROM PREVIOUS *HISTORIC DOCUMENTS*

Early Elections Called in Greece Ahead of Bailout

DECEMBER 8 AND 29, 2014

The breakup of Greece's coalition government toward the end of 2014 resulted in early elections being scheduled for January 25, 2015. While the immediate cause of the coalition collapse was the failure of Greece's parliament to elect a new president, the dominant political undercurrents were Greece's continuing economic challenges and its brief relations with the European Union (EU). Having received bailout packages worth €240 billion ($295 billion) since 2010 to avoid a catastrophic sovereign default on its debts, the Greek authorities made serious efforts to implement so-called austerity policies demanded of it by the EU. These included cuts in public spending and reforms of its economy to make it more competitive. These steps were starting to reap results, with an improved—albeit still fragile—economic picture as growth returned. But after five uninterrupted, devastating years of recession, there was an overwhelming appetite among the Greek public for austerity to end. The leader of the antiausterity movement, the left-wing Syriza party, seemed set to capitalize on this in the new elections. All sides meanwhile braced for a tough upcoming set of negotiations between the future Greek government and the European Union as the bailout-austerity program came up for review.

GREEK ECONOMY IMPROVES

The outgoing coalition government of Greece, led by Prime Minister Antonis Samaras from the center-right New Democracy party, was formed following the June 2012 elections. Samaras found it increasingly hard to keep his coalition together in the face of the pressures both from within Greece and outside, having to constantly meet the demands of his EU partners who provided Greece with a series of bailout loans from 2010 to 2012. Greece joined the EU's single currency area, the eurozone in 2001. Its membership had encouraged successive Greek governments to borrow too much, lulled into the false sense of security created by eurozone membership. When the financial crisis hit in 2008, Greece's debt-to-GDP ratio rocketed and its economy contracted severely. By the time Samaras took office in 2012, his government had limited margin to maneuver in setting policies. The Troika, a team of European Commission, European Central Bank (ECB), and International Monetary Fund (IMF) officials, had hammered out in the preceding years a set of policy prescriptions that Greece was bound to implement in return for being rescued from a sovereign default.

The Greek economy had shrunk more than 20 percent in five years and its unemployment rate soared to 26 percent. While some blamed the austerity policies for having made an already bad situation worse by stifling economic activity, others argued that these policies, painful as they may be, were necessary to put Greeks on a path of living within their means. Moreover, supporters of the austerity policies predicted that ultimately the country would reap benefits from them by becoming more competitive in the global economy. The Greek economy had indeed turned a corner by the end of 2014. It was registering growth again, and the jobless rate seemed to have at least peaked, although it was still far too high. On the public finance side, the picture was even more impressive, with the Greek government on course to register a significant primary surplus in 2015, a remarkable achievement considering that in 2009 Greece's public deficit stood at 15 percent of its GDP.

It was an achievement that EU officials in Brussels were keen to acknowledge, acutely aware of how unpopular the austerity policies were with Greeks and how they had damaged the EU's reputation there. The EU commissioner for economic and financial affairs, Pierre Moscovici, said in a speech on December 8 that "Greece has achieved very significant reforms and fiscal adjustment" and that the "Commission of course recognises this. And we are committed to supporting Greece." Moscovici said the Commission was in the process of clarifying the EU's Stability and Growth pact—the agreement that binds eurozone members to adhere to clearly prescribed debt and deficit targets—to examine how Greece could increase public investments without being in breach of those rules. After hearing that new elections had been called, Moscovici said on December 29 that "a strong commitment to Europe and broad support among the Greek voters and political leaders for the necessary growth-friendly reform process will be essential for Greece to thrive again within the Euro area."

Moscovici had only recently taken up his position on a new team of twenty-eight EU commissioners (one from each EU member country) who took office on November 1. Prior to that, Moscovici had been France's finance minister in a socialist government. This background and his initial statements gave some early indications that the commissioner was willing to show greater flexibility to Athens than, for example, Germany, which has consistently been at the vanguard of the pro-austerity camp. German finance minister from the center-right Christian Democratic Union was far frostier in his remarks about the upcoming ballot. "New elections change nothing about the agreements that the Greek government has entered into. Any new government must stick to the contractual agreements of its predecessors," said German finance minister Wolfgang Schäuble. As for the ECB, a member of the Troika that has been instrumental in bolstering the euro by such measures as buying up sovereign bonds from the markets, it struck a conciliatory tone. "We will wait for the views and suggestions of the Greek authorities on how to best proceed with the review [of the bailout-austerity program] and we will discuss this with the European Commission and the IMF," it said. The message conveyed by the IMF, whose managing director, Christine Lagarde, is a former French finance minister, was similar, stressing that the onus was on Greece to present concrete proposals.

Under its constitutional system, Greece elects its president not directly by its citizens but rather indirectly by its 300-member parliament. Prime Minister Samaras's favored candidate was Stavros Dimas, who had formerly been the EU environment commissioner. In the third round of voting on December 29, Dimas won 168 votes, falling just shy of the 180 votes that he needed to be elected. Under Greek law, new elections were required to be called. This in itself did not come as a great shock given how fragile Samaras's coalition had been, but it nevertheless generated jitters in financial markets, fearing another EU-Greece bailout-austerity showdown was pending, bringing with it the potential of Greece exiting from the eurozone, a so-called Grexit. The Athens stock market lost 5 percent of its value the day that the election was called, with yields on Greek government bonds increasing to 9.5 percent.

ANTI-AUSTERITY MOVEMENT SURGES

The eyes of Europe increasingly turned to the rising star of Greek politics, Alexis Tsipras, leader of Syriza, a left-wing antiausterity party that had enjoyed a meteoric growth in popularity following the financial crisis. In the previous two general elections, held in May and June 2012, Syriza narrowly missed coming in first place, scoring just a couple of percentage points less than Samaras's New Democracy party. Between 2012 and 2014, as the main opposition party, Syriza continued to grow in strength. In the May 2014 European Parliament elections, Syriza came in first place, winning 27 percent of the vote compared to 23 percent for New Democracy. The big loser in Syriza's rise was the Greek Panhellenic Socialist Movement (Pasok), which for decades had either held power or been the largest opposition party. By 2014, Pasok had been totally eclipsed by Syriza and was attracting only singles-digit percentage support from voters. On the far-right of the political spectrum, the neo-Nazi Golden Dawn party grabbed world headlines by winning seats in parliament. But when compared by actual vote share, Syriza has been far more successful than Golden Dawn, with the latter typically winning about 6 percent.

In the build-up to the election campaign, Tsipras maintained a stridently antiausterity line, pledging to reverse unpopular measures like the government's sale of state-owned assets to pay off debts and cuts in the minimum wage and pensions. At the same time, he made clear that his goal was for Greece to remain both inside the eurozone and the EU. But his number one priority was to secure some debt relief for Greece. The original 2010 bailout deal had already been revised a couple of times: the over sums increased, the calendar for when Greece had to pay back debts extended, the interest rate lowered, and private sector debt-holders were forced to accept some debt write-offs.

Nevertheless, at around 170 percent, Greece's debt-to-GDP ratio was worryingly high. Germany and like-minded austerity hawks in the European Union such as Finland and the Netherlands were keen to make Greece stick to its commitments, which include making the Greek economy more diverse and making a serious effort to reduce tax evasion. The Greeks were hoping, however, that other key players, notably the Commission and the IMF, would be willing to show greater flexibility.

JANUARY ELECTION

As anticipated, the elections on January 25, 2015, were a clear victory to Syriza, which took 36.3 percent of the vote, compared to 27.8 percent for New Democracy, 6.3 percent for Golden Dawn, and just 4.7 percent for Pasok. Winning 149 out of 300 seats in parliament, Syriza fell just shy of an overall majority, leading it to form a coalition government with a nationalist, right-wing party called Independent Greeks. Two days later, Tsipras, now prime minister, appointed fifty-three-year-old economist Yanis Varoufakis as his finance minister. Varoufakis was given the crucial and extremely difficult task of seeking more favorable terms from the EU and IMF for Greece's bailout programs.

Tsipras tried to curry support from the Commission president, Jean-Claude Juncker, in his pick for Greek president. Tapping the former interior minister, Prokopis Pavlopoulos, he snubbed a previously favored candidate, Dimitris Avramopoulos, the EU commissioner for immigration, to save Juncker the trouble of having to reshuffle his carefully constructed team of commissioners. The European Union embarked on some fence-mending, too, renaming the Troika as the "Brussels Group," aware of how the word Troika had become, for Greeks, synonymous with technocratic autocracy from Brussels.

Commission president Juncker tried to broker a compromise between Berlin and Athens, but by early spring of 2015, it was far from clear if Juncker could bridge the yawning gap between the two sides.

—Brian Beary

Following is a statement by European commissioner for economic and financial affairs, taxation and customs Pierre Moscovici on December 8, 2014, on fiscal reforms in Greece; and a second statement by Moscovici on December 29, 2014, on general elections in Greece.

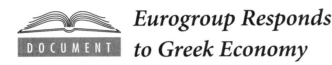 *Eurogroup Responds to Greek Economy*

December 8, 2014

Let me begin by underlining that Greece has achieved very significant reforms and fiscal adjustment in recent years, in the most difficult of circumstances for the Greek people.

The headline deficit has fallen from over 15% of GDP in 2009 to an estimated deficit of just 1.6% of GDP in 2014 and is expected to reach balance next year. The authorities are now targeting a primary surplus of 3.0% of GDP for 2015: indeed Greece now has the highest primary surplus in the euro area after Germany.

The European Commission of course recognises this. And we are committed to supporting Greece in taking forward this process of necessary change and modernisation of the economy. This requires that Greece also show continued commitment to both fiscal responsibility and further structural reforms.

We have been engaged in intensive discussions in recent days with the Greek authorities and with the IMF and ECB. Our approach has been firm but constructive, open but determined. Our aim is to conclude the current review with a credible, balanced set of reforms and fiscal measures to help strengthen Greece's economic recovery.

On the one hand, there has been clear progress in a number of areas. On the other hand, as you said Jeroen, this progress has not been as rapid as could have been hoped—or as would have been necessary to allow for a conclusion of the review in the coming days. We came to global agreement fast on this point.

That's why it has been agreed in principle, pending formal confirmation by Member States, that there will be a technical extension of the EFSF programme for two months. I really welcome this decision which in my view seems to be the wisest that was possible to take.

The Commission also welcomes Greece's intention to request an Enhanced Conditions Credit Line from the ESM. This will provide a sound support framework throughout 2015, ensuring that the reform process remains firmly anchored in a European and international support framework.

The Commission remains fully committed to concluding the review as soon as possible. In this context, technical teams will start work in Athens tomorrow focusing especially on fiscal issues.

[The French portion of the statement has been omitted.]

SOURCE: European Commission. "Commissioner Moscovici's remarks at the second press conference of the Eurogroup." December 8, 2014. http://europa.eu/rapid/press-release_SPEECH-14-2483_en.htm. © European Union.

Commissioner Moscovici on Greek Elections

December 29, 2014

Following the third vote on a new President in the Parliament today, the Greek government has just announced general elections on 25 January. Through this democratic process, the Greek people will once again decide on their future. A strong commitment to Europe and broad support among the Greek voters and political leaders for the necessary growth-friendly reform process will be essential for Greece to thrive again within the euro area.

SOURCE: European Commission. "Statement by Pierre Moscovici, Commissioner for Economic and Financial Affairs, Taxation and Customs, following the Greek parliament vote on the presidential candidate." December 29, 2014. http://europa.eu/rapid/press-release_STATEMENT-14-2900_en.htm. © European Union.

OTHER HISTORIC DOCUMENTS OF INTEREST

FROM PREVIOUS *HISTORIC DOCUMENTS*

Senate Committee Releases Report on CIA Detention and Interrogation Program

DECEMBER 9, 2014

In May 2009, the Senate Select Committee on Intelligence launched an investigation into the Central Intelligence Agency's (CIA) detention and interrogation program, through which the agency sought to apprehend suspected terrorists—and foil planned terrorist acts—during former president George W. Bush's administration. The investigation was reportedly prompted by revelations that Jose Rodriguez, director of the CIA's National Clandestine Service, had destroyed nearly 100 video recordings of detainee interrogations in 2005, leading the committee to suspect that he was attempting to hide illegal activity. The Senate committee completed its classified report in December 2013, but not until December 2014 did it publicly release portions of the report. The findings were highly critical of the CIA, concluding that the use of "enhanced interrogation techniques" such as waterboarding had been used more harshly and more frequently than previously believed, and that CIA officials had misled the White House and Congress about the program's efficacy and failed to provide sufficient oversight of its employees and secret prison facilities. The CIA challenged the report as "incomplete and selective"—an argument echoed by a number of Republicans and former intelligence officials—while others applauded the report for exposing troubling and potentially unlawful practices.

Examining the CIA

Committee chairman Dianne Feinstein, D-Calif., and vice chairman Kit Bond, R-Mo., initially projected that their investigation would take one year to complete, but the sheer volume of material provided by the CIA and several other challenges resulted in a delayed timeframe. Committee staff was given access to more than six million pages of records that they reviewed at a secure offsite location in Northern Virginia, only after a third-party contractor had first reviewed the materials. Notably, the committee's Republican staff withdrew from the investigation several months in, following Attorney General Eric Holder's announcement that the Justice Department was considering prosecutions against CIA employees who had been involved in enhanced interrogations.

The committee approved the final 6,400-page report by a vote of 9–6 during a meeting on December 13, 2013. The report was revised in April 2014, to include additional "minority views," as well as updated findings and conclusions, and was submitted to President Barack Obama for declassification. Then on December 9, 2014, Feinstein filed the full classified report with Senate president pro tempore Patrick Leahy, D-Vt., and publicly released 528 declassified pages. In a cover letter to Leahy, Feinstein wrote: "The full report should be used by the Central Intelligence Agency and other components of the Executive Branch to help make sure that the system of detention and interrogation described in this report is never repeated."

"Brutal" Interrogations, Agency Failures

The final report presented twenty key findings that provided a damning characterization of the CIA's interrogation tactics and mismanagement within the agency. All 119 individuals who had been held in CIA custody in the agency's network of secret prisons were named in the report—twenty of whom had never been acknowledged by the CIA. At least twenty-six of these prisoners had been "wrongfully held," according to the report, including one "intellectually challenged" man who was held as "leverage" to coax information from a family member. Others were reportedly held due to mistaken identity or bad intelligence, and the committee found that the CIA did not have sufficient evidence to justify keeping some of the detainees in custody.

Among its key findings, the report concluded that "the interrogations of CIA detainees were brutal and far worse than the CIA represented to policymakers and others." The report also identified other harsh interrogation techniques that had not been approved for use, including "rectal rehydration" or rectal feeding. In one instance, CIA documents outline how one prisoner's food was "'pureed' and rectally infused." At least five detainees were subjected to this practice without medical necessity. According to the report, "The CIA also used abdominal slaps and cold water dousing on several detainees during that period. None of these techniques had been approved by the Department of Justice. At least 17 detainees were subjected to CIA enhanced interrogation techniques without authorization from CIA Headquarters."

The report also cited evidence contradicting CIA claims that only three detainees had been waterboarded, including photos that showed worn waterboarding equipment at a secret site where the practice's use was never officially recorded. Additional evidence found that interrogators used some techniques, including waterboarding, in a manner different than had been authorized. While interrogating Khalid Sheikh Mohammed, the alleged mastermind of the September 11, 2001, terrorist attacks, CIA officers reportedly modified the waterboarding technique in such a way that caused him to ingest a significant amount of water and prompted one CIA medical officer to write that "we are basically doing a series of near drownings." In one particularly grim incident, employees at a secret location in Thailand reportedly broke down after witnessing the treatment of Abu Zubaida, the first person to be detained by the CIA after the program's implementation. Upon his transfer from Pakistan to Thailand, Zubaida was kept in isolation for forty-seven days. After this time, the CIA began a harsh interrogation program that included slamming him against walls, forcing him into a coffin-sized box, and waterboarding him until he had "involuntary spasms of the torso and extremities" for seventeen days. The waterboarding reportedly left Zubaida "completely unresponsive, with bubbles rising through his full, open mouth." The committee report included excerpts from internal CIA memos and e-mail, in which agency employees described their personal reactions to these and other interrogations. One CIA memo said that two or three employees who had been distraught by Zubaida's treatment and questioned its legality may request a transfer, contradicting previous assurances by high-ranking CIA officials that no agency personnel had expressed reservations about the interrogation program. Another officer described one of the CIA's secret prisons as a "dungeon" and said the interrogation techniques were leading to "psychological and behavioral issues, including hallucinations, paranoia, insomnia, and attempts at self-harm and self-mutilation" among the detainees. A total of thirty-nine detainees were found to have been subjected to enhanced interrogation.

The committee's investigation also found evidence suggesting that the CIA's own records on the program were full of errors, which in turn caused the agency to provide conflicting and inaccurate information to the White House and Congress. For example, former CIA director Michael Hayden testified before the committee in 2007 that the program had ninety-eight detainees throughout its history, though the committee later found documentation of 119 detainees. In 2009, a subordinate informed Hayden, who was preparing to brief President Obama, that the actual detainee number was higher. According to an e-mail the employee sent to himself, Hayden "instructed me to keep the detainee number at 98." This discrepancy was among a thirty-eight-page table that the committee included in the report that contrasted Hayden's public statements and congressional testimony to information included in CIA documents.

In some cases, the committee wrote, the CIA appeared to have deliberately deceived its overseers, or acted in a manner that conflicted with other agencies' missions. "The CIA withheld or restricted information relevant to these agencies' missions and responsibilities, denied access to detainees, and provided inaccurate information on the CIA's Detention and Interrogation Program to these agencies," the committee wrote. Among the examples provided to support this claim, the agency cited an incident in 2003, when a member of then-Vice President Dick Cheney's staff asked if the CIA had any recordings of Zubaida's interrogations. The agency's general counsel told him that no tapes were made, when in fact the CIA had recorded dozens of interrogations, including that of Zubaida. The tapes in question were the ones later destroyed by Rodriguez. Another CIA memo instructed officers not to tell then-Secretary of State Colin Powell about the interrogation program, lest he "blow his stack" about "what's been going on." In addition to these deceits, the report found that the CIA "impeded oversight" by the agency's inspector general and otherwise resisted oversight by Congress and requests for information about the program.

Regarding the program's "success," the report challenged CIA claims that its enhanced interrogation program had produced "unique" and otherwise unobtainable intelligence that had helped officials to prevent planned attacks or capture al Qaeda leaders, including Osama bin Laden. Seven of the detainees who faced enhanced interrogation tactics did not produce any intelligence while in custody, the report said. In some cases, intelligence was incorrectly attributed to detainees who had been harshly interrogated, when in fact the CIA had already obtained the information from other sources, or there was no viable terrorist threat. Of particular note, the committee found that the intelligence that had led the CIA to bin Laden's compound had been gathered before coercive interrogation measures were used.

THE CIA RESPONDS

Prior to releasing the report, the committee had submitted its findings to the CIA for comment. The agency responded in June 2013 with a 112-page report of its own, which was also released publicly in December 2014. The response acknowledged that the detention and interrogation program had some flaws, but denied that the agency had intentionally mislead the public or other officials about the interrogation program, and refuted all but a few of the committee's conclusions. CIA director John Brennan said that while the CIA had made mistakes, the committee's report was an "incomplete and selective picture of what occurred." He also noted that "no interviews were conducted of any CIA officers involved in the program, which would have provided Members with valuable context and perspective surrounding these events." The agency also continued to insist the program had gathered critical intelligence. "The intelligence gained from the program was critical to our understanding of al-Qa'ida and continues to inform our counterterrorism efforts to this day," Brennan said. The response included a fact sheet to help support these assertions and said the agency "takes no position" on whether the intelligence gathered through enhanced interrogation techniques could have been obtained another way. Brennan added, "In carrying out that program, we did not always live up to the high standards that we set for ourselves and that the American people expect of us. As an Agency, we have learned from those mistakes, which is why my predecessors and I have implemented various remedial measures over the years to address institutional deficiencies."

Hayden offered his own defense, stating in part that the discrepancy in the number of detainees between his remarks and other documents was a matter of how the detainees were counted; some counts included those who were captured before the start of the program. Hayden also criticized the committee's methods. "Maybe if the committee had talked to real people and accessed their notes we wouldn't have to have this conversation," he wrote in an e-mail to *The Washington Post*. "Take a stray 'fact' and claim its meaning to fit the desired narrative (mass deception)." Cheney also dismissed the report's findings as "a bunch of hooey" and claimed the interrogation tactics were "absolutely, totally justified," adding that "if I had to do it all over again, I would."

The committee's Republican members were also critical and released their own minority report on the program. They criticized the Democratic staff for spending $40 million of government money and diverting "countless CIA analytic and support resources" to conduct the investigation, but failing to offer recommendations for alternative, improved interrogation tactics. Republicans also claimed there were inaccuracies in the report and that because of "political considerations," the Democrats had created a "false impression that the CIA was actively misleading policy makers and impeding the counterterrorism efforts of other federal agencies."

President Obama, however, said the committee's report "documents a troubling program" and "reinforces my long-held view that these harsh methods were not only inconsistent with our values as a nation, they did not serve our broader counterterrorism efforts or our national security interests." He did applaud the CIA's counterterrorism efforts, but said the interrogation program "did significant damage to America's standing in the world and made it harder to pursue our interests with allies and partners."

Notably, the committee did not call for, nor is the government currently considering, further investigation or criminal prosecutions.

—Linda Fecteau Grimm

The following are the findings and conclusions from the Senate Select Committee on Intelligence report on the Central Intelligence Agency's detention and interrogation program, printed on December 9, 2014.

Senate Committee Releases
Report on CIA Detention Program

December 9, 2014

[The following pages have been excerpted from the 528 pages of declassified content from the Senate committee's full report, and reflect the key findings and conclusions.]

Findings and Conclusions

The Committee makes the following findings and conclusions:

#1: The CIA's use of its enhanced interrogation techniques was not an effective means of acquiring intelligence or gaining cooperation from detainees.

The Committee finds, based on a review of CIA interrogation records, that the use of the CIA's enhanced interrogation techniques was not an effective means of obtaining accurate information or gaining detainee cooperation.

For example, according to CIA records, seven of the 39 CIA detainees known to have been subjected to the CIA's enhanced interrogation techniques produced no intelligence while in CIA custody. CIA detainees who were subjected to the CIA's enhanced interrogation techniques were usually subjected to the techniques immediately after being rendered to CIA custody. Other detainees provided significant accurate intelligence prior to, or without having been subjected to these techniques.

While being subjected to the CIA's enhanced interrogation techniques and afterwards, multiple CIA detainees fabricated information, resulting in faulty intelligence. Detainees provided fabricated information on critical intelligence issues, including the terrorist threats which the CIA identified as its highest priorities . . . .

#2: The CIA's justification for the use of its enhanced interrogation techniques rested on inaccurate claims of their effectiveness.

The CIA represented to the White House, the National Security Council, the Department of Justice, the CIA Office of Inspector General, the Congress, and the public that the best measure of effectiveness of the CIA's enhanced interrogation techniques was examples of specific terrorist plots "thwarted" and specific terrorists captured as a result of the use of the techniques. The CIA used these examples to claim that its enhanced interrogation techniques were not only effective, but also necessary to acquire "otherwise unavailable" actionable intelligence that "saved lives."

The Committee reviewed 20 of the most frequent and prominent examples of purported counterterrorism successes that the CIA has attributed to the use of its enhanced interrogation techniques, and found them to be wrong in fundamental respects. In some cases, there was no relationship between the cited counterterrorism success and any information provided by detainees during or after the use of the CIA's enhanced interrogation techniques. In the remaining cases, the CIA inaccurately claimed that specific, otherwise unavailable information was acquired from a CIA detainee "as a result" of the CIA's enhanced interrogation techniques, when in fact the information was either: (1) corroborative of information already available to the CIA or other elements of the U.S. Intelligence

Community from sources other than the CIA detainee, and was therefore not "otherwise unavailable"; or (2) acquired from the CIA detainee prior to the use of the CIA's enhanced interrogation techniques . . . .

#3: The interrogations of CIA detainees were brutal and far worse than the CIA represented to policymakers and others.

Beginning with the CIA's first detainee, Abu Zubaydah, and continuing with numerous others, the CIA applied its enhanced interrogation techniques with significant repetition for days or weeks at a time. Interrogation techniques such as slaps and "wallings" (slamming detainees against a wall) were used in combination, frequently concurrent with sleep deprivation and nudity. Records do not support CIA representations that the CIA initially used an "an open, non threatening approach," or that interrogations began with the "least coercive technique possible" and escalated to more coercive techniques only as necessary.

The waterboarding technique was physically harmful, inducing convulsions and vomiting . . . .

Sleep deprivation involved keeping detainees awake for up to 180 hours, usually standing or in stress positions, at times with their hands shackled above their heads.

At least five detainees experienced disturbing hallucinations during prolonged sleep deprivation and, in at least two of those cases, the CIA nonetheless continued the sleep deprivation . . . .At least five CIA detainees were subjected to "rectal rehydration" or rectal feeding without documented medical necessity. The CIA placed detainees in ice water "baths." . . .

#4: The conditions of confinement for CIA detainees were harsher than the CIA had represented to policymakers and others. . . .

CIA detainees at the COBALT detention facility were kept in complete darkness and constantly shackled in isolated cells with loud noise or music and only a bucket to use for human waste. Lack of heat at the facility likely contributed to the death of a detainee. The chief of interrogations described COBALT as a "dungeon." Another senior CIA officer stated that COBALT was itself an enhanced interrogation technique.

At times, the detainees at COBALT were walked around naked or were shackled with their hands above their heads for extended periods of time. Other times, the detainees at COBALT were subjected to what was described as a "rough takedown," in which approximately five CIA officers would scream at a detainee, drag him outside of his cell, cut his clothes off and secure him with Mylar tape. The detainee would then be hooded and dragged up and down a long corridor while being slapped and punched. . . .

#5: The CIA repeatedly provided inaccurate information to the Department of Justice, impeding a proper legal analysis of the CIA's Detention and Interrogation Program.

From 2002 to 2007, the Office of Legal Counsel (OLC) within the Department of Justice relied on CIA representations regarding: (1) the conditions of confinement for detainees, (2) the application of the CIA's enhanced interrogation techniques, (3) the physical effects of the techniques on detainees, and (4) the effectiveness of the techniques. Those representations were inaccurate in material respects. . . .

#6: The CIA has actively avoided or impeded congressional oversight of the program.

The CIA did not brief the leadership of the Senate Select Committee on Intelligence on the CIA's enhanced interrogation techniques until September 2002, after the techniques had been approved and used. . . . The CIA restricted access to information about the program from members of the Committee beyond the chairman and vice chairman until September 6, 2006, the day the president publicly acknowledged the program, by which time 117 of the 119 known detainees had already entered CIA custody. Until then, the CIA had declined to answer questions from other Committee members that related to CIA interrogation activities. Prior to September 6, 2006, the CIA provided inaccurate information to the leadership of the Committee. . . .

#7: The CIA impeded effective White House oversight and decision-making.

The CIA provided extensive amounts of inaccurate and incomplete information related to the operation and effectiveness of the CIA's Detention and Interrogation Program to the White House, the National Security Council principals, and their staffs. This prevented an accurate and complete understanding of the program by Executive Branch officials, thereby impeding oversight and decision-making.

According to CIA records, no CIA officer, up to and including CIA Directors George Tenet and Porter Goss, briefed the president on the specific CIA enhanced interrogation techniques before April 2006. By that time, 38 of the 39 detainees identified as having been subjected to the CIA's enhanced interrogation techniques had already been subjected to the techniques. . . .

At the direction of the White House, the secretaries of state and defense—both principals on the National Security Council—were not briefed on program specifics until September 2003. An internal CIA email from July 2003 noted that" the WH [White House] is extremely concerned [Secretary] Powell would blow his stack if he were to be briefed on what's been going on." . . .

#8: The CIA's operation and management of the program complicated, and in some cases impeded, the national security missions of other Executive Branch agencies. . . .

The CIA withheld or restricted information relevant to these agencies' missions and responsibilities, denied access to detainees, and provided inaccurate information on the CIA's Detention and Interrogation Program to these agencies.

The use of coercive interrogation techniques and covert detention facilities that did not meet traditional U.S. standards resulted in the FBI and the Department of Defense limiting their involvement in CIA interrogation and detention activities. This reduced the ability of the U.S. Government to deploy available resources and expert personnel to interrogate detainees and operate detention facilities. The CIA denied specific requests from FBI Director Robert Mueller III for FBI access to CIA detainees that the FBI believed was necessary to understand CIA detainee reporting on threats to the U.S. Homeland. . . .

The CIA blocked State Department leadership from access to information crucial to foreign policy decision-making and diplomatic activities. The CIA did not inform two secretaries of state of locations of CIA detention facilities, despite the significant foreign policy implications related to the hosting of clandestine CIA detention sites and the fact that the political leaders of host countries were generally informed of their existence. . . .

#9: The CIA impeded oversight by the CIA's Office of Inspector General.

The CIA avoided, resisted, and otherwise impeded oversight of the CIA's Detention and Interrogation Program by the CIA's Office of Inspector General (OIG). The CIA did not brief the OIG on the program until after the death of a detainee, by which time the CIA had held at least 22 detainees at two different CIA detention sites. Once notified, the OIG reviewed the CIA's Detention and Interrogation Program and issued several reports, including an important May 2004 "Special Review" of the program that identified significant concerns and deficiencies.

During the OIG reviews, CIA personnel provided OIG with inaccurate information on the operation and management of the CIA's Detention and Interrogation Program, as well as on the effectiveness of the CIA's enhanced interrogation techniques. . . .

#10: The CIA coordinated the release of classified information to the media, including inaccurate information concerning the effectiveness of the CIA's enhanced interrogation techniques.

The CIA's Office of Public Affairs and senior CIA officials coordinated to share classified information on the CIA's Detention and Interrogation Program to select members of the media to counter public criticism, shape public opinion, and avoid potential congressional action to restrict the CIA's detention and interrogation authorities and budget. These disclosures occurred when the program was a classified covert action program, and before the CIA had briefed the full Committee membership on the program. . . . Much of the information the CIA provided to the media on the operation of the CIA's Detention and Interrogation Program and the effectiveness of its enhanced interrogation techniques was inaccurate and was similar to the inaccurate information provided by the CIA to the Congress, the Department of Justice, and the White House.

#11: The CIA was unprepared as it began operating its Detention and Interrogation Program more than six months after being granted detention authorities. . . .

The CIA was not prepared to take custody of its first detainee. . . . As it began detention and interrogation operations, the CIA deployed personnel who lacked relevant training and experience. The CIA began interrogation training more than seven months after taking custody of Abu Zubaydah, and more than three months after the CIA began using its "enhanced interrogation techniques." CIA Director George Tenet issued formal guidelines for interrogations and conditions of confinement at detention sites in January 2003, by which time 40 of the 119 known detainees had been detained by the CIA.

#12: The CIA's management and operation of its Detention and Interrogation Program was deeply flawed throughout the program's duration, particularly so in 2002 and early 2003.

The CIA's COBALT detention facility in Country began operations in September 2002 and ultimately housed more than half of the 119 CIA detainees identified in this Study. The CIA kept few formal records of the detainees in its custody at COBALT. Untrained CIA officers at the facility conducted frequent, unauthorized and unsupervised interrogations of detainees using harsh physical interrogation techniques that were not—and never became—part of the CIA's formal "enhanced" interrogation program. The CIA placed a junior officer with no relevant experience in charge of COBALT. On November 2002, a detainee who had been held partially nude and chained to a concrete floor died from suspected hypothermia at the facility.

#13: Two contract psychologists devised the CIA's enhanced interrogation techniques and played a central role in the operation, assessments, and management of the CIA's Detention and Interrogation Program. By 2005, the CIA had overwhelmingly outsourced operations related to the program.

The CIA contracted with two psychologists to develop, operate, and assess its interrogation operations. The psychologists' prior experience was at the U.S. Air Force Survival, Evasion, Resistance and Escape (SERE) school. Neither psychologist had any experience as an interrogator, nor did either have specialized knowledge of al-Qa'ida, a background in counterterrorism, or any relevant cultural or linguistic expertise.

On the CIA's behalf, the contract psychologists developed theories of interrogation based on "learned helplessness," and developed the list of enhanced interrogation techniques that was approved for use. . . . The psychologists personally conducted interrogations of some of the CIA's most significant detainees using these techniques. They also evaluated whether detainees' psychological state allowed for the continued use of the CIA's enhanced interrogation techniques, including some detainees whom they were themselves interrogating or had interrogated. . . .

#14: CIA detainees were subjected to coercive interrogation techniques that had not been approved by the Department of Justice or had not been authorized by CIA Headquarters.

Prior to mid-2004, the CIA routinely subjected detainees to nudity and dietary manipulation. The CIA also used abdominal slaps and cold water dousing on several detainees during that period. None of these techniques had been approved by the Department of Justice.

At least 17 detainees were subjected to CIA enhanced interrogation techniques without authorization from CIA Headquarters. Additionally, multiple detainees were subjected to techniques that were applied in ways that diverged from the specific authorization, or were subjected to enhanced interrogation techniques by interrogators who had not been authorized to use them. . . .

#15: The CIA did not conduct a comprehensive or accurate accounting of the number of individuals it detained, and held individuals who did not meet the legal standard for detention. The CIA's claims about the number of detainees held and subjected to its enhanced interrogation techniques were inaccurate. . . .

CIA statements to the Committee and later to the public that the CIA detained fewer than 100 individuals, and that less than a third of those 100 detainees were subjected to the CIA's enhanced interrogation techniques, were inaccurate. The Committee's review of CIA records determined that the CIA detained at least 119 individuals, of whom at least 39 were subjected to the CIA's enhanced interrogation techniques.

Of the 119 known detainees, at least 26 were wrongfully held and did not meet the detention standard in the September 2001 Memorandum of Notification (MON). . . . Detainees often remained in custody for months after the CIA determined that they did not meet the MON standard. CIA records provide insufficient information to justify the detention of many other detainees. . . .

#16: The CIA failed to adequately evaluate the effectiveness of its enhanced interrogation techniques.

The CIA never conducted a credible, comprehensive analysis of the effectiveness of its enhanced interrogation techniques, despite a recommendation by the CIA inspector general and similar requests by the national security advisor and the leadership of the Senate Select Committee on Intelligence.

Internal assessments of the CIA's Detention and Interrogation Program were conducted by CIA personnel who participated in the development and management of the program, as well as by CIA contractors who had a financial interest in its continuation and expansion. . . .

#17: The CIA rarely reprimanded or held personnel accountable for serious and significant violations, inappropriate activities, and systemic and individual management failures.

Significant events, to include the death and injury of CIA detainees, the detention of individuals who did not meet the legal standard to be held, the use of unauthorized interrogation techniques against CIA detainees, and the provision of inaccurate information on the CIA program did not result in appropriate, effective, or in many cases, any corrective actions. CIA managers who were aware of failings and shortcomings in the program but did not intervene, or who failed to provide proper leadership and management, were also not held to account. . . .

#18: The CIA marginalized and ignored numerous internal critiques, criticisms, and objections concerning the operation and management of the CIA's Detention and Interrogation Program.

Critiques, criticisms, and objections were expressed by numerous CIA officers, including senior personnel overseeing and managing the program, as well as analysts, interrogators, and medical officers involved in or supporting CIA detention and interrogation operations. . . . These concerns were regularly overridden by CIA management, and the CIA made few corrective changes to its policies governing the program. At times, CIA officers were instructed by supervisors not to put their concerns or observations in written communications. . . .

#19: The CIA's Detention and Interrogation Program was inherently unsustainable and had effectively ended by 2006 due to unauthorized press disclosures, reduced cooperation from other nations, and legal and oversight concerns.

The CIA required secrecy and cooperation from other nations in order to operate clandestine detention facilities, and both had eroded significantly before President Bush publicly disclosed the program on September 6, 2006. . . . With the exception of Country I, the CIA was forced to relocate detainees out of every country in which it established a detention facility because of pressure from the host government or public revelations about the program. . . .

By 2006, press disclosures, the unwillingness of other countries to host existing or new detention sites, and legal and oversight concerns had largely ended the CIA's ability to operate clandestine detention facilities.

#20: The CIA's Detention and Interrogation Program damaged the United States' standing in the world, and resulted in other significant monetary and non-monetary costs.

The CIA's Detention and Interrogation Program created tensions with U.S. partners and allies, leading to formal demarches to the United States, and damaging and complicating bilateral intelligence relationships. . . .

To encourage governments to clandestinely host CIA detention sites, or to increase support for existing sites, the CIA provided millions of dollars in cash payments to foreign government officials. CIA Headquarters encouraged CIA Stations to construct "wish lists" of proposed financial assistance to [entities of foreign governments], and to "think big" in terms of that assistance.

SOURCE: Senate Select Committee on Intelligence. "Report of the Senate Select Committee on Intelligence Committee Study of the Central Intelligence Agency's Detention and Interrogation Program." December 9, 2014. www.gpo.gov/fdsys/pkg/CRPT-113srpt288/pdf/CRPT-113srpt288.pdf.

OTHER HISTORIC DOCUMENTS OF INTEREST

FROM THIS VOLUME

FROM PREVIOUS *HISTORIC DOCUMENTS*

Nobel Peace Prize Awarded
to Two Child Rights Activists

DECEMBER 10, 2014

In 2014, the Norwegian Nobel Committee honored two individuals with the annual Peace Prize—Kailash Satyarthi and Malala Yousafzay, both crusaders for children's rights. The Nobel Committee received a record 278 separate nominations for the 2014 award, forty-seven of which were for organizations. Prior to the announcement of the winners in October 2014, speculation on potential winners included United Nations secretary general Ban Ki-moon, Pope Francis, Edward Snowden, and Denis Mukwege, a Congolese gynecologist who has pioneered treatments for sexual violence victims. Yousafzay was also an often-cited contender. According to the Nobel Committee, they purposely chose the combination of winners because the pair "join in a common struggle for education and against extremism," something that demonstrates "fraternity between nations," one of Alfred Nobel's founding criteria for the prize.

Malala Yousafzay Achieves Global Recognition

Yousafzay was born in Pakistan in 1997 to a Muslim family from the Pashtun tribe. In 2009, she began writing an online diary for BBC Urdu under the pen name Gul Makai, named after a heroine in Pashtun folklore. Her diary dealt mainly with her desire to ensure that she could continue her schooling, despite the constant threat from the Taliban. She wrote about the number of her friends who stopped coming to school, afraid that they would be targeted by the Taliban, and about her own fear that her school would be one of the hundreds that had already been closed.

Her father, Ziauddin, encouraged Yousafzay to begin writing the online diary. Her father owned a local private school and was a highly educated, well-respected leader in his community. However, he was constantly at odds with local authorities who he felt inadequately funded the basic needs of the people in the Swat Valley, where his family lived. According to one of Yousafzay's teachers, her father "encouraged Malala to speak freely and learn everything she could." When reporters came to her village to cover the onslaught from extremists in 2009, Yousafzay was sought out as someone who could add a personal narrative to the story. Yousafzay spoke under an assumed name and gave a speech titled "How the Taliban Is Trying to Stop Education," which was reported in the Urdu press. In it, she called on the international community for help: "This is our request to all the world. Save our schools. Save our world. Save our Pakistan. Save our Swat."

Shortly after appearing in a *New York Times* documentary, Yousafzay and her family fled Swat as the Taliban took control. A second video made by *The New York Times* followed Yousafzay and her father as they returned to their school in 2010 and found it destroyed. Villagers blamed the attacks on Ziauddin for speaking out. In the same video,

Yousafzay met with then–special envoy to Pakistan Richard Holbrooke. Yousafzay makes an impassioned plea for assistance from the United States to stop Taliban destruction of schools and allow the girls to return. Opponents used the footage of Yousafzay and Holbrooke as evidence that she was "a CIA spy."

After returning to Swat, Yousafzay began speaking much more freely in public about her beliefs, and it became known that she was the BBC Urdu blogger. The family began receiving Taliban threats, and the Pakistani government offered protection; however, Ziauddin refused. Close friends urged the family to leave the country but Yousafzay said that "does not fit with the code of bravery." On October 9, 2012, while on her way to school, a Taliban militant boarded Yousafzay's bus, called for her, and shot her in the head. The bullet failed to penetrate her skull, but Yousafzay required numerous surgeries and lengthy rehabilitation in Pakistan and the United Kingdom.

Yousafzay was discharged from the hospital in January 2013, and has since begun attending school in the United Kingdom. She has become a staunch advocate for girls around the world seeking an education. Her work has come with great accolades, including being named one of *Time* magazine's most influential people in 2013, winning the Sakharov prize for Freedom of Thought from the European Parliament, and being awarded the National Peace Award from the Pakistani government (the award was later renamed the National Malala Peace Prize).

The situation in Pakistan specifically for girls who seek an education remains grim. The nation allocates only 2.3 percent of its gross domestic product to education, and according to the United Nations, more than five million children do not attend school, the second highest rate in the world. Of those five million, two thirds are female. However, the government has announced that by the end of 2015, education for girls will be a compulsory legal right.

Yousafzay is the youngest awardee of any Nobel Prize in history. Upon learning of her award, she said that she was "honored" and that it made her feel "more powerful and courageous." She added, "I'm really happy to be sharing this award with a person from India."

Kailash Satyarthi's Activism

For decades, Satyarthi, an Indian activist, has used peaceful protest to elevate the rights of children around the world to stop exploitation and child labor. Satyarthi began his movement at age twenty-six when he left his job as an electrical engineer and became the leader of the Bonded Labor Liberation Front and began his own Bachpan Bachao Andolan (Save Childhood Movement). He began by organizing raids on factories that were often manned by child laborers and their families who were held against their will. Satyarthi and his supporters were often brutally wounded during the attacks, but they managed to free an estimated 80,000 children.

To further fulfill his aim, Satyarthi set up multiple international organizations that help former child laborers get an education and reintegrate back into society. One such organization is GoodWeave International, an organization of rug importers and exporters who voluntarily label and certify that their rugs were produced without the use of child labor. One of Satyarthi's largest efforts came in 1998, when he organized a march to the International Labor Organization (ILO) to encourage the body to adopt a convention against child labor. Seven million people joined the march, and by 1999, the ILO adopted the convention, which has been signed by 172 countries. Satyarthi's home nation of India, where there are approximately sixty million child laborers, has not yet signed the convention.

Satyarthi's work, which he says is aimed at wiping "away the blot of human slavery," has earned him a number of accolades around the world, including the U.S. Defenders of Democracy Award, the German Aachener International Peace Award, the Dutch Golden Flag Award, and recognition on the U.S. State Department's list of "Heroes Acting to End Modern Day Slavery." His work has also come at a price. He receives death threats and has been threatened with jail time. Two of his colleagues were murdered for their work. "It is a challenge definitely and I know that it is a long battle to fight, but slavery is unacceptable, it is a crime against humanity," Satyarthi said.

According to the Nobel Committee, the work Satyarthi has done has been instrumental in reducing the number of child laborers around the world. In 2000, there were approximately 246 million child laborers worldwide; by the time of his award, that number had fallen to 168 million. Upon learning of his award, Satyarthi said, "If with my humble efforts the voice of tens of millions of children in the world who are living in servitude is being heard, congratulations to all."

NOBEL AWARD CEREMONY

In announcing the award winners on October 10, the Nobel Committee said Satyarthi and Yousafzay were being jointly awarded "for their struggle against the suppression of children and young people and for the right of all children to education." According to the Committee, "[i]t is a prerequisite for peaceful global development that the rights of children and young people be respected," especially in conflict-ridden regions and the poorest nations.

During the December 10 award ceremony, Thorbjørn Jagland, the chairman of the Nobel Committee, said the importance of children's rights could not be understated, especially in regions where extremist groups like the Taliban, Islamic State of Iraq and the Levant (ISIL), and Boko Haram have taken hold. These groups, he said, "know that [education] is an important condition for freedom. Attendance at school, especially by girls, deprives Taliban, IS[IL], Boko Haram and similar movements of power."

Both awardees, Jagland said, followed the tradition of Mahatma Gandhi and respected the idea of nonviolent activism, and they also adhered to one of Alfred Nobel's central beliefs: unity between nations. "While it is in the nature of extremism to create enemies and frightening images, and to divide the world into us and them, the laureates show us something else," Jagland said. "A young girl and a somewhat older man, one from Pakistan and one from India, one Muslim, the other Hindu; both symbols of what the world needs: more unity."

Jagland called on leaders around the world to follow the example of Yousafzay and Satyarthi and work to "give the younger generation the hope which is probably our strongest defence against extremism. Young people must be able to see into the future instead of being trapped by dark thoughts and dark forces."

In her Nobel lecture, Yousafzay said she hoped everyone would stand up for the rights of young girls to receive an education. "I am here to stand up for their rights, to raise their voice . . . it is not time to pity them. . . . It is time to take action so it becomes the last time . . . that we see a child deprived of education." She spoke of her love of education and discovery and the anger and fear she felt when the Taliban came to Swat and began closing schools. "I had two options," she said. "One was to remain silent and wait to be killed. And the second was to speak up and then be killed. I chose the second one." She added of her attack, "[N]either their ideas nor their bullets could win. . . . I tell my story, not because it is unique, but because it is not. It is the story of many girls." She closed her speech calling on the audience to "let this be the last time that we see a child out of school" and "begin this ending . . . together . . . today . . . right here, right now."

Satyarthi began his speech saying that he could not give a lecture as instructed by the Nobel Committee because he was there to "represent . . . the sound of silence. The cry of innocence. And, the face of invisibility. I have come here to share the voices and dreams of our children . . . because they are all our children." He added, "There is no greater violence than to deny the dreams of our children." Satyarthi spoke of his travels around the world, meeting with children who were soldiers, laborers, and sold into slavery. He said he still has hope that if governments and international organizations can work together, these children will be given greater opportunity. He closed saying, "Let us democratise knowledge. Let us universalise justice. Together, let us globalise compassion, for our children!"

—Heather Kerrigan

Following is the text of the Nobel Peace Prize award ceremony presentation, delivered by Norwegian Nobel Committee chair Thorbjørn Jagland on December 10, 2014.

Nobel Peace Prize Ceremony

December 10, 2014

Your Majesties, Your Royal Highnesses, Excellencies, Ladies and Gentlemen,

A conscience exists in the world which extends beyond all national boundaries, and is independent of religion, culture and social adherence: it states that children have a right to childhood; they have a right to go to school instead of being forced to work. They are not to start life as the slaves of others.

This "world conscience" can find no better expression than through Kailash Satyarthi and Malala Yousafzai.

Dear Nobel Prize Laureates,

A stronger expression of Alfred Nobel's appeal for fraternity between nations would be difficult to find except through you two.

We are honoured to have you here.

Congratulations!

The road to democracy and freedom is paved with knowledge.

Taliban and IS dislike knowledge because they know that it is an important condition for freedom. Attendance at school, especially by girls, deprives Taliban, IS, Boko Haram and similar movements of power.

But nothing should be further from Islam than using suicide bombs against their co-religionists or shooting at a young girl whose only demand was to be allowed to go to school.

Violence and repression cannot be justified in any religion. Islam, Christianity, Judaism, Hinduism and Buddhism protect life and cannot be used to take lives.

The two whom we honour here today stand very firm on this point. They live according to a principle Mahatma Gandhi gave expression to. He said: "There are many purposes I would have died for. There are no purposes I would have killed for".

Satyarthi and Yousafzai are precisely the people whom Alfred Nobel in his will calls "champions of peace".

This they are not only behind a desk, but in practice.

Your Majesties, Your Royal Highnesses, ladies and gentlemen,

Kailash Sathyarthi's vision is quite simply to put an end to child labour. Since he abandoned a promising career as an electrical engineer in 1980, this has been Sathyarthi's overriding aim. He has worked at several different levels to achieve it. At grass-root level he has achieved the release of some 80,000 children, sometimes in very dramatic circumstances. He has often been brutally attacked. It takes little fantasy to imagine the reaction when he and his co-workers go into worn-down factory premises round about in India to set the children free. Powerful interests have profited from child labour. They do not give up without a struggle. Satyarthi himself has adhered to non-violence.

The child labourers are not infrequently recruited by kidnapping, but are often also hired out by parents who cannot manage their debts. Enslavement to debt remains very widespread, not only in India but also in many other countries.

Satyarthi insists that it is not poverty that leads to child labour. Child labour maintains poverty, carrying it on from generation to generation.

School attendance releases people from poverty.

Satyarthi has developed a model for how liberated children can be rehabilitated and provided with education. They must be provided with a basic education to enable them to some extent to function as normal citizens rather than as slaves. He has set up a number of different organizations which work both in India and internationally to fulfil children's rights. Bachpan Bachao Andolan is perhaps his most important instrument, taking direct action to set children free.

Satyarthi's struggle is marked by great inventiveness. Rugmark, established in 1994 (now Goodweave), is a striking example. It is an international consortium of representatives of countries which export and import rugs. We can all by simple means check that a rug has not been made by child labourers. A network of inspectors has been set up to ensure that the system works. The children get to go to school, and the adult workers earn a fair wage.

Exporters and importers pay a small fee to keep up this system of inspections and controls. Efforts are in hand to spread the scheme to other products often made by child labour, such as knitted goods and sports gear.

On the 17th of January 1998, Satyarthi embarked on his biggest project: The Global March Against Child Labour. Seven million children and adults took part in this march, which entered many different countries and regions. The march wound up at the ILO headquarters in Geneva. The following year the ILO convention against the worst forms of child labour was unanimously adopted. The convention has currently been ratified by 172 countries. No ILO convention has been ratified more quickly. ILO conventions 138 and 182, and the UN "Convention on the Rights of the Child", now form the basis of the world-wide struggle against child labour and for education.

Much nevertheless remains to be done. There are roughly 60 million child labourers in India alone, most of them in farming. If the country were to ratify the two ILO conventions, that would be a big step in the right direction.

There are currently 168 million child labourers worldwide. In the year 2000, the figure was 78 million higher. In this, as in so many other areas, things are thus moving in the right direction, and often much faster than we think. Satyarthi indeed believes that child labour can be more or less eliminated in his own lifetime.

Everyone here shares that hope.

Your Majesties, Your Royal Highnesses, ladies and gentlemen,

Malala Yousafzai is far and away the youngest Peace Prize Laureate of all time. Her story has nevertheless become known practically all over the world. When she was 11 or 12 she began under a pseudonym to write a blog for the BBC about what it was like to live in the Swat valley in northwest Pakistan, under heavy pressure from the Taliban and with only ambivalent support from the Pakistani authorities. The schools periodically had to close, especially girls' schools.

Malala Yousafzai's vision was clear right from the start. Girls had a self-evident right to education.

Her courage is almost indescribable. We all know what happened on the 9th of October 2012, when Malala was 15. A gunman climbed into the school bus and asked for Malala. He fired three shots at her, injuring her most severely. Her life was saved, and she decided to continue her struggle for girls' education, although Taliban have made no secret of their intention to try again.

Pakistan's population numbers nearly 200 million. One quarter are between 5 and 16 years old. The nation's constitution guarantees all these children free and compulsory education. But nearly half the 52 million do not go to school; a large majority of them are girls. And it is not just Taliban that seeks to keep the girls away from school. The authorities do so, too, having built schools without walls, without running water, and without toilets. And at least as important: indoctrination is sometimes more important than the skills and knowledge needed in order to cope in a modern world. The teachers, too, often lack the minimum qualifications needed.

Pakistani authorities have praised the award of the Peace Prize to Malala Yousafzai. The best gift they could give her would be dramatic improvements to the country's education system.

That would benefit the whole of Pakistan.

Few things provide a larger economic and social yield than investments in girls' education.

This logic applies all over the world. By placing the individual person at the centre of all politics, one will soon see that those "excluded" are not a burden and a threat, but an enormous unused resource. Here in Europe, too, such logic would work wonders. The problem here is not that children and adolescents receive no education or are obliged to work. Far too many find no use for their education or find no opportunities for work.

We need to leave this negative situation and instead give the younger generation the hope which is probably our strongest defence against extremism.

Young people must be able to see into the future instead of being trapped by dark thoughts and dark forces.

Ladies and gentlemen,

While it is in the nature of extremism to create enemies and frightening images, and to divide the world into us and them, the laureates show us something else:

A young girl and a somewhat older man, one from Pakistan and one from India, one Muslim, the other Hindu; both symbols of what the world needs: more unity. Fraternity between the nations!

The Laureates have underlined that if the prize can contribute to bringing Indians and Pakistanis, two people so near to one another and yet so distant, closer to one another, this would add an extra dimension to the prize.

We share this hope.

Ladies and gentlemen,

We need people like Satyarthi and Yousafzai to show that it helps to fight.

Few if any of us have had greater courage to live according to Mahatma Gandhi's principle that "I accept only one tyrant in the world, and that is the still small voice within me".

We others have perhaps become too accustomed to following the voices of others, pouring into our heads through the social media. We often forget to listen to our own voice, the one that talks to us about justice.

Freedom and justice have never been ceremonial. The world never progressed thanks to coldly calculating people. It advanced thanks to the efforts of people with warm hearts.

Your Majesties, ladies and gentlemen,

We live in an age in which the world, despite all the violence and extremism we see around us, is marked by an increasing humanity.

The author James Baldwin put it like this: "The people that once walked in darkness are no longer prepared to do so".

This has become an irrevocable part of our common awareness.

Persons like Kailash Satiarthi and Malala Yousafzai have brought us there.

They show that it helps to resist. Even under the most difficult conditions.

Dear Nobel Prize Laureates,

You will for all the future form part of the row of gold that forms our Nobel history—the row of campaigning people. People who have created the "global conscience" of which we can all be the bearers—the call for freedom and justice.

The most important thing of all is to have children and young people set free!

Thank you for your attention.

Source: The Nobel Foundation. "Award Ceremony Speech." December 10, 2014. www.nobelprize.org/nobel_prizes/peace/laureates/2014/presentation-speech.html. © The Nobel Foundation 2014.

Other Historic Documents of Interest

From this volume

■ Attack on Pakistani Military School, p. 614

From previous *Historic Documents*

Attack on Pakistani Military School

DECEMBER 16 AND 17, 2014

On the morning of December 16, Taliban militants entered a school for children of army members and indiscriminately killed 132 students. The attack was the worst carried out by the militant group in Pakistan. The Pakistani government quickly retaliated and began targeted airstrikes against Taliban militants along the Afghan border. The ongoing violence forced a growing number of Pakistanis from their homes and into refugee camps often filled with Afghan citizens. The threat of violence from the Taliban has kept aid organizations from delivering necessary food, water, and medical supplies, which has contributed to the spread of diseases such as polio.

TALIBAN MILITANTS TARGET ARMY SCHOOL

In early February 2014, newly elected prime minister Nawaz Sharif announced that peace talks were underway with Tehreek-e-Taliban Pakistan (TTP) in an effort to end years of deadly violence. Negotiations began to break down by the middle of the month when twenty-three Pakistani soldiers who were first captured in 2010 were executed by the Taliban. "We have warned the government time and time again . . . to stop the killing of our friends, who were in the custody of security forces, but the government continued killing our people," said Taliban commander Omar Khalid Khurassani. Sharif called such actions an attempt to sabotage the peace talks. Still, on March 1, 2014, both sides agreed to a ceasefire as a first step for another round of talks to continue. That ceasefire lasted until April 16 when the TTP formally withdrew its support for the measure. Any further effort to bring the two sides together ended on June 8 when TTP militants attacked the Jinnah Airport and killed more than twenty people. The Pakistan military subsequently launched a military assault against known TTP hideouts.

On the morning of December 16, 2014, militants dressed in Pakistani paramilitary uniforms scaled a wall and entered the Peshawar army school, located in the military cantonment area and attended by 1,000 students aged five to eighteen. The militants specifically targeted those students found hiding under desks or benches. Within fifteen minutes of the start of the attack, Pakistani military commandos arrived at the school and began engaging the terrorists. Local police and army troops cordoned off the area to prevent any of those responsible from escaping. The standoff with the attackers lasted for eight hours before the building was declared cleared. "The people of Pakistan are deeply shocked and grieved at the despicable act of terrorism in a Peshawar school this morning," said Pakistan's foreign minister, Mir Hazar Khan Khoso. "The terrorists have once again shown that they have no regard for human life and no respect for children." He added that "such cold blooded cowardly acts cannot weaken the resolve of the people of Pakistan."

The attack was the deadliest carried out by the Taliban in Pakistan. In total, 132 students and nine staff were killed. The students killed ranged in age from eight to eighteen. The seven terrorists who carried out the assault were also killed—some by detonating their suicide vests and others by Pakistan military responders. The identities of six of the terrorists and their nationalities were released following the attack. They included Abu Shamil, a Chechen; Nouman Shah Helmand and Wazir Alam Herat, both Afghans; Khatib al-Zubaidi, an Egyptian; Mohammad Zahedi, a Moroccan; and Jibran al-Saeedi, whose nationality was not known.

International reaction was swift. "There is not a belief system in the world that can justify this appalling act," said British prime minister David Cameron. Indian prime minister Narendra Modi called the attack "a senseless act of unspeakable brutality that has claimed lives of the most innocent of human beings—young children in their school." U.S. secretary of state John Kerry said the "gut-wrenching" attack was "an unspeakable horror" for which those responsible "must be brought to justice." United Nations (UN) secretary general Ban Ki-moon called the attack "an act of horror and rank cowardice." Seventeen-year-old Pakistani activist Malala Yousafzay, who had been awarded the Nobel Peace Prize less than one week earlier, said she was "heartbroken by this senseless and cold-blooded act of terror in Peshawar that is unfolding before us. Innocent children in their school have no place in horror such as this." But, she added, "we will never be defeated."

Pakistan Retaliates Against TTP Attack

TTP quickly claimed responsibility for the attack, which they said was carried out in retaliation for the Pakistan military offensive known as Operation Zarb-e-Azb against groups operating in North Waziristan, along the Afghan border. The ongoing offensive, which began in June 2014, had killed an estimated 1,000 militants. "We selected the army's school for the attack because the government is targeting our families and females," said Taliban spokesperson Mohammed Umar Khurasani. "We want them to feel the pain."

In response to the attack, Pakistan's military began a series of air strikes and ground assaults against the Pakistan Taliban in its strongholds. "Our resolve to tackle this menace has gotten a new lease of life. We will pursue these monsters and their facilitators until they are eliminated for good," said Pakistan's army chief General Raheel Sharif. Prime Minister Nawaz Sharif said the air attacks would continue "until terrorism is rooted from our land." He added, "At no stage there would be any discrimination between the good and bad Taliban and all would be dealt equally with an iron hand." In response to the ramped up attacks against the Taliban, TTP leader Maulana Fazlullah said that until the airstrikes stopped, his group would continue its own attacks. "You will forget the Peshawar school attack when you face more deadly attacks," he said, adding that the militants would continue to target the children of military families.

Pakistan's military leadership reached out to Afghan president Ashraf Ghani and his military leaders to discuss potential joint operations against the Taliban. Sources close to the talks indicated that Sharif told Ghani that while he respected Afghanistan's sovereignty, if the country was ineffective in rooting out terrorists along the border, Pakistan was prepared to step in, with or without permission. In response, the Afghan Ministry of Defense confirmed that in the wake of the school attack it had increased its own operations against Taliban militants operating within its borders. A few days after the school attack, it appeared that both Afghanistan and the U.S.-led coalition in the region were participating in attacks against terrorists in Pakistan. It was reported that a U.S. drone strike in northwestern Pakistan killed at least five militants; however, the United States did not confirm involvement. According to Sartaj Aziz, Sharif's national security adviser, Pakistan and Afghanistan "will supplement each others' operations by blocking the border during operations from one side so that anyone trying to escape could be arrested."

Pakistan's leader also reversed a moratorium on the death penalty for convicted terrorists, and in January 2015 went on to pass a constitutional amendment that would allow for quick trials of suspected terrorists. On December 19 and 21, 2014, six convicted militants were hanged, four of whom had been found guilty of a 2003 attempt to assassinate former military leader Pervez Musharraf. The move to lift the moratorium raised concerns among human rights groups, which point to Pakistan's record of having a weak judicial system that frequently relies on the terrorist label to convict individuals. According to a joint report by Reprieve, a UK-based legal charity, and the Justice Pakistan Project, approximately 86 percent of those convicted and sentenced under Pakistan's terrorism laws "had nothing to do with terror at all." Clive Stafford Smith, Reprieve's director, responded to the lifting of the moratorium saying, "While the slaughter of innocents in Peshawar was utterly reprehensible, it hardly solves the problem to kill someone who had nothing to do with it." Human Rights Watch also called on the government to stop killing convicted terrorists. "The government's death penalty spree is a craven politicized reaction to the Peshawar killings that will do nothing to bring the attackers to justice," said Phelim Kine, deputy director of the group's Asia Division. Amnesty International Asia-Pacific deputy director David Griffiths added, "Resorting to the death penalty is not the answer—it is never the answer. This is where the government should focus its energies, rather than perpetuating the cycle of violence with the resumption of executions."

Refugee Crisis Deepens in North Waziristan

After the school shooting, provincial governments inside Pakistan near TTP hideouts in North Waziristan began clearing refugee camps, searching through the Afghan refugees for possible TTP members or supporters. According to the UN high commissioner on refugees, Pakistan currently hosts nearly 1.5 million Afghan refugees. Many of the refugees in the camps had been there for decades since the Soviet Union took control of Afghanistan in the 1980s; others entered the camps during the tyrannical reign of Saddam Hussein's Baathist regime, or during the recent rise of the Islamic State of Iraq and the Levant (ISIL). Internally displaced Pakistanis have also become more common at the camps as their cities are witness to intense fighting between the Pakistan military and TTP.

As a result of the growing violence along the Afghan border, international aid agencies have had difficulty reaching those in need of assistance. One of the greatest concerns in the refugee camps since TTP has ramped up its presence in the area is the growing threat of polio. TTP banned vaccines in response to U.S. drone strikes in 2012, believing that vaccines are an attempt by Western governments to control the people of Pakistan and Afghanistan. Because of the lack of clean water and a stable, healthy food supply, the disease has spread quickly through the camps. The World Health Organization has been working to find the most common routes of passage to North Waziristan in an effort to vaccinate individuals before they enter the camps.

—Heather Kerrigan

Following is a press release issued on December 16, 2014, by Pakistan's Ministry of Foreign Affairs on the terrorist attack in Peshawar; and a December 17, 2014, statement from the Pakistan prime minister's office on actions against extremists.

Pakistan Foreign
Ministry on School Attacks

December 16, 2014

The people of Pakistan are deeply shocked and grieved at the despicable act of terrorism in a Peshawar school this morning. The terrorists have once again shown that they have no regard for human life and no respect for children.

In this hour of grief, our hearts go out to the families of these young children who embraced shahadat today. Such cold blooded cowardly acts cannot weaken the resolve of the people of Pakistan, the Government, and the Armed forces, to combat all terrorists. These terrorists are enemies of Pakistan, enemies of Islam and enemies of humanity.

We pay our homage to our brave soldiers who are engaged in a valiant effort to root out terrorism from the country.

The Pakistani nation stands united in condemning this heinous crime and remains resolute in its commitment to eliminate terrorism from the soil of Pakistan. Success will Inshallah be of our brave and indomitable people.

SOURCE: Pakistan Ministry of Foreign Affairs. "Terrorist Attack in Peshawar." December 16, 2014. http://www.mofa.gov.pk/pr-details.php?mm=MjQzMA,,.

Prime Minister Vows
Retaliation for School Attack

December 17, 2014

The national political leadership on Wednesday vowed to fight the extremists and terrorists without any discrimination so as to wipe out this scourge from the country.

"At no stage there would be any discrimination between the good and bad Taliban and all would be dealt equally with an iron hand," Prime Minister Muhammad Nawaz Sharif said while addressing a press conference along with national political leaders.

The Prime Minister read out a written statement agreed upon by the political leadership of the country, specifically gathered here at the Governor's House to deliberate upon a course of action following the horrific act of terrorism at a local school that left over 140 people dead, including 132 children.

While expressing deep grief and sorrow over the tragic Peshawar incident, the Prime Minister said the meeting agreed that the war against extremism and terrorism needed to be fought with national consensus and determination.

He said a number of terrorists had escaped towards Afghanistan and measures were afoot to apprehend them so that justice could prevail.

The Prime Minister said it was also decided to constitute a committee to finalize suggestions for preparing a "Plan of Action" that would be approved by the national political and military leadership and shared with the nation.

He said the committee, headed by the Interior Minister, would submit suggestions in seven days. Representatives of military and intelligence agencies would be included in the committee.

The meeting noted the supreme sacrifices of the law enforcement agencies during the operation Zarb-e-Azb and observed the attack on the school seemed to be a part of a plan of the fleeing terrorists.

He said the operation was going on with success and had achieved many of its stated objectives.

The Prime Minister said the hideouts and sanctuaries of the terrorists had been destroyed and they were on the run.

He said the national political leadership had discussed the critical issue of terrorism in detail and come up with solid suggestions.

To a question about his discussion with Pakistan Tehreek-i-Insaf chief Imran Khan, the Prime Minister said it was a beauty of democracy that all issues could be discussed amicably. He specially thanked Imran Khan for attending the meeting at a critical juncture while setting aside his differences.

The Prime Minister, when asked about the setting up of a judicial commission, said he himself had written a letter to the Supreme Court and also mentioned the recent decision of the apex court. The matter, he added, needed to be resolved amicably with consensus and to the satisfaction of the parties concerned.

Imran Khan on the occasion said the country was passing through a critical juncture and the entire leadership was together on one platform to address the issue of extremism and terrorism.

He said if the judicial commission was set up, his party would accept the decision whatever it took without any objection.

Imran Khan said in the wake of cold blooded murder of children, he had set aside his differences as the matter of terrorism was far more serious and needed urgent attention.

"It is a national cause and we stand fully with the federal government and give out a clear message that leaders of entire political spectrum stand together to express their resolve to defeat terrorism, once for all."

He termed the holding of the meeting a welcome step and said he would soon be going back to his container at D-Chowk to offer prayers for the departed souls.

The Prime Minister remarked he had to go to the hospital to inquire after the injured, otherwise he would too have joined Imran Khan on the container.

SOURCE: Office of the Prime Minister of the Islamic Republic of Pakistan. "Political Leadership Vows Indiscriminate Action Against Terrorists." December 17, 2014. www.pmo.gov.pk/press_release_detailes .php?pr_id=710.

OTHER HISTORIC DOCUMENTS OF INTEREST

FROM THIS VOLUME

FROM PREVIOUS *HISTORIC DOCUMENTS*

President Obama on Restoring Diplomatic Relations With Cuba

DECEMBER 17, 2014

Separated by just ninety miles, the United States and Cuba have a long history of diplomatic tensions that began shortly after Cuban leader Fidel Castro came to power in 1959. The practically nonexistent relationship since that time has prevented Americans from traveling to the island nation and stopped most trade. In mid-December 2014, President Barack Obama announced the intent of the two nations to begin working toward normalizing relations. The president admitted that the process would take time, but that it could have a far-reaching impact on Cuban society. "Cubans have a saying about daily life: 'No es facil'—it's not easy. Today, the United States wants to be a partner in making the lives of ordinary Cubans a little bit easier, more free, more prosperous," the president said.

HISTORY OF U.S.-CUBA RELATIONS

Castro came to power in 1959 after toppling the American-backed government of General Fulgencio Batista. The United States quickly recognized Castro as the legitimate ruler of Cuba, despite the methods used to gain power and his communist ideology. Cuba, however, began looking for new partners on the global stage, specifically the Soviet Union, then a fierce enemy of the United States. As Cuba increased its trade relations with the Soviet government, and in turn began raising taxes on American imports, the U.S. government began its own round of economic sanctions, including a complete embargo on all trade.

Diplomatic ties between the two countries officially ended in 1961, and the U.S. government followed with numerous attempts to overthrow Castro's government, including the infamous 1961 Bay of Pigs Invasion in which the Central Intelligence Agency oversaw an attack against Castro by 1,400 American-trained Cubans; the troops surrendered after less than twenty-four hours. Anger over the plan pushed Cuba to further strengthen its relationship with the Soviet Union, even allowing it to build a secret missile base in Cuba. The missile base set off the thirteen-day Cuban Missile Crisis during which then-President John Kennedy ordered a naval blockade around the island and demanded the removal of the base. To end the standoff, the United States agreed not to invade Cuba as long as the base was dismantled and further agreed to remove its own missiles from Turkey, which had been positioned against the Soviet Union.

After the agreement was reached, and even later after the fall of the Soviet Union in 1991, the United States did not lift its embargo against Cuba and made little effort to improve or restore relations. In 1992 and 1996, Congress passed the Cuba Democracy Act and the Helms-Burton Act, respectively, both of which further strengthened the embargo against the communist nation. Both pieces of legislation included language essentially disallowing the United States from lifting the embargo against Cuba until it held free, democratic elections in which the Castro family did not take part. In 1982, Cuba was added to the State Department's list of state sponsors of terrorism.

When Raúl Castro succeeded his ailing brother to become president in 2008, there was hope that he might make attempts to smooth the nation's relationship with the United States. During his first years in office, Castro worked to shore up the country's ailing economy by loosening economic restrictions including expanding opportunities in the private sector.

INTENT TO RESTORE DIPLOMATIC RELATIONS

When he took office in 2009, some of President Obama's first forays into international relations involved softening the U.S. approach toward Cuba and undoing some restrictions put in place by his predecessor, President George W. Bush. This included allowing Americans with Cuban relatives to make unlimited visits to the island nation and send financial aid and certain gifts to their families. The president also eased restrictions on wireless providers to allow them to setup cellphone and television services in Cuba. At the time, Obama's press secretary, Robert Gibbs, said the president's decision was aimed at helping Cubans be less dependent on the Castro regime. "The president would like to see greater freedom for the Cuban people. There are actions that he can and has taken today to open up the flow of information to provide some important steps to help that," Gibbs said. The goodwill was somewhat undone later in 2009 when Cuban officials arrested Alan Gross, a subcontractor for the U.S. Agency for International Development, who was on the island to help set up Internet access for Jewish residents. Gross was charged with an attempt to overthrow the Castro regime and sentenced to fifteen years in prison. Obama promised to both secure Gross's release and further restore ties with Cuba.

Over the course of eighteen months in 2013 and 2014, U.S. and Cuban officials met secretly to examine the potential of the normalization of the relationship. The talks were hosted mostly by Canada and supported by Pope Francis, and they resulted in a framework for restoring full diplomatic ties, as long as certain concessions were met. This included the release of the remaining three Cuban Five by the United States and the release of Gross and Rolando Sarraff Trujillo, a Cuban intelligence officer who spied on Cuba for the CIA and had been held by the Castro regime for two decades. Cuba also agreed to release fifty-three individuals being held in Cuban jails who were considered political prisoners by U.S. officials. "We will end an outdated approach that, for decades, has failed to advance our interests, and instead, we will begin to normalize relations between our two countries," President Obama said in an address on December 17, 2014, announcing the agreement. "Neither the American nor Cuban people are well served by a rigid policy that's rooted in events that took place before most of us were born," he continued. In announcing the intent of Cuba and the United States to begin normalizing relations, the president said the hope was "to create more opportunities for the American and Cuban people and begin a new chapter among the nations of the Americas."

The new approach to Cuban relations included fourteen key provisions: the establishment of diplomatic relations, the adjustment of relations to empower Cubans, expanded travel to Cuba, an increase in remittance levels, expanded commercial sales and exports to Cuba, the allowance of additional imports from Cuba, the facilitation of authorized transactions between the two countries, new efforts to help Cubans access communications technologies, an update to Cuban sanctions in third countries, a discussion of the maritime boundary in the Gulf of Mexico, a review of the State Department designation of

Cuba as a state sponsor of terrorism, seeking the allowance of Cuban civil society groups to participate in the 2015 Summit of the Americans in Panama, and a continuing commitment to human rights and democracy.

Raúl Castro appeared on state-run television in Cuba to announce the release of the remaining three Cuban Five members. During his speech, he also addressed the work that would be done to normalize relations with the United States. "This in no way means that the heart of the matter has been solved. The economic, commercial, and financial blockade, which causes enormous human and economic damages to our country, must cease," Castro noted. "While acknowledging our profound differences, particularly on issues related to national sovereignty, democracy, human rights and foreign policy, I reaffirm our willingness to dialogue on all these issues." The leader closed, "We must learn the art of coexisting with our differences in a civilized manner."

POTENTIAL BENEFITS AND REACTION TO REFORM

The announcement of a renewed relationship and release of the Cuban Five was met with cheers in the streets of Havana, Cuba's capital. Public opinion polls in the United States indicated a similar softening of opinion toward the nation. A Pew Research poll conducted after the president's announcement found 63 percent of those surveyed supported the resumption of diplomatic relations. In a similar *Washington Post*-ABC News poll, 74 percent of respondents said they would like to see the United States end the travel ban to Cuba. Cuban Americans, who for decades supported the increasing sanctions against Cuba, now support the normalization of relations with Cuba, according to a Florida International University poll. The latter point is of particular interest to politicians who were wary of alienating that portion of the electorate. Cuban Americans strongly supported Republican candidates until the 2012 election when support shifted to President Obama.

Republican lawmakers did not similarly agree with the president's decision. "Relations with the Castro regime should not be revisited, let alone normalized, until the Cuban people enjoy freedom—and not one second sooner," said Speaker of the House John Boehner, R-Ohio. Sen. Marco Rubio, R-Fla., a Cuban American, called the president's announcement "another concession to tyranny." Jeff Flake, R-Ariz., was one of few Republicans to support the president. U.S. policy on Cuba to date has "done more . . . to keep the Castro regime in power than anything we could have done," he said. Republicans in Congress have proposed a number of methods for keeping the president from normalizing relations with Cuba, including withholding funds for the opening of a U.S. embassy in Havana, voting down any bill that would open up travel, and ignoring executive requests to lift the trade embargo. "I will do all in my power to block the use of funds to open an embassy in Cuba," said Sen. Lindsey Graham, R-S.C. While Obama will have some ability to use his executive authority to implement some changes, he will require the approval of Congress for many, a difficult undertaking given that both houses were in the control of Republicans beginning in January 2015.

Many international analysts believe that the opening up of diplomatic relations between the United States and Cuba could lead to more democratic reforms on the island, something the United States has been keen to see. "Cuba is undertaking a process of economic reforms that will, I hope, lead to political reforms," said Organization of American States secretary-general José Miguel Insulza. Changes in Cuban human rights have been raised as an issue that will be closely followed as the United States and Cuba work to normalize relations.

According to Human Rights Watch, Cuba "continues to repress individuals and groups who criticize the government or call for basic human rights." The Castro brothers' governments have used wrongful imprisonment, beatings, and exile to silence their critics; however, some of those tactics have been used less frequently since Raúl Castro came to power. In his speech regarding normalization of relations, President Obama said, "The United States believes that no Cuban should face harassment or arrest or beatings simply because they're exercising a universal right to have their voices heard, and we will continue to support civil society there."

Raúl Castro has promised to leave office no later than 2018, at the end of his second term, and it remains to be seen whether he will be able to institute democratic and human rights changes before he steps down, or if it will be up to his successor to see through such changes.

—Heather Kerrigan

Following is the text of an address delivered by President Barack Obama on December 17, 2014, regarding the normalization of relations with Cuba.

President Obama
Addresses the Nation on Cuba

December 17, 2014

Good afternoon. Today the United States of America is changing its relationship with the people of Cuba.

In the most significant changes in our policy in more than 50 years, we will end an outdated approach that, for decades, has failed to advance our interests, and instead, we will begin to normalize relations between our two countries. Through these changes, we intend to create more opportunities for the American and Cuban people and begin a new chapter among the nations of the Americas.

There's a complicated history between the United States and Cuba. I was born in 1961, just over 2 years after Fidel Castro took power in Cuba and just a few months after the Bay of Pigs invasion, which tried to overthrow his regime. Over the next several decades, the relationship between our countries played out against the backdrop of the cold war and America's steadfast opposition to communism. We are separated by just over 90 miles. But year after year, an ideological and economic barrier hardened between our two countries.

Meanwhile, the Cuban exile community in the United States made enormous contributions to our country: in politics and business, culture and sports. Like immigrants before, Cubans helped remake America, even as they felt a painful yearning for the land and families they left behind. All of this bound America and Cuba in a unique relationship, at once family and foe.

Proudly, the United States has supported democracy and human rights in Cuba through these five decades. We've done so primarily through policies that aimed to isolate the island, preventing the most basic travel and commerce that Americans can enjoy anyplace else. And though this policy has been rooted in the best of intentions, no other nation joins us in imposing these sanctions, and it has had little effect beyond providing the Cuban Government with a rationale for restrictions on its people. Today, Cuba is still governed by the Castros and the Communist Party that came to power half a century ago.

Neither the American nor Cuban people are well served by a rigid policy that's rooted in events that took place before most of us were born. Consider that for more than 35 years, we've had relations with China, a far larger country also governed by a Communist Party. Nearly two decades ago, we reestablished relations with Vietnam, where we fought a war that claimed more Americans than any cold war confrontation.

That's why, when I came into office, I promised to reexamine our Cuba policy. As a start, we lifted restrictions for Cuban Americans to travel and send remittances to their families in Cuba. These changes, once controversial, now seem obvious. Cuban Americans have been reunited with their families and are the best possible ambassadors for our values. And through these exchanges, a younger generation of Cuban Americans has increasingly questioned an approach that does more to keep Cuba closed off from an interconnected world.

While I've been prepared to take additional steps for some time, a major obstacle stood in our way: the wrongful imprisonment, in Cuba, of a U.S. citizen and USAID subcontractor, Alan Gross, for 5 years. Over many months, my administration has held discussions with the Cuban Government about Alan's case and other aspects of our relationship. His Holiness Pope Francis issued a personal appeal to me, and to Cuba's President Raul Castro, urging us to resolve Alan's case and to address Cuba's interest in the release of three Cuban agents who've been jailed in the United States for over 15 years.

Today Alan returned home, reunited with his family at long last. Alan was released by the Cuban Government on humanitarian grounds. Separately, in exchange for the three Cuban agents, Cuba today released one of the most important intelligence agents that the United States has ever had in Cuba, and who has been imprisoned for nearly two decades. This man, whose sacrifice has been known to only a few, provided America with the information that allowed us to arrest the network of Cuban agents that included the men transferred to Cuba today, as well as other spies in the United States. This man is now safely on our shores.

Having recovered these two men who sacrificed for our country, I'm now taking steps to place the interests of the people of both countries at the heart of our policy.

First, I've instructed Secretary Kerry to immediately begin discussions with Cuba to reestablish diplomatic relations that have been severed since January of 1961. Going forward, the United States will reestablish an Embassy in Havana, and high-ranking officials will visit Cuba.

Where we can advance shared interests, we will: on issues like health, migration, counterterrorism, drug trafficking, and disaster response. Indeed, we've seen the benefits of cooperation between our countries before. It was a Cuban, Carlos Finlay, who discovered that mosquitoes carry yellow fever; his work helped Walter Reed fight it. Cuba has sent hundreds of health care workers to Africa to fight Ebola, and I believe American and Cuban health care workers should work side by side to stop the spread of this deadly disease.

Now, where we disagree, we will raise those differences directly, as we will continue to do on issues related to democracy and human rights in Cuba. But I believe that we can do more to support the Cuban people and promote our values through engagement. After all, these 50 years have shown that isolation has not worked. It's time for a new approach.

Second, I've instructed Secretary Kerry to review Cuba's designation as a state sponsor of terrorism. This review will be guided by the facts and the law. Terrorism has changed in the last several decades. At a time when we are focused on threats from Al Qaida to ISIL, a nation that meets our conditions and renounces the use of terrorism should not face this sanction.

Third, we are taking steps to increase travel, commerce, and the flow of information to and from Cuba. This is fundamentally about freedom and openness and also expresses my belief in the power of people-to-people engagement. With the changes I'm announcing today, it will be easier for Americans to travel to Cuba, and Americans will be able to use American credit and debit cards on the island. Nobody represents America's values better than the American people, and I believe this contact will ultimately do more to empower the Cuban people.

I also believe that more resources should be able to reach the Cuban people. So we're significantly increasing the amount of money that can be sent to Cuba and removing limits on remittances that support humanitarian projects, the Cuban people, and the emerging Cuban private sector.

I believe that American businesses should not be put at a disadvantage and that increased commerce is good for Americans and for Cubans. So we will facilitate authorized transactions between the United States and Cuba. U.S. financial institutions will be allowed to open accounts at Cuban financial institutions. And it will be easier for U.S. exporters to sell goods in Cuba.

I believe in the free flow of information. Unfortunately, our sanctions on Cuba have denied Cubans access to technology that has empowered individuals around the globe. So I've authorized increased telecommunications connections between the United States and Cuba. Businesses will be able to sell goods that enable Cubans to communicate with the United States and other countries.

These are the steps that I can take as President to change this policy. The embargo that's been imposed for decades is now codified in legislation. As these changes unfold, I look forward to engaging Congress in an honest and serious debate about lifting the embargo.

Yesterday I spoke with Raul Castro to finalize Alan Gross's release and the exchange of prisoners and to describe how we will move forward. I made clear my strong belief that Cuban society is constrained by restrictions on its citizens. In addition to the return of Alan Gross and the release of our intelligence agent, we welcome Cuba's decision to release a substantial number of prisoners whose cases were directly raised with the Cuban Government by my team. We welcome Cuba's decision to provide more access to the Internet for its citizens and to continue increasing engagement with international institutions like the United Nations and the International Committee of the Red Cross that promote universal values.

But I'm under no illusion about the continued barriers to freedom that remain for ordinary Cubans. The United States believes that no Cuban should face harassment or arrest or beatings simply because they're exercising a universal right to have their voices heard, and we will continue to support civil society there. While Cuba has made reforms to gradually open up its economy, we continue to believe that Cuban workers should be free to form unions, just as their citizens should be free to participate in the political process.

Moreover, given Cuba's history, I expect it will continue to pursue foreign policies that will at times be sharply at odds with American interests. I do not expect the changes I'm announcing today to bring about a transformation of Cuban society overnight. But I am convinced that through a policy of engagement, we can more effectively stand up for our values and help the Cuban people help themselves as they move into the 21st century.

To those who oppose the steps I'm announcing today, let me say that I respect your passion and share your commitment to liberty and democracy. The question is how we uphold that commitment. I do not believe we can keep doing the same thing for over five decades and expect a different result. Moreover, it does not serve America's interests or the Cuban people to try to push Cuba towards collapse. Even if that worked—and it hasn't for 50 years—we know from hard-earned experience that countries are more likely to enjoy lasting transformation if their people are not subjected to chaos. We are calling on Cuba to unleash the potential of 11 million Cubans by ending unnecessary restrictions on their political, social, and economic activities. In that spirit, we should not allow U.S. sanctions to add to the burden of Cuban citizens that we seek to help.

To the Cuban people, America extends a hand of friendship. Some of you have looked to us as a source of hope, and we will continue to shine a light of freedom. Others have seen us as a former colonizer intent on controlling your future. José Martí once said, "Liberty is the right of every man to be honest." Today I'm being honest with you. We can never erase the history between us, but we believe that you should be empowered to live with dignity and self-determination. Cubans have a saying about daily life: "No es facil"— it's not easy. Today, the United States wants to be a partner in making the lives of ordinary Cubans a little bit easier, more free, more prosperous.

To those who have supported these measures, I thank you for being partners in our efforts. In particular, I want to thank His Holiness Pope Francis, whose moral example shows us the importance of pursuing the world as it should be, rather than simply settling for the world as it is; the Government of Canada, which hosted our discussions with the Cuban Government; and a bipartisan group of Congressmen who've worked tirelessly for Alan Gross's release and for a new approach to advancing our interests and values in Cuba.

Finally, our shift in policy towards Cuba comes at a moment of renewed leadership in the Americas. This April, we are prepared to have Cuba join the other nations of the hemisphere at the Summit of the Americas. But we will insist that civil society join us so that citizens, not just leaders, are shaping our future. And I call on all of my fellow leaders to give meaning to the commitment to democracy and human rights at the heart of the Inter-American Charter. Let us leave behind the legacy of both colonization and communism, the tyranny of drug cartels, dictators, and sham elections. A future of greater peace, security, and democratic development is possible if we work together, not to maintain power, not to secure vested interests, but instead to advance the dreams of our citizens.

My fellow Americans, the city of Miami is only 200 miles or so from Havana. Countless thousands of Cubans have come to Miami, on planes and makeshift rafts, some with little but the shirt on their back and hope in their hearts. Today, Miami is often referred to as the capital of Latin America. But it is also a profoundly American city, a place that reminds us that ideals matter more than the color of our skin or the circumstances of our birth, a demonstration of what the Cuban people can achieve and the openness of the United States to our family to the South. Todos somos Americanos.

Change is hard, in our own lives and in the lives of nations. And change is even harder when we carry the heavy weight of history on our shoulders. But today we are making these changes because it is the right thing to do. Today America chooses to cut loose the shackles of the past so as to reach for a better future, for the Cuban people, for the American people, for our entire hemisphere, and for the world.

Thank you. God bless you, and God bless the United States of America.

SOURCE: Executive Office of the President. "Address to the Nation on United States Policy Toward Cuba." December 17, 2014. *Compilation of Presidential Documents* 2014, no. 00937 (December 17, 2014). www.gpo.gov/fdsys/pkg/DCPD-201400937/pdf/DCPD-201400937.pdf.

OTHER HISTORIC DOCUMENTS OF INTEREST

FROM PREVIOUS *HISTORIC DOCUMENTS*

Russian President on the State of Russia's Economy

DECEMBER 18, 2014

Having depreciated gradually against the dollar throughout 2014, Russia's currency, the ruble, experienced a far sharper decline on December 16, losing nearly a fifth of its value. This sudden tumble was largely the result of a downturn in Russia's economy, a consequence of a significant fall in oil prices combined with trade sanctions imposed on Russia by the United States and European Union (EU). The Russian central bank—the Bank of Russia—intervened to prevent the situation from further deterioration by raising interest rates to limit liquidity on the markets. Meanwhile, Russia's President Vladimir Putin gave a lengthy news conference on December 18 to assure the Russian public and the financial markets that he had things under control and that Russia's economy would soon bounce back.

EXTERNAL FORCES BLAMED FOR ECONOMIC WOES

"The current situation was obviously provoked primarily by external factors," Putin said, while praising the Bank of Russia for "moving in the right direction." The president assured viewers that "our economy will come out of this situation" within "a couple of years" in the worst-case scenario. He was quick to point out that Russia had more than $400 billion in foreign exchange reserves and that this would help it avoid the situation deteriorating into a systemic crisis. He admitted that Russia's economy needed to become more diverse and less reliant on oil and gas exports, but he insisted that this diversification would happen naturally as a matter of course. However, he could provide little in the way of detail as to how precisely Russia would diversify.

During a question-and-answer session, Putin was quick to steer the conversation toward what he viewed as the faults and failings of the EU and United States. For instance, asked about businesses in Russia being hampered by excessive bureaucracy, he deflected the question, saying that "there must be some people from the European Union here. If you ask them about red tape in Brussels, they will tell you all about it. Our bureaucracy is child's play compared to theirs." More at ease when discussing geopolitics, he lambasted the North Atlantic Treaty Organization (NATO), asking, "Didn't they tell us after the fall of the Berlin Wall that NATO would not expand eastwards? However, the expansion started immediately." He said that the EU and United States had "decided they were the winners, they were an empire, while all the others were their vassals, and they needed to put the squeeze on them." Since the 1990s, many former Soviet satellite countries in Central and Eastern Europe and the former Soviet republics of Estonia, Latvia, and Lithuania have joined NATO, much to the chagrin of Putin. He called the change of government in Ukraine that took place the spring of 2014 a "coup" and "a big mistake." Acknowledging that Russia has been turning its sights eastward lately, he explained that this was "because the East—that is, the Asia-Pacific region—shows faster growth than the rest of the world."

His exchanges with reporters at the news conference revealed how unshakable his personal grip on power in Russia had become. When one reporter asked how he could blame "external forces" for Russia's economic problems given that he had been Russia's leader for fifteen years, something critics from within his own circle had noted, Putin asked for the names of those critics. When a question was posed about elites in Russia, he claimed, "There are no elite people. You know what the Russian elite is. It's a worker. A farmer." The deferential manner in which one journalist addressed him was similarly telling. "Thank you for noticing me. This year you've enjoyed extremely high ratings and popularity among the public," she said, noting that the next most popular politician in Russia was only scoring between 2 and 4 percent in the polls. "Does this total pre-eminence and, therefore, loneliness in politics bother you?" she asked. Even Putin's fiercest critics accepted that his approval ratings among the Russian public remained very high, despite the economic downturn.

Ukraine Crisis

The single biggest cause of this increased popularity at home is the same cause of Russia's worsening relations with the West: his actions in neighboring Ukraine. In late 2013, Putin successfully pressured the pro-Russian president of Ukraine, Viktor Yanukovych, to cancel a planned signing of a free trade agreement with the EU. The pressure was applied because Putin did not wish Ukraine to be drawn into the West's orbit in the way that Central and Eastern European countries such as Lithuania and Poland have been; both countries are now members of the EU and NATO.

While the EU and United States were greatly dismayed by Yanukovych reneging on the trade deal at the last minute, the tables were turned in February 2014 when Yanukovych suddenly fled the Ukrainian capital Kiev. His unexpected departure came in response to weeks of pro-Western protests that were becoming more violent as protesters engaged in bloody clashes with security forces. Putin quickly exploited the power vacuum created by Yanukovych's departure by orchestrating the annexation of the Ukrainian province of Crimea bordering on the Black Sea. Crimea has an ethnic Russian majority and has great strategic and historic importance for Russia. The annexation was formalized in March following a hastily called referendum in Crimea, which overwhelmingly endorsed the annexation. The vote was condemned by the EU, United States, and the interim Ukrainian government as being neither free, fair, nor legal. The annexation has failed thus far to gain international acceptance.

Russia's seizure of Crimea triggered a spiral of sanctions between Russia and the West. These sanctions began in the form of travel bans and asset freezes imposed by the EU and United States on Russian officials connected to the annexation. However, within a few months it escalated into trade sanctions. An important turning point came in July after a Malaysia Airlines passenger plane was shot down as it was flying over Eastern Ukraine, killing all 298 people on board. By this time Ukraine had elected a new pro-Western government whose president, Petro Poroshenko, had quickly signed the free trade agreement which his predecessor had refused. Pro-Russian separatist militias, aided covertly by Russia, who supplied weapons and troops, captured territory in eastern Ukraine on the Russian border. These separatist militias were believed to have accidentally shot down the airliner, mistaking it for a Ukrainian military jet, although the separatists blamed the

Ukrainian military for the plane's downing. Almost 200 of the passengers who died were from the Netherlands, which had the effect of hardening the EU's stance on Russia and generating agreement among member states to impose economic sanctions, something they were reluctant to do before then. Russia responded by imposing a ban on imports of U.S. and EU meat, fruit, and vegetable products. Throughout this period, the EU closely coordinated its actions with the United States. The EU-Russian sanctions had the greater impact because the volume of trade between these two blocs was much greater than U.S.-Russia trade.

The souring of relations with the West triggered a significant decline in foreign investment in Russia. This was directly due to the sanctions but also more indirectly to the generally dismal state of relations between the West and Russia, coupled with uncertainty about what would happen in Ukraine where the separatist conflict continued escalating despite sporadic ceasefires. The European Central Bank estimated the total flight of capital from Russia at several hundred billion dollars. And it was not only foreign businesses that divested from Russia. Many Russian citizens shifted capital out of the country, with wealthy oligarchs opting to buy expensive properties in London, whereas middle-class Russians were more inclined to purchase condos in Spain. Creeping inflation inside Russia, a result of sanctions and the steadily depreciating ruble, led Russians to increase purchases of durable consumer goods.

OIL PRICE DROP ADDS TO ECONOMIC PROBLEMS

What many commentators called "a perfect storm" gathered in the fall of 2014 when crude oil prices started plummeting just as the sanctions began to bite. The price of crude decreased from $115 to $60 a barrel between summer and winter. Around half the Russian government's revenue is derived from oil exports, so this had an immediate impact on the country's public finances. The major oil exporting states including Saudi Arabia were partly responsible for the price plummet because they decided to maintain oil production at existing levels despite the increased global supply of oil from other countries such as the United States. When the International Monetary Fund (IMF) published its revised global economic outlook in January 2015, it made the biggest adjustments to the figures for Russia, whose growth prospects were revised downward by 3.5 points. Thus, instead of forecasting 0.6 percent growth in 2015, as it had done in October, the IMF now predicted that the Russian economy would contract by 3 percent over the coming year.

The Russian authorities took steps to alleviate the worsening economic climate. Interest rates were increased from 10.5 percent to 17 percent on December 16 by the central bank. That was the same day the ruble's value depreciated, with a dollar buying 58 rubles at the start of business and 70 rubles by the close. As major Russian businesses felt the pinch, the authorities intervened to prevent them going under. The large state-owned oil company, Rosneft, was given an $11 billion bailout loan to cover mounting debts. Retail bank Trust Bank received a $531 million bailout after it began running out of money, having previously offered depositors 8 percent interest on dollar-denominated accounts in a bid to attract customers.

As the year drew to a close there were two competing, very different, narratives about Russia's economic future. Western economists and commentators predicted a continuing slide given the cumulative effect of sanctions, low oil prices, and conflict. But President Putin maintained that the downturn would be temporary, that growth would soon return, and that Russia's economy would adapt to lower energy prices and become less reliant on hydrocarbon exports. The first few months of 2015 saw the situation stabilize a little, with the ruble recovering some of its lost value, oil prices creeping back up, and interest rates on Russian government bonds decreasing. But with little sign of an end to the conflict in eastern Ukraine and the Western sanctions likely to remain in force until at least the end of 2015, clear severe economic challenges lay ahead.

—Brian Beary

Following are excerpts from a press conference held by Russian president Vladimir Putin on December 18, 2014, on the state of Russia's economy.

President Putin Remarks on Russia's Economic Downturn

December 18, 2014

PRESIDENT OF RUSSIA VLADIMIR PUTIN: Good afternoon, colleagues.

I am very happy to see you in high spirits. As we did last time, I will begin by briefing you on the work done during the year and then I will try to answer your questions.

First the most important thing: the economic performance. In the first 10 months of this year, the gross domestic product grew by 0.7 percent, and the final figure may be around 0.6 percent. My colleagues and I met yesterday to finalise the figures. The trade surplus grew by $13.3 billion to reach $148.4 billion.

Industrial production picked up some speed after last year's lull. In the first 10 months of the year, it went up by 1.7 percent. Unemployment is also low: at times, it dropped to below 5 percent, and now it is around 5 percent, possibly 5.1 percent.

The agroindustrial complex is developing. I believe that by the end of the year growth there will amount to 3.3 percent. As you may know, this year we had a record crop of 104 million tonnes.

Despite the turbulent situation on the financial market, the federal budget this year will show a surplus. In other words, revenue will exceed expenses by 1.2 trillion rubles [over $20 billion], which is about 1.9 percent of the GDP. The Finance Ministry is still working on the final calculations, but the surplus is definite.

The main achievement of the year in the social sphere is of course the positive demographics.

Natural population growth in the first 10 months of the year was 37,100 people. The death rate is going down in this country, while the birth rate is increasing. This is a very good trend and we must make every effort to maintain it. As promised, we continued adjusting the maternity capital. In 2014 it amounted to 429,408.5 rubles.

We have met and exceeded the targets set for this year for salary rates for ten workforce categories. I am sure you know what I am talking about. First of all, these are teachers at schools and institutions providing supplementary education, counsellors, university faculty members, medical doctors, paramedics and nurses, and employees of cultural institutions. In 2014, we adjusted pensions to inflation twice: by 6.5 percent on February 1 and by an additional 1.7 percent on April 1.

We gave significant attention this year to enhancing the combat capability and efficiency of the Armed Forces. I will not go into detail here. I would only like to mention the social sphere. In 2014, 11,700 Defence Ministry servicemen received permanent housing and 15,300 received service housing. This is 100 percent of the year's target figures.

These are the numbers I wanted to begin with. Now a few words regarding the current situation. I believe we all know that the main issue of concern to this country's citizens is the state of the economy, the national currency and how all this could influence developments in the social sphere. I will try to briefly describe this situation and say how I expect it to develop. Basically, that is where we could end this news conference. (Laughter) However, if you have any further questions I will try to answer them.

The current situation was obviously provoked primarily by external factors. However, we proceed from the view that we have failed to achieve many of the things that were planned and that needed to be done to diversify the economy over the past 20 years. This was not easy, if at all possible, given the foreign economic situation, which was favourable in the sense that businesses were investing into areas that guaranteed maximum and fast profits. This mechanism is not easy to change.

Now, as you may know, the situation has changed under the influence of certain foreign economic factors, primarily the price of energy resources, of oil and consequently of gas as well. I believe the Government and the Central Bank are taking appropriate measures in this situation. We could question the timeliness or the quality of the measures taken by the Government and the Central Bank, but generally, they are acting adequately and moving in the right direction.

I hope that yesterday's and today's drop in the foreign currency exchange rate and growth of our national currency, the ruble, will continue. Is this possible? It is. Could oil prices continue falling and would this influence our national currency and consequently all the other economic indexes, including inflation? Yes, this is possible.

What do we intend to do about this? We intend to use the measures we applied, and rather successfully, back in 2008. In this case, we will need to focus on assistance to those people who really need it and on retaining—this is something I would like to highlight—retaining all our social targets and plans. This primarily concerns pensions and public sector salaries, and so forth.

Clearly, we would have to adjust our plans in case of any unfavourable developments. We would certainly be forced to make some cuts. However, it is equally certain—and I would like to stress this—that there will be what experts call a positive rebound. Further growth and a resolution of this situation are inevitable for at least two reasons. One is that the global economy will continue to grow, the rates may be lower, but the positive trend is sure to continue. The economy will grow, and our economy will come out of this situation.

How long will this take? In a worst-case scenario, I believe it would take a couple of years. I repeat: after that, growth is inevitable, due to a changing foreign economic situation among other things. A growing world economy will require additional energy resources. However, by that time I have no doubt that we will be able to do a great deal to diversify our economy, because life itself will force us to do it. There is no other way we could function.

Therefore, overall, I repeat, we will undoubtedly comply with all our social commitments using the existing reserves. Fortunately, this year they have even grown.

I would like to remind you that Central Bank reserves amount to $419 billion. The Central Bank does not intend to "burn" them all senselessly, which is right. The Government reserve, the National Wealth Fund, the Reserve Fund have grown this year by about

2.4-2.5 trillion rubles to a total 8.4 trillion rubles. With these reserves I am certain we can work calmly to resolve our main social issues and to diversify the economy; and I will repeat that inevitably the situation will return to normal.

I would like to end my introductory remarks here. As I have said, we could end the whole news conference here, but if you do have any questions, I am ready to answer them . . . .

VYACHESLAV TEREKHOV, INTERFAX: . . . There is something I would like to clarify, Mr President. Judging by the situation in the country, we are in the midst of a deep currency crisis, one that even Central Bank employees say they could not have foreseen in their worst nightmares.

Do you believe that things will get better in two years, as you mentioned, and we will recover from this financial and economic crisis? Criticism was piled on the Government and the Central Bank for the ruble's Black Monday and Tuesday. Do you agree with this criticism?

Thank you.

VLADIMIR PUTIN: I said that given the most unfavourable foreign economic situation this could last (approximately, because no one can say for certain) for about two years. However, it may not last that long and the situation could take a turn for the better sooner. It could improve in the first or second quarter of next year, by the middle of next year, or by its end.

Nobody can tell. There are many uncertain factors. Therefore, you could call it a crisis or something else, you can decide which word to use. However, I believe I made it quite clear that the Central Bank and the Government are generally taking appropriate measures in this situation. I believe some things could have been done sooner, and this is actually what the expert community are criticising them for.

What does the job involve, in my view? And what are the Central Bank and the Government actually doing? First, as you may know, they raised the key interest rate. I hope the rate will remain for the duration of these complicated developments connected with the foreign economic situation, and the economy will adjust one way or another.

What is the basis for my optimism? The idea that the economy is bound to adjust to life and work in conditions of low prices on energy resources. This will become a fact of life.

How soon will the economy adapt if the prices remain at the current level or even go below 60 [USD/barrel], 40, or whatever? For us it could be any figure, the economy would simply have to get structured. How fast will this happen? This is hard to say. But it is inevitable. I would like to highlight this. This will be a fact of life.

What is the Central Bank doing? They have raised the key interest rate. What else do they need to do? And what are they already doing? To stabilise the national currency they need to somewhat limit ruble liquidity and give economic entities access to foreign currency liquidity. This is exactly what the Bank is doing. Their foreign currency interest rate is quite low—0.5.

Overall, I think it is up to the Central Bank to decide whether to reduce the interest rate or not, they should see and react accordingly. They should not hand out our gold and foreign currency reserves or burn them on the market, but provide lending resources. And they are doing this as well.

The so-called repo is a well-known instrument here. They can be offered for a day, a week, 28 days, almost a month, or for a year. This is money that is returned, but it gives economic entities the opportunity to make use of the foreign currency. Everything is being done right.

They should probably move at least half a pace faster. Of course, I see the criticism levelled at the Central Bank and its Governor. Some of it is justified, some is not. The Government should also bear responsibility. They should work with exporters who have sufficiently high foreign currency revenues.

The Prime Minister met with heads of our major companies and we can see some results. Many of them have to return their loans and think of the condition their companies are in.

Every company, just like every individual, tries to save "for a rainy day". Is such behaviour economically justified? In terms of economic logic, it is not. Nevertheless, companies do it, and we now see a certain result, the "rebound" is happening.

The Government should be taking other measures as well. What do I mean? For instance, combatting inflation is of course the Central Bank's job. However, there are things that we have mentioned already, things I spoke of in public during our meetings with the Government.

For instance, the prices of petrol and food are something they should work on. Moreover, the current situation, whatever anyone says, requires a "hands on" approach. They have to meet with producers, those who are on the market, with retailers and with the oil companies that have significantly monopolised the market. The Federal Antimonopoly Service should function properly.

These actions have to be joint and reasonable, though without any violation of the individual competence of, say, the Central Bank or the Government. Nevertheless, they should coordinate their actions, and do so in a timely fashion.

Therefore, they can criticise Nabiullina [Central Bank Governor] all they like, but one should bear in mind that overall their policy is right. The Central Bank is not the only one responsible for the economic situation in the country . . . .

ALEXANDER GAMOV, KOMSOMOLSKAYA PRAVDA NEWSPAPER: . . . Since 2008, we have been talking about the need to get rid of our oil addiction and restructure our economy to make it more efficient. However, the developments of the past few days have shown that we did not manage to achieve this.

We are still addicted, and nobody knows how long this will last. Could you say openly what you personally think: will we be able to use this crisis for to our advantage, lose our addiction and rebuild the economy? I realise that this would take time . . . .

[Questions and answers about oil prices and prisoners have been omitted.]

ANTON VERNITSKY, CHANNEL ONE RUSSIA: Mr President, are the current economic developments the price we have to pay for Crimea? Maybe the time has come to acknowledge it?

VLADIMIR PUTIN: No. This is not the price we have to pay for Crimea. . . . This is actually the price we have to pay for our natural aspiration to preserve ourselves as a nation, as a civilisation, as a state. And here is why.

As I've already mentioned when answering a question from your NTV colleague, and as I've said during my Address to the Federal Assembly, after the fall of the Berlin Wall and the breakup of the Soviet Union, Russia opened itself to our partners. What did we see? A direct and fully-fledges support of terrorism in North Caucasus. They directly supported terrorism, you understand? Is that what partners usually do? I won't go into details on that, but this is an established fact. And everyone knows it.

On any issue, no matter what we do, we always run into challenges, objections and opposition. Let me remind you about the preparations for the 2014 Olympics, our inspiration and enthusiasm to organise a festive event not only for Russian sports fans, but for sports fans all over the world. However, and this is an evident truth, unprecedented and clearly orchestrated attempts were made to discredit our efforts to organise and host the Olympics. This is an undeniable fact! Who needs to do so and for what reason? And so on and so forth.

You know, at the Valdai [International Discussion] Club I gave an example of our most recognisable symbol. It is a bear protecting his taiga. You see, if we continue the analogy, sometimes I think that maybe it would be best if our bear just sat still. Maybe he should stop chasing pigs and boars around the taiga but start picking berries and eating honey. Maybe then he will be left alone. But no, he won't be! Because someone will always try to chain him up. As soon as he's chained they will tear out his teeth and claws. In this analogy, I am referring to the power of nuclear deterrence. As soon as—God forbid—it happens and they no longer need the bear, the taiga will be taken over.

We have heard it even from high-level officials that it is unfair that the whole of Siberia with its immense resources belongs to Russia in its entirety. Why exactly is it unfair? So it is fair to snatch Texas from Mexico but it is unfair that we are working on our own land—no, we have to share.

And then, when all the teeth and claws are torn out, the bear will be of no use at all. Perhaps they'll stuff it and that's all.

So, it is not about Crimea but about us protecting our independence, our sovereignty and our right to exist. That is what we should all realise.

If we believe that one of the current problems—including in the economy as a result of the sanctions—is crucial. . . . And it is so because out of all the problems the sanctions take up about 25 to 30 percent. But we must decide whether we want to keep going and fight, change our economy—for the better, by the way, because we can use the current situation to our own advantage—and be more independent, go through all this or we want our skin to hang on the wall. This is the choice we need to make and it has nothing to do with Crimea at all . . . .

[Questions and answers about Crimea and gas contracts have been omitted.]

GRIGORY DUBOVITSKY, RIA NOVOSTI: Mr President, I'd like to go back to the situation on the currency market, which changes from one day to another and is a great concern for millions of Russians. Many experts, including you, Mr President, have said the current situation could be blamed also on currency profiteers. Concrete companies and individuals have been named. Can you give us those names? Are they Russians or foreigners? And why can't they be stopped? Are they too strong? Or are we too weak?

I have a second question on the same subject, if I may. Do the Central Bank and the Government plan to peg or devalue the ruble?

VLADIMIR PUTIN: This is what our Ukrainian partners did, quite unsuccessfully. Are you asking if we plan to force our companies, our main exporters, who receive revenues in foreign currency, to sell it? They would just buy it back the next day, as it happened in Kiev and as it happens in other countries.

The next step in this case should be to set a limit on the purchase of foreign currency on the domestic market. We won't go this far, and so the Central Bank and the Government are not planning, quite correctly as far as I see it, to limit our exporters in this field.

This doesn't mean, though, that the Government should not act through its representatives on company boards. After all, these are our largest energy companies. They are partly state-owned, which means that we can influence their policies, but without issuing any directives or restrictions. This we won't do.

As for the so-called profiteers, it is not a crime to play on the currency market. These market players can be foreigners or various funds, which are present on the Russian market and have been operating quite actively there. Or they can be Russian companies. Overall, as I said at the beginning of this meeting, this is an accepted practice in a market economy. Profiteers always appear when there is a chance to make some money.

They don't show up to steal or to cheat but to make some money in the market by creating favourable conditions, by pushing, for example, as was done in the beginning of this process, like, in this particular case, the Central Bank of Russia was pushed to enter the market and start selling gold and foreign currency reserves in the hope of intervening and supporting the national currency.

But the Central Bank stopped, and it was the right thing to do. Perhaps it would have been better if it had been done earlier and in a tougher way. Then perhaps it wouldn't have been necessary to increase the rate to 17 percent. But that is a different matter. A matter of taste, so to speak. Although it is still rather significant. It is true. So, I told you who they are.

You know, two days ago I had a friendly telephone conversation with some of them and I asked, "So why are you holding back?" By the way, I didn't make them do anything. "Our loan payments are due soon," was the reply. Then I say, "I see. OK, if you scrape the bottom of the barrel, can you enter the market?" He took a minute and replied: "Well, I guess we have three billion dollars." They have three billion in reserves. See what I mean? It is not 30 kopeks. And this is just one company.

So if each company has three billion, in total it is not 30 but 300 billion. Still, we can't force them. Even top management of the companies with state participation must anticipate what will happen and ensure the stability of their companies. To this end, the Government must work very closely with them and ensure, along with the Central Bank, foreign currency and ruble liquidity whenever it is necessary. . . .

[Questions and answers about hospitals, Crimea, education, political opponents, the Olympic Games, amnesty, agriculture, housing, international relations, and the media, have been omitted.]

ALEXANDER KOLANDER, DOW JONES: Mr Putin, you said the ruble is falling and economic problems are emerging because of the declining price of oil. But the ruble began weakening in 2013, investment flows began shrinking even before that, and members of the Government responsible for economic matters spoke about economic problems even before the ruble began falling. The situation is similar to having a cold—a healthy person can go on ignoring the symptoms, while a sick person suffers much more from the same cold.

Don't you think that the economic problems are the result of the personnel decisions as well as domestic and foreign policy moves of the last two or three years? Do you think you are personally responsible for these moves, for the weakened ruble and economic problems?

And the last question—have you made a decision about running for another term, and will this decision depend on the ruble rate and the economic situation?

VLADIMIR PUTIN: It depends on the overall result of our performance—the president, the Government and the Central Bank. I would say it is too early for anyone to make any decisions about running in 2018 presidential elections. We must work our hardest for the sake of and in the interests of the Russian people, and then look at the results of this work and at the public sentiment to decide who should run in 2018. That's first.

Second, the head of state always bears responsibility for everything that happens in the country, as do officials throughout the government hierarchy. I have never tried to evade responsibility and I am not going to start now.

Finally, as for mistakes with personnel and so on—everyone makes mistakes. In general, I would repeat that personal accountability should be increased—all Central Bank and Government officials should be responsible for the work entrusted to them. At the same time, I believe that most administrative bodies, including the Government and the financial authorities, are coping with the issues facing Russia today.

I said this at the start, and I would like to repeat this in conclusion: we are indeed going through a difficult period. The difficulties are caused by a range of objective and perhaps subjective circumstances—meaning that certain steps could have been taken faster and more resolutely.

Overall, I think that the Central Bank and the Government are pursuing the right policies. This gives us grounds to believe that we can achieve the social targets set out in the 2012 executive orders and overcome the current problems in the medium term, if not in the near future, by maintaining macroeconomic stability and a healthy economy and by using available reserves.

I have already said why it will happen—because the economy will eventually adjust to low energy prices and will start to diversify.

And second, even if energy prices remain low or continue to decline, there will come a time when energy prices will resume growing again when the global economy and the demand for energy grow.

I'm absolutely confident that this will happen. But how will it happen? We will see how the authorities—the financial and managerial sectors and the Government—perform and evaluate them accordingly.

We can be absolutely sure that the worst will pass, and that we will overcome this very difficult situation, emerging from it stronger domestically, in the global economy and on the international stage. We have the necessary resources to meet our social commitments, to strengthen our defences, and to modernise the army and the navy, and we will definitely use them to implement our plans.

But our biggest priority is to guarantee people's wellbeing, to adjust pensions to inflation despite declining budget revenues. Can we do this? We certainly can. Next year, we will adjust pensions to actual, not estimated inflation.

We will focus our attention on the social wellbeing of our people in the upcoming period. And I'm confident that we will achieve all targets . . . .

SOURCE: President of Russia. "News conference of Vladimir Putin." December 18, 2014. http://eng.krem lin.ru/transcripts/23406.

OTHER HISTORIC DOCUMENTS OF INTEREST

FROM THIS VOLUME

FBI and North Korea
Respond to Sony Hack

DECEMBER 19 AND 21, 2014

In late November 2014, hackers accessed the Sony Pictures Entertainment computer networks, stealing information ranging from personal data to unreleased films. The Federal Bureau of Investigation (FBI), after researching the hack, determined that it was perpetrated by North Korean government hackers most likely in retaliation for the creation and release of the comedy film *The Interview,* which details an assassination plot against North Korean leader Kim Jong Un. North Korea denied any involvement in the hacking but threatened to attack the United States if it continued to place blame on North Korea. In response, the United States issued additional economic sanctions against the reclusive nation.

SONY COMPUTERS HACKED, DATA RELEASED

On November 24, hackers entered the computer system at Sony Pictures Entertainment, stealing personal information, e-mail, executive salary information, and unreleased movies including *Annie, Mr. Turner, Still Alice, To Write Love on Her Arms,* and the script of a still-to-be filmed James Bond movie. When Sony employees attempted to log into their computers, they were met with a screen that said: "Hacked By #GOP [Guardians of Peace]" and "We've already warned you, and this is just a beginning. We continue till our request be met. We've obtained all your internal data including your secrets and top secrets. If you don't obey us, we'll release data shown below to the world." The FBI immediately began looking into who was behind the attack. Much of its work centered on the North Korean government.

On December 16, the Guardians of Peace issued another message, this time threatening attacks against any theaters that chose to screen *The Interview,* a comedy starring Seth Rogen and James Franco depicting a CIA plot to assassinate Kim. The planned Christmas Day release of the movie was scrapped by Sony after a number of major theater chains, including Regal, AMC, and Cinemark, announced that they would not run the film in an effort to protect their customers. Two days before Christmas, the studio reversed its decision and said it would make the movie available online and would also have a limited 300-theater release. Rogen tweeted, "The people have spoken! Freedom has prevailed! Sony didn't give up!" The movie made $1 million on its first day of release.

President Barack Obama was critical of the decision by Sony to cancel the nationwide release of *The Interview*. In his annual end-of-year speech to the press corps, the president said movie producers should "not get into a pattern where you are intimidated by these acts." He added, "We cannot have a society where some dictator someplace can start imposing censorship here in the United States. Because if somebody is able to intimidate folks out of releasing a satirical movie, imagine what they start doing once they see a documentary they don't like, or news reports they don't like." Sony CEO Michael Lynton responded, saying, "We have not given in. And we have not backed down. We have always had every desire to have the American public see this movie."

LEAKED E-MAIL

In addition to releasing yet unseen movies, the hackers also published a series of e-mails sent by Sony executives. Some of those released caused massive fallout in the entertainment industry. In one leaked exchange between Hollywood producer Scott Rudin and Sony Pictures Entertainment chief Amy Pascal, the pair remarked on President Obama's potential movie preferences, noting that he would likely prefer a movie with black actors like *Django, 12 Years a Slave, Amistad,* and *The Butler.* In an apology, Rudin said his e-mail were in jest; however, "in the harsh light of a public forum, without context" they are indefensible. Pascal called her e-mails "insensitive and inappropriate." The pair also apologized for a separate exchange in which they referred to Angelina Jolie as a "minimally talented spoiled brat." Pascal ultimately resigned her position over the scandal.

U.S. BLAMES NORTH KOREA FOR THE CYBERATTACK

On December 19, the FBI announced that North Korea was likely the culprit behind the hack. According to the FBI, the "technical analysis of the data deletion malware used in this attack revealed links to other malware that the FBI knows North Korea previously developed. For example, there were similarities in specific lines of code, encryption algorithms, data deletion methods, and compromised networks." The FBI added that "several times . . . we could see that the IP addresses that were being used to post and to send the emails were coming from IPs that were exclusively used by the North Koreans." According to *The New York Times*, the FBI easily identified the source because in 2010, the United States began hacking into North Korean computer networks to track the activities of North Korea's government hackers.

While the FBI stood by its assertions that the hacking was carried out by North Korea, some cybersecurity experts speculated that disgruntled former Sony employees might instead have carried out the hack. "State-sponsored attackers don't create cool names for themselves like 'Guardians of Peace' and promote their activity to the public," said Lucas Zaichkowsky, a cybersecurity expert. Norse Corp., a cybersecurity firm, submitted the findings of its own independent investigation to the FBI. "Sony was not just hacked; this is a company that was essentially nuked from the inside. We are very confident that this was not an attack master-minded by North Korea and that insiders were key to the implementation of one of the most devastating attacks in history," said Kurt Stammberger, the company's senior vice president. He said that his organization had narrowed down possible suspects to six Sony employees, based on comments they made on message boards and their known skills. The FBI was briefed on the Norse review during a three-hour meeting, and in the end rejected the findings, noting that the group did not fully understand all the evidence the FBI had collected on the hack.

North Korea denied that it had any involvement in the hacking of Sony servers. "My country has nothing to do with the Sony hacking. It is out of sense to do that, and we very [much] want [the] United States to provide evidence," said An Myong Hun, the country's deputy UN ambassador. He further offered to assist the United States with a "joint investigation" to find out the true identity of the hackers. An unnamed North Korean official told Voice of America that "linking the DPRK to the Sony hacking is another fabrication targeting the country."

President Obama said that he would consider the appropriate response to the cyberattack: "We will respond proportionally and we will respond in a place and time and manner that we choose." One such response might include adding the nation back to the State Department's list of state sponsors of terrorism, from which it was removed in 2008 by then-President George W. Bush.

North Korea's Threats Lead to U.S. Sanctions

On December 22, North Korea's National Defense Commission issued a statement warning that if the United States continued to blame it for the cyberattack, it would strike "the whole U.S. mainland, that cesspool of terrorism." The statement said that North Korea's 1.2 million member army was prepared to attack the United States in multiple ways, but it offered no specific details. "Our toughest counteraction will be boldly taken against the White House, the Pentagon and the whole U.S. mainland . . . by far surpassing the 'symmetric counteraction' declared by Obama." While maintaining its innocence, the commission called the attack "righteous" and said it was likely carried out by "supporters and sympathizers with [North Korea]."

In its statement, the commission said that it had "clear evidence" that the U.S. government was behind the creation and release of *The Interview*, saying, "U.S. President Obama is the chief culprit who forced the Sony Pictures Entertainment to 'indiscriminately distribute' the movie and took the lead in appeasing and blackmailing cinema houses and theatres in the U.S. mainland to distribute the movie." The commission added, "Obama always goes reckless in words and deeds like a monkey in a tropical forest."

In late December, North Korea blamed the United States for a massive Internet outage that it claimed was done in retaliation for North Korean threats. "The U.S., a big country, started disturbing the Internet operation of major media of the DPRK," it said. The U.S. government refused to comment on the issue.

Sanctions Imposed on North Korea

In response to the cyberattack, in January 2015, the United States added additional sanctions to the long-list of those already targeting North Korea. The new sanctions would prevent government leaders from entering the United States and would try to further prevent North Korean entities from accessing the global financial markets. Specific companies targeted by the measures included the Korea Mining Development Trading Corporation (the North Korean agency responsible for arms trade and weapons sales), Korean Tangun Trading Corporation, and Reconnaissance General Bureau. Sanctions were also imposed on seven North Korean arms operatives in Africa, Iran, Russia, and Syria. The hope of the U.S. government was that by exposing the operatives' names, their business would be impacted. In a letter to Speaker of the House John Boehner, R-Ohio, Obama explained that imposing sanctions, instituted through executive order, "is not targeted at the people of North Korea, but rather is aimed at the government of North Korea and its activities that threaten the United States and others." He added that the sanctions were necessary because North Korea poses a "continuing threat to the national security, foreign policy and economy of the United States."

—Heather Kerrigan

Following is a December 19, 2014, press release from the Federal Bureau of Investigation on the outcome of its inquiry into the Sony hack; and a statement by North Korea's National Defence Commission on December 21, 2014, in response to allegations that it was behind the Sony attack.

FBI Announces
North Korea Behind Cyberattack

December 19, 2014

Today, the FBI would like to provide an update on the status of our investigation into the cyber attack targeting Sony Pictures Entertainment (SPE). In late November, SPE confirmed that it was the victim of a cyber attack that destroyed systems and stole large quantities of personal and commercial data. A group calling itself the "Guardians of Peace" claimed responsibility for the attack and subsequently issued threats against SPE, its employees, and theaters that distribute its movies.

The FBI has determined that the intrusion into SPE's network consisted of the deployment of destructive malware and the theft of proprietary information as well as employees' personally identifiable information and confidential communications. The attacks also rendered thousands of SPE's computers inoperable, forced SPE to take its entire computer network offline, and significantly disrupted the company's business operations.

After discovering the intrusion into its network, SPE requested the FBI's assistance. Since then, the FBI has been working closely with the company throughout the investigation. Sony has been a great partner in the investigation, and continues to work closely with the FBI. Sony reported this incident within hours, which is what the FBI hopes all companies will do when facing a cyber attack. Sony's quick reporting facilitated the investigators' ability to do their jobs, and ultimately to identify the source of these attacks.

As a result of our investigation, and in close collaboration with other U.S. government departments and agencies, the FBI now has enough information to conclude that the North Korean government is responsible for these actions. While the need to protect sensitive sources and methods precludes us from sharing all of this information, our conclusion is based, in part, on the following:

- Technical analysis of the data deletion malware used in this attack revealed links to other malware that the FBI knows North Korean actors previously developed. For example, there were similarities in specific lines of code, encryption algorithms, data deletion methods, and compromised networks.
- The FBI also observed significant overlap between the infrastructure used in this attack and other malicious cyber activity the U.S. government has previously linked directly to North Korea. For example, the FBI discovered that several Internet protocol (IP) addresses associated with known North Korean infrastructure communicated with IP addresses that were hardcoded into the data deletion malware used in this attack.
- Separately, the tools used in the SPE attack have similarities to a cyber attack in March of last year against South Korean banks and media outlets, which was carried out by North Korea.

We are deeply concerned about the destructive nature of this attack on a private sector entity and the ordinary citizens who worked there. Further, North Korea's attack on SPE reaffirms that cyber threats pose one of the gravest national security dangers to the United States. Though the FBI has seen a wide variety and increasing number of cyber intrusions, the destructive nature of this attack, coupled with its coercive nature, sets it apart. North Korea's actions were intended to inflict significant harm on a U.S. business and suppress the right of American citizens to express themselves. Such acts of intimidation fall outside the bounds of acceptable state behavior. The FBI takes seriously any attempt—whether through cyber-enabled means, threats of violence, or otherwise—to undermine the economic and social prosperity of our citizens.

The FBI stands ready to assist any U.S. company that is the victim of a destructive cyber attack or breach of confidential business information. Further, the FBI will continue to work closely with multiple departments and agencies as well as with domestic, foreign, and private sector partners who have played a critical role in our ability to trace this and other cyber threats to their source. Working together, the FBI will identify, pursue, and impose costs and consequences on individuals, groups, or nation states who use cyber means to threaten the United States or U.S. interests.

SOURCE: Federal Bureau of Investigation. "Update on Sony Investigation." December 19, 2014. www.fbi. gov/news/pressrel/press-releases/update-on-sony-investigation.

DOCUMENT *North Korea on Sony Hack Allegations*

December 21, 2014

The Policy Department of the National Defence Commission of the DPRK issued the following statement Sunday:

Strange thing that happened in the heart of the U.S., the ill-famed cesspool of injustice, is now afloat in the world as shocking news.

The Sony Pictures Entertainment, the biggest movie producer in the U.S., which produced the undesirable reactionary film "The Interview" daring hurt the dignity of the supreme leadership of the DPRK and agitating even terrorism and had a plan to distribute it, was exposed to surprisingly sophisticated, destructive and threatening cyber warfare and has been thrown into a bottomless quagmire after suffering property losses worth hundreds of millions of dollars.

The public in the U.S. is now describing this case as "disgrace suffered by Sony Pictures Entertainment," "very sorry thing caused by the U.S.," "Sony Pictures Entertainment showing a white flag before hackers" and the "unprecedented disaster suffered by the U.S."

Those who meted out a stern punishment of justice were reported to be cyber experts styling themselves "guardians of peace".

Seized with terrible horror and threat in face of their merciless hacking attack in retaliation against unjust actions, many movie and drama distributors in North America including 41 states of the U.S. and Canada immediately canceled the screening of the reactionary movie. And it was reported that the Sony Pictures Entertainment which directly sponsored its production and distribution hastily issued a statement on Dec. 25 that it would suspend the screening of the undesirable movie which had been planned in 63 countries.

The NDC of the DPRK highly estimates the righteous action taken by the "guardians of peace," though it is not aware of their residence.

It, at the same time, considers as fortunate the step taken by the Sony Pictures Entertainment to give up the overall distribution of the above-said movie due to the decision and strong pressure of the movie and drama distributors for stopping the screening of the reactionary movie, though belatedly.

This is an official stand of the army and the people of the DPRK on what happened in the heart of the U.S.

This stand is taken by the DPRK because the movie "The Interview" is an undesirable and reactionary one justifying and inciting terrorism which should not be allowed in any country and any region.

Another reason is that the movie is run through with a story agitating a vicious and dastardly method of assassinating a head of a legitimate sovereign state.

No wonder, even political and social circles of the U.S. commented that it is quite wrong to defame the head of the state for the mere reason that his politics is different from that of the U.S. and it is in the hostile relationship with the latter and, therefore, the Sony Pictures Entertainment got into a serious trouble and paid a due price.

For these reasons, the DPRK is more highly praising the "guardians of peace" for their righteous deed which prevented in advance the evil cycle of retaliation—terrorism sparks terrorism.

It is quite natural that the movie and drama producers should refrain from undesirable deeds contrary to the noble mission to lead morality and civilization.

But what matters is that the U.S. and its followers are groundlessly trumpeting that the recent cyber attack was made by the DPRK.

The FBI issued the results of the investigation into the hack at the Sony Pictures Entertainment on December 19.

According to them, it suffered tremendous losses.

One may say this is the due price incurred by wrong deed, the evil act of hurting others.

The U.S. released a statement asserting that this loss was caused by the DPRK.

No matter how big and disgraceful the loss may be, the U.S. should not pull up others for no reason.

The FBI presented a report on the results of technical analysis of hacking program used by the "guardians of peace" for this attack, citing it as the ground that the serious hacking was caused by the DPRK.

The report says the malignant code had access to north Korea's IP already known several times and the hacking methods applied in the "March 20 hacking case" and during cyber warfare against media and various other computer networks in south Korea in recent years are similar to that applied against the Sony Pictures Entertainment this time, being another ground that "this was done by the north".

The report, in particular, adds that the malignant code and algorithm applied during the attack are similar to what was used during the hacking attack on south Korea, citing it as a proof.

Not satisfied with those groundless "evidence", the FBI is letting loose ambiguous remarks that it is hard to fully prove due to the "protection of sensitive information sources."

This means self-acknowledgement that the "assertion about the north's deed" came from an intentional allegation rather than scientific evidence.

It is a common sense that the method of cyber warfare is almost similar worldwide.

Different sorts of hacking programs and codes are used in cyberspace.

If somebody used U.S.-made hacking programs and codes and applied their instruction or encoding method, perhaps, the "wise" FBI, too, could not but admit that it would be hard to decisively assert that the attack was done by the U.S.

Moreover, the DPRK has never attempted nor made a "cyber-attack" on south Korea.

The rumor about "cyber-attack" by the DPRK was a concoction made by the south Korean puppet regime and its plot.

After all, the grounds cited by the FBI in its announcement were all based on obscure sci-tech data and false story and, accordingly, the announcement itself is another fabrication. This is the DPRK's stand on the U.S. gangster-like behavior against it.

What is grave is that U.S. President Obama is recklessly making the rumor about "DPRK's cyber-attack on Sony Pictures" a fait accompli while crying out for symmetric counteraction, strict calculation and additionally retaliatory sanctions.

This is like beating air after being hit hard. A saying goes every sin brings its punishment with it. It is best for the guilty to repent of its evil doings and draw a lesson when forced to pay dearly for them.

The DPRK has clear evidence that the U.S. administration was deeply involved in the making of such dishonest reactionary movie.

It is said that the movie was conceived and produced according to the "guidelines" of the U.S. authorities who contended that such movies hurting the dignity of the DPRK supreme leadership and inciting terrorism against it would be used in an effective way as "propaganda against north Korea".

The U.S. Department of State's special human rights envoy went the lengths of urging the movie makers to keep all scenes insulting the dignity of the DPRK supreme leadership in the movie, saying it is needed to "vex the north Korean government".

The facts glaringly show that the U.S. is the chief culprit of terrorism as it has loudly called for combating terrorism everywhere in the world but schemed behind the scene to produce and distribute movies inciting it in various countries of the world.

It is not exaggeration to say in the light of the prevailing situation that the U.S. administration and President Obama looking after the overall state affairs of the U.S. have been behind the case.

Can he really cover up the crimes he has committed by trying so hard to falsify the truth and turn white to black.

So we watched with unusual attention what had been done by the "guardians of peace" to avert terrorism and defend justice.

Yet, we do not know who or where they are but we can surely say that they are supporters and sympathizers with the DPRK.

The army and people of the DPRK who aspire after justice and truth and value conscience have hundreds of millions of supporters and sympathizers, known or unknown, who have turned out in the sacred war against terrorism and the U.S. imperialists, the chieftain of aggression, to accomplish the just cause.

Obama personally declared in public the "symmetric counteraction", a disgraceful behavior.

There is no need to guess what kind of thing the "symmetric counteraction" is like but the army and people of the DPRK will never be browbeaten by such a thing.

The DPRK has already launched the toughest counteraction. Nothing is more serious miscalculation than guessing that just a single movie production company is the target of this counteraction. Our target is all the citadels of the U.S. imperialists who earned the bitterest grudge of all Koreans.

The army and people of the DPRK are fully ready to stand in confrontation with the U.S. in all war spaces including cyber warfare space to blow up those citadels.

Our toughest counteraction will be boldly taken against the White House, the Pentagon and the whole U.S. mainland, the cesspool of terrorism, by far surpassing the "symmetric counteraction" declared by Obama.

This is the invariable toughest stand of the army and people of the DPRK.

Fighters for justice including "guardians of peace" who turned out in the sacred drive for cooperation in the fight against the U.S. to defend human justice and conscience and to dismember the U.S. imperialists, the root cause of all sorts of evils and kingpin of injustice, are sharpening bayonets not only in the U.S. mainland but in all other parts of the world.

The just struggle to be waged by them across the world will bring achievements thousands of times greater than the hacking attack on the Sony Pictures Entertainment.

It is the truth and inevitability of the historical development that justice prevails over injustice.

Whoever challenges justice by toeing the line of the biggest criminal U.S. will never be able to escape merciless punishment as it is the target of the sacred drive for cooperation in the fight against the U.S.

The U.S. should reflect on its evil doings that put itself in such a trouble, apologize to the Koreans and other people of the world and should not dare pull up others.

Source: Korean Central News Agency. "U.S. Urged to Honestly Apologize to Mankind for Its Evil Doing before Groundlessly Pulling up Others." December 21, 2014. www.kcna.co.jp/item/2014/201412/news21/20141221-14ee.html.

OTHER HISTORIC DOCUMENTS OF INTEREST

FROM PREVIOUS *HISTORIC DOCUMENTS*

U.S.-NATO Coalition Officially Ends Combat Mission in Afghanistan

DECEMBER 28, 2014

After thirteen years of increasingly unpopular ground operations resulting in the deaths of more than 2,200 American soldiers, on December 28, 2014, the United States and the North Atlantic Treaty Organization (NATO) formally ended its coalition combat mission in Afghanistan. Thousands of troops would remain in the nation in a support role through the end of 2016 under the terms of an agreement forged with Afghanistan's newly elected president Ashraf Ghani.

INTERNATIONAL ACTION AND INCREASING ATTACKS

On September 18, 2001, seven days after the September 11 terrorist attacks in the United States, then-President George W. Bush signed a joint resolution that would allow the U.S. military to use force against anyone who had perpetrated the attacks on New York and Washington, D.C. Less than one month later, on October 7, the U.S. military launched Operation Enduring Freedom, which involved airstrikes against al Qaeda and Taliban strongholds. Ground forces entered Afghanistan by October 19, and in November, the central government collapsed. It was quickly replaced by an interim body led by Hamid Karzai. Major combat in the region was declared complete in 2003, and the first democratic vote was held in 2004. In 2009, newly elected president Barack Obama vowed to continue to support Afghanistan, even as he called for a complete troop withdrawal by the end of 2014. On May 1, 2011, the United States achieved arguably its greatest victory in the coalition effort when al Qaeda leader Osama bin Laden was killed by U.S. forces in Pakistan. A troop drawdown plan was announced one month later and was set to begin in the summer of 2012.

As troop drawdowns began, the Taliban ramped up attacks. In 2014 alone, an estimated 3,200 Afghan civilians were killed by militants, a 19 percent increase from 2013. According to data from the Afghan government, attacks by the Taliban in the nine-month period from April 2014 to December 2014 had increased between 15 percent and 20 percent when compared with the prior year. The United Nations stated that there was "a distinct increase in the activities and the visibility of al Qaida–affiliated entities in Afghanistan" in 2014. An Afghan security official said that increasingly the attacks have targeted Kabul, which he saw as "a message to the international community: 'You guys have failed. Despite what you did, you cannot guarantee security, we are able to attack.'" Many believe that peace talks between the Afghan government and Taliban are necessary to secure lasting peace; however, there is no indication that Taliban leadership would consider any arrangement.

BILATERAL SECURITY AGREEMENT SIGNED

In the latter years of its efforts in Afghanistan, the United States attempted to work with Karzai to reach an agreement that would allow American troops to remain in the country in a support role past 2014. In 2012, the United States and Afghanistan signed a strategic agreement that outlined the ongoing relationship between the two countries after 2014 and required the execution of a Bilateral Security Agreement (BSA), which would define the role of U.S. support after 2014. The United States said that its intent was to ensure that it was leaving behind a stable Afghan government that could continue to govern in a democratic fashion and avoid falling back under the control of terrorist elements. Negotiations on a BSA began in November 2012, and were tense from the beginning. Afghanistan demanded that part of the agreement include U.S. military support in the event that Afghanistan was ever attacked, something the U.S. government was wary to become involved with.

In June 2013, Karzai suspended negotiations on the BSA, his office stating, "In view of the contradiction between acts and the statements made by the United States of America in regard to the Peace Process, the Afghan government suspended the negotiations." To bring Afghan officials back to negotiations, Karzai's government demanded that the United States convince the Taliban to hold separate peace discussions with Afghanistan.

Negotiations reopened two months later, and by October, a draft agreement was announced, followed by a second draft on November 20 which U.S. secretary of state John Kerry said was nearly final. In the draft, the United States would assist in counterterrorism missions in Afghanistan and continue to train Afghan security forces. The draft was approved by the *loya jirga*, a group of elders responsible for making important determinations regarding the nation's governance, and they urged Karzai to quickly sign the agreement. Karzai balked, and the agreement went unsigned until a new president was elected. Karzai refused to sign the BSA, saying "My trust with America is not good. I don't trust them and they don't trust me."

Karzai was term limited in 2014. On June 14, 2014, candidates Ashraf Ghani and Abdullah Abdullah met in a runoff fraught with alleged voting fraud and delayed results. Abdullah fiercely contested the outcome, which put Ghani ahead with 56.44 percent of the vote. On September 21, the Independent Election Commission declared Ghani, a former World Bank official, the winner, at which point Abdullah signed a power-sharing agreement brokered by John Kerry, which named Abdullah the nation's chief executive officer. In this newly created position, Abdullah would handle the day-to-day running of the government.

On September 30, at Ghani's request, Afghan national security adviser Mohammad Hanif Atmar and U.S. Ambassador to Afghanistan James Cunningham signed the BSA. The agreement was the culmination of two years of work by representatives of both nations and would keep a set number of coalition troops in Afghanistan following the formal end of the combat mission. President Obama called the signing "an historic day in the U.S.-Afghan partnership that will help advance our shared interests and the long-term security of Afghanistan." Obama added, "We look forward to working with this new government to cement an enduring partnership that strengthens Afghan sovereignty, stability, unity and prosperity and that contributes to our shared goal of defeating al Qaeda and its extremist affiliates." Ghani called the BSA "good for the country," adding that "this agreement will pave the way for peace; it will not be an obstacle to peace." Following the signing of the BSA, NATO finalized its status-of-forces agreement, which will be the framework for the ongoing support mission.

Even with the BSA signed, international analysts have expressed doubt about how the instability created by the power sharing agreement might impact the fragile relationship between Afghanistan and the United States. "They have created a fabricated national unity government, and I don't think such a government can last," said Kabul University political analyst Wadir Safi. By the close of the year, Ghani and Abdullah had failed to seat a government. The United States and its international partners agree that a stable Afghani government is key to both mutually beneficial ongoing noncombat operations by coalition forces and halting the threat of terrorist groups in the region.

FORMAL END OF COMBAT MISSION

The end-of-mission ceremony on December 28, 2014, at the International Security Assistance Force (ISAF) headquarters in Kabul was kept secret until shortly before it began, for fear that Taliban militants might attempt to attack the building. "Today marks an end of an era and the beginning of a new one," U.S. general John Campbell, commander of the ISAF, said at the close of the joint mission. "We will continue to invest in Afghanistan's future," he added. "We are not walking away." Secretary of Defense Chuck Hagel echoed those remarks, stating, "The United States remains strongly committed to a sovereign, secure, stable, and unified Afghanistan. As we responsibly draw down our military presence, we will continue to partner together with Afghan forces to combat terrorism and create a better future for the Afghan people." During the ceremony, NATO secretary general Jens Stoltenberg said, "The security of Afghanistan will be fully in the hands of the country's 350,000 Afghan soldiers and police. But NATO Allies, together with many partner nations, will remain to train, advise and assist them." He added, "Many challenges remain, and there is much work still to do. The Afghan security forces will continue to need our help as they develop."

The Afghan government was represented at the ceremony by Atmar, who said the people of Afghanistan "recognize that you carried on the fight for us when we were not ready." He also expressed his confidence that Afghan forces were prepared to take over leadership of security and defense against al Qaeda and the Taliban, but said the nation appreciated the ongoing noncombat support that would be provided under the BSA. "We don't want or expect your support to be indefinite, but we need it now more than ever," Atmar said.

Approximately 12,500 to 13,500 coalition troops will remain in Afghanistan following the December end of combat missions, 9,800 of whom will be Americans. These troops will remain in Afghanistan for two years to provide training to Afghan security forces and help to root out al Qaeda and Taliban terrorists. The withdrawal of these troops will be gradual, and President Obama said he expected that the size of the U.S. force would be cut in half by 2015, before complete withdrawal by the end of 2016. Traditional U.S. embassy support troops would be allowed to remain in Afghanistan after 2016.

The necessity of continued involvement by coalition forces to assist in rooting out terrorists became clear immediately after the BSA was signed when Taliban spokesperson Zabiullah Mujahid posted on Twitter "Death to America!" and the Taliban issued a message reading, "We are certain that our nation will strengthen its jihad." The same message indicated that the end of combat missions signaled that the coalition had been "pushed to the brink of defeat."

—Heather Kerrigan

Following is the text of two statements, one from North Atlantic Treaty Organization secretary general Jens Stoltenberg, and one from U.S. secretary of defense Chuck Hagel, both released on December 28, 2014, in response to the end of formal combat missions in Afghanistan.

NATO Secretary General on End of Afghanistan Combat Mission

December 28, 2014

At the end of this year, we complete our combat mission in Afghanistan and open a new chapter in our relationship with Afghanistan.

The security of Afghanistan will be fully in the hands of the country's 350,000 Afghan soldiers and police. But NATO Allies, together with many partner nations, will remain to train, advise and assist them. This is what NATO and Afghan leaders agreed together. It has been made possible by the courage and capability of the Afghan National Security Forces, and by the dedication of the international forces who helped train them over the past years.

Many challenges remain, and there is much work still to do. The Afghan security forces will continue to need our help as they develop.

Our new mission, "Resolute Support," will bring together around 12,000 men and women from NATO Allies and 14 partner nations. The mission is based on a request from the Afghan government and the Status of Forces Agreement between NATO and Afghanistan. The United Nations Security Council unanimously welcomed the agreement between Afghanistan and NATO to establish the mission and stressed the importance of continued international support for the stability of Afghanistan.

We will also contribute to the financing of the Afghan security forces, and build an Enduring Partnership with Afghanistan which reflects our joint interests, shapes our joint cooperation and contributes to our shared security.

For over a decade, NATO and our partners have stood with Afghanistan. 51 nations have contributed forces to our effort—over a quarter of the countries of the world. The International Security Assistance Force (ISAF) has been the largest military coalition in recent history and represents an unprecedented international effort. The mandate of the United Nations Security Council was to help the Afghan authorities provide security across the country and develop new Afghan forces.

This mandate was carried out at great cost, but with great success. We will always remember the sacrifice of international and Afghan forces, who deserve our respect and our gratitude.

Thanks to the remarkable effort of our forces, we have achieved what we set out to do. We have made our own nations safer, by denying safe haven to international terrorists. We have made Afghanistan stronger, by building up from scratch strong security forces. Together, we have created the conditions for a better future for millions of Afghan men, women and children.

SOURCE: North Atlantic Treaty Organization. "NATO Secretary General's statement on a new chapter in Afghanistan." December 28, 2014. www.nato.int/cps/en/natohq/news_116341.htm?selected Locale=en.

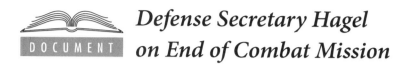

Defense Secretary Hagel on End of Combat Mission

December 28, 2014

At the end of this year, as our Afghan partners assume responsibility for the security of their country, the United States officially concludes Operation Enduring Freedom. Our combat mission in Afghanistan, which began in the aftermath of the September 11, 2001 attacks, will come to an end.

In 2015, we begin our follow-on mission, Operation Freedom's Sentinel, to help secure and build upon the hard-fought gains of the last 13 years.

I want to express my deep gratitude to all U.S. personnel, both military and civilian, who have served in Afghanistan since 2001, many on multiple deployments. I also thank the thousands more who were a part of the mission at home and around the world. In fighting America's longest war, our people and their families have borne a heavy burden, and some paid the ultimate price.

From my first trip to Afghanistan in 2002 to my visit earlier this month, I have seen firsthand the hard and heroic work done by American military and civilian personnel. That work and their sacrifices have made our world safer and given Afghanistan the opportunity to chart a secure, democratic, and prosperous future. I also want to thank and acknowledge our International Security Assistance Force partners for their indispensable work and sacrifice in helping strengthen Afghanistan.

In Operation Freedom's Sentinel, the United States will pursue two missions with the support of the Afghan government and the Afghan people. We will work with our allies and partners as part of NATO's Resolute Support Mission to continue training, advising, and assisting Afghan security forces. And we will continue our counterterrorism mission against the remnants of Al-Qaeda to ensure that Afghanistan is never again used to stage attacks against our homeland.

The United States remains strongly committed to a sovereign, secure, stable, and unified Afghanistan. As we responsibly draw down our military presence, we will continue to partner together with Afghan forces to combat terrorism and create a better future for the Afghan people. And through enduring security cooperation, we will continue assisting the Afghan government to build its capacity and self-sufficiency, as we transition to the next phase of the U.S.-Afghanistan defense relationship. We will continue to work with our Afghan partners to secure the great progress we have made since 2001 and to seize this defining moment of opportunity for Afghanistan's future.

SOURCE: U.S. Department of Defense. "Statement by Secretary of Defense Chuck Hagel on Operation Enduring Freedom and Operation Freedom's Sentinel." December 28, 2014. www.defense.gov/Releases/Release.aspx?ReleaseID=17091.

OTHER HISTORIC DOCUMENTS OF INTEREST

FROM THIS VOLUME

FROM PREVIOUS *HISTORIC DOCUMENTS*

Index

Names starting with al- or el- are alphabetized by the subsequent part of the name.